THE OXFORD HANDBOOK OF

HUMAN CAPITAL

THE OXFORD HANDBOOK OF

HUMAN CAPITAL

Edited by

ALAN BURTON-JONES

and

J.-C. SPENDER

OXFORD
UNIVERSITY PRESS

OXFORD
UNIVERSITY PRESS

Great Clarendon Street, Oxford OX2 6DP

Oxford University Press is a department of the University of Oxford.
It furthers the University's objective of excellence in research, scholarship,
and education by publishing worldwide in

Oxford New York

Auckland Cape Town Dar es Salaam Hong Kong Karachi
Kuala Lumpur Madrid Melbourne Mexico City Nairobi
New Delhi Shanghai Taipei Toronto

With offices in

Argentina Austria Brazil Chile Czech Republic France Greece
Guatemala Hungary Italy Japan Poland Portugal Singapore
South Korea Switzerland Thailand Turkey Ukraine Vietnam

Oxford is a registered trade mark of Oxford University Press
in the UK and in certain other countries

Published in the United States
by Oxford University Press Inc., New York

British Library Cataloguing in Publication Data

Data available

Library of Congress Cataloging in Publication Data

Data available

Typeset by SPI Publisher Services, Pondicherry, India
Printed in Great Britain
on acid-free paper by
MPG Books Group, Bodmin and King's Lynn

ISBN 978–0–19–953216–2

1 3 5 7 9 10 8 6 4 2

CONTENTS

PART I: THE NATURE OF HUMAN CAPITAL

PART II: HUMAN CAPITAL AND THE FIRM

PART III: HUMAN CAPITAL AND
ORGANIZATIONAL EFFECTIVENESS

PART IV: HUMAN CAPITAL INTERDEPENDENCIES

PART V: HUMAN CAPITAL IN THE FUTURE ECONOMY

Acknowledgments

The inspiration for this handbook came from David Musson, Business and Management Editor at Oxford University Press, who in late 2006 suggested to us the need for a volume that might throw fresh light on the subject of human capital from an organizational perspective. For some years we had been individually researching knowledge-based theories of management and organization and exchanging ideas on issues associated with the growing importance of 'knowledge capital', so we were delighted to have the opportunity to cooperate on this project. We set about attracting leading scholars from around the world—more than forty distinguished academics from multiple disciplines finally contributing to the twenty-five chapters in the handbook. Despite operating as co-editors at long range from one another, the editorial process was remarkably smooth, with electronic communications overcoming the tyranny of distance.

Three and a half years later we are pleased to have an opportunity to express in a formal way our thanks to all those who have helped to bring this handbook to fruition. David Musson has been a constant source of advice, encouragement, and guidance throughout the project, and the members of his team at Oxford University Press, particularly Emma Lambert and Matthew Derbyshire, have provided invaluable technical and administrative support. Most of all we would like to thank all the authors who have contributed to this volume for their patience and cooperation in dealing with our queries and suggestions, and for the commitment they have shown to making this handbook a success.

LIST OF FIGURES

LIST OF TABLES

FOREWORD BY GARY S. BECKER

The human capital 'revolution' began in the 1950s and early 1960s with the research of Theodore W. Schultz, Jacob Mincer, and myself. Schultz's most influential piece among many on human capital is his presidential address to the American Economic Association (Schultz, 1961). Mincer's pioneering study was his dissertation published in the *Journal of Political Economy* in 1958 (Mincer, 1958). He followed that up sixteen years later with his classic book *Schooling, Experience, and Earnings* (Mincer, 1974). Becker's most famous human capital studies are the various editions of his book *Human Capital* (Becker, 1964, 1975, 1993).

I do not use the word 'revolution' casually because the emphasis on investments in education, training, and other human capital radically changed the way economists and others interpreted many important economic, social, and policy issues. In this Foreword I discuss three of the most important fields affected by the human capital approach: the analysis of labor markets, explanations of the determinants of economic growth, and evaluations of the benefits from improved health and of the determinants of longer life and a better quality of life. I take each up in turn.

When I started my NBER research on human capital in 1957, my goals were modest. I had noticed from my study of discrimination against minorities in American labor markets that earnings of both white and black males rose significantly with their years of schooling. The main goal of my human capital study was to calculate rates of return on investments in education for different groups, after costs of education were netted out of the earnings benefits.

As my research progressed I began to realize that the human capital approach provided an entirely new way of looking at labor markets. Instead of assuming that differences in earnings mainly reflected whether workers held 'good' or 'bad' jobs, the human capital approach assumed that earnings mainly measure how much workers had invested in their skills and knowledge. According to this view, earnings would rise with the amount invested in education and training. On this interpretation, good jobs are mainly jobs held by workers who have invested a lot in their human capital.

This approach provided a broad range of implications about workers, including determinants of layoffs and quits, inequality in earnings, the effect of job experience on earnings—the so-called age–experience–earnings profiles—and on many other important characteristics of labor markets. Most importantly, the theory rather directly leads to methods that link implications of the theory to empirical evidence through earnings regressions, and in many other directions.

For example, Becker and Chiswick (1966) ran the first empirical regressions that related log of earnings to years of schooling for different age groups. They showed, 'under various simplifying assumptions', that the coefficient on years of schooling would equal the rate of return on investment in education. (Mincer, 1958, makes the unrealistic assumption that the present value of earnings is the same for all schooling groups when future earnings are discounted by the market interest rate.) However, Mincer (1974) made the major extension of the Becker–Chiswick approach by adding years of job experience to the right-hand side regressors, where job experience was measured by age minus years of schooling minus six years. This greatly improved the fit of log wage earnings regression, although it did not much change the coefficient on years of schooling.

Prior to Schultz's work on human capital, the emphasis in the economic development literature was on the accumulation of physical capital, as in the basic neoclassical growth model. Schultz helped shift some of the attention to investments in skills and knowledge because he demonstrated in various ways that these seemed crucial to economic development. He even argued that investment in human capital was more important than investment in physical capital (see Schultz, 1960). Many subsequent empirical and theoretical studies have built on Schultz's analysis, such as empirical studies of the factors behind economic growth (see for example, Mankiew *et al.*, 1992), and incorporations of human capital accumulation into models of economic growth (see for example, Lucas, 1988).

Health as human capital received its major push from the pioneering doctoral dissertation by Michael Grossman (see Grossman, 1972, for an article based on his dissertation). Grossman interpreted both the growth and decline of the quality and quantity of life as due to investments and disinvestments in human capital that improved health. Death occurred when health human capital fell below a certain level.

A related literature on human capital and health emphasizes the statistical value of life. This literature refers to how much individuals are willing to pay to increase their probability of surviving different ages (see for example, Rosen, 1988). A recent and important paper in that tradition (Murphy and Topel, 2003) estimates how much the population of the United States would be willing to pay for various reductions in the probabilities of dying from cancer, heart diseases, and other major ailments. They estimate that Americans would be willing to pay in the many trillions of dollars for even moderate reductions in these probabilities. I bring various strands of this literature together, and I also estimate the human capital cost of a major worldwide flu pandemic, in my Hicks lecture 'Health as Human Capital' (2007).

In the first several decades, human capital analysis was mainly concentrated at two universities: Chicago and Columbia. Since then it has spread to most universities and think tanks in the world, into other fields, such as sociology and political science, and among politicians and public officials. Politicians feel insecure unless they frequently mention the importance of investing in the human capital of their constituents. I certainly had not anticipated anything close to the eventual impact of the early research on investing in education, training, and other forms of human capital.

Human capital has remained a vital area of research for half a century because it has turned out to be so relevant in many different aspects of life. The research agenda has grown and expanded 'in my judgment' because, from the very early research on human capital, a close dialog developed between theory and empirical analysis. New theoretical developments generally stressed their empirical implications, and many of these implications have been tested with empirical and experimental data. Similarly, new empirical results have usually led to further theoretical insights, as in research that relates new empirical measures of the education levels of a labor force to issues like economic development, and studies of why women in richer countries are now considerably more likely than men to receive university degrees. Fields tend to become sterile when theorists refer mainly to the work of other theorists, with little attention to the empirical side, and when empiricists proceed with little concern for how their results relate to different theories.

The twenty-first century is clearly placing much greater emphasis than ever before on the importance of knowledge and information to the development of both countries and individuals. For example, the Internet provides access to a breadth of information that was unthinkable prior to its development, and growing knowledge of the role of different genes in affecting propensities to be vulnerable to different diseases makes personalized medicine a possibility rather than a pipe-dream. This means that it is more important than ever for both individuals and for nations to acquire knowledge, skills, and the experience to know how to acquire additional information. To me, this is the main explanation for the worldwide boom in higher education not only in the rich countries but also in developing and quite poor nations.

Therefore, I am optimistic that the vitality of human capital research will continue, and that its scope will expand further beyond the original emphasis on earnings into the effects of early childhood on the capacity to benefit from investments in human capital, the role of human capital in the sorting of men and women into different marriages, household production, and consumption decisions, such as habits and addictions, organizational structure, voting and political decisions, volunteer and other social activities, and other aspects of human behavior.

The chapters in the present volume provide an excellent example of the vibrant research that is currently taking place on human capital. These chapters discuss interactions between human capital and social capital, various links between human capital, entrepreneurship, and the theory of the firm, matching human capital of different individuals to different organizations, the growing role of human capital as globalization increases, and many other exciting topics. Readers should greatly benefit from studying and reflecting on the chapters that follow.

REFERENCES

Becker, G. S. (1993). *Human Capital: A Theoretical and Empirical Analysis, with Special Reference to Education* (3rd edn. Chicago: University of Chicago Press).

——(2007). 'Health as Human Capital: Synthesis and Extensions', *Oxford Economic Papers*, 59: 379–410.

——and Chiswick, B. R. (1966). 'Education and the Distribution of Earnings', *American Economic Review*, 56: 358–69.

Grossman, M. (1972). 'On the Concept of Health Capital and the Demand for Health', *Journal of Political Economy*, 80(2): 223–55.

Lucas, R. E. (1988). 'On the Mechanics of Economic Development', *Journal of Monetary Economics*, 22: 3–42.

Mankiw, N. G., Romer, D., and Weil, D. N. (1992). 'A Contribution to the Empirics of Economic Growth', *Quarterly Journal of Economics*, 107(2): 407.

Mincer, J. (1958). 'Investment in Human Capital and Personal Income Distribution', *Journal of Political Economy*, 66 (Aug.): 281–302.

——(1974). *Schooling, Experience and Earnings* (New York: Columbia University Press).

Murphy, K. M., and Topel, R. H. (2003). 'Diminishing Returns? Evidence on the Costs and Benefits of Improving Health', *Perspectives in Biology and Medicine*, 46(3) (summer): 108–28.

Rosen, S. (1988). 'The Value of Changes in Life Expectancy', *Journal of Risk and Uncertainty*, 1: 285–304.

Schultz, T. W. (1960). 'Capital Formation by Education', *Journal of Political Economy*, 68(6): 571–83.

——(1961). 'Investment in Human Capital', *American Economic Review*, 51(1): 1.

List of Contributors

Soon Ang (Ph.D. Minnesota) is Goh Tjoei Kok Endowed Chair and Professor of Management and is Head of the Division of Strategy, Management and Organization at the Nanyang Business School, Nanyang Technological University, Singapore. She is also the Executive Director of the Center for Leadership and Cultural Intelligence. Her research interests are in cultural intelligence, global leadership, and outsourcing. She has published extensively in *Academy of Management Journal, Journal of Applied Psychology, Organization Science, Management Science, Information Systems Research, MIS Quarterly,* and *Social Forces,* and serves on editorial boards including *Organization Science, Applied Psychology, Decision Science, MIS Quarterly,* and others. She pioneered and co-authored two foundation books on cultural intelligence (Stanford University Press) and co-edited the *Handbook of Cultural Intelligence* (M.E. Sharpe). She recently received the prestigious Distinguished International Alumni Award from the University of Minnesota for her academic leadership and scholarship record.

Margaret Mendenhall Blair is an economist who focuses on management law. She joined the Vanderbilt's Law and Business faculty in 2004. She was previously at Georgetown University Law Center, where she served as a Sloan Visiting Professor and Research Director for the Sloan-GULC Project on Business Institutions, from 2000 through June 2004. Prior to that, she was a Senior Fellow in the Economic Studies Program at the Brookings Institution, where she wrote about corporate governance and the role of human capital in corporations. Her current research focuses on team production and the legal structure of business organizations, legal issues in the governance of supply chains, and the role of finance in creating bubbles.

Rocio Bonet is an Assistant Professor at IE Business School in Madrid, Spain. Her research focuses on the effects of postgraduate education, in particular of the MBA degree, on individuals' career success. Bonet is also a sworn employee of the Census Bureau where she is conducting research on the effect of work organizational practices on employee welfare, especially on wage growth and promotions. She received her Ph.D. from the Wharton School of the University of Pennsylvania.

Peter Boxall is Professor of Human Resource Management and Associate Dean for Research in the Business School at the University of Auckland. His research is concerned with the links between HRM and strategic management and with the changing nature of work and employment systems. He is the co-author with John Purcell of *Strategy and Human Resource Management* (Palgrave Macmillan), co-editor with John Purcell and Patrick Wright of the *Oxford Handbook of Human Resource Management* (Oxford University Press), and co-editor with Richard Freeman and Peter Haynes of *What Workers Say: Employee Voice in the Anglo-American Workplace* (Cornell University Press).

Rhett Brymer is a Ph.D. student of strategic management at the Mays Business School at Texas A&M University. He received his M.B.A. and M.S. degrees from the Florida State University, and worked as an organizational change consultant for six years with firms such as Hewlett-Packard, Credit Suisse, BearingPoint, Citigroup, and Proctor & Gamble. He is a member of the Academy of Management and the Strategic Management Society. His research interests include human capital, strategy implementation, collective cognitions, strategic entrepreneurship, and acquisitions.

Alan Burton-Jones heads an international management consultancy practice headquartered in Brisbane, Australia, with affiliates in Asia and the UK, and is a senior visiting lecturer at New South Wales, Griffith and Bond Universities. He received his Ph.D. from the University of Canberra. His academic research focuses on the role of knowledge in organizations and the links between strategy, intellectual resources, and organizational effectiveness. He is the author of *Knowledge Capitalism: Business, Work and Learning in the New Economy* (Oxford University Press, 1999, Nikkei, 2002) and his writings have also been published in a number of leading international journals. He contributed to the Australian government report on the knowledge-based economy in APEC countries (DISR 2000), the first national Knowledge Management Framework published by Standards Australia, and the establishment of the Asia-Pacific Learning and Knowledge Management Council (pan-Pacific industry forum).

Andrew Burton-Jones is an Assistant Professor at the Sauder School of Business, University of British Columbia. He holds a Bachelor of Commerce and Master of Information Systems from the University of Queensland and a Ph.D. from Georgia State University. His first research stream seeks a deeper understanding of how well individuals and collectives use information systems. His second research stream seeks ways to improve methods for analyzing and designing systems in organizations. He has published in *Data and Knowledge Engineering, Database for Advances in Information Systems, Information Systems Research, and MIS Quarterly*, and he has received best paper awards from *MIS Quarterly* and the *International Conference on Information Systems*. Prior to his academic career he was a senior consultant in a Big-4 accounting/consulting firm.

Peter Cappelli is the George W. Taylor Professor of Management at The Wharton School and Director of Wharton's Center for Human Resources. He is also a Research Associate at the National Bureau of Economic Research in Cambridge, Massachussetts. He has degrees in industrial relations from Cornell University and in labor economics from Oxford, where he was a Fulbright Scholar. His work focuses on human resource practices, talent and performance management, and public policy related to employment. He is the author of over 100 papers in refereed journals and numerous book chapters. He serves on the editorial boards of *Organizational Dynamics, Journal of Industrial Relations, Industrial Relations, Administrative Science Quarterly, Employee Relations (UK)*, and *Industrial and Labor Relations Review*.

Thomas Clarke is Professor of Management at the University of Technology, Sydney, and Director of the Key University Research Centre for Corporate Governance research at UTS. He was awarded his doctorate in Industrial and Business Studies from the University of Warwick Business School, UK. He was previously DBM Professor of Corporate Governance at the Leeds Business School, UK, and Visiting Professor at the China Europe International Business School (CEIBS), Shanghai, the FGV Business School, Sao Paulo, Brazil, and UAM Business School, Mexico City. His broader research interests include management and business paradigms, globalization, international best practice in knowledge management, the knowledge economy, privatization and deregulation, management reform in China and SE Asia, sustainable enterprise, stakeholder management, media and communications, new organizational forms, and the governance of knowledge-based business. Professor Clarke has published a number of books including *Changing Paradigms: The Transformation of Management Knowledge for the 21ˢᵗ Century* (Profile Books, 2000), and over 120 book chapters and articles in refereed journals.

Russ Coff (Ph.D. UCLA) is an Associate Professor of Organization and Management at Emory University. He studies dilemmas associated with knowledge-based competitive advantages such as how buyers cope when acquiring human asset intensive targets, and value/rent appropriation from knowledge-based advantages. He served as the Chair for the Business Policy and Strategy Division of the Academy of Management, and currently sits on the editorial boards of the *Academy of Management Journal, Organization Science, Strategic Management Journal, Strategic Organization*, and *Journal of Strategic Management Education*.

Nicolai J. Foss is a Professor of Organization and Strategy at the Copenhagen Business School and the Norwegian School of Economics and Business Administration, and a visiting professor at Lund University and LUISS, Rome. His research interests are the theory of the firm, knowledge governance, and social science methodology. He is the author of more than 100 papers in reviewed journals, including the *Strategic Management Journal, Organization Science, Human Resource Management*, and others. He has edited or written several books on the theory of the firm and strategic management. He blogs on http://organizationsandmarkets.com.

Robert Grant holds the Eni Chair in Strategic Management at Bocconi University. He previously worked at Georgetown University, City University (London), California Polytechnic, University of British Columbia, London Business School, and St Andrews University, and was economic adviser to the British Monopolies Commission. His interests are in competitive and corporate strategy, and the theory of the firm. His textbook *Contemporary Strategy Analysis* is used in MBA programs worldwide. He serves on the editorial boards of *Strategic Management Journal, Journal of Management Studies, Long Range Planning, Strategy and Leadership*, and *European Management Review*.

James Guthrie is a Professor at Bologna University and an Honorary Professor at the University of Sydney. His research and teaching interests include public sector accounting, auditing, accountability and management, social and environmental reporting and auditing, management of knowledge and intellectual capital, and the measurement of intangibles. He has published 145 articles in both international and national refereed and professional journals, and over 35 chapters in books. He is also co-editor of eight public sector management and accounting books, and has presented his ideas and research findings to over 280 national and international gatherings.

Monika Hamori is Professor of Human Resource Management at IE Business School in Madrid, Spain. Her research focuses on the predictors of managerial and executive career success, on top executive and chief executive career paths, and on the role of executive search firms in the corporate hiring process. Her articles have been published in a number of refereed journals including the *Harvard Business Review, International Journal of Human Resource Management* and *Industrial and Labor Relations Review*. She was born in Hungary and pursued her undergraduate studies in Budapest. She received her Ph.D. from the Wharton School of the University of Pennsylvania.

James C. Hayton is Goldman Professor of Entrepreneurship at Newcastle University Business School. His research interests include the strategic management of human resources, organizational learning and innovation, and entrepreneurship and firm growth. He serves as Executive Editor of *Human Resource Management Journal*, and serves on the editorial board of *Entrepreneurship Theory and Practice, Journal of Business Venturing, European Management Review, Human Resource Management Review*, and *Journal of Management Studies*.

Michael Hitt is currently a Distinguished Professor of Management at Texas A&M University and holds the Joe B. Foster Chair in Business Leadership. He received his Ph.D. from the University of Colorado. A recent article noted that he was one of the top ten most cited authors in the management field over a 25-year period. He has served as an editor of the *Academy of Management Journal* and is currently co-editor of the *Strategic Entrepreneurship Journal*. He is a Fellow in the Academy of Management and in the Strategic Management Society, and received an honorary doctorate (Doctor Honoris Causa) from the Universidad Carlos III de Madrid. He is a former President of the Academy of Management and is the current Past President of the Strategic Management Society. He has received awards for the best article published in the *Academy of Management Executive, Academy of Management Journal* and the *Journal of Management*. He has received the Irwin Outstanding Educator Award and the Distinguished Service Award from the Academy of Management.

Thomas Kochan is George Maverick Bunker Professor of Management and Professor of Work and Employment Research at the MIT Sloan School of Management. He is an expert source on labor relations, collective bargaining, human resource management, regulatory policies, and unemployment. His recent work calls attention to the challenges facing working families in meeting their responsibilities at work and at home and in their communities. Through empirical research, he demonstrates that fundamental changes in the quality of employee and labor–management relations are needed to address America's critical problems in industries ranging from health care to airlines to manufacturing. He is the author of over 100 articles in refereed journals and over 40 book chapters.

Jeroen Kraaijenbrink is Assistant Professor at Nikos, the Dutch Institute for Knowledge Intensive Entrepreneurship at the University of Twente. He holds an M.Sc. and a Ph.D. in Industrial Engineering and Management and an M.Sc. in Public Administration from the University of Twente. His research focuses on knowledge-based and entrepreneurial explanations of the theory of the firm. Embracing the non-mainstream economic positions variously labeled Austrian, Knightian, evolutionary or otherwise 'non-equilibrium', and taking a pragmatist sociological perspective, he is working towards a subjectivist and dynamic theory of the firm with human imagination and judgment at its center. He teaches courses on strategy, knowledge management and entrepreneurship in the M.Sc. programs of Business Administration and Business Information Technology. He also teaches these topics to entrepreneurs within the VentureLab Twente and managers at the Twente School of Management (TSM).

Robin Kramar is a Professor and Deputy Dean and Director of Accreditation at MGSM, Macquarie University. She has a particular interest in human resource management, diversity management, and education for sustainability. She represents Australia in the Cranet Network which undertakes comparative, longitudinal research in more than 40 countries. She is Associate Editor of *Asia Pacific Journal of Human Resources*, and serves on the editorial board of *Journal of Chinese HRM* and *Asia Pacific Journal of Business Administration*. She has co-authored and co-edited eight books on Australian human resource management and has more than sixty publications in refereed journals and books.

David Lepak is Professor of Human Resource Management and Department Chair of the HRM department in the School of Management and Labor Relations at Rutgers University. His research focuses on strategic human resource management with an emphasis on employment sub-systems and the HR architecture, contingent labor, intellectual capital, and linking HR systems to important company outcomes. His research has appeared in a variety of outlets such as *Academy of Management Review, Academy of Management Journal, Journal of Applied Psychology, Journal of Management*, and *Human Resource Management*. He has co-authored a comprehensive textbook with Mary Gowan entitled *Human Resource Management* (Prentice Hall, 2008). He is currently associate editor of *Academy of Management Review*, and serves on the editorial boards of many other academic journals.

Peter Lewin (Ph.D. Chicago, 1979) was born and grew up in Johannesburg, South Africa, and emigrated to the United States in 1972. At the University of the Witwatersrand, in Johannesburg, he studied under Ludwig Lachmann, a German scholar specializing in capital theory deriving from the Austrian School of Economics. At the University of Chicago he completed his Ph.D. under the guidance of Gary Becker on *The Economics of Apartheid*, and acquired an interest in human capital and the Chicago approach human behavior. These two educational experiences provided the basis for his work in human capital as an aspect of capital theory more generally. In recent years his work has focused on applications of capital theory to business organization. He is a Clinical Professor of Economics at the University of Texas at Dallas, School of Management, where he has taught economics for the last 15 years.

Adam Seth Litwin is Assistant Professor and a founding member of the faculty at the Carey Business School at Johns Hopkins University. His research focuses on the interplay of employment practices and workplace technological change. His dissertation, completed at the MIT Sloan School of Management, examined the influence of the employment relationship on the adoption, diffusion, and effective deployment of health IT. Aside from his broad interests in employment relations and strategic HRM, he has recently focused on the effects of employee involvement programs in the healthcare industry as well as on the issue of employment practices in small business.

Brian Loasby was born in Kettering, Northamptonshire, and was educated in local schools and at Emmanuel College, Cambridge. After appointments at the Universities of Aberdeen, Birmingham and Bristol, and a year as Arthur D. Little Management Fellow during which he attended courses at Harvard Business School and the Sloan School of Management at MIT, he moved to the new University of Stirling where he is now Emeritus and Honorary Professor of Economics. His interests centre on the relationships between knowledge and organization, both conceived as distinctive structures of selected elements, and include human cognition, firm and interfirm relationships, decision processes, the history of economics (a major source of reusable ideas) and methodology. He has written five books, and well over a hundred articles and chapters in multi-authored volumes. *Knowledge, Institutions and Evolution in Economics* (Routledge 1999), developed from his Graz Schumpeter Lectures, was joint winner of the Schumpeter Prize in 2000. He holds an honorary doctorate from the University of Stirling, and is a Fellow of the British Academy and the Royal Society of Edinburgh.

Vijaya Murthy is a lecturer and a Ph.D. student at the Discipline of Accounting, University of Sydney. Vijaya's focus is on intellectual capital research; in particular, human capital. She is interested in developments in human capital accounting. She is currently doing research on the managerial use of non-financial performance information in practice, and is specifically examining how management uses information on workplace flexibility to mobilize the different elements of intellectual capital.

Janine Nahapiet is Emeritus Fellow, Green Templeton College, and Associate Fellow of the Saïd Business School at the University of Oxford, and specializes in the links between strategy and organization. Her co-authored paper 'Social Capital, Intellectual Capital and the Organizational Advantage' won the Academy of Management Review best paper award in 1998, and has been identified recently as the second most cited article in the last decade in the fields of economics and management and the fifth most influential strategic management article published in the last 26 years. Her research focuses on links between social capital, innovation and knowledge, the theory and practice of cooperation, and innovative forms of organizing. In 2006 she moved to a portfolio career in order to focus both her research and work with executives on the challenge of building organizational capabilities for the twenty-first century.

Kok-Yee Ng is Associate Professor in Management at the Nanyang Technological University, and Director of Research at the Center for Leadership and Cultural Intelligence. She received her Ph.D. in Organizational Behavior from Michigan State University. Her research interests include cultural intelligence, leadership, and teams. She has published in the *Academy of Management Journal, Journal of Applied*

Psychology, Management Science, Organizational Behavior and Human Decision Processes, and the *MIS Quarterly*.

Ikujiro Nonaka is a Professor Emeritus at the Graduate School of International Corporate Strategy, Hitotsubashi University, Xerox Distinguished Faculty Scholar, University of California, Berkeley, and also First Distinguished Drucker Scholar in Residence at the Drucker School and Institute, Claremont Graduate University. He has published many books and articles in Japanese and in English. Selected publications include *Managing Flow: A Process Theory of the Knowledge-based Firm* (Palgrave Macmillan, 2008, with co-authors), and *The Knowledge-Creating Company* (Oxford University Press, 1995, with H. Takeuchi).

David O'Donnell, of the Intellectual Capital Research Institute, Ireland, is an inter-disciplinary researcher in the fields of intellectual capital, governance, democracy studies, and critical management studies. A founding member of the New Club of Paris, he has conducted research for CIMA, CIPD, and Houses of the Oireachtas (Irish Parliament), and is actively involved in international collaborative research with like-minded colleagues. He serves on the editorial boards of *Corporate Governance International Review* and *Journal of European Industrial Training*, and has published widely since rediscovering The Frankfurt School after twenty-five years in various roles in Europe, Africa, and the Middle East. Living in rural County Limerick, he is an avid Munster Rugby Club supporter.

Seán Ó Riain is Professor of Sociology and Department Head at the National University of Ireland, Maynooth. He earned his Ph.D. in Sociology from the University of California, Berkeley in 1999, and taught at the University of California, Davis, before moving to NUI Maynooth. His research interests include globalization and the knowledge economy, the politics of the workplace, new state formations, life histories and social change in twentieth-century Ireland, and ethnography and public sociology. He is the author of *The Politics of High Tech Growth: Developmental Network States in the Global Economy* (Cambridge University Press, 2004), which was co-awarded the James S. Donnelly Prize for Best Book in History and the Social Sciences at the American Conference of Irish Studies in 2005. He is currently co-authoring (with Chris Benner) a book entitled *Re-Making the Information Economy: The Politics of Work in Silicon Valley and Ireland* (American Sociological Association Rose Series/ Russell Sage Foundation, under contract).

Vesa Peltokorpi is an Assistant Professor in human resource management at HEC School of Management, Paris. He has published various articles in management journals such as *Journal of Management Studies*, *International Business Review*, *International Journal of Human Resource Management*, and *Review of General Psychology*.

Mario Schijven is currently an Assistant Professor of management at Texas A&M University. He received his Ph.D. from Tilburg University, The Netherlands. His current research focuses on corporate development activities—most notably acquisitions, alliances, and organizational restructuring, which he studies using theories of organizational learning, behavioral decision-making, and evolutionary economics. His work has appeared in the *Academy of Management Journal* and the *Journal of Management*, among others.

Peter D. Sherer is an associate professor in the Haskayne School of Business at the University of Calgary. His research focuses on strategy and human resource management, principally in the context of professional service firms. He has published in a number of journals and research volumes including the *Academy of Management Journal, Industrial and Labor Relations Review, Industrial Relations, Journal of Labor Economics, Organization Science, Research in Organizational Behavior, Research in Personnel/Human Resources Management, Research in the Sociology of Organizations,* and *Trends in Organizational Behavior.* He was the lead author in an article on institutional change in law firms that received the Best Paper award of 2002 in the *Academy of Management Journal* by the Academy of Management. His chapter in this volume, on bringing organizations deeper into human capital theory, reflects his long-standing interest in integrating economics with organizational and behavioral theories. He is one of the founders of the Human Capital and Competitive Advantage Interest Group of the Strategic Management Society. He serves on the editorial board of the *Academy of Management Journal.* He received his Ph.D. from the University of Wisconsin–Madison.

J.-C. Spender served in experimental submarines in the Royal Navy, then studied engineering at Oxford (Balliol), worked as a nuclear submarine reactor engineer with Rolls–Royce & Associates, a sales manager with IBM (UK), a consultant with Decision Technology International (Boston), and as an investment banker with Slater–Walker Securities. His Ph.D. thesis (Manchester Business School) won the Academy of Management's 1980 A. T. Kearney Ph.D. Research Prize, later published as *Industry Recipes* (Blackwell, 1989). He served on the faculty at City University (London), York University (Toronto), UCLA, and Rutgers. He was Dean of the School of Business and Technology at SUNY/FIT before retiring in 2003. He now researches, writes, and lectures on organization theory, strategy, and knowledge management in the USA, Canada, and Europe, with Visiting Professor appointments at Lund University, ESADE, Cranfield University, Leeds University, and the Open University. He was awarded, jointly with Rob Grant, the SMJ Best Paper Prize for 2006 for the 1996 SMJ Special Issue on *Knowledge and the Firm.*

Juani Swart directs the Work and Employment research Centre (WERC) where she specializes in Managing Knowledge and Knowledge Workers. Her specific research interests include understanding the nature of knowledge in networked processes, strategic knowledge assets, and the links between the intellectual capital, HRM and performance debates. She has published widely in the area of people management in knowledge intensive firms, intellectual capital structures, systems approaches to knowledge management, and network influences on strategic choice in leading journals, and has co-authored two books: *People and Performance* and *Strategic Human Resource Development*. Her research publications also include policy-informing reports on performance in knowledge-intensive firms, managing professional knowledge workers, and managing across boundaries.

Riki Takeuchi is an Associate Professor in the Department of Management at the School of Business and Management, Hong Kong University of Science and Technology. He received his Ph.D. from the Robert H. Smith School of Business, University of Maryland at College Park. His research interests include expatriate adjustment and international human resource management, strategic human resource management, organizational justice, and organizational citizenship behaviors. His research has appeared in *Academy of Management Journal, Journal of Applied Psychology, Organization Science*, and *Personnel Psychology*, among others. He also received the Distinguished Early Career Contributions Award from SIOP in 2010. He currently serves on the editorial review board for *Academy of Management Journal, Academy of Management Review, Journal of Applied Psychology, Journal of International Business Studies, Journal of Management*, and *Personnel Psychology*.

Mei Ling Tan is a doctoral candidate in management at the Nanyang Business School, Nanyang Technological University. She holds the prestigious Nanyang President's Graduate Scholarship to pursue her doctoral studies at Nanyang Business School. To date, her research has been presented at the Academy of Management Meetings, and she has published in the fields of psychological contracts and cultural intelligence. Her current research interests include cultural intelligence, international experience, and managing international and diverse workforces.

David Teece is Tusher Professor in Global Business at the Haas School of Business at the University of California, Berkeley. He received his Ph.D. in economics from the University of Pennsylvania in 1975. He is the co-author of over 200 books and articles on topics in innovation strategy, intellectual property, and antitrust policy. He also holds four honorary doctorates. Two volumes of Professor Teece's published papers—*Economic Performance and the Theory of the Firm* and *Strategy, Technology and Public Policy*—were published in 1998 by the Edward Elgar (London) publishing house in its series 'Economists of the Twentieth Century.' Recent books include *Dynamic Capabilities and Strategic Management: Organizing for Innovation and Growth* (Oxford University Press, 2009). He is on the Accenture list of the Top

50 Living Business Intellectuals. Prizes include the 2002 Viipuri International Prize in Strategic (Technology) Management and Business Economics, and the 2003 Strategic Management Journal Best Paper Award. According to *Science Watch* (November/December 2005) he is the lead author of the most cited paper in economics and business 1995–2005, and is ranked number 10 in citations worldwide by the same source for the same time period. Dr Teece has also been an active consultant to corporations and governments worldwide for more than 25 years. He is also an active private equity investor.

Ryoko Toyama is a Professor at the Graduate School of Strategic Management, Chuo University, Tokyo. Her research interests include strategy, technological management, and knowledge creation. She has published books about knowledge management, such as *Managing Flow* (Palgrave), and articles in management journals such as *Industrial and Corporate Change* and *Long Range Planning*, co-authored with Ikujiro Nonaka.

Dr Jacqueline Vischer has degrees in psychology and architecture, and is an environmental psychologist who has specialized in the study of the impact on building users of physical aspects of contemporary work environments. She is Professor in the Faculty of Environmental Design at the Université de Montréal, where she founded the *Groupe de Recherche sur les Environnements de Travail* (New Work Environments Research Group). She has also worked extensively as a consultant to large organizations in North America and Europe. Vischer is author or coauthor of six published books and a seventh in press. She has also published numerous articles on the environmental psychology of workspace, building evaluation, users' needs in buildings, indoor air quality, user–manager communication, facilities management, and architectural programming.

Georg von Krogh is a Professor at ETH Zurich, where he holds the Chair of Strategic Management and Innovation. He is also the Head of ETH Zurich's Department of Management, Technology, and Economics. He specializes in competitive strategy, technological innovation, and knowledge management. He has conducted research in various industries including financial services, media, computer software and hardware, life-sciences, and consumer goods, and has coauthored books on strategic management, knowledge creation, innovation, and organization and management theory. His articles have been published in leading journals including *Management Science, Organization Science, Research Policy, Strategic Management Journal*, and *Harvard Business Review*. He is a Senior Editor of *Organization Studies*, and an editorial board member of a number of journals including *European Management Journal, European Management Review, MIT Sloan Management Review*, and *Long Range Planning*.

Martin W. Wallin is a post-doctoral researcher at the Department of Management, Technology, and Economics, ETH Zurich, Switzerland. He was born in Ludvika, Sweden, and was educated at Chalmers University of Technology, where he received his M.Sc. (Industrial Engineering and Management) and Ph.D. (Technology Management). His research is focused on the organizational and motivational implications of distributed innovation. His empirical research has been conducted in several industries, including information technology, software, chemicals, and professional services. He teaches strategy, industry analysis and marketing, and has been a visiting researcher at Stanford University. He is author of a number of peer-reviewed book chapters and articles in refereed journals, including *R&D Management*, *Organizational Dynamics*, *Research Policy*, and *Technovation*.

INTRODUCTION

ALAN BURTON-JONES
J.-C. SPENDER

CONCEPT AND RATIONALE:
WHY A HANDBOOK OF HUMAN CAPITAL?

This *Handbook* aims to show the importance of human capital for contemporary organizations: how it contributes to theories of the firm, how it affects organizational performance, and its role in the future economy. We identify human capital as the linchpin of social and other forms of capital. Central to our thesis is the systemic nature of human capital in organizations: how human capital interacts with and complements other organizational resources. We also show how applying the notion of human capital to organizations requires us to consider how human and other intangible intellectual forms of capital differ from more traditional forms, implying the need for a theory of the firm that accommodates a concept of dynamic, heterogeneous human capital.

Given human capital's vintage and subsequent developments in management theorizing some might ask whether the notion has been subsumed or possibly superseded by more recent concepts, such as the resource-based or knowledge-based views of the firm. Some may question whether human capital is analytically separable from other forms of intellectual capital, such as social and structural capital. Others may question how the dynamic, heterogeneous nature of human capital in the contemporary firm fits with the traditional neoclassical view of capital as a static, homogeneous stock. We address these and related issues in this Introduction.

We start with a brief review of how the concept of human capital evolved. As many contributors to this volume remind us, human capital is not a new concept. Adam

Smith in *The Wealth of Nations* (1776) wrote of an individual's acquisition of talents as 'a capital fixed and realized, as it were, in his person'. Related notions surfaced occasionally in the nineteenth and early twentieth centuries, the first use of the term human capital, being credited to Arthur Pigou (1928). Human capital became prominent in the late 1950s and early 1960s as leading economists, notably Mincer (1958), Schultz (1961), and Becker (1964), proclaimed it as much a form of capital as physical and financial capital, and emphasized its importance to future economic growth. Since the 1960s an illustrious group of economists, all at one time or other associated with the Chicago School of Economics—such as Becker, Mincer, Rosen, Grossman, Friedman, Lucas, Romer, and Heckman—have continued to research human capital in relation to economic growth, the labor market, education, health, marriage, and related macroeconomic and social issues in both the market and non-market sectors.

Microeconomic perspectives based on human capital emerged more slowly. Even Becker's distinction between firm-specific and general human capital has yet to be brought deeply into theorizing at the firm level (see Sherer, Chapter 22 below). As Spender notes (Chapter 7), interest in human capital at the organizational level may have been spurred as much or more by Drucker's predictions of the rise of the knowledge worker, Daniel Bell's (1973) prediction of a shift to a post-industrial knowledge-intensive economy, and Reich's discussion of symbolic analysts in *The Work of Nations* (1992) in which he pays homage to Smith's *The Wealth of Nations*— the same work that inspired Schultz and Becker. Certainly there was a confluence of ideas and theories during the 1980s and early 1990s linking information, knowledge, and human talent. Zuboff (1988) spoke of the 'automating' and 'informating' potential of the new information technologies—implicitly substitutes for and enhancers of human capital. The resource-based (Wernerfelt, 1984; Barney, 1991) and dynamic capabilities perspectives (Teece and Pisano, 1998) highlighted the attributes of firms' human resources as drivers of value and competitive advantage. During the mid-1990s the idea that an organization's knowledge had become its most important economic and strategic resource became widely accepted (OECD, 1996), leading to a view of the firm as an integrator of disparate human knowledge and an explosion of interest in a knowledge-based approach (Blackler, 1995; Nonaka and Takeuchi, 1995; Grant, 1996; Spender, 1993, 1996; Conner and Prahalad, 1996; Zack, 1999).

Knowledge-based and human capital perspectives appear complementary— albeit the opportunities for synthesis are underexplored in the literature. Staffing and recruitment strategies can be viewed from both knowledge and human capital perspectives: firms recruit and invest in individuals largely based on their current and potential value as human/knowledge capital suppliers (Lepak and Snell, 1999; Burton-Jones, 1999). For individuals the firm provides an enabling context for developing their knowledge capital through training and socially enabled practice (Kogut and Zander, 1992). Combining human capital and knowledge-based perspectives can help identify complementarities and tensions between individuals as knowledge suppliers and firms as knowledge buyers, help us to better appreciate issues such as human capital formation and mobility, and throw fresh light on the principal–agent relationship. (For a variety of perspectives on these and related issues see Chapters 4, 7, 10, 13, 14, and Part V.)

During the 1980s and 1990s two additional forms of intellectual capital came to prominence alongside human capital: social capital, derived from investments in relationships between the organization's stakeholders, and structural capital, derived from investments in systems, processes, brands, and other non-human resources (Brooking, 1996; Edvinsson, 1997; Sveiby, 1997). Strong reciprocal interdependencies have been indentified between social capital and human capital (Coleman, 1988; Burt, 1992; Lin, 2001). People need social networks, and networks depend on people to develop and use them. Strong interdependencies are equally evident between human capital and other forms of structural capital such as information systems (ISs) (Wade and Hulland, 2004; Youndt *et al.*, 2004). People are essential to information systems, and people depend on ISs to acquire and apply their human capital. While intellectual capital provides a simple typology of intangible forms of capital, all forms of intellectual capital including social and structural capital are arguably reducible to the human knower—human capital thus becoming the linchpin. (For a spectrum of views see Chapters 2, 7, 11, and Part IV.)

Human capital and other forms of intangible, intellectual capital in organizations are heterogeneous, dynamic, and notoriously difficult to measure and value, yet according to the prevailing neoclassical economic orthodoxy capital is homogeneous, quantifiable, and commensurable. For macroeconomists working at the aggregate level, the dynamic and heterogeneous aspects of human capital are not an issue. In organizations, however, such differences matter. Dean and Kretschmer (2007) argue that we need to accept that human, social, and structural capital are only metaphorically 'capital' and revert to resource-based or capabilities-based typologies, or alternatively develop a new theory of dynamic capital to account for them. Lewin, (Chapter 5) following the Austrian school of economics (Hayek, Kirzner, Lachmann), takes a radically different view, emphasizing that the concept of capital can apply to all productive resources including dynamic, heterogeneous human capital. According to this view all capital is knowledge-based, whether in the form of artifacts (knowledge representations) or people (embodied knowledge). Consequently capital itself is not a static stock of durable assets from past production but 'the ability of combinations of things and ideas to produce value over time' (Baetjer and Lewin, 2007: 28). A dynamic view suggests we may need both a new concept of capital and a new theory of the firm that more accurately reflects the nature and role of human capital in today's knowledge-based economy—ideas that are discussed in more detail later in this Introduction. Part II of this *Handbook* is devoted to an examination of human capital in relation to theories of the firm, and Part III addresses a range of issues associated with human capital management and organizational effectiveness.

It is apparent from this brief survey that human capital is alive and well—knowledge-based and intellectual-capital-based perspectives reinforce rather than diminish its organizational relevance. We also show that the interdependent and complementary nature of human capital in organizations increases rather than diminishes its strategic significance. Finally, to provide it with enduring foundations and maximize its value we show the need to move human capital in organizations from management heuristic to theory. To do that we need to rationalize our perspectives of human capital—from neoclassical to modern—and find a theory of the firm that will give it a proper home.

These are issues that to date have been the subject of a diffuse and fragmented set of literatures—from economics, sociology, and cultural studies to organization theory, psychology, HR, and accounting. There is an evident need to pull these literatures together to investigate the phenomenon of human capital in organizations. That is what we have aimed to do in designing this volume.

SCOPE AND DESIGN OF THE *HANDBOOK*

Of recent years there have been a number of authoritative works on particular aspects of human capital in organizations, such as employment practices (Blair and Kochan, 2000) and interfirm mobility (Pennings and Wezel, 2007). Few, however, have attempted a comprehensive analysis of the subject. We determined to address this gap in the literature by exploring human capital in organizations from multiple perspectives, combining overviews of prior research with critical and original insights. We decided to focus on five aspects of human capital: its conceptual underpinnings; its relevance to theories of the firm; its implications for organizational effectiveness; its interdependencies with other resources; and its role in the future economy.

Given this broad canvas, we were conscious of the need to maintain a sense of thematic coherence—an overarching theme being the systemic nature of human capital and its centrality to other organizational resources. To achieve our goals required a multidisciplinary approach; contributing authors, over forty in total, comprise experts from a diverse range of disciplines including philosophy, law, economics, sociology, strategy, international business, corporate governance, cultural studies, entrepreneurship, organizational behavior, human resource management, industrial relations, environmental psychology, accounting, and information systems.

STRUCTURE OF THE *HANDBOOK*

We divided the *Handbook* into five parts, each designed to offer a different perspective. Part I, 'The Nature of Human Capital', opens the work with a series of chapters probing the concept of human capital, its conceptual underpinnings, and its links to other forms of capital. Individual chapters explore the economic role of human capital in the firm (a topic further developed in Part II), the links between human and social capital, human capital and cultural intelligence, cognitive human capital, and the nature of human capital and its relationship with capital more broadly.

Part II, 'Human Capital and the Firm', focuses on the role of human capital in theories of the firm. Individual chapters review the role of human capital from a transaction cost perspective, an agency perspective, the resource-based view of the firm, in relation to theories of entrepreneurship and the firm, and from a knowledge-based perspective.

Part III, 'Human Capital and Organizational Effectiveness', continues the theme of human capital in the firm but shifts the focus to human capital and organizational effectiveness. Topics addressed in the five chapters include the role of strategic HR management, trends in human capital procurement, strategic alignment of people with organizations' needs, appropriating value from human capital, and developments in approaches to human capital accounting and measurement.

Part IV, 'Organizational Implications of Human Capital Interdependencies', investigates the nature of interdependencies between human capital and other resources and their implications for organizational effectiveness. Chapters explore interdependencies between people, people and their physical work environments, people and information systems, human and structural capital, and the implications of human capital as a distributed and dynamic concept for human capital development and organizational performance.

Part V, 'Human Capital in the Future Economy', focuses on the dynamic interplay between human capital and its environment in the context of the future economy. Topics discussed include the different types of human capital expected to be in demand in the twenty-first-century business enterprise, how investigating human capital mobility helps us to bring human capital theory closer into the firm, how different regions and nations are developing human capital policies and capabilities, lessons learnt from the recent history of human capital development in Asian countries, and the future of human capital from an employment relations perspective.

HUMAN CAPITAL IN THE KNOWLEDGE ECONOMY

Many of our authors point to the explosion of interest in human capital as an academic topic. A connection with the knowledge economy is suggested along with a way of defining it as an economy in which human capital is of qualitatively higher importance. But Becker's relating this to education raises questions, for instance, about educational policy; and we have touched on some already. His intuition that education is a determinant of economic growth, mediated by rising human capital, makes us wonder how education becomes economically useful at the national level. Is on-the-job training more important than general education? Is the hypothesis that education increases productivity actually valid (Berg, 2003)? Is education so intimately tied up with social and organizational capital that it simply reinforces prevailing social, institutional, and organizational structures? Does it exacerbate the theory–practice divide and distort productivity (Raelin, 2007)?

Our contributors probe these questions by contrasting static or 'stock' notions of capital against 'flow' or 'process' notions, and by considering the relationships between human capital and the other types of capital—financial, social, organizational, intellectual, and so on. In the background is an assumption that the explosion of interest is more than a fad and that it reflects qualitative changes in the global economy—typically seen as a sea change from tangible forms of capital to intangible forms. To clarify this, Reich's analysis and his distinction between high-value and high-volume economies are often cited; high-value production processes are information-intensive, hugely impacted by the Internet, and call for education in symbolic analysis (Reich, 1992). One can also point to the demands of an increasingly technologically penetrated workplace wherein all use increasingly complex tools. The interfaces between work and worker are increasingly data-intensive and symbolic, fly-by-wire rather than the hands-on feel of the materials or issues. There are attendant changes in the economic landscape as manufacturing moves from the US and Europe to India, China, and elsewhere (see Chapter 3), while we focus on design and innovation. How does a human capital approach provide additional insights?

We distinguish between the capital in general necessary for an economy to expand, and the need for human capital as a specific type of capital. The first is widely accepted; the second is central to this volume's contributions. An explanation obviously depends on how the distinction between human and other types of capital is made. The 'human capital as an individual's knowledge and skills' definition turns on the distinction between tangible and intangible assets. Thus some of our authors are interested in measuring intangible capital directly, the implication being that both can then be brought into the same analytic framework and managed according to the same principles of efficiency and maximization (for example, Blair and Kramar, Murthy and Guthrie). Others are interested in the implications for the theory of the firm or organization where the tangible and intangible interact to generate economic value. The managerial implication here is that their synthesis brings both into the same economic framework as a matter of practice—measurable in its outcomes—rather than as a matter of analysis—measurable as inputs.

At the same time, noting 'the explosion', there is some danger of falling into the conceit that economic activity prior to modern times did not require much human capital. Aside from natural modesty, the history of technology transfer, both industrial and military, shows this is untrue (Pacey, 1990). Likewise, an appreciation of the complexity of trade, production, and the financial instruments during the height of the Arab Empire shows how pre-European management was highly sophisticated (Chaudhuri, 1985). Knowledge has always been crucial to making good use of resources, and in this respect Penrose did not tell managers anything they did not already know.

But if we see qualitative rather than quantitative changes in the human capital being applied today we can also see the knowledge economy as qualitatively different. There is an undercurrent of this in many of our volume's chapters and, as noted earlier, we can address it directly by contrasting the concepts of capital in neoclassical theory with those proposed by some 'Austrian' economists, notably Lachmann. In the neoclassical framework, where everything has a price, the challenge is to bring what people know into the same market-based analysis as the other factors of production. This obviously hinges on use-value. Being measured by the same standard the human capital imagined is presumed homogeneous. Lachmann proposes something very different, focusing on the variety of resources that, when synthesized, produce economic value (Lachmann, 1977; Mathews, 2010). Here human capital is more about how to structure the synthesis than a stock or factor of production that is drawn into—and either consumed or regenerated—in the production process. In Lachmann's reading the knowledge economy is marked by an explosion in resource heterogeneity and in the corresponding managerial task of synthesis. Today's world is qualitatively more complex and less certain.

This argument's origin lies in Menger's intuition that progress should be framed in qualitative terms—better and more diverse products that more closely matched people's heterogeneous needs and so led to more appropriate pricing and resource allocations—rather than in the homogenizing neoclassical quantitative terms of GDP growth (Vaughn, 1994). His intuition was rephrased in Böhm-Bawerk's idea that progress and economic value were associated with increasing 'roundaboutness' in the production process. The knowledge age, then, is one in which complex production processes become paramount—and the human capital necessary to manage them becomes increasingly significant, both economically and theoretically. While Adam Smith stressed the division of labor and the crucial learning and task-oriented human capital to which it led, he paid little attention to the knowledge required for task integration and coordination. This knowledge is orthogonal to and qualitatively different from task-oriented knowledge. Managing is not producing. No question, qualitative changes in specialization, work measurement, and production communications since the 1950s have transformed the way we go about economic coordination. By way of illustration we might consider the cost and value differences between a low-tech approach to dealing with terrorists holed-up in Waziristan, massing a fully trained army and covering every inch of a territory versus a high-tech satellite intelligence-based remotely piloted Predator strike—the latter being hugely complex and management-intensive. It is brute force versus precision, the knowledge economy rewarding the second.

A knowledge economy distinguished by highly roundabout methods of production and highly customized goods and services exploits today's qualitatively different management tools—high-speed communications, data gathering and mining, supply chain management, customer relationship management, and so on. As Grant has often reminded us, competitive advantage is about integration, and there seems no question that there have been qualitative changes in our integrating practices and capacity over the last century, beginning with the telegraph (Grant, 1997). There is some irony here for Austrian economists, since the idea of a highly heterogeneous economy coordinated by increasingly powerful centralized management practices and technologies (and the human capital they imply) stands against the anti-centralizing impulses of Hayek and von Mises, whose approach to managing heterogeneity was to turn to the coordinating capacity of the market. A human capital-based approach to theorizing the knowledge economy could be powerful. It lets us probe the differences between the human capital that characterizes efficient markets and that which characterizes productive organizations, helping move us towards the human-capital-based theory of the firm sought explicitly by authors such as Coff, Foss, von Krogh and Wallin, Lewin, Kraaijenbrink and Loasby—but implicit in every chapter.

CONCLUSION

Our volume shows that human capital research and theory is in a fluid state. From one side it is supported by its economic roots; from the other by its practical nature. From economics we take human capital as a factor of production and the impulse to measure and value it. From practice we take the notion of human capital as the result of learning, whether in class, in training schemes, or by doing, whether individually or collectively. The economic approach seeks a general theory that defines human capital in abstract terms, and focuses on its interplay with less controversial factors of production. The practice-based approach emphasizes the situatedness and contingencies of bringing human capital into play. The economic angle looks to the managerially and theoretically significant differences between human capital as a factor of production and those factors or resources normally considered in microeconomic theory. It hews to maximization. The practical approach looks at human capital as an indicator of the dynamism of our socioeconomic situation, and the complexities of resolving the diversity of human goals and purposes.

Some will see human capital theory on the cusp between modernism and postmodernism. If so, it can serve as critical theory and engage many important projects. First, it is an attempt to move beyond the astringent rational maximizing individual on which much neoclassical analysis is based. The very notion of human capital presumes individuals who differ in what they know as well as in their utilities. It follows that non-market interactions with others come to the fore as individuals form relationships with others to compensate for the particularities of their knowledge endowment. All knowledge becomes firm- or situation-specific in Williamson's sense (Williamson, 1985). Management is extended from the modernist notion of rational goal-setting and performance measurement to include managing the interindividual relationships—and the infrastructure, such as IT, culture, and trust, that mediates these.

Second, human capital theorizing presumes individuals who learn. As mentioned earlier, learning is one of the strongest themes in our volume. But it remains a challenge to theorize. In business studies we have generally trailed other disciplines, such as developmental psychology or educational theory, in this area. The challenge to identify and measure human capital can move us beyond naïve learning models in which experience or communications lead to knowledge in an unproblematic way, onwards to the sounder empirically testable models on which these other disciplines are working.

Third, while our volume generally reinforces the Penrosian point that the value of resources is always dependent on knowledge, individual or managerial, human capital opens up new ways of thinking about technology and its social and economic impact. Referring to our time as the Information or Knowledge Age is often a trope to hide the more pressing evidence of how the ways we do things (our technologies) are changing our circumstances. The need for us to reshape our intellectual assumptions, from markets made as perfect as possible to tightly bounded finite systems, means we have to begin to inventory those systems and their processes of interaction. To address these challenges we need concepts and theories that more accurately reflect the systemic role of human capital in contemporary organizations.

CHAPTER SUMMARIES

Chapter 1

Part I's agenda is the definition of human capital. Margaret Blair's chapter opens by identifying two principal reasons for looking into this. Defining human capital broadly as the 'skills, knowledge and capabilities of the workforce', she argues, first, that these are critical inputs to production. Second, that resources expended on increasing them are investments like more conventional investments in resources, facilities, and equipment. While a person's possessing 'skills and knowledge' is an old idea, she argues that the recent history of human capital is its rehabilitation as an additional variable to help explain economic growth not otherwise explained by conventional macroeconomic analysis. Yet this approach is controversial. Many have objected to its characterization of people and how and why they act, seeming to deny our humanity. It also glosses the mechanisms connecting education and training to productivity. She reports that despite forty years of objections human capital has become central to macroeconomics, labor economics, growth theory, trade theory, development economics, the economics of education, the theory of the firm, human resource management, and strategy theory—a very significant impact.

Blair takes up two other analyses: (*a*) whether human capital is analogous to capital as economists understand it, and (*b*) how to relate human capital to other forms of capital. From an economic point of view capital comes into existence when, first, previous production is saved rather than consumed and, second, it contributes to later production. One difficulty is that human capital, unlike other forms of capital, cannot be separated from the workers who acquire it. It is inalienable and untradable. Ownership is problematic—is it the property of the worker who develops it or the investor who paid for its production? These differences between human capital and other forms of capital suggest differences in its management as well as its place in our theories. Some relations between these forms of capital have been explored via intangibles—goodwill, customer loyalty, trademarks, and so on. Other forms of business capital have also been considered—reputational, intellectual, organizational, social, and so on. Blair points out that these are often trickier, and perishable, requiring maintenance that tangible assets may not.

She goes on to consider the associated questions of measuring intangibles, noting four accounting criteria typically used to justify a resource's economic asset status: (*a*) sufficiently well defined to be distinguishable from other assets and so tradable, (*b*) subject to the firm's control, (*c*) valuable, the basis for predictable returns, and (*d*) sufficiently defined to measure if its value has been impaired. But given human capital's inalienability it cannot be traded, suggesting a conflict between these criteria and the core notions of capital. Nonetheless, many think measuring human capital in terms of educational attainment or the costs of training useful, even while raising questions about future value. 'Book to market' makes it possible to use the market's valuations. But these methods often work better in aggregate than in the particular—even though that is where value is actually created. Blair returns to Becker's distinction between general and firm-specific human capital. She analyzes the tension between employees and investors that emerges from such asset-specificity, giving rise to the 'hold up' problem and the challenges of bringing human capital into a theory of the firm. She concludes on the public policy issues around the creation, distribution, and control of human capital when firm-controlled on-the-job training is so material to its production.

Chapter 2

Janine Nahapiet's chapter begins by suggesting one must define human capital from a social perspective. Its value inevitably depends on a wide range of social factors and relationships. The focus should be on the relationship between human (individual) capital and social capital, and their impact on each other's development. She examines the concept of capital, drawing initially on the economics literature. Along with many of our authors she concludes that even though human capital fails to meet the criteria for capital evident in that literature, the concept's heuristic value has made it popular nonetheless. She quotes Schultz's telling point—that there is nothing in the concept of human capital contrary to the idea that it exists for the advantage of people, and by investing in themselves people enhance their choices and welfare. She notes that human capital's failure to meet the conceptual conditions of capital theory can be interpreted as a critical insertion of human values into the discussion. Leveraging from the 'Austrian' economists she urges the analysis from static concepts and to a more dynamic interactive frame.

Like many of our authors Nahapiet revisits the evolution of human capital analysis but with her own points in mind. She notes the OECD's influential shift from defining human capital as an individual's economically relevant knowledge and skills to one in which the knowledge and skills are related to an individual's overall social and personal wellbeing, extending beyond their economic rewards. This need to pay attention to this broader context is supported by other research into on-the-job training and its impact. Then, leveraging from Swedberg and Granovetter's economic sociology, she argues that economic activity is a form of social action, embedded in a socially constructed institutionalized context. It follows that the nature and value of human capital is shaped by this context, positing a type of contingency or historicism at human capital's core.

Nahapiet follows with an analysis of the social capital literature, arguing its core proposition is that 'social ties constitute a valuable resource for the conduct of social affairs, enabling individuals and social groupings to achieve outcomes they could not otherwise achieve'. The research divides into a program investigating networks and another about 'communities'. The first focuses on access and resource mobilization, the second on shared norms and cooperation. Social capital includes both, giving it a multidimensional nature. The argument is that social and human capitals are interrelated and interdependent. She discusses the literature that looks, first, at the determining effect of social capital on human capital, second at the determining effect of human capital on social capital. She argues that 'what is needed now is a clearer articulation of the ways in which human and social capital may be linked'. Citing the Austrian approach and the work of Lewin (in this volume), as well as Bourdieu's argument that the various forms of social capital can be transformed into each other, Nahapiet suggests a program of research into the various mechanisms by which both human and social capitals grow, converge, synthesize, and change. Each exhibits characteristics of (*a*) fungibility and convertibility, (*b*) substitutability, (*c*) complementarity, (*d*) co-evolution, and (*e*) interaction. This dynamic typology points to a rich and novel theory of the firm as the human/social context in which these various capital transformations take place.

Chapter 3

Kok-Yee Ng, Mei Lang Tan, and Soon Ang's chapter likewise concentrates on the firm as the context of human capital development and application, though their focus is on global firms. Their analysis reaches back into the urban sociology of Gouldner and Merton and adopts their classic distinction between 'locals' and 'cosmopolitans', the latter having several languages and travel experience to add to their human capital. Cosmopolitan human capital, they argue, is essential for firms competing in the globalized economy. Their intent is to understand how such human capital is developed. In a neat move they appropriate much of the human capital literature's thinking about the impact of parent attitudes, learning habits, and education on their children's educational development. They reposition the corporation as a form of intellectual parent, defined as the custodian or context of the relevant 'global cultural capital' and able to foster cosmopolitan human capital.

Taking off from Kanter's argument that travel alone does not make cosmopolitans, their analysis looks beyond postings in multiple countries to consider each individual's 'intercultural capabilities'. These imply a different kind of personal intelligence—the cultural intelligence (CQ) proposed by Bourdieu and Passeron— that parallels IQ and EQ (emotional intelligence). They draw on Sternberg and Detterman to argue that CQ's dimensions are: (*a*) metacognitive intelligence about the awareness and control of cognitions used to acquire and understand information, (*b*) cognitive intelligence about knowledge and knowledge structures, (*c*) motivational intelligence as the energy behind the engagement of intelligence, and (*d*) behavioral intelligence focused on individual capabilities at the action level. They report studies of the relationship between CQ and cultural adaptation and performance, expatriate effectiveness, interpersonal trust, team acceptance, and joint profits in intercultural negotiation dyads.

While the authors note that these effects are well known, they argue that little is known about how cosmopolitan human capital is developed. They turn to the international business literature to contrast different corporations' attitudes towards multicultural contexts. They note the firm's culture balances global integration and local responsiveness and the distinctions between 'parochial' and 'diffused' mindsets. They consider the literature on organizational routines to sketch out those that might increase CQ by (*a*) managing human capital flow globally, (*b*) developing intercultural talent, and (*c*) rewarding a global mindset. They conclude with a discussion of a program to test these notions empirically.

Chapter 4

Brett Rhymer, Michael Hitt, and Mario Schijven's chapter also focuses on managerial, operative, and corporate cognition. They argue that 'the transformation of knowledge into practice is mediated by the cognition of the firm's human capital'. They posit a mutually constituting reciprocal relationship between knowledge and behavior, the exchange being governed by cognition. They argue that managers are able to influence the firm's cognitive states even when these are path-dependent and contextualized. Managers set the strategic balance between 'learning' and 'using', between 'exploration' and 'exploitation', creating effective alignment between the environment and internal activity systems through adjustments to cognition. The authors cite empirical research showing a strong relationship between human capital, as measured by education and experience, and firm performance. They also presume that human capital can arise at both individual and collective levels, enabling them to explore the relationship between individual and collective cognition and the value of the firm's human capital. They surface the various difficulties confronting those managing the firm's knowledge, for it is dispersed and subject to market failure and agency problems.

They go on to argue that the 1960s concern with managerial behavior and decision-making marked by behavioral analysis was displaced by a more abstract focus on transaction cost economics, resource dependency theory, and population ecology. The pendulum has now swung back to the individual and to the microfoundations of organizational performance. The knowledge-based analyses of Kogut and Zander and Orlikowski are part of this trend, drawing cognition to the foreground. Likewise, the economy has shifted towards knowledge-intensive activity with the services sector now dominant.

The chapter continues with a model of the extraction of human capital value. The value of the firm's knowledge and cognitive capabilities is initially embedded and must be extracted by combining them with other resources. While these knowledge and cognitive resources can be regarded either as a stock or as embedded practices and routines, their value must be brought out through the cognitive activity of decision-making, communication, and action. This body of knowledge is dynamic, impelled by individual and collective learning. The result is path-dependent, for each period's knowledge builds on the previous period's knowledge. The strategic challenge is to find the 'sweet spot' that aligns the external demands on the organization with the activity systems its cognitions underpin. The means are either 'use' moderators that determine the extent to which knowledge is translated into cognition and behavior, or 'learning' moderators that determine the extent to which knowledge is reinforced or changed. The use moderators can be separated into 'recall' processes that bring stored knowledge into cognition, and 'enactment' processes that induce behavior from a cognitive state. The model integrates knowledge and practice, its core being the cognitions that broker, filter, and guide the 'generative dance' leading to performance outcomes.

Chapter 5

Peter Lewin's chapter reflects his interest in the 'Austrian' school of economics formulated by Menger, Böhm-Bawerk, Hayek, Lachmann, and others. Much of the contrast between the Austrian and neoclassical approaches revolves around their different notions of capital. Broadly speaking, Lewin claims that human capital cannot be treated adequately within the neoclassical tradition, while it fits naturally into the Austrian tradition. Lewin's argument proceeds first from the commitment (*a*) to define all resources as forms of capital based on the value-add of their application; that is, on knowledge of how to apply them. Capital is essentially embodied knowledge, whether in tools, symbols, or practices. Applying it entails combining it with other forms. Since the outcomes are subject to uncertainty, the values on which managers plan and act are expectations rather than determined facts. Resource-combining projects inevitably fail to meet their planned objectives, so open up previously unseen entrepreneurial opportunities. Thus (*b*) the theoretical task is to understand how resource combinations should be managed under conditions of uncertainty. Additionally Lewin argues that the defining difference between physical and human capital is that while the first can be traded, the second is inalienable. This distinction is merely one aspect of a more complex structuring of the socio-economy—one marked by heterogeneity of knowledge and thus of all forms of capital. An article of faith for 'Austrians' is that economic progress follows the increasing complexity of this structure, an increasing division of labor and knowledge, and a corresponding increasing heterogeneity of economically relevant capital. Lewin concludes that modularization is management's main tool to deal with this complexity.

Along with most of the economists who have adopted Austrian thinking, Lewin argues that absent Knightian uncertainty—the impossibility of making certain forecasts—there would be no economy as we understand it, no opportunity for entrepreneurship, rents, or profits. A Knightian world is explicitly heterogeneous, for there are no overarching insights into its fundamental nature such as scientific laws assert about the natural universe. There is no coherent or universal market that sets the price of everything. Resources must always be understood as specific to a particular use, tied to their application. Lewin quotes Lachmann's observation that something is a capital good not because of its physical form, but because of its economic function. Thus every capital good has an unknowable set of possible attributes and applications. It waits to be transformed into added value by some entrepreneur's judgment and expectations. Thus entrepreneurs lie at the center of the economic system, activating it, for there is no market that alone does that. 'The market' is no more than a term of art to describe the welter of heterogeneous processes arising as entrepreneurs pit their judgments against each other.

Lewin goes on to argue that capital goods embody our knowledge of their value, not simply about how to make them. The uncertainties here create the disjunction between cost and value that drives economic growth. A good hammer embodies subtle knowledge and skills, yet allows a vast range of applications that vary in their economic consequences. Some tools embody more knowledge than others—Lewin compares hammers and microscopes. This leads to realizing that capital is social, embodying the knowledge of many people. At the same time the analysis becomes dynamic, for situations change, and knowledge, such as embodied in tools, becomes obsolete. Who needs to know PC-DOS? Ultimately, capital is about structuring relationships between actors, knowledge, and entrepreneurial and social processes that are ever-changing across space and through time. In all, progress is marked by increasing complexity and heterogeneity.

As for many of our authors, the idea that the individual's human capital is inalienable leads Lewin to a discussion of hold-up and agency issues. He argues that the heart of the management dilemma lies in providing knowledgeable employees with decision rights optimal to the firm's performance—and we do not yet know how this might be done. Human capital management is thus differentiated from the management of other forms of capital by the agency problem, but the penetration of knowledge into all aspects of capital structure hugely increases its scope and significance. Lewin's answer is modularization. That knowledge and situations are heterogeneous opens up the possibility of finding some sympathy between the contextualized task, resources, and social boundaries—so modularizing economic activity. Modules, he suggests, are ideally self-defining and self-contained substructures whose inner workings are hidden from managers above. Lewin argues that this is what organizational design is about, bringing Hayek's ideas about the 'division of knowledge' together with Smith's ideas about the 'division of labor'.

Chapter 6

Part II's agenda is the relationship between human capital and the theory of the firm. There are, of course, several theories current in the literature today. Nicolai Foss's chapter focuses on the transactions cost view spearheaded by Williamson, a recent Nobel winner for this work, but also takes note of the property-rights approach of Grossman and Hart. Foss begins by defining human capital as 'the stock of valued skills, knowledge, insights, etc. controlled by an individual, the attributes of the individual that are valuable in an economic context'.

Theorists of the firm are not only concerned with defining firms by, for instance, contrasting them with markets or explaining their existence. They are also concerned with alternative forms of organizational governance—in the case of human capital, understanding whether it is most efficiently sourced through market transactions, employment relations, voluntary organizations, or households. Foss claims that transaction cost economics (TCE) has provided 'the first and still most comprehensive treatment of the organizational ramifications of human capital in economics'. Yet it is 'not at the same level of detail as the human capital literature'—'It does not tell Mrs Jones what to do on Monday morning'. Both the TCE and property-rights approaches 'provide a rather abstract understanding of the efficient matching of transactions and governance structures or property rights allocations'.

Underpinning TCE is Coase's intuition that if transactions were costless their mode of governance would be irrelevant. Types of organization should be evaluated by their relative costs. Williamson argues that a special category of cost arises because the employment relationship is marked by bounded rationality and opportunism. These are multitransactional, marked by frequency and asset specificity. So he sees six reasons why assets may be difficult to deploy: (*a*) they are attached to a brand, (*b*) the need to act quickly (temporal specificity), (*c*) market size (dedicated assets), (*d*) localization (spatial specificity), (*e*) physical characteristics, and (*f*) specialized knowledge (human capital specificity). Along the lines of our previous chapters, Williamson uses these terms to define the socioeconomic context of a transaction. Foss writes that asset specificity 'opens the door to opportunism'—a restatement of the hold-up and agency issues noted earlier. The implications of the TCE approach are that transactions involving highly specific assets should be internalized within the firm and not conducted across a market. Given that human capital is inalienable, it is especially specific in this respect.

Coase saw the employment relation as the essence of the firm. In the presence of uncertainty contingencies are costly to anticipate, and rather than renegotiate each one, firms make employment contracts. Coase defined these as arrangements under which the employee, for a specific remuneration, agrees to obey the directions of an entrepreneur within certain limits. The contract limits the entrepreneur's powers. Foss likens this view to Simon's notion of the employee's 'zone of acceptance', redefining managerial authority as the decision rights purchased through the employment contract. He concludes that the arrangement has little to do with knowledge asymmetry or human capital differences.

Foss argues that Williamson goes well beyond the Coase–Simon analysis. While they treat human capabilities as generic, Williamson pays attention to the heterogeneity of human capital and the problems this raises. His lever is that as the division of labor advances, so the worker's knowledge becomes increasingly specific and hold-up and agency issues intrude into the employment relation. Williamson sees four modes of labor contract: (*a*) sequential spot contracts—contract now for prescribed performance later, (*b*) contingent claims contracts—contract now for one of several prescribed performances, to be chosen later, (*c*) long-term contracting—determine performance later, and (*d*) establishing an authority relation alone—or 'fiat'. His concern differs from that of Lewin and the Austrian economists who see increasing complexity and a 'deepening' of human capital; rather, it is the capital's increasing specificity and the governance problems generated, the 'separability of work relations' and the attendant difficulty of measuring employee performance. The framework leads to an in-depth analysis of governance under conditions of uncertainty and opportunism, and Foss reports and summarizes extensive empirical research that confirms its power and relevance to management.

Foss then turns to the property-rights approach. This too stands on the incompleteness of the firm's contracts and deals with the need to allocate rights to residual assets; that is, those not allocated *ex ante* to employees or other agents. He notes that such controls determine the boundaries of the firm as a bundle of jointly owned assets. Under uncertainty, control goes beyond the explicitly contractible to include subtleties of motivation, trust, and reputation. Foss notes Ghoshal and Moran's belief that employees perform in accordance with incentives and the opportunities offered, but also from their 'feelings for the entity'. Thus motivations are both extrinsic and intrinsic, and the firm is seen as a 'carrier of reputational capital'.

TCE is a novel theory of the firm that offers a place for human capital within it. Williamson's focus is on the connections between its specificity and its governance. As in Lewin's analysis, Foss shows that the human capital management insights the TCE offers turn on its inalienability and the particular governance challenges this raises. While the debates around the TCE are extensive and complex, its contributions are substantial. Foss urges theorists to pay it considerable attention.

Chapter 7

While Foss locates human capital within the transaction cost theory of the firm and shows how its heterogeneity gives rise to problems that drive the choice of governance mechanism, Spender's chapter locates human capital within principal–agent theory. He argues that the agency problem can be defined as a human capital difference between principal and agent. The value of doing this is that the principal–agent relationship then describes a key feature of firms—the same employment relationship that Coase regarded as defining for the firm. We can first explore how a human capital approach might illuminate this theory of the firm. But second, a critical analysis of agency problem theorizing might illuminate our notions of human capital. Spender's emphasis is less on human capital's heterogeneity, as either Foss or Lewin describe it, and more on the principal's decision-making when facing the agency problem. But unlike Foss's chapter, which presents TCE as a coherent body of work to which human capital's heterogeneity is essential, Spender's approach is more critical. He argues that principal–agent theory is actually far from coherent and that its shortcomings help us see that human capital must be conceived more widely, extended beyond the customary 'knowledge and skills' notion to include the agent's ability to respond creatively to the uncertainties of practice. He implies a previously underconsidered dimension of human capital: an ability to deal with the unanticipated that must be added to the accepted ability to deal with the anticipated.

Spender begins by questioning the relationship between Becker's macrolevel analysis of human capital as the output of the educational system and human capital as most of our authors see it, at the level of the firm. He moves on to surface some of the inconsistencies between the classic contributions of Jensen and Meckling, and Fama. He argues that Jensen and Meckling's analysis is essentially incoherent in that it offers no rigorous solution in the absence of the perfect markets in which the various benefits to managers and owners can be priced. The paradox is that such markets can exist only under conditions of certainty; that is, when Knightian uncertainty is absent. But under such conditions, principal and agent can negotiate a complete contract. Thus the conditions in which Jensen and Meckling's analysis 'works' are the conditions in which no agency problem can arise to demand their solution. Fama's analysis 'works' quite differently. While he too indicates that solutions are contingent on an institutional context—which, as we have seen, is the real mark of human capital theory—his context does not comprise perfect markets. On the contrary, Fama appeals to the available imperfect markets for financial capital and management talent, in ways that cannot be modeled rigorously.

Spender argues that this discussion illustrates the difference between (a) a theory—in the conventional philosophy of science sense of an apparatus for generating predictions (dependent variables) from discoverable facts (independent variables)—and (b) a social–economic 'framework' which indicates the actual context into which executive agency must be projected in order to achieve conceptual closure and reasoned action. This is the entrepreneurial act. Conversely, the distinction illustrates how, under conditions of Knightian uncertainty, the application of human capital to any action, social or economic, must call for the actor's agentic capability. This argument stands opposed, as in Knight's analysis, to an analysis based on risk, population statistics, and the actor's risk propensity. Spender continues reviewing Mitnick's parallel approach to the principal–agent relationship. This turns on the notion of 'organizational slack', presuming some of the firm's resources are in an agentic 'potential' category, yet to be applied, just as some aspects of human capital are not applied until people are fully 'stretched'. Mitnick frames the interplay of tangible and intangible resources as a contextual aspect that must be addressed by calling up the actor's agentic capability.

As soon as agentic capability comes into the analysis, new theories of the firm open up. Spender discusses two—one advanced by Foss in 1996, and another by White in 1991. Both turn on the notion that markets are extremely flexible—prices adjusting to supply, demand, technological change, product redesign, consumer taste, and so on. In contrast, most theories of organization, presuming certainty, prioritize stability and rigidity. Foss proposes that 'rather than conceptualizing firms as entities primarily kept together by transaction cost minimization, it might be better to view firms as entities whose primary role is to acquire, combine, utilize and upgrade knowledge'. This is the never-complete process that defines the firm's human capital as dynamic, focused on learning and responsiveness to the unanticipated. Spender argues that this shows the innovative power of differences of perception, interest, and thus human capital between principal and agent, allowing for flexibility and even the role reversals of real principal–agent relationships. The conclusion is that the inherent flexibility of the principal–agent relationship under Knightian uncertainty can be contained only by agentic appeals—like Fama's—to the institutional apparatus that defines its context.

Chapter 8

The previous chapters in Part II probed the nature of human capital by locating it within a specific theory of the firm–transaction cost (Chapter 6) and principal–agent (Chapter 7). Jeroen Kraaijenbrink's chapter examines how human capital relates to the resource-based view of the firm (RBV). The RBV claims to explain sustained competitive advantage. Kraaijenbrink takes a critical stance and poses three questions that this kind of theory of the firm should be able to address. (*a*) What are the assets that claim to explain the firm's sustained competitive advantage? (*b*) What is their value? (*c*) How might rents be generated and sustained?

But first he deals critically with the RBV's evident weaknesses—especially its vague notions of resource and value. Most RBV authors include the employees' human capital, and sometimes that of suppliers, customers, and others, as among the resources to be managed with a view to extracting sustainable rents. Wernerfelt argued that 'anything which could be thought of as a strength or weakness of a given firm' would be an RBV-relevant resource. Likewise, Barney argued that the relevant resources would comprise 'all assets, capabilities, organizational processes, firm attributes, information, knowledge, etc. controlled by a firm'.

This seems fine, as far as it goes. But is anything excluded? Kraaijenbrink notes there is no analysis of how human capital might be differentiated from other types of resource, for the RBV treats all resources as conceptually equivalent. This contrasts with the view advanced by many of our authors, such as Lewin or Foss, who argue that it is precisely human capital's inalienability that leads to the special problems around managing it that our theorizing must address. Using human capital as a hammer, Kraaijenbrink chips away at the RBV's tautological notion of resource. He points out that an individual's human capital must often be shared with other entities, such as the family, and be applied under specific legal and institutional arrangements that limit the firm's usage—a reminder of Coase's theory of social cost. The RBV presumes full unproblematic title to the relevant resources.

Kraaijenbrink then turns to the RBV's notion of value—a theme running throughout the human capital discussion. While most of our authors see the value of distinguishing between input costs and output returns, the RBV is in special difficulties because of the tautology around identifying rent-earning resources by their ability to produce rents. In contrast, many of our authors argue that resources of all types only reveal their value when combined with other resources—which lifts the analysis from the component level to a project or a firm level. The RBV is dismissive of collective capabilities, and of the distinction between human and group or social capital, considering them conceptually identical to individual capabilities—just at another level of analysis.

Kraaijenbrink then focuses on his three questions and the way human capital might help address them. First, regarding identifying the assets, he cites literature that shifts attention from definitions of resources, such as those of Wernerfelt and Barney above, that are hopelessly tautological, and onto the specification of property rights, defining their economic nature and significance. He notes the importance of the knowledge and skills which individuals are able to draw in from outside the firm, problematizing the boundary around the firm as a bundle of resources. This would include intra-individual resources, such as the individual's own work relations, and the inter-individual resources drawn from their social network—their personally controlled social capital. He notes Bowman and Swart's typology of separable, embodied, and embedded capital.

Second, regarding valuing the assets, Kraaijenbrink deals with the literature that contrasts internal and external valuation. But he also argues that a resource's value ultimately depends on the context and infrastructure around its application. He observes how Barney's 1991 RBV formulation—VRIN, where N denoted non-substitutable—was replaced in 2002 by his VRIO formulation, where O denoted the organizational context into which the resource must be brought before value could be extracted. He reads this as an admission of failure to theorize value successfully as deriving from the resources alone. He also reminds us that some of the firm's resources lie beyond its zone of control. Finally, on the generation and appropriation of rents, Kraaijenbrink points out that it fails to recognize the human capital that enables people to generate rents with their creativity. Clearly his attempt to surface additional dimensions or features of human capital by locating it within the RBV discourse does not produce very much. But his chapter shows that the problem is less with his analysis than with the RBV itself, for it evidently lacks the power and integrity to illuminate human capital as a resource beyond the tautology on which all its resource definitions stand. Compared with the transactions cost and principal–agent approaches—which yield important insights into the nature of human capital—the RBV's weaknesses are such that this cannot happen.

Chapter 9

Brian's Loasby's chapter adopts the methodology of the previous chapters—seeing how human capital might be theorized in the context of a specific theory of the firm. But his focus is on the entrepreneurship literature—which implies rather than offers an articulate theory of the firm. As a respected contributor to our field he lays down several radical points. First, neoclassical theories have neither a place nor a need for an entrepreneurial theory of the firm—or a theory of the entrepreneurial firm. Neoclassical theory defines the firm as determined by external (market) forces—so is often labeled a theory of markets rather than of firms. A firm's modes of governance are irrelevant. Economic theory is not overly interested in firms, their internal arrangements, or even why they exist. Insofar as individuals are present in the analysis, standard explanations 'all rely on a reallocation of decision rights to resolve some conflict of incentives, and when this has been achieved everyone acts independently'. He observes that 'only Williamson's analysis, which postulates a complementary relationship between parties dependent on each other, envisages the solution as a hierarchy in which one person is partially controlled by another to the benefit of both'. But Williamson has yet to explain how this works. *Inter alia* it implies firms are little more than 'devices for validating the dominance of markets while ignoring the methods and costs of organizing such markets'.

Having thrown down the gauntlet Loasby reviews the entrepreneurial literature, suggesting entrepreneurship, human capital, and the theory of the firm form 'a natural grouping'. His point of departure is Knight's distinction between certainty, risk, and uncertainty. Under conditions of certainty decision-making is a purely logical matter, the conclusion fully determined by the data, and one decision-maker cannot be distinguished from another. The relevant human capital is shared and non-distinctive and is no more than the ability to think logically. Education might enhance this ability but cannot produce it. When there is a range of possible future values, each with a known probability of occurrence, the decision cannot be determined without knowing the decision-maker's attitude towards risk. The decision-maker's risk profile is her/his distinctive human capital. But under Knightian uncertainty neither the range of values nor their probability are known. The decision-making turns on conjectured possibilities, subjective expectations. It requires knowledge of both the risk preferences and the process by which expectations are arrived at. Loasby observes that the standard economic analysis bypasses this to presume the decision-maker is using the 'correct' probabilistic model of the economy—that known to the analyst. It follows that three major economic phenomena cannot be explained without the concept of uncertainty: profit, entrepreneurship as its pursuit, and the incomplete contracts which characterize firms. Thus the standard microeconomic analysis is incapable of explaining these.

In the face of Knightian uncertainty the analyst must appeal to the decision-maker's imagination, especially evident in Shackle's theory. But since it cannot be determined in the same way as reasoning, the challenge is to know how it might be shaped or directed. There must be both a source of intentionality and a mechanism for its action. Loasby turns to evolution and self-organization, citing Simon's speculations on 'decomposability' that parallel Lewin's notions of 'modularization'. Loasby concludes self-organization influenced by human ideas and intentionality grounds human capital. Crucial is the distinction between homogeneity and heterogeneity. Drawing on Marshall, Knight, and Barnard, Loasby argues intelligence and knowledge hinge on differences and their perception. Uncertainty-based economics is related because organization is then the context in which heterogeneities are synthesized into the novelties that drive economic growth.

The human capital needed to engage these processes implies cognitive capabilities that go well beyond those needed for rational choice. Loasby refers to Hayek's speculations about the neurological capabilities that make classification our deepest mode of consciousness. It follows that 'the qualities we attribute to experienced objects are strictly speaking not properties of that object at all, but a set of relations by which our brain classifies them'. Humanly constructed 'sensory order' is epistemologically distinct from the 'physical order' that characterizes the natural world—such as the arrangement of the planets. The tension between the two orders often leads to the interpretive breakdowns that, by presenting us with uncertainty and calling forth our imagination, become progress's drivers. While the resulting paradigm shifts are familiar from Kuhn's work, Loasby reminds us that Adam Smith thought this way too. Smith was also interested in the quality or aesthetics of the constructed order, and education can prepare us to be aware of these characteristics—giving us a form of 'absorptive capacity' as a dimension of our human capital.

On this basis Loasby analyzes various approaches to entrepreneurship—Cantillon, Kirzner, Richardson, Lachmann, Casson, Harper, Schumpeter, and so on. He concludes that these authors have yet to pin down the interplay of the imaginative process and the experience of failure. He turns back to the firm as an apparatus through which one individual may shape the cognitive processes of another, in their extent and their timing. Thus Shackle observed that the firm is 'a means by which choice can be deferred until a later and better informed time'. Being able to carry knowledge through time and apply it later defines it as a form of capital—especially evident in Penrose's theory of the growth of the firm. New combinations are discovered by trial and error but then recomprehended as opening up new economic opportunities. Loasby notes Marshall's and Penrose's attention to the relevant knowledge that lies outside the firm, available through networking and other modes of communication. It follows these systems must be bounded—for the cognitive resources comprising the various people's human capital are limited. But these boundaries are of our own construction and so artificial. They are sensory and in tension with our experience. Loasby concludes that uncertainty is the founding notion that makes it possible to articulate a theory of economic activity that embraces a natural grouping of entrepreneurship, human capital, and an evolutionary theory of the firm.

Chapter 10

In the final chapter in Part II Georg von Krogh and Martin Wallin look at human capital in the context of the knowledge-based view of the firm. While personal notions of knowledge as human capital are axiomatic, they also recognize collective or community processes. But their interplay is a problem, and von Krogh and Wallin argue there has been little attention to the microfoundational aspects of aligning the interests of the various individuals involved. Their chapter proposes a relationship between the individual and the firm that takes divergent interests into account. Taking Nonaka's thinking as their starting point they argue that 'organizations create knowledge through individuals and groups who make available and amplify their knowledge and crystallize and connect this knowledge to the organization's knowledge assets'. The processes are voluntary, so interests and motivations are key. They note Gottschalg and Zollo's call for a theory of interest alignment. Employees are also members of groups beyond the organization, so relating their human capital to the organization requires consideration of external knowledge resources.

Von Krogh and Wallin review the history of human capital theory, paying special attention to Becker's distinction between general and specific capital. They note Mincer's attention to on-the-job training. They go on to consider the relation between the individual knowledge-based human capital and that of the firm. They leverage from Florin and Schultze's analysis to distinguish three types of human capital: firm-specific, industry-specific, and individual-specific. Their interplay depends on the individual's voluntary decisions about how to allocate their time. Clearly the tension where individuals invest in themselves rather than contributing to the firm can be seen as a zero-sum game. But von Krogh and Wallin also see it can be mutually beneficial. This sets up a two-by-two matrix: win–win, lose–lose, win–lose, and lose–win. The bulk of their chapter is taken up with a detailed discussion of how each of these possibilities arises and might be influenced by management. They point to the tension between the knowledge-based firm literature, which presumes that the role of the individual is to increase the firm's knowledge, and the human capital literature which presumes the firm, as a context of activity-based learning, focuses on increasing the individual's knowledge. They also criticize principal–agent theorizing for its implicitly zero-sum assumption and neglect of the synergistic win–win possibilities. Theorizing these requires moving from a rivalrous currency, such as money, to a non-rivalrous currency—with which human capital must be described and measured.

They conclude that three important results emerge from a democratic and cooperative approach to management: firm-level knowledge results only when individuals contribute beyond the terms specifiable in their employment contract, non-pecuniary rewards are essential, and the motivational aspects become those that define the firm. The complexity and multiplicity of the individuals' relations means the firm can be regarded as a repository or 'safe haven' for the knowledge gathered through these processes. It gains competitive advantage as (*a*) a context for learning-by-doing, (*b*) because it can use training to create knowledge more economically than markets can, and (*c*) it can be entrepreneurial in capturing opportunities for learning. The subtlety of the balance between the firm and the individual raises questions about their separability and the management of their interaction. This cannot be comprehended if performance is defined only in terms of a single stakeholder.

Chapter 11

Part III continues the theme of human capital in organizations, shifting focus to the links between human capital and organizational effectiveness. Peter Boxall's chapter opens this part of the *Handbook* with the premise that human capital in organizations is dependent on social capital and exists within clusters or configurations of human, social, technological, and other resources—a view reflected by several authors here.

Boxall's second premise is that a firm's particular configuration of human and social capital may help it build and sustain superior performance. Noting that such concepts verge on truisms and that (acknowledging Penrose) merely possessing resources is not enough, he emphasizes the importance of resource management. He proceeds to highlight three strategic human resource management problems: (1) why the management of human capital is inherently problematic; (2) why firms' investments in human capital vary across critical contexts within and outside their boundaries; and (3) how firms can obtain a sustained advantage through their management of human capital.

In relation to the first problem Boxall identifies the main issues as deriving from firms' dependence on the employment relationship, the attendant problems of gaining access to required levels of skilled labor, and motivating workers, once hired, to contribute fully—the last problem accentuated by the discretionary nature of human knowledge. These challenges are compounded by the need to continue to motivate workers over time. Motivation in turn requires trust, and in this context Boxall refers to Hyman's (1987) ironic comment that capitalism requires workers to be '*both* dependable *and* disposable'. Boxall notes that while levels of trust will vary according to the nature of the exchange, breaches of trust are the issue. In extreme cases loss of trust may demand radical solutions such as relocation or outsourcing.

In relation to the second problem Boxall identifies three moderating variables. First, firms' investments in human capital vary according to the different value to them of employee groups, from managers to contract staff. A second factor is the technological context: low knowledge-intensive industries such as textiles and footwear demand less investment than high knowledge-intensive sectors such as professional services. A third factor relates to the cost-based or skill-based nature of service industries—the former demanding less human capital investment than the latter.

The 'cutting edge' of current strategic HRM research, however, according to Boxall, is concerned with the third question: how firms can obtain a sustained competitive advantage through their management of human capital. Here he notes the importance of distinguishing between labor-cost advantages and labor-differentiation advantages. The key to sustained advantage according to Boxall is via the 'human resource advantage', which he claims is derived from more rather than less investment in people (see also Sean O'Riain's comments on 'lean versus learning' approaches to staffing and human capital development in Chapter 23). While indicating potential solutions, Boxall's approach is essentially analytic, his main concern being to highlight some major problems contemporary organizations face in managing human capital. His chapter sets the scene for succeeding chapters in this part, which continue our exploration of the human capital—performance equation.

Chapter 12

Monika Hamori, Rocio Bonet, and Peter Cappelli address the question of how modern firms obtain the human capital they need. They focus on how workforce recruitment and hiring practices have changed since approximately the late 1980s, as firms, driven by external forces to improve efficiency and increase flexibility, have responded by flattening hierarchies, downsizing, and making greater use of external labor markets.

Hamori and her co-authors identify four key features of these strategic shifts: (1) a decrease in the importance of internal talent development; (2) an increase in external hiring practices; (3) increased use of alternative work arrangements such as part-time, temporary, and contract work; and (4) decreasing loyalty of employees to employers.

In a wide-ranging and insightful survey of current trends the authors describe these strategic shifts and their human capital implications. For individuals the most important implication appears to be the shift in responsibility for their human capital development from the firm to themselves: careers have become dissociated from specific employers or particular jobs. From the firm's perspective we can see an increasing need to achieve a balance between workforce flexibility and workforce continuity, the former required to survive and the latter to compete long term. Clearly not all human capital is of equal value—reinforcing the importance for HR practitioners of adopting contingent rather than universalistic approaches to human capital management—as noted by Lepak and his co-authors in Chapter 13.

In their analyses of current recruitment practices Hamori and her co-authors identify two key trends: the increased use of executive search agencies, and the growing use of the Internet as a recruitment medium. They show how executive search agencies typically recruit from a small number of top-tier firms in any industry, one result being to restrict firms' access to a restricted human capital pool. On the other hand, as they point out, lower-tier firms are likely to be the beneficiaries of such human capital transfer. One might also speculate on the implications for transfer of firm-specific human capital from larger to smaller firms (see for example, Peter Sherer's comments in Chapter 22).

The results of increased use of the Internet appear clearer cut; both firms and workers have more options but as a result have to invest more effort in filtering and evaluating the relevant data. Once hired, employees are still open to the lure of new jobs online while employers are left with the problems of staff retention. All parties clearly benefit from internet recruitment but, as the authors note, availability and use of the technology appears to have shifted the balance of bargaining power from human capital buyers to human capital suppliers, and recruitment power from the firm to the market.

Hamori and her co-authors highlight three conclusions from their research: (1) a need for firms to improve their personnel selection skills and methods, (2) a need to acknowledge the shift in responsibility for career management from firms to individuals, and (3) a need for firms to recognize that employee attitudes and turnover are increasingly driven by forces outside their boundaries.

This chapter raises some interesting questions. Will firms accept the recruitment challenge or outsource it to the market? Will individuals shoulder their career management or will new intermediaries emerge to assist them—enhanced roles perhaps for staffing agencies and business schools? Will firms combat the growing dissociation between jobs and careers by offering ever stronger incentives to retain their key suppliers of human capital?

Chapter 13

David Lepak, Juani Swart, and Riki Takeuchi focus on the question of how alignment between human capital and organizational strategy influences individual and organizational performance. The starting point for their chapter is the HR architecture proposed by Lepak and Snell (1999), which suggests that firms' decisions to build or buy in human capital are influenced by its strategic value and uniqueness. Lepak and Snell identify four types of employment relationship, each aligned with a different value/uniqueness configuration and a correspondingly different human resource management system. The model suggests that optimizing fit between employees' differential human capital, their work contracts, and organizational HR practices should positively influence firm performance.

Lepak and his co-authors note that while subsequent research has broadly validated Lepak and Snell's HR architecture, its performance implications have not been fully explored. It is also static in nature—that is, aimed at achieving alignment at a point in time, whereas organizations need to maintain fit over time and in changing contexts. The authors proceed to address both these issues.

In relation to performance implications the authors review possible relationships between employment type and organizational performance, identifying a range of potential effects. For example, a differentiated approach to employee management may positively influence a flexibility outcome while negatively influencing a cost outcome. Their analyses illuminate the complex web of relationships between fit and performance, including the effects of differentially targeted HR systems.

At the individual level of analysis the authors investigate the potential influence of job security/career prospects and the target of an individual's commitment on performance. In a wide-ranging analysis they question whether conventional goals of maximizing workforce commitment are necessarily desirable, given that, while core workers and firm's targets of commitment are likely to be in alignment, the targets of commitment for those in job/productivity relationships are more likely to align with their future careers outside the firm. Other topics explored in relation to each of the four generic employment groups include the performance effects of 'overinvestment' and 'underinvestment' strategies (for example, low- or high-commitment HR practices), perceived organizational support, and employee perceptions of fairness and equity.

Turning to the question of dynamic fit, Lepak and his co-authors explore temporal, social, and contextual factors. They canvass issues such as how to anticipate and dynamically adjust management practices to cope with human capital growth and decay over time, how to use social capital to leverage human capital, and how to maximize individuals' different value-adding capacities, noting that some may contribute value directly whereas others may be 'value enablers' or 'connectors'.

In their conclusion the authors speculate as to whether a firm's core knowledge workers (those with highly valuable and unique knowledge) might reside outside its boundaries; that is, not be in an employment relationship and thus not directly manageable, and if so how this would affect the firm's strategic freedom. They further ask whether an employee's attachment to clients or to their professions may surpass their commitment to the firm, and if so, how such preferences may affect their interest alignment with the firm (see also Chapter 10). These are clearly significant questions for future research. Coff picks up the topic of commitment in the next chapter.

Chapter 14

Russell Coff's chapter describes two dilemmas for organizations seeking to derive a competitive advantage from human capital (defined as knowledge derived from education, training, and experience). First, the very qualities such as knowledge tacitness and causal ambiguity that make employees' human capital valuable, inimitable, and a source of competitive advantage to firms, make it difficult for firms to acquire, organize, retain, and motivate those employees. Secondly, employees will inevitably seek to maximize their share of the rents accruing from organizational use of their capital through wages, expenses, and benefits, thus only a portion of the rents may flow to shareholders. Strategies to reduce dependency on employees' idiosyncratic human capital through knowledge codification and routinization risk increasing imitability. Firms must therefore address these human capital dilemmas directly.

Coff proceeds to analyze issues associated with gaining a competitive advantage from human capital. Employee turnover is one issue. Individuals with general human capital are considered attractive to other firms, but individuals with the ability to acquire firm-specific knowledge may also prove attractive in the external labor market (see also Peter Sherer's comments on this topic in Chapter 22). Competitors tend to seek individuals with socially complex human capital derived from relationships with suppliers and customers, such as members of high-performing work teams. General, firm-specific, and socially complex forms of human capital are thus all prone to turnover, implying a need for firm strategies to retain and motivate staff at all levels.

Other factors constraining firms' ability to realize a competitive advantage through their human capital include information issues related to social complexity and causal ambiguity. Effects on team performance of individual suppliers of human capital in complex social structures may prove causally ambiguous, not only to external observers but to firms' managers. Other information dilemmas reviewed by Coff include effects of adverse selection, issues of moral hazard relating to shirking and motivation, and issues of bounded rationality. In relation to bounded rationality issues, Coff notes that today's managers may have less knowledge than those they oversee, resulting in serious organization and motivation dilemmas (see also Chapter 7).

Coff proposes several 'coping' strategies to address turnover and information dilemmas. Retention strategies may reduce turnover by improving job satisfaction and creating firm-specific knowledge and routines. Organizational design strategies may be used to address motivational and informational issues; shared governance mechanisms may be used to overcome problems of asymmetric information and uncertainty; organic organization structures may be used to encourage lateral and face-to-face communication, and 'strong' cultures used to help firms cope with both turnover threats and information problems. Informational strategies suggested by Coff include use of labor market data to address adverse selection, and multi-rater feedback to evaluate employee performance.

Coff comments that even if coping strategies are applied successfully and the firm thereby gains a competitive advantage, the full value derived from the advantage may not necessarily flow to shareholders, because managers and other employees of the firm will seek to maximize their share of the rents. This brings us to the second of the two human capital–firm performance dilemmas. Coff identifies employees' ability to maximize the benefits of their human capital contributions for themselves as a function of their bargaining power. Such power is reflected in individuals' ability to act collectively, their access to key information, their replacement cost to the firm, and their ability to move to another firm. On all these dimensions he argues that employees may be in a strong bargaining position relative to external shareholders.

To address this bargaining imbalance Coff suggests that firms need effective value appropriation strategies. Mechanisms identified by him include the use of strong incentives, such as participation in decision-making, plus investments in firm-specific skills, the provision of firm-specific compensation, and routinizing tasks. He notes, however, that governance mechanisms that grant external shareholders bargaining power in terms of strong information and direct influence are probably the most effective means of ensuring optimal distribution of rents.

The chapter provides much food for thought. Coff's argument is that the more idiosyncratic the firm's human capital the greater its potential for generating competitive advantage, but equally the greater the challenges to firm-level appropriation and equitable distribution of its value. These considerations highlight the need to explore further the relationships between human capital, competitive advantage, and firm performance. We continue the exploration of the elusive human capital-performance relationship in Chapter 15.

Chapter 15

In Chapter 15 Robin Kramar, Vijaya Murthy, and James Guthrie discuss how the shift to a knowledge-based economy has propelled firms' human capital and associated intellectual resources to center stage. They note that while organizational researchers have highlighted the increasingly strategic role of human capital, and despite a growing realization among firms that their human knowledge resources are becoming more important, managerial awareness of the value of human capital remains low. The authors suggest that human capital management, measurement, and reporting are increasingly vital capabilities that all organizations will need to acquire. They proceed to analyze the nature of human capital, trace the evolution of human capital accounting, identify current accounting challenges, and describe contemporary frameworks that are seeking to address these challenges.

Kramar and her co-authors define human capital within organizations as 'employee capability, knowledge, innovation, adaptability and experience', noting that it is typically represented as one element in a tripartite framework of intellectual capital or 'knowledge flows', the other two being relational capital (relationships involving customers, suppliers, and others) and organizational capital (intellectual property and infrastructure assets). They describe six stages in the evolution of human capital accounting. In the 1960s human asset accounting sought to improve accounting for human capital in firms' balance sheets. During the 1970s and 1980s human resource accounting aimed at accounting for human resources as assets rather than expenses. During the 1990s an interdisciplinary management accounting perspective, human resource costing, and accounting was developed in Sweden, and separately Roslender and Dyer promoted the concept of human worth accounting.

Throughout the 1990s and early 2000s various attempts were made at accounting for human competences as a part of intellectual capital accounting frameworks, such as Sveiby's Intellectual Assets Monitor. The authors comment that the consensus among theorists and informed practitioners is that these and prior attempts at human capital accounting, mostly based on monetary valuation, have largely failed. They note a current trend away from reliance on monetary valuation to broader accounting frameworks, incorporating qualitative measures and financial and non-financial indicators.

Accounting-related challenges facing contemporary organizations include how to optimize human capital alignment with organizational needs, how to predict human capital requirements, how to measure the effects of human capital on organizational performance, and how to increase managerial awareness of people as assets rather than costs. The authors note that the tools that organizations are currently using to address these challenges, such as competency frameworks, benchmarking studies, human capital management systems, and engagement surveys, have so far been able to provide only partial solutions.

In light of the relative lack of success of human capital accounting and reporting to date, the authors suggest a need for fresh approaches. They cite recent moves to link human capital accounting to social accounting and new forms of accounts, including 'extended performance accounts' and 'global reporting initiatives'. In general they signal a shift to using a richer mix of financial and non-financial indicators and the use of narratives to help identify the value of human capital to organizations.

Chapter 16

Rob Grant and James Hayton's chapter helps to set the scene for Part IV with an examination of interdependencies among people in organizations. Defining human capital as the 'totality of human potential' available to an organization, they note that to realize this potential individuals must integrate their knowledge and activities, and that integration involves human interactions requiring both cooperation and coordination. Grant and Hayton review the relevant literature from three perspectives: the characteristics of the work people do (structures and processes), the characteristics of the organizations within which they interact (social capital, culture, and climate), and the characteristics of the individuals themselves (competencies).

The authors trace the evolution of structural and process perspectives on interdependencies, from sociotechnical systems thinking in the 1950s, through the work of Thompson in the late 1960s, to the work of Mintzberg in the 1970s, and Malone and others associated with the MIT Centre for Coordination Science in the 1990s. They highlight the work of Tjosvold during the 1980s, relating it to prior research, notably by Deutsch, in embracing not only the nature of work processes but culture, cognition, and social psychological factors. Grant and Hayton proceed to examine the literatures on organizational culture and climate. They argue that the organizational climate literature, given its focus on the impact of the organization's social system on individuals and groups, offers a particularly useful lens through which to study the effects of informal coordination and interdependencies. As an example they note how organizational climate may influence choice of autonomous versus team-based working, with consequent implications for social interaction. Social interactions bring into question the role of social capital. The authors argue that although social capital can be used to help explain human capital investments and how human capital creates value, from the viewpoint of managing interdependencies between people in organizations it is the structure and character of social interactions that matters; that is, networking rather than capital *per se*.

The authors turn next to the literature on individuals' characteristics and the role they play in human interactivity in organizations. They note that competency modeling has confirmed the role of four attributes: achievement motivation, self-awareness, social awareness, and self-regulation—factors associated with 'emotional intelligence'—as consistently characterizing high performers, and that these attributes have been claimed to be better predictors of job performance than traditional human capital determinants such as education, training, and experience. They suggest that while debates may continue over the value of emotional intelligence as a construct, effective human interaction is critical to job performance, and human competencies in this area are clearly related to individuals' control of their own emotions and their ability to sense and react appropriately to the emotions of others.

Grant and Hayton's review shows how task and process perspectives reveal differing types of interdependencies between people in organizations and their effects on knowledge integration. They also show that collective norms and values (culture) and individual competencies for interaction (particularly emotional intelligence) significantly influence the success of human interactions, thus the extent of integration achieved. Their findings remind us that for organizations to maximize returns on their human capital investments they will need to take into account all these elements.

Chapter 17

David O'Donnell explores interdependencies between human and structural capital in organizations, drawing on Kantian pragmatism and in particular the work of Jürgen Habermas. In common with many authors in this volume he identifies prevailing notions of human capital, along with other intangible, intellectual forms of capital in organizations, as an heuristic rather than a theoretical construct. He argues that currently accepted intellectual capital taxonomies are based largely on neo-positivist concepts borrowed from the natural sciences, which he claims have resulted in linear, static models with limited practical relevance. He highlights the need for more dynamic and theoretically grounded approaches to defining intangible capital and to exploring intra-organizational relationships between human and structural capital.

As a basis for developing a dynamic view of the human—structural capital relationship O'Donnell moves to the agency—structure question, drawing on Reed's (2003) reductionist, determinist, conflationist, and relationist/realist typology of competing perspectives. He discusses how the relationist/realist perspective fits the Kantian pragmatist worldview and aligns with the concepts of organizational lifeworld and Habermas's theory of communicative action. The firm in this context is conceived as a social community specializing in creating, developing, maintaining, and leveraging its processes of knowing through relations between people involved in communicative action. O'Donnell uses Habermas's 1987 typology to depict communicative relations between people in the firm (human capital in interaction) as dynamically interdependent with its cultural, social/community, and psychological social structures and their associated reproduction processes of cultural reproduction, social integration, and socialization (social structural capital). Dimensions of evaluation are defined as rationality of knowledge, solidarity of members, and personal responsibility.

O'Donnell emphasizes the importance to modern organizations of collaboration and thus linguistic competence. He prefaces a discussion of the linguistic validity claims, central to the theory of communicative action, by distinguishing between instrumental and communicative agency orientations. Whereas the former is oriented towards success or efficacy, communicative action is essentially concerned with reaching inter-subjective understanding. Following a discussion of the communicative relationship O'Donnell uses the organizational lifeworld typology to model the interplay between communicative action ('human capital in interaction with the validity claims within speech acts') and lifeworld structures and processes ('social structural capital') in organizations, citing real world examples. A key message for management is that anything that impedes critiques of validity claims within a set of communicative relations will negatively influence the firm as a knowing community. Another implication is that given agents and their lifeworlds are 'situated', communicative actors cannot transcend their own organizational lifeworlds, albeit the organizational lifeworld itself is inherently transcendental in character in that it provides the background of mutual intelligibility that makes communicative relations possible.

O'Donnell's chapter shows how Habermas's theory of communicative action and the lifeworld can be used to illuminate the dynamic interdependencies between the human capital inhering in communicative relations between people and the social structures and regenerative processes representing structural capital. He also reveals how a Kantian pragmatist approach, by regarding objectivity, intersubjectivity, and subjectivity as 'mutually irreducible' and 'equiprimordial,' overcomes the apparent limitations of intersubjective communication and that, as a result, validity claims within the communicative relation may be empirically verified both by internal participants and external observers.

Chapter 18

Ikujiro Nonaka, Ryoko Toyama, and Vesa Peltokorpi commence Chapter 18 with a review of perspectives on human capital from labor market economics, intellectual capital, and the transactions-cost and resource-based literatures. They conclude that although these perspectives shed light on what human capital is and how it contributes to firms' competitive advantage, they largely fail to explain how human capital is developed and utilized in organizations. The authors attribute this failure to perceptions of human capital as an aggregate notion and positivist philosophical concepts of organizations, which they criticize for allowing standardization and uniformity to take precedence over human variances. The authors argue the need for a concept of organizations as organic entities investing in dynamic and distributed human capital, and proceed to use the Aristotelian notion of phronesis to describe how human capital is developed and used within organizations and the implicit interdependencies involved.

Building on the notion of the firm as a knowledge-creating entity, Nonaka and his co-authors characterize knowledge creation as a social process that validates truth. Knowledge in organizations emerges through a collective validation of individuals' value judgments based on their values, ideals, aesthetic perceptions, and truth perceptions. These ideals, values, and aesthetic sensibilities create an organization's ontology or way of categorizing the world, helping to define its vision, its present existence, the knowledge it creates, and its perception of its environment. Phronesis is the practical capability to make the value judgments necessary for continuous knowledge creation. Citing Aristotle, the authors note there are three types of knowledge: *episteme*, universal truth that exists objectively, is context independent and can be described explicitly; *techne*, technique, technology, and art, is context dependent and represented in practical and tacit human skills; and phronesis is the ability to grasp the truth about what is good or bad in a particular situation and take appropriate action. The element of moral discernment reveals phronesis as an intellectual virtue, possessing an ethical component lacking in the other two types of knowledge. Key components of phronesis are practical wisdom and prudent and ethical decision-making ability.

Nonaka and co-authors posit phronesis as a capacity of organizations that exists at multiple levels and is an essential complement to other types of knowledge; for example, *techne* is knowledge of how to make a car properly, whereas phronesis is knowledge of what a good car is (value judgment) and how to build it (value realization). The authors propose that phronesis in a knowledge-creating company consists of six abilities: making a judgment on 'goodness'; sharing knowledge contexts; grasping the essence of situations and things; using language, concepts, and narratives to reconstruct particulars into universals, and vice versa; using the necessary political means well to realize concepts for the common good; and fostering phronesis in others. They describe these six abilities and the conditions necessary for fostering collective phronesis in organizations, using examples from leading organizations including Honda, Mitsui, Eisai, Seven Eleven, and Toyota.

The authors conclude that phronesis has fundamental implications for how organizations view their human capital and the strategies they adopt to develop and use it. Rather than simple investments in education and training, they note the importance of developing contextual and value-laden knowledge from individual, subjective interpretations produced and validated in a social context. The management of organizations and the development and use of human capital they describe as an emergent, distributed, phronetic process operating at multiple levels, rather than the domain of single entrepreneurs.

This chapter provides a further set of perspectives on human capital and its interdependencies. We see a different type of interdependency at work, involving the interplay of idiosyncratic human values and intentions and the reconciliation between them required for effective organizational functioning. Moving beyond scientific and technical concepts of knowledge, phronesis incorporates virtues of human character—intent on discerning what is 'good'. In an organizational context this implies good not just for the individual but for the collective. Such discernment requires human capital with the ability to identify the 'virtuous mean' among competing options, highlighting in turn the importance of experience, leadership, and political skills. Investments in and returns from human capital need to be geared to developing these aspects of human 'character', not merely epistemic knowledge or technical skills.

The chapter indicates that a phronesis-supporting environment (*ba*) aids distributed phronesis, thus inducing individuals to maximize contribution of their human capital. The use of phronetic narratives suggests how organizational appropriation of the value of individual's contributions may be enhanced (see Chapters 10 and 14). Phronesis also offers another lens through which to view Becker's firm-specific versus general human capital distinction (see in particular Chapter 22). Phronesis or practical wisdom suggests dimensions of firm-specificity extending beyond knowledge of firm-specific rules and routines to suggest how experienced and expert organizational actors may embody firm-specific history and values in decisions, policy-making, and development of procedural artifacts. The authors reveal how understanding phronesis can aid our understanding of human agency in the knowledge-creating firm.

Chapter 19

Jacqueline Vischer's chapter focuses on interdependencies between people and their physical work environment—the buildings they occupy and the spaces in which they work. She shows how these interdependencies affect employees' work attitudes and behaviors, thus organizational returns on human capital investments. She argues that an organization's physical environment affects its overall performance, through constraining or supporting achievement of its business objectives, the task environment, and intra-organizational relationships. She proceeds to review how work space influences each of these dimensions.

Vischer suggests that organizations and their members develop organization–accommodation (O–A) relationships with the land, buildings, workspaces, and information technology that they use that reflect their objectives and cultures. As with relationships between organizations and their employees, O–A relationships need to be aligned but also flexible so as to permit change over time. At different times O–A relationships may for example reflect a focus on 'exploration' or 'exploitation' strategies, structural coordination or interpersonal cooperation, and the differing needs of a mobile or static workforce. Vischer suggests that organizations need a workspace architecture, analogous to an HR architecture (see Chapter 13) that is designed to maintain fit over time between people and their physical environments.

On the subject of relationships between organizations and individuals, Vischer argues that along with the various HR elements in work contracts there is a 'socio-spatial' element involving promises regarding physical work conditions. Key elements of this (usually implicit) sociospatial contract are territoriality, environmental control, and job performance. Promises, however, may be breached. Vischer claims, for example, that 'homogenized' open-plan working conditions tend to send a message to workers that 'you are all the same to us'. Drawing on the theoretical and empirical literatures Vischer suggests that making workspace arrangements more explicit within the hiring process, and involving workers in accommodation decisions affecting them, can speed up employee acceptance and productive use of workspace, thus organizational returns on human capital investments.

Understanding how workspace features affect human behavior and how people interact with their workspaces, Vischer argues, is essential to negotiating the socio-spatial contract and to understanding and improving the O–A relationship. Synthesizing environmental psychology and human capital perspectives, she uses the notion of 'functional comfort' to suggest that workers struggling with arduous physical work environments are wasting human capital that might be better applied for the benefit of the organization. Expanding the concept of physical functional comfort to incorporate the virtual and mental concept of 'ba' and drawing on Nonaka, Nenonen, Heerwagen, and others, Vischer outlines a high-level workspace typology that identifies the various space requirements associated with differing levels of social collaboration (awareness, brief interaction, collaboration) at each stage in Nonaka's SECI model (socialization, externalization, combination, and internalization).

Vischer reveals the importance of the physical work environment in supporting or constraining workplace productivity and organizational performance. Her chapter illuminates linkages between the physical and virtual worlds of organizations and suggests how a better understanding of their interdependencies can assist organizations in obtaining more value from their human capital.

Chapter 20

In Chapter 20 Alan and Andrew Burton-Jones argue that while people and information systems (ISs) represent the two single largest areas of investment for many organizations and are increasingly interconnected resources, there has been very little research on the nature of their interdependencies and how these interdependencies affect their functioning and complementarity—thus organizational returns on investments in them and their effects on organizational performance.

Defining an IS as 'an artifact that provides representations of some domains in the world', and noting that 'the development and use of an IS depends on both technologies (infrastructure and applications) and people (developers, managers, users)', the authors examine the extent to which people and ISs can be regarded as forms of 'capital'. They find that both share many features traditionally associated with capital, and in addition both derive their value principally from individuals' knowledge. The authors conclude that human and IS capital are strongly interdependent forms of capital, requiring an holistic approach to their measurement and management.

From a review of the literature on interdependency in organizations the authors identify critical interdependencies involving people, systems, and tasks. They next introduce a model describing interdependencies between two types of resources—people and systems—and two types of activity and associated tasks: functional support activities and primary activities. Noting a paucity of research on such interdependencies in the organization science and IS literatures, the authors describe the results of two empirical studies of people–IS interdependencies that the first author conducted. These two studies differed in nature—one was inductive and the other was deductive—but both found strong interdependencies between people and ISs, providing further fuel to the authors' thesis that these interdependencies cannot be ignored or assumed away. Moreover, the studies identified several different ways in which these interdependencies can occur in practice.

The first study, involving a large inner-city hotel, measured the influence of the hotel workforce (people), hotel information systems and processes (IS), and the hotel brand standard on hotel performance. The authors report evidence of strong resource–resource dependencies, leading them to conclude that models positing an independent effect of people, brands, or systems on organizational effectiveness may be incomplete and possibly misleading. The second example, a deductive study, used a three-stage causal model to explain how functional support tasks affected the provision of resources used to perform work tasks that in turn influenced organizational effectiveness. The authors describe various interdependent relationship patterns involving HR and IS resources and support functions at each stage of the model.

The authors identify three main implications from their research. The first is that given the strong interdependencies observed between people and IS in their performance effects, models that seek to show how to use human capital to improve organizational performance should incorporate both people and IS, and model both resource fit and resource interdependency. The second implication is that people and IS are dependent on other forms of intellectual capital and that all forms of capital are ultimately knowledge-based (see also Chapter 5). The authors conclude from these multiple dependencies that researchers and practitioners should benefit from viewing all forms of capital in a more systemic and dynamic fashion. The third implication is a recommendation for more coordinated approaches to managing IS and people resources, which the authors note may involve reconceptualizing the relationships between people, IS, and knowledge as an active process in organizations.

Chapter 21

Part V looks to the future and the place of human capital in twenty-first-century economies, firms, and institutions. Various angles open up: the interaction of developed and developing economies, environmental and ethical concerns, globalization, and new forms of work. David Teece's chapter deals with organizational transformation, noting that twenty-first-century organizations are structured to extend delegation by the senior management team to those whose task-specific expertise (organizationally relevant human capital) is greater than their own. Citing McGirt, Teece describes Cisco as 'a distributed idea engine whose leadership emerges organically, unfettered by a central command'.

As ideas become more important, so does education. Teece reviews Marshall's comments on this, and some, we presume, helped shape Becker's views. The trend makes the people who absorb and generate these ideas more significant too. Teece labels these individuals 'literati and numerati'—the latter being skilled in numerate and symbolic analysis. These categories contrast with entrepreneurs, whose activity draws ideas into the economy. Teece shares the 'Austrian' theme echoed by many of our authors—Lewin and Loasby in particular. Like Loasby, Teece argues that neoclassical economics neglects ideas and entrepreneurial creativity. The twenty-first-century managerial challenge, he suggests, is to manage contributions by the literati and numerati who create and convey innovative ideas into the non-equilibrium-seeking and dynamic economies in which they generate value.

Teece reviews the literature on entrepreneurship, noting difference between the Schumpeterian entrepreneur's desire to innovate and disturb the economy, and the Kirznerian entrepreneur who spots the opportunities opened up and seizes the market's impulse to equilibrium in his/her favor. Teece fleshes out the management practices that lead to profit. One problem, as most recognize when discussing the measurement of human capital, is that it is difficult to know talent and to value it *ex ante*. Teece notes Lotka's 'power law'—that most of the important contributions to a field are made by a small percentage of those engaged in it—implying that *ex ante* measures miss the point. Talent must be both present and engaged for success. Teece sees organizations as the important means to achieve this, thus 'engines of economic progress with human capital as their pistons'.

To engage the literati and numerati Teece proposes that organizations need 'dynamic capabilities', about which he has written much. 'Dynamic capabilities have become the shorthand by which many understand the processes whereby, in fast-paced global environments, firms organize to develop sought-after new products and processes'. Or 'dynamic capabilities are those attributes of the business enterprise that enable it to orchestrate assets and organizational units, while remaining relevant to the market and other aspects of the business environment'. Teece argues that dynamic capabilities enable the firm to deal with (*a*) multi-trial contexts, (*b*) co-specialization of knowledge, and (*c*) the structures that engage the necessary human capital. He distinguishes the processes of creating and capturing value from those of sensing, seizing, and transforming the opportunities available, capturing the two dimensions in a two-by-three matrix.

Teece goes on to review some history of technological innovation and surface the conundrum managers face as they see that innovative activity does not necessarily lead to success—technological push cannot produce without demand pull—as success often depends on complementary products, services, and attitudes not under management's direct control. While such issues are external, the internal challenge of managing the literati and numerati into the push remains. Teece discusses the strategic balance between direction and delegation, and how this changes when managing experts. He offers a table distinguishing traditional teams from virtuoso teams—the second being more appropriate to literati and numerati. He concludes with critical comments about the failure of contemporary theories of the firm to engage these issues.

Chapter 22

Remarking on the lack of linkage between Becker's notion of general and firm-specific human capital and the organizational literature on inter-firm movement of talent, Peter Sherer discusses how these literatures may be reconciled and how synthesizing human capital and organizational perspectives can bring human capital deeper into organizational theory. He highlights the fact that Becker's proposition that firm-specific human capital should be of higher value in the firm, providing it and general human capital of equal value across firms takes no account of the role of the firm receiving the human capital. At Becker's (aggregate, national) level of theorizing this role was not important, but for organizational theorists it clearly is. Using examples from law firms and the semiconductor industry, and drawing on population economics, labor market theories, the resource-based view of the firm, and HR management theories, Sherer explores the dynamics of inter-firm talent transfer—in particular the role of the receiving firm and the implications of particular types of human capital for firm-level competitive advantage. He shows that in practice both firm-specific and general human capital may be critical to a firm's competitive advantage, and describes how and why the relative value and scarcity of each type may vary over time and across organizations.

From an organizational process perspective Sherer suggests that two alternative processes may occur when human capital is transferred from one firm to another: *Relocation* when general human capital is transferred, and *Replication* when firm-specific human capital is transferred. He presents a range of studies of *Relocation* and *Replication* effects, providing insights into the various factors constraining and supporting human capital transfer. While acknowledging that more research is required on population level transfers he suggests that the activities of individual organizations over time and involving transfers of differing forms of human capital must generate population level effects, which he categorizes as *Diffusion*, in which firm-specific human capital becomes more general as it spreads across a population; *Specification*, when general human capital becomes fragmented and its use becomes firm-specific; and *Drift*, when firm-specific human capital fragments into multiple versions.

Sherer's research on the inter-firm movement of talent suggests that, dependent on a range of factors, relocation and replication of general and firm-specific human capital may generate positive, negative, and no firm performance effects at the individual firm level. Human capital characteristics also appear to change as they diffuse over time across a population. While focusing on inter-firm transfer of human talent, Sherer's research clearly carries implications for knowledge transfer within firms, for organizational learning, innovation, and competitive advantage, and for industry evolution. His call for a research agenda, aimed at identifying how firms gain a competitive advantage through general and firm-specific human capital and for a better understanding of population processes, seems warranted and timely. Sherer's chapter helps us to appreciate both the value and the limitations of Becker's distinction between general and firm-specific human capital, and reinforces a central contention of this *Handbook* that organizations matter to human capital theory.

Chapter 23

Seán Ó Riain's chapter relocates managing human capital into the larger world of which firms are merely part. He goes beyond the relationship between human capital and education to embrace the knowledge-based workings of the state. A firm's production strategies work in an institutional framework that shapes how the benefits of education are distributed and the nature of skills, work, its control, and rewards.

Ó Riain builds a complex model of five elements: inputs from firms' production strategies, national welfare production regimes, pertinent labor norms and interests, the firms' goals and interests, and the political system—collectively determining a sixth, the politics of firm-level human capital formation. He contrasts notions of work, education, and welfare in Germany, Japan, Sweden, and the US and UK. The analysis stands on Esping-Andersen's distinction between modes of welfare capitalism: Liberal, Social Democratic, and Christian Democrat. The processes are dynamic and interactive—calls for change by one interest group, such as labor or the employers, often neglect the way situations institutionalize in self-reinforcing ways so that even the disadvantaged are loath to change.

Yet change occurs; there is convergence as much professional work—scientific research, computers, and so on—becomes standardized. Likewise, the EU's Bologna accord leads to a convergence on the approach to the European approach to human capital. There are also contrary tendencies as regional identities flourish. Many have suggested that national innovation systems are dissolving under the press of globalization—that it is not useful to compare, say, state-supported industrial training in Germany, traditionally strong, against the weaker US system. Riain reminds us that attempts to extract human capital management from its broader political context and thereby ignore the tussle between that society's interests groups misconstrues the kinds of human capital that matter economically and with which managers must actually deal.

Ó Riain contrasts production strategies, welfare strategies, political conditions, and human capital formation regimes in the three systems, and shows how the interplay of elements varies. He distinguishes the service and knowledge economy, and indicates how changes in the nature of work affect their interplay. He pays attention to the feminization of the labor force and to the impact of transnational production. He concludes by observing that the situation is ongoing—though it is clear that the distinctions and interactions that underpinned the 'Golden Age of Western Capitalism' are disappearing. This is of particular interest to human capital theorists given Ashton's argument that 'human capital theory is a product of the Fordist techniques that dominated that period. The use of narrow, tightly circumscribed job descriptions, a highly specialized division of labor, and command and control hierarchies, led to the treatment of skill as an attribute of the individual almost as if it were a possession of asset which could then be used at work for a specific return.' In this light, many chapters in our book can be understood as attempts to overcome this historical legacy and find a concept of human capital more fitting to our time.

Chapter 24

In Chapter 24 Thomas Clarke surveys the development of human capital in developing countries, focusing on the significance of the Asian experience. A central theme is how the countries of Asia have coped and will need to continue to cope in future with the shift to a globalized, knowledge-based economy. In this process of development Clarke identifies a central role for human capital while stressing the complementary nature of other forms of capital including social capital, financial capital, manufacturing capital, and natural capital.

Commenting on institutional and national cultural influences across the Asian region Clarke observes that on the surface India, with its technical skill-oriented educational system, and inheritance of the English language, might appear better prepared for the knowledge economy than China with its more classical tradition of education and emphasis on rote learning. Drawing on economic, sociological, and organizational research literature he suggests that the future knowledge economy is likely to require more broadly based and creative forms of human capital than the past. Citing Evans and Sen, he notes the importance of appropriate political, social, and educational institutions plus advanced information infrastructures and innovation systems.

Turning to economic growth trajectories and tracing the progression of several Asian countries from light to heavy industries through assembly industries such as electronics to innovation, information, and knowledge-intensive industries, Clarke questions whether Asian countries can leapfrog one or more of these stages of economic growth. Here he observes that Asian nations are already playing catch-up with their European and US counterparts via information technology and telecommunications. Not only advanced economies such as Japan but emerging economies in the region are investing in broadband networks and applying internet technologies across their industry sectors. India already has the largest concentration of IT skills in the world. Clarke also notes the efforts of countries across the region to ramp up manufacturing, hi-tech, and knowledge-based industries via clusters that fuse FDI with local research and producer services. A potential source of expert and well connected human capital that may aid this process is the large Asian entrepreneurial diaspora currently participating in North America who may be attracted home for cluster development in East Asia—providing, as Clarke notes, there is a welcoming institutional environment to which they can return.

Clarke observes that the spectacular growth enjoyed by several East Asian economies, previously led by Japan and now China and India, has demonstrated the region's huge potential for developing human capital. This growth has undoubtedly been fueled by significant public expenditure on education, with nine years of education compulsory across the region and increasing investment in vocational and tertiary education. As to whether the Asian model of rapid growth can be extended to the rest of the developing world Clarke is less sanguine, noting that poorer nations' struggle to climb out of poverty and progress towards a knowledge economy is unlikely to make progress until issues of international trade, foreign investment, and aid are resolved in a more balanced way. For the relatively few economies in East Asia and elsewhere that have developed the necessary human and other capital necessary to succeed in the knowledge economy, a future challenge will be to continue to develop the institutions and the business and educational relationships that will help them continue to compete with the West.

Chapter 25

Thomas Kochan and Adam Seth Litwin assess the future of human capital in organizations from an industrial relations perspective. They note that, paradoxically, while human capital has grown in importance in the shift to a knowledge-based economy, the externalization of work that has accompanied this shift and the consequent weakening of labor market institutions has reduced incentives and pressures on firms to invest in people. They suggest that this is a case of market failure. Resolving the paradox will require firms as well as unions, professional associations, staffing agencies, and the state to work together. The employment relationship thus becomes their unit of analysis, and they explore the variety of institutional support that will be necessary to rebuild and sustain that relationship in the future economy.

Kochan and Litwin start by discussing how traditional assumptions underpinning firm worker relations, such as protected national wage systems, a male dominated workforce, full-time employment, and its associated social contract, no longer apply. Similarly the institutions constructed to address three key labor market issues: human capital formation and development, work–life integration, and the role of women in the labor market, and the relationships between technology, technological change, and employment practices are now outmoded. The authors proceed to chart the changes that have occurred in each these three key areas. They describe how, when internal labor markets were strong and stable, firms could afford to invest in general human capital, whereas in today's markets such investments would make workers mobile and open to poaching— possibly a belated confirmation of Becker's thesis (see also Chapter 22). Similarly, whereas unions used to help keep workers' skill levels up to date, the shift to individualized and externalized work contracts has fragmented collective bargaining and union power.

Charting the evolution of work–life perspectives, the authors note that Henry Ford paid his male workers enough to allow their wives to look after home and family. As women became more educated the male breadwinner model of employment became progressively less viable, leading to pressures to utilize both male and female human capital in the workforce. While in the industrial era the state could safely devolve work–life integration problems to business this has become decreasingly viable. Kochan and Litwin discuss the differing approaches taken by nations to support work–life integration through paid maternity leave and other schemes, noting the USA's relatively poor showing compared to some EU nations. In relation to technological change the authors argue that whereas pacts between business and organized labor traditionally helped spread the positive and negative effects of technological progress across all the stakeholders, the balance now favors business, and state intervention is therefore required, in the form of worker retraining and similar schemes, to reduce human capital loss due to technological substitution.

Turning to the question of how to encourage the right type of work arrangements for the future economy, Kochan and Litwin emphasize the importance of trust-based relationships between business and both external and internal suppliers of human capital. Citing the literature on productivity from IT usage they note the importance of understanding the complementary roles played by people and IT in economic growth in order to maximize ROI in human and IT investments (see also Chapter 20). Given the continuing trend to externalized work arrangements the authors discuss the potential for professional associations and craft unions to help externalized workers acquire and maintain their skills and advocate a stronger role for government to avoid loss of human capital through market failures.

In making industrial relations the centerpiece of their chapter Kochan and Litwin bridge micro-, meso-, and macrolevel perspectives of human capital. They show that while the old industrial relations model is outmoded, a viable successor is not yet in place, and that new links and stronger connections between individual workers, firms, and networks of private and public institutions will be increasingly vital for human capital to flourish in the future economy.

REFERENCES

BAETJER, H., and LEWIN, P. (2007). '*Can Ideas be Capital: Can Capital be Anything Else?*' Working Paper, 83, Mercatus Center, George Mason University.

BARNEY, J. B. (1991). 'Firm Resources and Sustained Competitive Advantage', *Journal of Management*, 17(1): 99–120.

BECKER, G. S. (1964, 1993). *Human Capital* (Chicago: University of Chicago Press).

BERG, I. (2003). *Education and Jobs: The Great Training Robbery* (Clinton Corners, NY: Percheron Press).

BELL, D. (1973). *The Coming of Post-Industrial Society* (New York: Basic Books).

BLACKLER, F. (1995). 'Knowledge, Knowledge Work and Organizations: An Overview and Interpretation', *Organization Studies*, 16(6): 1021–46.

BLAIR, M. M., and KOCHAN, T. A. (2000) *The New Relationship: Human Capital in the American Corporation* (Washington, DC: Brookings Institution Press).

BROOKING, A. (1996). *Intellectual Capital* (London: Thomson Business Press).

BURT, R. S. (1992). *Structural Holes* (Cambridge, Mass.: Harvard University Press).

BURTON-JONES, A. (1999). *Knowledge Capitalism: Business Work and Learning in the New Economy* (Oxford: Oxford University Press).

CHAUDHURI, K. N. (1985). *Trade and Civilisation in the Indian Ocean: An Economic History from the Rise of Islam to 1750* (Cambridge: Cambridge University Press).

COLEMAN, J. S. (1988). 'Social Capital in the Creation of Human Capital', *American Journal of Sociology*, 94 (supplement): S95–S120.

CONNER, K. R., and PRAHALAD, C. K. (1996). 'A Resource-Based Theory of the Firm: Knowledge vs. Opportunism', *Organization Science*, 7: 477–501.

DEAN, A., and KRETSCHMER, M. (2007). 'Can Ideas be Capital? Factors of Production in the Postindustrial Economy: A Review and Critique', *Academy of Management Review*, 32(2): 573–94.

EDVINSSON, L. (1997). 'Developing Intellectual Capital at Skandia', *Long Range Planning*, 30(3): 366–73.

FELIN, T., and FOSS, N. J. (2004). *'Methodological Individualism and the Organizational Capabilities Approach,'* Working Paper 2004–5, Center for Knowledge Governance, Copenhagen Business School (http://www.cbs.dk/ckg).

GRANT, R. M. (1996). 'Toward a Knowledge-Based Theory of the Firm', *Strategic Management Journal*, 17 (Winter special issue): 109–22.

GRANT, R. M. (1997). 'Knowledge-Based View of the Firm: Implications for Management Practice', *Long Range Planning*, 30(3): 450.

HYMAN, R. (1987). 'Strategy or Structure? Capital, Labour and Control', *Work, Employment and Society*, 1(1): 25–55.

KOGUT, B., and ZANDER, U. (1992). 'Knowledge of the Firm, Combinative Capabilities, and the Replication of Technology', *Organization Science*, 3: 383–97.

LACHMANN, L. M. (1977). *Capital, Expectations, and the Market Process: Essays on the Theory of the Market Economy* (Mission, KS: Sheed Andrews & McMeel, Inc.).

LEPAK, D. P., and SNELL, S. A. (1999). 'The Human Resource Architecture: Towards a Theory of Human Capital Allocation and Development', *Academy of Management Review*, 24(1): 31–48.

LIN, N. (2001). *Social Capital: A Theory of Social Structure and Action* (Cambridge: Cambridge University Press).

MATHEWS, J. A. (2010). 'Lachmannian Insights into Strategic Entrepreneurship: Resources, Activities and Routines in a Disequilibrium World', *Organization Studies*, 31(2): 219–44.

MINCER, J. (1958). 'Investment in Human Capital and Personal Income Distribution', *Journal of Political Economy*, 66(4) (Aug.): 281–302.

NONAKA, I., and TAKEUCHI, H. (1995). *The Knowledge-Creating Company: How Japanese Companies Create the Dynamics of Innovation* (New York: Oxford University Press).

OECD (1996). *The Knowledge-Based Economy* (Paris: OECD).

PACEY, A. (1990). *Technology in World Civilization: A Thousand-Year History* (Cambridge, Mass.: MIT Press).

PENNINGS, J., and WEZEL, F. (2007). *Human Capital, Inter-Firm Mobility and Organizational Evolution* (Cheltenham: Edward Elgar Publishing).

PORTES, A. (1998). 'Social Capital: Its Origins and Applications in Modern Sociology', *Annual Review of Sociology*, 24: 1–24.

REED, M. (2003). 'The Agency Structure Dilemma in Organization Theory: Open Doors and Brick Walls', in H. Tsoukas and C. Knudsen (eds.), *The Oxford Handbook of Organization Theory: Meta-Theoretical Perspectives* (Oxford: Oxford University Press).

RAELIN, J. A. (2007). 'Toward an Epistemology of Practice', *Academy of Management Learning and Education*, 6(4): 495–519.

REICH, R. B. (1992). *The Work of Nations: Preparing Ourselves for 21st Century Capitalism* (New York: Vintage Books).

PIGOU, A. (1928). *A Study in Public Finance* (London: Macmillan).

SCARBROUGH, H. (1999). 'Knowledge as Work: Conflicts in the Management of Knowledge Workers', *Technology Analysis and Strategic Management*, 11(1): 5–16.

SCHULTZ, T. W. (1961). 'Investment in Human Capital', *American Economic Review*, 51: 1–17.

SMITH, A. (1776, 1904). *An Inquiry into the Nature and Causes of the Wealth of Nations* (2 vols. Everyman's Library; London: Dent & Sons).

SPENDER, J.-C. (1993). 'Competitive Advantage from Tacit Knowledge? Unpacking the Concept and its Strategic Implications', *Academy of Management Best Paper Proceedings*, 37–41.

SPENDER, J.-C. (1996). 'Making Knowledge the Basis of a Dynamic Theory of the Firm', *Strategic Management Journal*, 17 (Winter special issue): 45–62.

SVEIBY, K. E. (1997). *The New Organizational Wealth: Managing and Measuring Knowledge-Based Assets* (San Francisco, CA: Berrett-Koehler).

TEECE, D. J., and PISANO, G. (1998). 'The Dynamic Capabilities of Firms: An Introduction', in G. Dosi, D. J. Teece, and J. Chytry (eds.), *Technology, Organization and Competitiveness: Perspectives on Industrial and Corporate Change* (New York: Oxford University Press), 193–212.

VAUGHN, K. I. (1994). *Austrian Economics in America: The Migration of a Tradition* (Cambridge: Cambridge University Press).

WADE, M., and Hulland, J. (2004). 'The Resource-Based View and Information Systems Research: Review, Extension, and Suggestions for Future Research', *MIS Quarterly*, 28(1): 107–42.

WERNERFELT, B. (1984). 'A Resource-Based View of the Firm', *Strategic Management Journal*, 5: 171–80.

WILLIAMSON, O. E. (1985). *The Economic Institutions of Capitalism: Firms, Markets, Relational Contracting* (New York: Free Press).

YOUNDT, M. A., SUBRAMANIAM, M., and SNELL, S. A. (2004). 'Intellectual Capital Profiles: An Examination of Investments and Returns', *Journal of Management Studies*, 41(2): 335–61.

ZACK, M. H. (1999). 'Developing a Knowledge Strategy', *California Management Review*, 41(3): 125–44.

ZUBOFF, S. (1988). *In the Age of the Smart Machine—The Future of Work and Power* (New York: Basic Books).

PART I

THE NATURE OF HUMAN CAPITAL

CHAPTER 1

AN ECONOMIC PERSPECTIVE ON THE NOTION OF 'HUMAN CAPITAL'

MARGARET M. BLAIR

'HUMAN capital' is increasingly recognized as the most important factor of production and the most important source of economic wealth and engine of economic growth over time. The term 'human capital' is a shorthand name given by economists and other social scientists to the skills, knowledge, and capabilities of the workforce of a firm, or of the population of a country, as well as the organizational arrangements and networks of relationships those people have formed that enable them to be more innovative and productive. The phrase is meant to evoke two related ideas: that the capabilities of the workers are critical inputs into production, and that resources spent on education, training, team-building, and other forms of 'human capital investment' can be analyzed and understood in a way similar to the way economists and social scientists understand investments in physical capital, such as factories and equipment.

The idea that improvements in human capabilities are important to production goes back at least to Adam Smith (1937), who noted that the division of labor in a factory made it possible for some workers to specialize in certain tasks and thereby build up special skills and capabilities. Arthur Pigou (1928) may have been the first economist to use the phrase 'human capital', but the term became widely used by economists, social scientists, and business people after Gary Becker (1964) wrote his classic book on the subject, which examined the role of education and training in increasing the knowledge and skill resources of people, and thereby helping to explain differences in wages and salaries across different workers.

Despite its widespread use, the phrase, as well as the theories of labor productivity and wage determination that it represents, has been controversial. 'Passions are easily aroused on this subject and even people who are generally in favor of education, medical care, and the like often dislike the phrase 'human capital' and still more any emphasis on its economic effects', Becker acknowledged in the introduction to his book (1964: 10). The reasons are varied. At its essence, 'human capital theory' says simply that workers with different levels of knowledge and skill differ in their productivity and, therefore, earn different rates of compensation according to their skill level. Moreover, the theory explains that education and training are likely to increase the knowledge and skills of workers, thereby increasing their expected earnings. By analogy to investments in physical capital, expenditures on education and training, therefore, operate like investments in better and more efficient machines to increase labor productivity. Such investments, the theory says, can thus be analyzed in ways analogous to the way social scientists analyze investments in physical capital.

Some critics of the term have argued, however, that treating education and training as if they are like investments in physical assets is misleading because it directs attention away from the personal and cultural reasons that individuals seek out particular educational experiences or seek to master certain bodies of knowledge. Some social scientists regard these personal and cultural factors as more important than, or as important as, the economic reasons, and argue that education should be regarded as a 'consumption good', not an investment (Becker, 1964).

Others have argued that the expression and the idea it represents are demeaning because they reduce human experience to a type of commodity. A third criticism relates to the way the concept has been used in models explaining economic growth. This criticism emphasizes the importance of understanding the mechanism by which education and training can lead to increases in productivity and in economic output, and argues that simply referring to such activities as 'investments in human capital' tends to short-circuit the analysis that might uncover the mechanism and how it works (Blaug, 1987).

Although the phrase 'human capital' can obscure some important issues about how people and societies become more productive over time, the idea has proved to be an extraordinarily evocative and powerful way to frame economic discussions about factors that lead to economic growth or to better performance in firms. Hence, in the last forty years, human capital has become a central concept not only in labor economics, but also in macroeconomics, economic growth theory, development economics, trade theory, the economics of education, the theory of the firm, and the theory and practice of human resources management and strategic planning.

1.1 ANALOGY BETWEEN HUMAN CAPITAL AND PHYSICAL CAPITAL

The idea of 'capital' has a long and complex history in economic thought. For purposes of this discussion it is sufficient to note that neoclassical economic theorists have generally settled on a definition of 'capital' as a factor of production that is itself produced from other inputs. The 'primary' factors of production are understood to be 'land' (which is taken to include raw materials such as minerals and timber taken from the land) and 'labor', where labor is usually measured in terms of the amount of time that workers spend in production. In addition to these primary factors, some output from earlier production may be used in current production to enhance total current output per unit of labor input. These produced inputs—tools, machines, railroad tracks, steel sheets, textiles, semiconductors, and so on—are collectively called 'capital'. Capital comes into existence only if some of the output of prior rounds of production is not consumed immediately but is either used as is or traded for materials and tools that can increase productivity in later rounds. Farmers, for example, historically have had to save some of the grain from one harvest to plant in the next planting season and sell some of the grain to buy tools and fertilizer in order for the farmers' grain output to continue in perpetuity or even grow over time. This notion that 'capital' is an input or factor of production produced in earlier rounds of production, then, links economic growth and productivity in one period to savings and investments in prior periods to give a dynamic account of output and productivity.

Like land, capital inputs are owned by some party to the production process, and just as landlords must be paid 'rents' for the use of land, the owners/providers of capital must earn a return in the form of 'interest' or 'profits' for contributing their capital inputs. In contrast, labor inputs cannot be separated from the workers who contribute them and, in that sense, the inputs cannot be 'invested' in a lump sum into the production process but must be contributed over time as workers work. Workers must then be compensated with 'wages' as they contribute hours and days to productive activity. By analogy to physical capital, however, some workers have special knowledge or skills or better insights into how to organize the production process that they acquire through experience, education, and training, and these acquired traits, which we call 'human capital', enable them to produce more with the same inputs of land, machines, materials, and time than other workers could produce without those traits. Under standard neoclassical economic theory, when a worker has better physical capital to work with—more efficient machines, better raw materials, and so on—that worker is expected to have a higher productivity and thus to earn a higher wage. Similarly, economists say that if a worker has superior skills or other traits that enable her to produce more with the same time, tools, and raw materials as another worker, that worker also has a higher productivity (by definition), and thus earns a higher wage. Superior knowledge and skill—the 'human capital' of the worker—can be 'produced' if the worker defers consumption of leisure time and goods and invests some of those goods and time in acquiring new or better skills. Such an investment can lead to greater output in the future.

Human capital is thus like physical capital in that it can be produced by deferring consumption and devoting some of current output to improving the health, well-being, knowledge, and capabilities of workers. And it is like physical capital in that the worker who makes the investment in improved human capital may expect to earn a return on that investment because that worker will be more productive than she would otherwise be. Human capital is also like physical capital in that it can 'depreciate' over time if workers become ill, weaker, or less physically or mentally able as they age. It can also 'depreciate' if certain skills become obsolete (such as, for example, the ability to communicate via Morse code).[1]

But human capital is different from physical capital in a number of important ways. First of all, human capital is, obviously, a trait of the worker and cannot be separated or conveyed or traded to another party. For this reason, the capitalist (the party who invests to own or develop physical capital to contribute to production) generally cannot 'own' the human capital that works with the capitalist's goods and machines. This difference raises important questions about how work is organized and how output should be shared in order to provide incentives for all parties to make optimal investments. This issue will be discussed further below. But, in general, we note here that it is likely to be important to the party who makes an investment in capital, whether physical capital or human capital, to be able to control its use, to be sure that it is deployed in its highest and best use, and to be compensated adequately. For physical capital, the party who invests can 'own' the capital and control its use.

But the problem is much more complex in the case of investments in human capital. Even if an employer pays for training that enhances the human capital of its workers, the employer in no way 'owns' that new human capital. The employee in fact takes it with her if she goes to work for another employer. Thus, it turns out to be useful in many situations for employers and employees to form long-term relationships, or to develop contracts and legal rules to govern the circumstances under which employees and/or former employees can use knowledge acquired on the job.[2] This issue of providing incentives and protection for investments in human capital has been extremely important to organizational theory, contract theory, theory of internal labor markets, and theory of the firm, as will be discussed below and/or in other articles in this volume.

Secondly, human capital can only be contributed to production if the worker spends time in productive activity. Unlike the contributor of physical capital, who can invest, and then sit back and wait for the return, the contributor of human capital must actually work in the productive activity (Marx and Engels, 1952).[3]

Thirdly, while a worker's time may be used up in the production of some goods, that worker's skill and knowledge will probably not be used up. In fact, it may very well appreciate or grow over time as the worker 'learns by doing', using her special knowledge and skills in current production. In the process she may actually acquire new human capital, such as special insight into how the tasks might be accomplished more efficiently in future production. This also has implications for understanding the benefits that come from forming long-term relationships between employer and employee and for how economists model the contracting problem between them.

1.2 RELATIONSHIP BETWEEN HUMAN CAPITAL AND OTHER FORMS OF INTANGIBLE CAPITAL

Human capital takes many forms, including good health of the workers, their knowledge of popular culture, or machinery operations, their relationships with other parties internal and external to the enterprise, their ability to organize and lead other people, and their capacity to adjust and innovate in the face of changing conditions. In the last two or three decades, economists, policy analysts, and business practitioners have all come to understand that such non-physical or 'intangible' assets are of substantial and growing importance in economic activity (Blair and Wallman, 2001; Hand and Lev, 2003). Intangible assets that have been widely recognized as important to value creation by businesses include brands, trademarks, customer goodwill, and other forms of 'reputational capital'; patents, copyrights, business methods, customer lists, research and development in progress, innovations, and other 'intellectual capital', or 'knowledge capital'; and relationships, networks, trust, contracts, legal institutions, community goodwill, and other forms of 'organizational capital' or 'social capital'.

While these assets do not take a physical form, most of them are clearly 'capital', in the sense that they are created in the course of prior production, and they can contribute value in future production. Most are also clearly part of, expressions of, or deeply connected to human capital. A few of the assets listed above, such as brands, trademarks, patents, copyrights, and customer lists, could be separated from the people who created them and sold or conveyed, and hence are not properly thought of as 'human' capital, even though human capital was an input in creating them. But while a brand can be sold, it is not clear that a reputation can be conveyed with the brand. Rather, businesses must continually earn and protect their reputations and, over any significant period of time, the reputation of a firm depends on the character and behavior of the people carrying out the firm's business activities—the firm's 'human capital'. Likewise, patents, or the right to use the technology they represent, can be sold to a licensee, but even if the firm wanted to do so it would probably be difficult to sell the deep knowledge and capability—the human capital—that made it possible for the business to develop the new patented technology in the first place.

On the other hand, a firm that has developed a new technology can, over time, by teaching and consulting with a licensee, convey much of the knowledge and capability associated with the use of its patented technology to the employees of that licensee. In other words, the licensee can also acquire much of the relevant human capital. Moreover, once that knowledge has been conveyed, it will be very difficult in the future for the licensor firm to continue to control its use. Similarly, depending on the legal rules, a firm may be able to claim ownership of an idea that was developed by an employee if it can be proved that the employee developed the idea on company time while using company resources. For example (Pollock, 2008), a federal jury in the US decided that the designer of a popular doll brand had conceived the idea for the dolls while working for his prior employer and, as a result, the concept belonged to that prior company. An appeals court subsequently overturned this finding (Pettersson, 2010), demonstrating that it is difficult to prevent the employee from using general knowledge gained at the workplace to enrich himself or his new employer. These examples illustrate the point that such assets as 'knowledge', 'ideas', or 'reputation' are generally imbedded in people, and hence, unlike other forms of capital, may not be susceptible to being owned or controlled by any 'investor' other than the employees or workers in which they are imbedded.

1.3 Measuring Human Capital

This discussion of the many forms that 'human capital' can take is also relevant to the problem of identifying and measuring human capital, as well as measuring its contribution to productivity. In recent years, numerous reports and policy position papers have addressed the problems that arise because intangible assets in general are not measured well, which may cause individual investors and society as a whole to underinvest in such assets or to mismeasure macroeconomic growth and returns to capital in the economy as a whole (McGrattan and Prescott, 2007). Accounting principles, for example, establish four criteria that must be applied to determine whether something is considered an 'asset' on the books of a company with a positive value: the thing must be well-defined and sufficiently separate from other assets that it can be the object of a sales transaction; the firm must have effective control over it and be able to transfer that control to someone else;

it must be (reasonably) possible to predict the future economic benefits from it; and it must be (reasonably) possible to determine if its economic value has been impaired (Blair and Wallman, 2001: 52).

Among the intangible factors listed above, brands, trademarks, patents, copyrights, patentable business processes, customer lists, or other databases, as well as some business agreements, contracts, and franchises, probably meet all four criteria. Such assets are the product of efforts that are largely human capital investments, but once a brand, trademark, database, or contract has been created, documented, or otherwise converted to written, printed, or digital form, the law can assign property rights over such an asset's use, and the asset can then be separated from the individuals who created it and sold or conveyed to someone else. If such an asset is sold or conveyed, the price at which it is sold provides a strong indicator of its value, so assets that are the object of a sales transaction can be measured in terms of their value or potential value in a sale. But then, of course, such assets can no longer be regarded as human capital. The very characteristics that make it qualify as an 'asset' for accounting purposes—its ability to be separated and sold—disqualify it from being human capital.

Other intangibles, such as in-process research and development, reputation, or organizational competencies, may be proprietary to the firm but are inextricably tied up with the individual people who are employed by the firm. The firm may be able to exercise some control and influence over these 'assets', but because the firm cannot separate them out and sell them, they will not be assigned a value and will not be included on the balance sheet of the firm as assets. While economists and business practitioners would agree that such human capital assets are important and valuable to the business, there is no accepted way for the firm which deploys the 'assets' to measure and/or account for or fully control them.

Nonetheless, for a variety of policy and business reasons, economists, business theorists, and practitioners often try to find measures or proxies that can be used to model, forecast, or evaluate the role of human capital in economic activity. These attempts to measure human capital raise the question of what units should be used. One common approach is to measure the inputs required to acquire the human capital in terms of units of time, such as years of post-secondary education, years on the job, months of apprenticeship, or hours per week of training. An alternative method might be to itemize certain achievements, such as degrees obtained, languages learnt, or courses completed. The problem is that none of these units necessarily bears a close relationship to valuable skills or knowledge acquired. Should three years of community college count the same as three years at Massachusetts Institute of Technology? Is a bachelor's degree earned online equivalent to a bachelor's degree earned in residence at Ohio State University? If not, how can we aggregate or compare such indicators of human capital acquisition?

At the level of individual firms, an indicator of the dollar value of the firm's total capital (including intangibles) might be the amount that investors are willing to pay for financial claims on the firm—the equity shares plus the debt securities and other liabilities of the company. If one subtracts the cost of the firm's tangible capital and purchased intangibles (its 'book' value[4]) from the total value of the firm's capital measured as the sum of the value of financial claims, what remains can be interpreted as the value of the firm's intangible capital, including its human capital, which cannot be measured directly. Even this amount, however, may not be a good proxy for the value of the firm's human capital because this total includes some intangibles that are not human capital and because some of the value of the human capital in use in the firm is presumably captured by the employees in the form of higher wages, rather than by the investors in the financial securities of the firm.[5]

An alternative approach to measuring the value of human capital within a firm would be to attempt to directly measure the productivity and profit benefits of investments in training and in relationship-building. This has been done in aggregate terms using statistical analysis. For example, the National Center on the Educational Quality of the Workforce issued a report (Stewart, 1997: 85) in 1995 that estimated that, on average, a 10 percent increase in workforce education level led to an 8.6 percent gain in total factor productivity. This was after controling for other factors like the age of equipment, industry, and establishment size. A 10 percent increase in capital stock, by contrast, yielded just a 3.4 percent increase in productivity in the same sample of firms (Stewart, 1997: 85).

But while estimating these effects can be done statistically on a large sample of firms, it is difficult or impossible to try to quantify the value that a specific business enterprise can create through investments in employee training. Some management scholars and business consultants claim that metrics they have developed can serve as indicators of how well a firm is carrying out its human capital development activities, and that those indicators, in turn, can help to predict future profits (Gates, 2002). Numerous studies, reports, books, and articles have been published in the fields of management and labor relations that attempt to measure and assess a wide variety of human resource practices in firms, and identify and promote those that are considered 'best practices', in the sense that they are associated with better performance by the firm. This literature defines whole subfields of management and is addressed in Parts III and IV of this *Handbook*.

Measuring the cost of human capital might seem to be easier than measuring its value, and, indeed, standard measures of the cost of human capital usually include the direct costs of education and training, plus the opportunity cost a student or trainee incurs by not working while going to school, or the opportunity cost to the employer of having the worker spend time in training. These approaches provide only an indirect measure of human capital, such as the cost per unit of time that it takes the worker to go through specific learning experiences. But they do not directly measure actual knowledge or skills or other human capital acquired, so they cannot provide a measure of cost per unit of human capital acquired. And the approaches provide no measure of the cost of other types of human capital acquired in other ways, which include computer skills acquired by experience, public-speaking skills acquired through participation in civic clubs, or better health acquired through individual fitness programs.

At the individual level, labor economists have used data on education, training, and other activities that are commonly regarded as investments in human capital to try to measure the economic effects of such investments in terms of wages, salaries, and other forms of compensation for workers. In this way, economists have been able to estimate the average dollar value of additional years of schooling beyond some baseline level, such as a high-school diploma, for example (Card, 2001). But this approach cannot be used to estimate the economic value (let alone the personal or psychic value) for any one individual of obtaining an additional year of college education.

1.4 Role of Human Capital in Economic Growth and Development

At the macroeconomic level, most economists believe that the knowledge and skills of the labor force, as well as innovations in production technology, are important to economic growth and to the development of nations and regions. Until the late 1980s, neoclassical models of economic growth generally assumed that both labor and capital were subject to 'diminishing returns', meaning that the addition of more labor or capital to the model yielded progressively smaller increments in output (Solow, 1957). The rationale for this assumption was that ultimately the amount of land available for production was understood to be finite because land cannot expand at the same rate as labor and capital and, as a result, land becomes scarce, and labor and capital eventually become crowded and less productive. These early growth models, however, included a fourth factor: technological progress, or knowledge, that made it possible for existing labor and capital to produce more output on given quantities of land (Solow, 1957). The level and rate of change of this fourth factor was taken as exogenous to the model—knowledge simply expanded continuously on its own and not as a result of investments accounted for within the model (Solow, 1957).[6] But analyses of the possible sources of growth in national output over time showed repeatedly that this poorly understood and non-measurable factor, technological change, accounted for a very large share of total economic growth throughout the twentieth century (Denison, 1983).

Economists, of course, did not believe that knowledge grew on its own, and so some variations on this model allowed for the 'labor' input to grow not only by adding people and hours of work, but also by assuming that the human capital of the labor force could, effectively, grow through education and training (Harrod, 1948; Domar, 1957).[7] This approach is highly arbitrary, and, in the view of many economists, hardly better than simply treating technological change as a residual factor that 'explains' the part of economic growth that cannot be explained by growth in population or investment in physical capital.

In the 1980s, economists became interested in a modeling approach called 'New Growth Theory', which endogenizes the contributions of increases in human capital and in technological change. Beginning with the work of Paul Romer (1986), economists traced out the implications of assuming that knowledge is characterized by increasing returns rather than diminishing returns. This could be true because, unlike equipment or labor hours, knowledge is not 'used up' in the course of production, hence knowledge costs per unit of output decline with each additional unit of production. Moreover, many people can use the same knowledge at the same time without experiencing crowding or congestion. 'Knowledge' is not exactly the same in these models as human capital, although knowledge is developed by human capital and adds to human capital when it is acquired and used by workers. Some knowledge can be, and is, codified, and once it is, it is no longer part of human capital. But some knowledge is tacit. The sequence of notes that we recognize as Beethoven's Violin Concerto in D major, Op. 61, is codified knowledge (and this knowledge can be represented symbolically by musical notation), but the knowledge of how to play a violin to perform the concerto is mostly tacit knowledge, acquired by years and years of practice. Tacit knowledge is a part of human capital embedded in the individuals or communities that have the knowledge and share it among themselves.

The new interest on the part of economists in the creation, use, and codification of knowledge has encouraged economists to think more about the role played in economic welfare and growth by institutions which facilitate the creation, sharing, and use of knowledge, and the associated development of human capital.

1.5 ROLE OF HUMAN CAPITAL IN THE THEORY OF THE FIRM

The basic neoclassical economic model of a 'firm' is little more than a 'production function' that describes the amount of output that can be produced with different combinations of labor and capital. The model is a 'black box' in the sense that it does not describe how labor and capital actually work together to produce the output. Instead, it is simply assumed in these models that capital can be aggregated and measured, with, for example, K assigned to represent the quantity of capital, and that labor is undifferentiated, and measured simply as L person-hours to be used with K units of capital. For a given L and a given K, the model determines how much output Y can be produced.

This simple model provides a solution to the problem of how labor and capital should be compensated by positing that both factors should be paid at rates equal to their marginal productivity in the model—the additional amount of output that would be produced if one more unit of the input were added. Under certain assumptions,[8] this solution allocates all of the output and compensates all inputs at their opportunity costs. If labor and capital are employed up to the point where their marginal productivity equals their marginal opportunity cost, this also maximizes total output for given level of inputs and thereby leads to an efficient outcome.

Within the framework of this model, investments in generalized human capital are assumed to make workers more productive for all levels of physical capital, thereby shifting the production function up and out, and, for any given level of capital, K, raising the wages as well as the opportunity costs for the workers whose human capital has been enhanced. In other words, if workers enhance their human capital by additional education or training, this is modeled in the basic production-function model of a firm as if more units of L are added to the production process.

In his important treatise on human capital, however, Gary Becker (1964) noted that some human capital may be very generally useful (literacy, for example), while other types of human capital, such as specialized knowledge about how to use, maintain, and further develop an important database, may be unique or highly specific to a particular enterprise. Enterprise-specific human capital investments present a problem for the standard neoclassical model for a several reasons. By definition, they make the worker more productive when used in the current enterprise than he or she would be in alternative applications. This, in turn, drives a wedge between marginal productivity of each worker in the enterprise, and the opportunity cost to that worker of working in that particular enterprise. Economists call the extra output that results from specific investments 'rents'.

The allocation of such rents as between labor and capital cannot be determined purely through the 'invisible hand' of the market. If the employee with firm-specific human capital captures all of the rents, she would be paid more than her opportunity cost. But the employer does not have to let the employee capture all of the rents, because, presumably, the employee would want to continue to work at that job as long as she makes somewhat more than she could in alternative employment. Thus, the employer/capital-supplier could capture some of the rents from the employee's firm-specific human capital, even if the investments were made entirely by the employee. The reverse is also true. If the employer makes the investment to train the employee or teach her firm-specific skills, the employer-firm cannot guarantee that it will capture all of the rents because the employee, who can always quit and go to another firm where she would earn at least her opportunity cost, will be in a position to bargain for a share of the rents.

This means that both the wage level and the return to capital are indeterminate in situations where employees have firm-specific human capital that earns rents. In general, most economists believe that the rents would be shared in some way (Hashimoto, 1981). But the indeterminacy means that, absent such institutional mechanisms as contracts or hierarchical decision-making mechanisms, neither employees nor capital-suppliers can be sure that if they make investments to acquire specialized human capital, they will capture the return on that investment (Becker, 1964).

Economists describe this dilemma as a 'hold-up' problem—regardless of whether the workers or the capital-suppliers make the specific investments, either party can 'hold up' the other party by threatening to end the relationship unless he captures most of the rents. Since neither party can be sure of capturing the returns, they are both likely to have poor incentives to make significant investments in the first place. Thus, modern theories of the firm nearly all grapple in some way with explaining how institutional arrangements help solve the 'hold-up' problem associated with firm-specific human capital investments. These solutions generally involve some sort of long-term relationship between the employer and the employee, governed either by a relational contract or by hierarchical decision-making structure within a firm. Labor economists Peter Doeringer and Michael Piore (1971), for example, developed a theory of internal labor markets based on the idea that both firms and their employees would want to have a stable relationship over time to capture the full benefit of relationship-specific investments.

Relationship-specific investments, especially in human capital, are central to two different branches of theory of the firm literature: the transactions costs approach and the team production approach. Oliver Williamson (1985) has identified and defined many of the basic ideas in the transactions cost approach. He notes, for example, that if one party owns a coal mine and another party owns an electric power plant located near the mine mouth, and the power plant is designed to use the particular grade of coal from that mine, then the two parties are obviously better off if the power plant obtains its coal supply from the mine (Williamson, 1985; Williamson et al., 1975). But both are likely to try to capture the value of the efficiency gains from trading with each other, and the battle over the gains is likely to take the form of disputes over the price that the power plant owner should pay for coal from the mine.

If the power plant owner buys the coal mine, however, or the coal mine operator buys the power plant, the owner of the resulting vertically integrated enterprise would be able to maximize the joint return over the whole enterprise without wasting resources in haggling over the terms of trade between them. Thus, vertical integration is one way to solve the hold-up problem and reduce the 'transactions costs' that would be associated with the two operations attempting to trade with each other at arm's length.

This solution works, however, only if the specific assets in question are physical assets rather than human capital. If some of the firm-specific investments are in human capital, there may be no way to arrange for joint ownership of both specific physical capital and specific human capital since the latter is not transferable. If more than one person in the enterprise has significant specific human capital invested in the enterprise, then 'ownership' of that human capital cannot be consolidated in a single person. Williamson (1985) recognizes this problem and argues that many of the special arrangements we see in the relationship between corporations and their employees, such as severance pay, various forms of job security, and collectively bargained agreements that give certain benefits to employees with seniority, may serve as mechanisms for protecting employee investments in firm-specific human capital.

Sanford Grossman and Oliver Hart (1986) address these issues in a different way. Grossman and Hart's (1986) model considers a situation in which multiple participants in an enterprise must make investments in firm-specific human capital that are very difficult or impossible to contract over because, for example, they are not well-defined or observable to a third party (for contract enforcement purposes). Their model leads to the conclusion that ownership rights in the firm should go to the party whose firm-specific human capital investments add the most value to the enterprise but are the most difficult to contract over. Ownership rights over the firm itself—which, in Grossman and Hart's (1986) analysis give the owner the right to make decisions about the use of the firm's assets—provide some assurance for the party who must make specialized human capital investments that her claim to a share in the rents generated by the investments will not be expropriated by the other participants. But again, this solution fails to resolve the question of how rents are to be allocated when multiple persons must make firm-specific investments (Blair, 1999).

A second line of thinking about the role of firm-specific human capital in the theory of the firm emphasizes the importance of 'team production'. Armen Alchian and Harold Demsetz characterize team production as 'production in which (1) several types of resources are used and (2) the product is not a sum of separable outputs of each cooperating resource…[and] (3) not all resources used in team production belong to one person' (Alchian and Demsetz, 1972: 779). In the original Alchian and Demsetz (1972) model, the organizational problem that needs to be solved is simply the possibility that team members might shirk, or fail to work as hard and as diligently as expected. The team members solve this problem by choosing someone to serve as a monitor. In order to be effective, the monitor must have the power to hire and fire. In addition, the monitor should be entitled to keep any surplus or rents generated by the team, in order to assure that she has appropriate incentives to carry out her task diligently. The model thus provides an explanation for individual proprietorships in which the entrepreneur has decision-making authority, and captures the rent from joint production. Alchian and Demsetz's (1972) team members are not assumed to make any specialized human capital investments in the firm, however, and, in this article at least, the authors even argue that nothing in the model implies that the relationship between the monitor (employer) and the team members (employees) should even be long term.[9]

Demsetz (1991) has since adopted the view that longevity in the relationships between employees and employers is one of the key features of firms, and that to explain these it is important to consider enterprise-specific human capital investments. A team, then, is a group of participants who have specialized their human capital to work with each other, which implies that the human capital of all the team members is worth more when they work together than when they work in other contexts. Labor is not undifferentiated, as in the production function model of the firm—it matters who is on the team. Demsetz (1991) then defines a firm as 'a bundle of commitments to technology, personnel, and methods, all contained and constrained by an insulating layer of information that is specific to the firm, and this bundle cannot be altered or imitated easily or quickly' (1991: 165), thereby placing firm-specific investments, including investments in specialized human capital, at the center of his theory of the firm.

The difficulty that must be overcome in team production is that of giving each team member incentives to cooperate fully. When the output is a joint output, and the contributions of each team member are difficult to define, observe, or measure, there will be incentives for team members to shirk or free-ride on the efforts of other team members if they are all compensated with a flat wage determined before production begins. On the other hand, if the wage is to be determined based on the outcome in production, team members will have incentives to waste resources in attempting to make the output look more impressive than it is,[10] or make their own role look more important than it was.

Team production, then, presents exactly the same organizational problem as investments in specific human capital—how are the rents generated from team production to be divided among the team members so that each has an incentive to specialize their human capital and to cooperate fully with the other team members, and none have incentives to expend resources in squabbling over the allocation of the rents?

Recall that Alchian and Demsetz (1972) assumed away the specific-investment problem, identifying 'shirking' rather than rent allocation as the problem to be solved by the monitor. A subsequent line of articles, however, put specific investments back into the problem and also relied on a role for some sort of monitor to solve the rent allocation problem (Holmstrom, 1982; Rajan and Zingales, 1998; Blair and Stout, 1999). In a mathematical model of the team production problem, Bengt Holmstrom (1982) showed that there was no solution to the problem that allocated all of the output to team members, yet did not create perverse incentives. Holmstrom's proposed solution (1982) designated a role for an outsider who would capture all of the rents unless the total rents generated by the enterprise were high enough to demonstrate that none of the team members could have shirked.[11]

Raghuram Rajan and Luigi Zingales (1998) likewise modeled the problem, using a model that was similar to the one that Grossman and Hart (1986) had used, but designated a role for an 'owner' rather than for a monitor. In their model, output could be maximized if all of the members of the team made investments in human capital that were specialized to the particular physical assets owned by the 'owner'.[12] The owner, however, could capture some of the rents by selling the specialized asset, along with the opportunity to direct the team, to an outsider. If the potential gains from selling exceeded the potential gains from personally investing in specialized human capital, the owner would, presumably, sell. Rajan and Zingales's (1998) proposed solution involved having an outsider, who is not part of the team (that is, who does not need to invest in specialized human capital), be the owner of the physical asset. An outside owner would then give access to the specialized physical asset to the team that promises the highest total production, which could only occur if all of the team members make the necessary investments in specialized human capital. Rajan and Zingales (1998) interpret their model as providing an explanation for outside investors in publicly traded corporations.

Blair and Stout (1999) argue, however, that the actual role of outside shareholders in corporations is very different from the role of the so-called 'owner' in the Rajan and Zingales (1998) model. Outside shareholders in corporations have little or no direct legal control over the assets of a corporation and play no part in choosing the team that should have access (unless they hold more than 50 percent of the voting rights, in which case they would not be regarded as 'outside' shareholders). Instead, Blair and Stout (1999) note that the role described by Rajan and Zingales (1998) looks more like the actual legal role that boards of directors play in corporations. Directors have the legal right and responsibility to make or approve investment decisions and allocation decisions (directors are the only participants in firms who may initiate and approve of dividend payments, for example), and they must choose the management team to carry out their responsibilities. Otherwise, directors are rarely actively involved in day-to-day management of a company unless they are also officers of the company.

1.6 Unresolved Controversies

Although the potential 'hold-up' problem between employer and employee that is said to arise when firm-specific human capital is employed continues to be important in the theory of the firm literature, some labor economists have cast doubts on its importance in understanding labor market characteristics, institutions, and out-comes. The most important feature of labor markets that is generally thought to be explained by firm-specific human capital investments is the fact that tenure in a given firm seems to matter, as well as experience, in explaining wages across differ-ent employees. If employees were compensated only for general human capital, most, if not all, of the difference in wages among individual employees would be the result of education, training, and experience. We would not expect to find that employee wages go up with tenure in a given firm, after controling for these other factors. Wages, however, do rise with tenure—in fact, generally tenure is as impor-tant in explaining wage differentials as is experience or other measures of general human capital (Hutchens, 1989).

Labor economist Edward Lazear (2003) has offered several alternative theories to explain this empirical regularity, however. In situations where they cannot easily monitor workers, Lazear (1979) has argued, firms may offer workers 'delayed-payment' contracts, with below-market wages in the early years and above-market wages in the later years.[13] Agreeing to delayed payments serves as a mechanism by which workers 'bond' their performance and their commitment not to shirk because they accept below-market wages early in the relationship in exchange for a promise of more later, thereby giving the employer the opportunity to withhold the subse-quent reward if the employee shirks. Delayed payment contracts also result in an upward sloping wage-tenure curve, as we would also expect to find under the 'firm-specific human capital' theory (Lazear, 1979). More recently, Lazear (2003) has fur-ther criticized specific human capital theory by pointing out that empirical economists have had difficulty 'generat[ing] convincing examples where the firm-specific component approaches the importance of the general component' (2003: 1) of human capital. He has argued that another possible explanation for the observed empirical relationship between wages and tenure is what he calls 'skill-weights'. The idea here is that all skills are general, but that different firms use skills in different combinations, with different weights attached to different skills (Lazear, 2003). Lazear (2003) claims that the skill-weights explanation also clarifies several other features of labor markets that are hard to explain under the firm-specific human capital theory.

Although the mechanism might be different from the mechanism at work in theories that rely on firm-specific human capital investments, these alternative the-ories have similar implications for theories of the firm because they all imply that employees often have much to lose if they are separated from their current employer prematurely by layoffs or job cutbacks, and that they will tend to have more to lose the longer they have been with their current employer. This, in turn, implies that employees, as well as shareholders, have 'assets' (their stream of expected high wages) at risk in corporate enterprises. This fact makes it important that employee welfare be taken into account, alongside shareholder welfare, in the management and governance of corporations (Blair, 1995).

1.7 Contemporary Policy Issues

As mentioned at the beginning of this article, the concept of human capital has come to play an important role in labor economics, macroeconomics, economic growth theory, development economics, trade theory, the economics of education, the theory of the firm, and the theory and practice of human resources management and strategic planning. It is also a significant aspect of policy questions for which these theories are relevant.

Many economists and policy-makers have been troubled, for example, by the growing disparity in both incomes and wealth in the US and in some other developed countries in recent years, and have puzzled over the causes of this (Heckman and Krueger, 2004; Levy and Temin, 2007). If the distribution of wages across individuals is determined by the distribution of human capital, the growing income disparity would suggest either that education and training achievements per person are becoming much more disparate (Lazear and Shaw, 2007), or that some types of human capital may be losing value while other types are becoming more valuable. In particular, technological change might be causing manual labor skills to become less valued, while math- and science-related skills, particularly in certain areas such as finance or biotechnology or software development, might be becoming much more valuable (Goldin and Katz, 2007).[14]

But scholars who have studied the distribution of income have found that when people are grouped by factors that are commonly taken as indicators of human capital, such as years of education, or degrees earned, data on individual incomes indicate that the variance of incomes within each category is almost as great as the variance across categories (Karoly, 1998). This suggests several possibilities: (1) unobserved dimensions of skill account for the discrepancy of earnings within categories (Juhn et al., 1993); (2) factors other than human capital endowments are at work in determining income distribution (Levy and Temin, 2007); or (3) our measures or indicators of human capital are woefully inadequate. Or perhaps more than one of these possibilities is true.

Another important policy area has to do with the role played by human capital investments in economic development and growth. If the international community wants to facilitate growth in the world's poorest countries, what strategies should be adopted? Is it more important to invest in physical infrastructure in those countries, such as roads and dams, or to provide financial capital, or to invest in human capital in those countries by working to improve basic education systems and post-secondary education institutions and by improving access by young people to educational opportunities?

A related area in which human capital theories are important to policy questions has to do with the impact of the growing practice by large corporations in developed countries of 'outsourcing' increasingly skilled work to subsidiaries or to independent firms in developing countries. There seems to be no question about the goal of the multinational firms that are doing this—they are engaging in 'labor arbitrage' to take advantage of lower wages in developing countries. But there are significant questions about whether this arbitrage, over time, is reducing employment opportunities across the board in developed countries, thereby bringing down wages, or whether it simply moves less desirable opportunities offshore while leaving the highest-valued work for employees with sufficient human capital in the home country (Krugman, 2008). If the latter, then the best policy response may be to expand education and training in the home country so that low-skilled workers can acquire more human capital, and thereby qualify for the higher-end opportunities.

Finally, if the stock of human capital in developed countries is the most important source of national wealth and international competitiveness, as many economists and policy-makers now believe, will developed countries lose their current pre-eminence in the world economy as the stock of human capital in developing countries grows to look more and more like that in developed countries? Several recent studies suggest that a substantial slowdown in the rate of human capital acquisition in the US since 1970 has already allowed other developed countries to catch up and surpass the US in productivity, and that it is the failure of education to keep up with the pace of technological change, not outsourcing and globalization, that is causing the US to lose competitiveness, and income inequality to increase. Claudia Goldin and Lawrence Katz (2008) assembled educational achievement data over nearly a century and a half to show that the average level of education of adults in the US rose by 0.8 of a year per decade from 1870 to 1960, but then flattened out from 1970 onwards. In 1890 the average adult in the US had completed eight years of schooling, and by 1960 the average adult had completed nearly fourteen years of schooling. This pace of human capital development allowed the US to surge ahead of the rest of the world in productivity and wealth in the first seven decades of the twentieth century. By contrast, educational attainment stagnated from 1970 to 1990, as many countries in the rest of the world caught up with and passed the US in productivity and real incomes (Goldin and Katz, 2008).

1.8 CONCLUDING THOUGHTS

There are, of course, many reasons why it is a good thing to encourage and support education, training, and health care for the population of a given country or community. The theory of human capital focuses attention on one subset of reasons: the possibility of increasing the productivity and wealth-creating potential of the people. A broad range of activities that enhance the economic productivity of workers—from schooling, to formal and informal training, to apprenticeship programs, to immunization programs, and even health club memberships—can be regarded as investments in human capital. Although the idea of treating the skills, knowledge, and capabilities of the workforce as being analogous to physical or financial capital was controversial when first introduced, the idea has proved powerful enough in policy discussions about productivity, economic growth, distribution of incomes and wealth, and workplace organization, for use of the phrase to be growing and to seem unlikely to diminish any time soon.

Notes

1. Lewin (Ch. 5) explores how the Austrian view of capital leads to an understanding of capital as accumulated knowledge, embodied in tools or machines or institutional structures—a concept which perhaps links more naturally to the concept of human capital.
2. Kochan and Litwin (Ch. 25) examine some of the implications of the breakdown in social arrangements that historically resulted in long-term relationships between employers and employees.
3. Marx and Engels (1952) argued that, for this reason, theories that treat wages or salaries as if they were 'interest' earned on human capital are inherently misleading.
4. 'Book value' measures the purchase price paid for purchased assets and assets made within the firm, minus some allowance for depreciation, and may not reflect the actual current value of the assets. To the extent that actual value differs from book value, the resulting measure of the value of intangibles will also be mismeasured.
5. Measures of intangibles derived from measures of the market value of a firm's financial capital are also extraordinarily volatile, as the wide fluctuations in values in stock and equity markets in 2008 and 2009 demonstrated.
6. In fact, these models provided no way to measure technical change directly; it was simply assumed that the 'residual' portion of economic growth that could not be explained by increases in labor and/or capital was a product of the unmeasured technological change input.
7. The so-called Harrod–Domar growth models assumed that labor inputs could be measured in terms of 'efficiency units' of labor, which grew faster than the growth of the number of people in the labor force as a result of 'labor augmenting' technical change.
8. Such as competitive markets for labor and capital, and that the marginal productivity of labor is equal to the long run average productivity of labor.
9. Gibbons (2005) provides an excellent summary and comparison of various economic theories of the firm.
10. Consider, for example, the efforts expended by Enron employees in the late 1990s and early 2000s to make it appear that the company had more assets and higher profits than it actually would have had if the balance sheets of its so-called 'special purpose entities' had been fairly incorporated into the balance sheet of the enterprise as a whole. See Bratton (2001–2).

11. This peculiar solution does not look like any known organizational structures, probably because, in practice, it would create perverse incentives for the monitor to collude with one of the team members to keep production low. See Blair (1999).
12. Rajan and Zingales did not use the 'team production' language in their article, but the model is conceptually similar.
13. Economists call these delayed payment contracts 'efficiency wages'.
14. This explanation for growing wage disparity is commonly called the 'skill-biased technical change' hypothesis (Card and DiNardo, 2002).

References

ALCHIAN, A., and DEMSETZ, H. (1972). 'Production, Information Costs, and Economic Organization', *American Economic Review*, 62(5): 777–95.
BECKER, G. (1964). *Human Capital: A Theoretical and Empirical Analysis, with Special Reference to Education*, 2nd edn. (New York: National Bureau of Economic Research).
BLAIR, M. M. (1995). *Ownership and Control: Rethinking Corporate Governance for the Twenty-First Century* (Washington, DC: Brookings Institution Press).
——(1999). 'Firm-Specific Human Capital and Theories of the Firm', in M. M. Blair and M. J. Roe (eds.), *Employees and Corporate Governance* (Washington, DC: Brookings Institution Press), 58–90.
——and STOUT, L. A. (1999). 'A Team Production Theory of Corporate Law', *Virginia Law Review*, 85(2): 248–328.
——and WALLMAN, S. M. H. (2001). *Unseen Wealth: Report of the Brookings Task Force on Intangibles* (Washington, DC: Brookings Institution Press).
BLAUG, M. (1987). *The Economics of Education and the Education of an Economist* (New York: New York University Press).
BRATTON, WILLIAM (2001–2). 'Enron and the Dark Side of Shareholder Value', *Tulane Law Review*, 76: 1275–1361.
CARD, D. (2001). 'Estimating the Return to Schooling: Progress on Some Persistent Econometric Problems', *Econometrica*, 69(5): 1127–60.
——and DiNARDO, J. (2002). 'Skill-Biased Technological Change and Rising Wages Inequality: Some Problems and Puzzles', *Journal of labor Economics*, 20: 733–83.
DEMSETZ, H. (1991). 'The Theory of the Firm Revisited', *Journal of Law, Economics, and Organization*, 4(1): 141–61.
DENISON, E. F. (1983). 'The Interruption of Productivity Growth in the United States', *Economic Journal*, 93(369): 56–77.
DOERINGER, P. B., and PIORE, M. J. (1971). *Internal Labor Markets and Manpower Analysis* (Lexington, Mass.: D. C. Heath & Co.).
DOMAR, E. D. (1957). *Essays in the Theory of Economic Growth* (New York: Oxford University Press).
GATES, S. (2002). 'Value at Work: The Risks and Opportunities of Human Capital Measurement and Reporting', in J. Radzin (ed.), *The Conference Board Research Report* (New York: Conference Board).

GIBBONS, ROBERT (2005). 'Four Formal(izable) Theories of the Firm?', *Journal of Economic Behavior and Organization*, 58: 200–45.

GOLDIN, C., and KATZ, L. F. (2007). 'Long-Run Changes in the U.S. Wage Structure: Narrowing, Widening, Polarizing', *Brookings Papers on Economic Activity*, 2: 135–67 (Washington, DC: Brookings).

——and ——(2008). *The Race between Education and Technology* (Cambridge, Mass.: Harvard University Press).

GROSSMAN, S. J., and HART, O. D. (1986). 'The Costs and Benefits of Ownership: A Theory of Vertical and Lateral Integration', *Journal of Political Economy*, 94: 691–719.

HAND, J. R. M., and LEV, B. (2003). *Intangible Assets: Values, Measures, and Risks* (New York: Oxford University Press).

HARROD, F. (1948). *Towards a Dynamic Economics* (London: Macmillan).

HASHIMOTO, M. (1981). 'Firm Specific Human Capital as a Shared Investment', *American Economic Review*, 71(3): 475–82.

HECKMAN, J. J., and KRUEGER, A. B. (2004). *Inequality in America: What Role for Human Capital Policies* (Cambridge, Mass.: MIT Press).

HOLMSTROM, B. (1982). 'Moral Hazard in Teams', *Bell Journal of Economics*, 13(2): 324–40.

HUTCHENS, R. M. (1989). 'Seniority, Wages and Productivity: A Turbulent Decade', *Journal of Economic Perspectives*, 4(3): 49–64.

JUHN, C., MURPHY, K. M., and PIERCE, B. (1993). 'Wage Inequality and the Rise in Returns to Skill', *Journal of Political Economy*, 101(3): 410–42.

KAROLY, L. A. (1998). 'Growing Economic Disparity in the U.S.: Assessing the Problem and the Policy Options', in J. A. Auerbach and R. S. Belous (eds.), *The Inequality Paradox: Growth of Income Disparity* (Washington, DC: National Policy Association), 239–59.

KRUGMAN, P. (2008). 'Trade and Wages, Reconsidered', *Brookings Papers on Economic Activity* (spring): 103–37 (Washington, DC: Brookings).

LAZEAR, E. P. (1979). 'Why is there Mandatory Retirement?', *Journal of Political Economy*, 87(6): 1261–84.

——2003). *Firm-Specific Human Capital: A Skill-Weights Approach* (Cambridge, Mass.: National Bureau of Economic Research Working Paper 9679).

——and SHAW, K. L. (2007). *Wage Structure, Raises, and Mobility: International Comparisons of the Structure of Wages within and across Firms* (Mass.: National Bureau of Economic Research Working Paper).

LEVY, F., and TEMIN, P. (2007). *Inequality and Institutions in 20th Century America* (Cambridge, Mass.: Massachusetts Institute of Technology Working Paper).

McGRATTAN, E. R., and PRESCOTT, E. C. (2007). *Unmeasured Investment and the Puzzling U.S. Boom in the 1990s* (Cambridge, Mass.: National Bureau of Economic Research Working Paper).

MARX, K., and ENGELS, F. (1952). *Capital* (Chicago: Encyclopedia Britannica).

PETTERSSON, E. (2010). 'Matel Loses Bratz Doll Appeals Court Ruling to MGA', Bloomberg, http://www.bloomberg.com/news/2010-07-22/mattel-s-victory-on-rights-to-bratz-dolls-overturned-by-u-s-appeals-court.htm

PIGOU, A. (1928). *A Study in Public Finance* (London: Macmillan).

POLLOCK, D. (2008). 'Jury Rules Bratz Dolls Conceived at Mattel', San Francisco Gate, http://www.sfgate.com/cgi-bin/article.cgi?f=/n/a/2008/07/17/financial/f145521D42.DTL.

RAJAN, R., and ZINGALES, L. (1998). 'Power in the Theory of the Firm', *Quarterly Journal of Economics*, 113(2): 387–432.

ROMER, P. M. (1986). 'Increasing Returns and Long Run Growth', *Journal of Political Economy*, 94(5): 1002–37.

SMITH, A. (1937). *An Inquiry into the Nature and Causes of the Wealth of Nations* (New York: Modern Library).

SOLOW, R. W. (1957). 'Technical Change and the Aggregate Production Function', *Review of Economics and Statistics*, 39(3): 312–20.

STEWART, T. A. (1997). *Intellectual Capital: The New Wealth of Organizations* (New York: Doubleday).

WILLIAMSON, O. (1985). *The Economic Institutions of Capitalism: Firms, Markets, Relational Contracting* (New York: Free Press).

——WACHTER, M., and HARRIS, J. (1975). 'Understanding the Employment Relation: The Analysis of Idiosyncratic Exchange', *Bell Journal of Economics*, 6(1): 250–78.

....

CHAPTER 2

A SOCIAL PERSPECTIVE

EXPLORING THE LINKS
BETWEEN HUMAN CAPITAL
AND SOCIAL CAPITAL

....

JANINE NAHAPIET

2.1 INTRODUCTION

....

In this chapter I argue that it is essential to take a social perspective on human capital. To explore what this implies I use the lens of social capital—a concept of growing interest and salience in studies of social and organizational theory and practice.

In their search for theories to explain differences in social and economic outcomes at the individual, organizational, and societal levels scholars and policymakers have increasingly drawn upon the concept of capital. In the second half of the twentieth century, two applications of the term became part of the mainstream: human capital and social capital.

Research on human capital highlights the significance of individual knowledge, skills, and qualifications for economic and social outcomes across several levels of analysis, from micro to macro. Appearing as a strong research stream in the years following the Second World War, interest in human capital has deepened with the transition to a knowledge economy. Evidence for this exists in the work of governments and international bodies such as the OECD, in scholarly associations—for example, the creation of a new interest group on strategic human capital in the Strategic Management Society—and in professional bodies and work organizations, as shown by the amount of attention given to the topic of human talent in recent years. Such trends demonstrate a widespread consensus that if the creation and exploitation of knowledge are fundamental to success, then developing a profound understanding of the ways in which the knowledge, skills, and attributes of individuals become productive is critical.

As part of this endeavour, increasing attention is being paid to the ways in which contextual factors may shape the development and application of human capital. Human capital is essentially an individual asset, but its value in practice often depends on wider social factors. To examine these, some scholars have turned to research on social capital as providing a promising theory and perspective. These two constructs—human and social capital—and their interrelationships are the focus of this chapter.

The chapter is structured as follows. In the opening sections I discuss three central constructs: the concept of capital, followed by human and then social capital. In exploring their relationships I examine what research tells us first about the impact of social capital on human capital, and then the influence of human capital on social capital. Given the centrality of knowledge and learning in research in both fields, this provides a useful focus for exploring the more complex interrelationships between these two forms of capital. This leads to a more detailed consideration of the several mechanisms whereby these two types of capital are interlinked. The chapter ends with general conclusions and discussion of the implications for future research.

The literatures on human and social capital are large and growing fast. Partly this is because these two fields are of great interest not only to scholars across several disciplines but also to policy-makers. In what follows here, my primary focus will be on research insights and challenges—with only occasional reference to policy and practice issues. In discussing research I will examine core concepts and evidence across a broad range of social spheres, leaving more detailed consideration of organizational and managerial applications to later chapters in this volume.

2.2 CAPITAL IDEAS

There has been a growing trend to apply the economists' term 'capital' to a wide range of social and psychological phenomena, highlighting their role as potentially valuable intangible assets. The concept of human capital is perhaps the most well established (Schultz, 1961; Becker, 1964), but discussion of cultural capital (DiMaggio,

1982; Bourdieu, 1986), social capital (Coleman, 1988; Putnam, 1993), organizational capital (Prescott and Visscher, 1980; Tomer, 1987), and identity capital (Côté, 1997, 2005) among others, has led some scholars to lament both the tendency to refer to virtually every feature of social life as a form of capital and the resulting 'plethora of capitals' that is to be found in the literature (Baron and Hannan, 1994).

This trend is controversial for two main reasons. First, many are critical of the value associations of the concept, and second, there are strong reservations about whether or not these newly labelled intangible assets should be called capital as they fail to meet the criteria that define the concept in neoclassical economics. The debates continue today, though there is a growing body of scholars developing alternative models in which all resources are viewed as a type of capital. Moreover, many researchers argue that, notwithstanding its limitations, using the term 'capital' metaphorically has clear heuristic value, bringing fresh insights and producing important advances in both theory-building and policy across a number of fields.

Questions about value associations range from disciplinary concerns about the spread of economics into other fields, especially sociology, with 'capital' as a Trojan horse for economic imperialism, through to much wider questions about the implications and consequences of using economic concepts as a prism to interpret wider social phenomena (Hirsch et al., 1990; Fine, 2001; Fishman, 2009). In particular, how far does calling something 'capital' fundamentally imply viewing people and social relationships as instrumental, invested in for a return and in the service of economic value? Does it inevitably deny or underestimate the importance of actions and interactions that are intrinsically valuable to those engaged in them, or that have wider social and political consequences that should be considered independently and separately from their economic impact? These are enduring concerns explicitly discussed in Schultz's (1961) influential paper on human capital. He, along with others, argues that there is nothing in the concept of human wealth contrary to the idea that it exists for the advantage of people. Indeed, he argues that by 'investing in themselves people can enlarge the range of choice available to them. It is one way free men can enhance their welfare' (1961: 2). Indeed, some scholars argue that extending usage of the term to other phenomena, for example to social capital, has merit in that '*it reinserts issues of value into the heart of social scientific discourse*' by questioning the assumptions of individualizing notions of self-interest that underpin economic theory (Schuller et al., 2000: 36; italics as in original). What is clear is that theorizing individual and social phenomena as capital opens up the possibility of adopting a highly rational and instrumental model of people and relationships. However, depending on the theory of capital being adopted, usage of the term does not of itself require the acceptance of a narrow view of values, even within economics (van Staveren and Knorringa, 2007).

The second controversy centers on the validity of the concept when applied beyond the sphere of economics: how far is it 'really' capital and in what sense? (Lin, 2001; Adler and Kwon, 2002; Robison et al., 2002). In asking the question, 'can ideas be capital', Dean and Kretschmer (2007) propose two criteria that justify extension of a concept to new phenomena. First, application of the term must conform to the commonly held understanding of that concept—in this case, capital—and second, additional interpretive power should result from defining a construct as capital.

Although the concept of capital is central to the study of economics, there are important disagreements about its meaning and significance. Lewin lists five schools of thought, observing that it 'seems as if each generation of economists has invented its own notion of Capital and its own "capital controversy"' (Lewin, 2005: 145). However, he suggests that there are essentially two broad and exclusive views of capital: the quantitative and the structural. The former provides the commonly held understanding of the term, is rooted in neoclassical economics, and reflects what Lewin describes as 'the Ricardian frame of mind'. The list of the defining features of capital varies somewhat from author to author, in part depending upon whether they take as their benchmark physical or financial capital, but there is substantial overlap in their understanding. Blair, for example, in Chapter 1 above, defines capital as a factor of production that is itself produced from other inputs, characterized by ownership, investment, and returns on that investment and deferred consumption. Dean and Kretschmer (2007) see capital in traditional economic thought as consisting of durable assets, themselves the result of past production, linked to an economic actor, facilitating the creation of value and an element in a closed system. Many of the so-called hybrid forms of capital meet some but far from all of these definitional criteria. Accordingly, critics have argued that the capital metaphor is wrong and that its use should be abandoned in these contexts (Baron and Hannan, 1994; Arrow, 2000; Solow, 2000).

Other authors, however, defend the merits of using the term metaphorically. For example, in their review of social capital Adler and Kwon argue that it resembles some kind of capital and differs from others. However it 'falls squarely within the broad and heterogeneous family of resources commonly called "capital"' (2002: 22). For Dean and Kretschmer (2007), discussions of extended or hybrid forms of capital, such as human, social, and intellectual capital, have led to the emergence of a fundamentally different conceptualization of capital, and they contrast 'the older traditional economic concept in which capital is an immutable, measurable stock versus the new extended concepts in which "hybrid" forms of capital embody processes and are dynamic' (2007: 581). This change in the underlying concept of capital being used appears consistent with a shift towards the second theory of capital described by Lewin—the structural approach of the Austrian School and the work of Adam Smith and Carl Menger.

Whereas the neoclassical model assumes equilibrium in which the components of capital must be reduced to commensurable terms and quantifiable in some dimension so that we can talk unambiguously of capital accumulation and capital stocks, the structural approach reflects the belief that not only is this impossible, it has also been unduly limiting in its effects on the applications of economics. Two features are striking about what Lewin acknowledges is as yet a minority perspective on capital. First, the structural approach allows for a set of heterogeneous capital items, some tangible and some intangible, with all resources being seen as a type of capital. Second, it emphasizes capital structure rather than capital stock; that is, the importance of the pattern and connections between different types and forms of capital—in particular their complementarity and substitutability. Both these aspects will be important when we come to consider the relationship between human and social capital.

What then is the additional interpretive power and heuristic value that comes from using the term capital in this extended fashion, particularly in respect of human and social capital? First, it highlights the many ways in which individual and social factors may act as resources influencing important personal, social, and economic outcomes. In doing so, it points to the importance of both tangible and intangible assets in such outcomes and, most especially, to the structure or configuration of these assets. Second, it draws attention to the significance of investments in human, social, and institutional spheres, now widely regarded as central to major policy initiatives (OECD, 2001; Halpern, 2005; Ahn and Ostrom, 2008). Third, it provides a common language and perspective that can be applied across multiple levels of analysis—opening up the possibilities for exploring their interrelationships. Finally, it brings an important time dimension into our analysis—with capital viewed as the durable result of past activity—a form of accumulated history capable of transforming current and future interactions and outcomes (Bourdieu, 1986; Lewin, 2005 and Ch. 5; Fisher, quoted in Dean and Kretschmer, 2007). For Spender (2009), the term capital demands that we focus on what can be transferred from one time-space to another.

2.3 HUMAN CAPITAL

Neoclassical economists use the term human capital to refer to the stock of knowledge and skills that enables people to perform work that creates economic value. The field is widely acknowledged to have developed formally around the middle of the twentieth century, particularly, though not exclusively, through the contributions of Theodore Schultz (1961) and Gary Becker (1964). However, its central propositions were developed much earlier. For example, in his review of the foundations of the field, Sweetland (1996) suggests that the most prominent economists to address issues of human capital were Adam Smith, John Stuart Mill, and Alfred Marshall. One can recognize the foundations of the idea in Adam Smith's (1776) discussion of labor which he saw as a type of capital stock alongside other key productive resources—machines, building, and land—and in his exposition of the costs of and returns to investments in human talents both to the individual and society. His belief in the importance of 'the acquired and useful abilities' of people for economic activity and status of these abilities as 'a capital fixed and realised, as it were, in his person' remain at the centre of human capital theory today.

There is no consensus on a definition of human capital, though it is generally agreed that of the various forms of hybrid capital it is human capital that most closely aligns to the requirements of the neoclassical view (Woolcock, 2001; Bowman and Swart, 2007). The concept is multidimensional, but the features at the centre of most research on the economic benefits of human capital have been knowledge, skills, and, to a lesser extent, health (Keeley, 2007). According to Blaug (1976: 829):

The hard core of the human capital research program is the idea that people spend on themselves in diverse ways, not for the sake of present enjoyments, but for the sake of future pecuniary and non-pecuniary returns. All these phenomena—health, education, job search, information retrieval, migration, and in-service training may be viewed as investment rather than consumption—whether undertaken by individuals on their own behalf or undertaken by society on behalf of its members.

Although scholars identify diverse types of investment that increase human capital, from health to migration (Schultz, 1961), education consistently emerges as the prime focus for empirical analysis. There is now a substantial body of evidence demonstrating the economic returns to education at both the individual and societal level (Keeley, 2007). Benson (1978) suggests that human capital theory rests on two key assumptions: education helps develop skills of work—that is, improves the capacity of the worker to be productive—and earned income reflects marginal productivities of different categories of worker. However, these two assumptions are severely limiting. For example, educational credentials are a simple and readily measured proxy for skills and competence, but there are real limitations to this mode of assessing human capital. There is an acknowledged but as yet largely unmet need to look at actual knowledge and skills, not just time spent in education. Moreover, the field is still heavily oriented to the assessment of educational stocks; that is, statics rather than dynamics. More technically, there are widely differing approaches to assessing rates of return—both for the individual and society—that have major implications for policy and practice (Sweetland, 1996).

Over time, research on human capital has developed in significant ways—from a relatively narrow view of both the relevant attributes of workers and the performance outcomes of interest. First, the attributes of individuals included in some definitions of human capital have been extended to include innate talents and abilities as well as the skills and learning acquired through education and training (OECD, 2007). This represents a broader view of human potential, taking it beyond characteristics that are the result of investments and may be a step too far for those committed to that part of the definition of capital as something that is produced. It also touches on the enduring debate about nature–nurture interrelationships in human behavior and performance—a debate beyond the scope of this chapter, but likely to resurface strongly in response to emerging insights from neuroscience research. Second, there has also been a widening of the outcomes to be considered in analysing the impact of human capital. For example, the OECD defined human capital as 'the knowledge, skills, competence and other attributes embodied in individuals that are relevant to economic activity' (OECD, 1998: 9). Three years later, the OECD definition had become: 'the knowledge, skills, competencies and attributes embodied in individuals that facilitate the creation of personal, social and economic well-being' (OECD, 2001: 18). This is a significant shift to include personal and social wellbeing alongside economic returns. It also blurs the helpful distinction made by Sen (1999) between human capital and human capability. Sen suggests that, by convention, the focus of the human capital perspective is on the 'human qualities that can be employed as 'capital' in production (in the same way that physical capital is)'. He sees this view as different from but fitting into the wider concept of human capability which focuses 'on the ability—the substantive freedom—of people to lead the lives they have reason to value and to enhance the real choices they have' (Sen, 1999: 293).[1] This distinction is an important one; both human capital and human capabilities are of great interest, but conflating them into one construct is unlikely to be helpful in research or, indeed, policy-making.

Finally, there has been a gradual acceptance of the need to move beyond formal education and qualifications to study learning processes, combined with a resurgence of interest in wider contexts for learning, particularly on-the-job training (Schuller et al., 2004b; Eraut and Hirsh, 2007). The focus on learning in wider social settings, including the family and community groups, is consistent with Fabricant's (1959) early observation that human capital can be built deliberately or accidentally as by-products of efforts to reach other goals. It is also representative of a trend towards a more social view of human capital. Both philosophically and methodologically, the majority of mainstream work on human capital is still characterized by an undersocialized model of man—based on an individually instrumental view of investment in education and training and a model of knowledge and skills as developed and embodied within the individual person, and accessible, manifest, and transferable with minimal regard for context (Bowman and Swart, 2007; Ch. 23 below). As our understanding of knowledge and learning has evolved, and as research has focused on the dynamics of learning across different settings, there has been a growing recognition of the relevance and potential of taking a more social perspective on human capital. This insight parallels the reasoning of economic sociologists more generally who argue that it 'is important to open up the academic debate about the economy to include a genuinely social perspective and to set the interactions of real people at its center' (Swedberg and Granovetter, 2001: 1).

2.4 HUMAN CAPITAL: THE CASE FOR A SOCIAL VIEW

Swedberg and Granovetter (2001) identify three principles that underpin the development of a social perspective on economic phenomena. First, economic action is a form of social action. Second, economic action is socially situated or embedded. Third, economic institutions are social constructions. All three are relevant arguments for a social view of human capital.

Viewing economic action as a form of social action—behaviour that actors invest with a meaning and that is also oriented to other actors—presents important challenges to the reductionist neoclassical model of human capital in which individuals are presumed to invest on the basis of instrumental, self-maximizing motives. It implies that the motives of actors need to be researched and discovered rather than assumed, and that actors' definitions of the situation will be important (van Staveren and Knorringa, 2007). Moreover, it suggests that economic actions, such as investing in health or learning, may not be determined exclusively or even primarily by economic self-interest. Other motives such as the search for approval, status, sociability, or power cannot be separated from economic action—and need to be taken into account in theorizing and researching such action. Such themes emerge clearly in recent research on the benefits of learning in education (Schuller et al., 2004b) and in the workplace (Eraut and Hirsh, 2007). They highlight the general importance of understanding the social context for human capital.

Learning, skills development, and knowledge acquisition typically take place in a social context—whether it is the individual interacting online, working collaboratively solving problems or at play in the family or some community group. Understanding the significance of social context and the ways in which it affects the development of human capital is essential for both theory and practice. Moreover, much knowledge and many skills are manifest in a social setting. Indeed some can only be displayed in a relational context. These include communication and interpersonal skills, such as teamwork and leadership, as well as civic skills such as community participation and being a good neighbor. They are socially situated and embedded in social interaction and social practice and inseparable from them (Preston, 2004; Bowman and Swart, 2007). This implies that if we are to develop a richer understanding of human capital, we need to move our attention from exclusive interest in individual attributes to include the emergent features of social relations and social interaction.

Finally, what we view as human capital at any one time and place is socially constructed—it reflects the prevailing thinking about what constitutes important knowledge, talent, and skills in terms of social and economic outcomes. As thinking changes, so does the focus on human abilities—as evidenced by the growing emphasis on so-called 'soft skills', such as collaboration and teamwork, and on attributes such as emotional and cultural intelligence.

For these reasons, I argue that it is essential that we consider human capital from a more social perspective. The question therefore becomes: which social theories can help us do this? There are several contenders. For example, social constructionism has much to offer in understanding how what is measured and accounted for reflects social values (Burchell *et al.*, 1980; Nahapiet, 1988). Social identity theory offers important insights, for example showing how multiple representations of the self— individual, relational, and collective—can enrich our understanding of individu- als—their attributes and actions (Sedikides and Brewer, 2001). Much of the thinking here has now been drawn into a separate area: identity capital, discussed by Côté (1997, 2005) and by Schuller (2004), and explored elsewhere in this *Handbook*.

My suggestion here is that research on social capital provides a particularly prom- ising theory for moving towards a more social model of human capital, for several reasons. Most obviously, both areas of research draw on the concept of capital to highlight the potential of human qualities and social relationships as valuable resources. Second, the link between social and human capital has been established for some time, initially and prominently through the work of James Coleman (1988), who demonstrated the importance of family and school connections for the educa- tional attainment of children. Both fields have focused extensively on the signifi- cance of educational institutions for individual and social outcomes—though their analysis has differed in important ways. Beyond this, I suggest that social capital provides both theory and evidence to illuminate the ways in which connections and relationships shape the development and realization of human potential.

2.5 SOCIAL CAPITAL

If human capital is about the value of people's individual abilities, social capital is about the value of social connections and relationships. For Burt (2005), social capi- tal in the contextual complement to human capital in explaining advantage.

The social capital construct has become attractive to a wide range of economic and social science disciplines as they seek to highlight and explain the value of social relations and networks for individuals, groups, and society. Social capital became established as a clear field of study somewhat later than human capital. Reviewers typically refer to Bourdieu (1986), Coleman (1988, 1990), and Putnam (1993, 1995) as the key pioneers. However, as with human capital, the central ideas about the impor- tance of social connections were evident in much earlier writing. For example, in his analysis of the conceptual history of social capital, Farr (2004) refers to Hanifan's (1916) work on the significance of civic education as a form of community capital, and to Dewey's (1900) critical pragmatism with its emphasis on the value of associational life. Indeed, for Dewey 'the individual mind [is] a function of social life' (quoted in Farr, 2004: 17).

The core proposition of social capital theory is that social ties constitute a valuable resource for the conduct of social affairs, enabling individuals and social groupings to achieve outcomes that they could not otherwise achieve, or could do so only at extra cost (Coleman, 1988; Burt, 1992; Putnam, 1993, 1995). According to Adler and Kwon (2002), goodwill is the substance of social capital and its effects flow from the information, influence, and solidarity such goodwill makes available.

As with human capital, no universally accepted definition of social capital yet exists, though the differences between authors are greater. In part, this is because work on social capital draws on a wide range of theories. Woolcock (1998) suggests that social capital research can be linked to five traditions associated with the work of Marx, Weber, Simmel, Durkheim, and Bentham. Recent definitions and approaches to social capital in the organizational field draw heavily on two separate but interrelated perspectives: the study of networks (Baker, 1990; Burt, 2000, 2005; Lin, 2008) and of communities (de Tocqueville, 1832/1969; Putnam 1993, 1995; Fukuyama, 1995, 1999). The former focuses primarily on the consequences of network structure and the configuration of social ties for the access and mobilization of resources. The latter highlights the importance of shared norms and values for fostering and enabling social exchange and cooperation—and the consequences for communities when these are lacking. An interest in cooperation is also evident in a third, but as yet less prominent perspective, that has been especially important in the international development field: the institutional perspective (Ostrom, 1994, 2009; Ahn and Ostrom, 2008). Research in this tradition examines how diverse forms of institution, especially in the form of institutional rules, may enhance or inhibit norms of trustworthiness, trust, and reciprocity.

The definition of social capital that informs this chapter and has been influential in research in economics and management studies is that of Nahapiet and Ghoshal. They see social capital as 'the sum of the actual and potential resources embedded within, available through and derived from the network of relationships possessed by an individual or social unit. Social capital comprises both the network and the assets that may be mobilized through that network' (Nahapiet and Ghoshal, 1998: 243). This definition highlights both the potential of social connections and three ways in which they link to resources.

As with the other hybrid forms of capital, there continues to be a debate about the validity of using the term capital for the phenomenon of social connections (Baron and Hannan, 1992; Lin, 2001; Adler and Kwon, 2002; Robison *et al.*, 2002). To the extent that there is a consensus, and some such as Fine (2001) remain deeply critical, scholars appear to agree that, while social capital resembles other forms of capital in some respects, for example—it is a durable asset that can yield important benefits at both the individual and collective level—it does not comply with the neoclassical view of capital. Indeed, there are notable differences from such capital. For example, unlike physical capital and much human capital, social capital is a public good: the actor or actors who generate social capital often capture only a small part of its benefits (Coleman, 1988). Like physical capital and human capital, but unlike financial capital, social capital needs maintenance. It is not depleted and, in some circumstances, it is enriched by use. And most strikingly, 'social capital is unlike all other forms of capital in being "located" not in the actors but in their relationships with other actors' (Adler and Kwon, 2002: 22). Whereas human capital resides in individuals, social capital resides in relationships. Given these characteristics, most social capital research aligns more with the structural approach to capital.

Similar to human capital, social capital is a multidimensional construct and researchers have sought to identify key features and their interrelationships. Two frameworks have become prominent in research across several disciplines. One typology makes the distinction between bonding, bridging, and linking social capital to describe the attributes and consequences of different network structures (Halpern, 2005). The networks that underpin bonding social capital are typically relatively closed and inward-looking, with strong reciprocal ties between homogeneous members. They are usually characterized by high levels of trust and tend to reinforce exclusive social identities. Bridging networks span diverse groups, connecting normally separate people and communities, and are often associated with innovation and change. Linking social capital is a particular form of bridging social capital and represents the resources that are associated with networks of vertical connections to powerful institutions. A common finding across studies of network structures is the significance of network centrality—those actors that occupy central positions in networks typically do better across a wide range of performance criteria (Burt, 2005).

The second framework, developed in the context of research specifically exploring the links between social capital and intellectual capital, identifies three dimensions that are important in understanding the links between knowledge and relationships. They are the structural, the relational, and the cognitive (Nahapiet and Ghoshal, 1998). As the name suggests, the structural dimension refers to the overall pattern of connections between actors whereas the relational dimension describes the kind of relationships actors have in terms of such facets as trust, obligations, and emotional bonds. Research consistently identifies trust as one of the central dimensions of social relationships affecting a wide range of outcomes. The cognitive dimension captures the degree to which actors share common schemas and systems of meanings and thus shared understandings. All three dimensions have been shown to play an important role across a range of knowledge processes (Ferlie *et al.*, 2005; Inkpen and Tsang, 2005; Maurer and Ebers, 2006).

There has been a huge expansion of research on social capital in the last twenty years or so. This reflects the potential of the concept to bring insights not only across a range of disciplines but also to policy at the organizational, regional, national, and international levels. There remain major areas of debate within the field—about appropriate methodologies, the links between social capital at different levels, and most obviously, the variety of definitions that coexist and drive different lines of research. Nonetheless, two themes are clear. First, a contingency perspective now characterizes much research. The early debates about which forms of social capital are better—for example, bonding or bridging—are now being resolved with a greater recognition of their relative merits. What is effective in one context may be less so in another, but both are important (Hansen, 1999; Burt, 2005). Second, it is more widely recognized that social capital is not universally beneficial. It has a dark sides and can be a disadvantage as well as an advantage for individuals, groups, and communities. For example, what is beneficial for individuals or small groups may prove counterproductive for larger collectives, as is the case when in-group solidarity leads to wider social fragmentation. Understanding better who gains, who loses, and how, increasingly focuses attention on the implications of social capital at different levels of analysis.

2.6 Exploring the Relationships between Human and Social Capital

Exploring the relationships between human and social capital is a major challenge, not least because each of the concepts is itself complex and multidimensional. Both scholars and policy-makers acknowledge that there is still a need to understand better the relationships between the different dimensions within each domain—for instance, in the human capital field between health and education—and in the social capital field between bonding, bridging, and linking social ties. For example, Halpern (2005) argues that a healthy and effective community needs a blend of different types of social capital, just as a person needs a blend of different vitamins in their diet to be physically healthy. Thus, analyzing the evolution and consequences of different configurations within each type of capital constitutes a significant and ongoing area of research.

Alongside this there is a growing interest in how these two forms of capital may be interrelated. Some studies provide evidence for independent effects—initially demonstrating the influence of social capital on human capital, and more recently analyzing the ways in which human capital may shape social capital. However, increasingly research suggests that these two forms of capital are often highly interrelated and interdependent. This has important implications for research.

2.6.1 The Influence of Social Capital on Human Capital

If we focus first on the same outcomes as much of the human capital literature—school performance—then there is a substantial body of evidence that shows that social capital is a major influence on educational results.

As already noted, the classic work in the field is that of James Coleman (1988), who saw social capital as a parallel concept to financial, physical, and human capital. For Coleman, human capital is created by changes in persons that bring about skills and capabilities that enable them to act in new ways. Just as physical capital and human capital facilitate productive activity, so does social capital. For example, a group within which there is extensive trust is able to accomplish much more than a comparable group without trustworthiness and trust. Coleman's core argument is that social capital—in the family and the community—affects the creation of human capital in the next generation through processes such as physical presence and attention, social norms, and values that reduce drop-out rates and thus benefit learning and the achievement of qualifications. In brief, research suggests that schools which are an integral part of community life (Hanifan, 1916) nurture high parental involvement (Coleman, 1988) and expand the horizons of students (Morgan and Sorensen, 1999), and are more likely to help students achieve higher test scores. Belonging to a family or social network that has strong educational aspirations is a very good predictor of positive educational achievement (OECD, 2001; Schuller, 2007). In summary, it appears that both the structure of family relationships, such as the number of adults and children in a household, and the process aspects of family social capital, affect educational outcomes (Halpern, 2005).

Research also shows that acquiring social capital can make the biggest difference to people experiencing disadvantage; in other words, socially excluded people derive the greatest benefit from developing social capital (Prevalin and Rose, 2000). However, community strength is not universally positive in its effect. Field and Spence (2000) find that tight-knit communities can serve to inhibit the learning aspirations of adults, binding them into a low-skill economy and reinforcing the divide between those who achieve high qualifications in the initial educational phase and those that do not. Moreover, social capital can be used to exclude, or to limit participation in education, as well as to promote it (Field *et al.*, 2000).

It is not only the acquisition of knowledge and skills that is affected by social capital but also their deployment and impact. Bidner (2008), for example, has shown recently how workers' productivities are influenced by the skills of their co-workers, and the literature has long recognized the importance of networks in creating opportunities for skill deployment through job search and increased employment prospects.

If we take the broader perspective on human capital evident in the 2001 OECD definition, again there is substantial evidence for the importance of social capital. For example, as regards health, at the individual level there is a strong stream of evidence pointing to the links between social capital and a range of health measures, both physical and mental (OECD, 2001; McKenzie and Harpham, 2006). In his extensive review of the literature, Woolcock (2001) finds that, controling for other key variables, the well connected are more likely to be hired, housed, healthy, and happy. Specifically, they are more likely to be promoted faster, receive higher salaries, be favorably evaluated by peers, miss fewer days of work, live longer, and be more efficient in completing assigned tasks. He argues that the broader message rippling through the social capital literature is that how we associate with each other, and on what terms, has enormous implications for our individual and collective well-being, whether we live in rich or poor countries.

2.6.2 The Influence of Human Capital on Social Capital

Although the main aim of this chapter is to develop a social perspective on human capital, it is relevant to note the growing interest in the ways in which human capital may shape social capital. This interest reflects the desire to develop better accounts of the microfoundations of social phenomena in general and, more specifically, to include agency more strongly in considering social capital (Felin and Foss, 2005). While social capital is fundamentally a relational resource, residing in the connections between actors, nonetheless one of the under-researched questions in social capital is: what is the role of individual and human factors in shaping the creation and deployment of social capital?

If having an advantageous position in social networks is so important, scholars have begun to study the characteristics of people who reach these positions. Research shows that educational level is a good predictor of centrality in networks and thus high structural social capital. In their research on project teams, Klein *et al.* (2004) found that highly educated individuals with low neuroticism were high in advice centrality, high in friendship centrality, and low in adversarial centrality. The authors suggest that these individuals present a good bargain to their team-mates, offering benefits (education) at low cost (low neuroticism). Self-monitoring is another personality dimension that has been shown to be important in social capital, with high self-monitors more likely than low self-monitors to occupy central positions in social networks (Mehra *et al.*, 2001; Kilduff and Krackhardt, 2008).

The creation and maintenance of social capital depends on the actions and not just the attributes of individuals. For Kramer (2009) an important question is: why are people willing to invest in and contribute to the creation and maintenance of social capital when it often benefits the wider community as much or more than the individual? For, as Coleman (1988) pointed out, the public goods aspect of social capital, in which the actors who generate social capital ordinarily capture only a small part of its benefits, often leads to an under-investment in social capital. In answering the question, Kramer (2009) highlights the importance of the psychological embeddedness that comes through shared identity. He argues that the psychological ties that bond and bridge should be viewed as a supplement to structural and relational embeddedness. He identifies three relevant identities: personal, sub or in-group, and superordinate or collective—constructs that parallel the individual self, relational self, and collective self discussed by Sedikides and Brewer (2001). In Kramer's view, collective identification encourages peoples' cognitive, motivational and affective processes to shift the focus from 'I' to 'we', and consequently fosters their willingness to contribute to the development of social capital.

Over many years there has been an interest in the biological basis for social order. For example, Fukuyama (1999) sees the roots of social capital in human nature, and Felin and Hesterly (2007) draw attention to the significance of innate individual level knowledge. At the most basic level, humans appear to have a hard-wired tendency to cooperate and reciprocate. One of the newly emerging disciplines providing novel insights into this perspective is the field of neuroscience. An important recent discovery is that certain things leaders do—specifically, exhibit empathy and become attuned to each others' moods—literally affect both their own brain chemistry and that of their followers (Goleman and Boyatzis, 2008). Such findings are encouraging researchers to focus on the recursive cycles between social interactions and the processes in the brain that underlie or influence behaviors and interactions in the workplace and beyond (Ringleb and Rock, 2008). Although still at a very early stage, this work emphasizes again the importance of understanding the dynamics of social interaction and the complex interplay between human and social capital.

2.6.3 The Interactions between Human and Social Capital: The Case of Knowledge and Learning

Earlier in this chapter I noted that the majority of mainstream work on human capital is characterized by an undersocialized model of man—based on a view of knowledge and skills as developed and embodied within the individual person, and accessible, transferable, and actionable with minimal regard for context. As research has moved away from qualifications and accreditation to focus more on the dynamics of learning across a wider range of settings, this view of knowledge has been shown to be severely limited. Increasingly, scholars argue that we need to understand much more about the social contexts within which individual learning takes place and the enactment processes through which knowledge, learning, and skills are manifest.

In a parallel development, work in the knowledge-based perspective on organizations is also challenging the dominant paradigm of knowledge as something that people possess. Here too scholars propose that we need also to consider knowing in action; that is, how people interact with the social and physical world (Cook and Brown, 1999; Eisenhardt and Santos, 2002). The bridging of knowledge and knowing that is proposed implies that more attention should be paid to those social contexts, processes, and practices in which meaning and knowledge are created and sustained. As Spender suggests, 'knowledge is less about truth and reason and more about the practice of intervening knowledgeably and purposefully in the world' (Spender, 1996: 64). Moreover, an emphasis on knowing also indicates that we need to move to a richer view of social capital beyond the prevailing model which sees networks and ties primarily as conduits or pipes through which information and knowledge flow towards embracing a practice perspective on social capital (Nahapiet, 2009).

What becomes clear from these trends is that human capital and social capital are highly interrelated. Work on communities of practice consistently emphasizes that they have both knowledge and relational dimensions, and both are critical to their success (Lave and Wenger, 1991). In their research on mid-career learning, Eraut et al. (2007) found that most learning was informal learning within the workplace itself. It was mostly triggered by consultation and collaboration within the working group, consultation outside the working group, and the challenge of the work itself. Similarly, in her detailed study of product development practices, Orlikowski (2002) provides multiple insights into the ways in which everyday social practices, such as interacting face-to-face and learning by doing, foster social relations, learning, and knowledge exchange. As she observes, 'knowing is not a static embedded capability or a stable disposition of actors, but rather an ongoing social accomplishment, constituted and reconstituted as actors engage the world in practice' (Orlikowski, 2002: 268).

In previous work we identified the dialectical relationships between social and intellectual capital in an organizational context in which the two forms of capital frequently co-evolve (Nahapiet and Ghoshal, 1998). I am suggesting here that the links between human and social capital are often similarly complex, recursive, and dynamic. In such circumstances, a clear distinction between the two is difficult to establish and maintain. It is for this reason that scholars are raising fundamental questions about how far, and in what circumstances, these two forms of capital can be regarded as separate and what this implies for research (Healy, 2005; Keeley, 2007; Spender, 2009).

For research to progress, what is needed now is a clearer articulation of the main ways in which human and social capital may be linked. Building from the literature reviewed so far, this is the focus of the next section.

2.7 RESEARCHING THE RELATIONSHIPS BETWEEN DIFFERENT TYPES OF CAPITAL

In outlining the structural approach to capital, Lewin (2005), drawing on Lachmann (1978), emphasizes that it is the overall pattern of different types of capital that is important, and the ways in which they interact. He highlights in particular the importance of complementarity and substitutability. Scholars in both the human and social capital domains similarly suggest that their value is affected significantly by the ways in which they are linked to other forms of capital. We are still at a relatively early stage in understanding these linkages. However, research on human and social capital suggests the following possible mechanisms: fungibility, liquidity, and convertibility, substitutability, complementarity, co-evolution, and interaction. These are described briefly below. A high priority for research is to examine these mechanisms in detail—how they operate, in what contexts, and how they interconnect. Although discussed here in relation to human and social capital, they are likely to represent the patterns of linkage between many forms of hybrid capital.

2.7.1 Fungibility and Convertibility

The first two mechanisms—fungibility and convertibility—arise directly from using the concept of capital as a metaphor for understanding human and social assets. Within economics and finance, fungibility describes situations in which individual units of some commodity can substitute for each other without loss. In its strictest sense, it is about the interchangeability between goods and assets of the same type. Money is the archetypical fungible asset. By contrast, liquidity describes the speed and ease with which one form of capital is transformed or converted into another form. A good is liquid or convertible if it can be easily exchanged for money or another different good. How far and in what ways such exchanges and substitutions can happen with human and social resources are the focus for much debate. Clearly trust cannot be exchanged and traded in the same ways as physical goods. However, ideas of fungibility and convertibility are prominent in the work of leading human and social capital theorists.

Coleman discusses two aspects of fungibility—contextual specificity and substitution. He notes that 'like physical capital and human capital, social capital is not completely fungible—but fungible with respect to particular activities. A given form of social capital that is valuable in facilitating certain actions may be useless or even harmful for others' (Coleman, 1988: S98). That is, the value of both human and social capital is tied to particular contexts and not directly or readily transferable. He also suggests that different components of social capital can to some extent substitute for one another. Halpern (2005) reviews several studies demonstrating how norms, networks, and sanctions can partly compensate for each other, implying they have some form of functional equivalence.

It is the issue of liquidity and convertibility that has been the focus for more discussion. The idea that educational qualifications, knowledge, and learning are liquid at least to some degree is central to human capital theory. A key proposition in Bourdieu's discussion of different forms of capital—cultural, social, and economic—is the idea that one form of capital can be converted into another, and that this represents the real logic of the functioning of capital. For Bourdieu, whose work represents a strong form of the capital metaphor, the general science of the economy of practices seeks to establish 'the laws whereby the different types of capital...change into another' (Bourdieu, 1986: 243). He suggests that cultural and social capital can be derived from economic capital through an investment of time, say in sociability, and that cultural and social capital may themselves over time be converted to economic capital. For example, certain educational qualifications may convert to a particular monetary value and social connections may be a way of mobilizing economic capital, as is shown by research on business start-ups. There is ample evidence that educational credentials may deliver social capital through social prestige and access to high-status networks. The question of how far and in what circumstances social and human capital are convertible remains an important issue for both research and policy.

2.7.2 Substitutability

In the literature on capital more widely, it is clear that some forms of capital may substitute for others. This goes beyond the narrow view of fungibility in which different aspects of one type of capital may substitute for another of the same type. Coleman (1988) gives the example of Asian immigrant families in which the human capital of the parents was low, at least in terms of years of schooling, but the social capital—in terms of the commitment of the parents to spending time with their children helping them do well in school—compensated for the former. An acknowledged potential downside of social capital is that it substitutes inappropriately for human capital—giving the well-connected privileged opportunities over the well qualified. Amongst the most active areas of research analyzing substitutability are the fields of development and community studies. It has yet to feature significantly in management research.

2.7.3 Complementarity

Complementarity is perhaps the major feature identified by scholars who specifically discuss the relationship between human and social capital. Coleman is very clear on this point, arguing that 'if the human capital possessed by parents is not complemented by social capital embodied in family relations, it is irrelevant to the child's educational growth that the parent has a great deal, or a small amount, of human capital' (Coleman, 1988: S110). Schuller and his colleagues similarly stress complementarity: 'If people do not have the capacity to deploy their skills in collaboration with others, to exhibit and develop trust In their working relationships, it does not much matter how well qualified they are. Economic success depends, generally on a modicum of social competence as well as opportunity' (Schuller *et al.*, 2004*a*: 181). In his recent reflections on the use of social capital, Schuller (2000) concludes that if it is not linked to social capital, human capital is weakened both as an analytical tool and as an asset, since it is harder to acquire and its value harder to realize. He argues that in many contexts it is more important to focus on the dynamics of complementarity than the issue of fungibility.

2.7.4 Co-evolution

There is mounting evidence that human and social capital are highly and often reciprocally interrelated—co-evolving over time. The same social processes often build both social and human capital. At an institutional level, the family, schooling, and education provide contexts for both learning and the development of relationships. Indeed, the OECD (2001) suggests that the social impact of learning—in terms of health, crime, and social cohesion—could be as large as the impacts on economic productivity. At a more micro level, we have already noted how many social practices provide the locus for the emergence, development, and sustenance of both human and social capital. This co-evolution raises fundamental questions for research, both theoretically and empirically. As Spender notes, one difficulty is the idea that social capital can be conceived, measured, or theorized independently of the other: 'Social capital is about individuals and their interactions, just as human capital presupposes those interactions' (Spender, 2009: 9). Healy (2005) goes so far as to suggest that human capital and social capital cannot be juxtaposed as two separate types of capital to be completely distinguished empirically. Rather, social capital is a different optic on human capital—seeing it not simply as an attribute of individuals without context, culture, or meaning—but a deeply cultural and intersubjective property of systems in which individual parcels of knowledge and competence are based. In moving to this more social view of human capital, we face profound challenges in articulating our theories of both forms of capital and in finding ways to study them empirically.

2.7.5 Interaction

Finally, research on the impact of these two forms of capital shows that many outcomes appear to result from their interaction. For example, Teachman *et al.* (1997) found that social capital interacts with the financial and human capital of parents to determine school continuation. In their research programme on the wider benefits of learning, Schuller *et al.* (2004*b*) similarly show how the interactions between human, social, and identity capital produce better health, stronger social networks, and enhanced family life. A focus on these interactions is likely to be an increasingly important feature of future research.

2.8 SUMMARY AND CONCLUSIONS

There has been a marked trend towards applying the economists' term capital to a wide range of intangible assets. The trend remains controversial not only because of its value associations but also because many of these so-called hybrid capitals do not have the attributes associated with the neoclassical model of capital. Nonetheless, many scholars maintain that the heuristic value of the term justifies its continued use in areas such as human social identity and organizational capital. Moreover, alternative theories of capital—notably the structural approach—provide a stronger foundation for research on hybrid capitals. Specifically, the structural approach incorporates heterogeneous types of capital, both tangible and intangible, with all resources being seen as a form of capital. It also addresses the issue of change, adaptability, and flexibility in value creation. Of particular significance, the theory highlights the importance of capital structure and the pattern and connections between different types and forms of capital.

Research on human capital is now well established, demonstrating the significance of education, qualifications, and skill levels for economic outcomes at the individual, organizational, and societal levels. However, the dominant paradigm in which knowledge and skills are treated as relatively unproblematic attributes of the individual, accessible and transferable with limited regard for context, is coming under increasing scrutiny. Human capital may be an individual asset, but its value in practice depends on a wide range of social factors and social relations. It thus needs to be understood and analyzed within a more social paradigm. Social capital theory provides a powerful perspective for doing this—partly because it too adopts the capital metaphor as well as focusing on the importance of knowledge, learning, and education. There is now a growing body of evidence demonstrating the many ways in which social capital shapes the development and application of human capital. However, our review of this evidence shows that human and social capital are highly interrelated, often co-evolving over time in complex, dynamic, and recursive ways.

This has important implications for theory development as we go forward. In discussions of these two forms of capital, scholars generally identify the need for more consistency in definitions and better ways of measuring and assessing them in their multiple dimensions. While these are important, what is clear is that we need also to advance our ways of modeling their interrelationships and yet greater investment in studying the dynamics of their evolution over time. The complementarity and situatedness of human and social capital are frequently lost in conventional studies, yet are fundamental to understanding their development and impact. These are serious challenges that must be met if we are truly to develop a more social view of human capital.

NOTES

1. This specific usage of the term 'capabilities' differs from that of many authors, including Schultz (1961), who uses the terms 'human capital' and 'human capabilities' interchangeably.

REFERENCES

ADLER, P. S., and KWON, S.-W. (2002). 'Social Capital: Prospects for a New Concept', *Academy of Management Review*, 27: 17–40.

AHN, T. K., and OSTROM, E. (2008). 'Social Capital and Collective Action', in D. Castiglione, J. W. Van Deth, and G. Wolleb (eds.), *The Handbook of Social Capital* (Oxford: Oxford University Press), 70–110.

ARROW, K. J. (2000). 'Observations on Social Capital', in P. Dasgupta and I. Serageldin (eds.), *Social Capital: A Multifaceted Perspective* (Washington, DC: World Bank), 3–5.

BAKER, W. (1990). 'Market Networks and Corporate Behaviour', *American Journal of Sociology*, 96(3): 589–625.

BARON, J., and HANNAN, M. (1994). 'The Impact of Economics on Contemporary Sociology', *Journal of Economic Literature*, 32: 1111–46.

BECKER, G. S. (1964). *Human Capital* (Chicago: University of Chicago Press).

BENSON, C. S. (1978) *The Economics of Public Education* (3rd edn. Boston: Houghton Mifflin).

BIDNER, C. (2008). 'A Spillover-Based Theory of Credentialism', Working Paper of the University of British Columbia.

BLAUG, M. (1976). 'The Empirical Status of Human Capital Theory: A Slightly Jaundiced Survey', *Journal of Economic Literature*, 14: 827–55.

BOWMAN, C., and SWART, J. (2007). 'Whose Human Capital? The Challenge of Value Capture When Capital is Embedded', *Journal of Management Studies*, 44(4): 488–505.

BOURDIEU, P. (1986). 'The Forms of Capital', in J. G. Richardson (ed.), *Handbook of Theory and Research for the Sociology of Education* (New York: Greenwood), 241–58.

BURCHELL, S., CLUBB, C., HOPWOOD, A., HUGHES, J., and NAHAPIET, J. (1980). 'The Roles of Accounting in Organizations and Society', *Accounting, Organizations and Society*, 5(1): 5–27.

BURT, R. S. (1992). *Structural Holes: The Social Structure of Competition* (Cambridge, Mass.: Harvard University Press).

——(2000). 'The Network Structure of Social Capital', *Research in Organizational Behaviour*, 22: 345–423.

——(2005). *Brokerage and Closure: An Introduction to Social Capital* (Oxford: Oxford University Press).

COLEMAN, J. S. (1988). 'Social Capital in the Creation of Human Capital', *American Journal of Sociology*, 94: 95–120.

——(1990) *Foundations of Social Theory* (Cambridge, Mass.: Harvard University Press).

COOK, S. D. N., and BROWN, J. S. (1999). 'Bridging Epistemologies: The Generative Dance between Organizational Knowledge and Organizational Knowing', *Organization Science*, 10(4): 381–400.

CÔTÉ, J. E. (1997). 'An Empirical Test of the Identity Capital Model', *Journal of Adolescence*, 20: 577–97.

——(2005). 'Identity Capital, Social Capital and the Wider Benefits of Learning: Generating Resources Facilitative of Social Cohesion', *London Review of Education*, 3(3): 221–37.

DEAN, A., and KRETSCHMER, M. (2007). 'Can Ideas be Capital? Factors of Production in the Post Industrial Economy: A Review and Critique', *Academy of Management Review*, 32(2): 573–94.

DEWEY, J. (1900). 'The Psychology of the Elementary Curriculum', *The Elementary School Record* (Chicago: University of Chicago Press), 223, 225, 230, 231.

DE TOCQUEVILLE, A. (1832, 1969). *Democracy in America* (New York: Harper).

DIMAGGIO, P. (1982). 'Cultural Capital and School Success: The Impact of Status Culture Participation on Grades of U.S. High School Students', *American Sociological Review*, 47: 189–210.

EISENHART, K. M., and SANTOS, F. M. (2002). 'Knowledge-Based View: A New Theory of Strategy?', in A. Pettigrew, H. Thomas, and R. Whittington (eds.), *Handbook of Strategy and Management* (London: Sage Publications), 139–64.

ERAUT, M., and HIRSH, W. (2007). *The Significance of Workplace Learning for Individuals, Groups and Organisations* (Oxford and Cardiff: ESRC Centre on Skills Knowledge and Organizational Performance).

ERAUT, M., ALDERTON, J., COLE, G., and SENKER, P. (2007). 'Development of Knowledge and Skills at Work', in F. COFFIELD (ed.), *Differing Visions of a Learning Society*, i (Bristol: Policy Press), 231–62.

FABRICANT, S. (1959). *Basic Facts on Productivity Change* (New York: National Bureau of Economic Research).

FARR, J. (2004). 'Social Capital: A Conceptual History', *Political Theory*, 32(6): 6–33.

FELIN, T., and FOSS, N. J. (2005). 'Strategic Organization: A Field in Search of Micro-Foundations', *Strategic Organization*, 3(4): 441–55.

——and HESTERLY, W. S. (2007). 'The Knowledge-Based View, Nested Heterogeneity, and New Value Creation: Considerations on the Locus of Knowledge', *Academy of Management Review*, 32(1): 195–218.

FERLIE, E., FITZGERALD, L., WOOD, M., and HAWKINS, C. (2005). 'The Nonspread of Innovations: The Mediating Role of Professionals', *Academy of Management Journal*, 48(1): 117–34.

FIELD, J., and SPENCE, L. (2000). 'Social Capital and Informal Learning', in F. Coffield (ed.), *The Necessity of Informal Learning* (Bristol: Policy Press), 32–42.

——SCHULLER, T., and BARON, S. (2000). 'Social Capital and Human Capital Revisited', in S. Baron, J. Field, and T. Schuller (eds.), *Social Capital: Critical Perspectives* (Oxford: Oxford University Press), 243–63.

FINE, B. (2001) *Social Capital Theory Versus Social Theory: Political Economy and Social Science at the Start of the Millennium* (London: Routledge).

FISHMAN, R. M. (2009). 'On the Costs of Conceptualizing Social Ties as Social Capital', in V. O. Bartkus and J. H. Davis (eds.), *Social Capital: Reaching Out, Reaching In* (Cheltenham: Edward Elgar), 66–83.

FUKUYAMA, F. (1995). *Trust: The Social Virtues and the Creation of Prosperity* (London: Hamish Hamilton).

——(1999). *The Great Disruption: Human Nature and the Reconstitution of Social Order* (New York: Free Press).

GOLEMAN, D., and BOYATZIS, R. (2008). 'Social Intelligence and the Biology of Leadership', *Harvard Business Review*, 86(9): 74–81.

HALPERN, D. (2005). *Social Capital* (Cambridge: Polity Press).

HANIFAN, L. J. (1916). 'The Rural School Community Centre', *Annals of the American Academy of Political and Social Science*, 67: 130–8.

HANSEN, M. T. (1999). 'The Search Transfer Problem: The Role of Weak Ties in Sharing Knowledge across Organizational Subunits', *Administrative Science Quarterly*, 44: 82–111.

HEALY, T. (2005). 'In Each Other's Shadow: What has been the Impact of Human and Social Capital on Life Satisfaction in Ireland?', Ph.D. thesis, National University of Ireland.

HIRSCH, P., MICHAELS, S., and FRIEDMAN, R. (1990). 'Clean Models vs Dirty Hands: Why Economics is Different from Sociology', in S. Zukin and P. DiMaggio (eds.), *Structures of Capital* (Cambridge: Cambridge University Press), 39–56.

INKPEN, A. C., and TSANG, E. W. K. (2005). 'Social Capital, Networks and Knowledge Transfer', *Academy of Management Review*, 30(1): 146–65.

KEELEY, B. (2007). *Human Capital: How What You Know Shapes Your Life* (Paris: Organisation for Economic Co-operation and Development).

KILDUFF, M., and KRACKHARDT, D. (2008). *Interpersonal Networks in Organizations: Cognition, Personality, Dynamics and Culture* (Cambridge: Cambridge University Press).

KLEIN, K. J., LIM, B.-C., SALTZ, J. L., and MAYER, D. M. (2004). 'How do they Get There? An Examination of the Antecedents of Centrality in Team Networks', *Academy of Management Review*, 47(6): 952–63.

KRAMER, R. M. (2009). 'Social Capital Creation: Collective Identities and Collective Action', in V. O. Bartkus and J. Davis (eds.), *Social Capital: Reaching Out, Reaching In* (Cheltenham: Edward Elgar), 159–239.

LACHMANN, L. M. (1978). *Capital and its Structure* (Kansas City: Sheed, Andrews & McMeel; orig. publ. 1956).

LAVE, J., and WENGER, E. (1991). *Situated Learning: Legitimate Peripheral Participation* (Cambridge: Cambridge University Press).

LEWIN, P. (2005). 'The Capital Idea and the Scope of Economics', *Review of Austrian Economics*, 18(2): 145–67.

LIN, N. (2001). *Social Capital: A Theory of Social Structure and Action* (Cambridge: Cambridge University Press).

LIN, N. (2008). 'A Network Theory of Social Capital', in D. Castiglione, J. W. Van Deth, and G. Wolleb (eds.), *The Handbook of Social Capital* (Oxford: Oxford University Press), 50–69.

MCKENZIE, K., and HARPHAM, T. (eds.) (2006). *Social Capital and Mental Health* (London: Jessica Kingsley Publishers).

MAURER, I., and EBERS, M. (2006). 'Dynamics of Social Capital and their Performance Implications: Lessons from Bio-Technology Start-Ups', *Administrative Science Quarterly*, 51: 262–92.

MEHRA, A., KILDUFF, M., and BRASS, D. J. (2001). 'The Social Network of High and Low Self-Monitors: Implications for Workplace Performance', *Administrative Science Quarterly*, 46(1): 121–46.

MORGAN, S. L., and SORENSEN, A. B. (1999) 'Parental Networks, Social Closure and Mathematics Learning: A Test of Coleman's Social Capital Explanation of School Effects', *American Sociological Review*, 64(5): 661–81.

NAHAPIET, J. (1988) 'The Rhetoric and Reality of an Accounting Change: A Study of Resource Allocation in the NHS', *Accounting, Organizations and Society*, 13(4): 333–58.

——(2009). 'Capitalizing on Connections: Social Capital and Strategic Management', in V. Bartkus and J. Davis (eds.), *Social Capital: Reaching Out, Reaching In* (Cheltenham: Edward Elgar), 205–36.

——and GHOSHAL, S. (1998). 'Social Capital, Intellectual Capital and the Organizational Advantage', *Academy of Management Review*, 23: 242–66.

OECD (Organization for Economic Co-Operation and Development) (1998). *Human Capital Investment: An International Comparison* (Paris: OECD).

——(2001). *The Well-Being of Nations: The Role of Human and Social Capital* (Paris: OECD).

——(2007). 'Lifelong Learning and Human Capital', OECD Policy Brief, July.

ORLIKOWKI, W. J. (2002). 'Knowing in Practice: Enacting a Collective Capability in Distributed Organizing', *Organization Science*, 13(3): 249–73.

ORR, J. (1990). 'Sharing Knowledge, Celebrating Identity: Community Memory in a Service Culture', in D. Middleton and D. Edwards (eds.), *Collective Remembering* (London: Sage), 169–89.

OSTROM, E. (1994). 'Constituting Social Capital and Collective Action', *Journal of Theoretical Politics*, 6: 527–62.

OSTROM, E. (2009). 'What is Social Capital?', in V. O. Bartkus and J. H. Davis (eds.), *Social Capital: Reaching Out, Reaching In* (Cheltenham: Edward Elgar), 17–38.

PRESCOTT, E. G., and VISSCHER, M. (1980). 'Organization Capital', *Journal of Political Economy*, 88(31): 446–61.

PRESTON, J. (2004). 'A Continuous Effort of Sociability: Learning and Social Capital in Adult Life', in T. Schuller, J. Preston, C. Hammond, A. Brassett-Grundy, and J. Bynner (eds.), *The Benefits of Learning: The Impact of Education on Health, Family Life and Social Capital* (London: RoutledgeFalmer), 119–36.

PREVALIN, D. J., and ROSE, D. (2000) *Social Capital for Health: Investigating the Links between Social Capital and Health Using the British Household Panel Survey* (London: Health Development Agency).

PUTNAM, R. D. (1993). 'The Prosperous Community: Social Capital and Public Life', *American Prospect*, 13: 35–42.

——(1995). 'Bowling Alone: America's Declining Social Capital', *Journal of Democracy*, 6(1): 65–78.

RINGLEB, A. H., and ROCK, D. (2008). 'The Emerging Field of NeuroLeadership', *NeuroLeadership Journal*, 1: 3–19.

ROBISON, L. J., SCHMID, A. A., and SILES, M. E. (2002). 'Is Social Capital Really Capital?', *Review of Social Economy*, 60(1): 1–21.

SCHULLER, T. (2004). 'Three Capitals: A Framework', in T. Schuller, J. Preston, C. Hammond, A. Brassett-Grundy, and J. Bynner (eds.), *The Benefits of Learning: The Impact of Education on Health, Family Life and Social Capital* (London: RoutledgeFalmer), 12–33.

—— (2007). 'Reflections on the Use of Social Capital', *Review of Social Economy*, 65(1): 11–28.

—— BARON, S., and FIELD, J. (2000). 'Social Capital: A Review and Critique', in S. Baron, J. Field, and T. Schuller (eds.), *Social Capital: Critical Perspectives* (Oxford: Oxford University Press), 1–38.

—— HAMMOND, C., and PRESTON, J. (2004*a*) 'Reappraising Benefits', in T. Schuller, J. Preston, C. Hammond, A. Brassett-Grundy, and J. Bynner (eds.), *The Benefits of Learning: The Impact of Education on Health, Family Life and Social Capital* (London: RoutledgeFalmer), 179–93.

SCHULLER, T., PRESTON, J., HAMMOND, C., BRASSETT-GRUNDY, A., and BYNNER, J. (eds.) (2004*b*). *The Benefits of Learning: The Impact of Education on Health, Family Life and Social Capital* (London: RoutledgeFalmer).

SCHULTZ, T. W. (1961). 'Investment in Human Capital', *American Economic Review*, 51: 1–17.

SEDIKIDES, C., and BREWER, M. (2001). 'Individual Self, Relational Self and Collective Self', in C. Sedikides and M. B. Brewer (eds.), *Individual Self, Relational Self, Collective Self* (Philadelphia: Psychology Press), 1–3.

SEN, A. (1999). *Development as Freedom* (Oxford: Oxford University Press).

SMITH, A. (1776). *The Wealth of Nations Books I–III* (Repr. in Penguin Classics; London: Penguin Books, 1986).

SOLOW, R. M. (2000). 'Notes on Social Capital and Economic Performance', in P. Dasgupta and I. Serageldin (eds.), *Social Capital: A Multifaceted Perspective* (Washington, DC: World Bank), 6–12.

SPENDER, J.-C. (1996). 'Organizational Knowledge, Learning and Memory: Three Concepts in Search of a Theory', *Journal of Organizational Change*, 9: 63–78.

—— (2009). 'Organizational Capital: Concept, Measure or Heuristic?', in A. Bounfour (ed.), *Organizational Capital: Modelling, Measuring and Contextualizing* (Abingdon: Routledge), 5–23.

SWEDBERG, R., and GRANOVETTER, M. (2001). 'Introduction to the Second Edition', in M. Granovetter and R. Swedberg (eds.), *The Sociology of Economic Life* (Cambridge, Mass.: Westview Press), 1–28.

SWEETLAND, S. R. (1996). 'Human Capital Theory: Foundations of a Field of Inquiry', *Review of Educational Research*, 66(3): 341–59.

TEACHMAN, J. D., PAASCH, K., and CARVER, K. (1997). 'Social Capital and the Generation of Human Capital', *Social Forces*, 75(4): 1343–59.

TOMER, J. F. (1987). *Organizational Capital: The Path to Higher Productivity and Well-Being* (New York: Praeger).

VAN STAVEREN, I., and KNORRINGA, P. (2007). 'Unpacking Social Capital in Economic Development: How Social Relations Matter', *Review of Social Economy*, 65(1): 107–35.

WOOLCOCK, M. (1998). 'Social Capital and Economic Development', *Theory and Society*, 27: 151–208.

—— (2001). 'The Place of Social Capital in Understanding Social and Economic Outcomes', *Canadian Journal of Policy Research*, 65–88.

CHAPTER 3

GLOBAL CULTURE CAPITAL AND COSMOPOLITAN HUMAN CAPITAL

THE EFFECTS OF GLOBAL MINDSET AND ORGANIZATIONAL ROUTINES ON CULTURAL INTELLIGENCE AND INTERNATIONAL EXPERIENCE

KOK-YEE NG

MEI LING TAN

SOON ANG

> The conventional wisdom...places formal educational institutions in a central role as the main producers of the skills required by the modern economy. It neglects the crucial role of families and firms in fostering skill, and the variety of abilities required to succeed in the modern economy.
>
> (Heckman, 2000, on fostering human capital)

IN today's global and knowledge-intensive economy, a firm's human capital plays an increasingly strategic role in achieving and maintaining its competitive advantage

(Pfeffer, 1994). Research has established that variations in firms' human capital, defined as the education, experience, and skills of firms' employees, contribute to differences in firms' performance (for example, Daily *et al.*, 2000; Hitt *et al.*, 2001).

Given the importance of human resources to a firm's performance, and in the context of growing international trade, it is timely for research to reexamine the nature of human capital needed for individuals and organizations to be successful in the modern economy (Heckman, 2000). Kanter (1995) argued that for organizations to become world-class in today's global economy, they must develop a new breed of managers who can fulfil three important roles: 'integrators' who see beyond surface-level cultural differences to find common ground; 'diplomats' who resolve conflicts and influence locals to accept world standards; and 'cross-fertilizers' who help to transfer knowledge and best practices from one place to another (Kanter, 1999). Kanter (1995) termed these individuals 'cosmopolitans', borrowing the term from earlier sociological work of Gouldner (1957) and Merton (1957).

This chapter focuses on *'cosmopolitan' human capital*—the additional human capital needs required of global organizations to compete effectively in the world economy. Even though our focus is on organizations with international operations, we note that cosmopolitan human capital is similarly valuable to organizations operating primarily within one country, but with a culturally diverse workforce arising from the diversity of the country's population. Consistent with existing research, we define cosmopolitan human capital as the experience and skills that individuals possess that enable them to work effectively in many different cultures (Haas, 2006; Tung, 1998). Specifically, our key objective is to understand how cosmopolitan human capital in firms is developed internally. Why are some firms able to cultivate cosmopolitan human capital more effectively than other firms?

This is an important question for several reasons. First, two Economist Intelligence Unit (EIU) CEO briefings (2006, 2007), based on survey data from over 1,000 senior executives across forty nations, identified lack of high-quality talent that can operate in multiple cultures as the greatest challenge facing global organizations. As the demand for cosmopolitan human capital exceeds its supply, it is vital for firms to develop such global talent internally in order to sustain their competitive advantage. Second, given the social embeddedness of human capital (Chapters 2 and 16), cosmopolitan human capital involves some extent of firm-specific knowledge and skills, such as an understanding of the firm's global context and operations, and thus is not readily available in the open labor market (see Chapter 22). Given that cosmopolitan human capital is both valuable and unique to the firm, there is strategic incentive for organizations to develop these employees internally (Becker, 1964; Lepak and Snell, 1999).

We propose the concept of *global culture capital* to explain why some firms are more effective in developing cosmopolitan human capital. Our concept of global culture capital is drawn from sociologists Bourdieu and Passeron's (1990) concept of cultural capital. (We label our concept global *culture* capital, to avoid confusion with the sociological term *cultural* capital.) Specifically, our central thesis is that, just as educated parents are able to create a home environment that transmits values and habits to their children to aid them academically, we propose that organizations that possess global culture capital provide a work environment that fosters the development of human capital through the process of situated learning (Brown *et al.*, 1989; Lave and Wenger, 1991). Our view is consistent with Heckman's (2000) argument, illustrated in our opening quotation, that families and firms play a critical but under-examined role in fostering the human capital required of individuals to succeed in this modern economy.

In the following sections we first review relevant literatures to expound on the concepts of cosmopolitan human capital and global culture capital. We then describe how global culture capital affects the development of cosmopolitan human capital

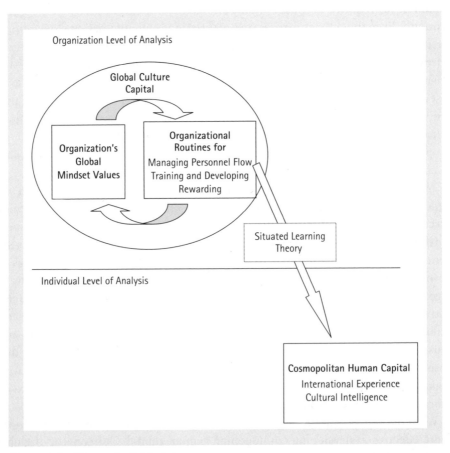

Figure 3.1. Conceptual Model

via situated learning theory (see Figure 3.1). We conclude the chapter with implications for future research.

3.1 COSMOPOLITAN HUMAN CAPITAL

Broadly, cosmopolitans refer to individuals who have the education, experience, and skills that enable them to work effectively in many different cultures (Haas, 2006; Kanter, 1995; Tung, 1998). By contrast, locals refer to individuals whose education, experience, and skills deal mostly with their original culture (Haas, 2006). The cosmopolitan–local distinction can be traced back to early sociological theories of role orientation by Merton (1957) and Gouldner (1957). In Merton's (1957) study of influential community members, he distinguished between leaders whose interests were restricted to their communities (locals) and leaders whose interests extended beyond their communities to relate to the world (cosmopolitans). Likewise, Gouldner's (1957) research in the context of organizations defined cosmopolitans as employees who were oriented toward external communities based on professional interests, versus locals who were oriented inwardly toward their organizations based on loyalty.

The study by Haas (2006) offered the most in-depth conceptual treatment and operationalization of the cosmopolitan–local distinction to date. Based on earlier research by Tung (1998), Haas (2006) distinguished cosmopolitans from locals along two attributes. Cosmopolitans are employees who have lived and worked in three or more countries, and who speak three or more languages, while locals are employees who have lived and worked in the project country, and who speak the local language. Hence, a primary feature of cosmopolitan human capital, as defined by Haas (2006) and others, is the amount of international experiences that individuals possess.

In this chapter we offer an expanded operationalization of cosmopolitans that goes beyond individuals' international experiences. Consistent with the general definition of human capital as consisting of both experiences and skills, we argue that an important but neglected aspect of cosmopolitan human capital is the capabilities that employees possess that enable them to be effective in dealing with diverse cultures. Incorporating a direct measure of employees' intercultural capabilities, as opposed to merely relying on a proxy measure of employees' international experience, would give a more accurate indication of how equipped the individual is in managing the challenges arising from the global workplace. This is consistent with Kanter's (1995: 23) assertion that 'it is not travel that defines cosmopolitans'. Likewise, research has shown that experience does not necessarily translate into knowledge or skills, and that individuals do not learn equally from their international experiences (Leslie and Van Velsor, 1996; Spreitzer et al., 1997). Studies have found that individual differences in cognitive abilities, self-esteem, personality traits, and competencies such as seeking and using feedback can affect the extent to which individuals learn from their expatriate assignments. Hence, we advance that a more complete operationalization of cosmopolitan human capital must take into account both the international experiences and the intercultural capabilities of the individuals.

3.1.1 Cultural Intelligence

Intercultural capabilities are captured by the construct of cultural intelligence (CQ; Ang and Inkpen, 2008; Ang and Van Dyne, 2008)—defined as a 'person's capability for successful adaptation to new cultural settings, that is, for unfamiliar settings attributable to cultural context' (Earley and Ang, 2003: 9). CQ provides a timely and relevant set of capabilities for enriching the cosmopolitan human capital construct. The theory of CQ is drawn from Sternberg and Detterman's (1986) framework of multiple intelligences, which integrates different perspectives of intelligence to propose four complementary ways of conceptualizing individual-level intelligence: (a) metacognitive intelligence refers to awareness and control of cognitions used to acquire and understand information; (b) cognitive intelligence refers to knowledge and knowledge structures; (c) motivational intelligence acknowledges that most cognition is motivated and thus focuses on the magnitude and direction of energy as a locus of intelligence; and (d) behavioral intelligence focuses on individual capabilities at the action level. This framework is noteworthy because it recognizes multiple forms of intelligence, unlike traditional research that has focused narrowly on linguistic, logical–mathematical, and spatial intelligence, while ignoring forms of intelligence related to self-regulation and interpersonal relations (Gardner, 1993).

Drawing on this multidimensional perspective of intelligence, Earley and Ang (2003) conceptualized CQ as a multidimensional construct with mental (metacognitive and cognitive), motivational, and behavioral components. Metacognitive CQ is the capability for consciousness and awareness during intercultural interactions. It reflects mental capabilities to acquire and understand culturally diverse situations and includes knowledge of and control over individual thought processes (Flavell, 1979) relating to culture. Relevant capabilities include planning, monitoring, and revising mental models. Those with high metacognitive CQ are consciously mindful of cultural preferences and norms—before and during interactions. They question cultural assumptions and adjust mental models during and after experiences (Nelson, 1996).

While metacognitive CQ focuses on higher-order cognitive processes, cognitive CQ focuses on knowledge of norms, practices, and conventions in different cultural settings, acquired from education and personal experiences. This includes knowledge of economic, legal, and social systems of different cultures (Triandis, 1994). Individuals with high cognitive CQ are able to anticipate and understand similarities and differences across cultural situations. As a result, they are more likely to have accurate expectations and less likely to make inaccurate interpretations of cultural interactions (for example, Triandis, 1995).

In addition to mental capabilities that foster understanding of other cultures, CQ also includes the motivational capability to cope with ambiguous and unfamiliar settings. Motivational CQ is the capability to direct attention and energy toward learning about and functioning in situations characterized by cultural differences. Based on the expectancy-value theory of motivation (Eccles and Wigfield, 2002), it includes intrinsic motivation (Deci and Ryan, 1985) and self-efficacy (Bandura, 1997). Those with high motivational CQ direct attention and energy toward cross-cultural situations based on intrinsic interest and confidence in cross-cultural effectiveness.

The fourth aspect of CQ recognizes that cultural understanding (mental) and interest (motivational) must be complemented with behavioral flexibility to exhibit appropriate verbal and non-verbal actions, based on the cultural values of a specific setting (Hall, 1959). Thus, behavioral CQ is the capability to exhibit situationally appropriate behaviors from a broad repertoire of verbal and non-verbal behaviors, such as being able to exhibit culturally appropriate words, tones, gestures, and facial expressions (Gudykunst et al., 1988).

Applying Sternberg and Detterman's (1986) framework of multiple intelligences to CQ provides a theoretical foundation that integrates the previously fragmented research on intercultural competencies. To date, there is a substantial body of research supporting the predictive validity of CQ (Ang et al., 2010). Studies have found that CQ is positively related to cultural adaptation and performance (Ang et al., 2007), expatriate effectiveness (Kim et al., 2008; Templer et al., 2006), adaptive performance (Oolders et al., 2008), interpersonal trust (Rockstuhl and Ng, 2008), and joint profits of intercultural negotiating dyads (Imai and Gelfand, 2010).

To recapitulate, we argue that a more comprehensive operationalization of cosmopolitan human capital should reflect employees' international experiences as well as their intercultural capabilities, embodied by the CQ construct. Based on this expanded definition, existing research has demonstrated that cosmopolitan human capital has an important impact on performance outcomes at different levels of analysis. At the firm level, several studies have found that cosmopolitan human capital, reflected in the international experience of CEOs, was positively related to the corporate financial performance of international firms (Carpenter et al., 2001; Daily et al., 2000; Sambharya, 1996). At the team level, Haas (2006) found that project teams with greater cosmopolitan human capital, indicated by the number of members who have lived and worked in multiple countries and who speak several languages, outperformed other teams with members who are primarily locals. At the individual level, Ang et al. (2007) found that managers with higher CQ were rated as more effective in their jobs.

Although research has clearly demonstrated the importance of cosmopolitan human capital for firm, team, and individual effectiveness, there is little understanding of how cosmopolitan human capital in firms is developed. (For an exception, see Gibbons and Waldman's (2004) process-oriented view of on-the-job human capital accumulation via task-specific learning by doing.) In the next section we expound on the concept of a firm's global culture capital, and how it affects the development of cosmopolitan human capital in the firm. Before we elaborate on the concept of global culture capital, we first review the extant literature on cultural capital, on which our concept of global culture capital is based.

3.2 CULTURAL CAPITAL

The concept of cultural capital was originally conceived by Bourdieu and Passeron (1977) to explain the higher education success rates of children of educated parents. In the original formulation, cultural capital was sketched in abstract terms as 'the cultural goods transmitted by the different family pedagogic actions, whose value qua cultural capital varies with the distance between the cultural arbitrary imposed by the dominant pedagogic actions and the cultural arbitrary inculcated by the family pedagogic actions within the different groups or classes' (Bourdieu and Passeron, 1990: 30). In other words, cultural capital refers to the legitimized knowledge acquired in the home environment that enables children to achieve more advantageous outcomes during the educational process.

A basic tenet of the cultural capital theory is that children of educated parents have higher cultural capital and, as a result, are more likely to achieve greater academic success because of their familiarity with the academic culture, which is also regarded as the dominant or legitimate culture in society. According to Bourdieu and Passeron (1977), school preferences are not neutral; rather, schools are essentially institutions that adopt and favor particular linguistic structures, authority patterns, types of curricula, and classroom practices that, at any historical period, represent the social and cultural experiences of the intellectual and economic elites. As such, parents who have gone through the education system should be familiar with the academic culture, and be able to impart it to their children.

The concept of cultural capital by Bourdieu and Passeron (1977) emphasized two key sets of elements that parents transmit to their children: parents' values and attitudes, and the habits and practices regarding education. Values and attitudes are intangible, subjective beliefs about the importance of education and how to achieve success in the academic environment. Vryonides (2007) found that professional middle-class parents have stronger beliefs about how they should participate in their children's education, compared to working-class parents who, due to their scant experience with education, are more likely to leave their children to manage their education process themselves.

Habits and practices are overt behaviors that reflect parents' beliefs about education. When parents are more involved in their children's education process, they are more likely to instill habits that will enable their children to perform better in school. Examples of habits and practices include employing appropriate study techniques and learning methods, reading newspapers and periodicals regularly, maintaining an interest in classical texts, music, film, theatre, and art appreciation (which help in humanities subjects) (Bourdieu and Passeron, 1979).

Through family socialization, cultural capital moulds human capital. Specifically, by modeling their educated parents, children are able to 'act the part' of a scholar and adopt attitudes and behaviors required for effective adaptation in schools. When these children display behaviors and mannerisms that are deemed appropriate by school teachers, they are evaluated and treated more favorably by the school system. Success in school, in turn, translates to higher human capital in the form of quality and quantity of education. Empirically, studies have shown a positive relationship between cultural capital and human capital (for example, Georg, 2004; Kurashi and Terano, 2008; van de Werfhorst and Hofstede, 2007). These findings support the theory that having cultural capital enables children to engage successfully in educational processes and institutions, thus influencing children's human capital in terms of educational attainment.

We propose that organizations, like parents, possess cultural capital which can help their employees secure advantages in the global economy. Applying the cultural capital construct to the organizational level may provide insights into the development of human capital within organizations. Whilst Bourdieu and Passeron (1977, 1979) focused on cultural capital of an academic orientation, we are interested in cultural capital with a global orientation. We term this bundle of elements as the firm's global culture capital, to distinguish it from individual-level cultural capital. We elaborate on the elements of 'global culture capital' below.

3.3 GLOBAL CULTURE CAPITAL

Consistent with Bourdieu and Passeron's (1979, 1990) concept of parents' cultural capital, we propose that a firm's global culture capital may be characterized by two major types of resources: the intangible cultural element in the form of organizational values toward globalization, and the overt cultural element in the form of organizational routines for promoting its global values. More specifically, we define the first element of global culture capital as a firm's *organizational values* that embrace a 'global mindset', and the second element of global culture capital as *organizational routines* that promote a global mindset within the organization. The two major elements of global culture capital are interrelated since the specific content of organizational routines is often derived from and should be consistent with the organizational values (Begley and Boyd, 2003; Chandler, 1962; Miles *et al.*, 1978). Moreover, organizational routines, when enacted over time, also serve to reinforce the values. Below, we elaborate on each element.

3.3.1 Organizational Values: A Global Mindset

A firm's mindset characterizes how it perceives and interprets its global environment, and has important implications for its business strategies (Gupta and Govindarajan, 2002). According to several scholars, a global mindset is one that recognizes, and strikes a balance between, global integration and local responsiveness (Begley and Boyd, 2003; Gupta and Govindarajan, 2002). This is contrasted with a 'parochial' mindset that emphasizes uniformity across cultures and markets; and a 'diffused' mindset that favors market segmentation and differentiation without a global picture (Javidan *et al.*, 2007).

The value of global integration comes from the headquarters' imperative to maintain centralized coordination and control to monitor strategy implementation. When integrating globally, the organization emphasizes standardization, leverages economies of scale, and achieves optimal resource deployment by reducing duplication of efforts. On the other hand, the value of local responsiveness is rooted in the diverse requirements and capabilities of different locals in different countries. By being locally responsive, the multinational corporation has to allow each subsidiary autonomy and independence to customize according to local requirements.

To embrace a global mindset, the organization has first to think globally; that is, recognize when it is advantageous to create a uniform global standard. Second, it also has to think locally by being in tune with local peculiarities. Lastly, and most essentially in the spirit of a 'global mindset', an organization has to think globally and locally concurrently, recognize situations in which demands from both global and local elements are compelling, and strike a fine balance between global uniformity and local sensitivity (Bartlett and Ghoshal, 1991; Begley and Boyd, 2003).

3.3.2 Organizational Routines

How do organizations achieve a global mindset in their international operations? Scholars have proposed a myriad of organizational routines that can help firms focus on both global integration and local sensitivity simultaneously (for example, Bartlett and Ghoshal, 1991; Gupta and Govindarajan, 2002). A routine is a repetitive, recognizable pattern of interdependent actions involving multiple actors through which work is accomplished in organizations (Cyert and March, 1963; Feldman and Pentland, 2003; Nelson and Winter, 1982). Scholars have likened organizational routines to an individual's habit (Nelson and Winter, 1982: 73) or programs and scripts that determine the sequence of actions to be taken (Cyert and March, 1963). Organizational routines are useful in that they guide organizational activity, create stability, and boost efficiency under normal circumstances.

Consistent with the knowledge-based view of the firm (Barney and Wright, 1998), we propose that routines for managing human resources play a particularly vital role in ensuring that firms are able to acquire local knowledge, and to integrate and utilize the information for global effectiveness. These human resource routines refer to the firm's established processes and procedures for hiring, deploying, rewarding, and training its human resources. Here we identify three types of routine that are critical in facilitating the firm's achievement of a global mindset.

Routines for Managing Personnel Flow Globally

To promote knowledge transfers across their subsidiaries, transnational firms need to manage their personnel flows effectively (Bartlett and Ghoshal, 1991). Traditionally, firms adopt two types of routine in managing their personnel flow. The first mode relies heavily on the use of expatriate managers in foreign subsidiaries because of their knowledge and experience of the parent organization (Black *et al.*, 1992). Organizations that adopt this mode of deployment often aim to achieve the purpose of control and coordination, while at the same time providing important international developmental experience for their high-potential managers (Black and Mendenhall, 1990). Scholars have termed this form of deployment as reflecting an exportive or ethnocentric orientation (Taylor *et al.*, 1996).

The second common mode of deployment is the use of host-country nationals to manage foreign subsidiaries. This form of deployment routine relies on locals with in-depth knowledge of the local culture to manage the firms' foreign operations. Typically, organizations that adopt this adaptive or polycentric approach exert only limited control from the parent organization, allowing the local subsidiaries to formulate their management policies and practices (Taylor *et al.*, 1996).

Both approaches, however, have important limitations that may impede the organization from achieving its global mindset values. A major criticism for the use of expatriates relates to their lack of local knowledge of the culture, which not only poses major difficulties for the expatriates' adjustment and performance (for example, Webb and Wright, 1996), but also impedes the organization's acquisition of local knowledge in service of its global operations. On the other hand, while the use of host-country nationals enables organizations to acquire diverse local knowledge, many of these host-country managers may be unable to share their knowledge because of the lack of knowledge of the operations and social networks in the parent company (Harvey *et al.*, 2001).

In response, research has promoted a third form of deployment routine that builds on the strengths of the earlier two forms of deployment. Rather than using expatriates or host-country nationals to manage subsidiary operations, the integrative approach emphasizes the use of the most qualified personnel regardless of nationality (Schuler *et al.*, 1993). This may include the use of third-country nationals— managers from neither the parent nor the host country—who have the requisite skills and experience to run the subsidiary.

More recently, Harvey *et al.* (2001) advocated the use of inpatriates as an important mechanism to achieve an integrative global human resource management orientation. Inpatriation refers to a formalized process of transferring either host-country or third-country nationals into the parent company on a semi-permanent or permanent basis. In doing so, inpatriation enables the parent company to acquire perspectives of its local markets and operations, while at the same time enabling the inpatriate managers to be socialized into their parent organization to understand the firm's global strategy. Hence, having inpatriates at headquarters not only facilitates the transfer and integration of local knowledge, but also increases the workforce diversity that is useful for innovation and the cultivation of social networks in the parent company (Harvey *et al.*, 2001).

In addition, several scholars have recently advocated an expanded variety of deployment options, including the use of contract expatriates, assignees on short- or medium-term overseas postings, international commuters, and virtual international employees (Briscoe and Schuler, 2004; Collings *et al.*, 2007). These options are particularly useful in cross-border team projects of short to medium lifespan, and where knowledge of local cultures is critical. Indeed, research is increasingly recognizing that short-term business travelers are important knowledge agents that facilitate the flow and use of information between headquarters and subsidiaries through providing formal training, informal mentoring, and social networking (Welch *et al.*, 2007).

Routines for Training and Developing

In a research involving sixty large multinational companies, Stroh and Caligiuri (1998) found that one of the three key aspects of people management identified as the most critical to the MNC's global competitiveness is the development of global leadership skills in its people. Organizational routines for developing global leaders range from didactic programs to intensive cultural experiences (Caligiuri, 2006). Didactic programs typically take the form of training programs aimed to equip individuals with specific knowledge, skills, and abilities (KSAs) such as greater awareness of cross-cultural differences, knowledge of appropriate behaviors when working with people from different cultures, and specific business knowledge such as international finance and project management, as well as the ability to converse in a different language. Intensive cultural experiences, on the other hand, aim to develop individuals more holistically by exposing them to the challenges of living and working in a foreign environment (Leung *et al.*, 2008). Short- and long-term international assignments are examples of such developmental programs, and are increasingly recognized by organizations as the most effective way to help their employees gain a global orientation in the firm's operations. The growing emphasis on experiential approaches to global leadership development may be attributed to the importance accrued to CEOs' international experience for firm performance (Carpenter *et al.*, 2001; Daily *et al.*, 2000; Sambharya, 1996).

Notwithstanding the crucial role that international assignments play in global leadership development, most organizations and research to date have focused on the performance of international assignees, rather than the development of their global leadership skills. Adopting a developmental as opposed to a performance focus in international assignments requires several changes in assumptions (Ng *et al.*, 2009). A major and obvious difference is the emphasis on learning effectiveness, rather than on work effectiveness. This shift acknowledges that failures during international assignments can present excellent learning opportunities that help individuals hone their global leadership skills (Hall *et al.*, 2001), and contrasts starkly with the traditional view of failures as undesirable outcomes to be avoided. The focus on learning outcomes also moves beyond expatriate research that has commonly focused on ways to staff and manage those in international positions, such as pre-departure cross-cultural training (Morris and Robie, 2001), role clarity, and relational skills (Bhaskar-Shrinivas *et al.*, 2005). Adopting a developmental perspective based on existing theories of learning (for example, Gagne, 1984; Kraiger *et al.*, 1993), Ng *et al.* (2009) proposed that global leadership self-efficacy, ethno-relative attitudes, accurate mental models of effective leadership across cultures, and flexibility of behavioral styles are key developmental outcomes that organizations and individuals should assess.

Following Ng *et al.*'s (2009) model, we argue that organizational routines that emphasize the development of their employees' global leadership competencies during overseas assignments (or any assignments involving intercultural interactions, such as virtual teams) are key to the global culture capital of the firms. Based on Kolb's (1984) four-stage theory of experiential learning (concrete experience, reflective observation, abstract conceptualization, and active experimentation), Ng *et al.* (2009) proposed several organizational routines and practices to encourage leader development through international assignments and other relevant global experiences.

First, organizations should encourage their leaders to get involved in the host culture to gain concrete experience. This can be achieved by emphasizing involvement and leadership development as important objectives of the assignment. This framing should help global leaders view the experience as more than just another task assignment (Oddou *et al.*, 2000). Organizations can also structure international assignments to facilitate interdependence with locals. Such routines not only provide leaders with more concrete and meaningful interactions with locals, but also aid the leaders in developing social networks and social capital. (For further discussion on the instrumentality of social capital in building human capital, see Chapters 2 and 16).

Second, to encourage leaders to engage in *reflective observation*, organizations can train and inculcate in their leaders the habit of documenting their cross-cultural experiences, insights, and learning points in a journal (Oddou *et al.*, 2000). By writing down their experiences and thoughts, leaders learn to reflect on past incidents to help them formulate theories and actions steps to be more effective in future interactions. Given that global leaders often have heavy workload and responsibilities, instilling the habit of reflection is critical for personal and professional effectiveness (Mintzberg and Gosling, 2002).

Third, Ng *et al.* (2009) suggest that organizations should provide training programs that focus on the development of inductive logic and reasoning skills to help global leaders make sense of, as well as translate, their concrete experiences and reflections into more abstract understanding of the culture. Currently, the majority of cross-cultural training programs focus on providing culture-specific knowledge to trainees (Earley and Peterson, 2004), which may have the adverse effect of promoting cultural stereotyping rather than help individuals develop a more dynamic approach to understanding and appreciating cultures (Osland and Bird, 2000).

Fourth, and consistent with the last stage of active experimentation in the experiential learning theory, organizations should encourage leaders to apply their newly acquired insights by providing resources that help them set specific and measurable developmental goals for exploration and experimentation. Cultural coaches, for instance, can work with individuals to set realistic and specific developmental goals, offer advice for implementation, and provide accountability for individuals to achieve their goals. Coaches or trainers could also facilitate virtual team interactions among global leaders in various locations and encourage them to share their experiences and sense-making with each other. All of these should promote active learning (for example, Oddou *et al.*, 2000).

Routines for Rewarding

Appropriate incentive systems must be in place for the deployment and training routines to achieve their purpose of facilitating a global mindset. For instance, research has shown that finding employees who are willing to accept long-term global assignments is one of the greatest challenges for organizations (Stroh and Caligiuri, 1998). Reasons range from the challenges of managing dual careers in the global assignment for married employees, family responsibilities, and repatriation issues that may adversely affect perceived career development prospects

(Collings *et al.*, 2007). Hence, organizations need to have appropriate incentive structures that overcome these challenges to motivate employees to accept global assignments. Specific practices include providing financial support for children's education overseas, income replacement for spouses or offering employment services to spouses, and offering significant rewards and a clear developmental path for employees who successfully complete a foreign assignment (for example, Briscoe and Schuler, 2004).

To encourage employees in international assignments to develop global leadership skills critical to the firm's success, it is important that reward systems for these employees do not overemphasize short-term business results at the expense of longer-term development of the employees. Apart from rewarding leaders for job performance, providing incentives for leaders to learn foreign languages and increase their knowledge of the local culture during their assignments should also facilitate and encourage cultural involvement (Oddou *et al.*, 2000).

Another set of incentive structures should focus on encouraging the transfer and utilization of knowledge across individuals from different subsidiaries. This is critical because the unwillingness of individuals and subsidiary units to share information (Szulanski, 1996) and to absorb and utilize new information (Cohen and Levinthal, 1990) can pose a serious barrier to achieving a global mindset and orientation for the firm. This problem usually arises because of asymmetry of goals between parent and subsidiary. While it is in the interest of the headquarters that a subsidiary shares its knowledge with other subsidiary units, the subsidiary may view the sharing of its knowledge as against its own interest.

To address this problem, MNCs can use a variety of mechanisms to align goals amongst units and individuals to facilitate the flow of knowledge. First, organizations should clearly specify performance evaluation criteria by which by individuals and units will be assessed, that are consistent with promoting a global mindset. Hence, to facilitate knowledge transfer and integration between units, it is imperative that headquarters formulate and communicate performance criteria that assess the extent of knowledge transfer and integration in their subsidiaries. The explicit specification of knowledge sharing across units as a performance criterion not only raises units' awareness of the headquarters' objectives, but also serves to address issues of goal conflict by aligning the goals of the units with the headquarters (Bjorkman *et al.*, 2004).

Besides clarifying the criteria for performance assessment, incentive systems that encourage knowledge transfer and integration will encourage subsidiary managers to cooperate with and to learn from other subsidiaries (see Stroh *et al.*, 1996). Bjorkman *et al.* (2004) gave the example of basing the subsidiary's management's bonuses not only on the subsidiary's performance, but also on the regional or global performance of the MNC. Since the regional or global performance of the MNC is likely to be enhanced by greater knowledge transfers and integration amongst its units, such an incentive system will align subsidiary's managers' interests with the interests of other managers, as well as with those of the headquarters.

In summary, we have argued that a firm's global culture capital consists of (1) organizational values of a 'global mindset'—that is, emphasizing the importance of achieving global integration and local responsiveness simultaneously—and (2) organizational routines that promote a global mindset orientation in its employees through systematic processes to manage its personnel flow globally, provide effective cross-cultural training and development, and build commitment through attractive reward systems.

3.4 GLOBAL CULTURE CAPITAL AND COSMOPOLITAN HUMAN CAPITAL

Building on our earlier arguments from sociological research on cultural capital, we argue that employees who work in firms with globally oriented culture capital are more likely to acquire cosmopolitan human capital in terms of international experience than those who work in firms with locally oriented culture capital. As firms with globally oriented culture capital emphasize the value of global mindset and are more likely to have in place organizational routines that promote the flow of people and knowledge across geographical locations, employees in these firms will therefore have more contact with people from different cultures, whether through overseas travel and assignments, or through virtual meetings and interactions, thus gaining more international experiences. Hence, our first proposition argues that:

> P1: The more 'globally' oriented the culture capital of the firm, the more likely employees will gain international experiences.

Situated learning theory also suggests that firms' global culture capital can affect employees' acquisition of CQ capabilities—the other aspect of cosmopolitan human capital. Specifically, situated learning theory emphasizes the importance of context and the exposure to 'authentic' activities as a powerful source of learning and skill acquisition (Collins *et al.*, 1989; Lave and Wenger, 1991). Authentic activities are 'the ordinary practices of the culture' (Brown *et al.*, 1989: 25); the concrete acts and practices that are anchored in culturally specific learning contexts (Fox, 2006; Hedegaard, 1998). Hence, unlike conventional learning theories that view knowledge and capabilities as abstract, theoretical entities that can be acquired in isolated, decontextualized settings, the situated learning perspective views acquisition of knowledge and capabilities as a result of interactions between learners and the context (both social and cultural) (Rogoff, 1995).

According to situated learning theory, authentic experiences are more effective than contrived activities devoid of the social context for learning skills and knowledge, for two key reasons. First, authentic activities provide problem-solving opportunities that require interpersonal and practical deliberations with immediate relevance to goal-directed activities. When efforts are goal-directed and grounded in specific situations, individuals are motivated to learn because the consequences are immediate and personal (Billet, 1996). Moreover, authentic activities provide holistic and complex experiences that allow development of cognitive, behavioral, and motivational capabilities. This contrasts with the dominant emphasis in traditional learning situations which focuses on cognitive knowledge (Anderson *et al.*, 1996). Thus, situated learning argues that more realistic experiences that are holistic and goal-directed are more likely to lead to internalization and enhanced capabilities that can be applied in other situations.

Second, authentic situations allow people to observe and compare themselves with others in the situation who have more experience. This follows from Lave and Wenger's (1991) idea of legitimate peripheral participation, which describes the processes whereby newcomers gain skills, knowledge, and habits and move toward becoming 'full' participants in the situation. Thus, by observing others who are more experienced, those in peripheral roles can pick up knowledge and skills through vicarious learning (Bandura, 1997) and practice their newly acquired knowledge and skills. These real-time practical experiences are sometimes termed 'social apprenticeship experiences' because they allow people to learn the knowledge, skills, and capabilities required in the situation. Situated learning, with its emphasis on real events embedded in social contexts, also provides opportunities for immediate feedback. For instance, the verbal and non-verbal reactions of others that occur in response to social interactions are important cues for assessing effectiveness and adjusting behaviors as necessary. This allows people to improve their knowledge and skills relative to specific situations (Billet, 1996).

By highlighting the importance of authentic activities and the social context for developing skills and capabilities, situated learning theory provides the theoretical link between a firm's culture capital and its employees' CQ. Firms that emphasize a global mindset and actively promote organizational routines that facilitate their employees' acquisition and integration of local knowledge (high in global culture capital) are in effect creating more opportunities for authentic intercultural interactions for their employees across different geographical locations to develop their CQ capabilities. Consistent with situated learning theory as well as social learning theory (Bandura, 1997), this acquisition of capabilities occurs through both direct experiences with people from different offices and cultures, and through indirect experiences by observing how others interact and manage cross-cultural working relationships. Below, we propose relationships for firm's global culture capital and each of the four CQ capabilities.

3.4.1 Cognitive CQ

We argue that through the multicultural activities and experiences that are more likely to occur in firms with higher global culture capital, individuals gain first-hand knowledge of how cultures differ in their economic and business systems, as well as values and behavioral norms that are important for effective cross-cultural interactions. As a result, they develop a richer schema of cultural concepts and systems (cognitive CQ).

> P2: The more 'globally' oriented the culture capital of the firm, the more likely employees will possess higher cognitive CQ.

3.4.2 Metacognitive CQ

Moreover, because of more exposure to multicultural experiences, individuals in firms with higher global culture capital are likely to have encountered more cultural surprises such as cultural paradoxes (Osland and Bird, 2000), defined as situations or interactions that involve contradictory norms or behaviors. To cope with and understand these cultural paradoxes, individuals are required to be flexible and open to disconfirming experiences, and to learn to interpret these situations. Through these experiences, they learn to hone their capabilities to question cultural assumptions, and to pick up and sense-make relevant cues in the situation (meta-cognitive CQ) (Triandis, 2006).

> P3: The more 'globally' oriented the culture capital of the firm, the more likely employees will possess higher metacognitive CQ.

3.4.3 Motivational CQ

Situated in an organization that emphasizes interactions and exchange of information between offices should enhance the motivation of the employees to be effective in their intercultural interactions, since this has important ramifications on their work performance. Moreover, social cognitive theory (Bandura, 1997) suggests that individuals with greater multicultural experience are more likely to be confident of their ability to manage cross-cultural interactions effectively because of their exposure to and experience with overcoming cross-cultural challenges. Also, international experiences can affect the amount of effort that individuals are willing to exert for international assignments (Feldman and Bolino, 2000), such as a willingness to relocate, the willingness to work with others from different cultures (Richard, 2000), and a willingness to communicate with the host-country nationals (Mendenhall and Oddou, 1985).

> P4: The more 'globally' oriented the culture capital of the firm, the more likely employees will possess higher motivational CQ.

3.4.4 Behavioral CQ

Finally, we argue that individuals in firms with globally oriented culture would have more opportunities to develop a larger repertoire of verbal and non-verbal behaviors, thus enhancing their behavioral CQ. Individuals with greater multicultural experiences have more opportunities to observe the different verbal and non-verbal styles across cultures, and to learn to respond appropriately. This is consistent with studies that have found that individuals with greater international experiences are more likely to learn how to communicate and negotiate effectively with people from different cultures (Gudykunst *et al.*, 1988) as well as learn to be more proficient in different languages (Mendenhall and Oddou, 1985).

> P5: The more 'globally' oriented the culture capital of the firm, the more likely employees will possess higher behavioral CQ.

3.5 CONCLUSION

Cultural capital is seldom evoked in organization studies; its relationship with human capital has rarely been explicitly considered. Instead, organizational researchers tend to devote most of their attention to human capital's relationship with capital in its economic or social form. In this chapter we have presented a framework that links firm-level global culture capital to culturally intelligent human capital in organizations. We hope to make several contributions to existing research.

First, we highlight the need for an expanded conceptualization of cosmopolitan human capital that goes beyond international experiences to include CQ capabilities, in order to reflect the nature of work and business environment in today's modern economy. Although previous work has attempted to capture the ability to function effectively in multicultural settings, a clear definition and operationalization of what this ability encompasses has not been well established. Empirical research has proceeded on the reliance on proxy measures such as international experience (Haas, 2006), organization tenure (for example, Hitt *et al.*, 2001), and work experience (for example, Hitt *et al.*, 2006). By incorporating CQ in the definition of cosmopolitan human capital, we propose a direct measure of intercultural capabilities that better reflects the ability of employees to overcome cross-cultural challenges of the global economy.

Second, we propose an organizational-level construct of global culture capital, based on Bourdieu and Passeron's (1990) concept of cultural capital, to explain why some firms are likely to achieve a greater competitive advantage in developing cosmopolitan human capital. Specifically, we argue that firms with a global mindset and organizational routines for managing their human resources to facilitate the achievement of a global mindset will create more authentic intercultural experiences for their employees that will enhance their cosmopolitan human capital.

The validity of our framework awaits empirical confirmation. Employees' CQ can be assessed with the Cultural Intelligence Scale (CQS)—a survey measure that assesses the four dimensions of CQ. The CQS has demonstrated discriminant validity as well as incremental validity over and above demographic characteristics, cognitive ability, and emotional intelligence in predicting individuals' cultural judgment and decision-making and interactional adjustment. The CQS has also demonstrated generalizability across samples, time, countries, and methods (self-report and peer-report) (Ang et al., 2007). However, global culture capital is a new construct with no existing measures. Thus, an immediate future direction for research is to develop and validate a measure of global culture capital.

Our framework also points to other interesting research questions. First, within an organization, are there inter-individual differences in the development of CQ? Given that individuals are products of the same routines within an organization, do some individuals develop CQ better and faster? If so, what are the individual differences that contribute to the different growth trajectories?

Second, is there a level of culturally intelligent human capital that is optimal? For optimal firm performance, does every individual in an organization need to be culturally intelligent? Haas (2006) found that teams with high proportions of cosmopolitans (individuals who have lived and worked in multiple countries and who speak several languages) delivered projects of higher quality, but that teams with very high proportions of cosmopolitans delivered projects of lower quality. This suggests that the relationship between CQ and firm performance could possibly be non-monotonic rather than linear. To determine the precise nature of the relationship, researchers need to consider the mean, variability, and concentration of CQ within a firm; short-term versus long-term perspectives; and multiple measures of firm performance.

Third, although we have made the case for the importance of developing cosmopolitan human capital internally, there are many dynamic factors such as the firm's stage of internationalization that will affect the appropriate mode of acquiring the needed cosmopolitan human capital for each firm (for example, Mayerhofer et al., 2004). Future research should explore the impact of these contextual factors that could moderate the decision to develop cosmopolitan human capital internally versus acquiring it externally (Lepak and Snell, 1999).

Our understanding of the relevance of CQ to human capital is still in its infancy. We have provided a theoretical framework and a research agenda to provide a link between the sociological concept of cultural capital and the economic literature on human capital. Whilst we have homed in global culture capital and cosmopolitan human capital, the cultural capital–human capital link can be further explored. Future organizational research should endeavour to uncover additional elements of firm-level culture capital that can contribute to specific dimensions of human capital. We hope to interest cultural capital and human capital scholars to pursue our line of inquiry and bring our understanding of these two forms of capital to maturity.

REFERENCES

ANDERSON, J. R., REDER, L. M., and SIMON, H. A. (1996). 'Situated Learning and Education', *Educational Researcher*, 25(4): 5–11.

ANG, S., and INKPEN, A. C. (2008). 'Cultural Intelligence and Offshore Outsourcing Success: A Framework of Firm-Level Intercultural Capability', *Decision Sciences*, 39(3): 337–58.

——and VAN DYNE, L. (eds.) (2008). *Handbook of Cultural Intelligence: Theory, Measurement and Applications* (New York: M. E. Sharpe).

————KOH, S. K., NG, K. Y., TEMPLER, K. J., TAY, C., and CHANDRASEKAR, N. A. (2007). 'Cultural Intelligence: An Individual Difference with Effects on Cultural Judgment and Decision Making, Cultural Adaptation, and Task Performance', *Management and Organization Review*, 3(3): 335–71.

————and TAN, M. L. (2010). 'Cultural Intelligence', in R. J. Sternberg and S. B. Kaufman (eds.), *Cambridge Handbook on Intelligence* (Cambridge: Cambridge University Press).

BANDURA, A. (1997). *Self-Efficacy: The Exercise of Control* (New York: Freeman).

BARNEY, J. B., and WRIGHT, P. M. (1998). 'On Becoming a Strategic Partner: The Role of Human Resources in Gaining Competitive Advantage', *Human Resource Management*, 37: 31–46.

BARTLETT, C. A., and GHOSHAL, S. (1991). *Managing across Borders: The Transnational Solution* (Boston: Harvard Business School Press).

BECKER, G. S. (1964). *Human Capital: A Theoretical and Empirical Analysis, with Special Reference to Education* (New York: Columbia University Press).

BEGLEY, T. M., and BOYD, D. P. (2003). 'The Need for a Corporate Global Mind-Set', *MIT Sloan Management Review* (Winter): 25–32.

BHASKAR-SHRINIVAS, P., HARRISON, D. A., SHAFFER, M. A., and LUK, D. M. (2005). 'Input-Based and Time-Based Models of International Adjustment: Meta-Analytic Evidence and Theoretical Extensions', *Academy of Management Journal*, 48(2): 257–81.

BILLET, S. (1996). 'Situated Learning: Bridging Sociocultural and Cognitive Theorizing', *Learning and Instruction*, 6(3): 263–80.

BJORKMAN, I., BARNER-RASMUSSEN, W., and LI, L. (2004). 'Managing Knowledge Transfer in MNCS: The Impact of Headquarters Control Mechanisms', *Journal of International Business Studies*, 35: 443–55.

BLACK, J. S., and MENDENHALL, M. (1990). 'Cross-Culture Training Effectiveness: A Review and Theoretical Framework for Future Research', *Academy of Management Review*, 15(1): 113–36.

——GREGERSEN, H., and MENDENHALL, M. (1992) *Global Assignments* (San Francisco: Jossey-Bass).

BOURDIEU, P., and PASSERON, J. (1977). *Reproduction in Education, Society and Culture* (2nd edn. London: Sage Publications).

——and——(1979). *The Inheritors: French Students and their Relations to Culture* (Chicago: University of Chicago Press).

BRISCOE, D. R., and SCHULER, R. S. (2004). *International Human Resource Management* (2nd edn. London: Routledge).

BROWN, J. S., COLLINS, A., and DUGUID, P. (1989). 'Situated Cognition and the Culture of Learning', *Educational Researcher*, 18(1): 32–42.

CALIGIURI, P. M. (2006). 'Developing Global Leaders', *Human Resource Management Review*, 16(2): 219–28.

CARPENTER, M. A., SANDERS, W. G., and GREGERSEN, H. B. (2001). 'Bundling Human Capital with Organizational Context: The Impact of International Assignment Experience on Multinational Firm Performance and CEO Pay', *Academy of Management Journal*, 44(3): 493–511.

CHANDLER, A. D., JR. (1962). *Strategy and Structure* (Garden City, NY: Doubleday).

COHEN, W. M., and LEVINTHAL, D. A. (1990). 'Absorptive Capacity: A New Perspective on Learning and Innovation', *Administrative Science Quarterly*, 35: 128–52.

COLLINS, A., BROWN, J. S., and NEWMAN, S. E. (1989). 'Cognitive Apprenticeship: Teaching the Crafts of Reading, Writing, and Mathematics', in L. B. Resnick (ed.), *Knowing, Learning, and Instruction: Essays in Honor of Robert Glaser* (Hillsdale, NJ: Erlbaum), 453–94.

COLLINGS, D. G., SCULLION, H., and MORLEY, M. J. (2007). 'Changing Patterns of Global Staffing in the Multinational Enterprise: Challenges to the Conventional Expatriate Assignment and Emerging Alternatives', *Journal of World Business*, 42(2): 198–213.

CYERT, R. M., and MARCH, J. G. (1963). *A Behavioral Theory of the Firm* (Englewood Cliffs, NJ: Prentice-Hall).

DAILY, C. M., CERTO, S. T., and DALTON, D. R. (2000). 'International Experience in the Executive Suite: The Path to Prosperity?', *Strategic Management Journal*, 21(4): 515–23.

DECI, E. L., and RYAN, R. M. (1985). *Intrinsic Motivation and Self-Determination in Human Behavior* (New York: Plenum).

EARLEY, P. C., and ANG, S. (2003). *Cultural Intelligence: Individual Interactions across Cultures* (Palo Alto, Calif.: Stanford University Press).

——and PETERSON, R. S. (2004). 'The Elusive Cultural Chameleon: Cultural Intelligence as a New Approach to Intercultural Training for the Global Manager', *Academy of Management Learning and Education*, 3: 100–15.

ECCLES, J. S., and WIGFIELD, A. (2002). 'Motivational Beliefs, Values, and Goals', in S. T. Fiske, D. L. Schacter, and C. Zahn-Waxler (eds.), *Annual Review of psychology*, 53 (Palo Alto, Calif.: Annual Reviews), 109–32.

Economist Intelligence Unit (2006). *CEO Briefing: Corporate Priorities for 2006 and Beyond* (London: Economist Intelligence Unit).

——(2007). *CEO Briefing: Corporate Priorities for 2007 and Beyond* (London: Economist Intelligence Unit).

FELDMAN, D. C., and BOLINO, M. C. (2000). 'Skill Utilization of Overseas Interns: Antecedents and Consequences', *Journal of International Management*, 6: 29–47.

FELDMAN, M. S., and PENTLAND, B. T. (2003). 'Reconceptualizing Organizational Routines as a Source of Flexibility and Change', *Administrative Science Quarterly*, 48: 94–118.

FLAVELL, J. H. (1979). 'Metacognition and Cognitive Monitoring: A New Area of Cognitive Inquiry', *American Psychologist*, 34(10): 906–11.

FOX, S. (2006). 'Inquiries of Every Imaginable Kind: Ethnomethodology, Practical Action and the New Socially Situated Learning Theory', *Sociological Review*, 54(3): 426–45.

GAGNE, R. M. (1984). 'Learning Outcomes and their Effects: Useful Categories of Human Performance', *American Psychologist*, 39(4): 377–85.

GARDNER, H. (1993). *Multiple Intelligence: The Theory in Practice* (New York: Basic Books).

GEORG, W. (2004). 'Cultural Capital and Social Inequality in the Life Course', *European Sociological Review*, 20: 333–44.

GIBBONS, R., and WALDMAN, M. (2004). 'Task-Specific Human Capital', *American Economic Review*, 94: 203–7.

GOULDNER, A. W. (1957). 'Cosmopolitans and Locals: Toward an Analysis of Latent Social Roles—I.' *Administrative Science Quarterly*, 2(3): 281–306.

GUDYKUNST, W. B., TING-TOOMEY, S., and CHUA, E. (1988). *Culture and Interpersonal Communication* (Newbury Park, Calif.: Sage).

GUPTA, A. K., and GOVINDARAJAN, V. (2002). 'Cultivating a Global Mindset', *Academy of Management Executive*, 16(1): 116–26.

HAAS, M. R. (2006). 'Acquiring and Applying Knowledge in Transnational Teams: The Roles of Cosmopolitans and Locals', *Organization Science*, 17(3): 367–84.

HALL, E. T. (1959). *The Silent Language* (New York: Doubleday).

HALL, D. T., ZHU, G., and YAN, A. (2001). 'Developing Global Leaders: To Hold on to Them, Let Them Go!', *Advances in Global Leadership*, 2: 327–49.

HARVEY, M., SPEIER, C., and NOVECEVIC, M. M. (2001). 'A Theory-Based Framework for Strategic Global Human Resource Staffing Policies and Practices', *International Journal of Human Resource Management*, 12(6): 898–915.

HECKMAN, J. J. (2000). 'Policies to Foster Human Capital', *Research in Economics*, 54(1): 3–56.

HEDEGAARD, M. (1998). 'Situated Learning and Cognition: Theoretical Learning and Cognition', *Mind, Culture and Activity*, 5(2): 114–26.

HITT, M. A., BIERMAN, L., SHIMIZU, K., and KOCHHAR, R. (2001). 'Direct and Moderating Effects of Human Capital on Strategy and Performance in Professional Service Firms? A Resource-Based Perspective', *Academy of Management Journal*, 44(1): 13–28.

————UHLENBRUCK, K., and SHIMIZU, K. (2006). 'The Importance of Resources in the Internationalization of Professional Service Firms: The Good, the Bad, and the Ugly', *Academy of Management Journal*, 49(6): 1137–57.

IMAI, L., and GELFAND, M. J. (2010). 'The Culturally Intelligent Negotiator: The Impact of Cultural Intelligence (CQ) on Negotiation Sequences and Outcomes', *Organizational Behavior and Human Decision Processes*, 112(2): 83–98.

JAVIDAN, M., STEERS, R. M., and HITT, M. A. (2007). 'Putting it All Together: So What is Global Mindset and Why is it So Important?', in M. Javidan, R. M. Steers, and M. A. Hitt (eds.), *Advances in International Management*, xix (Oxford: JAI Press Elsevier), 215–26.

KANTER, R. M. (1995). *World Class: Thriving Locally in the Global Economy* (New York: Simon & Schuster).

——(1999). 'Change is Everyone's Job: Managing the Extended Enterprise in a Globally Connected World', *Organizational Dynamics*, 28(1): 7–23.

KIM, K., KIRKMAN, B. L., and CHEN, G. (2008). 'Cultural Intelligence and International Assignment Effectiveness: A Conceptual Model and Preliminary Findings', in S. Ang and L. Van Dyne (eds.), *Handbook of Cultural Intelligence: Theory, Measurement, and Applications* (New York: M. E. Sharpe), 71–90.

KOLB, D. A. (1984). *Experiential Learning: Experience as the Source of Learning and Development* (Englewood Cliffs, NJ: Prentice-Hall).

KRAIGER, K., FORD, J. K., and SALAS, E. (1993). 'Application of Cognitive, Skill-Based, and Affective Theories of Learning Outcomes to New Methods of Training Evaluation', *Journal of Applied Psychology*, 78(2): 311–28.

KURASHI, S., and TERANO, T. (2008). 'Historical Simulation: A Study of Civil Service Examinations, the Family Line and Cultural Capital in China', *Advances in Complex Systems*, 11(2): 187–98.

LAVE, J., and WENGER, E. (1991). *Situated Learning: Legitimate Peripheral Participation* (Cambridge: Cambridge University Press).

LEPAK, D. P., and SNELL, S. A. (1999). 'The Human Resource Architecture: Toward a Theory of Human Capital Allocation and Development', *Academy of Management Review*, 24: 31–48.

LESLIE, J. B., and VAN VELSOR, E. (1996). *A Look at Derailment Today: North American and Europe* (Greensboro, NC: Center for Creative Leadership).

LEUNG, A. K., MADDUX, W. W., GALINSKY, A. D., and CHIU, C-Y. (2008). 'Multicultural Experience Enhances Creativity: The When and How', *American Psychologist*, 63: 169–81.

MAYERHOFER, H., HARTMANN, L. C., MICHELITSCH-RIEDL, G., and KOLLINGER, I. (2004). 'Flexpatriate Assignments: A Neglected Issue in Global Staffing', *International Journal of Human Resource Management*, 15(8): 1371–89.

MENDENHALL, M., and ODDOU, G. (1985). 'The Dimensions of Expatriate Acculturation: A Review', *Academy of Management Review*, 10: 39–47.

MERTON, R. K. (1957). *Social Theory and Social Structure* (2nd edn. Glencoe, Ill.: Free Press).

MILES, R. E., SNOW, C. C., MEYER, A. D., and COLEMAN, H. J., JR. (1978). 'Organizational Strategy, Structure, and Process', *Academy of Management Review*, 3(3): 546–62.

MINTZBERG, H., and GOSLING, J. (2002). 'Educating Managers Beyond Borders', *Academy of Management Learning and Education*, 1(1): 64–76.

MORRIS, M. A., and ROBIE, C. (2001). 'A Meta-Analysis of the Effects of Cross-Cultural Training on Expatriate Performance and Adjustment', *International Journal of Training and Development*, 5: 112–25.

NELSON, R. R., and WINTER, S. G. (1982). *An Evolutionary Theory of Economic Change* (Cambridge, Mass.: Harvard University Press).

NELSON, T. O. (1996). 'Consciousness and Metacognition', *American Psychologist*, 51(2): 102–16.

NG, K. Y., VAN DYNE, L., and ANG, S. (2009). 'From Experience to Experiential Learning: Cultural Intelligence as a Learning Capability for Global Leader Development', *Academy of Management Learning and Education*, 8(4): 511–26.

ODDOU, G., MENDENHALL, M., and RITCHIE, J. B. (2000). 'Leveraging Travel as a Tool for Global Leadership Development', *Human Resource Management*, 39(2–3): 159–72.

OOLDERS, T., CHERNYSHENKO, O. S., and STARK, S. (2008). 'Cultural Intelligence as a Mediator of Relationships between Openness to Experience and Adaptive Performance', in S. Ang and L. Van Dyne (eds.), *Handbook of Cultural Intelligence: Theory, Measurement, and Applications* (New York: M. E. Sharpe), 145–58.

OSLAND, J. S., and BIRD, A. (2000). 'Beyond Sophisticated Stereotyping: Cultural Sensemaking in Context', *Academy of Management Executive*, 14(1): 65–87.

PFEFFER, J. (1994). 'Competitive Advantage through People', *California Management Review*, 36: 9–29.

RICHARD, O. C. (2000). 'Racial Diversity, Business Strategy, and Firm Performance: A Resource-Based View', *Academy of Management Journal*, 43(2): 164–77.

ROCKSTUHL, T., and NG, K. Y. (2008). 'The Effects of Cultural Intelligence on Interpersonal Trust in Multi-Cultural Teams', in S. Ang, and L. Van Dyne (eds.), *Handbook of Cultural Intelligence: Theory, Measurement, and Applications* (New York: M. E. Sharpe), 206–20.

ROGOFF, B. (1995). 'Observing Sociocultural Activities on Three Planes: Participatory Appropriation, Guided Appropriation and Apprenticeship', in J. V. Wertsch, P. Del Rio, and A. Alverez (eds.), *Sociocultural Studies of the Mind* (Cambridge: Cambridge University Press), 139–64.

SAMBHARYA, R. B. (1996). 'Foreign Experience of Top Management Teams and International Diversification Strategies of U.S. Multinational Corporations', *Strategic Management Journal*, 17(9): 739–46.

SCHULER, R., DOWLING, P., and DE CIERI, H. (1993). 'An Integrative Framework of Strategic International Human Resource Management', *International Journal of Human Resource Management*, 4(4): 717–64.

SPREITZER, G. M., McCALL, M. W. JR., and MAHONEY, J. D. (1997). 'Early Identification of International Executive Potential', *Journal of Applied Psychology*, 82(1): 6–29.

STERNBERG, R. J., and DETTERMAN, D. K. (eds.) (1986). *What is Intelligence? Contemporary Viewpoints on its Nature and Definition* (Norwood, NJ: Ablex).

STROH, L. K., and CALIGIURI, P. M. (1998). 'Increasing Global Competitiveness through Effective People Management', *Journal of World Business*, 33(1): 1–16.

——— BRETT, J. M., BAUMANN, J. P., and REILLY, A. H. (1996). 'Agency Theory and Variable Pay Compensation Strategies', *Academy of Management Journal*, 39(3): 751–68.

SZULANSKI, G. (1996). 'Exploring Internal Stickiness: Impediments to the Transfer of Best Practices within the Firm', *Strategic Management Journal*, 17: 27–43.

TAYLOR, S., BEECHLER, S., and NAPIER, N. (1996) 'Toward an Integrative Model of Strategic International Human Resource Management', *Academy of Management Review*, 21(4): 959–85.

TEMPLER, K. J., TAY, C., and CHANDRASEKAR, N. A. (2006). 'Motivational Cultural Intelligence, Realistic Job Previews, and Realistic Living Conditions Preview, and Cross-Cultural Adjustment', *Group and Organization Management*, 31(1): 154–73.

TRIANDIS, H. C. (1994). *Culture and Social Behavior* (New York: McGraw Hill).

——— (1995). 'Culture Specific Assimilators', in S. M. Fowler (ed.), *Intercultural Sourcebook: Cross-Cultural Training Methods* (Yarmouth, ME: Intercultural Press), 179–86.

——— (2006). 'Cultural Intelligence in Organizations', *Group and Organization Management*, 31(1): 20–6.

TUNG, R. L. (1998). 'American Expatriates Abroad: From Neophytes to Comsmopolitans', *Journal of World Business*, 33(2): 125–44.

VAN DE WERFHORST, H. G., and HOFSTEDE, S. (2007). 'Cultural Capital or Relative Risk Aversion? Two Mechanisms for Educational Inequality Compared', *British Journal of Sociology*, 58(3): 391–415.

VRYONIDES, M. (2007). 'Social and Cultural Capital in Educational Research: Issues of Operationalization and Measurement', *British Educational Research Journal*, 33: 867–85.

WEBB, A., and WRIGHT, P. C. (1996). 'The Expatriate Experience: Implications for Career Success', *Career Development International*, 1(5): 38–44.

WELCH, D. E., WELCH, L. W., and WORM, V. (2007). 'The International Business Traveller: A Neglected But Strategic Human Resource', *International Journal of Human Resource Management*, 18(2): 173–83.

CHAPTER 4

....

COGNITION AND HUMAN CAPITAL

THE DYNAMIC INTERRELATIONSHIP BETWEEN KNOWLEDGE AND BEHAVIOR

....

RHETT A. BRYMER

MICHAEL A. HITT

MARIO SCHIJVEN

4.1 INTRODUCTION

....

The importance of knowledge as a crucial asset for firm performance has been of growing interest to organizational scholars over the last two decades (for example, Cook and Brown, 1999; Grant, 1996; Kogut and Zander, 1992; Nonaka and Takeuchi, 1995; Orlikowski, 2002; Spender, 1996). While it is commonly accepted that both institutional (Scott, 1995) and organizational (Nag *et al.*, 2007; Walsh and Ungson, 1991) structures can retain knowledge, a significant portion of this knowledge is also contained in the cognition of the firm's constituent employees and other stakeholders; that is, within its human capital (Hitt *et al.*, 2001; Tsoukas, 1996).

According to Webster's dictionary, cognition is the 'act of knowing', as the root of the word comes from the Greek *cognos*, 'to know'. From this etymological perspective, cognition is both the possession of knowledge by human agents and the mental processing, either conscious or unconscious, that is fundamentally involved in possessing knowledge. The act of knowing—which is necessarily performed by the mental processes of a firm's members—and the possessing of that knowledge by the firm's members, therefore, is a significant subset of the overall body of organizational knowledge.

Cognition, though, is at once more broadly defined than and fundamentally different from knowledge. While inextricably interrelated, cognition and knowledge are separate constructs even when considered within a person. Knowledge may be either explicit or tacit and reconstituted through action and practice (Orlikowski, 2002). In either case, the knowledge alone does not change and cannot interact with the environment of which it is a part. Cognition involves the mental processing that uses, changes, enacts, recalls, stores, senses, and transforms knowledge in a dynamic, recursive manner. To be cognizant is to be actively aware of a set of knowledge, including a framework within which such knowledge might be used, based on environmental or mental cues. In addition to the fact that cognition is a process, this dimension of awareness which maintains and transforms knowledge helps to distinguish it from conceptions of knowledge alone. Cognition involves 'rational, logical, ongoing, and especially *conscious* processing... [as well as] non-rational, schematic, and, in particular, *unconscious* processing' (Gioia, 1986: 342; italics in original). Thus, cognition discriminates between which knowledge to process, which knowledge to seek, which knowledge to discard, and which knowledge to enact.

The advance of knowledge work as the integral value creator of modern economies (Drucker, 2003) has led researchers to focus on the cognitive characteristics of employees within firms. From a resource-based view of the firm, the knowledge held by human capital (as measured by education and experience) has been demonstrated to have a strong positive effect on firm performance (Hitt *et al.*, 2001, 2006). The strategy literature has recognized that knowledge held by human capital is unique, socially complex, and capable of contributing to a sustained competitive advantage (Barney, 1991; Coff, 1997; Wright and McMahan, 1992). Likewise, research in organizational behavior and human resource management has shown the importance of cognitive capability for individual and team performance in organizational tasks (for example, Gottfredson, 1997; Pulakos *et al.*, 2003).

Cognitive human capital is present at both the individual and collective levels. In the context of an organizational resource, cognitive human capital includes the thoughts, schemas, heuristics, dispositions, and knowledge structures that, when bundled with resources and/or driven by strategic framing, produce actions and decisions that bring value to the organization. Whether held by an individual or a collection of individuals and whether conscious or unconscious, cognition is central to the processing of vast amounts of information necessary to navigate effectively in today's complex organizational environment. It provides the basis for all decisions and actions that determine firm resources, boundaries, the enacted environment, and performance. Consisting of active human beings, organizations can prosper or fail depending on the extent to which their cognitive human capital is aligned with the needs of the environment.

This chapter explores the relationship between both individual and collective cognition and the value of human capital within firms. In synthesizing the literature in this area, we address three broad, interrelated questions relevant to our understanding of this important concept. First, given the importance of both knowledge and behavior to firm performance, what role does cognition play with respect to both? Second, as organizational environments are dynamic, complex, and multilevel, what are the most salient determinants of cognitions that have been recognized by organizational researchers to date? Third, given the potentially fragile nature of cognitive human capital, what framework is useful for examining the managerial influences on their firms' cognitive processes? We develop a model in an attempt to offer answers to these questions. The chapter ends with a discussion of how this model contributes to the existing literature on human capital, and suggests further research.

4.2 BACKGROUND

4.2.1 The Nature of Human Cognition as Capital

Higher cognition of the human mind has been a topic of philosophical dialogue throughout the ages, from the Socratic concept of 'true belief', to the Cartesian connection with existence ('I think, therefore I am'), to the modern epistemological writing of Polanyi (1967). Recently, anthropologist Mark Hauser postulated that four enduring cognitive qualities of humans separate us from other lifeforms: the ability to combine different types of information, the application of rules and solutions to a new and different situation, the mental creation of symbolic representation for problem-solving, and the detachment of thought from raw sensory and perceptual input (Hauser, 2008). Although there is debate within the scientific communities about the extent to which these characteristics are accurate (Penn *et al.*, 2008), there is broad consensus that humans, as compared to other intelligent forms, possess higher cognitive abilities and that higher cognitive functioning is one of the defining characteristics of humankind.

Human capital is a unique type of capital. The traditional economic view is that capital represents a means of production—a way of improving the input-to-output ratio. Adam Smith originally conceived of human capital as follows: 'The improved dexterity of a workman may be considered in the same light as a machine or instrument of trade which facilitates and abridges labor, and which, though it costs a certain expense, repays that expense with a profit' (Smith, 1776: 377). Becker (1964) expanded on this concept by outlining the investment options in human capital, such as education, training, and medical treatment, while highlighting that human capital is unique in that it can never be owned by the firm. As Coff notes, 'The most obvious problem is a firm's [human] assets walk out the door each day, leaving some question as to whether or not they will return' (1997: 375).

The problem is compounded when considering the cognitive aspects of human capital. As knowledge is possessed by individuals dispersed throughout the organization (Grant, 1996; Hayek, 1945; Henderson and Clark, 1990; Tsoukas, 1996), there is a high likelihood that the knowledge will not be recognized fully. Partially because of this, the firm fails to optimize the total utility of knowledge. Information about others' knowledge can be difficult to assess, because some of the most valuable knowledge is tacit and difficult to articulate (Polanyi, 1967) and its outcomes are causally ambiguous (Coff, 1997; Lippman and Rumelt, 1982). Common agency problems, such as shirking, moral hazard (Jensen and Meckling, 1976), and dilution of firm rents through salary renegotiation (Spender, 1994; Coff, 1997), suggest that human actors might use (or not use) their knowledge in ways that advance their own goals rather than those of the firm. These problems are particularly insidious for cognitive aspects of human performance, as mental processes are impossible to observe directly and thus their effectiveness is exceedingly difficult to evaluate. Additionally, knowledge is notoriously susceptible to market failure. Interested parties require information about the knowledge to assess its value—information that the owner of the knowledge is reluctant to share, because sharing it inevitably provides the interested party with (part of) the knowledge at no cost (Arrow, 1962).

While human capital in the manufacturing context might be focused on productivity and utility in a narrowly defined task environment, the highest valued human capital commonly resides in managers and knowledge workers (Drucker, 2003). Unlike other forms of capital, human capital is capable of a number of autonomous value-adding functions, such as complex decision-making (March and Simon, 1958), creative activities and innovation (Leonard, 1995; Woodman *et al.*, 1993), purposeful enactment of one's environment (Weick, 1969), and social behavior that leads to unique configurations of interdependence (Thompson, 1967). These factors all involve cognitive functioning and thus rely on individuals' cognitive capabilities.

4.2.2 Strategy, Cognition, and Knowledge

The 1970s witnessed the development of several economic theories of the firm, from transaction cost economics (Williamson, 1975) to resource dependence theory (Pfeffer and Salancik, 1978) and population ecology (Hannan and Freeman, 1977).

Much of the focus was removed from individual managerial decision-making and behavior that had dominated the organizational literature previously (for example, March and Simon, 1958; Cyert and March, 1963).

In the last twenty years, however, the pendulum has swung back towards research with a stronger emphasis on the internal and microlevel determinants of firm performance (Hoskisson *et al.*, 1999). Further, a greater amount of research attention has focused on the cognitive aspects of firms, such as learning and decision-making. Perhaps the most dominant theory in recent organizational research is the resource-based view of the firm (Barney, 1991; Peteraf, 1993; Amit and Schoemaker, 1993), the foundations of which are from the work of Penrose (1959). Even in the early work using the resource-based tradition, human knowledge is central to the value derived from resources:

A firm is basically a collection of resources. Consequently, if we can assume that business-men believe there is more to know about the resources they are working with than they do know at any given time, and that more knowledge would likely improve the efficiency and profitability of the firm, then unknown and unused productive services immediately become of considerable importance, not only because the belief that they exist acts as an incentive to acquire new knowledge, but also because they shape the scope and direction of the search for knowledge. (Penrose, 1959: 77)

Cognitions of individual managers have also been regarded as resources (Barney, 1991); they are considered to be critical in transforming resources and capabilities into strategic assets through decision-making (Amit and Schoemaker, 1993). A related theoretical perspective is the knowledge-based view of the firm (Kogut and Zander, 1992, 1993), which suggests that the inter- and intraorganizational boundaries of the firm are predicated on the ease with which knowledge is transferred between individuals (Grant, 1996; Nickerson and Zenger, 2004; Szulanski, 1996; Lyles and Salk, 1996; Prahalad and Bettis, 1986).

Simultaneous to the resurgence of internally focused theories of firm performance, organizational learning theory also burgeoned in the management literature (for example, Cohen and Levinthal, 1990; Huber, 1991; Levitt and March, 1988; March, 1991; Senge, 1991; Walsh and Ungson, 1991). Although organizational knowledge, organizational learning, and organizational memory are not entirely cognitive phenomena, human embodied knowledge in the firm and the distribution and exchange of that knowledge are critical components of each (Cohen and Levinthal, 1990; Walsh and Ungson, 1991; Argyris and Schön, 1978).

More recently, organizational scholars have challenged the classification of knowledge as a resource that can be transferred and distributed throughout a collectivity. While tacit knowledge has long been recognized as difficult to articulate, and therefore difficult to exchange (Polanyi, 1967; Kogut and Zander, 1992), recent writings have extended the notion of knowledge to refer to more than an 'epistemology of possession'; rather, knowledge is conceived not only as a commodity to be exchanged, but also a recursive process that cannot be separated from action, practice, or behavior (Cook and Brown, 1999). Orlikowski (2002) highlights this 'knowing-in-practice' from the more traditional 'possessed' knowledge. Whereas knowledge has typically been conceptualized as a 'separate entity, static property, or stable disposition embedded in practice' (Orlikowski, 2002: 250), knowledge-in-practice can be thought of as an enacted entity that is reconstituted everyday by behavior. Therefore 'it does not make sense to talk about either knowledge or practice without the other' (Orlikowski, 2002: 250).

Consistent with the concept of a recursive knowledge–behavior relationship, organizational scholars have considered the ways in which knowledge and behavior interact to produce organizational outcomes. Cook and Brown (1999) suggest that the interaction of the two is similar to a 'generative dance' which allows better understanding of organizational learning, innovation, and effectiveness. Similarly, Tsoukas and Vladimirou (2001: 976) define organizational knowledge as 'the capability members of an organization have developed to draw distinctions in the process of carrying out their work...by enacting sets of generalizations'. Emphases on knowledge as a dynamic resource that both determines and relies on the actions by knowledgeable persons underline this new perspective.

Theoretical and empirical work has identified cognition as a broker of this knowledge–behavior interplay. The processes of behavioral change can be hindered by misalignment of collective cognitions and knowledge 'grafts' attempted (Nag *et al.*, 2007) and of the knowledge based on cognitions and changing incentives (Kaplan and Henderson, 2005). Bases of knowledge lead to the practices and related organizational outcomes through the cognitions of constituent employees. Examples include the accuracy and sharedness of transactive memory (Brandon and Hollingshead, 2004), cognitive affect in entrepreneurial activity (Baron, 2008), and sense-making (Thomas *et al.*, 1993), search (Gavetti and Rivkin, 2007), attention of top management (Ocasio, 1997), and knowledge structures (Kabanoff and Brown, 2007) in the formulation and execution of strategy. The relationship has also been theorized to be reciprocal, as cognitive heuristics and structural supports that guide the behaviors of learning, and lead to new knowledge and action (Holcomb *et al.*, 2009; Kang *et al.*, 2007).

In sum, the utility of human cognition as an integral component of firm strategy is clearly pertinent today. The emergence of the information age has made the proliferation of real-time communications and munificent information sources commonplace in industrialized economies. The rise of the service sector, especially in developed countries, has gradually come to dominate these nations' economies. For instance, the services industry represents approximately 80 percent of the GDP and employment base of the US (Ford and Bowen, 2008). These, coupled with the continued reliance on automation in the production of manufactured goods, have motivated organizations to better understand and use the cognitive capabilities of their human resources, such as decision-making, knowledge, and the ability to learn, as their most unique and valuable assets. A variety of corporate behemoths, including Microsoft and Google, have taken advantage of their talented workforces to rapidly create firm value based almost exclusively on the innovations and intangible assets built with their collective cognitive capabilities. These information-age technological forces have simultaneously leveled the playing field for access to information and access to markets (Porter, 1996). The increased competition that these changes have created and the speed at which markets change and need to be exploited underscore the importance of firms managing their cognitive capabilities effectively.

We argue that the management of these cognitive capabilities determines the realized value of human capital within the firm, and that this process serves to dynamically induce the appropriate changes in amount and content to ensure stability in cognitions at both the individual and collective levels of its human capital.

4.3 A Conceptual Model of the Extraction of Human Capital Value

Although knowledge and cognitive capabilities have potential value embedded in them, much like any other organizational resource, little or none of this potential value will be realized unless they are bundled with other resources. Organizational cognition and knowledge can be classified as a stock of resources that is at the disposal of organization members (Sirmon et al., 2007). Or, it can also be classified as a Penrosian embedded practice that services resources to improve their efficiency (Penrose, 1959; Spender, 1996). Regardless of one's perspective on the categorization of cognition and knowledge as value-creating entities, neither has value for an organization without transformation to practice, specifically through decision-making, communication, and action. The induced behavior may be thought of as a resource flow, because firm value is created or destroyed based on decision-making and the actions undertaken by employees to deliver a service or add value to a good.

Bandura's (1986) social-cognition theory suggests that the cognitive establishment of a goal and personal self-efficacy are mediators for the use of knowledge leading to behavior. As such, cognition is a necessary transformative process between possessed knowledge and action. While Bandura's theory was focused primarily on individual behavior, the relationship between possessed knowledge and practice is not restricted to any particular level of analysis. The link between individual cognition and individual behavior is well established in the management literature (for example, organizational behavior), with additional theories explicitly suggesting the mental processes required for an individual to act. Individual cognition, particularly in the upper echelons of the firm, can induce many types of collective behavior (for example, Barr et al., 1992). Conversely, collective cognitions that support norms, culture, socialization patterns, and routines necessarily affect individuals nested in such collectivities (for example, Geletkanycz, 1997). Additionally, collections of individuals, such as teams, divisions of organizations, and entire firms share cognitive structures that shape collective behaviors (for example, Weick and Roberts, 1993; Reger and Huff, 1993).

The knowledge held by individuals and organizations is dynamic. Although knowledge affects behavior via cognitive processes, behavior also influences and necessarily builds knowledge. Hence, a reciprocal interrelationship exists between organizational knowledge and behavior. Both learning based on prior experience and learning based on cognitive search (Gavetti and Levinthal, 2000) are predicated on the behaviors in which employees and managers engage (Lei et al., 1996). This individual and collective learning increases and/or changes the organization's possessed knowledge (Huber, 1991; Miller, 1996). Over time, the explicit and tacit knowledge within a firm tend to stabilize through learning processes, embedding the established normative behaviors. The stabilization of the firm's knowledge, in turn, also produces more stability in the behaviors of individuals and collectivities within the organization such that routines are refined and rendered more efficient (Nelson and Winter, 1982). This reciprocal reinforcement of stabilizing patterns between the cognitive knowledge and the individual and collective behaviors within the firm are inherently exploitative (March, 1991; Gupta et al., 2006). Stated differently, the learning that occurs over time becomes path dependent because it builds on current knowledge stocks and behaviors derived from them.

Conversely, more dynamic change of the firm's knowledge (and thus behaviors) can also occur through this process if the learning is less path dependent (Weick, 1969). For example, purposeful exploration of new knowledge content can produce unique knowledge (Gavetti and Levinthal, 2000; March, 1991). It can also result from naturally occurring random or at least unexpected events, such as voluntary turnover or change in the regulatory environment of the firm. Such exploration can lead to positive outcomes, such as innovations for new product markets or new technologies for use in new products. Too much of this cognitive variation, however, can produce excessive change because of sensory overload (Corley and Gioia, 2004) that, in turn, results in undesirable outcomes, such as ineffective sense-making (Weick, 1995) or inefficiencies in established routines (Brown and Eisenhardt, 1997). Thus, forces of cognitive change and stabilization are of critical importance to strategic management, as they dictate the quality of decisions and the efficiency of actions taken by the firm's human capital.

In a competitive environment, the extent to which a firm decides to engage in exploitative or exploratory strategies is pivotal (Gupta et al., 2006; Kang and Snell, 2009). A firm with a dominant market share in a stable industry and a small entrepreneurial firm in a dynamic industry are likely to have different strategic profiles of exploration and exploitation. A goal of management is to identify, achieve, and maintain a balance between the two approaches that is optimal for the context in which the firm must operate. In other words, the firm should try to achieve a 'sweet spot' that aligns the external demands on the organization and the activity systems which cognitions underpin. Because it constitutes a mutually reinforcing system, the cognition within firms can be managed to achieve the amount of stability and change of knowledge and behavior over time needed to attain this sweet spot.

Through the lens of systems theory, some organizational scholars have described this 'sweet spot' as the 'edge of chaos' (Brown and Eisenhardt, 1997; Stacey, 1996). It is the 'edge of chaos' where performance is optimized, creating the greatest value possible from the exploitation of established knowledge and the exploration of new knowledge in pursuit of innovations (Gupta et al., 2006; March, 1991). This edge of chaos depends on the demands of the external environment, which rewards variations of stable and disruptive behavior differently depending on industry, institutional environment, and customer requirements. Thus, a primary role of the manager is to understand these external demands and align the organization's knowledge, cognitions, practices, services, and products accordingly (Sirmon et al., 2007; Amit and Schoemaker, 1993).

How can a manager influence cognitions in such a way as to achieve (or approximate) this sweet spot—this appropriate mix of exploration and exploitation? What are the levers that management has available to develop the proper mix of cognitive change and stability, and the resultant knowledge and behavior outcomes? The management literature has identified a vast array of forces, decisions, and contextual factors that can stabilize or destabilize the knowledge–cognition–behavior relationship. These factors act in two distinct ways: first as 'use' moderators that determine the nature and extent to which knowledge is translated into cognition and then behavior, and second as 'learning' moderators that determine the extent to which knowledge is reinforced or changed based on behaviors. The use factors can affect processes that can be categorized into one of two groups: 'recall' processes—those that induce stored knowledge to be brought into cognition—and 'enactment' processes—those that induce behavior from a cognitive state. Likewise, learning factors can affect processes that can be grouped into 'observation' and 'memory' processes, as behavior can be both perceived in a cognitive state and stored as knowledge, respectively.

While use and learning factors may often have the same effect on their constituent processes—that is, the factors may stabilize or destabilize the reinforcing subprocesses of recall, enactment, observation, and memory—these moderating factors can also have diverging effects on the sub-processes. For example, a use factor can induce the recall of knowledge through the cognition of the employees of a firm at a faster rate than it induces enactment of knowledge. Cognition, then, plays a central controling role in the firm as a broker and filter between the possessed knowledge and the extent to which that knowledge is translated into practice. Figure 4.1

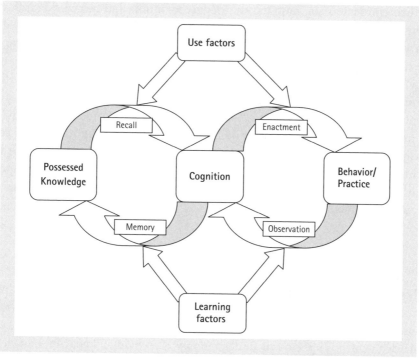

Figure 4.1. Use and Learning Factors in the Knowledge-Cognition-Behavior Interrelationship

presents a graphical illustration of our conceptual model, in which we equate the concepts of behavior and practice for purposes of this chapter.

The pursuit of a full understanding of the interplay between knowledge and practice, and all the factors that potentially moderate this complex relationship, inevitably build on a vast amount of literature, of which we only sample and summarize a representative portion. While appreciating the many factors that govern the processes through which knowledge may be used (or not used) and through which learning occurs, our model primarily attempts to synthesize these theoretical and empirical traditions to provide a more comprehensive understanding of the influences on the knowledge–cognition–behavior relationship.

The resulting model is naturally and inevitably multilevel (Hitt *et al.*, 2007). At any one level (for example, individual, group, organization, or industry), there is substantial evidence that knowledge and behavior are closely and causally related, and there is a growing number of studies that demonstrate cognition's mediating role. Moreover, there is a theoretical tradition and a growing body of empirical support showing that this relationship applies across levels; individual behavior can influence collective knowledge and collective knowledge can influence an individual's behavior, and either can occur through individual or shared cognitions.

Furthermore, it is common for knowledge, cognition, and behavior to influence multiple levels of one another. For instance, a collective behavior, such as socialization within a particular firm or profession, influences the shared cognitions, such as the shared values and norms within that collectivity, which in turn influence each individual's cognitive knowledge about his or her particular relationship to others within that firm or profession. Likewise, stabilizing/destabilizing factors of use and learning also commonly have multilevel effects. When considering the dynamic nature of the knowledge–cognition–behavior relationship, coupled with the complexity of constant multilevel influences of myriad schemas, behaviors, and use/learning moderators, the application of a more general and generic model to all levels of analysis simultaneously is, therefore, both parsimonious and necessary to advance our understanding.

4.3.1 Individual Use

Perhaps the most firmly established level of analysis dealing with the relationship of cognition and behavior within the management literature is that of the individual. Industrial/organizational psychologists and organizational behavior scholars have made rich contributions to our understanding of individual behavior, knowledge, and cognition.

Knowledge that is specific to any one person is unique, because each person's understanding and interpretation of the world is socially constructed (Tsoukas, 1996) and the result of path-dependent sense-making (Weick, 1995, 1969). The cognitive schemas—the maps or structures by which sense is made of incoming sensory input—held by an individual greatly influence the interpretation and storage of each piece of knowledge. Two individuals, because they each have unique schemas, can have largely different interpretations of the same observation, which then lead to unique knowledge held by each individual. Thus, variance in interpretations and reactions to the same information are common whenever two or more people interpret it. While variance can have some positive outcomes for firms, maintaining homogeneity in schemas can produce greater efficiencies on cooperative tasks (Weick and Roberts, 1993). Standardization of work and task schemas usually occurs through socialization processes (Corner *et al.*, 1994) and training within the firm (Ellis and Davidi, 2005; Ford and Kraiger, 1995). Subsequently, standardization of schemas is reinforced by organizational and industry culture (Harris, 1994; Phillips, 1994), along with the firm's dominant logic (Prahalad and Bettis, 1986; Bettis and Prahalad, 1995). Collective schemas are transformed into individual cognitive structures (Stacey, 1996; Langfield-Smith, 1992) through these processes. The stabilizing of individual schemas, after breaking initial cognitive inertia, potentially explains the observation that individuals are typically most productive and valuable within the firm by which they were initially hired (Hitt *et al.*, 2001).

Given a set of knowledge elements and a knowledge structure related to a particular behavior, several individual attributes, both states and traits, might affect the way that knowledge is translated into behavior. The following review represents a summary of potential catalysts for this transformation: personality, motivation, affect, social processes, and metacognition.

Personality, particularly the Five Factor Model (FFM), traits of conscientiousness and emotional stability, has been found to affect the performance of individuals in work contexts (Barrick and Mount, 1991). The behavior evoked by common knowledge, such as a particular meeting time, is more likely to be acted upon by more conscientious individuals than by less conscientious persons because of the different cognitive patterns inherent in personality characteristics. Other FFM personality traits, such as extroversion along with additional individual differences, can explain variance in success with particular jobs and tasks, such as selling a service (Barrick and Mount, 1991).

Motivational theories, such as goal orientation (Seijts et al., 2004), need for achievement (Steers, 1975), and self-efficacy (Judge et al., 2007), explain how otherwise unused or underutilized knowledge is activated through individual cognition, which subsequently induces behavior. Research shows that affect, moods, and emotions have effects on social activity (Watson et al., 1992), which in turn can determine the extent to which knowledge is shared among individuals. Affect, moods, and emotions also influence work performance, as cognitive processes are mediated by intermediary performance processes to shape behavior (Beal et al., 2005).

Knowledge held by individuals has been argued to be primarily co-created in communicative and social processes (Alvesson and Kärreman, 2001), reflecting the unique cultural–historical framework of symbolism created by prior generations (Spender, 1996; Vygotsky, 1978). Skills related to the sharing of such knowledge are, from this constructivist perspective, tantamount to the enactment of any given piece of knowledge by an individual. These include speaking, writing, listening, conversational, initiation, and cooperative abilities (Pulakos et al., 2005). These self-regulatory processes of transforming knowledge do not apply exclusively to socially constructed knowledge. Metacognition, defined as awareness and self-regulation of one's cognitive processes, is also an important predictor of how knowledge might be translated into action or choices (Brown, 1987). The efficacy of such cognitive processes as critical thinking, reasoning, information gathering, information integration, and problem-solving are all critical to the translation of basic knowledge into performance in mental tasks (Pulakos et al., 2005).

4.3.2 Individual Learning

The success with which newly learned knowledge is applied—known as the transfer of learning—depends both on metacognitive abilities of the individual and the contexts in which the new behavior was learnt and ultimately takes place (Ellis, 1964).

The transfer of learning is an important process, because it links learning (as a behavior), the processes of cognition, the storage of knowledge, and the retranslation of that knowledge to behavior. These dynamics of learning transfer within individuals are moderated both by use and learning factors (see Figure 4.1), which, jointly considered, help to explain the change and stability in knowledge and behavior. The efficiency and effectiveness by which this learning–performance progression is supported involves a person's general mental or cognitive ability, or simply 'g'. Scholars have argued that 'g', of which intelligence is often used as a proxy, represents the most central individual trait for predicting job performance (Schmidt and Hunter, 2004; Gottfredson, 1997).

The relationship between learning and formal work training is moderated by cognitive and contextual conditions (Gagné, 1965). These conditions also moderate the relationship between learning and the processes through which tacit knowledge is learnt (Polanyi, 1967), such as on-the-job training. Individuals must be cognitively primed to receive complex knowledge, such as having prerequisite knowledge (knowledge scaffolding) and sufficient capacity to consider novel information. The context of and the communication about the nature and relevance of the focal knowledge also influences the extent to which knowledge is learnt and retained within individuals (Gagné, 1965).

Learning from observing the behavior of others (Bandura, 1986; Holcomb et al., 2009)—or vicarious learning—and from interactions with others are important means by which individuals acquire knowledge and schema. Shared cognitions and routines are passed to individuals (Stacey, 1996; Nelson and Winter, 1982) and reinforced by social norms such as values (Langfield-Smith, 1992), culture (Harris, 1994; Phillips, 1994), language, discourse (Alvesson and Kärreman, 2000, 2001), and beliefs (Senge, 1991). Behavior is often transferred into personal learning events with performance feedback from superiors or other co-workers (Kluger and DeNisi, 1996). Individuals are also embedded in a variety of social groups (Barnard, 1938), and thus participate in several social networks, such as communities of practice, that can provide individuals with knowledge to which they are not exposed within the organization (Brown and Duguid, 2001). Thus, the combinations of individuals in work teams and formal leadership structures allow access by any one individual to the knowledge of other employees.

4.3.3 Collective Use

Polanyi (1967: 36) points out that 'each level is subject to dual control: first by the laws that apply to its elements in themselves, and second, by the laws that control the comprehensive entity formed by them'. In other words, collectivities of individuals (henceforth to refer to groups, organizations, and supra-organizational structures such as industries or nations) are governed by both individual behavior and emergent properties of the collectivity. Polanyi calls this multilevel phenomenon 'stratification' within 'hierarchies of human performances' (1967: 40), and explains that 'a higher operation may fail when the next lower operation escapes its control' (1967: 41). Thus, while individual phenomena can partially describe collective phenomena—particularly a collectivity's failure—there are emergent actions and organizing principles that dictate the behavior, cognitions, and knowledge of human capital collectivities. This emergence can cover a broad range, from isomorphic composition to discontinuous compilation as varying degrees of stabilization and change, respectively, wield influence over individual cognitions (Klein and Kozlowski, 2000).

The knowledge of a collectivity is dispersed among its constituents, and its contexts of action are based on the structural elements (relationships) of embedded individuals (Tsoukas, 1996). As no individual can hold the total of all knowledge embedded in an organization (Hayek, 1945; Tsoukas, 1996), the way in which knowledge is transferred between individuals determines, in large part, the way an organization is structured (Grant, 1996; Kogut and Zander, 1993). Indeed, Argote and Ingram (2000) argue that the efficiency with which information is transferred within an organization can be a source of sustained competitive advantage. This efficiency is affected by a number of factors, including shared schemas. For example, the collective mind of a work team within a high-reliability organization helps to minimize failure (Weick and Roberts, 1993), and transactive memory, or the shared cognition of those in the organization who have the knowledge to best perform a given task, is a predictor of group performance (Lewis et al., 2007; Brandon and Hollingshead, 2004). Exploratory and exploitative learning behaviors by the firm were suggested by March (1991). He argued that knowledge transfer rates and the inclusion of new knowledge (through turnover) had dramatic effects on a firm's knowledge stocks. The stability of such knowledge for exploitative behavior and the change of knowledge for exploratory behavior undergird the ability of an organization to enact such strategies (Crossan and Berdrow, 2003).

Different types of knowledge held by a collectivity can determine its performance. Architectural knowledge of a particular product system (versus simple component knowledge) can lead to more and higher-quality innovation with 'significant competitive implications' (Henderson and Clark, 1990: 9). The combination of knowledge in various inconspicuous ways allows the unique bundling of resources (Brown and Eisenhardt, 1997; Nonaka and Toyama, 2002; Jansen et al., 2005). The integration of different routines and tacit knowledge bases can create unique capabilities and allow organizations to effectively compete in highly competitive environments (Kogut and Zander, 1993; Teece et al., 1997; Sirmon et al., 2007). As these combinations become routinized (Nelson and Winter, 1982), the associated cognitive maps to compose strategic action are renewed (Barr et al., 1992).

The dominant logic of a firm is the shared cognition of decision-making heuristics within the firm (Prahalad and Bettis, 1986). While most decisions made within organizations are ultimately made by one or a few individuals (Staw, 1991), the influence of dominant logic is also beset by the influences of the collectivity that surrounds them. These influences include the shared knowledge (Nonaka and Takeuchi, 1995), normative forces (DiMaggio and Powell, 1983), external resource demands (Pfeffer and Salancik, 1978), and culture (Schein, 1988). Strategic decisions, such as acquisitions, diversification, alliances, or internationalization, often produce changed firm behavior, which in turn results in exposure to new types or knowledge. For example, acquiring another firm exposes the acquiring firm to potentially significant new knowledge held by the acquired firm, providing the potential for learning (Barkema and Schijven, 2008). How the collectivity handles and integrates that new knowledge into its activity systems is the topic of the next section.

4.3.4 Collective Learning

The role of cognition in collective learning (such as organizational learning) has been a topic of much theoretical interest for organizational scholars in the past two decades. There have been several attempts to describe the field of organizational learning through classic volumes (for example, Argyris and Schön, 1978; Senge, 1991), and many scholarly papers have examined theoretical bases of organizational learning, in particular (for example, Levitt and March, 1988; Huber, 1991; Miller, 1996; Barkema and Schijven, 2008).

A central theme in this work is the role of cognition in the process of collective learning. One stream of work suggests that cognition is not necessarily central to the way a collectivity changes and that learning can occur without the explicit recognition of the learning by its constituents. Fiol and Lyles (1985), for instance, distinguish between cognitive learning by collectivities and adaptation to an environment, which they argue is a phenomenon separate from learning. The mechanics of collective learning are not the sum of all constituent individuals' learning (Cohen and Levinthal, 1990) but also include social processes that can store collective thought (Weick and Roberts, 1993) and institutional practices such as routines, rules, and artifacts that can store new knowledge as memory (Levitt and March, 1988; Walsh and Ungson, 1991). One should be cautious about anthropomorphizing organizations, as collective and individual learning are fundamentally different (for example, Levitt and March, 1988).

Although organizational learning is not entirely predicated on cognition, cognition plays an important role in the way collectivities learn. Social organizing processes provide the framework by which information is interpreted (sense-making: Daft and Weick, 1984). The manner in which this information is observed and processed into knowledge occurs with cognitive mechanisms (Crossan *et al.*, 1999), even if the knowledge is obtained from hiring external individuals as a knowledge source (Miller *et al.*, 2006; March, 1991).

The schemas built on previous knowledge held by individuals are a primary source of an organization's absorptive capacity (Cohen and Levinthal, 1990). Cognitive structures within the organization such as dominant logic (Lane and Lubatkin, 1998) and shared interpretative schema (Zahra and George, 2002) determine the extent to which the absorptive capacity allows learning and the extent to which the new knowledge is used for creating new firm value. The ability of a collectivity to renew strategically, to explore different approaches to existing internal activity systems, depends on the cognitive maps that exist and new ones that emerge (Crossan and Berdrow, 2003; Barr *et al.*, 1992). As processes become routinized and integrated into the established relationships that exist within groups (Lewis *et al.*, 2007; Weick and Roberts, 1993), knowledge is

Table 4.1. Representative Use and Learning Factors: Managerial Levers of Cognitive Human Capital

Level of Cognition	Use Factors	Learning Factors
Individual	Motivation	General mental ability
	Personality	Knowledge scaffolding
	Affect	Discourse
	Social activity	Social norms
	Communication	Others' behavior (vicarious)
	Collective schemas	Organizational culture
	Organizational culture	Performance feedback
	Socialization	Communications
	Training	Training
Collective	Knowledge transfer	Social organizing processes
	Turnover	Hiring
	Resource bundling	Absorptive capacity
	Routines	Dominant logic
	Dominant logic	Cognitive maps
	Shared knowledge	Routines
	Normative forces	Constitutive practice
	External resource demands	Meta-learning competencies
	Strategic decisions (acquisitions, alliances, diversification, internationalization, and so on)	Strategic decisions (acquisitions, alliances, diversification, internationalization, and so on)

transformed from explicit to tacit (Nonaka and Takeuchi, 1995; Polanyi, 1967) and is deepened with the reconstitution of practice (Orlikowski, 2002). This allows collectivities to develop and sustain meta-learning competencies (Lei et al., 1996) and dynamic capabilities (Teece et al., 1997). These competences and capabilities, in turn, allow top performing firms to simultaneously exploit existing cognitive human capital and explore new combinations of knowledge, cognitions, and behavior.

4.4 DISCUSSION

The realized value of the human capital within a firm is based on the cognitive structures of the constituent individuals and collectivities within the organization. Utilization of the cognitive knowledge within an organization by effective decision-making and by implementation of those decisions leads to value relative to competitors. We have described several ways that the learning and use of knowledge, and the dynamic interplay between the two are catalyzed by a complex web of forces, contexts, cognitions, and behaviors that concurrently exist at the individual, group, organizational, and supra-organizational levels.

Using cognition as a focal point for the creation of firm value, this complex and interconnected array of forces is evident. Cognitive human capital exists both at the individual and collective levels, as do the knowledge and behaviors that reinforce it. Cognitions operate continuously, whether in conscious or unconscious states, enriching or changing the knowledge base and behavioral routines. They are a function of the history, strategic plans, internal and boundary-spanning relationships, the structure, the turnover patterns, the communication patterns, the shared beliefs, the culture, and the institutional environment of the organization.

The value derived from the cognitive human capital relies on an organization's ability to align with its environmental demands in order to solidify, incrementally alter, or significantly change existing patterns of knowledge and behavior. The composition of individual cognitions as a collection of both inherent (personality and intelligence) and path-dependent (experience and socially constructed norms) characteristics determines an organization's capacity to react to external demands in an effective manner. The value of cognitive human capital is continuously changing because the internal cognitive composition in an organization is dynamic and because the external environmental demands regularly change as well. The capabilities to understand these phenomena and respond to misalignments by leveraging knowledge use and learning factors appropriately is necessary for managers to maximize the cognitive resources that are, at least in part, under their influence.

4.4.1 Managerial Implications

Leadership and management play a critical role in unlocking the potential of and creating value from cognitive human capital. Managers need to achieve an effective balance between change and stability in the knowledge–cognition–behavior system. Effective balancing requires structures that support the correct mix of exploration and exploitation, simultaneously aligning the organization with the needs of the external environment and the needs of its stakeholders (Kang and Snell, 2009).

However, this is often a delicate balance to achieve. Managers must adjust to the array of forces that affect the cognition of organizational members—an inherently difficult task because of the ambiguity of cognitions, possessed knowledge, and outcomes of human action (Coff, 1997). To further complicate this matter, employees' individual agency precludes management from having significant control. Managers can only influence the cognitions and knowledge of their constituents (Gourlay, 2006; Alvesson and Kärreman, 2001) through use and learning factors. For instance, the proper alignment of structural, affective, and cognitive components within a human resource configuration is suggested to have a synergistic effect in supporting either an entrepreneurial (exploratory) or cooperative (exploitative) strategy (Kang et al., 2007). As there is disagreement in organizational science about (1) whether exploration and exploitation are orthogonal or continuous, and (2) whether firms can be ambidextrous or punctuated equilibrium causes sequential changes in the balance between exploration and exploitation over time (Gupta et al., 2006), the challenges faced by managers are clear. There is no recipe for success in managing the cognitive human capital within an organization. The knowledge–cognition–behavior interaction is fraught with contingencies, path dependencies, and individual differences that often change regularly. Managers who have success employing the use and learning factors to their advantage in creating alignment with their environment are likely experienced, intuitive, and observant. They are also likely to realize that most actions they take will have influence on those individuals and groups in the organization with whom they have an interdependent relationship.

It is incumbent on the organization's leaders to understand the needs of external stakeholders, the requirements for more stability or for change, and how these requirements are likely to interact with the current momentum of the internal knowledge–cognition–behavior systems. Leveraging use and learning factors to help align the organization with the external environment does not necessarily require using a multitude of tactics simultaneously, though we believe that alignment of structures, incentives, and culture toward a more stable strategic type would increase organizational effectiveness. Reinforcing systems can amplify the effects of a specific change through time, especially if a use and/or learning factor is consistently applied/reapplied. While systemic delays (such as resistance to change) in altering the dynamics of the knowledge–cognition–behavior processes are likely to emerge with a managerial change, diligence over an extended time horizon and an holistic approach improve the potential for unlocking and creating value from an organization's cognitive human capital.

4.4.2 Contributions and Future Research

This chapter has explored the value of cognitive human capital within firms, as both an individual and a collective construct. Based on prior research and our analyses, we have proposed a comprehensive model that integrates knowledge and practice—both important for creating value in firms. At the heart of this model is cognition, which brokers, filters, and guides the 'generative dance' (Cook and Brown, 1999) between knowledge and practice, leading to firm outcomes. This model extends our understanding of cognition in organizations generally. More specifically, this chapter provides theory that helps explain how cognition plays a critical role in the dynamic interrelationship between knowledge and practice. As organizations try to identify and achieve the right mix of exploratory and exploitative activities in order to maximize performance, cognition plays a central role in determining the extent to which both strategies are employed. The complexities of cognition and the agency of employees, however, allow for only partial influence over this balance. We have described a variety of managerial tools that can stabilize or destabilize cognitive structures, and, in turn, have similar effects on the knowledge and behaviors with which they are so tightly coupled. We have termed these contextual levers 'use' and 'learning' factors, with which managers influence the extent to which possessed knowledge becomes action, and how learning influences action.

We believe that this model contributes to our understanding of the value of human capital within organizations. The traditional conception of knowledge and expertise as relatively static assets held by individuals, amenable to independent measurement, may lead to erroneous conclusions about their value. The model proposed herein suggests that it is only through cognition and recursive practice that value from that knowledge or expertise can be realized. The model also suggests that while cognitions of the firm's workforce can never be completely controled, there is a variety of levers that managers can employ to create a more exploratory or exploitative strategy.

Future research is especially needed that examines the interrelationships among possessed knowledge, cognition, and behavior/practice. Further, we recommend empirical examination of the moderation of the interrelationships among these variables by use factors and learning factors. While most research is likely to focus on specific relationships and their moderation (such as the relationship between possessed knowledge and cognition), a more holistic examination of the model proposed herein is needed.

This is a rich and important area for further study. The value of understanding these relationships will not only enrich our theoretical understanding of the relationships but also affect managerial practice. Therefore, it has significant implications for the effective management of organizations.

REFERENCES

ALVESSON, M., and KÄRREMAN, D. (2000). 'Varieties of Discourse: On the Study of Organizations through Discourse Analysis', *Human Relations*, 53(9): 1125–49.

—— and —— (2001). 'Odd Couple: Making Sense of the Curious Concept of Knowledge Management', *Journal of Management Studies*, 38(7): 995–1018.

AMIT, R., and SCHOEMAKER, P. J. H. (1993). 'Strategic Assets and Organizational Rent', *Strategic Management Journal*, 14(1): 33–46.

ARGOTE, L., and INGRAM, P. (2000). 'Knowledge Transfer: A Basis for Competitive Advantage in Firms', *Organizational Behavior and Human Decision Processes*, 82(1): 150–69.

ARGYRIS, C., and SCHÖN, D. A. (1978). *Organizational Learning: A Theory of Action Perspective* (Reading, Mass.: Addison-Wesley).

ARROW, K. J. (1962). 'Economic Welfare and the Allocation of Resources for Invention', in R. R. Nelson (ed.), *The Rate and Direction of Inventive Activity: Economic and Social Factors* (National Bureau of Economic Research, Conference Series; Princeton: Princeton University Press), 609–25.

BANDURA, A. (1986). *Social Foundations of Thought and Action: A Social Cognitive Theory* (Englewood Cliffs, NJ: Prentice-Hall).

BARKEMA, H. G., and SCHIJVEN, M. (2008). 'How do Firms Learn to Make Acquisitions? A Review of Past Research and an Agenda for the Future', *Journal of Management*, 34(3): 594–634.

BARNARD, C. I. (1938). *The Functions of the Executive* (Cambridge, Mass.: Harvard University Press).

BARNEY, J. (1991). 'Firm Resources and Sustained Competitive Advantage', *Journal of Management*, 17(1): 99–120.

BARON, R. A. (2008). 'The Role of Affect in the Entrepreneurial Process', *Academy of Management Review*, 33(2): 328–40.

BARR, P. S., STIMPERT, J. L., and HUFF, A. S. (1992). 'Cognitive Change, Strategic Action and Organizational Renewal', *Strategic Management Journal*, 13 (Summer special issue): 15–36.

BARRICK, M. R., and MOUNT, M. K. (1991). 'The Big Five Personality Dimensions and Job-Performance: A Meta-Analysis', *Personnel Psychology*, 44(1): 1–26.

BEAL, D. J., WEISS, H. M., BARROS, E., and MacDERMID, S. M. (2005). 'An Episodic Process Model of Affective Influences on Performance', *Journal of Applied Psychology*, 90(6): 1054–68.

BECKER, G. S. (1964). *Human Capital: A Theoretical Analysis with Special Reference to Education* (New York: Columbia University Press).

BETTIS, R. A., and PRAHALAD, C. K. (1995). 'The Dominant Logic: Retrospective and Extension', *Strategic Management Journal*, 16(1): 5–14.

BRANDON, D. P., and HOLLINGSHEAD, A. B. (2004). 'Transactive Memory Systems in Organizations: Matching Tasks, Expertise, and People', *Organization Science*, 15(6): 633–44.

BROWN, A. (1987). 'Metacognition, Executive Control, Self Control, and Other Mysterious Mechanisms', in F. Weinert and R. Kluwe (eds.), *Metacognition, Motivation, and Understanding* (Hillsdale, NJ: Erlbaum), 65–116.

BROWN, J. S., and DUGUID, P. (2001). 'Knowledge and Organization: A Social-Practice Perspective', *Organization Science*, 12(2): 198–213.

BROWN, S. L., and EISENHARDT, K. M. (1997). *Competing on the Edge: Strategy as Structured Chaos* (Cambridge, Mass.: Harvard University Press).

COFF, R. W. (1997). 'Human Assets and Management Dilemmas: Coping with Hazards on the Road to Resource-Based Theory', *Academy of Management Review*, 22(2): 374–402.

COHEN, W. M., and LEVINTHAL, D. A. (1990). 'Absorptive-Capacity: A New Perspective on Learning and Innovation', *Administrative Science Quarterly*, 35(1): 128–52.

COOK, S. D. N., and BROWN, J. S. (1999). 'Bridging Epistemologies: The Generative Dance between Organizational Knowledge and Organizational Knowing'. *Organization Science*, 10(4): 381–400.

CORLEY, K. G., and GIOIA, D. A. (2004). 'Identity Ambiguity and Change in the Wake of a Corporate Spin-Off', *Administrative Science Quarterly*, 49(2): 173–208.

CORNER, P. D., KINICKI, A. J., and KEATS, B. W. (1994). 'Integrating Organizational and Individual Information-Processing Perspectives on Choice', *Organization Science*, 5(3): 294–308.

CROSSAN, M. M., and BERDROW, I. (2003). 'Organizational Learning and Strategic Renewal', *Strategic Management Journal*, 24(11): 1087–1105.

——LANE, H. W., and WHITE, R. E. (1999). 'An Organizational Learning Framework: From Intuition to Institution', *Academy of Management Review*, 24(3): 522–37.

CYERT, R. M., and MARCH, J. G. (1963). *The Behavioral Theory of the Firm* (Englewood Cliffs, NJ: Prentice-Hall).

DAFT, R. L., and WEICK, K. E. (1984). 'Toward a Model of Organizations as Interpretation Systems', *Academy of Management Review*, 9(2): 284–95.

DiMAGGIO, P. J., and POWELL, W. W. (1983). 'The Iron Cage Revisited: Institutional Isomorphism and Collective Rationality in Organizational Fields', *American Sociological Review*, 48(2): 147–60.

DRUCKER, P. F. (2003). *Managing in the Next Society* (New York: Macmillan).

ELLIS, H. C. (1964). *The Transfer of Learning* (New York: Macmillan).

ELLIS, S., and DAVIDI, I. (2005). 'After-Event Reviews: Drawing Lessons from Successful and Failed Experience'. *Journal of Applied Psychology*, 90(5): 857–71.

FIOL, C. M., and LYLES, M. A. (1985). 'Organizational Learning', *Academy of Management Review*, 10(4): 803–13.

FORD, J. K., and KRAIGER, K. (1995). 'The Application of Cognitive Constructs to the Instructional Systems Model of Training: Implications for Needs Assessment, Design, and Transfer', in C. L. Cooper and I. T. Robertson (eds.), *International Review of Industrial and Organizational Psychology*, 10 (Chichester: Wiley), 1–48.

FORD, R. C., and BOWEN, D. E. (2008). 'A Service-Dominant Logic for Management Education: It's Time', *Academy of Management Learning and Education*, 7(2): 224–43.

GAGNÉ, R. M. (1965). *The Conditions of Learning* (New York: Holt, Rinehart & Winston).

GAVETTI, G., and LEVINTHAL, D. (2000). 'Looking Forward and Looking Backward: Cognitive and Experiential Search', *Administrative Science Quarterly*, 45(1): 113–37.

——and RIVKIN, J. W. (2007). 'On the Origin of Strategy: Action and Cognition over Time', *Organization Science*, 18(3): 420–39.

GELETKANYCZ, M. A. (1997). 'The Salience of "Culture's Consequences": The Effects of Cultural Values on Top Executive Commitment to the Status Quo', *Strategic Management Journal*, 18(8): 615–34.

GIOIA, D. A. (1986). 'The State of the Art in Organizational Social Cognition: A Personal View', in H. P. Sims, Jr., and D. A. Gioia (eds.), *The Thinking Organization* (San Francisco: Jossey-Bass).

GOTTFREDSON, L. S. (1997). 'Why G Matters: The Complexity of Everyday Life', *Intelligence*, 24(1): 79–132.

GOURLAY, S. (2006). 'Conceptualizing Knowledge Creation: A Critique of Nonaka's Theory', *Journal of Management Studies*, 43(7): 1415–36.

GRANT, R. M. (1996). 'Prospering in Dynamically-Competitive Environments: Organizational Capability as Knowledge Integration', *Organization Science*, 7(4): 375–87.

GUPTA, A. K., SMITH, K. G., and SHALLEY, C. E. (2006). 'The Interplay between Exploration and Exploitation', *Academy of Management Journal*, 49(4): 693–706.

HANNAN, M. T., and FREEMAN, J. (1977). 'The Population Ecology of Organizations', *American Journal of Sociology*, 82(5): 929–64.

HARRIS, S. G. (1994). 'Organizational Culture and Individual Sensemaking: A Schema-Based Perspective', *Organization Science*, 5(3): 309–21.

HAUSER, M. (2008). Press release from Harvard University, 17 Feb.

HAYEK, F. A. (1945). 'The Use of Knowledge in Society', *American Economic Review*, 35(4): 519–30.

HENDERSON, R. M., and CLARK, K. B. (1990). 'Architectural Innovation: The Reconfiguration of Existing Product Technologies and the Failure of Established Firms', *Administrative Science Quarterly*, 35(1): 9–30.

HITT, M. A., BIERMAN, L., SHIMIZU, K., and KOCHHAR, R. (2001). 'Direct and Moderating Effects of Human Capital on Strategy and Performance in Professional Service Firms: A Resource-Based Perspective', *Academy of Management Journal*, 44(1): 13–28.

—— BIERMAN, L., UHLENBRUCK, K., and SHIMIZU, K. (2006). 'The Importance of Resources in the Internationalization of Professional Service Firms: The Good, the Bad and the Ugly', *Academy of Management Journal*, 49(6): 1137–57.

—— BEAMISH, P. W., JACKSON, S. E., and MATHIEU, J. E. (2007). 'Building Theoretical and Empirical Bridges across Levels: Multilevel Research in Management', *Academy of Management Journal*, 50(6): 1385–99.

HOLCOMB, T. R., IRELAND, R. D., HOLMES, R. M., and HITT, M. A. (2009). 'Architecture of Entrepreneurial Learning: Exploring the Link among Heuristics, Knowledge, and Action', *Entrepreneurship Theory and Practice*, 33(1): 167–92.

HOSKISSON, R. E., HITT, M. A., WAN, W. P., and YIU, D. (1999). 'Theory and Research in Strategic Management: Swings of a Pendulum', *Journal of Management*, 25(3): 417–56.

HUBER, G. P. (1991). 'Organizational Learning: The Contributing Processes and the Literatures', *Organization Science*, 2(1): 88–115.

JANSEN, J. J. P., VAN DEN BOSCH, F. A. J., and VOLBERDA, H. W. (2005). 'Managing Potential and Realized Absorptive Capacity: How do Organizational Antecedent's Matter?', *Academy of Management Journal*, 48(6): 999–1015.

JENSEN, M. C., and MECKLING, W. H. (1976). 'Theory of the Firm: Managerial Behavior, Agency Costs and Ownership Structure', *Journal of Financial Economics*, 3(4): 305–60.

JUDGE, T. A., JACKSON, C. L., SHAW, J. C., SCOTT, B. A., and RICH, B. L. (2007). 'Self-Efficacy and Work-Related Performance: The Integral Role of Individual Differences', *Journal of Applied Psychology*, 92(1): 107–27.

KABANOFF, B., and BROWN, B. (2007). 'Knowledge Structures of Prospectors, Analyzers, and Defenders: Content, Structure, Stability, and Performance', *Strategic Management Journal*, 29(2): 149–71.

KANG, S. C., and SNELL, S. A. (2009). 'Intellectual Capital Architectures and Ambidextrous Learning: A Framework for Human Resource Management', *Journal of Management Studies*, 46(1): 65–92.

KANG, S. C., MORRIS, S. S., and SNELL, S. A. (2007). 'Relational Archetypes, Organizational Learning, and Value Creation: Extending the Human Resource Architecture', *Academy of Management Review*, 32(1): 236–56.

KAPLAN, S., and HENDERSON, R. (2005). 'Inertia and Incentives: Bridging the Gap between Economics and Organizational Theory', *Organization Science*, 16(5): 509–21.

KOGUT, B., and ZANDER, U. (1992). 'Knowledge of the Firm, Combinative Capabilities, and the Replication of Technology', *Organization Science*, 3(3): 383–97.

——and —— (1993). 'Knowledge of the Firm and the Evolutionary-Theory of the Multinational Corporation', *Journal of International Business Studies*, 24(4): 625–45.

KLEIN, K. J., and KOZLOWSKI, S. W. J. (eds.) (2000). *Multilevel Theory, Research and Methods in Organizations: Foundations, Extensions, and New Directions* (San Francisco: Jossey-Boss).

KLUGER, A. N., and DeNISI, A. (1996). 'The Effects of Feedback Interventions on Performance: A Historical Review, a Meta-Analysis, and a Preliminary Feedback Intervention Theory', *Psychological Bulletin*, 119(2): 254–84.

LANE, P. J., and LUBATKIN, M. (1998). 'Relative Absorptive Capacity and Interorganizational Learning', *Strategic Management Journal*, 19(5): 461–77.

LANGFIELD-SMITH, K. (1992). 'Exploring the Need for a Shared Cognitive Map', *Journal of Management Studies*, 29(3): 349–68.

LEI, D., HITT, M. A., and BETTIS, R. (1996). 'Dynamic Core Competences through Meta-Learning and Strategic Context', *Journal of Management*, 22(4): 549–69.

LEONARD, D. (1995). *Wellsprings of Knowledge: Building and Sustaining the Source of Innovation* (Boston: Harvard Business School Press).

LEVITT, B., and MARCH, J. G. (1988). 'Organizational Learning', *Annual Review of Sociology*, 14: 319–40.

LEWIS, K., BELLIVEAU, M., HERNDON, B., and KELLER, J. (2007). 'Group Cognition, Membership Change, and Performance: Investigating the Benefits and Detriments of Collective Knowledge', *Organizational Behavior and Human Decision Processes*, 103(2): 159–78.

LIPPMAN, S. A., and RUMELT, R. P. (1982). 'Uncertainty Imitability: An Analysis of Interfirm Differences in Efficiency Under Competition', *Bell Journal of Economics*, 13(2): 418–38.

LYLES, M. A., and SALK, J. E. (1996). 'Knowledge Acquisition from Foreign Parents in International Joint Ventures: An Empirical Examination in the Hungarian Context', *Journal of International Business Studies*, 27(5): 877–903.

MARCH, J. G. (1991). 'Exploration and Exploitation in Organization Learning', *Organization Science*, 2(1): 71–87.

——and SIMON, H. A. (1958). *Organizations* (New York: Wiley).

MILLER, D. (1996). 'A Preliminary Typology of Organizational Learning: Synthesizing the Literature', *Journal of Management*, 22(3): 485–505.

MILLER, K. D., ZHAO, M., and CALANTONE, R. J. (2006). 'Adding Interpersonal Learning and Tacit Knowledge to March's Exploration–Exploitation Model', *Academy of Management Journal*, 49(4): 709–22.

NAG, R., CORLEY, K. G., and GIOIA, D. A. (2007). 'The Intersection of Organizational Identity, Knowledge, and Practice: Attempting Strategic Change via Knowledge Grafting', *Academy of Management Journal*, 50(4), 821–47.

NELSON, R., and WINTER, S. (1982). *The Evolutionary Theory of Economic Change* (Cambridge, Mass.: Belknap Press).

NICKERSON, J. A., and ZENGER, T. R. (2004). 'A Knowledge-Based Theory of the Firm: The Problem-Solving Perspective', *Organization Science*, 15(6): 617–32.

NONAKA, I., and TAKEUCHI, H. (1995). *The Knowledge-Creating Company* (New York: Oxford University Press).

—— and TOYAMA, R. (2002). 'A Firm as a Dialectical Being: Towards a Dynamic Theory of a Firm', *Industrial and Corporate Change*, 11(5): 995–1009.

OCASIO, W. (1997). 'Towards an Attention-Based View of the Firm', *Strategic Management Journal*, 18 (Summer special issue): 187–206.

ORLIKOWSKI, W. J. (2002). 'Knowing in Practice: Enacting a Collective Capability in Distributed Organizing', *Organization Science*, 13(3): 249–73.

PENN, D. C., HOLYOAK, K. J., and POVINELLI, D. J. (2008). 'Darwin's Mistake: Explaining the Discontinuity between Human and Nonhuman Minds', *Behavior and Brain Sciences*, 31(2): 109–30.

PENROSE, E. T. (1959). *The Theory of the Growth of the Firm* (New York: Wiley).

PETERAF, M. A. (1993). 'The Cornerstones of Competitive Advantage: A Resource-Based View', *Strategic Management Journal*, 14(3): 179–91.

PFEFFER, J., and SALANCIK, G. R. (1978). *The External Control of Organizations* (New York: Harper & Row).

PHILLIPS, M. E. (1994). 'Industry Mindsets: Exploring the Cultures of Two Macro-Organizational Settings', *Organization Science*, 5(3): 384–402.

POLANYI, M. (1967). *The Tacit Dimension* (New York: Doubleday).

PORTER, M. E. (1996). 'What is Strategy?', *Harvard Business Review*, 74(6): 61–72.

PRAHALAD, C. K., and BETTIS, R. A. (1986). 'The Dominant Logic: A New Linkage between Diversity and Performance', *Strategic Management Journal*, 7(6): 485–501.

PULAKOS, E. D., DORSEY, D. W., and BORMAN, W. C. (2003). 'Hiring for Knowledge-Based Competition', in S. E. Jackson, M. A. Hitt, and A. S. DeNisi (eds.), *Managing Knowledge for Sustained Competitive Advantage* (San Francisco: Jossey-Bass).

REGER, R. K., and HUFF, A. S. (1993). 'Strategic Groups: A Cognitive Perspective', *Strategic Management Journal*, 14(2): 103–23.

SCHMIDT, F. L., and HUNTER, J. (2004). 'General Mental Ability in the World of Work: Occupational Attainment and Job Performance', *Journal of Personality and Social Psychology*, 86(1): 162–73.

SCHEIN, E. H. (1988). *Organizational Culture* (Cambridge, Mass.: MIT Press).

SCOTT, W. R. (1995). *Organizations and Institutions* (Thousand Oaks, Calif.: Sage).

SEIJTS, G. H., LATHAM, G. P., TASA, K., and LATHAM, B. W. (2004). 'Goal Setting and Goal Orientation: An Integration of Two Different Yet Related Literatures', *Academy of Management Journal*, 47(2): 227–39.

SENGE, P. M. (1991). *The Fifth Discipline: The Art and Practice of the Learning Organization* (New York: Doubleday).

SIRMON, D. G., HITT, M. A., and IRELAND, R. D. (2007). 'Managing Firm Resources in Dynamic Environments to Create Value: Looking Inside the Black Box', *Academy of Management Review*, 32(1): 273–92.

SMITH, A. (1776). *The Wealth of Nations* (New York: Random).

SPENDER, J.-C. (1994). 'Organizational Knowledge, Collective Practice and Penrose Rents', *International Business Review*, 3(4): 353–67.

——(1996). 'Making Knowledge the Basis of a Dynamic Theory of the Firm', *Strategic Management Journal*, 17 (Winter special issue): 45–62.

STACEY, R. D. (1996). *Complexity and Creativity in Organizations* (San Francisco: Berrett-Koehler).

STAW, B. M. (1991). 'Dressing up like an Organization: When Psychological Theories Can Explain Organizational Action', *Journal of Management*, 17(4): 805–19.

STEERS, R. M. (1975). 'Effects of Need for Achievement on Job Performance Job Attitude Relationship', *Journal of Applied Psychology*, 60(6): 678–82.

SZULANSKI, G. (1996). 'Exploring Internal Stickiness: Impediments to the Transfer of Best Practice within the Firm', *Strategic Management Journal*, 17 (Winter special issue): 27–43.

TEECE, D. J., PISANO, G., and SHUEN, A. (1997). 'Dynamic Capabilities and Strategic Management', *Strategic Management Journal*, 18(7): 509–33.

THOMAS, J. B., CLARK, S. M., and GIOIA, D. A. (1993). 'Strategic Sensemaking and Organizational Performance: Linkages among Scanning, Interpretation, Action, and Outcomes', *Academy of Management Journal*, 36(2): 239–70.

THOMPSON, J. D. (1967). *Organizations in Action: Social Science Bases of Administrative Theory* (New York: McGraw-Hill).

TSOUKAS, H. (1996). 'The Firm as a Distributed Knowledge System: A Constructionist Approach', *Strategic Management Journal*, 17 (Winter special issue): 11–25.

——and VLADIMIROU, E. (2001). 'What is Organizational Knowledge?', *Journal of Management Studies*, 38(7): 973–93.

VYGOTSKY, L. S. (1978). *Mind and Society: The Development of Higher Mental Processes* (Cambridge, Mass.: Harvard University Press).

WALSH, J. P., and UNGSON, G. R. (1991). 'Organizational Memory', *Academy of Management Review*, 16(1): 57–91.

WATSON, D., CLARK, L. A., McINTYRE, C. W., and HAMAKER, S. (1992). 'Affect, Personality, and Social Activity', *Journal of Personality and Social Psychology*, 63(6): 1011–25.

WEICK, K. E. (1969). *The Social Psychology of Organizing* (Reading, Mass.: Addison-Wesley).

——(1995). *Sensemaking in Organizations* (Thousand Oaks, Calif.: Sage).

——and ROBERTS, K. H. (1993). 'Collective Mind in Organizations: Heedful Interrelating on Flight Decks', *Administrative Science Quarterly*, 38(3): 357–81.

WILLIAMSON, O. E. (1975). *Markets and Hierarchies: Analysis and Antitrust Implications* (New York: Free Press).

WOODMAN, R. W., SAWYER, J. E., and GRIFFIN, R. W. (1993). 'Toward a Theory of Organizational Creativity', *Academy of Management Review*, 18(2): 293–321.

WRIGHT, P. M., and McMAHAN, G. C. (1992). 'Theoretical Perspectives for Strategic Human Resource Management', *Journal of Management*, 18(2): 295–320.

ZAHRA, S. A., and GEORGE, G. (2002). 'Absorptive Capacity: A Review, Reconceptualization, and Extension', *Academy of Management Review*, 27(2): 185–203.

CHAPTER 5

A CAPITAL-BASED APPROACH TO THE FIRM

REFLECTIONS ON THE NATURE AND SCOPE OF THE CONCEPT OF CAPITAL AND ITS EXTENSION TO INTANGIBLES

PETER LEWIN

5.1 INTRODUCTION AND SUMMARY

Human capital is a concept of relatively recent vintage, though hints at its essence can be found throughout the history of economic thought. Conceived by T. W. Schultz (1981)[1] in the 1950s and extended by Gary Becker (1964), Jacob Mincer (1974), and their collaborators at Columbia University and the University of Chicago in the 1960s and 1970s, it was, at first, frowned upon by most within the economics profession, and even more so by those in contiguous disciplines such as sociology, political science, and social psychology. Human beings, it was argued, should not be thought of as 'mere' capital, and to do so was to run the risk of obscuring their individuality and humanity. Before long, however, human capital penetrated all branches of economic investigation in all of the various schools of economics including neoclassical economics,

Austrian economics, and behavioral economics. And it is now an indispensable conceptual tool in sociology and the other social sciences. Most recently it has become a stock in trade in the various fields of management studies, including most notably corporate-governance and entrepreneurship.

In this chapter I will investigate the nature of human capital through its relationship to the concept of capital more broadly. I will show that a 'proper' understanding of capital suggests that human capital is a logical component of the capital structure of the economy and the organizations that comprise it. In contrast to classical, neoclassical (and by implication the Marxist) view of capital, the Austrian view naturally embraces human capital and other forms of 'intangible' capital such as intellectual and social capital. The relationship of human capital to other forms of capital is subtle and is investigated here in some detail. Finally, I will examine how an all-embracing, fundamentally sound understanding of capital provides one with a flexible framework for the examination of a wide-ranging set of issues, including the relationship between production structures and organizational structures, the phenomenon of modularity (in production and organization), and the connection between planning and entrepreneurship.

To be more specific, the topics covered in this chapter may be identified briefly as follows:

1. Emphasis on resources in general as 'capital' in the economic sense of the word. This means seeing resources in terms of *the value they add over time* to the productive venture.

2. Given that time is involved and that different people appraise the value of these capital resources differently, and, therefore, appraise the value of the entire productive project that this capital combination represents differently, most productive plans will fail, at least in part. The disequilibrium that this represents is a necessary part of a dynamic economic process in which entrepreneurial visions are exercised and profits are earned. The question arises, how are capital combinations made and managed over time? To investigate this an examination of the types of capital goods and their differences is necessary.

3. The crucial difference between physical and human capital (and any other kind of capital, such as social and intellectual capital) lies not in the fact that the latter involves knowledge. *All* capital is intricately involved with knowledge—is a form of 'embodied knowledge'. The crucial difference lies rather in the alienability of physical capital (together with its embodied knowledge) and the inalienability of human capital.

4. This means that the management-organization of physical and human capital presents different challenges and opportunities.

5. Management-organization skills and abilities (a type of human capital) must evolve in a world in which the capital structure at all levels is evolving and becoming more complex. The increasing complexity of the capital structure is an

implication of the increasing heterogeneity of capital, which itself is a result of an increasing complexity of the division of labor and knowledge that comes with economic development over time. In a dynamic economy, design and production are inextricably linked as they co-evolve.

6. It is becoming increasingly clear that the only way to cope with this increasing complexity is by implementing, consciously and unconsciously, the principle of modularity. The modular nature of the capital structure is mirrored by the modular nature of the organizational structure which is really, in essence, a matter of knowledge management.

This is spelt out further in what follows.

5.2 CAPITAL

5.2.1 Capital and Production in an Uncertain World

The production[2] of every valuable good or service entails the performance of certain necessary (and jointly sufficient) tasks or activities over time. This is an essentially human phenomenon. These activities do not occur automatically; at some level they need to be organized.

This production of valuable goods and services over time implies the economic relationship known as 'capital' (Lewin, 2005). The resources involved in this process are capital assets; they form a capital structure—a structure or ordered set of items that yield services over time resulting (if successful) in the production of products that consumers value. These capital resources derive their value from the value of the products their services help to produce, in the absence of which they would have no value. *Capital value* is thus the result of forward-looking processes undertaken by the entrepreneurs who plan them. There must be a production plan if the activities of these resources are to have any meaning. These production plans reflect the *knowledge and expectations* of the planners and the human resources employed. Knowledge is an important and complex dimension of every production plan. Capital accumulation involves learning—it involves change—as the knowledge-base (human capital) of workers and planners is enhanced. Capital accumulation and technological change are thus intertwined (Menger, 1981; Böhm-Bawerk, 1959; Lachmann, 1978; Lewin, 1999).

In a world without radical uncertainty (real Knightian uncertainty as distinct from probabilistically known risks), the necessary complementary productive activities would be relatively easy to organize and evaluate. Knowledge about how they fit together to produce the desired good or service would be generally available. Teamwork could be directed by any team member. It is a world of shared mental models of the production process; there is no cognitive heterogeneity. In such a world, values could be fairly easily imputed to the heterogeneous resources that combine to produce the product, on the basis of their known 'contribution' to that value. Such values would become the basis for the prices of those resources (and the services they yield) that are traded on the market. In such a world, payments to resource owners would exhaust the value of the product produced and there would be no surplus value, no profit. The rental payments to resource owners would leave no room for earnings in excess of the market value (the opportunity cost) of the productive resources. In order to explain profits, entrepreneurship, and sustained competitive advantage, one must therefore take account of the fact that the real world is an uncertain world (a disequilibrium world) in which change is endemic (Lewin and Phelan, 2002; Lewin, 2008).

To be sure, the world as we know and experience it could be no other way. It is a world characterized by necessary economic and cognitive heterogeneity. Productive resources are heterogeneous because they are constructed for specific purposes— they have a limited range of applications. Heterogeneity is to be understood essentially in terms of function rather than form. As Ludwig Lachmann maintains, something is a capital good not because of its physical form, but rather because of its economic function (Lachmann, 1978).[3] This is not to say that physical form is irrelevant. But it is the economic function for which such form is appropriate that is the essential aspect of a capital good. It may happen that two capital goods with different physical forms could perform identical tasks in a given production process, and equally well. They would then possess no essential economic heterogeneity. By the same token, two capital goods of identical form may be deployed in different capital combinations with other complementary goods, and perform very different and differentially valued tasks. Thus the heterogeneity of capital goods refers to their economic functions.

Each capital good may be said to possess a set of attributes (potentially) useful in the production process (Barzel, 1997). These attributes determine the services that the capital good can yield. Sometimes they are deliberately constructed with these attributes in mind. Other times these attributes may be revealed only after being used in combination with other resources. In either event, the entire set of valuable attributes of capital goods and combinations of capital goods is not likely to be obvious to every observer. Different evaluators see them differently. Capital goods combinations have to be subjectively appraised according to the value of the product they are expected to yield; that is, according to the revenue streams they are expected to generate in changing circumstances (Mises, 1949; Kor et al., 2007). Account must be taken of the future actions of both competitors and producers of complementary products (Richardson, 1960). Different appraisers will thus have different expectations. The cognitive models will be heterogeneous (Klein, 2008). In forming specific capital combinations, it is the role of the entrepreneur to bring to bear on the production process her particular appraisal—her vision (Penrose, 1959; Lachmann, 1978). It is unavoidable, therefore, that in many spheres of human action, notably in the sphere of economic competition, expectations will be mutually inconsistent. Rival economic models are the essence of the competitive process—for example, in predicting standards, fashions, brand appeal, price–quality trade-offs, and so on. And where expectations are mutually inconsistent, at most one person can be right (Lachmann, 1978; Lewin, 1997, 1999). *Disparate expectations* mean inevitable errors. They are a normal part of the experimental nature of the market process. Entrepreneurs pit their judgments against each other. Such judgment is necessary in a world where resource values are uncertain (Knight, 1921). The more successful the judgment, the appraisal, the more surplus value (over the payments (or opportunity costs) of the employed resources) will be earned by the entrepreneur. In a world of uncertainly, profit is not difficult to explain.

In sum, *production occurs through the formation of capital structures in which heterogeneous capital goods are combined in real time by ambitious entrepreneurs in an uncertain world in the hope of earning a profit as a result of the superior judgment of the value of those combinations—or, equivalently the value of the produced product.*

In order to investigate some of the principles that govern the making and management of capital combinations we need to examine the different types of capital goods and how they fit together. The glue holding it all together is (production-relevant) knowledge.

5.3 Human and Other Forms of Capital

5.3.1 Knowledge about the Knowledge in Capital

In order to use capital goods we have to know what they can do.[4] The attributes a capital good possesses can be thought of as useful (productive) knowledge. Different capital goods 'know' how to do different things. Capital heterogeneity (of economic function) is a reflection of the division of labor—we might say it is a 'division of capital'. This division of labor, whereby different parts of the production structure are devoted to specialized activities, is an organizing principle (Loasby, 2007) based on what Hayek called a 'division of knowledge' (Hayek, 1945; Tsoukas, 1996). In order to understand this principle one needs to take account of the various ways in which knowledge enters the production process.

There is a fundamental relationship between knowledge and capital. Indeed, capital goods are useful because they *embody* knowledge about productive processes and how they may be carried out (Baetjer, 1998, 2000). In practice, much of our knowledge is to be 'found' not in our heads, but in the capital goods we employ.[5] In particular, capital equipment (tools) embodies knowledge of how to accomplish some purpose.[6] Of course, much of our knowledge of the causal relationships between things, and of how to achieve the changes we desire, is tacit knowledge. Adam Smith speaks of the 'skill, dexterity, and judgment' of workers (1982: 7); these attributes are a kind of knowledge, a kinesthetic 'knowledge' located in the hands rather than in the head. The improvements these skilled workers make in their tools are embodiments of that knowledge. The very design of the tool passes on to a less skilled or less dexterous worker the ability to accomplish good results. Consider how the safety razor enables those of us unskilled in the barber's craft to shave with the blade always at the correct angle, rarely nicking ourselves. The skilled barber's dexterity has been passed on to us, as it were, embodied in the design of the safety razor.

To emphasize, the knowledge aspect of capital goods is the fundamental aspect. Any physical aspect is incidental. A hammer, for instance, is physical wood (the handle) and metal (the head). But a piece of oak and a chunk of steel do not make a hammer. The hammer is those raw materials infused with the knowledge embodied in the precise shape of the head and handle, the curvature of the striking surface, the proportion of head weight to handle length, and so on. (We leave aside, for now, all the additional knowledge required to shape the oak into a handle and the steel into a head.) Even with a tool as bluntly physical as a hammer, the knowledge component is of overwhelming importance. With precision tools such as microscopes and calibration instruments, the knowledge aspect of the tool becomes more dominant still. We might say, imprecisely but helpfully, that there is a greater proportion of knowledge to physical material in a microscope than in a hammer.

The case of computer software ('intellectual capital') provides both a compelling *analogy* for general understanding and a particular *case* of the nature of capital. Software is less tied to any physical medium than are most tools. Because we may with equal comfort think of a given program *as* a program, whether it is printed out on paper, stored on a hard drive, or loaded into the circuits of a computer, we have no difficulty distinguishing the knowledge aspect from the physical aspect with a software tool. Of course, to *function* as a tool the software must be loaded and running in the physical medium of the computer, and there are definite physical limits to computation. Nevertheless, it is in the nature of computers and software to separate clearly the *knowledge* of how to accomplish a certain function from the *physical embodiment* of that knowledge.

Because the knowledge aspect of software tools is so clearly distinguishable from their physical embodiment, in investigating software capital we may distinguish clearly the knowledge aspects of capital in general. While software may seem very different from other capital goods in this respect, when we think in terms of the capital structure, there is no fundamental difference between software tools and conventional tools. What is true of software is true of capital goods in general. What a person actually uses is not software alone, but software loaded into a physical system—a computer with a monitor or printer or plotter, a Space Shuttle, or whatever. The computer is the multipurpose, tangible complement to the special-purpose, intangible knowledge that is software. When the word-processor or computer-assisted design (CAD) package is loaded in, the whole system becomes a dedicated writing or drawing tool. But there is no important difference in this respect between a word-processor and, say, a hammer. The oaken dowel and molten steel are the multipurpose, tangible complements to the special-purpose, intangible knowledge of what a hammer is. When that knowledge is imprinted on the oak in the shape of a smooth, well-proportioned handle, and on the steel in the shape, weight, and hardness of a hammerhead; and when the two are joined together properly, then the whole system—raw oak, raw steel, and knowledge—becomes a dedicated nail-driving tool.

All tools are thus a combination of knowledge and matter. They are knowledge imprinted on or embodied in matter. Software is to the computer into which it is loaded as the knowledge of traditional tools is to the matter of which those tools are composed. If this is true, then knowledge is the key aspect of all capital goods, because the matter is, and always has been, 'there'.

In sum: a significant proportion of the knowledge we use in production is not in any person or even group, but in the tools we use. I who use the hammer know nothing of ergonomics, and have not the slightest idea of the 'correct' ratio of head weight to handle length. Nevertheless, when I drive a nail I can tell if the hammer feels right. Thus I use that knowledge. The knowledge is 'built into' my hammer. *Capital goods, then, are embodied knowledge of how to accomplish productive purposes.*

5.3.2 The Social Character of the Valuable Knowledge in Capital

The knowledge of *many people* is combined in capital goods; capital development is a process of *social* interaction, not a matter of individuals working autonomously. Most individual capital goods are manifestations of a far-flung division of knowledge—an almost incomprehensibly extensive sharing of the knowledge and talents of thousands of people across time and space. *The ever-changing pattern of relationships among these capital goods*—the capital structure as a whole—is an essential aspect of what Hayek called 'the extended order of human cooperation'. Capital goods and the capital structure at any time result from a tremendously rich social interaction through which the knowledge of many has been combined.

The division of labor is best understood as the whole pattern of cooperation in production—direct and indirect. The indirect contributions—in the form of tools and processes developed elsewhere—are, in an advanced economy, the most significant. The crucial 'labor' is the creative effort of learning how, and the embodying of that learning in the design of a tool that can be used by others, who themselves lack the knowledge in any other form. Through the embodiment of knowledge into an extending capital structure, each of us is able to take advantage of the specialized knowledge of untold others who have contributed to that structure. *Thus, this structure becomes increasingly more complex over time, as the pattern of complementary relationships extends.*[7]

In capital-intensive modern production processes, the division of knowledge and labor is to be found not in the large number of people at work in a particular production process, but in the tools used by a relatively few people who carry out that process. The knowledge contribution of multitudes is embodied in those tools, which give remarkable productive powers to the individual workers on the spot, though, as explained above, these productive powers have to be organized by the discerning judgment of the entrepreneur (Knight, 1921). In a fundamental sense, all economies are 'knowledge-economies' and all firms are 'knowledge-based'.

When we say that a capital good 'knows' how to accomplish a certain set of activities, what we mean is that, when used by someone who *knows* what he is doing, these activities can be successfully accomplished because at some earlier time someone else *knew* how to design this capital good to perform the way it does when used properly. The latter knowledge is, in a sense, more comprehensive in that the designer of the equipment, in addition to understanding at a more fundamental level the workings of the designed equipment, would also have to possess the knowledge of how to use it. This deeper knowledge has to be retained by someone if such expertise in design is to be retained in the economy at all, and if progress in design is to occur, but it can be dramatically economized to the extent that it is unnecessary for the routine operation of the capital good. Most of the users do not have and do not need to have that knowledge.

Underlying the physical form of machine and human lies the intricate structure of knowledge embodied in capital goods and complemented by the knowledge of how to use such goods in the minds of workers. The development of capital goods brings to bear increasing amounts of knowledge on the productive process over time. *Economic growth and development entails the increasing complexity of knowledge, one aspect of which is the increasing ratio of knowledge to 'stuff' embodied in capital structures.* We may refer to this as the *complexification* of production. It is this complexification that has given rise to the challenges of the so-called 'knowledge-economy'.[8]

5.3.3 Managing in the Knowledge-Intensive Economy

Agency and hold-up problems: the crucial difference
between human and other capital

Understanding that below the surface of the physical phenomena of production lies the knowledge necessary to accomplish planned activities (embodied in physical capital assets or the human capital of the team members) leads to the realization that management is always 'knowledge-management'. The crucial difference between *physical* capital and *human* capital is not that the latter is about knowledge and the former is not. Both are about knowledge, albeit in different forms. The crucial difference is that human capital is *not alienable*. Human capital ownership cannot be alienated from its original owner. Its services can be rented, but the capital itself always remains the 'property' of the original 'owner'.[9] This means that use and development of human capital by firms is necessarily governed by human relationships. And human relationships are characterized by numerous agency-type problems.

Williamson's 'hold-up' problem (Williamson 1985), for example, occurs because expected performance (the making of an investment in firm-specific human and physical capital) is 'relationship'-specific—it depends on the motivations of human capital owners who become tied in to an economic relationship by its specific nature. Hold-up is thus a possibility on both sides of the transaction. This is similar to the making of an investment by a firm in the specific human capital of one of its employees who may quit and take the human capital with her (Becker 1964; for more on this see Chapter 6 below).

Similarly, managing knowledge-rich human assets *inside* the firm has to take account of agency problems—trying to get the worker to use her knowledge as you, the principal, would use it if you were as knowledgeable as she. Since you do not have the knowledge necessary to fully judge the performance of activities, you have to resort to attempts at adequate incentive alignment to safeguard against moral hazard on the job. This monitoring problem is greater the greater the knowledge intensity (or complexity—of which more below) of the job. Complexity is thus another dimension governing internal agency problems.

Providing knowledgeable employees with decision rights optimal to the performance of required activities, and the development of necessary future knowledge needed to remain competitive, is at the heart of the management dilemma (Jensen and Meckling, 1992). Finding the right combination of 'high-powered' incentives (associated with ownership and market) and centralized direction is an ongoing challenge that determines both the boundaries of the firm and its internal organization.

Knowledge-problems

Much of the difficulty of managing (whether to accomplish routine activities or to plan and implement activities directed to growth and innovation) relates to the very nature of knowledge as a phenomenon. Considered as an input into the production process, knowledge is peculiar in that 'having it' means 'knowing'. To have knowledge one has to learn; one cannot simply buy it as one buys an automobile. Knowledge of knowledge is not the same thing as having the knowledge in the first place. And, as is well known, the knowledge-transfer problem is exacerbated by the fact that tacit knowledge is particularly difficult to transfer. Thus Hayek's (1945) *knowledge-problem*—the problem of planning in a world in which the planner has to deploy and make use of knowledge which he himself does not (and cannot) have, so that he cannot form an opinion as to the value of knowledge-assets in various production combinations—*exists as much in regard to physical as human capital assets*. Also, the *manner of interaction* of capital assets that is crucial to the outcome, much of which is not predictable, is subject to learning; that is, the accumulation of new knowledge. Insofar as capital assets are embodied knowledge (indeed we might say they are types of 'knowledge modules') and insofar as that knowledge is brought to bear in combination with other capital (physical and human) assets, the central planner of the firm faces a Hayekian knowledge-problem in regard to *all* of the firm's assets.

The severity of that problem is related not to the distinction between human and non-human assets, but rather to the *knowledge intensity* of the assets, whatever their form. And, as explained, above, since knowledge intensity is related to capital accumulation and capital accumulation implies the complexification of the (physical and human) capital structure, it is the *complexity* of capital broadly understood that intensifies the Hayekian knowledge-problem. This is an implication of Lachmann's (1978) reconstitution of Böhm-Bawerk's famous assertion that wisely chosen 'roundabout' methods of production are more productive. In effect, Lachmann replaced 'increased roundaboutness' with 'increased complexity'.

Thus, the perception that the 'information-age' economy is one that requires different types of economic organizations—smaller, flatter, more democratic, and so on—can be understood in terms of the increased complexity of knowledge rather than of the existence of 'knowledge-workers' as such.[10] Both physical and human assets become more complex with economic growth and capital accumulation, increasing the severity of Hayekian knowledge-problems and encouraging greater use of market decentralization where the market is thick enough to possess the necessary specialized and complex capital assets (Langlois and Robertson, 1995). This becomes more likely with economic growth. Where activities are relatively simple, are of low knowledge intensity, vertical integration is easier to manage, such as in assembly-line manufacturing.

Table 5.1 indicates the relationship between the dimensions of complexity and alienability and the two commonly mentioned types of management problem. The cell entries indicate whether the problem (knowledge or incentive) is affected by the dimension of alienability and/or complexity. Incentive-problems apply only to human (non-alienable) capital, and complexity makes it worse. But knowledge-problems apply to *all* assets, whether alienable or not, and are also exacerbated by the degree of complexity.

Table 5.1. The Dimensions of Management Problems

	Human Capital (not alienable)	Physical Capital (alienable)
Knowledge-problems	Yes	Yes
Incentive-problems (hold-up and agency)	Yes	No
Affected by knowledge complexity	Yes	Yes

One way to understand the firm boundary decision is in these terms. Integrating the capital assets of independent firms removes the incentive-problems associated with cooperation between separate owners of *physical* capital, though it may also dilute incentives if ownership is more dispersed. At the same time it exacerbates the knowledge-problem by increasing the extent of centralization, and imports incentive-problems associated with the new human capital acquired.

5.3.4 The Organization of Production

The Task of Organizing

The approach to the firm offered here—a capital-based view (CBV)—considers the problem of organizing (and managing) production to be the formation, maintenance, and adaptation of profitable capital combinations. The ingredients of any production project are the (human and physical) capital assets in capital combinations, characterized by their economic heterogeneity and complementarity (and also by their substitutability/specificity in the face of change). Though capital goods are heterogeneous, they do not come together in an 'amorphous heap'; rather, they are ordered in a coherent structure (Schumpeter, 1954). The capital goods of an economy compose a structure within which exist a multitude of substructures. At the level of the economy the capital structure is a result of the spontaneous workings of the market. Firm-level structures, by contrast, have to be planned and maintained, though their adaptive mutations are governed by unpredictable, emergent knowledge phenomena (Baldwin and Clark, 2000[11]).

Heterogeneity of capital resources is a reflection of the division of labor—of the specialization of knowledge and function. As emphasized, different capital goods 'know' how to do different and complementary things. Thus, the greater the degree of specialization the more heterogeneous the capital structure. Furthermore, heterogeneous capital implies *heterogeneous knowledge*. And, since the extent of the market and of economic growth is crucially related to the degree of specialization,

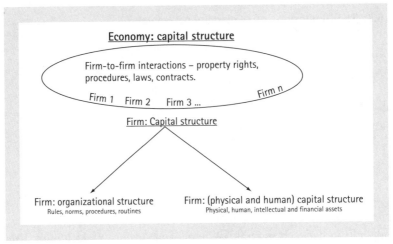

Figure 5.1. Structures and Substructures

heterogeneity will increase with economic growth and development—as will complexity, as explained above. The greater the heterogeneity of resources, the greater the complexity of the organizational task. Organization of heterogeneous knowledge assets into productive combinations requires organizing ability and an organizational structure. The organizational structure of the firm can be thought of as an aspect of the firm's general capital structure. The firm has 'social' capital in the useful (knowledge-economizing) rules, customs, norms, and so on, that it develops. And leadership will be required for non-routine situations. The value of leadership lies in the ability of the leader to organize complementary activities; for example, by aligning belief-systems (Foss, 2001: 357).

See Figure 5.1.

Modularity

As knowledge becomes more complex (heterogeneous), knowledge-management strategies can be expected to develop. One of the most ubiquitous is increased modularization (Baldwin and Clark, 2000; Garud *et al.*, 2003; Langlois, 2002).

Resource management requires structure. To view a set of resources as simply a quantity of heterogeneous items reveals nothing about them. They are simply quantities of various categories of resources. Unless they are a structure, they remain an amorphous list of sets of quantities of incommensurable items, devoid of meaning for productive purposes. Modularity is relevant to the relationship between quantities and structures. A structure can be described by a list of items that stand in a certain orientation to one another. Complex structures are composed of many items with many interactions. A structure as opposed to simply a list of the structure's elements (which, as explained, could be unmanageably detailed and devoid of meaning) is distinguished by the fact that one can infer properties about the whole list from a description or observation of just a few component (or typical) parts together with an articulation of the principles of interaction. It is an important strategy for economizing in knowledge about knowledge. Modules are self-contained substructures, whose inner workings are hidden from the high-level observer (manager).[12]

It can be readily seen that the modular design of knowledge structures is organizational design. Organizations must be designed by deciding what managers need to know and need not know (Spender, 2006). They need some knowledge of the knowledge of others. What do we really know when we have knowledge about knowledge? We move to successive levels of abstraction (modularization) (Baldwin and Clark, 2000; Tulloh and Miller, 2006) in order to economize on what we need to know. Successful management thus depends on finding the right level of abstraction—knowing enough to make correct judgments about the deployment of assets (human and physical) that know more (about their specialized activities) than the managers do, in productive combinations, but not seeking to know so much as to tie up managers' time and energies in the process of learning and understanding. The managers' 'big picture' must be accurate yet not too detailed. This is an important task of organizational design.[13]

5.4 CONCLUSION

A capital-based view of the firm sees the firm as a capital structure composed of ordered physical and human capital assets. Capital value relates to time. It is an assessment of the *prospective* services of productive assets at a single point in time.[14] Capital combinations can be understood (derive their meaning) from the production plan of which they are/were a part. Capital implies planning. The task of the planning entrepreneur is the formation of productive capital combinations. The firm can be seen as a productive capital combination. Aspects of the firm, its boundaries, its organizational structure, its growth, and management can all be fruitfully analyzed from this central capital-based perspective.

ACKNOWLEDGMENTS

I am grateful to J. C. Spender for comments on earlier versions of this chapter.

NOTES

1. Though the term may have been used earlier by Arthur Pigou.
2. Here we understand 'production' very broadly to include all activities from the initiation of the production process to the final delivery to the consumer, including manufacture, transportation, distribution, marketing, and so on—all the stages in the supply chain.
3. Lachmann: 'The generic concept of capital without which economists cannot do their work has no measurable counterpart among material objects. Beer barrels and blast furnaces, harbor installations and hotel-room furniture are capital not by virtue of their physical properties but by virtue of their economic functions. Something is capital because the market, the consensus of entrepreneurial minds regards it as capable of yielding an income' (1978: p. xv). Compare this with: 'In general, an artifact's value or worth in society is determined by its functions, and not by its [physical] structure' (Baldwin and Clark, 2000: 29).
4. This section borrows liberally form Baetjer and Lewin (2008).
5. Consumption goods also have a knowledge aspect, of course. Indeed, knowledge is a necessary aspect of any economic good, if by economic good we mean something that people value. It is only because of our knowledge that something will satisfy some purpose—in either consumption or production—that we consider it a good. Hence we may reasonably say that consumption goods embody knowledge of what will directly satisfy our wants.
6. In a wonderful passage Friederich Hayek writes: 'Take the concept of a "tool" or "instrument," or of any particular tool such as a hammer or a barometer. It is easily seen that these concepts cannot be interpreted to refer to "objective facts," that is, to things irrespective of what people think about them. Careful logical analysis of these concepts will show that they all express relationships between several (at least three) terms, of which one is the acting or thinking person, the second some desired or imagined effect, and the third a thing in the ordinary sense. If the reader will attempt a definition he will soon find that he cannot give one without using some term such as "suitable for" or "intended for" or some other expression referring to the use for which it is designed by somebody. And a definition which is to comprise all instances of the class will not contain any reference to its substance, or shape, or other physical attribute. An ordinary hammer and a steam-hammer, or an aneroid barometer and a mercury barometer, have nothing in common except the purpose for which men think they can be used' (1979: 44).
7. I use the term 'complexity' in this chapter in its intuitive common-sense meaning. A system (structure) becomes more complex as the number of components it contains increases *and* the number of types of interface (interconnections) increases with it. Its increased complexity means that it is more difficult to figure out, to comprehend, though it is clear there is a coherent structure to it.
8. A different though complementary discussion of the role and types of knowledge in organizations can be found in Chapter 9.
9. Even in a slave economy, where the human embodiment of the human capital (say acquired skills) could be sold, the slave would still be in crucial control over the use of his brain in a way that a machine is not, thus posing very different management problems.
10. In fact this perception may be mistaken, or, at least, simplistic. Complexity may require greater 'hierarchy' in the form of modularity—though intramodular interaction may

be more 'democratic' to encourage creativity. See Beinhocker, 2007: ch. 6. More on modularity below.

11. 'Indeed, products and technologies and firms and markets evolve interactively over time to create a *complex adaptive system*': Baldwin and Clark, 2000: 2–3; italics added.

12. The M-form corporation is a particular form of modularization, in which the divisions form large modules (Sautet, 2001).

13. Of course there are other aspects of modularity, such as adaptability and resilience in the face of change, that are not examined here. See for example, Lewin, 2008.

14. Erroneous views of capital have led to an underappreciation of the centrality of the concept for understanding production, the firm, entrepreneurship, and the like (see Dean and Kretschmer, 2007, for an example, and Baetjer and Lewin, 2008, for a critique). Perhaps the most egregious mistake is to think of capital as necessarily physical in nature and to exclude human, social, and intellectual capital from the category of capital—confining them to a special and very different category. To the contrary, these are all part of capital generically speaking—part of the capital structure, though the non-alienability of human capital does imply specific management issues.

REFERENCES

BAETJER, H. (1998). *Software as Capital: An Economic Perspectives on Software Engineering* (Los Alamos, NM: IFEE Computer Society).

——(2000). 'Capital as Embodied Knowledge: Some Implications for the Theory of Economic Growth', *Review of Austrian Economics*, 13(1): 147–74.

——and LEWIN, P. (2008). 'Can Ideas be Capital: Can Capital be Anything Else?', http://www.utdallas.edu/~plewin/Can%20Ideas%20be%20Captal.pdf.

BALDWIN, C. Y. (2007). 'Where do Transactions Come from? Modularity, Transactions, and the Boundaries of Firms', *Industrial and Corporate Change*, 17(1): 155–95.

——and CLARK, K. B. (2000) *Design Rules* (Cambridge, Mass.: MIT Press).

BARZEL, Y. (1997). *Economic Analysis of Property Rights* (2nd edn. Cambridge: Cambridge University Press).

BECKER, G. S. (1964). *Human Capital: A Theoretical and Empirical Analysis, with Special Reference to Education* (Chicago: University of Chicago Press; 3rd edn. 1993).

BEINHOCKER, E. D. (2007). *Origin of Wealth: Evolution, Complexity, and the Radical Remaking of Economics* (Cambridge, Mass.: Harvard Business School Press).

BÖHM-BAWERK, E. VON (1959) *Capital and Interest* (3 vols. in 1; South Holland: Libertarian Press; orig. pub. 1881).

DEAN, A., and KRETSCHMER, M. (2007). 'Can Ideas be Capital? Factors of Production in the Postindustrial Economy: A Review and Critique', *Academy of Management Review*, 32(2): 573–94.

FOSS, N. J. (2001). 'Leadership, Beliefs and Coordination', *Industrial and Corporate Change*, 10: 357–88.

GARUD, R., KUMARASWAMY, A., and LANGLOIS, R. N. (eds.) (2003). *Managing in the Modular Age: Architectures, Networks, and Organizations* (Malden, Mass.: Basil Blackwell).

HAYEK, F. A. (1941). *The Pure Theory of Capital* (Chicago: University of Chicago Press).

—— (1945) 'The Use of Knowledge in Society', *American Economic Review*, 35(4).

—— (1979). *The Counter Revolution of Science* (Indianapolis: Liberty Press).

JENSEN, M. C., and MECKLING, W. H. (1992) 'Specific and General Knowledge, and Organizational Structure', in Lars Werin and Hans Wijkander (eds.), *Contract Economics* (Oxford: Blackwell), 251–74.

KLEIN, P. G. (2008). 'Opportunity and Discovery: Entrepreneurial Action and Economic Organization', *Strategic Entrepreneurial Journal*, 2: 175–90.

KNIGHT, F. H. (1921). *Risk, Uncertainty and Profit* (Boston: Houghton Mifflin Co.).

KOR, Y. Y., MAHONEY, J. T., and MICHAEL, S. C. (2007). 'Resources, Capabilities and Entrepreneurial Perceptions', *Journal of Management Studies*, 44(7): 1187–1212.

LACHMANN, L. M. (1978). *Capital and its Structure* (Kansas City: Sheed, Andrews & McMeel; orig. pub. 1956).

LANGLOIS, R. N. (2002). 'Modularity in Technology and Organization', *Journal of Economic Behavior and Organization*, 49(1): 19–37; repr. in Nicolai Foss and Peter Klein (eds.), *Entrepreneurship and the Theory of the Firm* (Cheltenham: Edward Elgar).

—— and ROBERTSON, P. L. (1995). *Firms, Markets, and Economic Change: A Dynamic Theory of Business Institutions* (London: Routledge).

LEWIN, P. (1997). 'Capital in Disequilibrium: A Re-examination of the Capital Theory of Ludwig M. Lachmann', *History of Political Economy*, 29(3): 523–48.

—— (1999). *Capital in Disequilibrium: The Role of Capital in a Changing World* (London and New York: Routledge).

—— (2005). 'The Capital Idea and the Scope of Economics', *Review of Austrian Economics*, 18(2): 145–67.

—— (2008). 'The Firm in Disequilibrium: Contributions from the Austrian Tradition', *Advances in Austrian Economics*, 11: 167–92.

—— and PHELAN S. E. (2002). 'Rent and Resources: A Market Process Perspective', in N. J. Foss and P. G. Klein (eds.), *Entrepreneurship and the Firm: Austrian Perspectives on Economic Organization* (Aldershot: Edward Elgar), ch. 11.

LOASBY, B. J. (2007). 'The Ubiquity of Organization', *Organization Studies*, 28(11): 1729–59.

McCLOSKEY, D. N. (1985). *The Rhetoric of Economics* (Madison, Wis.: University of Wisconsin Press).

MENGER, C. (1981). *Principles of Economics* (New York: New York University Press; orig. publ. 1871).

MINCER, J. (1974). *Schooling, Experience and Earnings* (New York: Columbia University Press).

MISES, L. (1949). *Human Action* (San Francisco: Fox & Wiles).

PENROSE, E. (1959). *The Theory of the Growth of the Firm* (London: Basil Blackwell).

RICHARDSON, G. B. (1960 [1997]). *Information and Investment: A Study in the Working of the Competitive Economy* (Oxford: Oxford University Press).

SAUTET, F. (2001). *An Entrepreneurial Theory of the Firm* (London: Routledge).

SCHULTZ, T. W. (1981). *Investing in People: The Economics of Population Quality* (Berkeley, Calif: University of California Press).

SCHUMPETER, J. A. (1954). *History of Economic Analysis* (New York: Oxford University Press).

SMITH, A. (1982) *An Inquiry into the Nature and Causes of the Wealth of Nations*, ed. R. H. Campbell and A. S. Skinner (Indianapolis, Ind.: Liberty Classics; orig. pub. 1776).

SPENDER, J.-C. (2006). 'Method, Philosophy and Empirics in KM and IC', *Journal of Intellectual Capital*, 7(2): 12–28.

TSOUKAS, H. (1996). 'The Firm as a Distributed Knowledge System: A Constructionist Approach', *Strategic Management Journal*, 17: 11–25.

TULLOH, B., and MILLAR M. S. (2006). 'Institutions as Abstraction Boundaries', in J. High (ed.), *Humane Economics: Essays in Honor of Don Lavoie* (Northampton, Mass.: Edward Elgar), ch. 5.

WILLIAMSON, O. E. (1985) *The Economic Institutions of Capitalism* (New York: Free Press).

PART II

HUMAN CAPITAL AND THE FIRM

CHAPTER 6

HUMAN CAPITAL AND TRANSACTION COST ECONOMICS

NICOLAI J. FOSS

6.1 INTRODUCTION

Human capital may be defined as the stock of valued skills, knowledge, insights, and so on, controlled by an individual—the attributes of the relevant individual that are valuable in an economic context. Human capital yields services such as labor services, management services, or entrepreneurship. As slavery is almost universally prohibited, the issue from the point of view of comparative economic organization is not one of allocation of ownership to human capital; rather, it concerns whether the services of human capital are supplied through market transactions, transactions in an employment relation (Coase, 1937), in club-like organization (Buchanan, 1965), or within households (Becker, 1964, 1991). A key issue in the body of microeconomic thought commonly referred to as 'organizational economics' or the 'theory of the firm' concerns the efficient organization of such transactions, specifically across contracts and governance structures. By supplying instruments of coordination and providing incentives, contracts and governance structures coordinate human capital services, and provide incentives for investments in human capital. Under a norm of efficiency (value maximization) the specific contracts or governance structures with which human capital is matched depends on the characteristics of the latter.

While this overall perspective cuts across organizational economics perspectives, such as transaction cost economics, property rights/incomplete contracts theory, and agency theory, the specific terminology ('transactions', 'governance structures', and so on) applied here is particular to transaction cost economics (TCE). Arguably, giving TCE terminology pride of place is warranted, as TCE has provided the first and still most comprehensive treatment of the organizational ramifications of human capital in economics. The present chapter surveys TCE as it pertains to human capital, concentrating on the work of TCE's most prominent flag-bearer, Oliver Williamson, the precursors of his work (Coase, 1937; Simon, 1951), and the various operationalizations and extensions of his approach. Also briefly discussed is the property rights approach (Hart, 1995); like TCE, it rests on the notion of incomplete contracting and the need to safeguard transactions under such conditions.

Human capital plays a key role in these approaches as an important component in the explanation of important aspects of economic organization, notably the boundaries of the firm. To be sure, these approaches contain many implications for understanding the employment relation, such as the sources of the employer's power in such a relation, the implications of an employee holding outside options, the *raison d'être* of internal job markets, and so on (Milgrom and Roberts, 1992). These are all issues that are relevant to general management. However, TCE and the property rights approach are simply not on the same level of detail as, for example, the human resource management literature. As Loasby (1995) observes, neither carry any particular implications regarding what to 'tell Mrs Jones what to do on Monday morning'. TCE and the property rights approach are concerned with providing a rather abstract understanding of the efficient matching of transactions and governance structures/allocations of property rights at a point of time. They are not taken up with process analysis, managerial decision premises, and so on. There is little or nothing on standard HR practices such as hiring or training employees, and in fact rather little detail on compensation issues (which is treated more comprehensively in agency theory). Like most of economics, these theories make heavily simplified assumptions concerning the motivation and cognition of agents.[1] Still, TCE is an important source theory for many fields in management, because it supplies an economizing logic, explaining the matching of transactions and governance structures, and therefore offers relatively clean predictions. However, it has also been subject to heavy criticism from management scholars who have indicted the theory for purportedly being 'bad for practice'. Other critiques on the part of management scholars concern the neglect of differential firm-level capabilities, and the basis of such capabilities in human capital. Such critiques are briefly discussed at the end of this chapter.

6.2 The Role of Human Capital in Transaction Cost Economics

6.2.1 Transaction Cost Economics: Overall

The foundations of contemporary transaction cost economics were laid by Ronald Coase (1937, 1960). The logical starting point for a transaction cost approach to governance and organizational issues is Coase's (1960) insight that if it were not for transaction costs, all gains to trade would be exhausted, and this could take place under any organizational arrangement. This connects to Coase's earlier paper (1937) for the argument that the assessment of the net benefits of organizational and governance alternatives must proceed in terms of a comparative analysis of the costs of transacting under the relevant alternatives (Barzel and Kochin, 1992).

In a string of influential contributions, Williamson (1971, 1973, 1975, 1985, 1996) has built a theory that while based on Coasian foundations also incorporates ideas from psychology and contract law. The behavioral starting points in Williamson's theorizing are bounded rationality and opportunism. Simon's notion of bounded rationality implies the presence of contractual incompleteness and, consequently, a need for adaptive, sequential decision-making. Opportunism is defined as 'self-interest seeking with guile'—the relevant implication being that contracts will often need various types of safeguards, such as 'hostages' (for example, the posting of a bond with the other party). The unit of analysis in Williamson's work is the multidimensional transaction. In addition to uncertainty (which is kept constant at an intermediate level), the dimensions of the transaction that create transaction costs are frequency and asset specificity. In an early contribution, Klein *et al.* (1978: 297) linked asset specificity to the concept of appropriable quasi-rent:

Assume an asset is owned by one individual and rented to another individual. The quasi-rent value of the asset is the excess of its value over its salvage value; that is, its value in its next best *use* to another renter. The potentially appropriable specialized portion of the quasi-rent is that portion, if any, in excess of its value to the second highest-valuing *user*.

Following Klein *et al.*, asset specificity has increasingly become the central character in Williamson's analysis. Williamson (1996) now identifies six different reasons why assets may be costly to redeploy: attachment to a brand name, a need to take quick actions ('temporal specificity'), market size ('dedicated assets'), localization, physical characteristics, and specialized knowledge (human capital specificity).

Asset specificity opens the door to opportunism. If contracts are incomplete due to bounded rationality, it may be necessary to renegotiate them as uncertainty unfolds, and if a party to the contract (say, a supplier firm) has incurred sunk costs in developing specific assets (including human capital), that other party can opportunistically appropriate an undue part of the investment's pay-off ('quasi-rents') by threatening to withdraw from the relationship. This situation leads to a Pareto-inferior outcome; for example, a no-trade outcome. Efficiency dictates the internalization within a firm of transactions that involve highly specific assets. More generally, Williamson (1985: 68) argues that variety in contracts and governance structures 'is mainly explained by underlying differences in the attributes of transactions'. The general design principle of discriminating alignment dictates aligning transactions that differ in the dimensions of uncertainty, frequency, and asset specificity with governance structures which differ in the capacities to handle different transactions (see the earlier mention of governance structures and governance mechanisms) in transaction cost discriminating way. Thus, specific constellations of (values for) the uncertainty, frequency, and asset specificity variables map directly into specific governance structures. This is the main predictive content of Williamsonian TCE.

So far, all that is special about human capital is that it cannot be traded; otherwise, it is just a capital asset like any other which may be more or less specialized to specific uses and/or users. It may explain variation in the organization of transactions across markets, hybrids, and hierarchies, exactly as, for example, physical assets may. However, it is important to bear in mind that Williamson not only emphasizes that transactions differ in the three mentioned dimensions; he is also adamant that alternative governance structures have differential capacities for governing different transactions. And it is here that (specific) human capital becomes of particular importance in Williamson's thought, for it relates directly to the employment relation and the understanding of the costs and benefits of hierarchical governance. To see this it may be instructive to look at the precursors of Williamson's analysis of the employment relation: Coase (1937) and Simon (1951).

6.2.2 Coase and Simon on the Employment Relation

In his classic paper, Coase (1937) essentially defines the firm as the employment relation. In the presence of uncertainty, Coase argues, contingencies are costly to anticipate and describe in advance, and rather than negotiating on a spot market basis over each contingency as they arise, an employment contract is concluded. The latter is defined as 'one whereby the factor, for a certain remuneration (which may be fixed or fluctuating) agrees to obey the directions of an entrepreneur *within certain limits*. The essence of the contract is that it should only state the limits to the powers of the entrepreneur. Within these limits, he can therefore direct the other factors of production' (p. 242).

Simon (1951) defines authority as obtaining when a 'boss' is permitted by a 'worker' to select actions, $A^0 \in \mathbf{A}$, where $\mathbf{A}$ is the set of the worker's possible behaviors. More or less authority is then defined as making the set A^0 larger or smaller. The boss then selects the action that he prefers, and directs the worker to that action which—for the latter to accept the assignment—must lie within his or her 'zone of acceptance'. A worker's zone of acceptance is defined by Simon as that set of actions where the worker's expected costs of carrying out these actions do not exceed the agreed-upon wage. An important feature of authority is that the authority of a superior is constrained by the acceptance of the subordinate of the authority. 'A subordinate may be said to accept authority', Simon (1951: 22) explains, 'whenever he permits his behavior to be guided by a decision reached by another, irrespective of his own judgment as to the merits of that decision'. In contrast, in a market contract, the parties negotiate *ex ante* about the actions that the agent can take in response to various contingencies so as to fulfil the contract. Thus, the principal's flexibility under market contracting is limited compared to what it would be under authority.

Clearly, Simon's explanation of authority and the employment relation is quite akin to Coase (1937). To both of them, authority is a decision right that an employer acquires through contracting, because he expects to obtain only *ex post* contracting the relevant information that will make it possible for him to pick his preferred actions within a specified subset of actions, which he will then direct the employee to carry out. Knowledge and knowledge asymmetries (notably, the employer possessing superior knowledge) are not explicit parts of either story (as they are in Demsetz, 1991, for example). Thus, in Simon symmetric knowledge is consistent with the authority relation; it is sufficient for the existence of that relation that one contracting party for whatever reason stands to gain more than the other from picking the actions once contingencies materialize. The thrust of Coase's discussion, however, seems to indicate that the employer is clearly the informed party who picks well-defined actions from a set of discrete actions on the basis of knowledge about contingencies that is superior to that of the employee, but this is not a central point and at any rate not the fundamental reason why the employment contract, and hence the firm, emerges. The absence of considerations of knowledge is also indicated by the fact that in both treatments the employer grants no discretion with respect to the choice of actions to the employee; such delegation would be warranted (*ceteris paribus*) if the employee possesses superior knowledge about contingencies, actions, or the matching of contingencies and actions. In other words, characteristics of human capital are not included in Coase and Simon's theories of the employment relation, where employees are implicitly taken to be homogeneous.

6.2.3 Williamson on Human Capital and the Employment Relation

While Williamson accepts Coase's emphasis on authority as a defining characteristic of the firm, he goes very significantly beyond the Coase–Simon analysis. He does so by taking more explicit account of the heterogeneity of human capital, by examining the transaction cost ramifications of human capital specificity, and by emphasizing the distinct informational advantages of the hierarchy in dealing with specific human capital. While Coase had stressed the savings of transaction costs attendant upon changing a spot labor transaction to an employment contract, Williamson locates the relevant transaction costs in the opportunism problem that may arise under small-numbers bargaining.

Williamson's first reflections on these issues from what we may recognize as a distinct TCE perspective appear in his 1975 paper with Wachter and Harris (Williamson *et al.*, 1975; reproduced with modifications as ch. 4 in Williamson, 1975). Williamson begins by declaring that he

is concerned with the implications of an extreme form of non-homogeneity—namely, job idiosyncrasy—for understanding the employment relation…The purpose is to better assess the employment relation in circumstances where workers *acquire*, during the course of their employment, significant job-specific skills and related task-specific knowledge. (1975: 57; emphasis in original)

In a footnote, he observes that 'the employment relation is not an isolated case of idiosyncratic exchange conditions. The vertical integration problem turns in no small degree on these same considerations' (p. 57 n.). In other words, in 1975 Williamson's reasoning on the employment contract proceeds by extension of the theoretical mechanism that he had developed in his 1971 and 1973 papers on vertical integration.

Explicitly drawing on Becker's work on human capital, as well as on labor law and the internal labor market literature (Doeringer and Piore, 1971), Williamson identifies four different modes for contracting labor services in a comparative manner, by (1) sequential spot contracts (contract now for specific performance); (2) contingent claims contracts (contracting now for the specific performance of x_i in the future depending contingent on e_i obtaining); (3) long-term contracting (wait until the future unfolds and contract for the appropriate specific action); and (4) the authority relation (as in Coase, 1937; Simon, 1951). This identification of the relevant contractual alternatives allows Williamson to take issue with Alchian and Demsetz (1972) and with Simon (1951).

Alchian and Demsetz famously argued that talk of 'authority' is a 'deceptive way of noting that the employer continually is involved in renegotiation of contracts on terms that must be acceptable to both parties' (Alchian and Demsetz, 1972)—an argument, Williamson (1975: 67) observes, that seems to involve zero or negligible transition costs associated with employee turnover, and which therefore corresponds to contracting alternative (3) above (rather than to the authority relation). Simon (1951) is criticized for only confronting alternatives (1) and (4), which means that 'the terms are rigged from the outset' (Williamson 1975: 71). As contractual alternative (1) lacks adaptability, transactions requiring such adaptability will naturally lead to the choice of the employment contract in Simon's model. However, there are numerous contractual alternatives that do allow for adaptability, so adaptability cannot be the (main) explanation for the choice of the authority relation. That choice rather depends on 'task idiosyncrasies'.

Drawing on Doeringer and Piore (1971), Williamson outlines various sources of such idiosyncrasies, which are to be understood as different manifestations of human capital specificity. Thus, such specificity may arise through workers acquiring knowledge about non-standard equipment (Penrose, 1959), specialized processes (Nelson and Winter, 1982), the capabilities of other employees (Alchian and Demsetz, 1972), and firm-specific communication channels and values (Arrow, 1974). The problem with task idiosyncrasy/specific human capital is that 'workers are strategically situated to bargain opportunistically' (Williamson, 1975: 74). Such opportunistic bargaining may cause alternative (4) to be the preferred mode of organizing the supply of labor services. The employment relation, Williamson argues, means making use of a collective bargaining system where 'wages rates are attached mainly to jobs rather than to workers. Not only is individual wage bargaining thereby discouraged, but may even be legally foreclosed…The incentives to behave opportunistically…are correspondingly attenuated' (1975: 74).

Williamson's 1985 book expands on labor organization and emphasizes opportunism and asset specificity to a much larger extent, compared to the treatment in the 1975 book. This reflects the increasing 'hardening' of Williamson's research program around the problem of hold-up in the presence of specific assets as the apparently universal mechanism that explains choices between markets, hybrids, and hierarchies. Thus, Williamson explains that what is at issue in explaining the organization of work is not the deepening of human capital, but its specificity; while both have implications for productivity, only the latter have direct implications for organization.

However, to nuance his analysis Williamson adds one more dimension: 'separability' of 'work relations'. The latter is an attempt to capture the issues of inputs and output measurability highlighted in agency theory. (Williamson specifically refers to Alchian and Demsetz, 1972.) Accordingly, the separability of work relations depends on how costly it is to measure individual outputs. Armed with the dimensions of specificity and separability, Williamson constructs a 2×2 matrix that maps the organization of human capital services (1985: 247). Non-specific separable human assets, such as migrant farm workers, certain kinds of engineer, IT specialists, and so on, can move between employers without loss of productivity; there is therefore no efficiency interest in maintaining a specific relation. The 'primitive team' obtains when human assets are non-specific, but their outputs are difficult to measure on an individual basis. As analyzed by Alchian and Demsetz (1972), this kind of work organization motivates monitoring of inputs. The 'obligational market' in turn obtains when human assets are specific but separable. Under these conditions both firms and employees have an interest in maintaining the relation, and various devices, such as severance pay and employee benefits such as non-vested retirement, arise to discourage arbitrary dismissal or unwanted quits. Under the final conditions—high specificity and non-separability—the 'relational' team organization arises, characterized by strong implicit contracts that can sustain cooperation. Williamson refers to Ouchi's (1980) notion of 'clan organization' and to the Japanese corporation (*anno* 1985) to exemplify the relational team.

6.2.4 Forbearance and the Informational Advantages of Hierarchy

In his later work Williamson placed much less emphasis on collective bargaining than he did in his 1975 book, and instead emphasized the informational advantages of the authority relation and the hierarchical organization in which it is embedded. However, the theme of the informational advantages of hierarchy has been present in Williamson's work at least since his 1971 paper. As he argues there, the hierarchy possesses certain inherent advantages over market contracting: 'When conflicts develop, the firm possesses a comparatively efficient resolution machinery. To illustrate, fiat is frequently a more efficient way to settle minor conflicts (say differences of interpretation) than is haggling or litigation' (Williamson, 1971: 114). This advantage has come to play an increasing role in Williamson's work. Thus, he has placed increasing emphasis on the argument that organizational governance is characterized by its own implicit contract law, which he calls 'forbearance'. To illustrate, whereas divisions will not normally be granted standing for a court, corporate headquarters and headquarters function as the firm's 'ultimate court of appeal'. For example, Williamson (1991) points out that disputes which arise within the firm, for example, between different divisions, may be easier to resolve than disputes arising between firms which sometimes require the use of the court-system. Thus, managerial authority partakes of an important role as arbitrator in the face of conflicts and disputes over unforeseen contingencies; in other words, Williamson's extension of the Coasian view of authority is to analyze it as a 'private ordering', a private legal institution (Williamson, 2002). Part of that argument is Williamson's assertion that there are qualitative and quantitative differences between the information structures that are available under market contracting and those that are available in the firm—an argument put to work in Williamson's work on the M-form as an internal capital market (Williamson, 1975).[2]

6.2.5 Employee and Employer Opportunism

According to Coase (1937), the key reason why firms exist lies in the exercise of managerial authority in response to changes in the environment being an efficient mode of organization for certain transactions. In this view, echoed in countless other contributions to organization theory and the theory of the firm, managerial intervention is implicitly always seen as beneficial.[3] However, in actuality, managerial intervention will typically override existing instructions of employees. Moreover, in firms where employees are given considerable discretion, managerial intervention may amount to overruling decisions that employees have made on the basis of decision rights that have been delegated to them (Baker *et al.*, 1999). This suggests that employee utility may be harmed by managerial intervention, particularly when employees perceive opportunistic intentions behind such intervention (Foss, 2003). Negative firm-level effects may result when employees put in less effort and/or undertake less investment in specific human capital.

Contrary to the common claim that Williamson puts all the explanatory emphasis on employee opportunism (for example, Dow, 1987), he has in fact never been blind to the possibility of employer opportunism. Thus, Williamson (1996: 150–1) points out that the option to intervene 'can be exercised both for good cause (to support expected net gains) and for bad (to support the subgoals of the intervenor)'. This raises a series of fundamental incentive problems that are rooted in the fact that it may be difficult to verify the nature of the cause, and that promises to only intervene for good cause are hard to make credible as they are not enforceable in a court of law. There remains a problem of '*credibly* [promising] to respect autonomy save for those cases where expected net gains to intervention can be projected' (Williamson, 1993: 104). An important problem therefore concerns how managerial intervention for good cause (value-increasing intervention) may be promoted, while intervention for bad cause (value-destroying intervention) is avoided. The practical relevance of this issue is underscored by a series of empirical studies that suggest that management breaking the psychological contract with employees is a phenomenon of frequent occurrence (Rousseau and Parks, 1992; Coyle-Shapiro and Kessler, 2000). While Williamson himself has not dealt with the issue in any detail, subsequent work has pointed to various mechanisms, such as implicit contracts (Kreps, 1990; Baker *et al.*, 1999), explicit credible commitments, or organizational structure (Aghion and Tirole, 1997; Foss *et al.*, 2006) that may reduce the incidence and severity of value-destroying managerial interventions.

6.2.6 Empirical Application

There is a now a huge body of empirical literature examining various issues in transaction cost economics. Many empirical studies have examined the make-or-buy decision, focusing mainly on the transaction cost approach.[4] The empirical TCE literature is surveyed and summarized in Shelanski and Klein (1995) and Macher and Richman (2006), and the bulk of the evidence is interpreted as consistent with the predictions of TCE (see David and Han, 2003, for a contrary view).

Despite challenges associated with the measurement and definition of key variables, the role of asset specificity, comparison with rival theories, and causality, the transaction cost model seems to have straightforward empirical implications, such that observed forms of organizational governance can be explained in terms of asset specificity, uncertainty, and frequency.

Indeed, much of the success of Williamson's formulation of TCE lies exactly in his identification of the key attributes that determine governance costs (Masten, 1996: 45). In Coase (1937), the decision rule/prediction is that $GS^* = GS_1$, if $GC_1 < GC_2$ and $GS^* = GS_2$, if $GC_1 > GC_2$ ('GS' is governance structure, 'GC' is governance cost). From the empirical point of view, Williamson's contribution is to specify the cost relations, $GC_1 = \beta_1 X + e_1$ and $GC_2 = \beta_2 X + e_2$, X being the vector of observable attributes that impact governance costs, yielding testable reduced form relations by means of qualitative choice models (for example, probit models).

Early empirical work in TCE all took this approach (Monteverde and Teece, 1982; Anderson and Schmittlein, 1984; Masten, 1984; John and Weitz, 1988). Monteverde and Teece draw on Teece's (1980) earlier work on how firm-specific human capital may help shape the horizontal boundaries of the firm (diversification). They examine how firm-specific 'industrial know-how', represented by the applications engineering effort (rated on a 1–10 scale) associated with the development of a given automobile component, shapes the incentives to engage in vertical integration. Anderson and Schmittlein (1984) examine whether or not the function of personal selling (as opposed to mass communication) is integrated, in the sense of whether a manufacturer's representative is used or rather an employed salesperson. The human capital specificity of the sales person is indicated by variables measuring, for example, the difficulty of the salesperson learning the ins and outs of a company, including learning about accounts, the importance of customer loyalty, and so on. John and Weitz (1988) measured the specificity of human capital investments by the time required for a newly hired salesperson with industry experience to familiarize himself with a given firm's products and customer base.

Since these classic studies, numerous studies in industrial organization and regulation (for example, Crocker and Masten, 1996; Saussier, 2000), alliance organization (Dyer 1997), international business, and marketing (for example, Anderson, 1985; Heide and John 1988) have examined the impact of human capital specificity on governance and contractual choice. Most confirm the TCE prediction(s). However, in a provocative paper Masten et al. (1991) suggest that standard TCE may have misconstrued the reason for this consistent finding. The standard story (Williamson, 1975, 1985) has specific human capital being associated with employment contracts because the costs of organizing the sourcing of the relevant services through market contracting are too high. However, it may be, Masten et al. argue, that it is simply less costly to manage workers with more specific skills; thus, firm organization (employment contracts) is preferred for organizing the services of specific human capital—not because the costs of using the market for organizing such assets are too high, but because internal costs of organization are low. This argument clearly smacks of the knowledge-based approach to the firm (particularly Kogut and Zander, 1992) rather than of TCE.

However, as Poppo and Zenger (1999) point out, the standard empirical research designs do not discriminate between TCE and competing approaches, such as the measurement approach (Barzel, 1997) or knowledge-based approaches (for example, Arrow, 1974; Demsetz, 1991; Kogut and Zander, 1992). All three approaches will, roughly, predict that specific human capital and firm organization are highly correlated. Poppo and Zenger develop and test a model of comparative institutional performance rather than institutional choice, and thereby examine the degree of support for the three competing explanations of boundary choice. For their sample of firms, they disconfirm the Masten *et al.* hypothesis. However, they also conclude that the evidence points to a need for eclectically combining the three theories for a satisfactory understanding of the boundaries of the firm.

6.3 PROPERTY RIGHTS APPROACHES AND HUMAN CAPITAL

6.3.1 Property Rights and Incomplete Contracts

The property rights approach was initiated in Grossman and Hart (1986) and explicitly motivated as an attempt to model Klein *et al.* (1978) and Williamson's ideas on asset specificity, using game theoretical modeling conventions (see Hart, 1995, for an accessible introduction).[5] However, the outcome of that attempt was essentially a new theory.[6] The basic logic of the approach is as follows. As in Williamson's work, a central assumption is that real-world contracts must necessarily be incomplete in the sense that the allocation of control rights cannot be specified for all future states of the world (Grossman and Hart, 1986). Ownership is defined as the possession of residual rights of control; that is, rights to control the uses of assets under contingencies that are not specified in the contract. Residual rights over human capital cannot be transferred. Control implies the ability to exclude other agents from deciding on the use of certain assets; for example, the owner has the right to pull out the assets he owns from a relation. Such ownership rights can confer bargaining power, and play an important role in the determination of the efficient boundaries of the firm. Thus, control rights determine the boundaries of the firm, which is defined as a collection of jointly owned assets. Obviously, the relevant assets are alienable assets plus, possibly, the owner's inalienable human capital.[7]

Asset ownership is important because the willingness of an agent to undertake a non-contractible investment (notably an investment in human capital) which is specific to the non-alienable asset(s) in the relation depends on who owns the asset(s). If the agent who undertakes the investment does not own the asset, she may, as in Williamson's work, be subject to a hold-up by the owner. On the other hand, the ability to deprive an agent of the piece of capital with which she works (and to which she may be heavily specialized) provides room for authority. Efficiency then dictates that the agent who is to make the most important (non-contractible) asset-specific investment should own the asset. It is not that opportunism can be avoided by internal organization/integration *per se*. Integration may shift incentives for opportunistic behavior, but it does not remove such incentives. Given this, one should choose the ownership arrangement that *via* its impact on incentives minimizes the consequences of opportunism. In sum, the property rights approach is a theory of the efficient allocation of ownership to alienable assets in the presence of investments—typically in human capital—that may be important to value creation, but are non-contractible.

6.3.2 Extensions: Access, Implicit Contracts, and Organization Ownership

Employees are not, strictly speaking, part of the firm, because employees cannot be owned. However as Rajan and Zingales (1998: 388) point out, 'there is a sense in which employees "belong" to an organization ... This sense of belonging arises from the expectation "good citizens" of an organization have that they will receive a share of future organizational rents.' This sort of belonging can be explained within the confines of the property rights approach by invoking the concept of 'access'. This means that agents are allowed to work with critical resources, specialize themselves relative to these resources, and make themselves valuable in this way. Since a specialized employee can control her own specialized human capital, she now has additional power, although she does not possess more residual rights of control. As Rajan and Zingales show, access may sometimes provide better incentives for making efficient effort choices or investments in human capital than direct ownership.

Incentives may also be provided by even softer means. When it is difficult to write complete state-contingent contracts—for example, when certain variables are either *ex ante* unspecifiable or *ex post* unverifiable—people often rely on 'unwritten codes of conduct'; that is, on implicit contracts. These may be self-enforcing, in the sense that each party lives up to the other party's (reasonable) expectations from a fear of retaliation and breakdown of cooperation. In an early extension of the property rights approach, Kreps (1990) argues that employers and employees may be seen as playing a prisoners dilemma game, that with repeated plays a cooperative norm (interpreted as corporate culture) may be established, and that this established norm tells employees (as well as outside contractors) that firm management will not opportunistically take advantage of them. The firm is seen in Kreps' paper, not as a collection of physical assets as in Grossman and Hart (1986), but rather as a carrier of reputation capital. Baker *et al.* (2002) also merge ideas on self-enforcing contracts with property rights, showing how the allocation of ownership influences which relational contracts are feasible. Klein (1991) takes a different approach. He argues that, rather than focusing on individual human or physical assets in the analysis of the boundaries of the firm, attention should be directed to what he calls 'organization ownership'. Thus, Klein argues that vertical integration may imply a certain degree of ownership of human capital after all. For an organization can obtain ownership of another organization's organization capital; that is, the firm-specific knowledge embodied in the organization's team of employees (its capabilities). This can alleviate the hold-up problem, for the reason that it is (post integration) hard for the now integrated team to hold up the acquiring organization. The costs of collective action may be prohibitive, and/or the hold-up attempt may be illegal according to labor law.

6.4 TRANSACTION COST ECONOMICS AND OTHER PERSPECTIVES ON HUMAN CAPITAL

Since its take-off in the mid-1970s, TCE has continuously been subject to strong criticism—in the beginning mainly from Marxists (Marglin, 1974) and sociologists (Perrow, 1986), but lately, increasingly from management scholars (for example, Kogut and Zander 1992; Ghoshal and Moran, 1996). The treatment in the theory of the employment relation and human capital has been particularly criticized. It is characteristic of TCE that human capital is treated like any other asset, and not even its inalienability is emphasized. (In contrast, the inalienable character of human capital is a key point in the property rights approach.) While theoretical generality is to be strived for, there is, of course, the fundamental distinction between human capital and other assets that only human capital is characterized by intention, rationality, motivation, and so on. Implicitly, this recognition lies underneath many of the critiques of TCE.

6.4.1 TCE and Bounded Rationality

As mentioned, bounded rationality is a behavioral starting point for TCE. 'But for bounded rationality', Williamson argues (1996: 36), 'all issues of organization collapse in favor of comprehensive contracting of either Arrow-Debreu or mechanism design kinds.' More generally, Williamson argues that taking more account of the relevant psychological literature will improve the understanding of organization 'as an instrument for utilizing varying cognitive and behavioral propensities to best advantage' (Williamson, 1998: 12).

In spite of his insistence on the necessity of assuming boundedly rational behavior, Williamson is in actuality rather vague on bounded rationality. He notes that '[e]conomizing on bounded rationality takes two forms. One concerns decision processes and the other involves governance structures. The use of heuristic problem-solving…is a decision process response' (Williamson, 1985: 46). The latter 'form' is not central, however, in transaction cost economics, which, Williamson argues, 'is principally concerned…with the economizing consequences of assigning transactions to governance structures in a discriminating way'. Thus, Williamson is interested in making use of bounded rationality for the purpose of explaining the existence and boundaries of firms and therefore the choice between alternative governance structures rather than for the purposes of explaining 'administrative behavior', as in Simon (1947).

However, it is open to some debate whether it makes much sense to separate bounded rationality as an important ingredient in the understanding of governance structures from bounded rationality as the starting point for the understanding of decision processes, as different governance structures probably exhibit different decision process properties (March and Simon, 1958). Clearly, from an organizational theory point of view, the lack of concern with decision processes means that the important possibility that bounds on rationality may be endogenous to organization is not inquired into. Moreover, even from a mainstream TCE position, interest in more far-reaching notions of bounded rationality seems warranted. Thus, while TCE seems to presuppose that organization is highly flexible and plastic, the existence of, for example, endowment effects (Heath et al., 1993) among employees may complicate organizational change and make such change sluggish (for more speculation on these issues, see Foss, 2001).

6.4.2 TCE and Employee Motivation

While the role of bounded rationality in the theory of the firm has given rise to a fair amount of debate (for example, Furubotn and Richter, 1997; Foss, 2001), it is nothing compared to the enormous amount of critical writings on the motivational assumptions in the theory. In particular, opportunism has been a favourite *bête noire*. Some such criticisms (for example, that the theory assumes all agents to be opportunists) can be dismissed as demonstrably false. However, according to a recent critique, which is not so easily dismissed, a primary problem with the treatment of motivation in TCE is not opportunism *per se*, but rather that modern economic approaches assume that all motivation is of the 'extrinsic' type (Ghoshal and Moran, 1996; Osterloh and Frey, 2000). In other words, all behavior is understood in terms of encouragement from an external force, such as the expectance of a monetary reward. (In contrast, when 'intrinsically' motivated, individuals wish to undertake a task because it is inherently interesting to do so.) These arguments do not necessarily deny the reality of opportunism, moral hazard, and so on, but assert that there are other, more appropriate ways to handle these problems than providing monetary incentives, sanctions, and monitoring. The arguments are often based on social psychological research (Deci and Ryan, 1985) and on experimental economics (for example, Fehr and Gächter, 2000).

In one version of the argument, Ghoshal and Moran (1996) argue that the theory of the firm misconstrues the causal relation between motivation (such as the tendency to shirk) and the surrounding environment (the type of governance structure in place). They claim that individuals within an organization perform not according to the incentives and opportunities offered, but to their 'feelings for the entity'. 'Hierarchical' controls, they state, reduce organizational loyalty and thus increase shirking. Reliance on internal governance in the presence of relationship-specific investments, they hold, causes the very problems it is designed to alleviate: Williamson's approach becomes a 'self-fulfilling prophecy', and is therefore 'bad for practice'. Osterloh and Frey (2000) ask which organizational forms are conducive to knowledge creation and transfer. They note that elements of market control (such as high-powered incentives) are often introduced into firms to accomplish this. However, Osterloh and Frey argue that this only works to the extent that there is no 'motivation crowding-out effect' in which extrinsic motivation does not crowd out intrinsic motivation (Deci and Ryan, 1985).

While these critiques are subtle and founded on important research from motivational psychology, it is somewhat questionable how much bite they really have as a critique of TCE. To be sure, intrinsic motivation and so on is not usually raised as an issue by TCE scholars. However, it has been a recurrent theme in TCE that the incentives that characterize internal organization are—and, indeed, generally should be—low-powered (Williamson, 1996). While the mechanism that supports this conclusion may be different (namely, multi-tasking agency theory; Holmström and Milgrom, 1991), the conclusion is the same as the one obtained by psychology-based arguments.

6.4.3 TCE and the Capabilities View

A recurring critique of TCE has concerned its neglect of productive capabilities (for example, Kogut and Zander, 1992). Differential capabilities give rise to different production costs, and such cost differentials may crucially influence the make-or-buy decision: firms may internalize activities because they can carry out these activities in a more production (not transaction) cost-efficient way than other firms are capable of. The factors that make capabilities distinctive and costly to imitate—for example, complexity and tacitness—also mean that such differences in production costs may be long-lived. Knowledge-based writers also claim that the existence of the firm can be explained in knowledge-based terms and without making use of the assumption of opportunism (Hodgson, 2004). Kogut and Zander (1992) argue that firms exist because they can create certain assets—such as learning capabilities or a 'shared context'—that markets purportedly cannot create (Kogut and Zander, 1992: 384). The problem with this argument is that it does not sufficiently characterize *firms*: markets can cultivate learning capabilities and shared context (as in industrial districts) as well. If these assets are indeed largely internalized in firms, it is, from the TCE point of view, exactly because they are firm-specific assets that yield an appropriable quasi-rent. Teece's (1982) early work on diversification, which merged Penrosian arguments (Penrose, 1959) with TCE, made exactly this point.

While TCE scholars may take issue with specific knowledge-based explanations, the view does point to some weak points in the theory of the firm. For example, differential capabilities probably do play a role in determining the boundaries of the firm (Walker and Weber, 1984; Monteverde, 1995; Argyes, 1996). However, there are two major problems in this area that may hinder progress. The first is that the nature of the central construct (capabilities) itself is highly unclear. It is not clear how capabilities are conceptualized, dimensionalized, and measured, and it is not clear how capabilities emerge and are changed by individual action (Abell *et al.*, 2008). The second problem partly follows from the first: the mechanisms between capabilities and economic organization are unclear. This points to a need for understanding in a detailed manner how specific human capital assets combine inside firms to constitute firm-level capabilities.

6.5 CONCLUSIONS

TCE represents the first systematic attempt in the economics and management literatures to explore the organizational ramifications of human capital for economic organization; that is, the choice between alternative contractual and governance structures. While they are certainly taken up with the rationale of the employment contract, Coase and Simon take no particular interest in what we would nowadays call human capital; specifically, they implicitly treat human capital as homogeneous. In contrast, Williamson, building on earlier contributions by Gary Becker and labor market economists, argues that the services of specific human capital would tend to be organized through employment contracts. His treatment of such assets is not fundamentally different from his treatment of other specific assets; the 'fundamental transformation' and so on may obtain for human capital as well as for any other kind of productive asset. However, Williamson clearly recognizes that the law regulating labor transactions is different from the law regulating other transactions.

The property rights approach presents a complementary logic, based on the inalienability of human capital.

TCE is first and foremost intended by its creator(s) as an economics-based theory of the efficient choice of contractual and governance structures. It is not a management theory of, for example, human resource management, although the theory obviously does hold implications for strategic management and organization issues, such as vertical integration, diversification, and so on. However, in actuality, TCE has emerged as one of the important source theories for much theorizing in management. This suggests that the critiques that have been leveled against the theory over at least the last two decades for an inadequate treatment of, particularly, cognition and motivation need to be taken seriously. For example, a more adequate treatment of bounded rationality may lead to the identification and conceptualization of other sources of transaction costs than opportunism (Foss, 2001), transaction costs that are relevant to economic organization. A more sophisticated treatment of motivation, going beyond the extrinsic type that is the sole type of motivation in TCE, may considerably help to nuance TCE explanations (cf. Lindenberg and Foss, 2009).

Acknowledgments

I am grateful to Alan Burton-Jones and J.-C. Spender for comments on an earlier version of this chapter.

Notes

1. But for attempts to take TCE and PPR in a managerial direction, see Rubin (1987) and Milgrom and Roberts (1992).
2. These are claims that have been disputed by what is often referred to as the property rights theorists of the firm. In the words of Grossman and Hart (1986: 691), 'the transaction cost-based argument for integration does not explain how the scope for such behavior changes when one of the self-interested owners becomes an equally self-interested employee of the other owner'.
3. However, as Williamson (1996: 150) points out, this raises the 'puzzle' of the 'impossibility of selective intervention'; namely, '[w]hy can't a large firm do everything that a collection of small firms can and more?' Thus, a large firm could replicate the market and only selectively intervene when there would be expected net gains from this, so that 'the firm will do at least as well as, and will sometimes do better than, the market'. Consequently, firms can grow without limits. As this is absurd, the answer to the question of what are the

efficient boundaries of the firm must involve an understanding of why selective intervention of this kind is impossible—a theory of managerial and hierarchical failure.

4. Comparatively little empirical work deals with agency theory (excepting corporate finance and governance applications), the resource-based view, and the property-rights approach.

5. Indeed, Williamson (1996: 372–3) argued that TCE had progressed from 'pre-formal' (Coase's work) to 'semi-formal' (Williamson's own work) and 'fully formal' (the new property rights view) stages. However, in a later discussion Williamson (2000) finds the new property rights substantially different from his own framework in several key respects.

6. Klein *et al.*, as well as Williamson, have unforeseen contingencies at the heart of their stories. The main problem is the haggling that arises when contracts are pushed outside of their self-enforcing range by unforeseen contingencies. What matters is the *ex post* action. In contrast, most of the incomplete contracting approach assumes that *ex post* bargaining is efficient, and that actions (for example, with respect to investment) are taken immediately after the contract is signed. Thus, what drive these models are misaligned *ex ante* incentives, particularly with respect to investment in vertical buyer–supplier relationships.

7. The basic distinction between an independent contractor and an employee—between an interfirm and an intrafirm transaction—turns on who owns the physical assets which the agent utilizes in his work. An independent contractor owns his tools and so on, while an employee does not.

References

ABELL, P., FELIN, T., and Foss, N. J. (2008). 'Building Micro-Foundations for the Routines, Capabilities, and Performance Links', *Managerial and Decision Economics*, 29: 489–502.

AGHION, P., and TIROLE, J. (1997). 'Formal and Real Authority in Organization', *Journal of Political Economy*, 105: 1–29.

ALCHIAN, A. A., and DEMSETZ, H. (1972). 'Production, Information Costs, and Economic Organization', *American Economic Review*, 62: 772–95.

ANDERSON, E. (1985). 'The Salesperson as Outside Agent or Employee: A Transaction Cost Analysis', *Marketing Science*, 3: 234–54.

——and SCHMITTLEIN, D. C. (1984). 'Integration of the Sales Force: An Empirical Examination', *Rand Journal of Economics*, 15: 3–19.

ARGYRES, N. S. (1996). 'Evidence on the Role of Firm Capabilities in Vertical Integration Decisions', *Strategic Management Journal*, 17: 129–50.

ARROW, K. J. (1974). *The Limits of Organization* (New York: Norton).

BAKER, G., GIBBONS, R., and MURPHY, K. J. (1999). 'Informal Authority in Organizations', *Journal of Law, Economics and Organization*, 1: 56–73.

—— —— ——(2002). 'Relational Contracts and the Theory of the Firm', *Quarterly Journal of Economics*, 117: 39–83.

BARZEL, Y. (1997). *Economic Analysis of Property Rights* (Cambridge: Cambridge University Press).

——and KOCHIN, L. A. (1992). 'Ronald Coase on the Nature of Social Cost as a Key to the Problem of the Firm', *Scandinavian Journal of Economics*, 94: 19–31.

BECKER, G. (1964). *Human Capital: A Theoretical and Empirical Analysis with Special Reference to Education* (3rd edn. Chicago: University of Chicago Press).

——(1991). *A Treatise on the Family* (Cambridge, Mass.: Harvard University Press).

BUCHANAN, J. M. (1965). 'An Economic Theory of Clubs', *Economica*, 32: 1–14.

COASE, R. H. (1937). 'The Nature of the Firm', in N. J. Foss (ed.), *The Theory of the Firm: Critical Perspectives in Business and Management*, ii (London: Routledge, 1999).

——(1960). 'The Problem of Social Cost', *Journal of Law and Economics*, 3: 1–44.

COYLE-SHAPIRO, J., and KESSLER, I. (2000). 'Consequences of the Psychological Contract for the Employment Contract: A Large-Scale Survey', *Journal of Management Studies*, 7: 903–30.

CROCKER, K. J., and MASTEN, S. E. (1996). 'Regulation and Administered Contracts Revisited: Lessons from Transaction-Cost Economics for Public Utility Regulation', *Journal of Regulatory Economics*, 9: 5–39.

DAVID, J. R., and HAN, S. (2003). 'A Systematic Assessment of the Empirical Support for Transaction Cost Economics', *Strategic Management Journal*, 1: 39–58.

DECI, E. L., and RYAN, R. M. (1985). *Intrinsic Motivation and Self-Determination in Human Behavior* (New York: Plenum).

DEMSETZ, H. (1991). 'The Theory of the Firm Revisited', in O. E. Williamson and S. G. Winter (ed.), *The Nature of the Firm* (Oxford: Blackwell, 1993).

DOERINGER, P. B., and PIORE, M. J. (1971). *Internal Labor Markets and Manpower Analysis* (Lexington, Mass.: Heath Lexington Books, D. C. Heath & Co.).

DOW, G. K. (1987). 'The Function of Authority in Transaction Cost Economics', *Journal of Economic Behaviour and Organization*, 1: 13–38.

DYER, J. (1997). 'Effective Interfirm Collaboration: How Firms Minimize Transaction Costs and Maximize Transaction Value', *Strategic Management* Journal, 18: 535–56.

FEHR, E., and GÄCHTER, S. (2000). 'Fairness and Retaliation: The Economics of Reciprocity', *Journal of Economic Perspectives*, 3: 159–81.

FOSS, K., and FOSS, N. J. (2001). 'Assets, Attributes and Ownership', *International Journal of the Economics of Business*, 8: 1937.

—— ——and VAZQUEZ, X. H. (2006). 'Tying the Manager's Hands: Constraining Opportunistic Managerial Intervention', *Cambridge Journal of Economics*, 5: 797–818.

FOSS, N. J. (2001). 'Bounded Rationality in the Economics of Organization: Present Use and Future Possibilities', *Journal of Management and Governance*, 5: 401–25.

——(2003). 'Selective Intervention and Internal Hybrids: Interpreting and Learning from the Rise and Decline of the Oticon Spaghetti Organization', *Organization Science*, 3: 331–49.

FURUBOTN, E., and RICHTER, R. (1997). *Institutions and Economic Theory* (Ann Arbor, Mich.: Michigan University Press).

GHOSHAL, S., and MORAN, P. (1996). 'Bad for Practice: A Critique of the Transaction Cost Theory', *Academic Management Review*, 21: 13–47.

GROSSMAN, S. J., and HART, O. (1986). 'The Costs and Benefits of Ownership: A Theory of Vertical Integration', *Journal of Political Economy*, 94(4): 691–719.

HART, O. (1995). *Firms, Contracts, and Financial Structure* (Oxford: Oxford University Press).

HEATH, C., KNEZ, M., and CAMERER, C. (1993). 'The Strategic Management of the Entitlement Process in the Employment Relationship', *Strategic Management Journal*, 14(8): 75–93.

HEIDE, J. B., and JOHN, G. (1988). 'The Role of Dependence Balancing in Safeguarding Transaction-Specific Investments', *Journal of Marketing*, 52: 20–35.

HODGSON, G. (2004). 'Opportunism is Not the Only Reason Why Firms Exist: Why an Explanatory Emphasis on Opportunities may Mislead Management Strategy', *Industrial and Corporate Change*, 13(2): 403–20.

HOLMSTRÖM, B., and MILGROM, P. R. (1991). 'Multitask Principal-Agent Analysis: Incentive Contracts, Asset Ownership, and Job Design', *Journal of Law, Economics and Organization*, 7: 24–52.

JOHN, G., and WEITZ, A. (1988). 'Forward Integration into Distribution: An Empirical Test of Transaction Cost Analysis', *Journal of Law, Economics, and Organization*, 2: 337–55.

KLEIN, B. (1991). 'Vertical Integration as Organizational Ownership: The Fisher Body/ General Motors Relationship', in O. E. Williamson and S. G. Winter (eds.), *The Nature of the Firm: Origins, Evolution, and Development* (Oxford: Oxford University Press).

—— CRAWFORD, R., and ALCHIAN, A. (1978). 'Vertical Integration, Appropriable Rents, and the Competitive Contracting Process', *Journal of Law and Economics*, 21: 297–326.

KOGUT, B., and ZANDER, U. (1992). 'Knowledge of the Firm: Combinative Capabilities, and the Replication of Technology', *Organizational Science*, 3: 383–97.

KREPS, D. M. (1990). 'Corporate Culture and Economic Theory', in J. G. Alt and K. Shepsle (eds.), *Perspectives on Positive Political Economy* (Cambridge: Cambridge University Press), 90–143.

LINDENBERG, S., and N. J. Foss (2009). 'How Firms Work? A Goal-Framing Theory of the Firm', unpublished manuscript.

LOASBY, B. J. (1995). 'Running a Business: An Appraisal of Economic Change by Milgrom and Roberts', *Industrial and Corporate Change*, 2: 471–89.

MARCH, J. G., and SIMON, H. A. (1958). *Organizations* (New York: Wiley).

MACHER, J., and RICHMAN, B. (2006). 'Transaction Cost Economics: An Assessment of Empirical Research in the Social Sciences', unpublished manuscript, Georgetown University.

MARGLIN, S. (1974). 'What do Bosses Do?', *Review of Radical Political Economics*, 2: 60–112.

MASTEN, S. (1984). 'The Organization of Production: Evidence from the Aerospace Industry', *Journal of Law and Economics*, 27: 403–17.

——(1996). 'Empirical Research in Transaction Cost Economics: Challenges, Progress, Directions', in John Groenewegen, *Transaction Cost Economics and Beyond* (Boston: Kluwer), 93–164.

—— MEEHAN, J. W., and SNYDER, E. A. (1991). 'The Costs of Organization', *Journal of Law, Economics, and Organization* 7: 1–25.

MILGROM, P., and ROBERTS, R. (1992). *Economics, Organization, and Management* (Englewood Cliffs, NJ: Prentice-Hall).

MONTEVERDE, K. (1995). 'Technical Dialog as an Incentive for Vertical Integration in the Semiconductor Industry', *Management Science*, 10: 1624–38.

——and TEECE, D. J. (1982). 'Supplier Switching Costs and Vertical Integration in the Automobile Industry', *Bell Journal of Economics*, 13: 206–13.

NELSON, R. R., and WINTER, S. G. (1982). *An Evolutionary Theory of Economic Change* (Cambridge, Mass.: Harvard University Press).

OSTERLOH, M., and FREY, B. S. (2000). 'Motivation, Knowledge Transfer and Organizational Form', *Organization Science*, 11: 538–50.

OUCHI, W. (1980). 'Markets, Bureaucracies, and Clans', *Administrative Science Quarterly*, 25: 129–41.

PENROSE, E. (1959). *The Theory of the Growth of the Firm* (New York: Wiley).

PERROW, C. (1986). *Complex Organizations: A Critical Essay* (3rd edn. New York: Random House).

POPPO, L., and ZENGER, T. (1999). 'Testing Alternative Theories of the Firm: Transaction Cost, Knowledge-Based, and Measurement Explanations for Make-or-Buy Decisions in Information Services', *Strategic Management Journal*, 19: 853–77.

RAJAN, R. G., and ZINGALES, L. (1998). 'Power in a Theory of the Firm', *Quarterly Journal of Economics*, 113: 387–432.

ROUSSEAU, D. M., and PARKS, J. M. (1992). 'The Contracts of Individuals and Organizations', in B. M. Staw and L. L. Cummings (eds.), *Research in Organizational Behavior*, 15 (Greenwich, Conn.: JAI Press), 1–43.

RUBIN, PAUL H. (1987). *Managing Business Transactions* (New York: Free Press).

SAUSSIER, S. (2000). 'Transaction Costs and Contractual Incompleteness: The Case of Électricité de France', *Journal of Economic Behavior and Organization*, 42: 189–206.

SHELANSKI, H., and KLEIN, P. G. (1995). 'Transaction Cost Economics: A Review and Assessment', *Journal of Law, Economics and Organisation*, 11: 334–61.

SIMON, H. A. (1947). *Administrative Behavior* (New York: Macmillan).

—— (1951). 'A Formal Theory of the Employment Relationship', in Simon, *Models of Bounded Rationality* (Cambridge, Mass.: MIT Press, 1982).

TEECE, D. J. (1980). 'The Diffusion of an Administrative Innovation', *Management Science*, 5: 464–70.

—— (1982). 'Towards an Economic Behaviour and Organization', *Journal of Economic Behavior and Organization*, 3: 39–63.

WALKER, G., and WEBER, D. (1984). 'A Transaction Cost Approach to Make-or-Buy Decisions,' *Administrative Science Quarterly*, 3: 373–91.

WILLIAMSON, O. E. (1971). 'The Vertical Integration of Production: Market Failure Considerations', *American Economic Review*, 61: 112–23.

—— (1973). 'Markets and Hierarchies: Some Elementary Considerations', *American Economic Review*, 2: 316–25.

—— (1975). *Markets and Hierarchies* (New York: Free Press).

—— (1985). *The Economic Institutions of Capitalism* (New York: Free Press).

—— (1991). 'Comparative Economic Organization: The Analysis of Discrete Structural Alternatives', *Administrative Science Quarterly*, 36: 269–96.

—— (1996). *The Mechanisms of Governance* (Oxford: Oxford University Press).

—— (1998). 'Human Behavior and Transaction Cost Economics', unpublished manuscript.

—— (2000). 'The New Institutional Economics: Taking Stock, Looking Ahead', *Journal of Economic Literature*, 38: 595–613.

—— (2002). 'The Lens of Contract: Private Ordering', *American Economic Review*, 92 (Papers and Proceedings): 438–43.

—— WACHTER, M. L., and HARRIS, J. E. (1975). 'Understanding the Employment Relation: The Analysis of Idiosyncratic Exchange', *Bell Journal of Economics*, 6: 250–80.

CHAPTER 7

HUMAN CAPITAL AND AGENCY THEORY

J.-C. SPENDER

A connection between human capital and agency theory seems obvious enough. As Jensen and Meckling told it, principal–agent theory (PAT) examines the difficulties facing principals (owners) investing in the economic activity of agents (managers) whose knowledge and interests differ from their own; they wondered why modes of corporate governance that separate ownership and control were so prevalent (Jensen and Meckling, 1976: 330). When principal and agent are defined by their human capital (HC), the 'agency problem' can be framed by the difference. Other economists, suggesting HC is information, define the agency problem in terms of information asymmetries between principal and agent (for example, Arrow, 1991: 44). But agency is about more than knowing and deciding on another's behalf; it is also about acting knowledgably and intentionally in the world, bringing one's own HC to bear in a particular situation that is neither fully known nor fully determined by 'causes' (for example, Emirbayer and Mische, 1998). People are then boundedly rational, their situations open to change through their action. HC expands from 'know what' to cover 'know how' and 'know why'—for how we know something depends on our intentions and utilities (Ryle, 1954; Urmson, 1988: 20). We admit 'risk propensity' as a dimension of 'know how'. The embeddedness of social and network capital indicates 'know who'. Agency also suggests something of 'know when'—awareness of the passage of time and the moment of appropriate action—and 'know where'—a spatial appreciation of the situation.

   We can use this richer concept of HC to do an analysis of PAT that takes us beyond the simplicity of *homo economicus*—but it might hide HC's own problems, to which I turn first. We can also frame PAT as a 'thought experiment' about colliding different kinds of 'capital'—financial (what owners put up) with human (what labor brings to the activity)—to be enriched with social, organizational, and institutional capitals contributed from outside the principal–agent relationship. While Adam Smith's mix of land, labor, and financial capitals leads to enterprise, treating HC as different from financial capital raises questions about capital theory yet to be fully addressed (Dean and Kretschmer, 2007; Harvey, 1982). There are also questions about whether we should treat HC as a theoretical construct or as an heuristic for illuminating management's practical problems (Spender, 2009). Clearly HC is more than a rhetorical flourish to draw attention to the people involved in socioeconomic processes. Its boundedness and contextuality means its value depends on its application—and value is not the same as cost. Proposals to 'measure' HC in some way other than *ex post* by its economic impact, stand on heroic assumptions that trump any weakness in the 'instrument' chosen (for example, AVSI, 2008; Bassi and McMurrer, 2008; Castello and Domenech, 2002; Weisbrod, 1961). There are also connections between an individual's HC and the infrastructure of its application. The value of what one person knows depends on what others know—like driving on the right side of the highway—leading to 'externalities'. Plus, at the firm level, if application is crucial to estimating value, where do we fit in the manager's (principal's) knowledge about how to get her/his employees (agents) to apply their HC appropriately—as a separate body of 'managerial' HC or as an aspect of what makes the employees' HC of value in the first place? Given a division of labor, every individual's HC admits the possibility that the coordinator's HC may be more valuable than the employees'—undermining the claim that theirs is 'the firm's most strategic asset'. Such nostalgia may be no more than a trope in the capitalist process. But accepting the difference between principal and agent as axiomatic means HC is framed as heterogeneous and its value contingent on the context of its application—and these contexts vary widely from the national and firm level to the individual.

Our volume is directed toward the business school community wherein many presume HC is at the level of the individual—mobile, potentially measurable, and perhaps inalienable. Yet a glance at Becker's *Human Capital* volume, or the *American Economic Review* and *Journal of Political Economy* papers that preceded it, confirms that his target was the relationship between education and economic growth at the national level (Becker, 1959, 1962, 1993). His individuals are 'representative', their attributes stated in formulae, age, levels of or years of schooling, or on-the-job training, and so on, their educational choices presumed to 'maximize their well-being'. He did not consider how education would lead to economic success. Others extended his analysis, adding how representative students might differ in other ways: social class, parental education attainments, family connections, and so on. His program's data are not about individual-level HC; they are at the macrolevel relating national policies and outcomes, hence there is no substantial connection between Becker's analysis and our current use of HC at the individual level or the presupposition that HC might be a firm-level resource.

Becker's inquiry into the determinants of national economic growth was in a tradition that goes back at least to Sir William Petty's seventeenth-century speculations about labor as a factor of production and the UK's inventory of human capital as a significant part of its wealth (Ehrlich and Murphy, 2007; Spiegel, 1971: 126). Becker sought an economics of education following Schultz's and Mincer's initiatives (Becker, 1993: p. xxii, foreword). His contemporaries, such as Enke, Schultz, and Weisbrod, also explored measuring national capital (Enke, 1960; Schultz, 1961a, 1961b; Weisbrod, 1961). Becker hypothesized the growth not explained by rising workforce numbers, physical capital (such as plant), or technology sprang from a residual category of production factors, 'labor quality'—relabeled 'human capital' after some hesitation (Becker, 1993: 16). The links between national policies on education—and health care (Becker, 1962: 9 n., foreword)—and such economy-driving HC seemed common sense, but ignored the fact that much education is of no obvious economic relevance; for example, the study of ancient languages or the history of art. But if educational inputs are not valuable *ex definitio*, their value must be established through their application—and agency issues are entailed. Becker's interest in formal education also made him aware of the amount of on-the-job training, drawing both public and private sector institutions into his analysis as socioeconomic entities that consumed the outputs of the educational system but made investments themselves. His HC-based theory of the firm—an apparatus to take up and generate HC, and to transfer earnings from younger employees to older holders of accrued job-specific HC—seems forgotten (Becker, 1962: 48; Topel, 1991). But his sense of HC as non-rivalrous supported Clark's earlier 'knowledge is the only instrument of production that is not subject to diminishing returns' (Clark, 1923), helping open up thinking about endogenous growth—the possibility that an individual's, a firm's, or a nation's learning might return substantially more than its cost (Lucas, 1988; Romer, 1994).

In this chapter I consider the 'obvious' relationship between HC and agency theory (AT) with two goals in mind. First, to show how principal–agent theory (PAT)—the AT variant most understand by agency theory—clarifies HC as a way of describing individuals in the organizational context. Second, to explore how PAT's own shortcomings illuminate possibilities implicit but underexplored in the HC literature, for while a workplace relationship between PAT and HC seems obvious, it is conceptually complicated. I begin with a review of the two concepts' history and the research programs from which they emerged. After considering the PAT/HC interaction I show how HC might contribute to the theory of the firm. Many see the firm as a socioeconomic context in which HC and agency issues collide under management's direction as other forms of capital enter the mix. Foss's and Loasby's chapters remind us there are many intuitions about what firms are and why they exist: bureaucracy, team production, transaction costs analysis, property rights, nexus of contracts, and so on (Furubotn and Pejovich, 1972; Gibbons, 2005; Holmstrom and Tirole, 1989; Mahoney, 1992; Pitelis and Teece, 2009; Williamson and Winter, 1991). In this handful PAT stands out by treating the management of interindividual differences of interest and information as central, offering a more formal analysis than anything available within the behavioral and organization theory (OT) traditions. In the background lies the great and almost forgotten project of bringing the divergent discourses of economics and OT—as in 'markets and hierarchies'—together again into a practical theory of the firm (Cyert and March, 1963: 16; Prendergast, 1999; Weber, 1968).

Today's thinking about HC at the macrolevel is relatively novel, in spite of Petty's speculations. That individuals are heterogeneous, making it important for others to judge an individual's skills and learning, is as old as human history. Likewise the notion of 'human capital' is as old as the Chinese proverb about teaching a man to fish, so feeding him for a lifetime, rather than giving him a single fish. Lane framed capital as the recognition of the value of making a hay-rake before setting out to stack the hay (Lane, 1969: 5). Adam Smith wrote of HC as one of four types of 'fixed capital'—land, finance, labor power, and knowledge—and an early *QJE* article noted the problems of considering people's knowledge as capital (Walsh, 1935). Those who presume an individual's 'natural rights' and think of HC metaphorically or ideologically as 'inalienable', may overlook HC's complex history. In the Europe and US of Smith's time, and well into the nineteenth century, human labor could be legally owned by another and also traded (Schmidt, 1998; Steinfeld, 1991). Employment law often gives firms rights over their employees' labor, if only to deny it to others. Thus, while Becker adopted Marshall's observation that 'the most valuable of all capital is that invested in human beings' as *Human Capital*'s epigraph, by no means did Marshall have in mind today's de-historicized 'inalienable' notion. The ownership, investment, and use of HC are always aspects of the social and legal systems of their time. What HC means is a matter of situated practice, constrained by employment and contract law, institutional, religious, and professional mores and so on—complexities matched by the difficulties of analyzing the consequences of HC's application. Pigou, one of Marshall's students, noted that the benefits of an individual's investments in education, such as piano lessons, often blur with those in consumption, such a piano playing (see also Schultz, 1961*a*).

In the light of these HC forerunners the novelty of Becker's work lay in its attempt to formalize a macrolevel approach towards an economic and social issue previously discussed anecdotally at the individual or class level. His formalization can be traced to Lewis's 'two-sector' macromodel theorizing the movement of labor from the agriculture sector into manufacturing (Lewis, 1954). Likewise, Schultz looked for an 'economics of agriculture' and paid attention to the post-war recoveries of both Germany and Japan that he argued were education-driven (Johnson and Mellor, 1961). A glance at Ehrlich and Murphy's opening editorial for the *Journal of Human Capital* or at Fleischhauer's recent summary of the state of HC theory shows that current HC research is more a continuation of Becker's macrolevel project rather than evidence of new attention to an HC-based theory of the firm or its management (Ehrlich and Murphy, 2007; Fleischhauer, 2007).

In contrast, many of our volume's authors echo variations of the 'human capital is the firm's most important asset' mantra, implying the need for an HC-based theory of the firm. It may be this idea does not come from Becker at all, but from Adam Smith and Marx, via Bell and his influential *The Coming of Post-Industrial Society* (Bell, 1999). Following Weber's notion of the 'disenchantment of the world' Bell surmised that an epochal transformation was under way, destroying traditional socio-economic patterns and transferring power into the hands of an emerging technocratic elite and professionalized 'meritocracy'. In a democratic capitalist system, corporations and legal and financial institutions are this elite's loci of action. Economic organizations, businesses, agencies, and bureaucracies are rising in importance while religious, academic, and voluntary institutions are declining, leading to changes in individuals' HC as they adapt to this new environment. Bell reconstituted Marx's labor theory of value and class around the distinction between professional and blue-collar work within the narrow contexts of firms and social institutions. His arguments paralleled those of contemporary sociologists (for example, Kerr *et al.*, 1964; Mills, 1959; Mumford, 1967; Wiener, 1967; Young, 1994). They extended Weber's arguments to the popular notion of a 'knowledge-based economy' (for example, Reich, 1992), reinforced by Drucker's influential writings (for example, Drucker, 1988, 1992). Becker's somewhat tangential interest in firm-specific training and his distinction between general and specific on-the-job training picked up on Pigou's analysis of firms' free-riding on public goods and the debate about whether firms should be rewarded for providing vocational training that could be useful to others (Stevens, 1999). In general the Becker program still focuses on the national education system and its macro-economic impact (for example, Hartog and van den Brink, 2007).

A first conclusion, then, is that to make sense of HC we must be explicit about its application context. This varies from the national level—Becker's program—to the firm or institutional level—Bell's program—and then, perhaps, to the individual level. Likewise, HC's 'obvious' connections to agency differ according to level—to differences of information and interest between individuals, organizations, institutions, or nations. But nowhere can HC stand on its own as an abstraction; its application context must be recognized. Of course, knowledge of context is not all there is to HC, but it is clearly material to its value. Measured in terms of its real-world impact, HC points to the agent's (individual, firm, or nation) ability to note, negotiate, and manipulate a specific situation. Likewise, it presupposes a socioeconomy open to manipulation by agents with relevant HC—a point made in many other chapters (for example, Nahapiet, Chapter 2) that HC presupposes social, organizational, or structural capital, that it is simply one of several 'capitals' that are mutually constituting and defining (Coleman, 1988; Spender, 2009).

If all capitals are interconnected it makes little sense to separate individually held capital from the interpersonal or 'relational'. The much-cited typology of 'intellectual capitals', of human, relational, and organizational types, points less towards the possibility of defining or measuring them separately than to restating their mutual constitution and definition—the impossibility of one without the others (Stewart, 1997; Sveiby, 1997). Thus the 'obvious' connection between HC and AT, and thereby to the human capital of others, is but one aspect of its contextualized nature. PAT suggests one application context, albeit stylized and minimalist. It follows that HC as knowledge about purposive human action in a specific socio-economic context differs from impersonal 'scientific' knowledge of Nature. Not only can HC not stand on its own; it necessarily hangs within frames shared with others who differ from us. So while AT implies HC, so HC implies AT. In the next section I review the emergence of AT. In particular, I expose contradictions in its literature that have important implications for HC and its application in organizational contexts.

7.1 PRINCIPAL–AGENT THEORY

Just as HC is an old concept newly refashioned into a 'revolution' in micro-economics (Ehrlich and Murphy, 2007; Jensen, 1983), agency theory has been recently refashioned. Princes, merchants, and estate owners long relied on agents to make decisions on their behalf, and the troubles this leads to are equally well known. Machiavelli proposed Draconian pre-emptive measures should agents not heed their masters' bidding (Williamson, 1993). Throughout books 4 and 5 of the *Wealth of Nations*—those discussing (*a*) the economic challenges of managing the British colonies and (*b*) the inherent weaknesses of the joint-stock companies then being formed, such as the South Sea Company—Smith devoted attention to the utility and perils of using agents. He advised against rigid regulations to prevent the servants of overseas corporations, such as the East India Company or the African Company, trading on their own behalf. Generally he urged aligning the interests of the agents with those of the parent company via its arrangements for defense and credit. He was less concerned with the agent's technical competence, and more with how their interests intruded into the company's affairs—a lesson for today. If alignment could be achieved, the agents would see themselves as corporate entrepreneurs despite not being owners of the main enterprise. Instead, they would own a small dependent subsidiary (their night-job). Analyzing the same challenges, Adams noted the overseas agents' dependencies; the lack of a labor market or of alternative positions obliging agents to share risks with their directors—so comprising a mode of governance (Adams, 1996).

Smith was thoroughly familiar with the centuries of accumulated experience of using agents in the Arabian, Indian, and China trades from the time of the rise of

Islam (for example, M. G. S. Hodgson, 1974; Labib, 1969; Risso, 1995) as well as in England from before the time of the Magna Carta (for example, Danziger and Gillingham, 2003). He was also familiar with the economic forces separating owner-ship and control as the precursor to raising capital, expanding trade, and growing the economy (Chaudhuri, 1985: 203). This separation was common by the twelfth century—evident, for instance, in Shakespeare's *The Merchant of Venice*—with at least three effects. First, before secure government investments such as T-Bills were available, when the opportunities in their own businesses were exhausted, success-ful traders had to invest surplus funds to protect them from theft or royal seizure—as in Marlowe's *The Jew of Malta*. This meant delegating a degree of control to others. Second, expanding trade required new methods of gathering funds for projects more costly than traders alone could afford, requiring a means of governance of the resources of others. Third, it became crucial to distinguish individuals from their money, socially and legally, so setting the stage for the distinction between an indi-vidual's own capital and that which, although in his possession, was owned by another, and thus for double-entry book-keeping—all additional preconditions for a capital market (Labib, 1969).

Thus the stylized principal–agent theory that emerged from Jensen and Meckling was far from the whole of our experience of this 'profoundly sociological' relation-ship (Shapiro, 2005). In an academic sense, Jensen and Meckling took off from a discussion of 'moral hazard' (for example, Mirrlees, 1999; Spence and Zeckhauser, 1971) and another about incentives and the trade-off with risk (Prendergast, 1999; Sappington, 1991; Shavell, 1979; Simon, 1951). The agency relationship was defined as 'one in which one or more persons (principals) engaged others (agents) to perform some service on their behalf which involved delegating some decision-making authority to the agent' (Jensen and Meckling, 1976: 308). Economists saw quickly that this opened up the 'black box' of the firm by presuming two categories of indi-vidual within and drawing attention to the problematics of their relationship. Kiser's definition was looser: 'Agency theory is a general model of social relations involving some delegation of authority and generally resulting in problems of control' (1999: 146). There was an associated body of contract law governing an agent's legal obliga-tions and the principal's remedies that varied across time and place, and changing social and institutional norms governing collaborative behavior, especially among professionals (Hart and Moore, 1990; Williamson, 2002). Sociology likewise dealt with interindividual relations and social order.

PAT's appeal to theorists of the firm and its management lay in the way it formal-ized an elemental relationship that differed from both a market relationship and a direct power relationship. Many previous OT theorists sought neo-Weberian theo-ries based on power—present in organizations (as in bureaucratic theory) but absent in perfect markets (a nod to 'methodological individualism'). Transaction cost economics, in contrast, focused on cost differences, presupposing the existence of both firm and market and dealing with the firm's boundary and size, rather than its reason for existing (Casson, 1982; Dosi and Marengo, 2007; Pitelis, 1993; Williamson, 2005). Agency theory's focus on information and interest differences tempted some to see PAT as an information-based theory of organization—an 'informated' bureaucratic theory perhaps (Eisenhardt, 1989). Yet the reasons why principal and agent come together in the first place remained unclear. An agent may well be more skilled than the principal whose capital comes from elsewhere, and an agent might also have more timely information, especially if opportunities for new deals were arising 'on the spot'. But, equally, the agent might be less competent, putting the principal's capital at risk beyond that agreed to, or engage in non-transparent non-productive behavior, calling for monitoring by the principal or by a second overseer-agent.

Many proclaimed PAT a new theory of the firm that offered insights about organizations large and small, for-profit and not-for-profit, commercial and academic (Fama and Jensen, 1983a: 301; Jensen and Meckling, 1976: 327). It was of special significance to business educators because of its impact on our core concepts, for it redefined the manager's role as the shareholders' agent, charged to maximize their wealth rather than the firm's productivity, its decision-making capability, or even its customers' satisfaction (Jensen, 1983). Many sharply criticized this shift from efficiency, arguing that it transformed 'managerial' capitalism into 'shareholder' capitalism (for example, Donaldson, 1990a, 1990b; Dore et al., 1999; Williams, 2000) and, as a result, overemphasized the owners' interests at the expense of the managers', the employees', the public's, or those of various other 'stakeholders' (Freeman, 1984; Ghoshal and Moran, 1996; Khurana, 2007; Lazonick and O'sullivan, 2000; Pfeffer and Fong, 2004). Organizational sociologists such as Perrow argued that PAT misrepresented both the nature of individuals and our understanding of their interactions and organizations (Perrow, 1986). Clearly, in today's climate of executive excess and widespread political malfeasance, it is tempting to pillory PAT and its proponents for seeming to validate these ethical and moral lapses, however legal they are (McCloskey, 2006; Pirson et al., 2009).

It is not clear whether these charges are warranted. Jensen and Meckling (1976: 307) and Fama (1980: 288) were explicit in presenting PAT as a push-back against popular but loose 'behavioral' or 'managerialist' theorizing, especially that coming out of Carnegie Tech. The Rochester and Chicago argument was that such views led to misunderstandings about corporate social responsibility, viable governance structures, and the separation of ownership of control and, in many cases, seemed to reject fundamental economic principles of maximizing (such as satisficing) and formal modeling. So the early PAT papers were less about the ethical implications of the principal–agent relationship than about getting back on track towards real (formal) economics. These writers noted that the separation of ownership and control went back 'at least' to Adam Smith and Berle and Means (1968; Fama and Jensen, 1983b), but overlooked Veblen's *Theory of the Business Enterprise* (1904: Veblen, 1965). Veblen argued that a business can be viable only when there is a gap between what the firm's managers know and what its owners and customers know—when there are differences in their HCs (Veblen, 1965: 148 n.). Veblen not only recognized the 'agency problem'; he made it fundamental to his theory of the firm.

PAT presumed two classes of individual with idiosyncratic knowledge and interests. Rather than interact through the market, they interacted within the firm in ways captured in the language of economics rather than of power. Jensen and Meckling's analysis was specifically of investment situations wherein (*a*) managers can draw both financial and non-financial benefits (perquisites) and (*b*) owners, whose benefits are solely financial, can expend funds to monitor them. They went beyond the agency costs associated directly with bounded rationality—monitoring, surveillance, or bonding—to consider the less direct costs when things did not turn out as agreed and led to 'residual loss' (Jensen and Meckling, 1976: 308). As they sought an economic optimum, their analysis turned on the role played by efficient markets 'characterized by rational expectations' (Jensen and Meckling, 1976: 345). These provided the prices that enabled them to draw their graphs and offer determinative solutions. Retaining the agent's self-interested choosing, suppressed in a bureaucracy, the firm was redefined in terms close to two-person game theory with a two-currency (two-interest) payoff.

Fama argued that Alchian and Demsetz's and Jensen and Meckling's 'striking insight' opened up the 'black box' to view the firm as a 'set of contracts among the factors of production' (Fama, 1980: 289). But Fama thought this did not go far enough—for while the firm was a 'nexus of contracts' for the factors of production, their coordination was also about allocating the firm's risks (Shavell, 1979). When these are shared between owners, managers, and even employees, simple concepts of entrepreneurship and ownership collapse. Indeed, noting 'the ownership of capital should not be confused with ownership of the firm', Fama argued that the latter should be abandoned and with it much of the talk about separating ownership and control. Real-world contracts are often open-ended or incomplete (Hart, 1991) and in many situations non-existent (Macaulay, 1963). Viewing the PAT relationship as an elemental firm, Fama separated the overall task of entrepreneurship into its constituent parts. Admitting differences of interest between individuals, he also distinguished the practice of 'management' (a knowledge-based coordination and control activity) from that of 'risk bearing' (typically but not necessarily involving up-front funding). Skipping traditional HC definitions as 'knowledge and skills' he defined the manager's HC as an outcome, the stream of her/his future wages following their knowledge and skills' application (Fama, 1980: 297). Fama's model presumed multiple periods and the consequences of managing and risk-bearing, and was thus more realistic than Jensen and Meckling's market-price-dependent single period model (Jensen and Meckling, 1976: 351). *Inter alia*, Fama's model made space for the theory of employment suggested by Coase in which unenterprising employees sought 'insurance' against the uncertainties of being jobless even while realizing their labor would benefit others (the risk-bearing security-holders) (Coase, 1991).

Fama also realized that the separation between his two types of HC—'managing' and 'risk-bearing'—was institutionally contingent, workable only because (a) residual risk-bearers—and claimants—could trade the various risks they took into specialized capital markets, and (b) owners could use the external labor market for managers to 'discipline' the non-risk-bearing managers' behavior—a restatement of the Smith and Adams points mentioned earlier. Such capital and labor markets are institutional in the sense of being time-full ongoing interactions wherein memory and expectations play a crucial role. They are not spot markets that equilibrate and clear in a timeless instant. Fama took the idea that an external labor market might influence the firm's managers, so providing owners with control beyond that in the Jensen and Meckling analysis, from Alchian and Demsetz (Fama, 1980; 294). At the same time, even though risk-bearers could use the capital markets, the added safety of a portfolio of investments would incline them to diversify their risks away from the one firm. Fama concluded the 'efficient allocation of risk-bearing seems to imply a large degree of separation of security ownership from control of a firm' (Fama, 1980: 291). Even given adequate internal monitoring and transparency, the signals provided by the labor and capital markets could act powerfully on the various agents' decisions and make it possible to integrate the 'nexus of contracts' into the viable economic entity then open to the further market 'discipline' provided by competing firms.

In this way Fama distanced his theory from that of Jensen and Meckling and of Alchian and Allen (1969) and Alchian and Demsetz (1972). In later papers together with Jensen, Fama seemed to retreat from his initial institutionally contingent model in the pursuit of more generic mathematical models (Fama and Jensen, 1983a, 1983b). They argued that the adoption of the 'nexus of contracts' model of the firm allowed a restatement of the 'agency problem': 'An important factor in the survival of organizational forms is control of agency problems. Agency problems arise because contracts are not costlessly written and enforced' (Fama and Jensen, 1983a: 327). Were a set of 'complete contracts' available, the agency problem would disappear, for the firm could not then be distinguished from an efficient market. While the later Fama and Jensen definition differed from their earlier one—indeed they did not even try to define the cause of the agency problem—PAT's significance lay in how it distinguished a firm from an efficient market or pure power relationship, entwining the agency problem in the nexus of contracts approach. As a firm embraced multiple agents, so different interests were drawn in. If these did not differ, the agency problem would be reduced to one of information asymmetry alone, and so priceable, as without differences of interest there is no agency problem. Fama showed that when these are present, rational individuals cannot resolve the agency problem unless they share and submit to a common institutional context. Second, while Fama's model seemed to make risk axiomatic, it actually brought Knightian uncertainty into the analysis (Knight, 1965). Knightian risk can be priced, as in the Jensen and Meckling model, but in the Fama model risk cannot, for it includes Knightian uncertainty.

7.2 UNCERTAINTY

Uncertainty perplexes and cannot be theorized—else it would no longer be uncertain. However, it can be illuminated (Spender, 1989: 43). Both Knight and Keynes argued that much economic activity involves our 'simply not knowing' (Keynes, 1937: 214; Knight, 1965). This need not end the discussion, for there are several ways of 'not knowing'. Knowledge has proved a puzzle to those interested in it as a component of human capital; we often claim HC is 'knowledge and skills'. While it seems easy to define HC this way, it is difficult to understand the implications, for knowledge is an unusually opaque term. Unlike many other terms such as 'hot' or 'left' we cannot understand knowledge by pointing to its 'opposite', such as 'cold' or 'right'. We cannot 'know' the opposite of 'knowledge'—'un-knowledge'. Luhmann urged us to appreciate the difference between 'externally referenced' and 'self-referenced' terms—we can know the opposites of the former but not the latter (Luhmann, 2002). 'Ignorance' is meaningless until we know what we are ignorant of and thus define it as a knowledge absence framed by the known—a discovered inability to ride a bicycle, perhaps. For this reason, theories of knowledge (epistemologies) have generally turned on typologies of knowledge rather than on definitions of knowledge, so breaking up the self-referencing notion knowledge (which actually means no more than the experience of consciousness) into contrasting constituents. The Ancient Greeks distinguished, for example, between *episteme*, *techne*, *sophia*, and *phronesis*. Kant theorized differences between synthetic and analytic, Locke those between rationality and judgment. These distinctions turn on our experience of being in the world. In modern times we have tried to grasp knowledge using practical distinctions such as individual versus organizational, explicit versus tacit, embodied versus embrained, and so on (Blackler, 2002; Spender, 1996a, 2002).

While uncertainty seems different from knowledge, it can be considered a condition of knowledge absence—but this of no help if we cannot grasp either notion securely enough to locate and make meaning from their contrast. Knight introduced uncertainty into contemporary economics by contrasting it with risk as a type of socially embedded unknowing. He argued that risks were eventualities against which one could acquire insurance, while uncertainties were those for which one could not (Knight, 1921). We need population statistics before we can define a risk. When we have no such data we have uncertainty. More importantly, uncertainty means neither does anyone else, so there is no market in which we can lay off uncertainties as risks—as we do when taking fire insurance. Knight's definition was an empirical test of the socioeconomic context—backward economies being those that do not have well-functioning insurance markets or other social institutions that enable businesses to lay off a significant portion of their uncertainties as insurable risks in the manner which Fama presumed. Under such circumstances businesses have to carry all risks themselves and are less likely to be formed. Knight did not unpack uncertainty beyond arguing that it reframed business management as an art form—a matter of personal judgment—rather than as a science (Knight, 1923).

We can unpack uncertainty with a typology of knowledge absences by contrasting epistemologies—especially by contrasting positivism against subjective or constructivist interpretivism. This provides us with at least three distinct ways in which to capture our awareness of 'not knowing'. We can adopt a positivistic stance, which presumes a logical and knowable world, and confront it to discover a specific ignorance in terms of our inability to know the natural world well enough to manipulate it predictably. Positivism seeks to reveal Nature in ways that help us forecast the results of our manipulations. While inductively generated heuristics are a start towards codified effective practice, empirical science is an inventory of our rigorously and statistically justified successes (Kuehn and Hamburger, 1970). In spite of the positivist dispositions so evident in our journals, PAT's target is not Nature but the social world and our relations with others who have attributes similar to but different from our own, such as utilities and interests. As Knight noted, enquiries here must be conducted in a very different manner (Knight, 1923: 24). As we confront and interact with like others we experience two quite different ways of 'not knowing'. First, we discover time and the uncertainty associated with our inability to anticipate fully the actions of others. Shubik, a seminal game theorist, labeled this type of uncertainty 'indeterminacy' (Shubik, 1954). Since B does not know what A is going to do, nor even how he is going to interpret A's action, there is no sense in A attempting to forecast B's reaction. Game theory, of which PAT might be thought a version, addresses some of these issues and 'works' under sharply defined conditions of full or asymmetric knowledge. It breaks down under Knightian uncertainty, when A and B 'simply do not know'. A makes a judgment, and takes a guess at B's response; but that has to be based on something less than a complete determination derived from B's previous actions, declarations, the presence of influential others, and so on—factors that might support A's grasp of the situation but can never lead to a certain forecast. In the absence of complete knowledge, we are 'agentic'—thus Knight's analysis took us beyond contextual analysis into a consideration of A's action as a projection of her/his self into the situation as a quite different means of dealing with uncertainty: agentic proaction rather than incompletely determined reaction.

Through our agentic actions under Knightian uncertainty we discover our identity and bounded rationality—and the fact that others may well differ and have different views that may be irreconcilable. This is 'incommensurability' (Spender, 1989: 43). PAT brought indeterminacy and incommensurability into the analysis—along with ignorance (asymmetric information)—as it adopted the axiomatic distinction of principal and agent. Game theory only provides solutions when these uncertainties are eliminated by, for instance, sharing knowledge of the payoff matrix. It offers no solutions when the interindividual indeterminacy is unresolved; multi-period learning and mutual adjustment is required. Incommensurability is political theory's basic problematic—to be resolved by the exercise of power, as in Hobbes's *Leviathan*, or by negotiation and reconciliation, De Tocqueville's solution: the extremes of hierarchy and market. Social institutions arise in the middle ground to help us manage the uncertainties of our interactions collectively (North, 1990). The bottom line is that if agency theory does not admit uncertainty it is trivial: 'the problem acquires interest only when there is uncertainty as some point' (Arrow, 1991: 37). When the uncertainty is nothing but risk, PAT is a variant of game theory. Fama's principal point was that when there are Knightian uncertainties—such as irreconcilable differences of interest—then the PAT relationship breaks down absent an agentic appeal to some extra-relationship institutional apparatus.

7.3 From PAT to HC

What can we draw from this discussion of principal–agent theory? For neoclassical economists PAT was unquestionably revolutionary in that it got into the 'black box'—displacing notions of the firm as either a single entrepreneur or an inanimate production function. It did not do this by shifting the analysis into a sociological or organization theory (OT) frame where it would abandon the axiom of economic rationality and hinge on a division of labor and a power-based system of coordination—or through any political or evolutionary or organismic version of that (Morgan, 1986). It entered into the firm by redefining it as an interaction between individuals with differing HC. But there could be no solution until that HC difference was contained by its relationship to some social or institutional capital—in which case equilibrium solutions are no longer available. Ironically, as an equilibrium theorist, Arrow noted the need to consider social embeddedness as he observed the evident differences between real agency relations and those prescribed by PAT (Arrow, 1991: 48).

Once uncertainty is admitted and equilibrium theorizing is abandoned there is more to agency theory than the HC differences between security holders, managers, and employees. In Fama's initial and Fama and Jensen's later formulations, the separation of management and risk-bearing would remain beyond analysis were the firm not embedded in an institutional and historical context. Then the agency-problem-addressing manager would have to identify the specific far-from-perfect markets for capital and managerial HC actually available and make arrangements through them to promote organizational order. Pushing into the black box also meant pushing into the real options available in the firm's markets and noting their imperfections. Thus the principal–agent model of the firm presupposes both imperfect people (with heterogeneous and boundedly rational HC) and imperfect markets. In their edited compendium of the TCE and AT literature, Barney and Ouchi surmised: 'Organization theory cannot explain why firms exist because it includes no concept of a market as an alternative to organization for governing exchanges' (1986: 212); that is, there is nothing theoretically significant lying outside the firm's boundaries. Barnard also remarked on the way social scientists approached the market at the edge of the organization, only to retreat (1938: p. ix). Barney and Ouchi traced this tendency to ignore the market's distinctive nature (or the consumers' behavior) to the work of Chandler and his interest in a contingent 'fit' between strategy (the firm's market engagements, defined in terms of its various products and services) and its structure (its resource dispositions and administrative arrangements) (Barney and Ouchi, 1986: 15; Chandler, 1962, 2009). Again Barney and Ouchi missed the institutional program in which Veblen and Commons played key parts (Commons, 1957). Whether 'organizational economics', as they defined it, falls within today's 'new institutional economics' is a separate issue (Furubotn and Richter, 1991; G. M. Hodgson, 1989, 2004; North, 1986; Williamson, 2000). But there was a clear step from Jensen and Meckling's abstract and decontextualized model to Fama's overtly institutional discussion of judicious agentic appeals to the external markets for (*a*) specialized types of capital and (*b*) specialized managerial expertise.

Fama introduced time, history (multiple time periods), Knightian uncertainty, and expectations into his analysis—giving the actors' HC new dimensions. Jensen and Meckling expressly ignored these, presuming a single-period analysis, in which case expectations would be irrelevant, there would be no uncertainty, learning would be impossible, and the relevant HC could be no more than information for a rational individual to compute (Jensen and Meckling, 1976: 314). Rational Man cannot learn, being no more than a superfast biocomputer. In contrast, Fama's individuals are bounded, rational, have divergent interests, a sense of the multi-dimensioned institutional context in which they are embedded—comprising both time and space—and have expectations that their experience might or might not alter. They mull over their decisions.

Readers of the *Academy of Management Review*, rather than economists and sociologists who look to their own journals, might note that Eisenhardt's much-cited PAT review missed PAT's extra-organizational institutional dimensions and, with them, the resulting interplay of history, bounded rationality, memory, expectation, and learning. Even Demski and Feltham's (1978) analysis of PAT in accounting caught the importance of a multi-period model. Thus Eisenhardt's remarks about the parallels between PAT and other OT theories were way off the mark. She observed, correctly, that when agents shoulder part of the principal's risk the agency problem diminishes—a tautology. She leveraged Jensen's problematic distinction between positive and normative theorizing (Jensen, 1983: 320) and concluded 'the heart of principal–agency theory is the trade-off between

(a) the cost of measuring behavior and (b) the cost of measuring outcomes' (Eisenhardt, 1989: 61). This completely ignored the uncertainties that powered Fama's analysis and the way institutional embeddedness might help contain the uncertainty-generating differences of interest. Her analysis merely rephrased one of OT's oldest problematics: under the circumstances of incomplete control are managers to insist on rule-following conformance (working to rule) even when that leads to suboptimal outcomes, or to set output targets and ignore how workers actually meet them? The agent's freedom to choose—axiomatic to PAT—was excised. Ignoring the organization's institutional context, she fell to Barney and Ouchi's critique of ignoring the market. Curiously, while she dismissed Barney and Ouchi's emphasis on the ways capital markets affect the firm (Eisenhardt, 1989: 57) she cited Wolfson's analysis of this very matter (Eisenhardt, 1989: 68; Wolfson, 1991).

We can summarize how agency theory, as considered above, helps define the HC necessary to the viable firm. Organization theory's focus on the role-occupant's knowledge and responsibilities is less helpful than it appears at first. Yes, there is a division of labor and a need to see HC as heterogeneous. But, as noted previously, identifying this does not explain why firms exist nor the managerial knowledge and skills required to bring differing individuals together into a viable firm. As Grant has reminded us, like Barnard before him, the theory of the firm must address coordination and integration (Grant, 1996). OT's emphasis on power as the sole means of coordinating others' capabilities does not help identify the specific HC managers must bring to bear—managers, security-holders, and employees are more than their power. PAT draws attention to (a) the heterogeneity of the actor's HC, (b) the need for coordination and governance, (c) the boundedness and time and space contingencies of the context, and (d) the uncertainties around the process. The micro-economists' conceit is that the risks and uncertainties the leader must resolve are always economic in nature and that the capital markets can price them. This is an *ex post* view in which prices follow the success or failure of the coordination process. For the entrepreneur, risks are *ex ante*, multidimensional, and comprehensive; not merely financial. This world is one of uncoordinated heterogeneous resources, land, and labor (and technology), as well as cash, in which profit is the score, not the process; an uncertain world in which the relations between things and the consequences of their interactions can never be fully foreseen. In general, along with Simon, we can argue that any actor's engagement with another entails a degree of Knightian uncertainty and thus calls for leadership (Spender, 2008). Thus Fama's PAT is something of a donut—an open-ended 'theory' with a hole in the middle, only made complete and determinative by an act of entrepreneurial agency. Loasby (Chapter 9) reminds us that neoclassical economics, looking only to the market and ignoring production and ignoring uncertainty and agency, has neither a need nor space for such leadership.

7.4 Mitnick's Agency Theory

The preceding section illustrated how PAT broadens HC to embrace uncertainty resolution, for it can never be only about an individual's knowledge, whether explicit or tacit. It is also about the human capability to deal agentically with the knowledge absences that arise during application. But bringing uncertainty into the discussion demands close attention to the methodologies adopted. PAT admitted bounded rationality and information asymmetry but held fast to rational maximization and 'classical forms of economic behavior, with each factor motivated by its self-interest'—without which the analysis would no longer have been economics. Thus PAT, along with its cousin, transactions costs economics (TCE), was allied to Becker's broader project to create not just an economics of education, but an economics of marriage, child-rearing, emotion, and much else besides. Many saw this as microeconomics' push to 'colonize' the other social sciences—politics (Miller, 1997), sociology (Beckert, 1996; Hirsch et al., 1987), psychology, and so on. A disciplinary crisis in the 1960s led micro-economists away from theorizing market behavior and towards applying their disciplined 'economic approach' to matters central to politics, sociology, and psychology (Becker, 1976). Fine and Perrow were especially critical, observing that just as the other social sciences were retreating from the extremes of post-modernism and searching for the practical, micro-economics plunged into these same areas riding on the abstractions of methodological individualism (Donaldson, 1990a; Fine, 2000, 2008; Fine and Green, 2000; Perrow, 1986).

This colonizing move was also felt beyond mainstream economics (Kiser, 1999; Shapiro, 2005). Shortly before Jensen and Meckling's paper appeared in 1976, Mitnick published the first of a succession of papers in which he modeled the principal–agent relationship (Mitnick, 1975, 1976, 1997). Less mathematical than the PAT mainstream, his model brought different ideas to bear. Leveraging from the behavioral theory of the organization (for example, Cyert and March, 1963) Mitnick probed the resources to be managed, and presumed an agent would often have effective control of some 'organizational slack'—uncommitted resources which she/he could deploy to increase her/his own rewards (Mitnick, 1975: 37). Realizing this, the principals might divert some of the 'excess' resources into policing the agent, normally with negative consequences—suggesting a 'paradox of policing', a PAT form of suboptimal managing. While Mitnick's model did not appeal to external markets as Fama's did, he raised new questions about the heterogeneity of organizational resources and the zone of discretion an agent might be able to find. Operating within this zone, unbeknownst to the principal, agents would be able to meet their principal's expectations with fewer resources than they actually had available and divert the benefits of the rest towards their own goals. Mitnick's model was a more formal statement of Smith's earlier cautions against overpolicing corporation agents found trading on their own behalf.

The contrast between Mitnick's model and those of Jensen, Meckling, and Fama was not merely about where their articles were published and the different disciplinary consequences. Mitnick raised questions about the heterogeneity of the firm's resources that were glossed by the PAT mainstream. At the start of this chapter I simply assumed the relevance of HC. Now, having unpacked the notion, we see how it has to be expanded to involve intangibles such as information, skill, interest, and entrepreneurial agency. For many economists such things are not resources at all until they have a market price. Inside the black box things are less transparent, and the tangible/intangible distinction blurs even as the interactions are crucial. Monitoring consumes tangible resources and produces information—something intangible. Yet this is of economic consequence as it helps shape tangible profit. PAT was radical in pushing beyond priceable resources and was a clear move towards the HC-based theory of the firm. But Mitnick's model drew attention to their interplay, so introducing a new source of uncertainties to be resolved.

That slack intangible resources might have economic value draws attention to their potential, something unrealized, and to the necessary link to some tangible resources through which their value might be realized (G. M. Hodgson, 2008). Intangible resources can never have value on their own; a complementary tangible resource is required if they are to realize value. Expertise, as an intangible, must act on or through something tangible in the practical world of things, such as tools, and actions, such as hammering, and the mental world of language, ideas, and decisions about where and when to hammer (Chi *et al.*, 1988). There is no need to recapitulate a Wittgenstinian or Habermasian analysis of the relationship between language and practice in order to bring these worlds together. We can see that the intangible resources to which the HC literature draws attention cannot be considered economically valuable absent the interplay Mitnick considered. Penrose's much-quoted 'it is never resources themselves that are the inputs in the production process, but only the services that the resources can render' (1995: 25) spoke directly to the relationship between tangible and intangible resources—the intangible resource being the knowledge with which her 'management team' transformed tradable resources into what the firm takes up as value-adding services. A link between resources and their value lies in the coordinator's knowledge of how to engage the tangible and intangible resources with each other. Both principal and agent help identify, select, and engage these resources (Bester and Krähmer, 2008) whose economic value is always underdetermined, contingent on knowing how to bring them into the value-generating process. Only under conditions of certainty (and space- and timelessness) can a resource's 'value' be fully determined and stated. Thus the heterogeneity of HC arises out of the variety of tangible resources that enable its value to be realized.

The methodological shift from neoclassical place- and time-free goods and services, to the dynamic and contingent space and time contexts of HC that make us think of it as valuable, highlights learning—its acquisition along with its application. Fama moved learning toward the center of his early thinking, but it disappeared from his later PAT work. At the same time, while in Becker's model HC is explicitly about education and learning at the national level, there is surprisingly little discussion of learning in the individual-level HC literature. Learning, central to Penrose's analysis, must also be central to any analysis that engages the notion of intangible resources (Spender, 1994). Thus PAT was further radical in embracing learning via attention to (*a*) how principals and agents learn about the relevant institutional constraints that help their relationship continue, such as laws, capital markets, social customs, and norms, and (*b*) how they might, over multiple time periods, learn about doing business together, signaling to each other and enter into a state of 'trust' that reduced the need for monitoring, bonding, and so on, and (*c*) individually, as they went about their different business, learn from dealing with their various situational uncertainties they encountered and thereby extend their HC.

Rather than analyze and critique the vast literature on learning and its place as a component of HC (for example, Argyris, 1982; Bahk and Gort, 1993; Bilodeau, 1968; Darrah, 1996; Dodgson, 1993; Engeström, 2001; Gagné, 1985; Lamoreaux *et al.*, 1999; Lewicki *et al.*, 1987; Nicolini *et al.*, 2003; Pawlowsky, 2001; Prichard *et al.*, 2000; Spender, 1996*b*), I focus on one aspect which every HC-based theory of the firm must consider. As mentioned earlier, Rational Man (RM) has many deficiencies along with his powerful attributes. One is that he neither learns nor needs to, just as a computer does not learn; a computer only computes, as opposed to being a beige box full of prettily colored cables and components, when a program has been inserted. The programmer changing the program is the one learning, not the computer (Dreyfus, 1979). Likewise RM only needs inputs—including an objective function—and enough consciousness to compute them. The person who 'learns' is someone other than RM. Learning hinges on imagination—a quality of mind that stands opposed to that of reasoning. This is explicit in constructivist theories of knowledge and learning (Fosnot, 1996; Lave and Wenger, 1992; Poerksen, 2004; Steffe and Gale, 1995; Steffe and Thompson, 2000; Tharp and Gallimore, 1988; von Glasersfeld, 1995, 2002). Non-Platonic theories of learning (those that do not presume that learning is about uncovering and bringing into consciousness essences that are genetically given and already known at some deeper level) presume a model of man quite unlike Rational Man. This other model presumes that we possess both reason (RM's defining attribute) and imagination (which agency demands). As Locke observed, when our reason fails us we call on our imagination, linking the experience of knowledge absence to acts of innovation and learning (Locke, 1997).

The other part of agency theory, hidden from the analysis whenever RM is made axiomatic, is that which brings our imagination and its engagement with Knightian uncertainty into focus. There is a huge literature here, often referred to as the 'structure and agency' debate (Archer, 2000; Bandura, 1989; Heugens and Lander, 2009; G. M. Hodgson, 2004; Korsgaard, 2008). To be an agent an individual has to have some freedom of choice and action. We thereby become responsible for our actions and thoughts. Human agency implies a philosophical position in which our creativity stands between the forces acting on us, and our actions (Emirbayer and Mische, 1998). It underpins Enlightenment beliefs about identity, personal freedom, and methodological individualism. Agency is the identity-defining contribution an agent makes in underdetermined circumstances (Korsgaard, 2009). It is about us 'making a difference'. It differs from 'free will' because in any stable space–time socioeconomic domain an agent's freedom is constrained and less than complete, as the quip about 'Not having the freedom to shout "Fire!" in a crowded theater' reminds us. But once human agency is made axiomatic to the analysis, attention must be shifted to the structures that constrain it and channel its realization.

It is interesting to see how the PAT literature fails to clarify why the principal and agent enter into a relationship in the first place. Under conditions of certainty, any needs the principal might have that he cannot satisfy on his own can be handled across the market and through contracts between principals–agency is irrelevant. But under conditions of uncertainty the imagination must be brought into play. While the neoclassical or positivist approach attempts to explain everything in terms of determinable causes and their effects, imagination demands a different analytical framework. The principal turns to an agent when she/he cannot or does not wish to provide the needed imaginative component of HC—perhaps lacking the relevant experience, information, or location from which to learn how to deal with the uncertainties arising, or through laziness or being overstretched. The impetus behind the principal–agent relationship is the principal's recognition of (a) the situation's uncertainties and (b) the boundedness of his/her own imagination, together with (c) an ultimately unwarrantable trust in the agent's capabilities.

This section has explored PAT, showing that it only makes sense under uncertainty, over multiple time periods, with a learning engagement that calls forth previously unconsidered dimensions of HC. HC is expanded into a dynamic concept or process. In the next section I deal with some of the challenges raised by allowing imagination into the analysis. My emphasis will be on (a) the flexibility which this introduces and (b) the attendant problems of its containment. PAT ultimately demands attention for the presumption that we are all agentic and that our imagination rather than our rationality is the source of all progress—and the nation's wealth.

7.5 FLEXIBILITY

In a 1996 paper Foss sketched a theory of the firm that differed from the PAT, TCE, team production, property rights, and nexus of contracts approaches. Rather than 'economizing' in an equilibrium framework, he suggested that a better answer might lie in firms' greater flexibility of organizational arrangements. 'Rather than concep-tualizing the firm as an entity that is primarily kept together by transaction cost minimization, [we] extend the view of the firm as an entity whose primary role is to acquire, combine, utilize and upgrade knowledge' (Foss, 1996: 17). It was also clear that flexibility, a mark of functioning markets, seems eliminated in most organiza-tion theory; bureaucracies adapt only by redesign. Foss positioned his theory of the firm in a 'hybrid' region somewhere between hierarchy and market, absorbing some of the market's flexibility into his theory. Goal-oriented learning that flowed from successful problem-solving within a structure of incomplete contracts constrained by centralized control was crucial.

Many organization theorists have struggled against the supposed inertia of bureaucratic theory by invoking 'the learning organization' (for example, Garratt, 1987; Nonaka, 1994; Senge, 1990). But, while presuming the presence of human (or even organizational) imagination, they typically overlooked how it must be gov-erned towards productive learning rather than mere disorder. Many ignored indi-viduals and their HC altogether. A methodological individualist, Foss made individuals and their learning axiomatic, and envisioned a flexible mode of govern-ance based on the interplay of central direction and individual learning. He argued that markets were not, as in the neoclassical model, efficient incentive mechanisms. Rather they were 'embodiments of options'—places of heterogeneous trading opportunities that purposive firms selected, took up, and wove into profitable activ-ity. Foss noted Loasby's aphorism that 'firms provide contracts for future options whereas markets provide options for future contracts' (Loasby, 1994). But options presume uncertainty and underdetermination and for markets to function there must be some means to contain this. Foss cited Kreps' notion that 'corporate culture is essentially reputation capital that tells the employees of the firm and its external suppliers how the firm will react to unforeseen contingencies' (Kreps, 1990, 1992). Firms existed because their hierarchy offered 'better bargaining costs relative to the market'. Here Foss took up Marengo's observation that coordination would be impossible without contractual incompleteness, and noted 'the superior flexibility that hierarchy may obtain relative to market contracting in influencing input-own-ers' actions in response to partly unexpected developments and new learning' (Conner and Prahalad, 1996; Marengo, 1992).

Thus while most PAT theorists take opportunism as axiomatic, to be tamped down by the principal, Foss adopted it as a core reason for the firm's existence, as Veblen had done before him (Veblen, 1965). The firm was reconceived as an appara-tus to capture the fruit of the various incompletely contracted agents' imaginations as they struggled with unforeseen uncertainties within the general constraints of the firm's strategic goals. The managing which Fama distinguished from risk-bear-ing did not shut down the agent's imagination; it directed it. In this way Foss's model also penetrated the black box. Both principal and agent provided focused imagina-tion of the boundary-spanning sort in Thompson's influential analysis, itself derived from Barnard's (Thompson, 2001). This achieved results far beyond those of Alchian and Demsetz's modest model of collaborative labor. The principal's risk-bearing burden was shared, not only with other investors, as in Fama's model, stressing the financial capital markets, but also within the firm, among those whose better experience, learning, and HC investments were attuned to dealing with the plethora of non-financial uncertainties at hand. Even though Foss's model lacked an explanation of how individuals' agency was to be shaped by the centralized governance system, for he stressed the economic value of flexibility rather than of control, implying a return to Smith's kind of agent, the profit-pursuing employee doing his best to be open to new conditions and exploit unforeseen options.

In a parallel historical analysis White leveraged from Isaacs's 1925 *HBR* article on agency and Llewellyn's analysis to stress the complementary flexibility and institutionalized embeddedness of agency relations (Isaacs, 1925; Llewellyn, 1930). 'Agency is an ancient device for getting business done which remains fresh and in common use. It is intensely social in its mechanism since it gets one person to do something for another vis-à-vis a third person, but only with heavy reliance on the lay of the social landscape. Opportunity and flexibility, in both the short and the long term, are key to agency's perennial robustness' (White, 1991: 187). He argued that the purpose of the agency relationship is control, and that it is a solution rather than a problem, a kind of social plumbing intermediate between market and hierarchy; more than a tie, a context for ties that cast shadows of commitment. At one extreme was *shaliach*—the Old Testament notion of the person sent not only 'in the name' of the principal but 'in his person', whose action unalterably committed the principal. At the other extreme was the minimal tie of mutual acknowledgment of civil existence needed to establish relations in a market. In between lay the firm wherein an employee has less say in the specifics of action than an agent, but a more fixed reward (White, 1991: 189).

White's analysis showed how flexibility and learning destabilized the principal–agent relationship. In contrast to the mainstream PAT assumption that the roles of principal and agent were fixed and inviolable, an historical analysis shows that as circumstances change and the various parties adjust, the roles might well reverse; those used to controlling might find themselves being controlled (White, 1991: 205) given which—Jensen and Meckling's notions of bonding turn out to be unrealistic and simplistic. In practice, various types of 'reverse bonding' occur. Medieval kings would bind barons to them by requiring them to 'borrow' large sums which the king 'loaned' to them—more than they could ever repay—before allowing them to take up their hereditary titles, estates, and associated revenues (Danziger and Gillingham, 2003). Here money was merely an instrument of control, not a resource. Reverse bonding can arise in other ways. White compared the Roman Empire as a system held together by *clientela*, family-allegiance-based patronage, with how US CEOs often hold corporate systems together with their personal patronage—a seldom discussed feature of executive life (White, 1991: 198). The *Godfather* films showed similar systems at work.

As we admit the dynamism of the principal–agent relationship and the possibility of its reversal we uncover the power relations which economists are often determined to hide—and the possibility of power as a dimension of HC once it is embedded in a social context. Perrow pointed to huge lacunae in the PAT literature, that principals are opportunistic too and equally likely to take advantage of the agent's ignorance, especially when it comes to breaking employment contracts or engaging in non-transparent but highly consequential financial dealings such as mergers and acquisitions (Perrow, 1986: 14). The principal–agent relationship is inevitably bilateral rather than unilateral, as the mainstream PAT writers would have it. In a capitalist system, legal rights and social power normally go with the money. In the extreme, money overpowers the agent's knowledge, skills, and learning; financial capital trumps human capital, the shareholders' rights trump the employees'. White's more general point was that fluid and shifting agentic relations between those involved overlaid structures of delegation, authority, and control in all organizations, ancient or modern, commercial or political, religious or academic. He argued that matrix structures were a modern instance, legitimated in part because 'formal' systems were typically 'insufficiently fine-grained'—providing general directions but not the detailed specifics and trade-offs necessary to keep the organization moving (White, 1991: 201). Agency theory reveals how 'informal' agentic relations lubricate the organization's functioning so that market and hierarchy interpenetrate and cannot be separated (White, 1991: 208).

Patronage is but one aspect of a social context in which it is possible for power-holders to channel their agents' imaginations towards organizational goals. Other lacunae in the PAT literature concern the ticklish matter of selecting agents. Sappington offered a rare exception, though some of Jensen and Meckling's thoughts on signaling and bonding addressed selection (Sappington, 1991). White's historical examples were based on family, ethnicity, or religion. Today business schools underpin structures of economic patronage; indeed this may be their chief deliverable given the criticisms and questions about the value of the training (Khurana, 2007; Mintzberg, 2004; Spender, 2007; Whitley et al., 1981). The MBA selection process's focus may really be on testing the aspirant's attitude toward the hiring firm's uncertainties, so demonstrating that she/he could be an agent of the right 'type' (Holmstrom, 1989; Kiser, 1999). Getting 'on the team' means more than having the necessary competencies; it means internalizing the organization's intentionality. A profession's 'ethics' are similar, revealed in the members' agentic actions whenever uncertainty makes choosing the appropriate rule problematic (Abbott, 1988; Sharma, 1997). Absent alignment at this level the aspirant's agency is unlikely to be manageable.

But selection alone does not guarantee alignment; governance must be present. Both Fama and White took an 'institutionalist' tack, looking to the organization's context to provide appropriate guidance to handling uncertainty, now known as 'new institutionalism' (Hechter, 1990; Powell and DiMaggio, 1991). But as Veblen suggested, the viable firm is not simply an actualization of contextually available options; meeting a market's demand may not generate profit. That requires 'competitive advantage'—the result of a managed agentic engagement with the context's uncertainties. Eventually we see that management's principal tool to make this happen, when the uncertainties mean rule-based systems of incentives and accountability cannot be established, is their talk—their leadership and rhetoric (Spender, 2008). An organization's flexibility ultimately stands on the flexibility of its agents and on management's being able to shape that agency to their own vision. Thus a final component of HC is the individual's ability to persuade others and, in complementary manner, her/his willingness to be persuaded.

7.6 CONCLUSION

My chapter's focus was the interplay of HC and AT. My intent was to show that neither makes sense in a static framework; both must be considered dynamic and active. The analysis of PAT, framed as a difference in HC between principal and agent, shows we should understand HC as more than knowledge and skills—as in 'know what', 'how', 'who', 'when', 'where', and so on—to embrace agency, our evident ability to deal imaginatively and productively with the uncertainties of our economic world as well as our social, natural, and technological worlds. Embedded in the social HC must also be the rhetorical capacity to 'know talk', to engage productively in the world of human discourse and persuasion. HC is an abstraction until we frame it. One possibility is to frame it in dynamic social and discursive relations with others. Then the value of any actor's HC must be realized in a specific space–time context and through other tangible resources. All too often we use the term HC loosely, assuming it is transportable but paying no attention to its context, thus ignoring both the practical challenges of moving it around and the boundaries to its relocation.

Principal–agent theory is a powerful way of examining how HC might work in practice, for it provides a minimalist theory of the firm and of the context in which HC might be of value. Probing this takes us beyond the 'obvious' stereotype of PAT as one person directing another, to a realization that agents are not dumb tools to be directed and manipulated by principals but human beings who (*a*) reason for themselves, (*b*) bring their imagination into play to get the job done, and (*c*) are open to being persuaded to act in the principal's interest. We end up radically reshaping the notion of HC—and its management. Instead of being an intangible resource 'ready to hand' like a hammer, whose application only seems unproblematic to those unskilled in its practicalities (Crawford, 2009; Harper, 1987), HC becomes the appearance in the world of our agentic capability to make something unexpected happen as we respond to the possibilities of our uncertain space–time situation.

References

ABBOTT, A. (1988). *The System of Professions: An Essay on the Division of Expert Labor* (Chicago: University of Chicago Press).

ADAMS, J. (1996). 'Principals and Agents: Colonialists and Company Men. The Decay of Colonial Control in the Dutch East Indies', *American Sociological Review*, 61(1): 12–28.

ALCHIAN, A. A., and ALLEN, W. R. (eds.) (1969). *Exchange and Production: Theory in Use* (Belmont, Calif.: Wadsworth).

—— and DEMSETZ, H. (1972). 'Production, Information Costs, and Economic Organization', *American Economic Review*, 62(5): 777–95.

ARCHER, M. S. (2000). *Being Human: The Problem of Agency* (Cambridge: Cambridge University Press).

ARGYRIS, C. (1982). *Reasoning, Learning and Action: Individual and Organizational* (San Francisco: Jossey-Bass).

ARROW, K. J. (1991). 'Economics of Agency', in J. W. Pratt and R. J. Zeckhauser (eds.), *Principals and Agents* (Boston: Harvard Business School), 37–51.

AVSI (2008). *Human Capital: A Resource for Development. The Experiences in the World of Three Italian NGOs; AVSI, ICU and Montserrate* (Milan: AVSI—Italia).

BAHK, B.-H., and GORT, M. (1993). 'Decomposing Learning by Doing in New Plants', *Journal of Political Economy*, 101(4): 561–83.

BANDURA, A. (1989). 'Human Agency in Social Cognitive Theory', *American Psychologist*, 44(9): 1175–84.

BARNARD, C. I. (1938). *The Functions of the Executive* (Cambridge, Mass.: Harvard University Press).

BARNEY, J. B., and OUCHI, W. G. (1986). *Organizational Economics: Toward a New Paradigm for Understanding and Studying Organizations* (San Francisco: Jossey-Bass).

BASSI, L. J., and MCMURRER, D. P. (2008). 'Toward a Human Capital Measurement Methodology', *Advances in Developing Human Resources*, 10(6): 863–81.

BECKER, G. S. (1959). 'Under-Investment in Education?', *American Economic Review, Papers and Proceedings*, 6 (May): 348–89.

—— (1962). 'Investment in Human Capital: A Theoretical Analysis', *Journal of Political Economy*, 70(5/2): 9–49.

—— (1976). *The Economic Approach to Human Behavior* (Chicago: University of Chicago Press).

—— (1993). *Human Capital: A Theoretical and Empirical Analysis, with Special Reference to Education* (3rd edn. Chicago: University of Chicago Press).

BECKERT, J. (1996). 'What is Sociological about Economic Sociology? Uncertainty and the Embeddedness of Economic Action', *Theory and Society*, 25: 803–40.

BELL, D. (1999). *The Coming of Post-Industrial Society: A Venture in Social Forecasting* (Special anniversary edn. New York: Basic Books).

BERLE, A. A., and MEANS, G. C. (1968). *The Modern Corporation and Private Property* (New York: Harcourt, Brace & World).

BESTER, H., and KRÄHMER, D. (2008). 'Delegation and Incentives', *Rand Journal of Economics*, 39(3): 664–82.

BILODEAU, E. A. (1968). 'Learning: Acquisition of Skill', in D. L. Sills (ed.), *International Encyclopedia of the Social Sciences* (New York: Macmillan), ix. 173–7.

BLACKLER, F. (2002). 'Knowledge, Knowledge Work, and Organizations', in C. W. Choo and N. Bontis (eds.), *The Strategic Management of Intellectual Capital and Organizational Knowledge* (New York: Oxford University Press), 47–62.

CASSON, M. C. (1982). 'Transaction Costs and the Theory of the Multinational Enterprise', in A. M. Rugman (ed.), *New Theories of the Multinational Enterprise* (New York: St Martin's Press), 24–43.

CASTELLO, A., and DOMENECH, R. (2002). 'Human Capital Inequality and Economic Growth: Some New Evidence', *Economic Journal*, 112(478): C187.

CHANDLER, A. D. (1962). *Strategy and Structure: Chapters in the History to the American Industrial Enterprise* (Cambridge, Mass.: MIT Press).

——— (2009). 'History and Management Practice and Thought: An Autobiography', *Journal of Management History*, 15(3): 236–60.

CHAUDHURI, K. N. (1985). *Trade and Civilisation in the Indian Ocean: An Economic History from the Rise of Islam to 1750* (Cambridge: Cambridge University Press).

CHI, M., GLASER, R., and FARR, M. J. (eds.) (1988). *The Nature of Expertise* (Hillsdale, NJ: Lawrence Erlbaum Associates).

CLARK, J. M. (1923). *Studies in the Economics of Overhead Costs* (Chicago: Universwity of Chicago Press).

COASE, R. H. (1991). 'The Nature of the Firm' (1937), in O. E. Williamson and S. G. Winter (eds.), *The Nature of the Firm; Origins, Evolution and Development* (New York: Oxford University Press), 18–33.

COLEMAN, J. S. (1988). 'Social Capital in the Creation of Human Capital', *American Journal of Sociology*, 94 (supplement): S95–S120.

COMMONS, J. R. (1957). *Legal Foundations of Capitalism* (Madison, Wis.: University of Wisconsin Press).

CONNER, K. R., and PRAHALAD, C. K. (1996). 'A Resource-Based Theory of the Firm: Knowledge versus Opportunism', *Organization Science*, 7(5): 477–501.

CRAWFORD, M. B. (2009). *Shop Class as Soulcraft: An Inquiry into the Value of Work* (New York: Penguin Press).

CYERT, R. M., and MARCH, J. G. (1963). *A Behavioral Theory of the Firm* (Englewood Cliffs, NJ: Prentice-Hall).

DANZIGER, D., and GILLINGHAM, J. (2003). *1215: The Year of Magna Carta* (London: Hodder & Stoughton).

DARRAH, C. N. (1996). *Learning and Work: An Exploration in Industrial Ethnography* (New York: Garland Publishing).

DEAN, A., and KRETSCHMER, M. (2007). 'Can Ideas be Capital? Factors of Production in the Postindustrial Economy: A Review and Critique', *Academy of Management Review*, 32(2): 573–94.

DEMSKI, J. S., and FELTHAM, G. A. (1978). 'Economic Incentives in Budgetary Control Systems', *Accounting Review*, 53(2): 336–59.

DODGSON, M. (1993). 'Organizational Learning: A Review of Some Literatures', *Organization Studies*, 14: 375–94.

DONALDSON, L. (1990*a*). 'The Ethereal Hand: Organizational Economics and Management Theory', *Academy of Management Review*, 15(3): 369–81.

—— (1990*b*). 'A Rational Basis for Criticisms of Organizational Economics: A Reply to Barney', *Academy of Management Review*, 15(3): 394–401.

DORE, R., LAZONICK, W., and O'SULLIVAN, M. (1999). 'Varieties of Capitalism in the Twentieth Century', *Oxford Review of Economic Policy*, 15(4): 102–20.

DOSI, G., and MARENGO, L. (2007). 'On the Evolutionary and Behavioral Theories of Organizations: A Tentative Roadmap', *Organization Science*, 18(3): 491–502.

DREYFUS, H. L. (1979). *What Computers Can't Do: The Limits of Artificial Intelligence* (Rev. edn. New York: Harper & Row).

DRUCKER, P. F. (1988). 'The Coming of the New Organization', *Harvard Business Review*, 66(1): 45–53.

—— (1992). 'The New Society of Organizations', *Harvard Business Review*, 70(5): 95–104.

EHRLICH, I., and MURPHY, K. M. (2007). 'Why does Human Capital Need a Journal?', *Journal of Human Capital*, 1(1): 1–7.

EISENHARDT, K. M. (1989). 'Agency Theory: An Assessment and Review', *Academy of Management Review*, 14(1): 57–74.

EMIRBAYER, M., and MISCHE, A. (1998). 'What is Agency?', *American Journal of Sociology*, 103(4): 962–1023.

ENGESTRÖM, Y. (2001). 'Expansive Learning at Work: Toward an Activity Theoretical Reconceptualization', *Journal of Education and Work*, 14(1): 133–56.

ENKE, S. (1960). 'The Economics of Government Payments to Limit Population', *Economic Development and Cultural Change*, 8/1 (July): 342.

FAMA, E. F. (1980). 'Agency Problems and the Theory of the Firm', *Journal of Political Economy*, 88: 288–307.

—— and JENSEN, M. C. (1983*a*). 'Agency Problems and Residual Claims', *Journal of Law and Economics*, 26(2): 327–49.

—— and —— (1983*b*). 'Separation of Ownership and Control', *Journal of Law and Economics*, 26(June): 301–26.

FINE, B. (2000). *Social Capital versus Social Theory: Political Economy and Social Science at the Turn of the Millennium* (London: Routledge).

—— (2008). 'Vicissitudes of Economics Imperialism', *Review of Social Economy*, 66(2): 235–40.

—— and GREEN, F. (2000). 'Economics, Social Capital, and the Colonization of the Social Sciences', in S. Baron, J. Field, and T. Schuller (eds.), *Social Capital: Critical Perspectives* (Oxford: Oxford University Press), 78–93.

FLEISCHHAUER, K.-J. (2007). 'A Review of Human Capital Theory: Microeconomics', *University of St. Gallen Department of Economics, Discussion Paper 2007-1*.

FOSNOT, C. T. (ed.). (1996). *Constructivism: Theory, Perspectives, and Practice* (New York: Teachers College Press).

FOSS, N. J. (1996). 'Firms, Incomplete Contracts and Organizational Learning', *Human Systems Management*, 15(1): 17–26.

FREEMAN, R. E. (1984). *Strategic Management: A Stakeholder Approach* (Marshfield, Mass.: Pitman Publishing Co.).

FURUBOTN, E. G., and PEJOVICH, S. (1972). 'Property Rights and Economic Theory', *Journal of Economic Literature*, 10: 1137–62.

——and RICHTER, R. (1991). 'The New Institutional Economics: An Assessment', in E. G. Furubotn and R. Richter (eds.), *The New Institutional Economics* (College Station, Tex.: Texas A. and M. University Press), 1–32.

GAGNÉ, R. M. (1985). *The Conditions of Learning* (4th edn. New York: Holt, Rinehart, & Winston).

GARRATT, B. (1987). *The Learning Organization: And the Need for Directors Who Think* (London: Fontana/Collins).

GHOSHAL, S., and MORAN, J. (1996). 'Bad for Practice: A Critique of Transaction Cost Theory', *Academy of Management Review*, 21(1): 13–47.

GIBBONS, R. (2005). 'Four Formal(izable) Theories of the Firm?', *Journal of Economic Behavior and Organization*, 58: 200–45.

GRANT, R. M. (1996). 'Toward a Knowledge-Based Theory of the Firm', *Strategic Management Journal*, 17 (Special Winter): 109–22.

HARPER, D. A. (1987). *Working Knowledge: Skill and Community in a Small Shop* (Chicago: University of Chicago Press).

HART, O. D. (1991). 'Incomplete Contracts and the Theory of the Firm', in O. E. Williamson and S. G. Winter (eds.), *The Nature of the Firm: Origins, Evolution and Development* (New York: Oxford University Press), 138–58.

——and MOORE, J. (1990). 'Property Rights and the Nature of the Firm', *Journal of Political Economy*, 98(6): 1119–58.

HARTOG, J., and VAN DEN BRINK, H. M. (eds.) (2007). *Human Capital: Advances in Theory and Evidence* (Cambridge: Cambridge University Press).

HARVEY, D. (1982). *The Limits to Capital* (Chicago: University of Chicago Press).

HECHTER, M. (1990). 'The Emergence of Cooperative Social Institutions', in M. Hechter, K.-D. Opp, and R. Wippler (eds.), *Social Institutions: Their Emergence, Maintenance and Effects* (New York: Aldine de Gruyter), 13–33.

HEUGENS, P. P. M. A. R., and LANDER, M. W. (2009). 'Structure! Agency! (And Other Quarrels): A Meta-Analysis of Institutional Theories of Organization', *Academy of Management Journal*, 52(1): 61–85.

HIRSCH, P., MICHAELS, S., and FRIEDMAN, R. (1987). '"Dirty Hands" versus "Clean Models"', *Theory and Society*, 16(3): 317.

HODGSON, G. M. (1989). 'Institutional Economic Theory: The Old Versus the New', *Review of Political Economy*, 1(3): 249.

——(2004). *The Evolution of Institutional Economics: Agency, Structure and Darwinism in American Institutionalism* (London: Routledge).

——(2008). 'The Concept of a Routine', in M. Becker (ed.), *The Handbook of Organizational Routines* (Cheltenham: Edward Elgar), 15–29.

HODGSON, M. G. S. (1974). *The Venture of Islam: Conscience and History in a World Civilization*, ii.—*The Expansion of Islam in the Middle Periods* (Chicago: University of Chicago Press).

HOLMSTROM, B. R. (1989). 'Agency Costs and Innovation', *Journal of Economic Behavior and Organization*, 12: 305–27.

——and TIROLE, J. (1989). 'The Theory of the Firm', in R. Schmalensee and R. D. Willig (eds.), *Handbook of Industrial Organization* (Amsterdam: North-Holland), 61–133.

ISAACS, N. (1925). 'On Agents and "Agencies"', *Harvard Business Review*, 3(3): 265–74.

JENSEN, M. C. (1983). 'Organization Theory and Methodology', *Accounting Review*, 58(2): 319–39.

——and MECKLING, W. H. (1976). 'Theory of the Firm: Managerial Behavior, Agency Costs, and Ownership Structure', *Journal of Financial Economics*, 3(4): 305–60.

JOHNSON, B. F., and MELLOR, J. W. (1961). 'The Role of Agriculture in Economic Development', *American Economic Review*, 51(4): 566–93.

KERR, C., DUNLOP, J. T., HARBISON, F., and MYERS, C. (1964). *Industrialism and Industrial Man: The Problems of Labor and Management in Economic Growth* (New York: Oxford University Press).

KEYNES, J. M. (1937). 'The General Theory of Employment', *Quarterly Journal of Economics*, 51(2): 209–23.

KHURANA, R. (2007). *From Higher Aims to Hired Hands: The Social Transformation of American Business Schools and the Unfulfilled Promise of Management as a Profession* (Princeton: Princeton University Press).

KISER, E. (1999). 'Comparing Varieties of Agency Theory in Economics, Political Science, and Sociology: An Illustration from State Policy Implementation', *Sociological Theory*, 17(2): 146.

KNIGHT, F. H. (1921). *Risk, Uncertainty and Profit* (Boston: Houghton Mifflin Co.).

——(1923). 'Business Management: Science or Art?', *Journal of Business*, 2(4): 5–24.

——(1965). *Risk, Uncertainty and Profit* (New York: Harper & Row).

KORSGAARD, C. M. (2008). *The Constitution of Agency: Essays on Practical Reason and Moral Psychology* (Oxford: Oxford University Press).

——(2009). *Self-Constitution: Agency, Identity, and Integrity* (Oxford: Oxford University Press).

KREPS, D. M. (1990). 'Corporate Culture and Economic Theory', in J. E. Alt and K. E. Shepsle (eds.), *Perspectives on Positive Political Economy* (Cambridge: Cambridge University Press).

——(1992). 'Static Choice in the Presence of Unforeseen Contingencies', in P. Dasgupta, D. Gale, O. D. Hart, and E. Maskin (eds.), *Economic Analysis of Markets and Games: Essays in Honour of Frank Hahn* (Cambridge, Mass.: MIT Press).

KUEHN, A. A., and HAMBURGER, M. J. (1970). 'A Heuristic Program for Locating Warehouses', in L. A. Welsch and R. M. Cyert (eds.), *Management Decision Making* (Harmondsworth: Penguin Books), 228–58.

LABIB, S. Y. (1969). 'Capitalism in Medieval Islam', *Journal of Economic History*, 29(1): 79–96.

LAMOREAUX, N. R., RAFF, D. M. G., and TEMIN, P. (eds.). (1999). *Learning by Doing in Markets, Firms, and Countries* (Chicago: University of Chicago Press).

LANE, F. C. (1969). 'Meanings of Capitalism', *Journal of Economic History*, 29(1): 5–12.

LAVE, J., and WENGER, E. (1992). *Situated Learning: Legitimate Peripheral Participation* (New York: Cambridge University Press).

LAZONICK, W., and O'SULLIVAN, M. (2000). 'Maximizing Shareholder Value: A New Ideology for Corporate Governance', *Economy and Society*, 29(1): 13–35.

LEWICKI, P., CZYZEWSKA, M., and HOFFMAN, H. (1987). 'Unconscious Acquisition of Complex Procedural Knowledge', *Journal of Experimental Psychology: Learning, Memory and Cognition*, 13: 523–30.

LEWIS, W. A. (1954). 'Economic Development with Unlimited Supplies of Labour', *The Manchester School*, 22(2): 139–91.

LLEWELLYN, K. N. (1930). 'Agency', *Encyclopedia of the Social Sciences* (New York: Macmillan), i. 483.

LOASBY, B. (1994). 'Understanding Markets', *University of Stirling Working Paper 94/4*.

LOCKE, J. (1997). *An Essay Concerning Human Understanding*, ed. Roger Woolhouse (London: Penguin Books).

LUCAS, R. E. (1988). 'On the Mechanics of Economic Development', *Journal of Monetary Economics*, 22: 3–42.

LUHMANN, N. (2002). *Theories of Distinction: Redescribing the Descriptions of Modernity*, tr. J. O'Neil, E. Schreiber, K. Behnke, and W. Whobrey (Stanford, Calif.: Stanford University Press).

MACAULAY, S. (1963). 'Non-Contractual Relations in Business: A Preliminary Study', *American Sociological Review*, 6: 55–66.

MCCLOSKEY, D. N. (2006). *The Bourgeois Virtues: Ethics for an Age of Commerce* (Chicago: University of Chicago Press).

MAHONEY, J. (1992). 'Organizational Economics within the Conversation of Strategic Management', *Advances in Strategic Management*, 8: 103–55.

MARENGO, L. (1992). *Structure, Competence, and Learning in an Adaptive Model of the Firm* (European Study Group for Evolutionary Economics, 9203).

MILLER, G. J. (1997). 'The Impact of Economics on Contemporary Political Science', *Journal of Economic Literature*, 35(3): 1173.

MILLS, C. W. (1959). *The Power Elite* (New York: Oxford University Press).

MINTZBERG, H. (2004). *Managers Not MBAs: A Hard Look at the Soft Practice of Managing and Management Development* (San Francisco: Berrett-Koehler Publishers).

MIRRLEES, J. A. (1999). 'The Theory of Moral Hazard and Unobservable Behaviour: Part I', *Review of Economic Studies*, 66(226): 3–21.

MITNICK, B. M. (1975). 'The Theory of Agency: The Policing "Paradox" and Regulatory Behavior', *Public Choice*, 24(Winter): 27–42.

——(1976). 'A Typology of Conceptions of the Public Interest', *Administration and Society*, 8(1): 5–28.

——(1997). 'Agency Theory', in P. Werhane and R. E. Freeman (eds.), *The Blackwell Encyclopedic Dictionary of Business Ethics* (Oxford: Blackwell Publishers), 12–15.

MORGAN, G. (1986). *Images of Organization* (Newbury Park, Calif.: Sage Publications).

MUMFORD, L. (1967). *The Myth of the Machine: Technics and Human Development* (New York: Harcourt, Brace & World).

NICOLINI, D., GHERARDI, S., and YANOW, D. (2003). 'Introduction: Toward a Practice-Based View of Knowing and Learning in Organizations', in D. Nicolini, S. Gherardi, and D. Yanow (eds.), *Knowing in Organizations: A Practice-Based Approach* (Armonk, NY: M. E. Sharpe), 3–31.

NONAKA, I. (1994). 'A Dynamic Theory of Organizational Knowledge Creation', *Organization Science*, 5(1): 14–37.

NORTH, D. C. (1986). 'The New Institutional Economics', *Journal of Institutional and Theoretical Economics*, 142: 230–7.

——(1990). *Institutions, Institutional Change, and Economic Performance* (Cambridge: Cambridge University Press).

PAWLOWSKY, P. (2001). 'The Treatment of Organizational Learning in Management Science', in M. Dierkes, A. B. Antal, J. Child, and I. Nonaka (eds.), *Handbook of Organizational Learning and Knowledge* (Oxford: Oxford University Press), 61–88.

PERROW, C. B. (1986). 'Economic Theories of Organization', *Theory and Society*, 15(1/2): 11–45.

PFEFFER, J., and FONG, C. T. (2004). 'The Business School "Business": Some Lessons from the US Experience', *Journal of Management Studies*, 41: 1501–20.

PIRSON, M., VON KIMAKOWITZ, E., SPITZECK, H., AMANN, W., and KHAN, S. (2009). 'Introduction: Humanism in Business', in H. Spitzeck, M. Pirson, W. Amann, S. Khan, and E. von Kimakowitz (eds.), *Humanism in Business* (Cambridge: Cambridge University Press), 1–11.

PITELIS, C. (1993). 'Transaction Costs, Markets and Hierarchies: The Issues', in C. Pitelis (ed.), *Transaction Costs, Markets and Hierarchies* (Oxford: Blackwell), 7–19.

——and TEECE, D. J. (2009). 'The (New) Nature and Essence of the Firm', *European Management Review*, 6: 5–15.

POERKSEN, B. (2004). *The Certainty of Uncertainty: Dialogues Introducing Constructivism*, tr. A. R. Koeck and W. K. Koeck (Exeter: Imprint Academic).

POWELL, W. W., and DiMAGGIO, P. J. (1991). *The New Institutionalism in Organizational Analysis* (Chicago: University of Chicago Press).

PRENDERGAST, C. (1999). 'The Provision of Incentives in Firms', *Journal of Economic Literature*, 37: 7–63.

PRICHARD, C., HULL, R., CHUMER, M., and WILLMOTT, H. (eds.) (2000). *Managing Knowledge: Critical Investigations of Work and Learning* (Basingstoke: Macmillan).

REICH, R. B. (1992). *The Work of Nations: Preparing Ourselves for 21st Century Capitalism* (New York: Vintage Books).

RISSO, P. (1995). *Merchantgs and Faith: Muslim Commerce and Culture in the Indian Ocean* (Boulder, Colo.: Westview Press).

ROMER, P. M. (1994). 'The Origins of Endogenous Growth', *Journal of Economic Perspectives*, 8(1): 3–22.

RYLE, G. (1954). *Dilemmas: The Tarner Lectures, 1953* (Cambridge: Cambridge University Press).

SAPPINGTON, D. E. M. (1991). 'Incentives in Principal-Agent Relationships', *Journal of Economic Perspectives*, 5(2): 45–66.

SCHMIDT, J. D. (1998). *Free to Work: Labor Law, Emancipation, and Reconstruction 1815–1880* (Athens, Ga.: University of Georgia Press).

SCHULTZ, T. W. (1961a). 'Investment in Human Capital', *American Economic Review*, 51(1): 1.

——(1961b). 'Investment in Human Capital: Reply', *American Economic Review*, 51(5): 1035–9.

SENGE, P. M. (1990). *The Fifth Discipline: The Art and Practice of the Learning Organization* (New York: Doubleday).

SHAPIRO, S. P. (2005). 'Agency Theory', *Annual Review of Sociology*, 31(1): 263–84.

SHARMA, A. (1997). 'Professional as Agent: Knowledge Asymmetry in Agency Exchange', *Academy of Management Review*, 22(3): 758–98.

SHAVELL, S. (1979). 'Risk Sharing and Incentives in the Principal and Agent Relationship', *Bell Journal of Economics*, 10(1): 55–73.

SHUBIK, M. (1954). 'Information, Risk, Ignorance and Indeterminacy', *Quarterly Journal of Economics*, 68(4): 629–40.

SIMON, H. A. (1951). 'A Formal Theory of the Employment Relationship', *Econometrica*, 19(3): 293–305.

SPENCE, M., and ZECKHAUSER, R. (1971). 'Insurance, Information, and Individual Action', *American Economic Review*, 61(2): 380–7.

SPENDER, J.-C. (1989). *Industry Recipes: The Nature and Sources of Managerial Judgement* (Oxford: Blackwell).

SPENDER, J.-C. (1994). 'Organizational Knowledge, Collective Practice and Penrose Rents', *International Business Review*, 3(4): 353–67.

——(1996a). 'Competitive Advantage from Tacit Knowledge? Unpacking the Concept and its Strategic Implications', in B. Moingeon and A. Edmondson (eds.), *Organizational Learning and Competitive Advantage* (Thousand Oaks, Calif.: Sage Publications), 56–73.

——(1996b). 'Organizational Knowledge, Learning and Memory: Three Concepts in Search of a Theory', *Journal of Organizational Change Management*, 9(1): 63–79.

—— (2002). 'Knowledge Management, Uncertainty, and the Emerging Theory of the Firm', in C. W. Choo and N. Bontis (eds.), *The Strategic Management of Intellectual Capital and Organizational Knowledge* (Oxford: Oxford University Press), 149–62.

——(2007). 'Management as a Regulated Profession: An Essay', *Journal of Management Inquiry*, 16(1): 32–42.

—— (2008). 'Can Simon's Notion of "Bounded Rationality" Give us New Ideas about Leadership?', *Leadership*, 4: 95–109.

——(2009). 'Organizational Capital: Concept, Measure or Heuristic?', in A. Bounfour (ed.), *Organizational Capital: Modelling, Measuring and Contextualising* (London: Routledge), 5–23.

SPIEGEL, H. W. (1971). *The Growth of Economic Thought* (Durham, NC: Duke University Press).

STEFFE, L. P., and GALE, J. (eds.) (1995). *Constructivism in Education* (Hillsdale, NJ: Lawrence Erlbaum Associates).

——and THOMPSON, P. W. (2000). *Radical Constructivism in Action: Building on the Pioneering Work of Ernst von Glasersfeld* (London: Falmer Press).

STEINFELD, R. J. (1991). *The Invention of Free Labor: The Employment Relations in English and American Law and Culture, 1350–1870* (Chapel Hill, NC: University of North Carolina Press).

STEVENS, M. (1999). 'Human Capital Theory and UK Vocational Training Policy', *Oxford Review of Economic Policy*, 15(1): 16.

STEWART, T. (1997). *Intellectual Capital: The New Wealth of Organisations* (London: Nicholas Brealey).

SVEIBY, K. E. (1997). *The New Organizational Wealth: Managing and Measuring Knowledge-Based Assets* (San Francisco: Berrett-Koehler).

THARP, R. G., and GALLIMORE, R. (1988). *Rousing Minds to Life: Teaching, Learning, and Schooling in Social Context* (Cambridge: Cambridge University Press).

THOMPSON, J. D. (2001). *Organizations in Action: Social Science Bases of Administrative Theory* (New Brunswick, NJ: Transaction Publishers).

TOPEL, R. (1991). 'Specific Capital, Mobility, and Wages: Wages Rise with Job Seniority', *Journal of Political Economy*, 99(1): 145.

URMSON, J. O. (1988). 'Prichard and Knowledge', in J. Dancy, J. M. E. Moravcsik, and C. C. W. Taylor (eds.), *Human Agency: Language Duty, and Value* (Stanford, Calif.: Standford University Press), 11–24.

VEBLEN, T. (1965). *The Theory of the Business Enterprise* (New York: Augustus M. Kelley).

VON GLASERSFELD, E. (1995). 'A Constructivist Approach to Teaching', in L. P. Steffe and J. Gale (eds.), *Constructivism in Education* (Hillsdale, NJ: Lawrence Erlbaum & Associates).

——(2002). *Radical Constructivism* (London: Routledge/Falmer).

WALSH, J. R. (1935). 'Capital Concept Applied to Man', *Quarterly Journal of Economics*, 49(2): 255–85.

WEBER, M. (1968). *Economy and Society: An Outline of Interpretive Sociology*, tr. G. Roth and C. Wittich (New York: Bedminster Press).

WEISBROD, B. A. (1961). 'The Valuation of Human Capital', *Journal of Political Economy*, 69(5): 425–36.

WHITE, H. (1991). 'Agency as Control', in J. W. Pratt and R. J. Zeckhauser (eds.), *Principals and Agents: The Structure of Business* (Boston: Harvard Business School Press), 187–212.

WHITLEY, R. D., THOMAS, A., and MARCEAU, J. (1981). *Masters of Business? Business Schools and Business Graduates in Britain and France* (London: Tavistock Publications).

WIENER, N. (1967). *The Human Use of Human Beings: Cybernetics snd Society* (New York: Avon Books).

WILLIAMS, K. (2000). 'From Shareholder Value to Present-Day Capitalism', *Economy and Society*, 29(1): 1–12.

WILLIAMSON, O. E. (1993). 'Opportunism and its Critics', *Managerial and Decision Economics*, 14(2): 97–107.

—— (2000). 'The New Institutional Economics: Taking Stock, Looking Ahead', *Journal of Economic Literature*, 38(3): 595–613.

—— (2002). 'The Theory of the Firm as a Governance Structure: From Choice to Contract', *Journal of Economic Perspectives*, 16(3): 171–95.

—— (2005). 'Transaction Cost Economics: The Process of Theory Development', in K. G. Smith and M. Hitt (eds.), *Great Minds in Management* (Oxford: Oxford University Press), 485–508.

—— and WINTER, S. G. (eds.) (1991). *The Nature of the Firm: Origins, Evolution, and Development* (New York: Oxford University Press).

WOLFSON, M. A. (1991). 'Empirical Evidence of Incentive Problems and their Mitigation in Oil and Gas Tax Shelter Programs', in J. W. Pratt and R. J. Zeckhauser (eds.), *Principals and Agents: The Structure of Bsuiness* (Boston: Harvard Business School Press), 101–25.

YOUNG, M. (1994). *The Rise of the Meritocracy*, with a new introduction by the author (Paterson, NJ: Transaction Publishers).

CHAPTER 8

HUMAN CAPITAL IN THE RESOURCE-BASED VIEW

JEROEN KRAAIJENBRINK

8.1 INTRODUCTION

The resource-based view (RBV) is one of the most influential theories for explaining a firm's sustained competitive advantage (SCA). Its basic idea is that firms can attain an SCA when they possess and control valuable, rare, and inimitable assets and have an organization in place that is equipped to handle them (Barney, 1991, 1994, 2002). Since the RBV's origin in the mid-1980s, scholars have emphasized the importance of intangible assets—such as knowledge, intellectual capital, and human capital—as sources of SCA. Because of their idiosyncratic and hard-to-imitate nature, it is argued, intangible assets are the most important assets for a firm (Drucker, 1992; Quinn, 1992). Strikingly, despite everyone agreeing that intangible assets—and human capital in particular—are the strategically most important for a firm, the RBV does not handle them well. As will be argued in this chapter, the RBV with its Ricardian logic of rent generation needs amendments if its embrace is to include human capital (Coff, 1997, 1999; Foss *et al.*, 2007a, 2008; Mahoney, 1995).

The relation between human capital and the RBV has been explored in the literature on strategic human resource management (Barney and Wright, 1998; Becker and Gerhart, 1996; Boxall, 1996; Boxall and Purcell, 2000; Hitt *et al.*, 2001; Kamoche, 1996; Lado and Wilson, 1994; Richard and Johnson, 2001; Wright *et al.*, 2001). That literature typically uses the RBV as a backdrop and seeks to frame HRM questions into the RBV framework. This approach can be well understood. Compared to the

RBV's predecessor—the industrial organization (IO) view with Bain (1968) and Porter (1979, 1980, 1985) as some of its main proponents—the RBV has provided the HRM discipline with legitimization. With its focus on the internal sources of SCA, and particularly on human and intangible assets, the RBV provides HRM a more central position than did the IO view. Moreover, the two dominant HRM approaches of universalistic best practices and the contingency perspective of fitting HR practices to the firm's strategy (Boxall, 1996; Colbert, 2004) make it almost natural to seek how HRM can fit into the RBV framework.

The RBV though has received broad and severe criticisms, and were we merely to seek to fit work on human resources into the RBV framework we would inherit its limitations and miss opportunities for further enhancement. This chapter therefore follows a different approach. Rather than taking the RBV as a given it starts from critiques to the RBV and explores what the literature on human capital has to offer in addressing them. In their review, Kraaijenbrink et al. (2010) distinguish eight types of critique to the RBV. Three of these threaten the RBV's status as a core theory: the indeterminate nature of two concepts fundamental to the RBV—resource and value—plus the RBV's narrow explanation of a firm's SCA. I take these critiques as a starting point, and will address three questions concerning the role of human capital in the RBV. What are the assets? What is their value? How might firms generate and appropriate sustained above normal rents? From this analysis and selected contributions to the literature on human capital (such as Chadwick and Dabu, 2009; Coff, 1997, 1999; Kor and Leblebici, 2005; Lepak and Snell, 1999) suggestions for future research are derived.

8.2 ASSESSING THE RBV ON HUMAN CAPITAL

Human capital has been defined as: (a) individuals' knowledge and abilities that allow for changes in action and economic growth (Coleman, 1988; Dakhli and De Clercq, 2004); and (b) the stock of knowledge, know-how, expertise, and education residing in individual workers, brought to bear in their productive work but distinct from their capacity to do manual labor (Becker, 1964; Dean and Kretschmer, 2007). These definitions express that human capital refers to the knowledge and skills of individual people in so far as these exceed their capacity to do manual labor. As Coleman's definition furthermore indicates, unlike other types of resources, human capital is explicitly associated with change and growth. Further characteristics of human capital appear when it is compared to other types of resource. Coff (1997) nicely illustrates this by comparing human assets to oil fields: 'Like human assets, an oil field may be a strategic asset. However, once acquired, an oil field 1) cannot quit and move to a competing firm, 2) cannot demand higher or more equitable wages, 3) cannot reject the firm's authority or be unmotivated, and 4) need not be satisfied with supervision, coworkers, or advancement opportunities' (Coff, 1997: 374). These differences indicate how agency issues such as intentionality and motivation are characteristics unique to human capital. As we will see in this chapter, these characteristics bring in difficulties but also opportunities concerning the RBV's demarcation of assets, its notion of resource value, and its explanation of a firm's SCA.

8.2.1 What are the Assets?

In the RBV, resources are defined broadly as 'anything which could be thought of as strength or weakness of a given firm' (Wernerfelt, 1984: 172) and 'all assets, capabilities, organizational processes, firm attributes, information, knowledge, etc. controlled by a firm that enable the firm to conceive of and implement strategies that improve its efficiency and effectiveness' (Barney, 1991: 101; 2002: 155). As these definitions indicate, the RBV recognizes various types of resource as important for firms—assets, capabilities, processes, and the like. Elsewhere in his seminal paper, Barney (1991) points this out more clearly by explicitly distinguishing between physical, human, and organizational capital. Despite these distinctions the RBV treats all types of resource in the same way. This means the typologies so far offered are mere labels for which the same basic logic of the RBV holds (Barney and Clark, 2007).

By its one-size-fits-all logic, the RBV avoids theorizing on the specific character of the various types of resources and their contribution to a firm's SCA. In particular for human capital this is problematic. In the RBV, managers are assumed to pick resources and bring these into the firm (Makadok, 2001). If we consider the individual person as the basic unit holding the human capital this is still unproblematic—individual persons can be clearly demarcated, selected, and hired. Such a simple notion of human capital however, does not capture some of the subtleties involved in demarcating and owning human capital. With its assumption of full control and ownership over resources, the RBV neglects, for example, that a firm will always have to share some property rights with other firms (Coase, 1960; Demsetz, 1967). One firm may have the right to consume a resource, even while another has the right to obtain income from that same resource, and yet another has the right to alienate some of the resource's attributes. Things become even more delicate when they concern human capital. Putting aside situations of slavery and oppression, human capital cannot be owned in the same sense as tangible assets can be owned. Rather than being owned, people work for a firm voluntarily and can decide to leave at any moment. Firms then will only be able to make use of part of the knowledge and skills of individual people in a particular time frame (Bowman and Swart, 2007; Coff, 1997). Other knowledge and skills may never be put to use for the firm—or even against the firm. This means the human capital that can be deployed to a firm's advantage is narrower than the RBV assumes.

In another sense the human capital at the firm's disposal may be broader than assumed. The RBV implicitly accepts people have no life beyond working for the firm, or at least that this life is irrelevant. While this may apply to the specific labor they contribute to the firm—which following the definitions above is not part of human capital—it does not apply to their broader knowledge and skills. In their private lives, people may gain important knowledge and skills that can be useful for the firm. These are well recognized and taken into account by firms when they hire personnel. With its assumption of distinct organizational boundaries, however, the RBV omits these forms of human capital from the analysis.

The RBV's understanding of human capital is narrow in another sense as well. By its focus on the component level, the RBV assumes that knowledge resides in individual people and is therefore subjective and embodied (Grant, 1996a, 1996b). It largely ignores the collective aspects of knowledge that reside in organizational routines, structures, and culture, and those that remain when the individuals would leave the firm (Baetjer and Lewin, 2008; Bowman and Swart, 2007; Hayek, 1945; Spender, 1994, 1996). While not denying the importance of the collective level (for example, Barney, 1986; Barney and Wright, 1998), the RBV avoids theorizing on it. Other than by referring to the notions of social complexity and organization, it does not explain how value can be created from anything other than clearly demarcated resources and capabilities.

A final issue here is that the RBV does not distinguish between types of human capital. It does not acknowledge, for example, a distinction between those types of human capital that serve as inputs to the firm, those that enable the firm to select, deploy, and organize such inputs, and those that enable the firm to conceive of and envision new directions and strategies. We may refer to these three types as operational, tactical, and strategic human capital. While these are all human capital, their contributions to a firm's SCA are different in terms of time frame, scope, and scale. For example, while operational human capital can provide the firm with an immediate advantage of limited scope, strategic human capital can provide it with an advantage of wide scope in the long run. While the basic VRIN/O logic of the RBV could perhaps be applied to all types of human capital, we lose much of the subtle and substantial differences between them when we do so. This suggests that typologies of resource are not mere labels for which the same basic RBV logic applies but distinct categories with their own rent-generating logic.

8.2.2 What is their Value?

The RBV's initial conceptualization of resource value was broad: 'Resources are valuable when they enable a firm to conceive of or implement strategies that improve its efficiency or effectiveness' (Barney, 1991: 105). When considering that Barney (2002) defines SCA in line with Porter (1985) in terms of improved efficiency (reducing cost) and effectiveness (increasing value), we see that the RBV's notion of value is also tautological: value appears in both *explanans* and *explanandum*. In an attempt to clarify, several scholars have invoked the 'value–price–cost' framework, which distinguishes between perceived use value, total monetary value, and exchange value (Bowman and Ambrosini, 2000; Hoopes *et al.*, 2003; Peteraf and Barney, 2003). While these clarifications have helped to better understand the notion of value in the RBV, they are not sufficient to clarify the value of human capital.

In the RBV, the value of a resource is assumed to be determined exogenously by the market (Barney, 2001; Priem and Butler, 2001). This, however, does not fully hold for human capital. While, as for other resources, there is a market that determines the price of human capital—the job market—this price is not necessarily related to the value of human capital for a particular firm (Penrose, 1959). Since human capital can be highly firm- and industry-specific, its value depends on the characteristics of a particular firm and industry. Firms recognize this in their recruitment and selection procedures. They take great care to make sure there is a match between newly hired human capital and the human capital already in the organization. The matching goes beyond the intellectual capabilities of an individual and includes a matching of culture, social skills, attitudes, and expectations. This indicates that in the case of human capital there is at least a large component of the value that is determined endogenously, by the firm.

A related issue is the RBV's assumption that the locus of resource value lies at the component level, at the level of the individual resource. Criticism here has come in several varieties, drawing attention to the set of productive opportunities (Penrose, 1959), integrative capabilities (Grant, 1996*a*), interdependencies (Kor and Leblebici, 2005), and asset co-specializations and complementarities (Teece, 2007) as sources of SCA. The common denominator of these criticisms is that it is not the value of an individual resource that matters, but the synergistic combination of resources created by the firm. While this is not denied by the RBV's originators (for example, Barney, 1986; Barney and Wright, 1998), the RBV does not include notions of value that exceed the component level of analysis.

Another issue pertaining particularly to the value of human capital is that there can be a substantial difference between its potential value and its actual value (Hodgson, 2008). Because of their agency, individual persons have their own intentions and motivations. These do not automatically match those of the firm. This means that employees who could be extremely valuable for a company because of their skills could turn out to be of no value at all—or even harmful—when they are not willing to act in line with the organization's goals. This is a unique characteristic of human beings that complicates the notion of value in the RBV.

Finally, the RBV assumes that resources are only valuable when they are owned by the firm. In the 'relational view' of the RBV it is recognized that it can be beneficial not to own the resources themselves, but to collaborate with other firms (Dyer and Singh, 1998). This view expands the RBV from single organizations to dyads. Yet it leaves a specific characteristic of human capital unaddressed: the mobility of people across different firms. In their lifetime most people work for different organizations and often in different industries. The risk associated with this is recognized in the RBV by focusing on mechanisms that hinder the mobility of resources. The fact that employees leave a firm, however, does not always mean that their value to the firm is lost. Paradoxically, a particular person may be most valuable for a company when he or she has left, for example, to a potential customer. The active alumni policies of larger firms show that firms are aware of this. The RBV though, is silent about this aspect of human capital.

8.2.3 How to Generate and Appropriate Sustained Above Normal Rents?

The key proposition of the RBV is that SCA can be achieved by applying resources and capabilities when these are valuable, rare, inimitable, and non-substitutable (VRIN) plus when there is an appropriate organization in place (O) (Barney, 1991, 1994, 2002). While the RBV does not say much about the application of resources, it is recognized that merely possessing resources is not sufficient: it is only by being able to deploy these that SCA can be attained and rents are generated (Makadok, 2001; Peteraf and Barney, 2003). How and whether such SCA can be appropriated by firms and turned into profits, though, is left unspecified. It is sometimes suggested that rents follow more or less automatically (Amit and Schoemaker, 1993; Peteraf and Barney, 2003). Others have argued that the RBV was formulated to explain why firms will generate rent—not who will appropriate it (Coff, 1999; Wernerfelt, 1984). In either case it follows that the RBV does not explain how and by whom rents are appropriated. When it concerns human capital, rent appropriation is a complex issue. As Coff (1999) reminds us, it is not organizations that appropriate rents, but individuals such as owners, managers, and employees. These individuals are also the firm's source of human capital. The specific complication here is that the characteristics that make individual persons valuable for the company also provide these persons with bargaining power in the process of rent distribution (Bowman and Swart, 2007; Coff, 1999). Lacking an explanation of rent appropriation, the RBV is not equipped to deal with such issues.

A second issue with the RBV's explanation of rent generation and appropriation stems from the RBV's factor market logic of scarcity and efficiency. It argues that firms should compete for resources and deploy them efficiently in order to attain above normal rents. This may apply to tangible resources and even to persons, but not necessarily to human capital. Human capital is a non-rivalrous resource, the value of which may increase when it is used for multiple purposes and by multiple firms (Chadwick and Dabu, 2009; Winter and Szulanski, 2001). For such resources, the RBV's factor market logic does not fully apply, implying that we have to look beyond the RBV to explain how human capital can serve as a firm's source of SCA.

More generally this concerns the RBV's focus on Ricardian rents. As Chadwick and Dabu (2009) summarize, the RBV explains traditional and to some extent non-traditional Ricardian rents—referring respectively to the superior access to inherently heterogeneous resources and the heterogeneity through path dependence, social complexity, and causal ambiguity. What it does not capture, though, are more subjective and creative sources of rents that can be called 'entrepreneurial rents' or Penrose rents (Spender, 1994). As Foss *et al.* (Foss *et al.*, 2007a, 2007b; Foss and Ishikawa, 2007; Foss and Klein, 2005), Kor *et al.* (2007), and Alvarez and Busenitz (2001) argue, the practical assessment and evaluation of resources involves subjectivism, knowledge creation, and entrepreneurial judgment. These non-Ricardian sources of rent are to be found in the human capital of the firm. The RBV though, is not well-equipped to explain how firms can generate such endogenous rents.

A third issue—pertaining not only to human capital but also to other types of resource—is that the RBV does not explain the processes by which rents are generated and appropriated. Clearly, some of the RBV literature distinguishes resources from dynamic capabilities (Eisenhardt and Martin, 2000; Teece *et al.*, 1997; Winter, 2003). A limitation of the capabilities approach, however, is that the processes of resource development and deployment are—like the resources themselves—conceptualized as capacities, inclining us to think in terms of their possession rather than in terms of integration and application. The issue here is that the RBV does not distinguish capacity from action (or process) explicitly.

Finally, with its focus on resources, the RBV explicitly looks for the internal sources of SCA and aims to explain why firms in the same industry might differ in performance. While attractive for its simplicity, the separation of industry-based and firm-based explanations of SCA becomes problematic when it concerns human capital. Human capital can move more freely and more frequently between firms than other types of resource. Whether one firm has a human capital-based competitive advantage over another firm depends upon the temporary division of knowledge between firms in the industry (Baetjer and Lewin, 2008; Hayek, 1945). When employees move from one firm to another in the same industry and have a great deal of industry-specific knowledge it is not sufficient to focus on either firm-level or industry-level explanations of SCA.

8.3 FUTURE DIRECTIONS

The above review has shown that the RBV provides unsatisfactory answers to three central questions when we seek for an explanation of human capital as a source of SCA. In the remainder of this chapter I shall provide some suggestions on how we can move forward in future theorizing and research.

8.3.1 What are the Assets?

The first comment above was that the RBV neglects the complexities associated with the ownership of human capital. Scholars have suggested that to better understand ownership issues of tangible and some intangible resources such as patents, the RBV should incorporate insights from property rights theorizing (Kim and Mahoney, 2005; Spender, 1983). Their incorporation in resource-based theorizing helps to shift the attention away from resources *per se* and to the specific rights associated with them. Since human capital cannot be owned in the same sense as tangible assets, property rights theory may not be fully apply here. A similar shift though can be made with contract theory, which refers to theorizing on formal legal-economic contracts (for example, Bolton and Dewatripont, 2005; Coff, 1999; Jensen and Meckling, 1976), but also to theorizing on more informal social contracts between the various stakeholders of a firm (Donaldson and Dunfee, 1994; Keeley, 1980; Mahoney *et al.*, 1994; Rousseau, 1968). Like property rights theory, contract theory focuses on what can be expected from a resource rather than on a resource itself. Contract theory furthermore recognizes that the several individuals in the firm have bargaining power and that negotiations take place to determine which contributions individuals will make to the firm—and thus what human capital the firm will have at its disposal. By its focus on individuals and their goals and bargaining positions, contract theory can help to bring human agency into resource-based theorizing and thereby stimulate theorizing beyond the notion of organizations as bundles of resources.

The second comment was that the RBV does not explicitly consider the knowledge and skills that people may gain outside the firm. Since these can be valuable for the firm, it is important that the RBV includes them. Arguing that such knowledge and skills should be obtained and deployed does not work, since in most societies today people can decide themselves what they do in their private lives. Hence we must find other ways to incorporate this aspect of human capital in resource-based theorizing. To a large extent the distinction between what individuals do for the firm and what they do in their private lives lies in the controllability of people's behaviors by the firm. While the firm has relatively much influence on what individuals do within the boundaries of the firm, it has less influence on what individuals do in their private lives or for other firms. To recognize this distinction it may be useful in future RBV theorizing and research to consider resource controllability as a factor that affects how firms can build an SCA from human capital. In a sense this suggests tightening the connection between the RBV and resource dependence theory (Pfeffer and Salancik, 2003). Different, though, is that where resource dependence theory focuses on the meso- and macro-level of the environment of the organization, resource controllability concerns the micro-level of individual resources.

A third comment made about the RBV was that it does not sufficiently cover the collective level of human capital and resources in general. A similar comment has appeared in the literature on human capital. Baetjer and Lewin (2008), for example, have argued that the term human capital is unfortunate since it suggests that all knowledge resides in individual human beings. Several attempts have been made to further understand the various levels at which human capital may reside. Typically, scholars have conceptualized human capital as one specific type of intellectual capital, the other types being organizational or structural capital, and social or relational capital (Bontis, 1998; Coleman, 1988; Subramaniam and Youndt, 2005; Youndt *et al.*, 2004). An illuminating contribution to the understanding of these distinctions comes from Bowman and Swart (2007), who distinguish between separable, embodied, and embedded capital:

In a firm manufacturing gearboxes the lathes and milling machines would be examples of *separable* capital. They are *capital* insofar as they are critical to the processes of efficient production, and they are *separable* insofar as they can exist in a form separate from the individuals that work with them. (Bowman and Swart, 2007: 4–5; original italics.)

In contrast, *embodied* capital cannot exist in a form separated from individuals or teams (Bontis, 1998), and would include the skills or tacit knowledge that are often cited as being 'resources' in the resource-based view of the firm. These forms of capital may enable the firm to compete more effectively, and they interact with other forms of capital to create value.(Ibid.)

Embedded capital exists as a *gestalt*; a complex agglomeration of human and separable capital that resists separation into the constituent parts that combine to produce it. This is usually a function of the nature of the synergies between the assets in the configuration that are difficult to identify, and due to causal ambiguity perceived by management, they are difficult to manage. (Ibid. 8.)

Of the three types, separable capital is the simplest form and easiest to manage because it can be clearly demarcated and separated. Embodied and embedded capital are more complex. As a *gestalt*, particularly embedded capital can be difficult to manage; it cannot be separated into parts and it therefore needs to be taken as a whole. Along similar lines, Baetjer and Lewin (2008) have argued that tangible and intangible capital cannot be separated. As they conclude, 'capital is naturally, and at least since Adam Smith has been, conceived of as part of a dynamic value-creating process, in which individual capital items are heterogeneous, complementary components of an extensive, but everchanging, structure of production' (Baetjer and Lewin, 2008: 28). Tangible capital, then, is embodied knowledge of productive processes and how those processes may be carried out. Using the example of a hammer, Baetjer and Lewin argue:

The point here is more radical than simply that capital goods have knowledge in them. It is rather that capital goods *are knowledge*, knowledge in the peculiar state of being embodied in a form ready to hand for use in production. The knowledge aspect of capital goods is the fundamental aspect. Any physical aspect is incidental. A hammer, for instance, is physical wood (the handle) and metal (the head). But a piece of oak and a chunk of iron do not make a hammer. The hammer is those raw materials infused with the knowledge embodied in the precise shape of the head and handle, the curvature of the striking surface, the proportion of head weight to handle length, and so on. (Baetjer and Lewin, 2008: 8; original italics)

Baetjer and Lewin stress the social and dynamic character of knowledge by arguing that the knowledge of many people is combined in capital goods and that capital development is a process of social interaction. Through the embodiment of knowledge into a capital structure, people are able to take advantage of the specialized knowledge of others who have contributed to that structure. With this Hayekian view of knowledge (Hayek, 1945), they stress that the notion of human capital is better conceived of as a dynamic structure than as a stock. I suspect that taking Bowman and Swart's and Baetjer and Lewin's notions of human capital as a starting point rather than the traditional neoclassical and Ricardian view of resources will have broad implications for the RBV and provide a fruitful direction for future research.

The final comment made on the RBV's notion of assets was that the RBV treats all types in the same way and thereby overlooks relevant differences between them. It has already been suggested that operational, tactical, and strategic human capital are substantially different and that rivalrous resources should be distinguished from non-rivalrous resources because they involve a different rent-generating logic. An additional suggestion here is to explore further types of human capital from the perspective of their distinct contribution to a firm's competitive advantage. In this respect, research on imaginative skills, persuasion skills, relational skills, and coordinative skills can be worth conducting. For each of these types, the VRIN/O logic may still apply. However, by further translating this logic into resource-specific notions of value, rarity, imitability, substitutability, and organization, the RBV can be made more precise.

8.3.2 What is their Value?

The question whether the value of resources is determined endogenously or exogenously has generated broad discussion. To further clarify this discussion it can be fruitful to consider the distinction between the industry-specificity, firm-specificity, and individual-specificity of human capital (Dakhli and De Clercq, 2004; Kor and Mahoney, 2004). Industry-specific human capital pertains to knowledge derived from experience specific to an industry. It develops through intimate communication between firms in the industry and through the tacit know-how present in existing technology (Dakhli and De Clercq, 2004). Given its specificity it is only valuable within a particular industry and much less so in other industries. Moreover, given its industry-level it seems likely that its value is largely determined exogenously. The shared nature of industry-specific human capital, though, makes it improbable as a source of SCA (Barney, 1991, 1994, 2002). Firm-specific human capital concerns the knowledge and skills that are only valuable to a specific firm. For example, managers' experience with firm-level resources leads to firm-specific knowledge about the productive opportunities of these resources (Kor and Mahoney, 2004; Penrose, 1959). Since it is unique to the firm, this type of human capital may give the firm an advantage over other firms. Therefore, its value is likely to be determined mainly endogenously. Finally, individual-specific human capital pertains to the individual's knowledge and skills that are applicable to a broad range of firms and industries. It includes general and broad education and experience, and is highly mobile across firms and across industries. As such, the RBV would not consider it to be a source of SCA. However, looking at the compensations that are sometimes given to individual persons it is this type of human capital that firms seem to value most. Executives moving from one firm to another have individual specific knowledge and skills that is not limited to a particular industry or firm. At the same time, though, they are considered to be of the highest value to the firm, which is inconsistent with the RBV's predictions. Further research should clarify how the three types of human capital should be valued and how they contribute to a firm's SCA.

A further suggestion to address the endogenous–exogenous discussion is that the management's own assessment of the value of human capital can be as determining its possible value to the firm as any reasoning or quality inherent to the human capital itself (Kraaijenbrink et al., 2010; Mahoney, 1995; Penrose, 1959). Along these lines we may want to consider that the processes of value assessment include those of conceiving ways to create and capture novel value through specific human capital. This moves us into a humanly constructed world in which value creation starts from our imaginings. The key difference here from the current RBV is that in environments that are not highly predictable and mature, the locus of value creation may lie within the firm—within the imaginative and creative capabilities of the people involved in it—rather than in the market.

Given the tight connections between individual and collective aspects of human capital, assessing its value requires reasoning beyond the component level. There are at least two manners in which to do so. First, along a similar line as Kor and Leblebici (2005) and Bowman and Swart (2007), it can be worthwhile to look at the leveraging effects that can occur when various types of human capital are combined within the firm. As their example of law firms illustrates, firms effectively leverage the human capital of senior partners by assisting them with more junior associates. By doing so, the partner can focus on the highest value-creating activities while the associates perform time-consuming, less value-creating activities. By the leveraging effect that takes place as such, the value of both the partners and the associates increases for the firm. When further investigated in future research, this leveraging effect would help us to better understand from where the value of human capital and other types of resource derives.

Second, and in line with Boxall and Purcell (2000), Colbert (2004), Delery and Doty (1996), and Youndt et al. (1996), it may also prove useful to distinguish between a universalistic, contingency, configurational, and complexity perspective on resource-based theorizing. Current resource-based theorizing is mainly of a universalistic or 'best practice' nature. This means that it is assumed that certain independent–dependent variable relationships hold across whole populations of organizations. Barney's (1991) canonical VRIN model is a typical example of this. By adding the 'organization' factor to this model, Barney (2002) forms an attempt to move to a contingency perspective. That is, it is assumed that the value of resources depends on the extent to which there is an organization in place that is equipped to handle them. Though it has not been developed extensively, the addition of this contingency variable enables theorizing at the collective level of the value of human capital. Further enhancements can be made when resource-based theorizing adopts a configurational and complexity perspective. A configurational approach to the RBV would follow a holistic principle of inquiry and would be concerned with how patterns of multiple interdependent resources relate to a firm's SCA (Meyer et al., 1993). It would allow for different configurations of resources as explanations of SCA. While a configurational approach still assumes some decomposability of the firm into separate parts—patterns—a complexity perspective does not, which makes it a truly holistic perspective. It assumes that organizations are self-organizing, emergent, and unique, and that they thrive at far from equilibrium states (Colbert, 2004). Organizations are assumed to be comprised of a large number of interacting agents and stable, observable properties that emerge due to the collective behavior of these agents. With its emphasis on (human) agency, interactions, and disequilibrium, we suspect that further research on human capital in the RBV using a complexity perspective will yield important new insights.

As noted, there may be a substantial difference between the potential value of human capital and its realized value. The suggestion of incorporating contract theory into resource-based theorizing may help to deal with this issue. By focusing on the legal/economic and social contracts in a firm a more accurate explanation can be given of the actual value of human capital for the firm. To further explore the distinction between potential and realized value of human capital it can also be useful to consider the opportunity, motivation, and ability that people have to realize their potential in the firm (Adler and Kwon, 2002). Whereas Adler and Kwon use the 'opportunity–motivation–ability' framework to explain the distinction between potential and realized social capital, its applicability can be extended to human capital. Opportunity in this respect would refer to the access that the firm has to human capital within and outside its boundaries. Motivation then would refer to the willingness and intention of individuals to put their human capital at the disposal of the firm. Ability would refer to the capacity of the individual to apply its knowledge and skills to the advantage of the firm.

The final comment concerning the RBV's notion of value is that human capital can be valuable even when it resides outside the firm. I gave the example of how firms deal with former employees as alumni that can be valuable to the firm in the future. For further research this implies that we may want to investigate how human capital outside the firm can contribute to a firm's SCA. Also here social contract theory can be a useful starting point. Although not bounded to the firm by a formal contract, a firm's alumni may still feel strongly associated with the firm and may be inclined to favor deals with the firm above deals with other firms. In such a case, the relationship between the focal firm and the firm the alumnus works for now is not merely transaction-based. Rather it involves personal and social aspects such as trust, liking, and commitment. Blyler and Coff's (2003) work is an example of a study that includes this.

8.3.3 How to Generate and Appropriate Sustained Above Normal Rents

Concerning the RBV's explanation of rent generation and rent appropriation, several comments have been made. The above suggestions on assets and value should help to address some of these. This last section provides additional suggestions on how the RBV may be better equipped to explain SCA based on human capital.

It has been suggested that the RBV's notion of a resource can be clarified when the distinctions between embedded, embodied, and separable resources are considered (Baetjer and Lewin, 2008; Bowman and Swart, 2007). This distinction can also help to develop the RBV's position on rent appropriation. In the case of embodied human capital, individual employees possess the valuable knowledge. This provides them with a bargaining position by which they can appropriate a substantial share of the rents (Coff, 1999). In the case of embedded human capital, knowledge resides at the organizational level and there is ambiguity surrounding the rent-creating contributions of individual people. This means that rents may be more likely appropriated by its managers than by the individual employees. Finally, when knowledge is separable from people, it resides in the firm's tangible assets and in such cases it may be the shareholders who appropriate most of the rents. As Bowman and Swart (2007) point out, the way rents are appropriated will differ across industries. In more traditional industries (such as pharmaceuticals) the owners of firms have control over the critical forms of capital, which tend to be separable, like equipment. Knowledge-intensive industries, though, are characterized by some control being exerted over the deployment of valuable human capital resources by the employees themselves. While some pioneering work has been done here, further research is needed to incorporate such ideas into the RBV.

As touched upon in the discussions above on resources and on their value, contract theory can help to both clarify the notion of human capital and its value. As such, it also provides a promising basis for further developing the RBV's explanation of rent generation and appropriation. The particular challenge here is that there is a tension between the two—that it may be the same characteristics of human capital that generate rents that also complicate the appropriation of rents. This means that appropriate mechanisms must be found to let the firm appropriate rents without reducing its ability to generate rents. While largely left unexplored in the RBV literature, the HRM literature may provide a starting point. Dealing with such issues, Lepak and Snell (1999, 2002) have suggested that the strategic value and uniqueness of human capital varies across individuals. Based on these differences they suggest four types of employment mode (internal development, acquisition, contracting, and alliance) and corresponding employment relationships (organizational, symbiotic, transactional, and partnership) and HR configurations (commitment-based, productivity-based, compliance-based, and collaborative). Lepak and Snell's framework has enhanced the understanding of how the tension between rent generation and rent appropriation of human capital could be managed. Further research could establish whether this framework can also be applied to other types of resource.

As argued above, the RBV is not well equipped to deal with entrepreneurial rents (Chadwick and Dabu, 2009), Penrose rents (Spender, 1994), and rents originating from non-rivalrous resources (Kraaijenbrink *et al.*, 2010). Based on strategic factor market logic, the RBV assumes that resources—including human capital—are scarce and that firms must compete to obtain the best. In the case of non-rivalrous resources there is no scarcity. When human capital increases after deployment, a firm could benefit from other firms' deploying it. This implies that collaboration and co-development rather than strict competition may be effective ways of generating a human capital-based SCA. As multiple firms are involved in this, the generation and appropriation of rents are more complex. Also, the management of non-rivalrous human capital differs greatly from the management of rivalrous resources. If human capital can be used only once, managers must focus on its efficiency in use. But if it is increased by its deployment, human capital should probably be deployed as widely and frequently as possible. Further theorizing and research on learning-by-doing and learning-curve implications of the RBV may prove fruitful here (Kraaijenbrink *et al.*, 2010; Yelle, 1979).

Concerning the generation and appropriation of entrepreneurial rents, Chadwick and Dabu (2009) have argued that more attention is needed to notions such as entrepreneurial alertness and exceptional foresight as sources of SCA. Along these lines, RBV theorists may want to consider that the rents derived from human capital include those of imagining ways to create and capture novel value from resources. Merely imagining value, though, is not sufficient. For actual rent generation, firms will need all kinds of resources to help turn their ideas into reality—including having other firms or people value what has been produced. Therefore, the role of the entrepreneurs cannot be limited to foreseeing or imagining value that others do not see. It must embrace bringing the resources together in such a way that the value they imagine is delivered. This implies that rent generation involves all kinds of internal and external social influence mechanisms, including the use of rhetoric, power, and bargaining (Coff, 1999).

The RBV does not explicitly distinguish the rent-generating capacity residing in human capital from the processes of rent generation and appropriation. Future theorizing would benefit from distinguishing explicitly between building or acquiring human capital, on the one hand, and the processes of deploying that human capital, on the other hand. By doing so, a more practical resource-based theory about what human capital to deploy and what to keep in reserve might be developed. So far, empirical studies on the RBV have primarily adopted a variance approach. Typically, these take a set of independent variables and performance or SCA as the dependent variable, leaving the processes by which resources are obtained and deployed black-boxed. Understanding how rents are generated and appropriated, however, requires a more process-based approach (for example, Van de Ven, 2007; Van de Ven and Polley, 1992). The literature on HRM provides some useful starting points for this. It has put much effort into understanding how the potential residing in human capital can by unleashed to the firm's potential. HRM activities put forward include attracting, motivating, developing, coordinating, deploying, and retaining employees (Boxall and Purcell, 2000; Chadwick and Dabu, 2009). Given that these activities have been broadly researched in the HRM literature and that the RBV literature mostly lacks a process perspective, it is worthwhile to explore how these HRM activities can be woven into the RBV. Particularly, Chadwick and Dabu's (2009) work may prove relevant here since it argues how the various HRM activities can contribute to the generation of different types of rent.

It was suggested above that to better understand human capital and its value, further attention needs to be given to industry-specific, firm-specific, and individual-specific aspects and to individual and collective aspects of human capital. Furthermore it was suggested that social contract theory can help to better understand how human capital residing outside the firm may be valuable to the firm. These suggestions can also contribute to further develop the relationship between internal and external aspects of rent generation and appropriation. Along these lines, two further directions for future research can be exemplified. The first relates to the observation that human capital can be valuable even when it resides outside the firm. The RBV focuses on isolating mechanisms to prevent other firms from imitating or obtaining the firm's resources. If human capital is valuable when residing outside the firm, isolating mechanisms may become less important. Rather than preventing the outflow of human capital, firms in some cases may want to actively promote such outflow. If so, proactive mobility rather than immobility can be a source of SCA. Further research is needed in order to find out under which circumstances this would be the case and how firms could manage it. The second direction concerns the notion of agency. One of the primary differences between human capital and other types of resource is that human beings have intentions and motivations that may differ from the firm's. The extant literature focuses on the negative aspects of this: because of agency involved, human capital is more difficult to obtain and retain, and people need to be satisfied and motivated in order to be valuable for the firm. Yet, this same agency also has a positive side: employees can decide to work for a firm or stay with a firm in cases where the market would predict they would not. People have several reasons why they want to work for a particular firm. They may live nearby, like other persons working there, or like the image and reputation of a firm. Such reasons imply that the repertoire of mechanisms to obtain, deploy, and retain human capital is broader than assumed in the RBV. They also imply that some of the earlier mentioned tensions between rent generation and rent appropriation can be dealt with by non-monetary HRM activities. As the RBV does not yet include these, future research is needed.

8.4 Conclusion

This chapter has explored how the extant RBV literature deals with the notion of human capital and how it may want to move forward. Rather than taking the RBV as a given and considering how the literature on human capital could fit into it, I have taken a critical approach to the RBV and suggested how the literature on human capital and HRM provides clues for further development. In some places I have oversimplified and may have put the RBV up as a straw man that can be easily attacked. This approach was chosen to separate and magnify problems in the RBV. By doing so I hope to have illuminated the problems and potential involved in theorizing and researching the role of human capital in the RBV.

Despite their breadth, many of the comments and suggestions are related. Together they point to a fundamental limitation of the RBV: that it does not recognize the unique and social character of human capital. This chapter suggests that firms should respect and nourish their peoples' agency and should strive to create conditions under which it can be applied effectively. This suggests that firms should both leave latitude for individual and collective action to deal with the unexpected and ensure that contributing agentic behavior is rewarded. These prescriptions, inherently different from the RBV's, are deeply humanist in the face of the RBV's economizing and focus on economic objects.

References

ADLER, P. S., and KWON, S.-W. (2002). 'Social Capital: Prospects for a New Concept', *Academy of Management Review*, 27(1): 17–40.

ALVAREZ, S. A., and BUSENITZ, L. W. (2001). 'The Entrepreneurship of Resource-Based Theory', *Journal of Management*, 27(6): 755–75.

AMIT, R., and SCHOEMAKER, P. J. H. (1993). 'Strategic Assets and Organizational Rent', *Strategic Management Journal*, 14(1): 33–46.

234   JEROEN KRAAIJENBRINK

BAETJER, H., and LEWIN, P. (2008). 'Can Ideas be Capital? Can Capital be Anything Else?', *George Mason Mercatus Center Working Paper*, 83.

BAIN, J. S. (1968). *Industrial Organization* (New York: John Wiley).

BARNEY, J. B. (1986). 'Organizational Culture: Can it be a Source of Sustained Competitive Advantage?', *Academy of Management Review*, 11(3): 656–65.

——(1991). 'Firm Resources and Sustained Competitive Advantage', *Journal of Management*, 17(1): 99–120.

——(1994). 'Bringing Managers Back In: A Resource-Based Analysis of the Role of Managers in Creating and Sustaining Competitive Advantages for Firms', in *Does Management Matter? On Competencies and Competitive Advantage* (The 1994 Crafoord lectures; Lund: Institute of Economic Research, Lund University), 1–36.

—— (2001). 'Is the Resource-Based "View" a Useful Perspective for Strategic Management Research? Yes'. *Academy of Management Review*, 26(1): 41–56.

—— (2002). *Gaining and Sustaining Competitive Advantage* (Englewood Cliffs, NJ: Prentice Hall).

——and CLARK, D. N. (2007). *Resource-Based Theory: Creating and Sustaining Competitive Advantage* (Oxford: Oxford University Press).

——and WRIGHT, P. M. (1998). 'On Becoming a Strategic Partner: The Role of Human Resources in Gaining Competitive Advantage', *Human Resource Management*, 37(1): 31–46.

BECKER, B., and GERHART, B. (1996). 'The Impact of Human Resource Management on Organizational Performance: Progress and Prospects', *Academy of Management Journal*, 39(4): 779–801.

BECKER, G. S. (1964). *Human Capital: A Theoretical and Empirical Analysis, With Special Reference to Education* (New York and London: Columbia University Press).

BLYLER, M., and COFF, R. W. (2003). 'Dynamic Capabilities, Social Capital, and Rent Appropriation: Ties that Split Pies', *Strategic Management Journal*, 24(7): 677–86.

BOLTON, P., and DEWATRIPONT, M. (2005). *Contract Theory* (Cambridge, Mass.: MIT Press).

BONTIS, N. (1998). 'Intellectual Capital: An Exploratory Study that Develops Measures and Models', *Management Decision*, 36(2): 63–76.

BOWMAN, C., and AMBROSINI, V. (2000). 'Value Creation versus Value Capture: Towards a Coherent Definition of Value in Strategy', *British Journal of Management*, 11(1): 1–15.

——and SWART, J. (2007). 'Whose Human Capital? The Challenge of Value Capture When Capital is Embedded', *Journal of Management Studies*, 44(4): 488–505.

BOXALL, P. (1996). 'The Strategic HRM Debate and the Resource-Based View of the Firm', *Human Resource Management Journal*, 6(3): 59–75.

——and PURCELL, J. (2000). 'Strategic Human Resource Management: Where have we Come from and Where should we be Going?', *International Journal of Management Reviews*, 2(2): 183–203.

CHADWICK, C., and DABU, A. (2009). 'Human Resources, Human Resource Management, and the Competitive Advantage of Firms: Toward a More Comprehensive Model of Causal Linkages', *Organization Science*, 20(1): 253–72.

COASE, R. (1960). 'The Problem of Social Cost', *Journal of Law and Economics*, 3: 1–44.

COFF, R. W. (1997). 'Human Assets and Management Dilemmas: Coping with Hazards on the Road to Resource-Based Theory', *Academy of Management Review*, 22(2): 374–402.

——(1999). 'When Competitive Advantage doesn't Lead to Performance: The Resource-Based View and Stakeholder Bargaining Power', *Organization Science*, 10(2): 119–33.

COLBERT, B. A. (2004). 'The Complex Resource-Based View: Implications for Theory and Practice in Strategic Human Resource Management', *Academy of Management Review*, 29(3): 341–58.

COLEMAN, J. S. (1988). 'Social Capital in the Creation of Human Capital', *American Journal of Sociology*, 94: S95–S120.

DAKHLI, M., and DE CLERCQ, D. (2004). 'Human Capital, Social Capital, and Innovation: A Multi-Country Study', *Entrepreneurship and Regional Development*, 16(2): 107–28.

DEAN, A., and KRETSCHMER, M. (2007). 'Can Ideas be Capital? Factors of Production in the Postindustrial Economy: A Review and Critique', *Academy of Management Review*, 32(2): 573–94.

DELERY, J. E., and DOTY, D. H. (1996). 'Modes of Theorizing in Strategic Human Resource Management: Tests of Universalistic, Contingency, and Configurational Performance Ppredictions', *Academy of Management Journal*, 39(4): 802–35.

DEMSETZ, H. (1967). 'Toward a Theory of Property Rights', *American Economic Review*, 57(2): 347–59.

DONALDSON, T., and DUNFEE, T. W. (1994). 'Toward a Unified Conception of Business Ethics: Integrative Social Contracts Theory', *Academy of Management Review*, 19(2): 252–84.

DRUCKER, P. F. (1992). 'The New Society of Organizations', *Harvard Business Review*, 70 (Sept.–Oct.): 95–104.

DYER, J. H., and SINGH, H. (1998). 'The Relational View: Cooperative Strategy and Sources of Interorganizational Competitive Advantage', *Academy of Management Review*, 23(4): 660–79.

EISENHARDT, K. M., and MARTIN, J. A. (2000). 'Dynamic Capabilities: What are They?', *Strategic Management Journal*, 21(10/11): 1105–21.

FOSS, N. J., and ISHIKAWA, I. (2007). 'Towards a Dynamic Resource-Based View: Insights from Austrian Capital and Entrepreneurship Theory', *Organization Studies*, 28(5): 749–72.

FOSS, N. J., and KLEIN, P. G. (2005). 'Entrepreneurship and the Economic Theory of the Firm: Any Gains from Trade?', in R. Agarwal, S. A. Alvarez, and O. Sorensen (eds.), *Handbook of Entrepreneurship: Disciplinary Perspectives* (Norwell, Mass.: Kluwer), 55–80.

FOSS, K., FOSS, N. J., and KLEIN, P. G. (2007a). 'Original and Derived Judgment: An Entrepreneurial Theory of Economic Organization', *Organization Studies*, 28(6): 1–20.

FOSS, K., FOSS, N. J., KLEIN, P. G., and KLEIN, S. K. (2007b). 'The Entrepreneurial Organization of Heterogeneous Capital', *Journal of Management Studies*, 44(7): 1165–86.

FOSS, N. J., KLEIN, P. G., KOR, Y. Y., and MAHONEY, J. T. (2008). 'Entrepreneurship, Subjectivism, and the Resource-Based View: Toward a New Synthesis', *Strategic Entrepreneurship Journal*, 2(1): 73–94.

GRANT, R. M. (1996a). 'Prospering in Dynamically-Competitive Environments: Organizational Capability as Knowledge Integration', *Organization Science*, 7(4): 375–87.

——(1996b). 'Toward a Knowledge-Based Theory of the Firm'. *Strategic Management Journal*, 17 (Winter): 109–22.

HAYEK, F. A. (1945). 'The Use of Knowledge in Society', *American Economic Review*, 35(4): 519–30.

HITT, M. A., BIERMAN, L., SHIMIZU, K., and KOCHHAR, R. (2001). 'Direct and Moderating Effects of Human Capital on Strategy and Performance in Professional Service Firms: A Resource-Based Perspective', *Academy of Management Journal*, 44(1): 13–28.

HODGSON, G. M. (2008). 'The Concept of a Routine', in M. C. Becker (ed.), *The Handbook of Organizational Routines* (Cheltenham: Edward Elgar), 15–29.

HOOPES, D. G., MADSEN, T. L., and WALKER, G. (2003). 'Guest Editors' Introduction to the Special Issue: Why is there a Resource-Based View? Toward a Theory of Competitive Heterogeneity', *Strategic Management Journal*, 24(10): 889–902.

JENSEN, M., and MECKLING, W. (1976). 'Theory of the Firm: Managerial Behavior, Agency Costs, and Capital Structure', *Journal of Financial Economics*, 3(4): 305–60.

KAMOCHE, K. (1996). 'Strategic Human Resource Management within a Resource-Capability View of the Firm', *Journal of Management Studies*, 33(2): 213–33.

KEELEY, M. (1980). 'Organizational Analogy: A Comparison of Organismic and Social Contract Models', *Administrative Science Quarterly*, 25(2): 337–62.

KIM, J., and MAHONEY, J. T. (2005). 'Property Rights Theory, Transaction Costs Theory, and Agency Theory: An Organizational Economics Approach to Strategic Management', *Managerial and Decision Economics*, 26(4): 223–42.

KOR, Y. Y., and LEBLEBICI, H. (2005). 'How do Interdependencies among Human-Capital Deployment, Development and Diversification Strategies Affect Firms' Financial Performance', *Strategic Management Journal*, 26(10): 967–85.

——and MAHONEY, J. T. (2004). 'Edith Penrose's (1959) Contributions to the Resource-Based View of Strategic Management', *Journal of Management Studies*, 41(1): 183–91.

—— MAHONEY, J. T., and MICHAEL, S. C. (2007). 'Resources, Capabilities, and Entrepreneurial Perceptions', *Journal of Management Studies*, 44(7): 1187–1212.

KRAAIJENBRINK, J., SPENDER, J. C., and GROEN, A. J. (2010). 'The Resource-Based View: A Review and Assessment of its Critiques', *Journal of Management*, 36(1): 349–72.

LADO, A. A., and WILSON, M. C. (1994). 'Human Resource Systems and Sustained Competitive Advantage: A Competency-Based Perspective', *Academy of Management Review*, 19(4): 699–727.

LEPAK, D. P., and SNELL, S. A. (1999). 'The Human Resource Architecture: Toward a Theory of Human Capital Allocation and Development', *Academy of Management Review*, 24(1): 31–48.

——and —— (2002). 'Examining the Human Resource Architecture: The Relationships among Human Capital, Employment, and Human Resource Configurations', *Journal of Management*, 28(4): 517–43.

MAHONEY, J. T. (1995). 'The Management of Resources and the Resource of Management', *Journal of Business Research*, 33(2): 91–101.

——HUFF, A. S., and HUFF, J. O. (1994). 'Toward a New Social Contract Theory in Organization Science', *Journal of Management Inquiry*, 3(2): 153–68.

MAKADOK, R. (2001). 'Towards a Synthesis of Resource-Based and Dynamic Capability Views of Rent Creation', *Strategic Management Journal*, 22(5): 387–402.

MEYER, A. D., TSUI, A. S., and HININGS, C. R. (1993). 'Configurational Approaches to Organizational Analysis', *Academy of Management Journal*, 36(6): 1175–95.

PENROSE, E. T. (1959). *The Theory of the Growth of the Firm*. (1995 edn. New York: John Wiley & Sons).

PETERAF, M. A., and BARNEY, J. B. (2003). 'Unraveling the Resource-Based Tangle', *Managerial and Decision Economics*, 24(4): 309–23.

PFEFFER, J., and SALANCIK, G. R. (2003). *The External Control of Organizations: A Resource Dependence Perspective* (Stanford, Calif.: Stanford University Press).

PORTER, M. E. (1979). 'How Competitive Forces Shape Strategy', *Harvard Business Review* (Mar./Apr.): 137–45.

——(1980). *Competitive Strategy: Techniques for Analyzing Industries and Competitors* (New York: Free Press).

——(1985). *Competitive Advantage* (New York: Free Press).

PRIEM, R. L., and BUTLER, J. E. (2001). 'Tautology in the Resource-Based View and the Implications of Externally Determined Resource Value: Further Comments', *Academy of Management Review*, 26(1): 57–66.

QUINN, J. B. (1992). *Intelligent Enterprise: A Knowledge and Service Based Paradigm for Industry* (New York: Free Press).

RICHARD, O. C., and JOHNSON, N. B. (2001). 'Strategic Human Resource Management Effectiveness and Firm Performance', *International Journal of Human Resource Management*, 12(2): 299–310.

ROUSSEAU, J. J. (1968). *The Social Contract* (New York: Penguin Group USA).

SPENDER, J.-C. (1983). *Strategic Management: A Property Rights Approach* (Los Angeles, Calif.: UCLA Working Paper).

——(1994). 'Organizational Knowledge, Collective Practice, and Penrose Rents', *International Business Review*, 3(4): 353–67.

——(1996). 'Making Knowledge the Basis of a Dynamic Theory of the Firm', *Strategic Management Journal*, 17 (Special issue): 45–62.

SUBRAMANIAM, M., and YOUNDT, M. A. (2005). 'The Influence of Intellectual Capital on the Types of Innovative Capabilities', *Academy of Management Journal*, 48(3): 450–63.

TEECE, D. J. (2007). 'Explicating Dynamic Capabilities: The Nature and Microfoundations of (Sustainable) Enterprise Performance', *Strategic Management Journal*, 28(13): 1319–50.

—— PISANO, G. P., and SHUEN, A. (1997). 'Dynamic Capabilities and Strategic Management', *Strategic Management Journal*, 18(7): 509–33.

VAN DE VEN, A. H. (2007). *Engaged Scholarship: A Guide for Organizational and Social Research* (Oxford: Oxford University Press).

—— and POLLEY, D. (1992). 'Learning While Innovating', *Organization Science*, 3(1): 92–116.

WERNERFELT, B. (1984). 'A Resource-Based View of the Firm', *Strategic Management Journal*, 5(2): 171–80.

WINTER, S. G. (2003). 'Understanding Dynamic Capabilities', *Strategic Management Journal*, 24(10): 991–5.

——and SZULANSKI, G. (2001). 'Replication as Strategy', *Organization Science*, 12(6): 730–43.

WRIGHT, P. M., DUNFORD, B. B., and SNELL, S. A. (2001). 'Human Resources and the Resource Based View of the Firm'. *Journal of Management*, 27(6): 701–21.

YELLE, L. E. (1979). 'The Learning Curve: Historical Review and Comprehensive Survey', *Decision Sciences*, 10: 302–28.

YOUNDT, M. A., SNELL, S. A., DEAN, J. W., JR., and LEPAK, D. P. (1996). 'Human Resource Management, Manufacturing Strategy, and Firm Performance', *Academy of Management Journal*, 39(4): 836–66.

——SUBRAMANIAM, M., and SNELL, S. A. (2004). 'Intellectual Capital Profiles: An Examination of Investments and Returns', *Journal of Management Studies*, 41(2): 335–61.

CHAPTER 9

HUMAN CAPITAL, ENTREPRENEURSHIP, AND THE THEORY OF THE FIRM

BRIAN J. LOASBY

9.1 OVERVIEW

One could read a great many articles in major economic journals without encountering any substantive discussion of entrepreneurship. Since all outcomes are described as the equilibrium results of the rational choices of optimizing agents, there is no need for this hypothesis. Firms, by contrast, frequently appear: in price theory they provide the supply side in goods markets and the demand side in labour markets. However, these firms are treated as unitary agents, and the 'theory of the firm' traces the effects of different kinds and degrees of competition on their optimal choices (including optimal choices among technological options which are public knowledge), and thus on equilibrium prices. Their internal arrangements are irrelevant to this theory, since firms must conform to external pressures. These may include the pressures of the stock market, which enforce the maximization of net present value in every public company. Therefore, a 'representative firm' is often sufficient for theorists.

Why there should be firms as organizations is a minor issue in economic theory, and the standard explanations all rely on a reallocation of decision rights to resolve some conflict of incentives. In most versions, once this reallocation has been achieved everyone acts independently. Only Williamson's analysis, which postulates a closely complementary relationship between two activities which would leave one party dependent on the other, actually envisages the solution as a hierarchy, in which one person's actions are partially controlled by another, to the benefit of both. Williamson has not sought to explain how this hierarchy might work, though he has assured us that it is unlikely to produce 'surprises, victims, and the like' because, although imperfect, it is the product of far-sighted contracting which is explicitly designed to avoid undesirable outcomes (Williamson, 1996: 46). This exiguous conception of organization serves as a device for validating theories which assume the dominance of market effects while ignoring the methods and costs of organizing markets.

Nevertheless, there have been important contributions to a theory of entrepreneurship and to a theory of the firm as an organization; and not all of these are recent. The primary objective of this chapter is to explore the basis for these more substantive treatments, and incidentally to explain their neglect by most economists. We shall consider the explanatory role of 'human capital' in this enquiry, arguing that this role requires a particular interpretation of the concept which rests on the characteristics of the human mind. These characteristics may then be used to provide microfoundations for theories of entrepreneurship and the firm which will locate them within a distinctive theory of evolutionary economics that has been developing quite rapidly in recent years.

9.2 INTRODUCTION

We begin by suggesting that entrepreneurship, the firm, and human capital form a natural grouping because they have a common foundation. This foundation is clearly displayed in the work of Frank Knight (1921), who distinguished between certainty, risk, and uncertainty, with particular reference to decision-making. If future events, and the consequences of any decision, can be predicted with absolute confidence, we have certainty—by which decision-making is a strictly logical operation in which choices are directly derived from the data. These data include individual preferences, and if these are known then decisions can be predicted by anyone. Indeed, decisions can be made by anyone, and so the outcomes of independent choices and benevolent central planning are observationally equivalent, as economists discovered long ago.

If there is a range of possible futures, but these are all known and the likelihood of each can be precisely specified (as can, for example, the relative chances of the eleven possible total scores, between 2 and 12, which may result from rolling a pair of dice), we have risk. Individuals may now make different choices because of their varying attitudes towards risk. We cannot then foretell what people will do without knowing their particular risk preferences; and although this is a modest addition to the knowledge of individual preference sets it may pose important problems—notably for theories which rely on the concept of a representative agent. However, once this risk preference is specified there is only one logically correct decision; and decisions may be safely delegated if the person taking the decision is given appropriate incentives to conform to the delegator's preferences. Moving from certainty to definable risk enlarges the scope of theory, and may give an impression of greater realism but it poses no theoretical challenge. The system is closed, and logical operations are sufficient to derive all the implications that are inherent in the data.

However, if there is no demonstrably correct method of distributing probabilities over a set of possible outcomes there can be no demonstrably correct method of making decisions. Now we have uncertainty. It is, of course, possible to check whether any particular decision is consistent with a set of conjectured probabilities, but that is not at all the same thing; conjectured probabilities (even when calculated according to some approved theory) may turn out to be seriously awry—as has often been shown. Now prediction requires knowledge not only of risk preference but of the process by which the probabilities are conjectured. The assumption of an optimizing agent is not enough. In addition there is no reason to believe that a set of individual decisions based on diverse assessments of probabilities will support a sustainable equilibrium. The standard response among economists has been to assume that the decision-maker is using the correct (probabilistic) model of the economy—which is, of course, known to the analyst.

A known set of possibilities with unknown probabilities, moreover, is a relatively mild form of uncertainty. Often there is no demonstrably correct method of enumerating all relevant possibilities; then uncertainty extends beyond the assignment of probabilities to the structure of the problem with which we are trying to deal. Many decisions have turned out badly because people failed to identify as a possibility what actually occurred. There are even many examples of eminent scientists denying possibilities which were later realized within their own field—sometimes within a few years. This has been abundantly illustrated by Sir John Meurig Thomas, who did not conceal his own predictive failures as an adviser to government (Thomas, 2007). Structural uncertainty is pervasive, and it has important consequences. Thomas focused on the implications for understanding the growth of science and for science policy. There will be tangential references to such implications in this chapter, but it is another, but related, set of consequences which provides its theme.

For these we return to Knight, who demonstrated that three major economic phenomena could not be explained without invoking uncertainty. The first is profit. Since, as already noted, in a world without uncertainty everyone can use demonstrably correct procedures to make the same deductions from the data, there can be no source of advantage to any optimizing agent other than control of a distinctive resource. Any gains from such control should analytically be treated as rent; recording them as profit in an accounting statement would be a simple misnomer. Calculable risk is a cost, and what might be a situation-specific risk for one person can be bundled with similar risks faced by many others into a contract for insurance at a price which reflects the known probabilities.

Second, if there are no sources of individual advantage there can be no scope for entrepreneurship; all productive opportunities are open to everyone. It is this assumption that underlies the concept of a 'representative agent'. Moreover, the twin fundamental theorems of welfare economics—that every perfectly competitive equilibrium is a Pareto optimum, and every Pareto optimum may be instantiated by a perfectly competitive equilibrium—carries the natural implication that differentiation between agents, which is essential to any theory of entrepreneurship, is a threat to welfare. Entrepreneurship is thus both difficult to incorporate into a theory of rational choice equilibrium and also inherently undesirable. The rarity of its appearance in microeconomics is therefore easy to explain.

Third, if all contingencies are already known, and their likelihood calculable by agreed procedures, then all economic activities can be coordinated by contracts for the provision of goods and services. These can include specific labour services to be supplied on particular occasions; but there is no reason for the kind of incompletely specified contract which creates an employment relationship. There may well be firms in the simple sense of individual providers of goods and services, who may buy in other goods and services in order to produce what they sell; but these would be unitary agents in practice and not just for analytical convenience.

Knight's analysis demonstrates that the standard apparatus of optimization and equilibrium cannot be the appropriate basis for analysing entrepreneurship and firms, although it leaves room for logic and for a modest notion of equilibrium as a position of balance, which may be disturbed either by outside influences or by the consequences of its own existence. That is also the practical judgment of Chester Barnard, who included in his exploration of business management a lecture in which he asserted that 'much of the error of historians, economists, and all of us in daily affairs arises from imputing logical reasoning to men who could not or cannot base their actions on reason' (Barnard, 1938: 305). This suggests a substantial shift of focus—for example, from equilibrium to emergent order (and its decay), from preference functions to underlying motivations, from production sets to the endogenous development of knowledge, and from logic to 'mental processes of the type that can handle contingencies, uncertainties and unknowables' (Barnard, 1938: 312). Perhaps most important, it suggests, as Barnard (1938: 317) argues, that we pay far more attention to complex structures at many levels from the human brain to national systems of innovation—a range which, as we shall see, was covered by Alfred Marshall.

The paradox of a theoretical system which explains all outcomes as the consequence of rational choices is that these choices are actually determined by their own outcomes. Knight (1921: 268) argued that in a world without uncertainty all adjustments would be mechanical and all organisms automata: 'It is doubtful whether intelligence itself would exist in such a situation'. This implicit contrast between rationality and intelligence may be compared with Niels Bohr's rebuke to those who relied on purely formal arguments: 'You are not thinking. You are merely being logical' (Frisch, 1979: 95). This is not a novel idea; indeed many thinkers have been worried by the notion of a fully determined universe as the ultimate goal of science, in which 'though there is a place for everything, there is no place for man' (Koyré, quoted by Prigogine, 2005: 63). To restore a place for man Prigogine invokes the inherent unpredictability which is ensured by thermo-dynamics, and which implies a world which 'is ruled both by laws and by events' (Prigogine, 2005: 69). Thus although uncertainty presents problems, both for eco-nomic theory and for people in economic (and other) systems, it also presents opportunities for both.

It now matters who makes what decisions, and how, because people may differ, not merely in their assessment of what is probable, but even in their assessment of what is possible. The advantages of uncertainty were noted by Knight; but it is George Shackle above all others who has insisted on the intimate connection between uncertainty and imagination, and its deep significance for individuals and for economic systems. (He insisted that his last book (Shackle, 1979) should be called *Imagination and the Nature of Choice*.) The environment in which people develop particular knowledge and skills may have a powerful influence on what possibilities are envisaged and the confidence to try to realize them. We shall there-fore focus on entrepreneurship in its various contexts, and on firms as distinctive environments within which knowledge and skills are developed, and as systems within which they are applied.

However, although our central task is to explain the emergence and establish-ment of novelty, we should be clear that successful innovation is not easy, either for individuals or organizations. Indeed, if we look at the evidence with any care, what we observe is the frequency of failure. Most new ideas, in science or in business, do not work, most new products are rejected (usually being discarded before launch), most new businesses quickly succumb, and almost all businesses eventually disap-pear. It was Barnard's recognition that the organizations of his time were a surviv-ing remnant that stimulated him into considering the institutions and processes by which some might be sustained.

Within standard economics, 'failure' is normally 'market failure' (though some-times 'government failure'). Everyone optimizes according to the logic of the situa-tion, but some situations do not permit beneficial outcomes. In particular, benefits which require cooperation may not be realized, because every potential cooperator will do better by defaulting. (This is the classic 'tragedy of the commons'.) Market failures may also occur because information is deficient, but not because people simply get things wrong. In macroeconomics, the great exception is Keynes' theory, which rested on the impossibility of assigning a correct probability distribution to future income streams, leaving investment decisions to be guided by 'animal spir-its'—and their collapse. However, the response to Keynes demonstrates how uncomfortable most economists feel about the corrosive effect of uncertainty on their theoretical structures.

If one is looking for guidance in developing a theory in which the most common outcome of action is failure, but which can also explain remarkable success, then an obvious possibility is Darwinism. However, as has been frequently pointed out, neither principal element in the specific neo-Darwinian model of random genetic mutation and selection by differential genetic inheritance is appropriate. Although we wish to escape the restrictions of rational choice, neither entrepreneurship nor the firm can be satisfactorily analyzed without a concept of intentionality. In economic evolution, trial and error is typically guided by conjectures which are intended to produce particular results, although (like genetic mutations) most conjectures are refuted, and some produce outcomes which were never intended. The diffusion of ideas and practices in economic systems, which are also social systems, is much more complex than a precisely defined process of replication. Adoption is often guided by intentionality, and (partly for this reason, but also because of different interpretations of what is being adopted) it often results in further change.

In addition, the neo-Darwinian model tends to divert attention from an operating principle which seems to characterize all kinds of evolution. This principle, which Prigogine explicitly links with unpredictability, is that of self-organization—the formation of systems in which a set of elements is connected in a particular way. This principle clearly applies to all living creatures, but it is more immediately apparent in the formation of chemical compounds, which was a precondition of biological evolution, and in the allocation of responsibilities within a firm. (However, evolutionary biologists have recognized the insufficiency of any attempt to ascribe each specific effect to the organization of a specific gene.) Self-organization has the great advantage that it may work in various ways—including the construction of entrepreneurial projects and the design of organizational forms, as well as the emergence of economic systems.

Because evolutionary processes (not least in economics) depend on interaction, evolution is inherently co-evolution. However, within each particular process these interactions are typically limited. Indeed, an elaborate system in which every element is directly connected to every other element is necessarily extremely resistant to change. Selective connections are the norm; in other words, structure matters. The sequence of evolution, as presently understood, has allowed increasing complexity to be mitigated by a high degree of decomposability between levels; thus each chemical compound functions as a single entity within a living creature, and each person functions as an identifiable individual within a group. Herbert Simon (1969) suggested that decomposability is essential to the 'architecture of complexity'. It is a great help in coping with uncertainty, because it allows us to restrict the problem-space. However, as Simon also observed, decomposability between levels is not complete, and the assumption that it is (often buttressed by experience) can lead to trouble, or even disaster. Because some connections are activated by cumulative effects, or by lengthy chains, their consequences may be very slow to appear. As the clinical psychologist George Kelly observed, *'time provides the ultimate bond in all relationships'* (1963: 6; italics in original). These bonds are the most difficult to anticipate, and the most tempting to ignore; but there is abundant evidence that apparently successful systems may eventually degrade or suffer catastrophic failure.

9.3 HUMAN CAPITAL

Self-organization influenced by human ideas and human intentionality provides a basis for exploring what we may choose to call human capital; and the notion of quasi-decomposability suggests that individual capitals may be important, especially when interacting with other individuals within particular structures. However, we should not simply assume that the established sense of 'capital', with its accumulated associations, can be safely transferred to another context. Transfers between contexts are a common feature of human intelligence, and they are often productive; but there are potential dangers. We have just seen that the transfer of 'evolution' from biology to economics requires reinterpretation, and there is reason to expect something similar with 'capital'.

In economics, usage capital became associated with land and labour as the three factors of production. All three factors were believed to be measurable, and the resulting output could be attributed to them according to some specific functional relationship. Economic growth could then, it was hoped, be explained by increased inputs, and this could be done at the level of the economy. However, attempts to do so left a discomfortingly large element of growth unexplained. A succession of attempts has been made to fill the gap, of which the current favorite seems to be a concept called 'total factor productivity'. This is understood to include improvements in labor quality, which it is convenient to attribute to investment in education and training, including learning by doing. Since investment is capital formation, the inputs to production may therefore include human capital as well as physical capital.

If we are interested in entrepreneurship and firms, such manipulation of aggregates is not helpful. Human capital needs to be disaggregated in order to explain how particular changes come about. However, the need for disaggregation is not produced by the switch from physical to human capital. Indeed, it was in objecting to the notion of measuring the quantity of physical capital that Shackle (1966: 288) observed that 'capital by its nature consists of a countless diversity of incommensurable objects'. Attempts to compute any aggregate measure of capital obstruct an understanding of this nature and its significance. Physical capital is necessarily heterogeneous. Individual items of capital are typically most effective in particular combinations for particular purposes, and may be effective in very different ways in different combinations. Lachmann (1978) emphasized this multi-specificity and its implications: the significance of capital as a factor of production results from the variety of capital elements and the many ways in which they may be arranged—which are not natural givens, and so offer scope for individual initiative. Elements and structure together explain both the composition and efficiency of output, and changes in both elements and structures have an essential role in producing economic change. All this is also true of human capital.

Heterogeneity and structure thus imply similarities between physical and human capital. They also imply close complementarities; the particular pattern of connections which creates an effective combination of items of physical capital is itself the product of a specific structure of human capital. The ability to create new combinations may provide a basis for entrepreneurial actions, of many different kinds and on many different scales—and by no means only in business. Particular combinations of human capital for particular purposes may constitute differentiated firms, which have value only if the human capital of the organization is greater than the sum of its elements (Barnard, 1938: 317) because of the connections, both formal and informal, between those elements. Sometimes it may be less; in particular, a combination of closely complementary elements, if thoroughly embedded and reinforced by success, may lead to dangerous rigidities. As Richardson (1960: 87) observed, 'close complementarity between investments is equivalent to a conductor of error'; and because escape from such close complementarities may require simultaneous but unfamiliar actions by many participants it may also be a major barrier to change, and so contribute to the record of organizational failure which attracted Barnard's attention.

The crucial importance of heterogeneity and structure was emphasized by Alfred Marshall, and subsequently forgotten, or discarded, by his successors as an obstacle to their theoretical ambitions. 'Capital consists in a great part of knowledge and organization...Knowledge is our most powerful engine of production...Organization aids knowledge' (Marshall, 1920: 138). Marshall is noted—and even notorious—for his reluctance to draw sharp distinctions; but he did suggest that organization might be treated as 'a distinct agent of production' (Marshall, 1920: 139), and allotted it five chapters out of thirteen on 'the agents of production'. Organization aids knowledge by providing a particular context within which particular knowledge can be developed, tested, and applied; and because knowledge, like other forms of capital, is multi-specific, requiring different connections for different purposes, its development and use is enhanced if there are multiple forms of organization to provide a variety of contexts. Marshall was well aware, because of his early exploration of the problems and possibilities of human knowledge, that knowledge itself is a form of organization in which elements are connected in particular ways, and that what connections are formed depends on the context (Raffaelli, 2003).

9.4 Microfoundations

In contrast to the apparent simplicities of rational choice—which, as we have seen, are dependent on a closed system within which unambiguous conclusions may be deduced from premises that are known to be correct—cognitive operations in conditions of uncertainty require deeper microfoundations within the human brain. As Simon has pointed out, the assumption of universal rational choice implies that cognition is not a scarce resource. As soon as we allow for cognitive limitations, we face the need to explain what is identified as a problem, what short-cuts can be used to reduce the cognitive demands so that we can move on to the next problem, and what is acceptable as a solution. These are issues familiar from the work of Simon and his associates. We also need to explain the process by which we develop and amend knowledge. In order to do this we need to consider human motivation as something more than the desire to maximize the value of a preference function which is itself unexplained.

Underlying these cognitive limitations is a physical difficulty, the significance of which was pointed out by Hayek.

Any apparatus of classification must possess a structure of a higher degree of complexity than is possessed by the objects that it classifies...therefore, the capacity of any explaining agent must be limited to objects with a structure possessing a degree of complexity lower than its own. (Hayek, 1952: 185)

The human brain cannot fully understand its own operations, let alone the context within which it functions. It must make do with representations, each of which is likely to have substantial deficiencies. Sight provides a powerful example. Although a substantial part of the brain is allotted to it, what we 'see' is not a record of the light falling on the eyes but a neural construction. Hence the phenomenon of illusions, some of which persist even when we know that they are illusions: indeed, the acceptance of illusions is essential to classical painting and photography, which require configurations of paint or pixels to be interpreted as places and people. Other kinds of representation are allotted much smaller shares of the brain's resources. That many of them work well within limits may be attributed to the prevalence of decomposability in our universe; but since decomposability is incomplete there will always be such limits, which may not be easy to recognize. Uncertainty is therefore inherent in our representations. It is especially likely in times of change; and as has often been observed, all economic problems arise because of change from some established condition (for example, Hayek, 1937: 35; Knight, 1921: 313).

As we have noted, Knight identified uncertainty as a precondition of intelligence. But if intelligence cannot be 'rationality', what is it? This is Knight's answer: 'To live intelligently in our world...we must use the principle that things similar in some respects will behave similarly in certain other respects even when they are very different in still other respects' (Knight, 1921: 206). A simple corollary, added by Knight, is that what similarities matter, and what differences do not, depends on 'the purpose or problem in view'. Here is another example of multi-specificity: one phenomenon may be linked with a (possibly diverse) range of other phenomena in constructing representations for a (possibly diverse) range of applications. This conception of intelligence is strikingly similar to Kelly's proposition that we cope with complexity by constructing patterns that we try to impose on particular events, and that alternative constructions are, in principle, possible. Kelly's overriding 'principle of similarity', in explicit contradiction to the categorical distinction between professional psychologists and their patients, is that of 'man-as-scientist'; and it is notable how frequently the ideas of created representations and pattern-making occur in accounts of science by its practitioners. (For an especially lucid exposition, see Ziman, 1978.)

In what may now be regarded as a pioneering contribution to neuroscience, Hayek (who had dissected brains during his early studies in psychology) identified 'the transmission of impulses from neuron to neuron within the central nervous system...as the apparatus of classification' (1952: 53); thus 'the qualities which we attribute to experienced objects are strictly speaking not properties of that object at all, but a set of relations by which our brain classifies them' (Hayek 1952: 143). Because these attributed qualities are not imprinted by the environment but constructed representations, they may incorporate distortions which can lead to error (Hayek, 1952: 145–6)—as we have already noted with the most elaborate of human sensory systems. Such means of creating and imposing order provide a mechanism for Knight's principle of intelligence; and this is not surprising, because Hayek's motivation in developing his neurological theory was to explain how it was possible for 'the physical sciences...to define the objects of which this world exists increasingly in terms of the observed relationships between these objects, and more and more to disregard the way in which these objects appear to us' (Hayek, 1952: 2–3). Since the sensory order emerged as elements of tacit 'knowledge how' and the physical order as 'knowledge that', they were addressed to different problems. Therefore, we should not be surprised either by this mismatch or by the persistence of both classification systems.

Not only are the sensory and physical orders applied to different problems; they appear to have emerged in different ways. Because sensory orders of similar kinds seem to have appeared at a very early stage of animal evolution it is reasonable to assume that human sensory orders are genetically programmed. Physical orders, however, although dependent on genetically endowed potential, are a much later development in human history. They rely heavily on language and mathematics, and have evolved and gained acceptance much more rapidly than could be explained by the slow processes of mutation and differential inheritance. The two orders have different cognitive domains and are embedded in different neural networks.

We might think that the presence of multiple domain-limited systems within a single brain would be inefficient, but if we consider the creation and operation of such systems this can be seen as an economizing device. Because the creation of physical orders, and other forms of 'knowledge that', makes much greater demands on cognitive resources, including conscious thought, than the sensory order, their emergence is dependent on the pre-existing sensory order in three ways. First, the almost-automatic operations of that order enable people to function effectively with low cognitive input, and thus release cognitive power for this new purpose; second, the well-established practice of classification by neural structures is available for exaptation to organizing the new kinds of patterns which constitute Knightian intelligence and scientific theories; and third, these newly formed neural structures, once established, can be maintained at low cognitive cost, thus releasing resources for further exploration.

As Kelly (1963: 68–72) argues, all interpretative systems have a limited range of application; many may not work at all, and those that do may fail in conditions not previously experienced. Because each provides a framework for both perception and action it restricts options, and this may deter people from entering new fields, while comparable constraints give them some protection against competition from outsiders. But if this protection fails, people may, as Kelly recognized, find it very hard to abandon a system on which they have come to rely and to invent or accept an alternative. That failure is a normal element in progress is a pervasive theme of this chapter; and failure may precipitate breakdown. The attempts by many members of an organization to avoid the breakdown of their own individual but interlinked interpretative frameworks when their structure no longer matches its environment may cause the disintegration of that organization.

Now, if the principles of similarity on which categories should be based, or interpretative systems constructed, differ between domains, then we should expect people in different circumstances, even if born with equivalent cognitive potential, to develop different categories and therefore to think and act in different ways. Path dependence will be common, though this is very unlikely to extend to path determination, because the boundaries of interpretative systems are typically not well defined and categories may be modified in various ways. That specialization between domains, leading to the emergence of domain-limited connecting principles, is the principal means of enlarging the knowledge and capabilities of a society is Adam Smith's ([1776] 1976b) fundamental principle of economic development, linked to his theory of the growth of knowledge (Smith, [1795] 1980).

The human brain has an extraordinarily wide potential for organizing new systems in many different fields and consolidating them into automatic procedures; and although the realization of this potential is limited for each individual, orderly specialization is a very effective way within a quasi-decomposable economic system of exploiting the opportunities which, as Shackle above all recognized, are inherent in uncertainty. In his typically qualified fashion, Marshall's theory of economic development rested on a combination of specialization between fields and variation within each—a double differentiation between individuals which could be stimulated and channeled by a combination of forms and levels of organization.

The propensity to seek opportunities in uncertainty has allowed humans to create new ways of exploiting their environment—ways which emerge and diffuse far more rapidly than the slow products of random genetic mutation followed by differential inheritance. The incentives which activate this propensity therefore deserve particular attention. Like Marshall and Hayek in the succeeding centuries, Adam Smith took an early interest in the process of knowledge creation; and all produced versions of a theory in which knowledge consists of schemes of order which are created within the brain and prove serviceable as means of economizing on cognition. Smith ([1795] 1980), however, began by identifying the motives which 'lead and direct' this process. These are the discomfort, or worse, experienced when confronted with phenomena which do not fit within any established pattern and delight in the realization that some novel pattern encompasses them.

Ziman (2000: 120) implicitly endorses Smith's analysis by insisting that 'the human capability for pattern recognition is deeply embedded in scientific practice'; and the mathematician Atiyah (2008) insists that pattern-making, not logic, is the mathematician's supreme delight. For Smith, Ziman, and Atiyah, imagination is the key to knowledge: it is the imagination which is disturbed by the inexplicable, and which seeks to invent a new pattern of 'harmony and proportion' (to use Copernicus's account of his own motivation, to which Smith ([1795] 1980: 71) drew attention). Smith recognized both that this was a process of trial and error, and also that any apparent success was a human invention and therefore provisional, exemplifying these points in his account of the development of astronomy—especially in his comments on the status of Newton's theory (Smith, [1795] 1980: 104–5).

The association between science and beauty therefore has deep foundations. However, the association between beauty and truth is not entirely reliable—even in science. That the imagination may be deceived by appearances is a theme that recurs in Smith's work—sometimes in contexts which are particularly relevant to this chapter. The 'poor man's son, whom heaven in its anger has cursed with ambition', imagines the splendor of the rich man's life, but finds it a miserable reward for his sacrifices; nevertheless, Smith adds, this deception is a major stimulus to economic development (Smith [1759] 1976a: 181, 182, 183). Here is a useful warning against any simple association between economic development and either rationality or Pareto improvements. However, Smith ([1759] 1976a: 185) also suggests a more straightforward case: 'the same love of system, the same regard to the beauty of order, art and contrivance' may be more effective in gaining support for schemes of public benefit than any contemplation of their advantages for the beneficiaries.

The aesthetic appeal of schemes of order is a powerful inducement to accept schemes which have been developed by others, often without understanding why they might be expected to work. Underlying this inducement is the human capacity and propensity to imitate apparently successful behavior. This is an extremely effective means of enhancing human capital. Of particular importance is the adoption of rules of behavior that seem to work for others, which saves the trouble of working out such rules for oneself. Such rules are the basis of the 'institutions' which regulate interactions.

Because the acceptance, like the creation, of new knowledge relies on some connection with existing knowledge, particular importance attaches to the points of contact for such acceptance. The requirement for linkage has been given salience in the notion of 'absorptive capacity'; since, like all kinds of knowledge and capabilities, this is domain-limited, such capacity is specific to each individual. A major function of education is to develop absorptive capacity in selected fields; and as we shall see, it is a major issue in considering the development of human capital within a firm.

The last psychological factor to be mentioned in this section is the degree of determination with which the search for knowledge, and for new applications of knowledge, is pursued. This is likely to be associated with each person's view of the chances of success for a particular scheme. There seems to be a good deal of evidence that these chances may be systematically overestimated; and if self-organization must proceed through trial and error, it seems likely that factors which expand the range of trials will generally increase the rate of progress.

9.5 ENTREPRENEURSHIP

The first significant treatment of the entrepreneur anticipates Knight's proposition that both entrepreneurship and profit are consequences of uncertainty. Richard Cantillon (1755) identified the impossibility of predicting the price of annual crops as a problem for producers and also as an opportunity for anyone willing to contract for such a crop in the hope of selling at a higher price. That such deals could result from voluntary exchange required differences in willingness or ability to take a chance, or different assessments of this chance. Their effect was to improve the allocation of resources. Such differences might be traced to differences in human capital, and so it might be claimed that it is differentiated human capital which is more effectively used.

This conception of entrepreneurship might seem to fit comfortably into a theoretical structure that emphasizes the efficiency of exchange. However, as the theoretical emphasis of economics became increasingly focused on the refinement of equilibrium theory, the role for intermediaries tended to disappear, especially as economists made stronger assumptions about the knowledge available to economic agents. Just as production became part of the theory of equilibrium, and no longer justified any attention to the role of managers, so the overall coordination of economic activities became a logical problem which could be resolved without the entrepreneur.

However, the optimization postulate which allows an equilibrium to be defined makes it impossible to specify a process for attaining that equilibrium: out of equilibrium someone must be failing to optimize, and there are no prescriptions for non-optimizing behavior. Although most economists have been prepared to ignore this difficulty, those of the 'Austrian' school are inclined to take processes seriously. Israel Kirzner (1973), influenced by Ludwig von Mises' ideas of 'human action' as a continual search for improvement, identified entrepreneurship as a prime resource for identifying and realizing newly emerging potential gains from trade. For Kirzner as for Cantillon, the entrepreneur is an intermediary, but instead of acting as an intermediary between producers and consumers he links isolated markets through arbitrage.

It is by increasing agents' knowledge that Kirzner's entrepreneur moves an economy closer to equilibrium; and what makes this possible is domain-specific alertness. Opportunities for gain do not advertise themselves. Everyone will take a clear opportunity for gain, once perceived; but perception depends on distinctive absorptive capacity which results from particular interests and knowledge of both goods and localities. Thus there is a division of entrepreneurial labor. Kirzner illustrates his argument by postulating a commodity which is being sold at different prices in two locations because of some difference in circumstances. Only someone who is particularly interested in this commodity and who happens to visit these two locations will notice this disparity, and this perception is immediately registered as a specific opportunity, unrecognized by anyone else, to make a profit by buying in the cheaper market and selling in the dearer. In Kirzner's striking phrase, the ten-dollar bill is found to be lying in the hand—because of the entrepreneur's specific human capital. The entrepreneur's action sends a clear signal to traders in both markets that their opportunity sets have changed, and this improved knowledge leads to further price adjustments which enhance economic performance.

In Kirzner's theory, entrepreneurial behavior is highly differentiated in time and space; but its application is potentially universal, and so the localized activities of many entrepreneurs, each moving a market towards its own partial equilibrium, allow the economy as a whole to accommodate change by the continuous creation of spontaneous order.

Unfortunately, the plausibility of Kirzner's argument declines as he seeks to extend it to complex opportunities, such as the reorganization of production processes to take advantage of new techniques or lower-cost sources of inputs. As Richardson (1960: 105) observed, 'production functions exist unknown to entrepreneurs only in the sense that musical tunes await discovery'. What is now required is not a simple application of existing categories but an act of imagination which creates new knowledge. But as we have seen, any such act of imagination is a conjecture; and such conjectures are usually wrong. We cannot reasonably assume that every entrepreneurial act improves order, and we may be sceptical (as Richardson was) about any proposal to select a single entrepreneur to organize the order-enhancing change. We may also note that introducing such complex reorganizations requires particular kinds of human capital (especially a working knowledge of production) that are quite unnecessary to achieve simple adjustment of market prices.

Lachmann (1986) has pointed out that even simple price adjustment may create problems. The immediate effect of the entrepreneur's action is to reduce the incomes of buyers and expand the incomes of sellers in the low-price market, and to produce the opposite effects in the high-price market, thus violating the assumptions on which their actions had been based. Unlike conventional 'rational optimisers', actual buyers and sellers may have to search for alternative arrangements; and the results may be surprising. Some may imagine novel possibilities and increase their human capital, while others may suffer the breakdown of deeply embedded routines as their human capital is destroyed. Lachmann allows for both. Like Shackle, he recognizes that uncertainty permits both the imaginative creation of knowledge which may enhance economic performance and the disruptions which generate Keynesian problems.

The role of the entrepreneur as the creator of knowledge is central to Casson's ([1982] 2003) theory of entrepreneurship, though his emphasis is on entrepreneurial success in 'acting intelligently' (he acknowledges Knight's influence) by constructing interpretative systems which allow the efficient use of information in deciding how to allocate resources. As already noted, even price signals require interpretation. Casson recognizes the importance of reducing the costs of customers' access to markets, especially new markets, which had been emphasized by Young (1928) as a necessary element in economic development. Casson examines the obstacles to creating customers for a new business and the means by which they may be overcome, and is less concerned with the maintenance of a business and adjustment to further change. Harper's (1996) distinctive contribution is his emphasis on entrepreneurial fallibility, and his Popperian recommendation to treat new business ideas as conjectures which should be subjected to rigorous testing before any substantial commitment. Willingness to abandon or modify projects in accordance with persuasive evidence may be no less important than the determination to succeed.

From Kirzner's simplest case in which the perception of a problem or opportunity carries with it the perception of the appropriate response, we can trace a succession of cases in which this connection is progressively weakened, first to a range of possible responses, then to possible elements for responses, and finally to some apparent requirements for a response. Along this sequence of increasingly ill-defined problems it becomes increasingly unlikely that there can be any formula for matching entrepreneurs to situations. It is here that competition can be most valuable. This is not the competition of homogeneous agents but competition between different ways of organizing thoughts and experiments—in other words, exploiting the advantages of differentiated human capital.

If a problem is not well-defined a definition must be imposed, and the result of such a definition may be an innovation which does not merely respond to some change but creates change through the imagination of the entrepreneur. Large-scale innovations of this kind are the central phenomena in Joseph Schumpeter's theory of economic development. The 'new combinations' which he lists are transformations rather than adaptations—a new good, a new method of production, a new market, a new source of supply, and a new organization of an industry (Schumpeter, 1934: 66)—and must therefore be the product of some new combination of ideas. Thus, what Schumpeter (1934: 63) calls change 'from within' is not only change which arises within the economic system but also change which originates within the brain of the entrepreneur.

Because a given set of elements can deliver radically different results by rearranging the connections between them, even extensive new combinations can be created without introducing novel elements; and Schumpeter's insistence that invention is not necessary for innovation suggests that his entrepreneur's crucial function is to recognize the potential of some novel way of connecting what is already available, and then to convert that potential into a successful business. Even if there are no new elements, the effect is not simply attributable to the sum of individual effects: there is also an effect of structure (which if the entrepreneur gets things wrong—as many do—will be negative). However, we should also note that some of the elements may be changed as a consequence of their new connections. Since human intelligence operates by the creation and application of categories and patterns which serve as representations for problems and projects already encountered, it is not unlikely that a new problem or project will lead to some modification of these representations. This is a feature of the development of science.

Schumpeter partitions economic activity between innovation and routine, leaving no space for rational choice, though there will be an appearance of rationality 'if things have time to hammer logic into men' (Schumpeter, 1934: 80). He suggests, almost in passing, that the cognitive economy of behavior which is predominantly automatic is essential for everyday existence. He also points out that the prevalence of such behavior provides the assurance which the entrepreneur needs to calculate profitability. However, it also provides a double challenge to the entrepreneur, who must overcome both economic and social opposition to the innovation and also expend great mental effort and willpower in working out the details of the project and selecting and convincing those whose cooperation is essential for carrying it out. This is 'the phenomenon of leadership' (Schumpeter, 1934: 84). It is not surprising that such an entrepreneur must be driven by some grand ambition, as Schumpeter argues. We have already noted that human motivation is not well represented by conventional ideas of preference, and we should heed Schumpeter's reminder of these often neglected constituents of human capital.

It is now common to distinguish two versions of Schumpeter's theory: the earlier version (Schumpeter, 1934) in which the entrepreneur is the outsider, displacing established businesses, and the later version (Schumpeter, 1943) in which the entrepreneur is the controler of a large and currently profitable business, but must create and install a succession of new combinations if that business is to survive the challenges of other entrepreneurial firms. What is missing from Schumpeter's conception of the big company entrepreneur is any substantial discussion of the management of such a business. His assertion that 'teams of specialists...turn out what is required and make it work in predictable ways' (Schumpeter, 1943: 132) seems to trivialize the problems of managing innovation, in striking contrast to his exposition of the cognitive and emotional obstacles to individual entrepreneurship. Schumpeter does not mention the possibility of entrepreneurial failure, or the personal failure that may accompany success, to which Adam Smith drew attention. Perhaps that is because his focus is on economic development and not individual satisfaction.

9.6 THE FIRM

To analyse management we need a theory of the firm as a form of organization. Knight not only identified uncertainty as a precondition for firms, but explained them as means by which 'the confident and venturesome...."insure" the doubtful and timid' (Knight, 1921: 259), not only by providing an income, as in Cantillon's theory, but also by assuming the responsibility for deciding many of their actions. Willingness to accept someone else's *prescription of some, but not all, of the premises that enter into an individual's choice of behaviors* (Simon, 1982, 2: 345; italics in original) within a firm is a natural extension of the motivation to look to others for guidance in many of our activities, which was a principal element in Smith's ([1776] 1976a) *Theory of Moral Sentiments* and more recently of Choi's (1993) exposition. A 'sense of order and consistency' (Shackle, 1967: 286) has both a cognitive and an aesthetic appeal, which can crowd out opportunism. Entrepreneurs can provide this appeal (Witt, 1998), and its maintenance is a prime function of management (Barnard, 1938). A firm is a sense-making system (Nooteboom, 2001; Weick, 1995).

Acceptance of authority offers a major cognitive economy together with emotional relief, as Adam Smith was well aware. But as Barnard (1938: 163) recognized, whether any communication is authoritative is determined by its recipient, not its author. Indeed no organization and no society can function unless its members are willing to accept as authoritative many communications from people with whom they have no formal relationship (Ménard, 1994); and even within an organization people must accept many messages from those who are not their subordinates. Acceptance of authority is a matter of trust—not only in the intentions of others but also in their competence within particular fields. So in organizations as in markets, we need to discover who will serve us well for particular purposes. This is a crucial element of our working knowledge, and in both fields trustworthiness is most readily assessed through regular contacts. It is a major potential merit of formal organizations that they can provide a context for the development and maintenance of trust relationships which support coherent and effective action, and for the incubation of institutions which legitimate particular interpretations, procedures, and critieria.

Coase (1937) implicitly defines the creation of an organization called a firm as an entrepreneurial act. (See also Witt, 2000.) Arguing that uncertainty is a necessary but not a sufficient condition, he claimed that the incentive is provided by the recurrent costs of repeated contracting in markets. An efficient alternative may be created by forming a new combination which is both a decision-making system and a productive system—an ordered array of human capital designed for a cluster of problems and purposes. The firm is 'a means by which choice can be deferred until a later and better informed time' (Shackle, 1972: 160).

Shackle's definition was originally applied to money. Both means of deferring choice rely on incompletely specified contracts: it is essential that the uses to which money and resources (both productive and cognitive) will be put are left for future decision, even though this increases the uncertainty faced by others. In contrast to the usual presumption in economics, incompletely specified contracts are not a problem but a solution. However, it is a solution that leads to further problems—as is often the way with solutions. Postponing decisions is valuable only if this enables one to be better prepared for them; and the organizational structure of the firm makes this possible, but does not ensure it.

Carl Menger ([1871] 1976) noted the advantages of a variety of reserves which provide both financial and real options; and the firm is an instrument for developing reserves in the form of specialized human capital which may be deployed in contingencies which may be specifically identified or more broadly envisaged. What array of reserves to develop for each particular firm may reasonably be classified as an entrepreneurial choice. Ansoff's (1965) pioneering exploration of corporate strategy was intended to help those responsible for strategic choices to identify the major uncertainties which are relevant to their particular business, and to provide the resources—especially the human resources—to cope with them. More recently, Shell developed the use of scenarios, which are explicitly not forecasts, to encourage greater openness among their managers to the opportunities as well as the threats of uncertainty (Jefferson, 1983).

Coase's explanation of the firm clearly locates it in time; and as time passes, knowledge changes. Since human knowledge is constructed within the human brain, we are active participants in the growth of knowledge, and every firm is a major influence on this process for all its members, not least because of the patterns of connections between them, which are partly prescribed and partly selected. (Studies suggest, not surprisingly, that there is a strong association between working and personal relationships but also a notable—and sometimes crucial—amount of spontaneity.) Marshall tells us a good deal about the firm as an incubator of knowledge; but the classic exposition was provided by Edith Penrose (1959), inspired by her membership of a research team which was seeking to locate the results of an empirical study of firms within an appropriate theoretical framework, only to find that no such framework existed. Penrose (1995: foreword) later realized that Marshall had already provided the necessary elements.

By accepting the common view that business management was outside the remit of economic theory, Penrose gained freedom to reject the standard assumption that consumers are equipped with complete preference functions and producers with a full knowledge of all the production possibilities which are relevant to their activities. Instead she produced a new combination. Her firms exhibit small-scale versions of Schumpeterian entrepreneurship, which is distributed among their members (Penrose, 1959: 36). Adopting Kenneth Boulding's (1956) concept of an image in the entrepreneur's mind (Penrose, 1959: 5), she envisages a two-stage process. The first stage is to conceive of new services which might be supplied by the firm's resources, which include equipment, individual knowledge, and capabilities, and existing and potential connections between them. The second is to conceive of novel productive opportunities to which these services might be directed.

Both the design and the introduction of a new venture require substantial effort by managers, and by many other members of the firm: new combinations even of familiar elements are likely to require the development of new practices, and even of changes in these elements. But if successful, the result will be significant changes in the capabilities and understanding of individuals, and in their capabilities of deriving value from particular combinations. The resource base will have changed; and as the new practices become established, both cognitive and emotional resources will become available for a new round of innovation through new combinations.

This sequence of cognitive-intensive innovation, its installation in routines which economize cognition, and the use of modified cognitive resources for further innovation, can be traced back to Marshall's (1994) early thought experiment. There too may be found the principle that learning, even within initially identical 'brains', is shaped by context. Moreover, for those working in a firm a substantial, and sometimes dominant, part of this context is provided by the internal organization of the firm, both formal and informal. That is the significance of Penrose's (1959: 142) definition of the firm as 'a pool of resources the utilization of which is organized within an administrative framework'. The organization of activities influences the organization of thought and of capabilities, and changes in organization may have powerful effects, intended or unintended.

A notable example is the destructive effect of diversification on the effectiveness of Du Pont's carefully designed structure of organization by function. The similarities within functions across the product range rapidly diminished as that range expanded, while managing the domain-specific complementarities between functions for each product became increasingly difficult as it became increasingly critical. The established pattern of connections impeded new uses of existing human capital and prevented the creation of new capital. Replacing a function-based with a product-based system transformed the growth and application of knowledge— but not immediately, because people had to discover how to work with new colleagues with different knowledge and skills (Chandler, 1962).

Although this chapter focuses on the structures of human capital within each firm and the differences between firms, it must not be forgotten that a significant part of the human capital on which members of each organization can draw exists outside that organization, provided that they cultivate the appropriate connections. Two broad categories may be distinguished. One is the complementary capital embodied in suppliers, customers, and other sources of support, such as investors, banks, and various public authorities. Marshall was so impressed by the importance of such relationships in creating and running a successful business that he referred to them as a firm's 'external organization', in which an entrepreneur might need to invest considerable time and effort in order to establish mutual trust in intentions and competence, and compatible—though not identical— frames of reference.

The other category, which Marshall also emphasized, is the human capital in other businesses in the same trade. Precisely because the history and circumstances of no two firms (and no two people) are exactly alike, they do not operate in exactly the same way, and they try different experiments. Now, although any single experiment by a rival may put a firm at a disadvantage, the results of a range of experiments can improve knowledge for all. If competition is to be a discovery procedure in a context of Knightian uncertainty, then it is essential that 'the participants hold uncertain and divergent beliefs about their chances of success' (Richardson, 1975: 359) based on their differentiated human capital and their differentiated interpretative frameworks. 'The tendency to variation is a chief cause of progress; and the abler are the undertakers in any trade the greater will this tendency be' (Marshall, 1920: 355).

The benefits of this tendency to variation may be explicitly recognized in an industrial district, where members of various firms meet, formally and informally, to discuss ideas. It may also be recognized by members of a large firm, who understand that their rivals can be a valuable resource because each firm is constrained by the ways of thinking that result from its members' interpretation of its particular history and its internal and external connections. If it is to maintain cohesion, any organization can tolerate only a modest amount of variety; otherwise uncertainty, as perceived by each of its members, will not be sufficiently bounded to allow them to function effectively. This inherent limitation is overlooked by those who see virtue in supporting a 'national champion' for an industry. By contrast, Marshall (1919) surveyed the characteristics of the French, German, and American economies and identified what would now be called 'national systems of innovation'.

9.7 CONCLUSION

A world for which rational choice theory were sufficient would have no place for entrepreneurship or firms. Both rely on human intelligence, which creates forms of spontaneous order by using imagination to build patterns. It is implicit in Knight's conception of 'acting intelligently' that 'the boundedness of uncertainty is essential to the possibility of decision' (Shackle, 1969: 224); and these boundaries must be created. There are many ways in which this may be done, and many levels at which to do it; all depend on finding some credible basis for decomposing a system which is ultimately too complex to be accurately represented by any human brain. Every entrepreneurial project, and every firm, assumes some such basis; many of these assumptions are false, and none can claim more than provisional success. Once 'the compass of potential knowledge…has been split up into superficially convenient sectors, there will be no knowing whether each sector has a natural self-sufficiency….Whatever theory is then devised will exist by sufferance of the things which it has excluded' (Shackle, 1972: 353–4).

The bounds of uncertainty are always artificial, and what has been excluded by these bounds may invalidate apparently well-proven procedures and well-ordered projects, thus destroying much human capital. If there is no alternative structure of human capital available, then Kelly's remedy for the collapse of an interpretative framework—construct or adapt an alternative—may be unfeasible. Then the outcome will be irremediable organizational breakdown, and for some people perhaps personal breakdown as well. Schumpeter's theory of entrepreneurship recognized that change, however beneficial, is necessarily destructive of established practice, of established connections, and of human capital.

However, without uncertainty there is no scope for imagination, which creates new patterns and so shapes the development of human knowledge in science, the economy, and society. Challenging the conventional self-sufficiency of a sector may create a new pathway of knowledge, and even a new industry. Such developments are evolutionary in the sense that they are conjectured forms which may diffuse or disappear; and we cannot foretell which. However, human intelligence does allow us to devise systems which encourage the generation of patterns within particular fields, efficient selection among them, and some protection for those who are threatened by novelty. Evolution proceeds by self-organization, and formal organizations, no less than market systems, are forms of spontaneous order.

REFERENCES

ANSOFF, H. I. (1965) *Corporate Strategy* (New York: McGraw-Hill).
ATIYAH, M. (2008) 'Mind, Matter and Mathematics', Presidential Address to the Royal Society of Edinburgh (royalsoced.org.uk/events).

BARNARD, C. I. (1938) *The Functions of the Executive* (Cambridge, Mass.: Harvard University Press).

BOULDING, K. E. (1956) *The Image* (Ann Arbor, Mich.: University of Michigan Press).

CANTILLON, R. (1755) *Essai sur la Nature du Commerce en General* (London: Fletcher Gyles).

CASSON, M. ([1982] 2003) *The Entrepreneur: An Economic Theory* (Cheltenham: Edward Elgar).

CHANDLER, A. D., JR. (1962) *Strategy and Structure* (Cambridge, Mass., and London: MIT Press).

CHOI, Y. B. (1993) *Paradigms and Conventions: Uncertainty, Decision Making, and Entrepreneurship* (Ann Arbor, Mich.: University of Michigan Press).

COASE, R. H. (1937) 'The Nature of the Firm', *Economica*, NS 4: 386–405.

FRISCH, O. (1979) *What Little I Remember* (Cambridge: Cambridge University Press).

HARPER, D. A. (1996) *Expectations and the Market Process* (London and New York: Routledge).

HAYEK, F. A. (1937) 'Economics and Knowledge', *Economica*, NS 4. Repr. in *Individualism and Economic Order* (Chicago: University of Chicago Press, 1948), 33–56.

—— (1952) *The Sensory Order* (Chicago: University of Chicago Press).

JEFFERSON, M. (1983) 'Economic Uncertainty and Business Decision-Making', in J. Wiseman (ed.), *Beyond Positive Economics?* (London and Basingstoke: Macmillan), 122–59.

KELLY, G. A. (1963) *A Theory of Personality* (New York: W. W. Norton).

KIRZNER, I. (1973) *Competition and Entrepreneurship* (Chicago: University of Chicago Press).

KNIGHT, F. H. (1921) *Risk, Uncertainty and Profit* (Boston: Houghton Mifflin).

LACHMANN, L. M. (1978) *Capital and its Structure* (Kansas City: Sheed, Andrews & McMeel).

—— 1986) *The Market as an Economic Process* (Oxford: Basil Blackwell).

MARSHALL, A. (1919) *Industry and Trade* (London: Macmillan).

—— (1920) *Principles of Economics* (8th edn. London: Macmillan).

—— (1994) 'Ye Machine', *Research in the History of Economic Thought and Methodology: Archival Supplement 4* (Greenwich, Conn.: JAI Press), 116–32.

MÉNARD, C. (1994) 'Organizations as Co-ordinating Devices', *Metroeconomica*, 45: 224–47.

MENGER, C. ([1871] 1976) *Principles of Economics*, tr. J. Dingwall and B. F. Hoselitz (New York: New York University Press).

NOOTEBOOM, B. (2001) 'From Evolution to Language and Learning', in John Foster and S. Metcalfe (eds.), *Frontiers of Evolutionary Economics: Competition, Self-organisation and Innovation Policy* (Cheltenham and Northampton, Mass.: Edward Elgar).

PENROSE, E. T. (1959) *The Theory of the Growth of the Firm* (Oxford: Basil Blackwell).

—— (1995) *The Theory of the Growth of the Firm* (3rd edn. Oxford: Oxford University Press).

PRIGOGINE, I. (2005) 'The Rediscovery of Value and the Opening of Economics', in K. Dopfer (ed.), *The Evolutionary Foundations of Economics* (Cambridge: Cambridge University Press), 61–9.

RAFFAELLI, T. (2003) *Marshall's Evolutionary Economics* (London and New York: Routledge).

RICHARDSON, G. B. (1960) *Information and Investment* (Oxford: Oxford University Press).

—— (1975) 'Adam Smith on Competition and Increasing Returns', in A. S. Skinner and T. Wilson (eds.) *Essays on Adam Smith* (Oxford: Clarendon Press), 350–60.

SCHUMPETER, J. A. (1934) *The Theory of Economic Development* (Cambridge, Mass.: Harvard University Press).

——(1943) *Capitalism, Socialism and Democracy* (London: Allen & Unwin).

SHACKLE, G. L. S. (1966) *The Nature of Economic Thought: Selected Papers 1955–64* (Cambridge: Cambridge University Press).

——(1967) *The Years of High Theory: Invention and Tradition in Economic Thought* (Cambridge: Cambridge University Press).

——(1969) *Decision, Order and Time in Human Affairs* (2nd edn. Cambridge: Cambridge University Press).

——(1972) *Epistemics and Economics* (Cambridge: Cambridge University Press).

——(1979) *Imagination and the Nature of Choice* (Edinburgh: Edinburgh University Press).

SIMON, H. A. (1959) 'Theories of Decision-Making in Economics and Behavioural Science', *American Economic Review*, 49: 253–83.

—— ([1962] 1969) 'The Architecture of Complexity', in *The Sciences of the Artificial* (Cambridge, Mass., and London: MIT Press).

—— (1982). 'Economics and Psychology', in *Models of Bounded Rationality*, ii. *Behavioral Economics and Business Organization* (Cambridge, Mass., and London: MIT Press), 318–55.

SMITH, A. ([1759] 1976*a*) *The Theory of Moral Sentiments*, ed. A. L. Macfie and D. D. Raphael (Oxford: Oxford University Press).

——([1776] 1976*b*) *An Enquiry into the Nature and Causes of the Wealth of Nations*, ed. R. H. Campbell, A. S. Skinner, and W. B. Todd (Oxford: Oxford University Press).

—— ([1795] 1980) 'The Principles Which Lead and Direct Philosophical Inquiries: Illustrated by the History of Astronomy', in *Essays on Philosophical Subjects*, ed. W. P. D. Wightman and J. C. Bryce (Oxford: Oxford University Press), 33–105.

THOMAS, JOHN M. (2007) 'The Unpredictability of Science', lecture delivered at the Royal Society of Edinburgh (royalsoced.org.uk/events).

WILLIAMSON, O. E. (1996) *The Mechanisms of Governance* (New York: Oxford University Press).

WEICK, K. E. (1995) *Sensemaking in Organizations* (Thousand Oaks, Calif.: Sage).

WITT, U. (1998) 'Imagination and Leadership: The Neglected Dimension of an Evolutionary Theory of the Firm', *Journal of Economic Behavior and Organization*, 35: 161–77.

——(2000) 'Changing Cognitive Frames—Changing Organizational Forms: An Entrepreneurial Theory of Organizational Development', *Industrial and Corporate Change*, 9: 733–55.

YOUNG, A. (1928) 'Increasing Returns and Economic Progress', *Economic Journal*, 38: 527–42.

ZIMAN, J. M. (1978) *Reliable Knowledge* (Cambridge: Cambridge University Press).

——(2000) *Real Science: What it is and What it Means* (Cambridge: Cambridge University Press).

CHAPTER 10

....

THE FIRM, HUMAN CAPITAL, AND KNOWLEDGE CREATION

....

GEORG VON KROGH

MARTIN W. WALLIN

10.1 INTRODUCTION

....

In recent years the field of strategic management has seen the emergence of a knowledge-based view of the firm. This view is a collection of theories portraying the firm as an institution that creates knowledge and innovates (Nonaka and Takeuchi, 1995), coordinates and integrates specialist knowledge (Grant, 1996), connects and transfers knowledge of individuals (Kogut and Zander, 1992, 1996; von Krogh et al., 1994), and protects knowledge from uncompensated spill-over to third parties (Liebeskind, 1996). The firm consists of a set of knowledge assets and the strategies to manage them (Boisot, 1998; Chou and He, 2004; Nonaka et al., 2006), which provide the firm with a certain level of economic rent. These theories conceptualize the firm as a social community, providing a sense of belonging and a shared identity for its organizational members (Kogut and Zander, 1996), not as merely a mechanism for reducing transaction costs or solving principal–agent problems. The purpose of knowledge-based theories is to uncover these firm characteristics and the principles by which they function; for example, the process of organizational knowledge creation (Nonaka and Takeuchi, 1995). Units of analysis predominantly cover the nature of the firm, including its divisions, departments, groups, or communities. However, scholars writing about knowledge-based theory seldom discuss the microfoundations of their perspective and often fail to conceptualize individual interests, actions, decisions, and the consequences of individual knowledge for competitive advantage.

The human capital literature may inspire scholars to achieve a greater understanding of the function and competitiveness of the firm by homing in on the relationship between the firm and the individual in knowledge creation. Recently, scholars have argued that one weakness in knowledge-based theory is its neglect of individuals' interests and motivation to learn, create, share, and apply knowledge (Gottschalg and Zollo, 2007; Osterloh and Frey, 2000). Clearly, individuals who learn, play, experiment, solve tasks, make decisions, collaborate, and so on, form a necessary condition for firms to create the knowledge assets that bring competitive advantage. As Grant (1996) shows, while individual efforts are necessary for a firm to function and deliver value to its stakeholders, on their own they are not sufficient to explain competitive advantage. Firms also need effective and efficient mechanisms to integrate individual knowledge. Historically, knowledge-based theories focused more on the latter condition than the former, with important consequences. For example, knowledge-based theories have tended to neglect the relative contributions to a firm's knowledge assets of individuals who are more or less motivated and fully, partly, or not at all employed by the firm (for example, Dahlander and Magnusson, 2005; Dahlander and Wallin, 2006).

Clearly, there is a need to understand better the relationship between the firm and the individual in organizational knowledge creation. That is the motivation behind this chapter, in which we discuss the indispensability of the concept of interest alignment to this relationship. While there are areas of interest alignment between the firm and the individual—for example, an individual acquires general management skills in return for a higher salary or a better career—there are also prevalent and immediate areas of conflict. A firm's competitive advantage might stem from unique and hard-to-imitate knowledge assets (Barney, 1991), and sustaining that advantage might require individuals to internalize specific knowledge that holds little value for other firms attracting talent in the labor market. As a result, people may be less motivated to acquire such skills.

In this chapter we develop a framework to analyze a knowledge-creation relationship between the individual and the firm that takes into account the possibility of each party having diverging or converging interests. We draw on the literature on human capital and on the knowledge-based view of the firm; in particular, organizational knowledge creation theory, which explains when, why, and how firms create knowledge assets for competitive advantage (Nonaka 1994; Nonaka et al., 2006; Nonaka and von Krogh 2009), and what assets they create. It is well suited to investigating the contributions of individuals to a specific process in the firm, and vice versa. An important contribution of the human capital literature was to bring individual knowledge to the center of economic analysis (Becker, 1964; Blaug, 1970; Mincer, 1962).

We see organizational knowledge creation theory as a conduit between the more static and firm-focused streams of knowledge-based theories and the human capital tradition, which is concerned with individual decision-making. We show that some findings and frameworks in the human capital literature can contribute to the understanding of the relationship between the firm and the individual. We are interested in conditions under which individuals contribute to the creation of knowledge within the firm and when the firm contributes to an individual's human capital development—addressing organizational knowledge creation that serves both individual and firm interests. We argue that there is a tension between the firm as an allocator of rewards, individuals who provide human capital, and the accrual of knowledge assets at firm level that needs to be managed. Integral to our argument is the idea that the firm allocates not only monetary rewards, like salaries, to participating individuals, but also non-pecuniary types of value, such as increases in human capital. This tension might be due to the lack of alignment, between the firm's and individuals' interests (Gottschalg and Zollo, 2007). We devise some options for ways in which firms might deal with conflict of interest and the mismatch of knowledge. Our ideas are based on the concept of interest alignment, and aim to contribute to our understanding of organizational knowledge creation within the firm, and to shed some light on knowledge creation and knowledge sharing that extends beyond firm boundaries.

We begin with a brief review of the knowledge-based view of the firm and organizational knowledge creation theory, and go on to examine some central contributions to the theory of human capital. We next discuss knowledge of the firm in relation to human capital, and follow this with a framework for understanding the relationship between the individual and the firm in a knowledge-creation context. Our concluding discussion calls for a human-capital-inspired knowledge-based theory of the firm.

10.2 KNOWLEDGE OF THE FIRM: THE NEED FOR MICROFOUNDATIONS

In the field of strategic management, a major purpose of theorizing is to explain performance differences between firms. The knowledge-based view of the firm consists of theories that attempt to explain competitive advantage and firm performance in terms of the firm's knowledge asset endowment. The predecessor of the knowledge-based view, the resource-based theory of the firm (Barney, 1991; Conner, 1991; Peteraf, 1993; Wernerfelt, 1984), proposed that costly-to-imitate resources such as knowledge constitute sources of competitive advantage. The knowledge-based view complemented the resource-based theory by providing a more fine-grained analysis: knowledge in the firm is dynamic, process-related, individual, collective, tacit, and explicit (Grant, 1996; Kogut and Zander, 1992; Nonaka, 1994; Spender, 1996). Winter (1987) proposed that tacit knowledge, which is costly to create and share, is the most important 'knowledge asset' in the context of the competitive implications of all the firm's resources. Later work built on this idea and found empirical evidence for the relationship between tacit and explicit knowledge assets and the firm's competitive advantage (for example, De Carolis and Deeds, 1999; Poppo and Zenger, 1998). Knowledge assets originate in organizational knowledge creation (Nonaka et al., 2006) and can be put to productive use in the firm. They include routines, procedures, rules, documents, databases, simulation models, patents, expertise, teamwork, and so on (Nonaka and Konno, 1998; for a more extensive discussion, see for example, Diaz-Diaz et al., 2009). Because firms do not compete only on existing knowledge assets, but rejuvenate and create entirely new assets, strategic management needs a dynamic, process-oriented theory of knowledge creation (Nonaka et al., 2008; Nonaka and von Krogh, 2009). Based on a recent definition (Nonaka et al., 2006), organizations create knowledge through individuals and groups who amplify and crystallize their knowledge, make it available to others, and connect it to the organization's overall knowledge assets. The individual is instrumental in this process. The knowledge-based view and organizational knowledge creation theory emphasize the social complexity of knowledge assets and argue that they are embedded in the interaction patterns of individuals as well as in culture, identity, policies, routines, documents, and systems (Kogut and Zander, 1992). Competitive advantage is created by firms' capabilities to create and share knowledge through social interaction (Nahapiet and Ghoshal, 1998). Kogut and Zander (1992) suggest knowledge is organizationally relevant if it can be translated into capabilities that enhance the firm's growth and survival. This means that individuals bring to bear their tacit and explicit knowledge when solving tasks, making decisions, generating and exploring ideas, developing and justifying concepts, acting on routines, and so on.

While individuals are critical to knowledge assets, the knowledge-based view of the firm and organizational knowledge creation theory have paid limited attention to microfoundations (see for example, Loewendahl and Revang, 1998; Tywoniak, 2007). In other words, scholars have explored individuals' motives for contributing to knowledge creation, knowledge assets, and competitive advantage far less than the nature of such assets and strategies for managing them. However, a number of contributions have shown that the problematic relationship between the individual and the firm in organizational knowledge creation warrants attention. For example, von Krogh et al. (1994) argue that knowledge sharing and creation within an organization is a fragile process, due to conflict of interest between individuals. Von Krogh et al. (2000) argue that individuals may be inclined to defect from organizational knowledge creation because the process or its outcome may depreciate the value of their own knowledge, create a bad self-image, endanger their position, or lower their perception of future value. Osterloh and Frey (2000) suggested that extrinsically motivated individuals, who act to achieve a separable outcome, such as pay or career, are unlikely to promote the interest of the firm by sharing their tacit knowledge. Doing so would diminish their bargaining power and, ultimately, private benefits accruing from their private investment in knowledge acquisition. In Osterloh and Frey's view, problems stem from omitting the relationship between the individual and the firm from the analysis. For example, while the knowledge-based view has proposed many structural solutions to the problem of knowledge creation and sharing, including new divisions, groups, or networks among organizational members (for example, Hedlund, 1994), these solutions cannot be effective unless they are supported by motivated individuals.

Wezel *et al.* (2006) suggested that the labor market provides self-interested individuals with the opportunity to make use of their knowledge in competing firms *and* to replicate higher-order organizing principles of former employers (Kogut and Zander, 1992) across firms in the industry. In effect, neglecting the relationship between individual and firm knowledge and interests is fatal to the notion of competitive advantage. As we indicated at the beginning of this chapter, scholars should aim to develop a framework that aligns the interests of firms and individuals in organizational knowledge creation and includes knowledge that individuals can bring to bear on the process (von Krogh *et al.*, 1999; see also Chen and Edgington, 2005, who develop a simulation model that looks at this). A similar conclusion was reached recently by Gottschalg and Zollo (2007), who argue that we need a 'theory of interest alignment' between the individual and the firm to understand better how firms can compete, based on individual and collective contributions to the firm's knowledge and other assets.

Finally, it should be noted that the knowledge-based view of the firm and organizational knowledge creation theory have been criticized for being too inward-looking and for giving inadequate consideration to characteristics of the firm's environment. In the knowledge-based view, firms exist because they outperform markets in creating and sharing knowledge. Knowledge is held at both individual and organizational level, in the form of higher-order organizing principles, knowledge assets, routines, and other elements. A popular image of the firm is that of a social community operating according to organizing principles (Kogut and Zander, 1992). While recognizing that employees are often part of multiple communities within and outside the firm, the knowledge-based view has not been able to explain how the firm's knowledge assets are affected by the presence of a labor market for skilled individuals (although there is abundant evidence from economic geography about this relationship; see Saxenian, 1994). For example, many scholars (Dahlander, 2006; Franke and Shah, 2003; Hienerth, 2006; Lüthje, 2004; Jeppesen, 2005; Lakhani and von Hippel, 2003) suggest that employees spend a significant amount of spare time developing products both for their own amusement and for the benefit of their employer. The knowledge-based view and organizational knowledge creation theory need to be able to explain knowledge creation and sharing that extends beyond firm boundaries. Kogut and Zander (1996) pointed out that knowledge could reside in networks between firms. Thus, scholars have taken steps to include relational aspects of firm knowledge and have suggested that productive resources may be located both inside and outside the firm (Dyer and Singh, 1998). The latter needs to be accessed through different relationships that facilitate or impede various kinds of firm-level outcomes (Powell *et al.*, 1996), some of which include relationships with individuals who participate in knowledge creation and sharing and who work for one or both firms. Limited interest has been devoted to how the knowledge acquisition opportunities of individual employees shape the capabilities of the firm. Kogut and Zander (1992, 1996) assume that social relationships important for knowledge assets do not exist outside the firm (or its networks) but offer no explanation for how external knowledge enters the firm. Yet, individuals who are endowed with human capital are an important source of new knowledge for the firm. In the next section we briefly present the human capital theory.

10.3 THE HUMAN CAPITAL THEORY

Human capital theory can explain a great deal about individual decision-making, incentives, and knowledge acquisition under various economic conditions inside and outside the firm. For a long time, though, knowledge and human capital were tangential to economic analysis. Classical economists, such as Adam Smith, David Ricardo, and John Stuart Mill, tried to explain wealth differentials in terms of access to various production factors, such as land, labor, and capital. Although it is true that Smith pointed to the improved skills and dexterity of every 'workman' following the division of labor (Smith, 1776), later developments focused less on human aspects and chose to treat labor as a factor of production. However, after the Second World War, development economists observed the difference in economic recovery across nations. Among them, Theodore Schultz suggested that economic recovery was supported by a healthy and well-educated population and could be achieved by investment in human capital. Schultz argued that 'much of what we call consumption constitutes investment in human capital' (1961: 1). In effect, he suggested that human capital, like any other kind of capital, is subject to investment and profits. However, 'although it is obvious that people acquire useful skills and knowledge, it is not obvious that these skills and knowledge are a form of capital'.

The modern human capital literature that emerged with Gary Becker and Theodore Schultz tried to explain the wealth differentials of individuals (as well as groups of individuals and nations) in terms of the knowledge they possessed—so-called human capital. A core question is how investment in human capital rendered subsequent profits. In the general human capital model, individuals make informed (or semi-informed) human capital investment decisions. A thoroughly researched area is the link between investment in schooling and subsequent earnings (Becker, 1964; Mincer, 1962, 1974; Schultz, 1961), where education is treated as an investment rather than consumption, which was previously the case (such as for higher education). The theory predicts declining investments in human capital formation with increasing age; that is, lifetime earnings are concave from below. Indeed, when Mincer (1974) analyzed private returns to schooling, he found a curvilinear relationship between years of schooling and a significant drop in earnings. As with all investments, the opportunity cost had to be factored in, which became a key feature of contemporary human capital models. Here, the individual is assumed to acquire more and different sets of knowledge not for its own sake, but in order to achieve a separable economic outcome; for example, a higher salary. A key feature of human capital, which distinguishes it from other factors of production, is its inseparability from the owner. Land and physical capital, such as machinery, can be transferred easily from one owner to another. This is not the case with human capital, which rests with the individual and can be only temporarily used for the purpose set out by an employer in agreement with the employee. As Becker (1964: 16) writes: 'expenditures on education, training, medical care...produce human, not physical or financial, capital because you cannot separate a person from his or her knowledge, skills, health, or values the way it is possible to move financial and physical assets while the owner stays put'. So human capital is the economic value derived from individuals' sets of skills, and differs qualitatively and quantitatively across individuals and with improvement potential derived from investments.

Becker (1964) distinguished between 'general' and 'specific' human capital. General human capital, such as literacy and simple arithmetic skills, is useful to all employees. Specific human capital refers to skills useful only within a single firm, industry, or nation. Human capital theory predicts that employers should only pay for employee-specific training, leading to skills that are directly and exclusively applicable to the firm. The individual pays for general training. The theory also predicts that rational firms match their competitors when compensating employees with general human capital. However, they should pay their employees with specific human capital more than their competitors (especially when assuming that the employee pays for general training). Specific training is often on-the-job. Mincer (1962) showed that on-the-job training is a very large component of total investment in education in the US, estimated in the range of 50 to 100 percent of formal schooling. His study also showed that on-the-job training had grown much faster at higher skills levels than at lower skills levels.

One reason for firms to supply on-the-job training relates to how the firm can access the human capital of its employees. Human capital skills cannot be accessed without the explicit permission of the individual, creating an incentive for the firm to invest in training demanded by the employee (Becker, 1964). Another reason for providing training is that employees perceive it as compensation, which should increase the firm's likelihood of accessing the human capital. This argument is familiar to scholars who write about a firm's absorptive capacity (for example, Cohen and Levinthal, 1990). Absorptive capacity deals with R&D investments necessary to access and interpret external knowledge. In a similar vein, training is an investment, necessary for access to employees' human capital. Through training, employers may hope to increase the human capital of the employees' knowledge and stimulate possible spillovers to other, less able, employees during and after training. Training can, therefore, increase the bargaining position of the firm in relation to the individual.

To summarize, human capital theory represents a long tradition that seeks to explain the outcomes and antecedents of individual investment in education, training, and—as we will argue later—organizational knowledge creation. In the next section we discuss human capital in relation to firm knowledge.

10.4 HUMAN CAPITAL AND KNOWLEDGE OF THE FIRM

There are two important attributes of the human capital theory, which are of particular relevance to the knowledge-based theory of the firm. First, individuals make decisions about human capital investments, which are assumed to lead to a subsequent payoff. Second, individuals allocate their time to work and leisure. In the knowledge-based theory of the firm, individuals in organizations use their knowledge to solve tasks, make decisions, and create change. In human capital theory the individual invests in human capital for private returns, but this plays a secondary role in the knowledge-based view of the firm (for example, Liebeskind, 1996; see also Lado and Wilson, 1994; Lepak and Snell, 1999). The implicit appropriation model for the individual in the knowledge-based view of the firm is one where future opportunities rest with the success of the firm and not, as in the human capital tradition, with the attractiveness of the individual on the labor market. As we said earlier, the knowledge-based theory has been criticized for not explaining how external knowledge enters the firm. One answer to this critique is that the human capital embodied in new employees is an important source of knowledge (for example, March, 1991). This complements the knowledge-based view, which historically has been concerned with how the organization unfolds from within; that is, on how employees learn from each other through their participation in groups, networks, and communities (Grant, 1996; Kogut and Zander, 1992; Tsoukas, 1996). The issue of how firms differ in terms of their attractiveness to potential employees by augmenting their human capital is critical to understanding how firms compete for talented individuals. We also need to understand how individuals' human capital, gained through their employment, makes them valuable to current and future employers, and competitive in the labor market.

The distinction between general and specific capital can be refined further into three types of human capital: firm-specific, industry-specific, and individual-specific (Florin and Schultze, 2000). Firm-specific human capital is the least valuable to the individual in the labor market because it lowers labor mobility. Conversely, it is the most valuable for the firm as it is non-transferable and gives rise to competitive advantage (Grant, 1996). Firm-specific human capital could relate to knowledge of a budgeting process, product descriptions, human resource procedures, and so on (see Skaggs and Youndt, 2004). Industry-specific human capital stems from experience accumulated within a specific industry; for example, from the supra-individual cognitive structures found in what Spender (1989) called 'industry recipes'. This type of capital has an intermediary-level benefit for both the firm and the employee. While it may be necessary to be knowledgeable about the context in which the firm operates, that knowledge is not a sufficient factor to differentiate firms within the industry. Firms may need employees with industry-specific human capital to achieve parity with competitors (Barney, 1991), but that may not be enough to outperform them. This type of human capital may refer to supply-chain management, alternative product technologies, market structures, customer preferences, and so forth. Finally, individual-specific human capital is specific only to one individual, but it is generally applicable across firms and industries and may refer to knowledge of mathematics, modeling, simulation, languages, leadership, and so forth. Such human capital is valuable to the individual and enhances employee mobility in the labor market, enabling employees to make productive use of their knowledge elsewhere; but it is more problematic for the firm to build competitive advantage from it. At the same time, increased individual-specific human capital may become a competitive advantage of the firm, if the labor market is not perfect; for example, when various geographical clusters compete against each other for talented individuals.

The degree to which non-firm-specific knowledge is embodied in employees is important for the knowledge-based view, because it impacts on knowledge flows (spillovers) between firms. These knowledge flows are partly regulated by calculating individuals and labor market conditions. For example, with regard to training, Becker (1964) argued that the likelihood that a firm will pay for any training (even specific as opposed to general training) depends on labor turnover. The reason for this is the fixed cost associated with any new employee joining the firm—any investment in training is wasted if the employee leaves the firm. Becker also argued that it is more difficult for firms to invest in specific training in competitive labor markets, whereas all human capital investments become firm-specific for firms holding a monopoly in the labor market.

Although variation in labor market conditions, including the availability of skilled labor, may not affect the existence of knowledge-based firms, it will affect their boundaries. For example, individuals' decisions about how they allocate their time are dependent on factors such as the relative price of labor. According to the human capital prediction, in an economy with high marginal taxes, employees are less motivated to work and so contribute less to the firm's knowledge assets. However, the firm can compensate for this effect by offering rewarding tasks, knowledge acquisition opportunities, social integration, peer recognition, and the like. Intrinsically motivated employees are likely to contribute more to the firm's knowledge assets (Osterloh and Frey, 2000), and the institutional tax setting may be of less concern.

While scholars adopting a knowledge-based view of the firm assume employees only contribute to knowledge assets in their work time (see Werr and Stjernberg, 2003), the human capital literature draws attention to human capital generated through both work and leisure. Writers on human capital recognized early on that individuals and firms share the investment in human capital, and so the literature conceptualized two 'spheres of time': the working and non-working time sphere, known as leisure time. Becker (1965) argues that leisure time (understood as nonworking time) is becoming an increasingly larger share of total time. What employees do during their leisure time increases in importance for the kind and quantity of human capital they accumulate, which is underscored by the fact that employees have idiosyncratic preferences about how to allocate work and leisure time (Rapoport et al., 2002).

In the next section we use these two attributes of human capital theory, and their consequences for the knowledge of the firm, to examine the relationship between the individual and the firm in organizational knowledge creation.

10.5 THE INDIVIDUAL IN ORGANIZATIONAL KNOWLEDGE CREATION

Let us begin by summarizing our argument so far. The knowledge-based view of the firm proposes and demonstrates that knowledge assets impact on competitive advantage. Organizational knowledge creation theory points to the microfoundations of the knowledge-based view, by suggesting that the creation of new knowledge assets and the sustainability of competitive advantage require individual efforts. Human capital theory shows that individuals invest in their knowledge and strive to appropriate economic returns from that investment. Education and on-the-job training are often cited as examples of human capital investments. However, the relationship between individuals' interests and knowledge and the firm's interest in accruing knowledge assets is an open issue that we address in this section, proposing a new framework that captures the relationship.

Working time	Non-working time	
Salaried Work	Unpaid Work	Working activity
Shirking	True Leisure	Non-working activity

Figure 10.1. Working Time and Working Activity

As we discussed in the previous section, human capital theory raises important questions about the ways employees choose to allocate their time. In a simple world, employees have two different types of time: working and non-working (leisure). The knowledge-based view seeks to explain the boundary of the firm; that is, the scale and scope of the firm's activities (Grant, 1997; von Krogh and Grand, 2002). If we imagine these two dimensions—activity, either work-related or non-work-related, and time, either work time or non-work time—there are four distinct ways in which employees can choose to use their time (see Figure 10.1). They can choose to do work-related activities during work time (salaried work). They can choose not to work during work time (shirking). They can choose to work during non-work time (unpaid work). Finally, they can choose not to work during non-work time. This is leisure.

Most theories of the firm are concerned with activities performed during work time, although many work-related activities can be performed outside work time. However, the knowledge-based view does not make a distinction between the times when individual knowledge is created. Instead, it is assumed that all relevant knowledge benefits the firm for the period the employee is bound by the work contract (Liebeskind, 1996). Nor does the literature acknowledge the potential conflict between activities performed in off-the-job hours and those performed in on-the-job hours throughout the duration of the contract. For example, employees could choose to take non-paid schooling in their off-the-job time for the benefit of the firm. But they could also choose to enjoy genuine leisure or to embark on competitive activities. These observations have implications for firm existence as well as firm boundaries. The boundary question is the most obvious, as the inclusion of the dimension of time allocation points to the fact that employees are part of multiple communities; for example, work-time and non-work-time communities. These communities can be coupled to various degrees, as has been demonstrated in studies of open source software development (Bonaccorsi et al., 2006; Roberts et al., 2006).

The human capital literature raises an important question about who actually pays for advancing knowledge assets, claiming that employers only pay for (firm)-specific training (such as budgeting procedures) while employees pay for generally applicable training (such as education in mathematics). Yet employees' general and specific skills both matter for the total knowledge assets of the firm. Organizational knowledge creation relies on the input of individuals (Nonaka, 1994). Taking into account the role of human capital, Chen and Edgington (2005: 280) defined a knowledge creation process as 'a unit of activity, either instructed or self-administered, undertaken for the purpose of improving upon individual or organizational tasks with respect to quality or efficiency'. Thus, a knowledge creation process is an assigned or unassigned activity with future tasks, for which an increased benefit is expected (Mincer, 1962); and complementary to training and education, employees can augment their human capital through participation in knowledge creation, either individually or within the organization. As this definition and other studies of knowledge creation confirm (Nonaka *et al.*, 2006), the process often relies on an individual to choose whether or not to contribute. Nonaka (1994) and Chen and Edgington (2005) argue that the autonomy of teams of individuals, coupled with slack resources, timing, and a clear goal orientation, is needed for optimal knowledge asset accrual. Thus, individual employees and firms might benefit mutually from knowledge creation. Firms provide processes, resources, and a context for knowledge creation, making it possible for individuals to contribute, learn new things, and collaborate in the process. In other words, organizational knowledge creation may enable the accrual of individual-, industry-, and firm-specific human capital. At the same time, knowledge creation draws out and crystallizes individual knowledge, and we can expect knowledge creation where there is alignment of knowledge and interest and human capital and knowledge assets can be simultaneously accrued. See the framework of alignment illustrated in Figure 10.2.

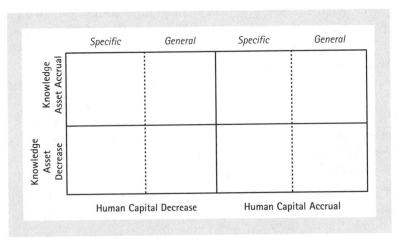

Figure 10.2. Human Capital and Knowledge Assets

10.5.1 Human Capital Accrual–Knowledge Assets Accrual

In this situation, firm benefits stem from knowledge creation that leads to augmented knowledge assets. This is a direct outcome of the knowledge and expertise brought in by individuals. In turn, individuals benefit from enhanced individual-specific and industry-specific human capital, as well as firm-specific human capital. For example, an engineer who knows computer-aided design (CAD) contributes to a product development project. While working on the project, the engineer learns to use and modify a new CAD system (programming skills). Because this system is widely used in the industry, the new expertise benefits the engineer. At the same time, firm-specific human capital related to the product development process is also enhanced. Where there is limited conflict of interest, as here, firms will compensate individuals directly for their involvement in the organizational knowledge creation process, and the individuals concerned might use some of their leisure time on an interesting project. As far as the increase in specific human capital is concerned, one of the main challenges for the firm is to keep individuals motivated by constantly providing interesting and challenging tasks. This is working from the assumption that individuals are largely motivated by the task itself rather than the potential leverage they can achieve in the firm (see Frey and Osterloh, 2000; and, for a contrasting view, Roberts *et al.*, 2006).

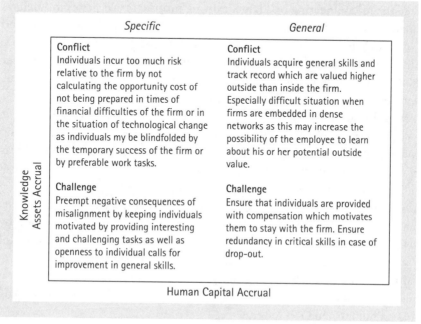

Figure 10.3. Human Capital Accrual–Knowledge Assets Accrual

However, a potential conflict can arise when individuals are not motivated by the task. In this case they will seek other forms of compensation—perhaps financial—or demand access to increased general human capital (financial compensation could, of course, be used for general training during leisure time). Although initially favorable to them, this situation is characterized by uncertainty, since individuals may be 'blindfolded' by the combination of preferred tasks and the temporary success of the firm. In effect, individuals do not always calculate the opportunity cost of being unprepared for a firm's financial difficulties, or technological change. One of the main general human capital challenges for the firm is retention—how to ensure that people stay with the firm and prevent them from switching to competitors or creating spin-off initiatives of their own. The situation is especially uncertain when firms are embedded in dense networks with other organizations and individuals, which can increase employees' appreciation of their potential outside value.

10.5.2 Human Capital Decrease–Knowledge Assets Accrual

In this situation the firm benefits directly from the knowledge brought in by individuals, and in the process accrues knowledge assets. However, the human capital decreases, largely due to opportunity costs. This can happen if individuals bring to bear their individual- and industry-specific human capital, but the investment in firm-specific capital (represented by the time spent by individuals on knowledge creation) outweighs investment in the two other forms of capital. For example, let us take the re-engineering of a large, existing proprietary legacy computer system for managing financial transactions. The proprietary nature of the system and the use of archaic programming languages may diminish the engineers' human capital. In response, engineers might defect from organizational knowledge creation, seek other work in the organization, or leave for another employer. The firm has various options to counter this uncertainty: increase salary to compensate for the reduction in human capital; keep salary at the same level while accepting more non-work-related activities (such as open source software development) designed to increase human capital; increase training in human capital relevant areas; or offer a portfolio of other organizational knowledge-creation activities that restores the alignment of firm and individual interests.

A decrease in specific human capital is generally of little economic significance to the individual, although it may be demotivating—unless accompanied by an increase in general human capital. The decrease in general human capital has different implications depending on each individual's position in the career cycle. Although it may be demotivating not to increase one's human capital, it may be preferable for those approaching retirement age, when the opportunity cost of decreased human capital is lower.

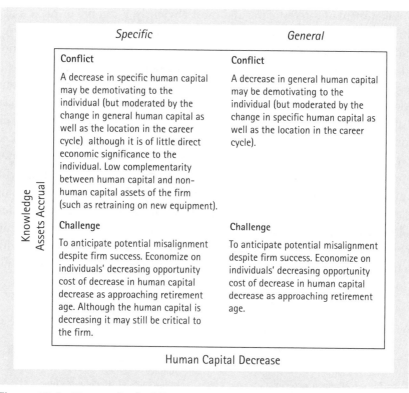

Figure 10.4. **Human Capital Decrease–Knowledge Assets Accrual**

10.5.3 Human Capital Accrual–Knowledge Assets Decrease

In this situation the firm does not benefit enough from the knowledge brought in by people—individual contributions do not convert into knowledge assets accrual. The individuals, however, augment their individual-, industry-, and (perhaps) firm-specific human capital. Organizational knowledge creation often involves considerable experimentation where failure is always a possible outcome (Thomke, 2003). While individuals learn a great deal through the process, the firm's knowledge assets may not improve, and there is no apparent effect on competitive advantage—which can happen if, say, a team innovates a failed prototype. Alternatively, because of the decentralized nature of knowledge creation (Nonaka, 1994), and the high cost of monitoring individual efforts (Osterloh and Frey, 2000), individuals can co-opt organizational knowledge creation to serve their specific human capital needs (shirking). For example, they may spend an excessive amount of time gaining general and industry-relevant knowledge, such as market characteristics or modeling skills, while neglecting the final outcome for the firm. The firm has some options to restore alignment of interest. First and most obviously, it can fire or make a plausible threat to fire individuals, since human capital cannot be put to productive use. Second, it can reduce salaries and lower expectations of individuals' allocation of time to knowledge creation, while restoring the objectives and governance of the process. Third, in the case of project failure, the firm can restart organizational knowledge creation with the specific aim of reusing knowledge and human capital for a specific purpose. Although the increase in specific human capital may be pleasant for the individual, it is obviously not sustainable if it is not mirrored by knowledge accrual at firm level: the firm should be expected to take action over non-productive tasks. However, it is essential to distinguish between individuals performing essentially non-productive tasks and experimentation that has not yet translated into firm benefits. Individuals working in isolation effectively hinder the knowledge sharing that is essential for organizational knowledge creation. Similarly, where general human capital increases, the firm essentially carries the cost without expecting any returns (unless the accumulation of general human capital is necessary for experimentation).

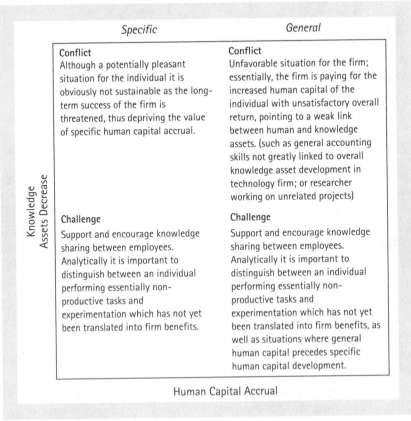

Figure 10.5. Human Capital Accrual–Knowledge Assets Decrease

10.5.4 Human Capital Decrease–Knowledge Assets Decrease

In this scenario, individual knowledge does not lead to knowledge asset accrual, and organizational knowledge creation also fails to augment human capital. There is an inherent mismatch: restoring alignment might require the firm to recruit individuals with entirely different human capital. Ensuring the supply of human capital might entail a hefty increase in salary, career prospects, or education and training levels. Alternatively, the firm might need to re-examine knowledge creation to identify how labor market conditions can match the need for human capital in the process. It is possible that the firm will find that it can only recruit the required talent where knowledge creation offers individuals significant advancement of individual- and industry-specific human capital. One example of the latter is the development of highly sophisticated software in the field of bioinformatics. Many firms compete in this space, but expertise that combines knowledge of biology/biotechnology and computing is rare. To compete successfully for talented individuals, the firm might need to offer them significant basic research and development activities.

As we argued earlier, a decrease in specific human capital is of little economic significance to the individual if substituted with an increase in general human capital, although it may be very demotivating. It may also signal that the firm has simply recruited the wrong people, with the wrong skills, who do not fit the firm. The

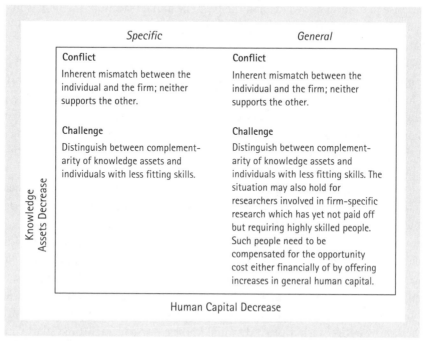

Figure 10.6. Human Capital Decrease–Knowledge Assets Decrease

importance of the time lag again becomes obvious; general (and specific) human capital may decrease in the short run, for example, when researchers are involved in firm-specific research that requires highly skilled individuals but has not yet paid off. Such people, especially when limited in supply, need to be compensated for the opportunity cost either financially or by increases in human capital.

10.6 Discussion

Although the concept of knowledge is central to both the human capital tradition and the knowledge-based view of the firm, it is used quite differently and for different purposes. Take level of analysis, for example. In the human capital tradition, the individual has a prominent role. In empirical terms, both independent and dependent variables can be at individual level; for example, when trying to explain how individual investments in human capital impact on wage levels. In the knowledge-based view of the firm, however, it is the nature of the firm and its knowledge assets that are of interest, and the specific knowledge and interest of the individual (microfoundations) are rarely taken into account. This view aims to explain firm-level performance, rather than individual-level performance, through firm-level investment in knowledge. In the knowledge-based view, the individual is mainly a means to increase firm-level knowledge; in the human capital tradition, the firm is mainly a means to increase individual human capital and subsequently the individual's private returns. And herein lies the chance to investigate what opportunities a human capital perspective can provide for the knowledge-based view of the firm. One opportunity consists in marrying key insights from both streams of literature, and focusing on the relationship between the firm and the individual. In the preceding section we let this relationship play out to the point where we could identify tensions and the implications of a lack of interest alignment. In the following section we discuss some implications for organizational knowledge creation theory within the knowledge-based view of the firm.

It is tempting to start our discussion of interest alignment by turning to adjacent literature on incentives, conflicts of interest, and well-known principal–agent problems (see Jensen and Murphy, 1990; Holmstrom and Milgrom, 1991). The commonly held view is that alignment occurs when the firm motivates employees to behave in a particular way, according to what is contractually stipulated. However, our discussion differs in two main ways. First, we argue that organizational knowledge creation occurs when the participating individuals contribute beyond what is specified in a labor or service contract—because the contractor can neither know entirely what the individual knows, nor contract for systemic interaction effects between individuals and the firm. Second, like Grant (1996), we argue for a less hierarchical and managerially dominated firm, in favor of a more demo-cratically managed firm. Interestingly, Rousseau and Shperling (2003) report on the issue of employee ownership as a particular characteristic of knowledge-intense firms, due to the mobility of highly skilled workers and the subsequent power of labor. But we argue in favor of a broader understanding of what motivates individuals to contribute in a firm setting, beyond the purely financial incentives that are the common focus.

At one extreme, the knowledge-based firm can be conceptualized and rationalized through the eyes of the calculating individual who emerges from the human capital tradition. The challenge for scholars contributing to the literature on the knowledge-based theory of the firm is to provide an image of the firm rooted in the creation, application, and appropriation of organizational knowledge, and in individuals' desire to achieve pecuniary and non-pecuniary benefits. We must first assume that individuals are compensated either through monetary or human capital. We must also assume that the monetary capital can be either consumed or invested. Individuals may choose to invest the monetary capital in activities to enhance their own human capital. As we have learned, compensatory human capital can come in various degrees of specificity and is always accompanied by an opportunity cost. Human capital cannot be acquired without giving up some other activity related to work or leisure. For the purpose of clarity we also assume a firm whose only asset is knowledge, with various degrees of specificity. It should now be clear that the research challenge is to explain what the firm provides for the individual. The assumptions provide one half of the answer; the firm provides pecuniary and non-pecuniary benefits. But as demand from individuals is subjective and varying, so are the benefits that firms provide.

The knowledge-based view has established that both close and distant social interaction between employees (shared language, information, knowledge, routines) set firms apart from markets for knowledge and expertise. The firm is therefore conducive to organizational knowledge creation and individual knowledge acquisition. Here the interests of the firm and the individual may meet (as explained in the human capital literature), improving their human capital. However, as we argued earlier, there are occasional tensions between the interests of firms and individuals. As a result, our framework suggests that managerial action needs to be directed precisely at this tension, where management has a reward allocation structure at its disposal. However, the firm cannot simply acquire human capital through transaction.

When a firm 'acquires' an employee through an employment or service contract, it can only benefit from the outcome produced and appropriated. For the sake of argument, if compulsory service was permitted, the firm would still face challenges about actual production; that is, whether or not employees put human capital to the best possible use (from the firm's perspective). This is a more fundamental problem than monitoring and measuring output (see Alchian and Demsetz, 1970). Management may not know all solutions to this problem, because the human capital is inseparable from the human being. The contract between the firm and the employee usually only covers either a specific period of time served or a specific work outcome. But the firm cannot contract for the best use of the employee's human capital, as this is known only to the individual. Instead, in order to align the interests of firms and individuals, managers may need to use the reward structure of the firm to induce contributions along the lines of Barnard's (1938) plea for cooperative management, as opposed to the top–down authoritarian model that characterizes classical organization theory. Three important results emerge from cooperative, democratic management. First, firm-level knowledge accrual necessitates that individuals contribute human capital beyond what is explicitly and contractually stipulated. Second, delivering non-pecuniary rewards, such as increased human capital, might induce contributions. Third, aspects of individual motivation to participate, contribute, share, and acquire knowledge become critical aspects of the firm. These are related issues that we will explore further.

Earlier in this chapter we suggested that the firm is not the only context where individuals can acquire knowledge. Individuals are part of multiple communities, whether they are professional societies, sport clubs, or loosely organized groups of friends. However, the firm must have something more to offer beyond such communities (pay and knowledge, for example), to have become the prominent institution it is today. We suggest that this is the firm's image as a temporary 'safe haven' for ideas and salary, drawing our proposition from the link we have made between the key insight from human capital literature (that individuals invest in their own human capital for later private return) with insights from the knowledge-based view of the firm, which sees social interaction as conducive for organizational knowledge creation (and thus human capital). For the employee, the firm provides a security function by paying a salary. The basic safety this provides enables employees to pursue other desires and invest in their human capital. The firm also provides a knowledge-enabling context, where ideas can materialize into subsequent human capital. Thus, the firm becomes a knowledge acquisition platform for the individual—but it is this combined with some financial reward that makes it a safe haven and an environment conducive to experimentation and innovation. Of course, the employee can acquire skills outside the firm, in time and space, but the firm has created an environment that satisfies the desire to optimize the reward function consisting of both direct financial as well as long-term human capital related rewards. The knowledge-based view has focused on the knowledge a firm creates and from which it can profit. Inspired by the human capital literature, it becomes evident that employee knowledge is crucial as well. This knowledge is therefore a form of compensation in itself, along with the salary provided by the firm. The efficient co-creation of knowledge assets and human capital through the provision of a temporary safe haven for ideas and salary makes the firm a highly important institution.

There is a threefold competitive advantage that stems from the firm's ability to produce human capital: first, learning-by-doing that grows as the firm creates its knowledge assets, and feeds directly into the products and services provided to customers; second, the firm's ability to produce training below the price that employees can acquire in markets; and third, the firm's ability to provide new knowledge acquisition opportunities, resulting from the competitive dynamics in the industry.

The concept of the firm as a 'temporary safe haven' leads to two important ideas. First, the firm may only be valuable to individuals for as long as it delivers services (human capital increase) to them. Second, the firm provides security for the human capital of the individual. The human capital perspective may reverse the rationale of the firm, and brings insights to the knowledge-based view, which may now explain the function of the firm from the perspective of the individual who is part of it, or could become so. It may be useful to ask not just what the individual does for the firm, but what the firm does for the individual. In other words, the question of how the firm protects and appropriates firm-specific knowledge assets needs to be complemented with the question of how it protects and enhances the human capital of its employees. The scale and scope of the firm can be viewed somewhat differently. The output of the firm depends not only on its paying customers, but also on what its employees demand; in other words, the firm's activities are partly regarded as compensation by its employees (Pfeffer and Salancik, 1978). The relative importance of this compensation scheme is moderated by labor market conditions; that is, individuals' external options. We cannot understand the functioning of the knowledge-based firm without understanding labor market conditions. The specific labor market conditions surrounding the firm impacts how it will compensate its employees, through money or human capital. For example, Mincer (1962) argued that labor markets need to be sufficiently competitive to allow private investment in human capital to materialize into private returns. Within the firm, individuals' knowledge can be protected and leveraged in ways that are not possible if they remain outside the firm.

This brings us to the difficult question of whether or not the individual and the firm are really separable entities. In the human capital tradition, they are clearly distinguishable, whereas in the knowledge-based understanding of the firm, they are not so easy to distinguish. We believe the question is somewhat misstated. The crucial question is to what degree the individual is part of the firm, suggesting that work effort and the kind of knowledge the individual decides to share with the firm probably depend on the individual's perception of the firm's ability to protect and nurture human capital. For example, studies of open-source software development have shown that firms sometimes try to access the complementary assets endowed in the community (Bonaccorsi et al., 2006; Dahlander and Wallin, 2006; Henkel, 2006). However, the firm cannot control this community of non-employees and cannot derive profits by traditional means of ownership. Instead, the firm needs to find other means to access the desired human capital. As a result, it is necessary to analyze what motivates individuals voluntarily to contribute to knowledge asset accrual in the firm. For example, intrinsically motivated individuals would be interested in any challenging tasks a firm could provide, whereas more extrinsically motivated individuals would emphasize financial compensation or tasks that increase their general human capital and by extension improve their attractiveness on the labor market. Thus, a knowledge-based understanding of the firm may benefit from incorporating a microlevel understanding of the differential motivation of individuals as well as the specific labor market conditions in which the firm and the individual are embedded.

10.7 CONCLUSION

In this chapter we have offered a framework to analyze tensions arising from the potentially differentiating interests of the individual and the firm. We have briefly presented work on the knowledge-based view of the firm, organizational knowledge creation theory, and human capital. We have suggested that organizational knowledge creation rests on the premise of individuals voluntarily contributing their human capital beyond contractual stipulations. We have also argued that individual motivation to participate, contribute, share, and learn are critical aspects of the functioning of a firm. Delivering non-pecuniary rewards, such as increased human capital, is one measure that might induce such behavior. As a result, managerial actions ought to be directed to the tensions caused by the misalignment of employees' and firms' interests. Here, the carrot may be more effective than the stick as a means of motivating individuals inside and outside the firm, as well as being more efficient in alleviating tensions between the firm and the individual. In this vein, the firm is only socially and economically valuable as long as it delivers value to its main stakeholders—a group in which its employees should be considered on a par with its shareholders.

REFERENCES

ALCHIAN, A. A., and DEMSETZ, H. (1970). 'Production, Information Costs, and Economic Organization', American Economic Review, 62(5): 777–95.

BARNARD, C. I. (1938). The Functions of the Executive (Cambridge, Mass.: Harvard University Press).

BARNEY, J. (1991). 'Firm Resources and Sustained Competitive Advantage', Journal of Management, 77: 99–120.

Becker, G. S. (1964). *Human Capital: A Theoretical and Empirical Analysis* (New York: National Bureau of Economic Research).

——(1965). 'A Theory of the Allocation of Time', *Economic Journal*, 75(299): 493–517.

Blaug, M. (1970). 'The Empirical Status of Human Capital Theory: A Slightly Jaundiced Survey', *Journal of Economic Literature*, 14(3): 827–55.

Boisot, M. H. (1998). *Knowledge Assets Securing Competitive Advantage in the Information Economy* (Oxford: Oxford University Press).

Bonaccorsi, A., Giannangeli, S., and Rossi, C. (2006). 'Entry Strategies under Competing Standards: Hybrid Business Models in the Open Source Software Industry', *Management Science*, 52(7): 1085–98.

Chen, A. N. K., and Edgington, T. M. (2005). 'Assessing Value in Organizational Knowledge Creation: Considerations for Knowledge Workers', *MIS Quarterly*, 29(2): 279–309.

Chou, S., and He, M. (2004). 'Knowledge Management: The Distinctive Roles of Knowledge Assets in Facilitating Knowledge Creation', *Journal of Information Science*, 30(2): 146–64.

Cohen, W. M., and Levinthal, D. A. (1990). 'Absorptive Capacity: A New Perspective on Learning and Innovation', *Administrative Science Quarterly*, 35(1): 128–52.

Conner, K. R. (1991). 'A Historical Comparison of Resource-Based Theory and Five Schools of Thought within Industrial Organization Economics: Do we have a New Theory of the Firm?', *Journal of Management*, 17(1): 121–54.

Dahlander, L. (2006). *Managing beyond Firm Boundaries: Leveraging User Innovation Networks* (Göteborg: Chalmers University of Technology).

——and Magnusson, M. G. (2005). 'Relationships between Open Source Software Companies and Communities: Observations from Nordic Firms', *Research Policy*, 34(4): 481–93.

——and Wallin, M. W. (2006). 'A Man on the Inside: Unlocking Communities as Complementary Assets', *Research Policy*, 35(8): 1243–59.

De Carolis, D., and Deeds, D. (1999). 'The Impact of Stocks and Flows of Organizational Knowledge on Firm Performance: An Empirical Evaluation of the Biotechnology Industry', *Strategic Management Journal*, 20: 953–68.

Diaz-Diaz, N. L., Aguiar, I., and De Saa-Perez, P. (2008). 'The Effect Of Technological Knowledge Assets on Performance: The Innovative Choice in Spanish Firms', *Research Policy*, 37(9): 1515–29.

Dyer, J. H., and Singh, H. (1998). 'The Relational View: Cooperative Strategy and Sources of Interorganizational Competitive Advantage', *Academy of Management Review*, 23: 660–79.

Florin, J., and Schulze, W. (2000). 'Social Capital and Fundability of High Potential New Ventures', Academy of Management Meeting, Toronto.

Franke, N., and Shah, S. (2003). 'How Communities Support Innovative Activities: An Exploration of Assistance and Sharing among End-Users', *Research Policy*, 32: 157–78.

Gottschalg, O., and Zollo, M. (2007) 'Interest Alignment and Competitive Advantage', *Academy of Management Review*, 32(2): 418–37.

Grant, R. (1996). 'Toward a Knowledge-Based Theory of the Firm', *Strategic Management Journal*, 17 (Winter special issue): 109–22.

——(1997). 'The Knowledge-Based View of the Firm: Implications for Management Practice', *Long Range Planning*, 30(3): 450–4.

Hedlund, G. (1994). 'A Model of Knowledge Management and the N-Form Corporation', *Strategic Management Journal*, 15: 73–90.

HENKEL, J. (2006). 'Selective Revealing in Open Innovation Processes: The Case of Embedded Linux'. *Research Policy*, 35(7): 953–69.

HIENERTH, C. (2006). 'The Commercialization of User Innovations: The Development of the Rodeo Kayak Industry', *R&D Management*, 36(3): 273–94.

HOLMSTROM, B., and MILGROM, P. (1991). 'Multitask Principal–Agent Analyses: Incentive Contracts, Asset Ownership, and Job Design', *Journal of Law, Economics and Organization*, 7: 24–52.

JENSEN, M. C., and MURPHY, K. J. (1990). 'Performance Pay and Top-Management Incentives', *Journal of Political Economy*, 98(2): 225–64.

JEPPESEN, L. B. (2005). 'User Toolkits for Innovation: Customers Support Each Other', *Journal of Product Innovation Management*, 22: 347–62.

KOGUT, B., and ZANDER, U. (1992). 'Knowledge of the Firm, Combinative Capabilities, and the Replication of Technology', *Organization Science*, 3(3): 383–97.

——and —— (1996). 'What Firms Do? Coordinations, Identity, and Learning', *Organization Science*, 17(5): 502–18.

LADO, A. A., and WILSON, M. C. (1994). 'Human Resource Systems and Sustained Competitive Advantage: A Competency-Based Perspective', *Academy of Management Review*, 19(4): 699–727.

LAKHANI, K., and VON HIPPEL, E. (2003). 'How Open Source Software Works: "Free" User-to-User Assistance', *Research Policy*, 923–43.

LEPAK, D., and SNELL, S. A. (1999). 'The Human Resource Architecture: Towards a Theory of Human Capital Allocation and Development', *Academy of Management Review*, 24(1): 31–48.

LIEBESKIND, J. P. (1996). 'Knowledge, Strategy, and the Theory of the Firm', *Strategic Management Journal*, 17 (Winter special issue): 93–107.

LOEWENDAHL, B., and REVANG, O. (1998). 'Challenges to Existing Strategy Theory in a Post-Industrial Society', *Strategic Management Journal*, 19(8): 755–74.

LÜTHJE, C. (2004). 'Characteristics of Innovating Users in a Consumer Goods Field: An Empirical Study of Sport-Related Product Consumers', *Technovation*, 24: 683–95.

MARCH, J. G. (1991). 'Exploration and Exploitation in Organizational Learning', *Organization Science*, 2(1): 71–87.

MINCER, J. (1962). 'On-the-Job Training: Costs, Returns, and Some Implications', *Journal of Political Economy*, 70(5): 50–79.

——(1974). *Schooling, Experience and Earnings* (New York: Columbia University Press).

NAHAPIET, J., and GHOSHAL, S. (1998). 'Social Capital, Intellectual Capital and the Organizational Advantage', *Academy of Management Review*, 23(2): 242–66.

NONAKA, I. (1994). 'A Dynamic Theory of Organizational Knowledge Creation', *Organization Science*, 5(1): 14–37.

——and KONNO, N. (1998). 'The Concept of "Ba": Building a Foundation for Knowledge Creation', *California Management Review*, 40(3): 40–54.

——and TAKEUCHI, H. (1995). *The Knowledge-Creating Company* (Oxford: Oxford University Press).

——and VON KROGH, G. (2009). 'Perspective: Tacit Knowledge and Knowledge Conversion: Controversy and Advancement in Organizational Knowledge Creation Theory', *Organization Science*, 20(3): 635–52.

—— VON KROGH, G., and VOELPEL, S. (2006). 'Organizational Knowledge Creation Theory: Evolutionary Paths and Future Advances', *Organization Studies*, 27: 1179–1208.

——Toyama, R., Hirata, T., Bigelow, S. J., Hirose, A., and Kohlbacher, F. (2008). *Managing Flow: A Process Theory of the Knowledge-Based Firm* (New York: Palgrave Macmillan).

Osterloh, M., and Frey, B. S. (2000). 'Motivation, Knowledge Transfer, and Organizational Form', *Organization Science*, 11: 538–50.

Peteraf, M. A. (1993). 'The Cornerstones of Competitive Advantage: A Resource-Based View', *Strategic Management Journal*, 14(3): 179–91.

Pfeffer, J., and Salancik, G. R. (1978). *The External Control of Organizations: A Resource Dependence Perspective* (New York: Harper & Row).

Poppo, L., and Zenger, T. (1998). 'Testing Alternative Theories of the Firm: Transaction Cost, Knowledge-Based, and Measurement Explanations for Make-or-Buy Decisions in Information Services', *Strategic Management Journal*, 19: 853–77.

Powell, W. W., Koput, K. W., and Smith-Doerr, L. (1996). 'Interorganizational Collaboration and the Locus of Innovation: Networks of Learning in Biotechnology', *Administrative Science Quarterly*, 41(1): 116–45.

Rapoport, R., Bailyn, L., Fletcher, J. K., and Pruitt, B. H. (2002). *Beyond Work–Family Balance: Advancing Gender Equity and Workplace Performance* (San Francisco: Jossey-Bass).

Roberts, J. A., Hann, I.-H., and Slaughter, S. A. (2006). 'Understanding the Motivations, Participation, and Performance of Open Source Software Developers: A Longitudinal Study of the Apache Projects', *Management Science*, 52(7): 984–99.

Rousseau, D. M., and Shperling, Z. (2003). 'Pieces of the Action: Ownership and the Changing Employment Relationship', *Academy of Management Review*, 28(4): 553–70.

Saxenian, A. (1994). *Regional Advantage: Culture and Competition in Silicon Valley and Route 128* (Cambridge, Mass.: Harvard University Press).

Schultz, T. H. (1961). 'Investment in Human Capital', *American Economic Review*, 51 (Mar.): 1–17.

Skaggs, B. C., and Youndt, M. (2004). 'Strategic Positioning, Human Capital, and Performance in Service Organizations: A Customer Interaction Approach', *Strategic Management Journal*, 25(1): 85–99.

Smith, A. (1776). *An Inquiry into the Nature and Causes of the Wealth of Nations* (Repr. London: Penguin Classics, 1986).

Spender, J.-C. (1989). *Industry Recipes: The Nature and Sources of Managerial Judgment* (Oxford: Blackwell).

——(1996). 'Making Knowledge the Basis of a Dynamic Theory of the Firm', *Strategic Management Journal*, 17 (Winter special issue): 45–62.

Thomke, S. (2003). *Experimentation Matters: Unlocking the Potential of New Technologies for Innovation* (Cambridge, Mass.: Harvard Business School Press).

Tsoukas, H. (1996). 'The Firm as a Distributed Knowledge System: A Constructionist Approach', *Strategic Management Journal*, 17: 11–25.

Tywoniak, S. A. (2007). 'Knowledge in Four Deformation Dimensions', *Organization*, 14(1): 53–76.

von Krogh, G., and Grand, S. (2002). 'From Economic Theory towards a Knowledge-Based Theory of the Firm: Conceptual Building Blocks', in C. W. Choo and N. Bontis (eds.), *The Strategic Management of Intellectual Capital and Organizational Knowledge* (New York: Oxford University Press), 163–84.

——Roos, J., and Slocum, K. (1994). 'An Essay on Corporate Epistemology', *Strategic Management Journal*, 15: 53–71.

von Krogh, G., and Lyles, M., Mahnke, V., and Rogulic, B. (1999). 'Preparing the Organization for New Competencies: A Process Perspective of Integrating Knowledge and Competence', in J. F. Porac and R. Garud (eds.), *Cognition, Knowledge, and Organizations* (Advances in Managerial Cognition and Organizational Information Processing Series; Stamford, Conn.: JAI Press), 57–78.

——Ichijo, K., and Nonaka, I. (2000). *Enabling Knowledge Creation: How to Unlock the Mystery of Tacit Knowledge and to Release the Power of Innovation* (New York: Oxford University Press).

Wernerfelt, B. (1984). 'A Resource-Based View of the Firm', *Strategic Management Journal*, 5(2): 171–80.

Werr, A., and Stjernberg, T. (2003). 'Exploring Management Consulting Firms as Knowledge Systems', *Organization Studies*, 24(6): 881–908.

Wezel, F. C., Cattani, G., and Pennings, J. M. (2006). 'Competitive Implications of Interfirm Mobility', *Organization Science*, 17: 691–709.

Winter, S. G. (1987). 'Knowledge and Competence as Strategic Assets', in D. J. Teece (ed.), *The Competitive Challenge* (Cambridge, Mass.: Ballinger Publishing Co.), 159–84.

PART III

HUMAN CAPITAL AND
ORGANIZATIONAL
EFFECTIVENESS

CHAPTER 11

HUMAN CAPITAL, HR STRATEGY, AND ORGANIZATIONAL EFFECTIVENESS

PETER BOXALL

11.1 INTRODUCTION

Strategic human resource management (HRM) is a management discipline concerned with analysing strategic problems, choices, and outcomes in the management of work and people in organizations (Boxall and Purcell, 2008). Organizations of all sizes—small, medium, and large—can be analysed from a strategic HRM perspective because all depend on some kind of 'human resourcing' process (Watson, 2005). The aim of this chapter is to analyze the role of human capital from a strategic HRM perspective. It starts by outlining basic premises about the nature of human capital. It then examines three questions that are important for the analysis of human capital and its relationship with firms' HR strategies and performance. The first is concerned with strategic HR problems: why is the management of human capital inherently problematic? The second examines strategic choices in human capital: why do firms' investments in human capital vary across critical contexts, both within the organization and across diverse external environments? The third question enters the debate around the prized outcome of sustained competitive advantage: when and how can firms establish sustained advantage through their management of human capital?

11.2 BASIC PREMISES: HUMAN CAPITAL, ORGANIZATIONAL VIABILITY, AND SUPERIOR PERFORMANCE

Our starting point must be that human capital—the knowledge, skills, and aptitudes embodied in people—is a *sine qua non* of organizational activity. Human capital has the same significance for organizations as water has for fish: it is not possible to imagine one without the other. Organizations—whether private, public, or voluntary—cannot exist without people leading them and supplying them with productive services, as Penrose (1959) emphasized long ago in her landmark study of the growth of the firm. The idea of the human-free organization is absurd: it is science fiction, not science. Even in the most machine-dominated organizations, some human intelligence and creative effort is needed to devise goals, locate capital, establish operating systems, and, if the organization's owners wish their creation to survive, monitor performance.

Here, we are not simply talking about the need for individual creativity and effort. We are also, in nearly all situations, talking about collaborative human activity: about the interactions and networks that enable an organization with diverse inputs or distinctive departments to function effectively as a whole. As elsewhere in this *Handbook* (see, for example, Chapter 2), individual human capital should be understood as operating within the context of *social* capital.

Managers, therefore, need to build appropriate levels of human and social capital in order for their organization to be viable (Boxall and Purcell, 2008). Another way of putting this is to say that in every industry in which a firm competes, it requires 'table stakes': a set of goals, resources, and capable, cooperating people—both managers and managed—that are relevant to the industry concerned (Boxall and Steeneveld, 1999; Hamel and Prahalad, 1994: 226). In banking, for example, firms require the products, capital resources, information technologies, and skilled, networked people who can deal effectively with the lenders and borrowers which the bank's directors are targeting (Boxall and Purcell, 2008). Without a cluster of goals, resources, and human capabilities that suppliers and customers regard as credible in the industry, a bank is doomed before it starts.

While an adequate level of human and social capital is necessary for the viability of any organization, our second basic premise is that a firm's particular configuration of human and social capital may help it to build and sustain superior performance. Although firms emulate 'industry recipes' (Spender, 1989) and need a high degree of functional equivalence to be recognized as legitimate members of a particular industry, they inevitably build some degree of idiosyncrasy in their goals, resources, and capabilities. As Penrose (1959: 74–8) emphasized, firms competing in the same domain remain 'heterogeneous' in important respects. Her understanding of the quality of the firm's human resources placed emphasis on the knowledge and experience of the management team and their subjective interpretation of the firm's environment. Faced with the same environment, different management teams will perceive somewhat different risks and opportunities, adopt somewhat different resource deployments, and enact somewhat different competitive postures.

The resource-based view of the firm, which has now risen to such prominence within the theory of strategic management (Barney, 1991; Wernerfelt, 1984; this *Handbook* Chapter 8), has made the point more general: the distinctive nature of a firm's total human resource pool, and not simply its senior managers, creates a large terrain for idiosyncrasy and, with it, the potential for superior performance or sustained competitive advantage (Wright *et al.*, 1994). The resource-based view (RBV) is deeply concerned with the conditions that give rise to valuable, inimitable resources (with inimitability covering both direct and indirect forms of copying) (Hoopes *et al.*, 2003). By its very nature, the RBV is laced with *human resource* issues: barriers to imitation, such as asset specificity and social complexity, are essentially about decisions that people make, and processes they build, over time.

But none of this gets us very far. The contentions that (1) a firm needs an appropriate cluster of human and social capital to secure its viability in its chosen industry (or industries), and (2) that this cluster has idiosyncratic features that may help create a source of sustained competitive advantage, are not seriously disputed. After all, these two premises verge on truism. The interesting and important issues start to emerge when we explore three important and complex questions in relation to human capital:

- What makes the management of human capital problematic for firms?
- In what ways do firms' investments in human capital vary across internal and external contexts?
- When and how can firms build sustained competitive advantage through human capital?

The rest of this chapter is structured around a discussion of these three questions.

11.3 WHAT MAKES THE MANAGEMENT OF HUMAN CAPITAL PROBLEMATIC?

As a management discipline, strategic HRM is concerned with identifying and analyzing the critical problems associated with managing work and people in organizations. An analytical approach to the subject starts from the problems which firm face and from research on how managers try to tackle them, not from inappropriate prescriptions about 'best practices' (Boxall and Purcell, 2008).

What, then, makes the management of human capital inherently problematic? The answer lies in the fact that the human capital of managers and workers is accessed via employment relationships, and bargaining is endemic to such relationships (Boxall, 1996; Edwards and Ram, 2006). It is useful to think of the employment relationship as an inherently fragile 'wage–work bargain'. There are two key aspects to this—one concerned with labor scarcity or the need to compete for access to labor in an external and increasingly globalized labor market, and the other concerned with bargaining for people's services within the firm's internal 'labor process'. We will consider each dimension in turn, and in so doing examine the reasons why some firms perform better than others in this critical bargaining process.

11.3.1 The Problem of Labor Scarcity

Labor scarcity refers to the fact that firms must compete in labor markets to secure appropriately skilled staff (Coff, 1997; Windolf, 1986). There are always business victors and victims in this process, for two simple reasons. The first is that human abilities and job performances are not inherently equal: on the contrary, they vary enormously (Wright *et al.*, 1994). In fact, as job complexity increases, so does the range of human performance (Hunter *et al.*, 1990). Thus, as we move up from low-complexity work (such as routine clerical work) to jobs where greater ambiguity is involved in decision-making, differences in skill and judgment become more pronounced and their consequences are more fateful for organizations. The second reason is a fundamental legal and practical constraint: aside from some part-time arrangements, employees cannot generally work for more than one company at the same time. In certain cases, restraint of trade clauses also prevent them from doing so in the future or for a defined period of time after resignation. Putting these two facts together means that some firms will hire better talent than others, and these decisions will have strategic consequences.

Why do some firms cope better with labor scarcity than others? A large part of the answer is that well-resourced and well-recognized organizations are able to pay wage premia and offer better development opportunities, and thus tend to disproportionately attract talented individuals (Boxall and Purcell, 2008). Firms which are undercapitalized or lacking in wider recognition can remain fragile organizations whose recruitment problems compromise their abilities to build adequate levels of human capital (Hendry *et al.*, 1995; Hornsby and Kuratko, 2003; Storey, 1985). Firms with these problems struggle to build the capabilities they need to meet business objectives. In the extreme, the tensions associated with labor scarcity can become a full-blown 'capability crisis', which can fatally compromise the firm's viability.

It is important to recognize that labor scarcity is not simply a problem for under-capitalized firms or new firms struggling for recognition, but can afflict entire industries which have undesirable features from a worker perspective. There are both unattractive firms and unattractive industries, which suffer disabling weaknesses in a hot labor market. In the British trucking industry, for example, there are major shortages of drivers because of difficult working conditions: drivers have responsibility for valuable vehicles and loads, work long hours in dangerous conditions, and are often away from home (Marchington *et al.*, 2003). Many people who hold the appropriate driving qualifications prefer not to drive trucks but to work in a local factory or in another service sector where their lifestyle can be more normal. The existence of such alternative sources of employment affects the performance of a whole host of firms trying to survive in this industry.

It is also important to realize that competition for human capital has global dimensions. The problems of firms cannot be understood simply at the level of the firm (Rubery and Grimshaw, 2003). Firms are not isolated entities but exist in societies which provide them with varying levels of support and regulate their activities to varying degrees (Boxall and Purcell, 2008). In terms of the labor market, different societies are engaged in a multilevel competitive game—a kind of 'regime competition'—which affects their firms at diverse levels. In high-tech industries, firms in first-world societies such as the USA, Germany, Japan, France, and the UK, with extensive research capabilities in both public and private sectors, are inherently advantaged. The scientific talent pools they train, and on which they can draw, are much deeper than those available to small economies such as Australia or New Zealand. On the other hand, high-wage first-world societies are no longer competitive in the labor market for production work in such industries as textiles, clothing, and electronics assembly. Here, China and India, and a host of smaller developing economies, are the economic giants, providing highly cost-competitive labor forces. Over time, the competition between regimes shifts across levels. China, hugely successful in low-cost manufacturing, is increasingly up-skilling its workforce and investing in science in order to develop a first-world labor market.[1]

11.3.2 Employee Motivation: the 'Labor Process' Problem

Bargaining with workers is not, however, simply about gaining their membership in the organization. The wage–work bargain is complicated by the need to motivate appropriate types of employee behaviour if and when individuals are actually hired. In what Marxists call the 'labor process' (Braverman, 1974; Thompson and Harley, 2007), the problem is one of how firms convert labor potential into productive labor—a problem that pertains to any firm, no matter how powerful or prestigious in the labor market. In order for workplace performance to occur, workers must choose to apply their capabilities with some level of effort and consistency: *motivated* capability is the quality that firms most need from individuals (Boxall and Purcell, 2008). Motivation is never simply a matter of command. While employment law gives employers the right to issue what are commonly known as 'lawful and reasonable orders', the simple fact is that control of the behavior of other human beings is always limited (Keenoy, 1992). The ability of employees to exercise their discretionary judgment is never fully circumscribed (Bendix, 1956).

All of this means that firms must offer workers sufficient incentives to attend work and do, at the least, an adequate job within a cost that the firm can afford. They need to engage in an ongoing process of incentive alignment or bargaining with their employees (Coff, 1999; Gottschalg and Zollo, 2007). Like the employer, the employee is motivated to enter an employment relationship when the benefits of doing so (such as wages, intrinsic enjoyment, and social standing) outweigh the costs (such as increased stress, fatigue, and travelling costs) and in the light of alternatives to that employment (such as alternative job offers). Firms are likely to fail if the incentives that workers seek, and are able to pursue elsewhere, are unaffordable within the firm's resources.

We can start to get a sense of why some firms fail to achieve economic levels of interest alignment when we look at research on the content of individual employee motivations. In a chapter like this we can only cite such research very selectively, but Table 11.1 lists results from a survey of some 7,000 British workers conducted in 1999–2000, showing the top five factors which they rated as their priorities in searching for a job (Rose, 2003).

As we might expect, the nature of the work itself is very important in whether British workers are attracted to particular jobs: 45 percent of people give it as either their first or their second priority. Research suggests that people like jobs which they personally find interesting, but more than this is involved; they also tend to prefer a high degree of autonomy in how they do the work, and enjoy work that take places in a supportive social context (Gallie, 2005; Karasek, 1979; Wood, 2008). Finding the work interesting for oneself (and this does not necessarily mean for others), being

Table 11.1. Job Facet Priorities of British Workers

Job Facet Priorities	Chosen First	Chosen Second
	%	%
The actual work	27	18
Job security	25	18
Pay	22	26
Using initiative	10	13
Good relations with manager	8	13

Source: Adapted from Rose (2003).

able to exercise one's initiative in work processes and methods, and having good relationships with managers and co-workers, are all part of the mix.

Other research by Rose (1994) helps to explain the role of skills in this picture: in a study of some 4,000 British employees, he finds that people are satisfied in their jobs (and more loyal to their companies) when the skills they use in their job match the skills they actually have. His study indicates that people who feel that their talents are underemployed at work are the most unhappy, while those where talents needed and possessed are equivalent are generally satisfied with their work. As time goes by, of course, people grow in their capabilities, prompting them to seek new challenges. Better quality jobs, therefore, are those which use the individual's skills and capacity for decision-making, have a fair level of work demands, and enable them to achieve the personal growth which they desire (Rose, 2000).

But the problem of recruiting and retaining talented individuals cannot be confined to addressing these intrinsic motivators: extrinsic rewards such as pay and job security are also highly valued, rated either first or second priority in Table 11.1 by 48 and 43 percent of employees respectively. A primary motive for changing jobs is to obtain higher levels of income (for example, Griffeth *et al.*, 2000; Guthrie, 2007) and, notwithstanding contemporary rhetoric about the 'end of the career', many people are motivated by the desire for employment security because of their private commitments to mortgages, spousal support, or dependent children. So, here is the rub: firms fail to recruit and retain in competitive labor markets because they cannot provide the mix of intrinsic and extrinsic factors that talented managers and workers are seeking. Their 'employment proposition' is inherently weak. They may not be able to meet the income expectations of high-productivity workers, or provide sufficient avenues for the deployment of an individual's skills, or meet expectations for personal growth once workers have mastered the immediate job, or be able to provide secure employment conditions, and so on. People often leave employers for a mix of such reasons (Boxall *et al.*, 2003). Employers face a major challenge in matching what they can offer with what the worker seeks in intrinsic and extrinsic rewards as they develop over the course of their career life-cycle.

To this challenging picture of the individual motivators that affect the firm's ability to recruit and retain human capital, we need to add an understanding of process issues, which affect not only individuals but also the social climate in which they are embedded. The social climate of an organization—including the level of trust between management and employees and among peers—is a critical dimension of its social capital. One metaphor used to help explain trust dynamics is the notion of the 'psychological contract' (Schein, 1978). Those writing on psychological contracting draw on concepts of 'social exchange' (Blau, 1964; Gouldner, 1960) to argue that employees reciprocate the kind of treatment they receive from management as the employment relationship unfolds (Grant, 1999; Whitener *et al.*, 1998). The critical principle at stake here is that employee trust in management and commitment to the firm tend to be based on their perceptions of fairness in HR practices and their assessment of managerial trustworthiness (Guest, 2007; Macky and Boxall, 2007). If firms are only interested in a short-term exchange (for example, so much money for a small task or a very finite project), this is not so much of an issue. Where, however, management wants to generate longer-term loyalty and productivity growth, there is always an issue with trust (Fox, 1974). Trust improves when the management team behaves in ways that are consistent with its promises.

Figure 11.1, modified from the work of Guest (2007), underlines the key insights involved here. It makes an important distinction between management's espoused values and HR policies on the one hand, and the HR practices enacted by managers on the other. Workers are sensitive to inconsistencies between managerial rhetoric and the reality of the management behavior which they experience (Legge, 2005). If workers consider that managers have reneged on their promises, their trust and commitment is undermined (Guest, 2007). It is important to recognize that there are important asymmetries with trust: once trust is undermined because the firm's leaders have reneged on an important commitment to the workforce, low trust levels can sour the employee relations climate and depress performance for some considerable time (Grant, 1999). In the extreme, workplaces or production sites that suffer from chronically poor industrial relations climates can only be dealt with by a strategy of 'escape': movement of work sites to 'greenfields' locations where a new approach is taken from the outset (Walton *et al.*, 1994).

In general, then, firms whose managers foster higher levels of trust will perform better in retaining employees with valuable human capital, and will enhance the social climate in which it is deployed and developed. Here the tables can be turned between large and small firms. Small firms, which typically have resource weaknesses, can be at an advantage where trust is concerned because of the capacity of owners to

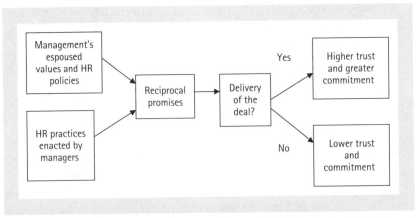

Figure 11.1. Promises, Trust, and Commitment in the Psychological Contract (modified from Guest, 2007)

deal both personally and consistently with individual employees over time (Edwards and Ram, 2006). In large firms, on the other hand, trust is a more fragile variable. Trust is only high in large firms when senior management's espoused values closely align with their own actions and with the actions of the various layers of line and specialist managers who report to them (Boxall and Purcell, 2008). Those large firms which suffer from frequent changes in senior leaders or in their leadership philosophies are particularly unlikely to develop positive social climates.

Even with skilful management, trust is naturally at risk when heightened competitive pressures require firms to foster greater organizational flexibility (Streeck, 1987). It is at risk during corporate mergers and acquisitions and whenever the leadership of a firm decides to use downsizing, deunionization, outsourcing, or offshoring to restructure labor costs (Boxall and Purcell, 2008). These events underline the fact that in capitalist societies the commitment of firms to workers is not unlimited: in Hyman's (1987: 43) memorable phrase, capitalism is a system in which 'employers require workers to be *both* dependable *and* disposable'. Firms need to be able to obtain the motivated behavior which they need from managers and workers within a cost structure that they can afford. Individual executives whose value is less than the remuneration and benefits they seek are inherently problematic, as are workforces whose productivity levels or capacities for learning are no longer economic. Employers want to be able to rely on employee loyalty to achieve stable production of products or services, but they also need to be able to dismiss individuals, or transfer production sites to cheaper locations, when the firm's survival or financial performance demands it.

In sum, firms depend for their human and social capital on a process of interest alignment through the employment relationship or wage–work bargain. This is an inherently problematic process, involving issues of labor scarcity, motivation, and cost, which some firms undertake much more successfully than others. Firms vary in their ability to manage the bargaining that is inherent in labor markets and labor processes. When relationships go sour, there is often a 'stickiness' about them that prevents easy change and may eventually require a radical solution such as relocation or outsourcing.

11.4 WHY DO FIRMS' INVESTMENTS IN HUMAN CAPITAL VARY ACROSS CRITICAL CONTEXTS?

As noted above, we know that all firms need a baseline of relevant human and social capital in order to be viable. However, is more human capital always better for firm performance? Or are there important contingent variables which moderate or nuance firms' investments in human capital? The answer to this latter question is 'yes': research indicates that firms differentiate their investments in people across a range of different internal and external environments. This section highlights three types of differentiation in particular.

11.4.1 Differentiation within Firms

Let us begin with the differentiation in labor management that we observe across employee groups within firms. Research shows that firms rarely maintain an egalitarian policy of investment in their diverse human capital (Osterman, 1987; Pinfield and Berner, 1994). Human capital is an element in HR strategy, and it is helpful to think of the HR strategy of the firm as a cluster of HR systems, each concerned with organizing the work and managing the employment of a particular group, as depicted in Figure 11.2 (Boxall and Purcell, 2008). Requirements for socially legitimate employment practices and internal political pressures mean there will usually be overlaps in HR practices across HR systems within an organization (Boxall and Purcell, 2008): for example, there may be common ways of handling leave entitlements and disciplinary procedures. In large organizations, claims for internal equity across occupational groups will often lead to a number of standardized employment policies in employment contracts or in the employee handbook. However, when we look more closely at critical variables such as work organization (including how much discretion is given to employees), at pay levels (in which variation has been increasing between those at the top and those at the bottom), and at investments in further training and education, it is typical for a substantially different approach to be taken across employee groups of different value or organizational status: for example, across managers, permanent non-managerial employees, and temporary and 'contract' staff (Green, 2008; Harley, 2001; Kalleberg et al., 2006).

It is not hard to see why such internal variation is so often the case. Managers need greater discretion in order to carry out their work—in order to lead others and solve non-routine problems. Their skills are typically scarcer, and they demand a higher level of rewards or a greater share of economic 'rents'—Coff, 1999). Similarly, core workers who are central to the firm's value creation process both underpin its viability and offer it the possibility of building sources of competitive advantage. If firms are to ensure these outcomes, they need to protect these workers from labor market competition through HR practices that build higher levels of commitment (Lepak, and Snell 1999, 2002, 2007; Ch. 13 below). For their part, core workers are likely to appreciate their centrality to competitive success and bargain for higher remuneration (Coff, 1999; Osterman, 2006). We should not thus be surprised that investment in human capital is rarely egalitarian: both firms and critically located workers have reasons to foster differential investments in human capital.

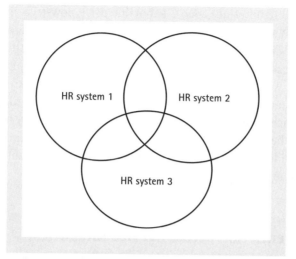

Figure 11.2. An Organization's HR Strategy as a Cluster of HR Systems (Boxall and Purcell, 2008: 60)

11.4.2 Differentiation across Technological Contexts

Differentiation in human capital investments is not only a feature within the boundaries of firms. It is also a feature of firm behavior across different technological contexts. In manufacturing, the level of investment in operating workers tends to be related to industry characteristics, including critical differences in technological choices. Blauner's (1964) study of work in four different technological environments—craft, machine-minding, assembly-line, and continuous process industries—remains the classic analysis of this point, but subsequent research confirms it. Snell and Dean's (1992) study of 512 US metal manufacturing plants shows that heavier investments in individual employees, including more extensive screening and training practices, are associated with plants using advanced technologies such as computer-integrated manufacturing systems. When a manufacturing firm has expensive investments in advanced technology, which requires highly skilled and careful handling, managers are likely to spend money building employee competencies and fostering employee commitment (Godard, 1991; Steedman and Wagner, 1989). In effect, where there are high 'interaction risks' between specialized capital assets (in which the firm has major 'sunk costs') and the behavior of workers, managers are likely to adopt employment models that foster greater expertise and buy greater loyalty and care (Boxall and Purcell, 2008). They want, after all, to maximize machine up-time.

The value of such investments, however, is likely to be questioned by managers when the industry they are operating in is characterized by a stable, low-technology environment (Kintana *et al.*, 2006). Labor-intensive, low-tech manufacturing is much more likely to be associated with pressures to outsource production to low-wage countries where firms have found that they can achieve the same or better levels of effectiveness for a much lower investment in human capital. This is abundantly evident in such industries as textiles, clothing, footwear, toy manufacturing, and home-appliance assembly (Boxall and Purcell, 2008). Offshoring production to countries in which labor costs are markedly lower, and labor regulations are less demanding, has become one of the preferred HR strategies of multinational companies in these industries (Cooke, 2001, 2007). In many cases, established firms have ceased manufacturing altogether in high-wage countries.

11.4.3 Differentiation across Service Industries

A similar process of differentiation in HR strategy is apparent in the service sector where investments in employees vary enormously from low-skill employment regimes in mass low-margin services to high-skill models in professional services (Boxall, 2003). In mass service markets, such as gas stations, fast food outlets, and supermarkets, key managers or franchisees have critical knowledge but general labor uses limited—mostly generic know-how. Customers are price-sensitive, and because costs, including labor costs, are in competition, firms do not generally pay above market-clearing wages unless persuaded to do otherwise by unions and state regulation (Hunter, 2000). In their quest to survive in a cost-conscious environment, firms substitute labor for technology and self-service. They also pursue outsourcing and offshoring of service or back-office operations which are not geographically sensitive to production sites which are more cost-effective (CIPD, 2006).

The dynamics of cost-based competition in mass services have the effect of imposing major constraints on the HR strategies of firms and, thus, limiting their investments in human capital. At the other extreme, in professional services, such as law, medicine, accountancy, and professional engineering, work organization has always involved high levels of employee discretion, and firms typically invest heavily in building employee skills. They recruit selectively, offer high pay levels, and provide opportunities to participate in decision-making and, ultimately, in ownership (Boxall, 2003). In the most esoteric forms of professional services, customers are heavily dependent on the knowledge and skills of professionals who are able to charge heavy premiums for the engagement of their idiosyncratic human capital.

The difference in human capital investments between mass and professional services is easy to demonstrate, but variation in such investment is also readily apparent in service industries which lie between these extremes. One excellent illustration is found in Batt's (2000) analysis of four segments in call-center work in the US telecommunications industry. These segments differ in terms of the complexity and value of the employee–customer interaction. At the low end there are low-margin interactions of short duration, typically with predetermined scripts and with strong technological monitoring of call-center workers. At the high end there are high-margin, low-volume interactions relying far more on employee skill and discretion where technology is much more of an enabler than a monitor. One statistic alone is telling: at the low-margin end, operators deal with an average of 465 customers per day—in the two mid-range segments they deal with 100 and 64, and at the top end they deal with an average of 32 (Batt, 2000: 550). Batt (2000) finds significant differences in the contours of HR strategy across these market segments with skill requirements, the degree of discretion allowed to employees, and pay levels all higher among firms competing at the high-margin end of the call-center market. Other compelling examples of differentiated investments in human capital can be found in US studies of rest homes (Eaton, 2000; Hunter, 2000) where investments in training, pay, career structures, and staffing levels are greater in firms that target higher-value niches and in studies of hotels where those at the luxury end invest more heavily in their staff in order to deliver superior customer service (Haynes and Fryer, 2000; Knox and Walsh, 2005; Lashley, 1998).

Overall, then, there is compelling evidence that firms vary their investments in human capital, both inside their 'skins' and across divergent contexts in both manufacturing and services. In the dynamic picture, when productive sites are potentially mobile, we see firms shifting to environments which offer the same or better functionalities at lower costs.

11.5 WHEN AND HOW CAN FIRMS BUILD SUSTAINED COMPETITIVE ADVANTAGE THROUGH HUMAN CAPITAL?

We have argued so far that while all firms need relevant types of human and social capital, there are important differences in the extent to which they invest in people across diverse contexts. This enables us to return to the 'truism' we noted at the outset: idiosyncrasy in human resources offers firms the opportunity to build enviable, hard-to-copy sources of advantage. No one seriously denies that idiosyncrasy exists in firms: the interesting questions turn on when and how idiosyncrasy in human and social capital is valuable and hard to imitate.

In thinking about this question, it is helpful to distinguish between labor-cost advantages and labor-differentiation advantages (Boxall and Purcell, 2008). The sort of production offshoring that we currently observe in labor-intensive manufacturing industries is primarily done for reasons of cost, including labor costs. This, however, is more likely to enhance survival or viability than it is to bring about a sustained advantage: the firms that do it first enjoy some temporary advantages but, as others follow suit, profits typically return to normal. Labor differentiation is mainly what people mean when they think of sustained advantage through human resource management or 'human resource advantage' (Boxall, 1996; Boxall and Purcell, 2008). This turns on a much higher level of investment in people and in their interactions with one another. Differentiation stems from employing smarter people and enhancing their teamwork, communication, and problem-solving in order to foster innovation and high quality. Labor differentiation is clearly the goal for much of the workforce in capital-intensive or high-tech manufacturing, as we noted in the previous section, and it can also be the goal for the inner core of research, marketing, and design functions in labor-intensive manufacturing that are not actually offshored but retained in high-wage countries (Boxall and Purcell, 2008). In the service sector, the goal of HR advantage is much more of a possibility in differentiated service markets where a group of more affluent customers is prepared to pay a premium for esoteric knowledge or better service quality (Boxall, 2003). This often happens, as the previous section indicates, in professional services and in such services as luxury hotels and premium banking.

The critical question in the HRM literature has turned on how the HRM process can build sources of sustained advantage when firms in these contexts choose to pursue this goal. Theoretical attention is focused on the complex competencies and relationships that people develop inside organizations over significant periods of time. These are the kind of path-dependent, socially complex, and causally ambiguous assets that can create barriers to imitation (Barney, 1991). The key argument is that firms trying to create such assets in their structures of human and social capital need to pay close attention to how they construct and enhance their HR systems (Boxall and Purcell, 2008). HR systems—the whole bundle of work and employment practices relating to a major employee group—rather than individual policies or practices, are the focus of current interest (Lepak *et al.*, 2006).

Much of the contemporary research on this question is going forward under the rubric of 'high-performance work systems' (Appelbaum and Batt, 1994) or, perhaps more aptly, *highly performing* HR systems. Firms face two challenges if they are to build exceptional HR systems (Boxall and Macky, 2007). One focuses on the make-up of such systems to serve particular management goals in different contexts. At the risk of stating the obvious, the specific policies and practices that are well adapted to enhancing employee performance in steel manufacturing, which cater well for the typical work structures and employee relations climates in this industry, will not necessarily create high performance in hotels or in professional services. There is a challenge in each industry, and for each organization, to learn to customize the content of its HR systems. This puts a premium on the insights and skills of senior managers, including, where they exist, HR directors (Boxall, 1998). The second challenge is associated with managing the key mediators between policy intentions and outcomes that exist inside the 'black box' of any firm's HRM, irrespective of its specific

HR policies (Purcell *et al.*, 2003). There are two critical mediators or linking elements in any sizable organization: one is the way in which first-line managers interpret and filter the policies and personal signals of higher-level managers, and the other is the way in which employees respond to the mix of messages that they receive from senior managers and from their direct line managers. It is actually very hard for any large organization to develop consistent transmission from senior management's intentions through line-manager behaviors to employee responses, and thus the management of this chain of links can become a source of competitive advantage or, conversely, can function as a source of competitive *dis*advantage (Purcell, 1999). Purcell and Hutchison's (2007) study of the British retail organization Selfridges is a case in point. It underlines the value of senior management taking a much greater interest in the selection, development, support, and motivation of front-line managers so that they, in turn, manage front-line employees in ways that enhance their satisfaction and commitment and that lead on to the important store-level outcomes of enhanced customer satisfaction and retention. Thus, research on how firms can build sustained advantage in HRM is concerned with both the astute adaptation of HR systems to management's goals in specific contexts and with the superior management of implementation processes—particularly in large and cumbersome organizations.

11.6 CONCLUSIONS

Human and social capital is a fundamental part of what makes firms successful. Firms are simply not viable without the willing cooperation of people who have the kind of knowledge and skills that are relevant to their industry. On top of this, human and social capital is always somewhat idiosyncratic. As the resource-based view of the firm emphasizes, it also offers the potential to build sources of sustained competitive advantage. These premises, however, do not take us far beyond the basic fundamentals.

This chapter has attempted to move the debate beyond these truisms to focus on three more important questions: (1) what is inherently problematic about human capital management, (2) how does investment in human capital vary across contexts, and (3) when and how can firms build competitive superiority through their human and social capital? A long tradition of research on the first question argues that firms wrestle with a major bargaining or interest-alignment problem in HRM stemming from the problems of labor scarcity and motivation. Some firms evolve better ways of handling the external problem of competition *for* labor and the internal problem of cost-effective cooperation *with* labor. In respect of the second question, a careful review of research shows that firms differentiate their investments in people in various ways, including across employee groups of different value, across different technological contexts, and across different types of service. The cutting edge of current research in strategic HRM is very much concerned with the third question. It turns on how we define the contours of highly performing HR systems in different industries and organizations, and how managers can better handle the processes within the 'black box' of the firms that foster them. To develop sustained advantage through HRM, firms must learn to customize their HR systems in astute ways and must manage a fragile chain of links from management intentions through line-manager behaviors and employee responses to performance outcomes. Insight into this process, and the stamina, skills, and political coordination needed for follow-through, are valuable and rare attributes. Human resource advantages are much easier to talk about than to achieve.

Notes

1. The Chinese Government's national guideline on its long-term programme for science and technology development: http://www.gov.cn/english/2006-02/09/content_212363.htm (accessed Mar. 2008).

References

Appelbaum, E., and Batt, R. (1994). *The New American Workplace* (Ithaca, NY: ILR Press).

Barnard, C. (1938). *The Functions of the Executive* (Boston: Harvard University Press).

Barney, J. (1991). 'Firm Resources and Sustained Competitive Advantage', *Journal of Management*, 17(1): 99–120.

Batt, R. (2000). 'Strategic Segmentation in Front-Line Services: Matching Customers, Employees and Human Resource Systems', *International Journal of Human Resource Management*, 11(3): 540–61.

Bendix, R. (1956). *Work and Authority in Industry* (Berkeley, Calif.: UCLA Press).

Blau, P. (1964). *Exchange and Power in Social Life* (New York: Wiley).

Blauner, R. (1964). *Alienation and Freedom: The Factory Worker and his Industry* (Chicago: University of Chicago Press).

Boxall, P. (1996). 'The Strategic HRM Debate and the Resource-Based View of the Firm', *Human Resource Management Journal*, 6(3): 59–75.

——(1998). 'Achieving Competitive Advantage through Human Resource Strategy: Towards a Theory of Industry Dynamics', *Human Resource Management Review*, 8(3): 265–88.

——(2003). 'HR Strategy and Competitive Advantage in the Service Sector', *Human Resource Management Journal*, 13(3): 5–20.

——and Macky, K. (2007). 'Commentary: High-Performance Work Systems and Organisational Performance. Bridging Theory and Practice', *Asia Pacific Journal of Human Resources*, 45(3): 261–70.

——MACKY, K., and RASMUSSEN, E. (2003). 'Labour Turnover and Retention in New Zealand: The Causes and Consequences of Leaving and Staying with Employers', *Asia Pacific Journal of Human Resources*, 41: 195–214.

——and PURCELL, J. (2008). *Strategy and Human Resource Management* (2nd edn. Basingstoke and New York: Palgrave Macmillan).

——and STEENEVELD, M. (1999). 'Human Resource Strategy and Competitive Advantage: A Longitudinal Study of Engineering Consultancies', *Journal of Management Studies*, 36(4): 443–63.

BRAVERMAN, H. (1974). *Labor and Monopoly Capital* (New York: Monthly Review Press).

BROWN, C., and REICH, M. (1997). 'Micro-Macro Linkages in High-Performance Work Systems', *Organization Studies*, 18(5): 765–81.

Chartered Institute of Personnel and Development (CIPD) (2006). 'Offshoring and the Role of HR'. URL:http://www.cipd.co.uk/subjects/corpstrtgy/general/_offshrgrolhr.htm?IsSrchRes=1 (accessed Mar. 2008).

COFF, R. (1997). 'Human Assets and Management Dilemmas: Coping with Hazards on the Road to Resource-Based Theory', *Academy of Management Review*, 22(2): 374–402.

——(1999). 'When Competitive Advantage Doesn't Lead to Performance: The Resource-Based View and Stakeholder Bargaining Power', *Organization Science*, 10(2): 119–33.

COOKE, W. N. (2001). 'The Effects of Labor Costs and Workplace Constraints on Foreign Direct Investment among Highly Industrialised Countries', *International Journal of Human Resource Management*, 12(5): 697–716.

——(2007). 'Multinational Companies and Global Human Resource Strategy', in P. Boxall, J. Purcell, and P. Wright (eds.), *The Oxford Handbook of Human Resource Management* (Oxford: Oxford University Press), 489–508.

EATON, S. (2000). 'Beyond "Unloving Care": Linking Human Resource Management and Patient Care Quality in Nursing Homes', *International Journal of Human Resource Management*, 11(3): 591–616.

EDWARDS, P., and RAM, M. (2006). 'Surviving on the Margins of the Economy: Working Relationships in Small, Low-Wage Firms', *Journal of Management Studies*, 43(4): 895–916.

FOX, A. (1974). *Beyond Contract: Work, Power and Trust Relations* (London: Faber).

GALLIE, D. (2005). 'Work Pressure in Europe 1996–2001: Trends and Determinants', *British Journal of Industrial Relations*, 43(3): 351–75.

GODARD, J. (1991). 'The Progressive HRM Paradigm: A Theoretical and Empirical Re-examination', *Relations Industrielles*, 46(2): 378–400.

GOTTSCHALG, O., and ZOLLO, M. (2007). 'Interest Alignment and Competitive Advantage', *Academy of Management Review*, 32(2): 418–37.

GOULDNER, A. (1960). 'The Norm of Reciprocity: A Preliminary Statement', *American Sociological Review*, 25: 161–78.

GRANT, D. (1999). 'HRM, Rhetoric and the Psychological Contract: A Case of "Easier Said than Done"', *International Journal of Human Resource Management*, 10(2): 327–50.

GREEN, F. (2008). 'Leeway for the Loyal: A Model of Employee Discretion', *British Journal of Industrial Relations*, 46(1): 1–32.

GRIFFETH, R., HOM, P., and GAERTNER, S. (2000). 'A Meta-Analysis of the Antecedents and Correlates of Employee Turnover: Update, Moderator Tests, and Research Implications for the Next Millennium', *Journal of Management*, 26(3): 563–88.

Guest, D. (2007). 'Human Resource Management and the Worker: Towards a New Psychological Contract?', in P. Boxall, J. Purcell, and P. Wright (eds.), *The Oxford Handbook of Human Resource Management* (Oxford: Oxford University Press), 128–46.

Guthrie, J. (2007) 'Remuneration: Pay Effects at Work', in P. Boxall, J. Purcell, and P. Wright (eds.), *The Oxford Handbook of Human Resource Management* (Oxford: Oxford University Press), 344–63.

Hamel, G., and Prahalad, C. (1994). *Competing for the Future* (Boston: Harvard Business School Press).

Harley, B. (2001). 'Team Membership and the Experience of Work in Britain: An Analysis of the WERS98 Data', *Work, Employment and Society*, 15(4): 721–42.

Haynes, P., and Fryer, G. (2000). 'Human Resources, Service Quality and Performance: A Case Study', *International Journal of Contemporary Hospitality Management*, 12(4): 240–8.

Hendry, C., Arthur, M., and Jones, A. (1995). *Strategy through People* (London and New York: Routledge).

Hoopes, D., Madsen, T., and Walker, G. (2003). 'Guest Editors' Introduction to the Special Issue: Why is there a Resource-Based View? Toward a Theory of Competitive Heterogeneity', *Strategic Management Journal*, 24: 889–902.

Hornsby, J., and Kuratko, D. (2003). 'Human Resource Management in US Small Businesses: A Replication and Extension', *Journal of Developmental Entrepreneurship*, 8(1): 73–92.

Hunter, J. E., Schmidt, F. L., and Judiesch, M. K. (1990). 'Individual Differences in Output Variability as a Function of Job Complexity', *Journal of Applied Psychology*, 75(1): 28–42.

Hunter, L. (2000). 'What Determines Job Quality in Nursing Homes?', *Industrial and Labor Relations Review*, 53(3): 463–81.

Hyman, R. (1987). 'Strategy or Structure? Capital, Labour and Control', *Work, Employment and Society*, 1(1): 25–55.

Kalleberg, A., Marsden, P., Reynolds, J., and Knoke, D. (2006). 'Beyond Profit? Sectoral Differences in High-Performance Work Practices', *Work and Occupations*, 33(3): 271–302.

Karasek, R. (1979). 'Job Demands, Job Decision Latitude, and Mental Strain: Implications for Job Redesign', *Administrative Science Quarterly*, 24: 285–308.

Keenoy, T. (1992). 'Constructing Control', in J. Hartley and G. Stephenson (eds.), *Employment Relations: The Psychology of Influence and Control at Work* (Oxford: Blackwell).

Kintana, M., Alonso, A., and Olaverri, C. (2006). 'High-Performance Work Systems and Firms' Operational Performance: The Moderating Role of Technology', *International Journal of Human Resource Management*, 17(1): 70–85.

Knox, A., and Walsh, J. (2005). 'Organisational Flexibility and HRM in the Hotel Industry: Evidence from Australia', *Human Resource Management Journal*, 15(1): 57–75.

Lashley, C. (1998). 'Matching the Management of Human Resources to Service Operations', *International Journal of Contemporary Hospitality Management*, 10(1): 24–33.

Legge, K. (2005). *Human Resource Management: Rhetorics and Realities* (Basingstoke and New York: Palgrave Macmillan).

Lepak, D., and Snell, S. (1999). 'The Strategic Management of Human Capital: Determinants and Implications of Different Relationships', *Academy of Management Review*, 24(1): 1–18.

——and ——(2002). 'Examining the Human Resource Architecture: The Relationships among Human Capital, Employment, and Human Resource Configurations', *Journal of Management*, 28: 517–43.

——and —— (2007). 'Employment Sub-Systems and the "HR Architecture"', in P. Boxall, J. Purcell, and P. Wright (eds.), *The Oxford Handbook of Human Resource Management* (Oxford: Oxford University Press), 210–30.

——LIAO, H., CHUNG, Y., and HARDEN, E. (2006). 'A Conceptual Review of Human Resource Management Systems in Strategic Human Resource Management Research', *Research in Personnel and Human Resources Management*, 25: 217–71.

MACKY, K., and BOXALL, P. (2007). 'The Relationship between High-Performance Work Practices and Employee Attitudes: An Investigation of Additive and Interaction Effects', *International Journal of Human Resource Management*, 18(4): 537–67.

MARCHINGTON, M., CARROLL, M., and BOXALL, P. (2003). 'Labour Scarcity and the Survival of Small Firms: A Resource-Based View of the Road Haulage Industry', *Human Resource Management Journal*, 13(4): 3–22.

OSTERMAN, P. (1987). 'Choice of Employment Systems in Internal Labor Markets', *Industrial Relations*, 26(1): 46–67.

—— (2006). 'The Wage Effects of High Performance Work Organization in Manufacturing', *Industrial and Labor Relations Review*, 59(2): 187–204.

PENROSE, E. (1959). *The Theory of the Growth of the Firm* (Oxford: Blackwell).

PINFIELD, L., and BERNER, M. (1994). 'Employment Systems: Toward a Coherent Conceptualisation of Internal Labour Markets', in G. Ferris (ed.), *Research in Personnel and Human Resources Management* (Greenwich, Conn.: JAI Press), xii. 41–78.

PURCELL, J. (1999). 'The Search for "Best Practice" and "Best Fit": Chimera or Cul-de-Sac?', *Human Resource Management Journal*, 9(3): 26–41.

——and HUTCHINSON, S. (2007). 'Front-Line Managers as Agents in the HRM-Performance Causal Chain: Theory, Analysis and Evidence', *Human Resource Management Journal*, 17(1): 3–20.

——KINNIE, N., HUTCHINSON, S., SWART, J., and RAYTON, B. (2003). *Understanding the People and Performance Link: Unlocking the Black Box* (London: CIPD).

ROSE, M. (1994). 'Job Satisfaction, Job Skills, and Personal Skills', in R. Penn, M. Rose, and J. Rubery (eds.), *Skill and Occupational Change* (Oxford: Oxford University Press), 244–80.

—— (2000). 'Work Attitudes in the Expanding Occupations', in K. Purcell (ed.), *Changing Boundaries in Employment* (Bristol: Bristol Academic Press), 209–40.

—— (2003). 'Good Deal, Bad Deal? Job Satisfaction in Occupations', *Work, Employment and Society*, 17(3): 503–30.

RUBERY, J., and GRIMSHAW, D. (2003). *The Organization of Employment* (New York and Basingstoke: Palgrave Macmillan).

SCHEIN, E. (1978). *Career Dynamics: Matching Individual and Organizational Needs* (Reading, Mass.: Addison-Wesley).

SNELL, S., and DEAN, J. (1992). 'Integrated Manufacturing and Human Resources Management: A Human Capital Perspective', *Academy of Management Journal*, 35(3): 467–504.

SPENDER, J.-C. (1989). *Industry Recipes* (Oxford: Blackwell).

STOREY, D. J. (1985). 'The Problems Facing New Firms', *Journal of Management Studies*, 22(3): 327–45.

STEEDMAN, H., and WAGNER, K. (1989). 'Productivity, Machinery and Skills: Clothing Manufacture in Britain and Germany', *National Institute Economic Review* (May): 40–57.

STREECK, W. (1987). 'The Uncertainties of Management in the Management of Uncertainty: Employers, Labour Relations and Industrial Adjustment in the 1980s', *Work, Employment and Society*, 1(3): 281–308.

THOMPSON, P., and HARLEY, W. (2007). 'HRM and the Worker: Labor Process Perspectives', in P. Boxall, J. Purcell, and P. Wright (eds.), *The Oxford Handbook of Human Resource Management* (Oxford: Oxford University Press), 147–65.

WALTON, R., CUTCHER-GERSHENFELD, J., and McKERSIE, R. (1994). *Strategic Negotiations: A Theory of Change in Labor-Management Relations* (Boston: Harvard Business School Press).

WATSON, T. (2005). 'Organizations, Strategies and Human Resourcing', in J. Leopold, L. Harris, and T. Watson (eds.), *The Strategic Managing of Human Resources* (Harlow: Pearson Education), 17–38.

WERNERFELT, B. (1984). 'A Resource-Based View of the Firm', *Strategic Management Journal*, 5(2): 171–80.

WHITENER, E. M., BRODT, S. E., KORSGAARD, M. A., and WERNER, J. M. (1998). 'Managers as Initiators of Trust: An Exchange Relationship Framework for Understanding Managerial Trustworthy Behaviour', *Academy of Management Review*, 23(3): 513–30.

WINDOLF, P. (1986). 'Recruitment, Selection, and Internal Labour Markets in Britain and Germany', *Organization Studies*, 7(3): 235–54.

WOOD, S. (2008). 'Job Characteristics, Employee Voice and Well-Being in Britain', *Industrial Relations Journal*, 39(2): 153–68.

WRIGHT, P., McMAHAN, G., and McWILLIAMS, A. (1994). 'Human Resources and Sustained Competitive Advantage: A Resource-Based Perspective', *International Journal of Human Resource Management*, 5(2): 301–26.

CHAPTER 12

HOW ORGANIZATIONS OBTAIN THE HUMAN CAPITAL THEY NEED

MONIKA HAMORI

ROCIO BONET

PETER CAPPELLI

12.1 THE TRADITIONAL 'BUILD' MODEL OF ACQUIRING AND DEVELOPING HUMAN CAPITAL

Since the turn of the nineteenth century, employers in the United States have tried to control their supply of human capital by bringing skill development inside the organization. Companies typically hired their employees at the entry level, without previous business experience or business skills—most often straight from college campuses—and would develop their skills inside the organization through a series of formal training programs and on-the-job training. More specifically, within the traditional enterprise internal labor market, jobs were grouped in mobility clusters that shared related skills or work experience, similar levels of job content, functional or departmental organization, and a single focus of work (Doeringer and Piore, 1971; Slichter *et al.*, 1960). Upward mobility took place within clusters that were characterized by natural skill progressions. Usually, the training required for any given job in the progression was acquired on the job below it. The internal labor market was then made up of a series of job ladders with several entry ports (Kerr, 1954). As a result, the careers inside the large employers were a series of increasingly important responsibilities where the greatest reward for good performance was promotion. Organizations provided lifetime security in return for loyalty and adequate performance (Cappelli et al., 1997; Cappelli, 1999).

IBM's lifetime model of career development is a good illustration for this way of developing human capital. IBM hired from twenty or so of the best colleges. The divisions were evaluated on how many of their hires came from those schools. Candidates were brought into functional tracks, given specialized training in that function, and then evaluated within two years to make the move into first-line management, supervising a group of about twelve people. Management training would follow, as would evaluation by the business units to be nominated based on job performance for advancement. The Division Presidents would evaluate those nominees and decide which ones to send up to the company Management Committee. (It is remarkable in contemporary terms to think that the operating committee of a huge multinational company would spend time mapping out the development of these 450 or so candidates, most of whom were still under age 30.) Each move meant significant increases in salary and responsibility, lots of additional training (the best-known was the requirement that each manager receive forty hours of formal training on managerial issues each year) and relocation. At its peak, IBM relocated 7,000 of its 50,000 managerial employees every year. IBM managed the careers of its managers to retirement. It required all its officers to retire at age 60 to help open up opportunities for internal advancement and to make career planning more predictable, reducing the disruptions caused by early retirement for executives (Cappelli, 2008).

12.2 THE EROSION OF THE 'BUILD' MODEL

12.2.1 The Driving Force behind the Changes

The erosion of the traditional 'build' model was a result of a series of socioeconomic changes—most notably, changes in the competitive environment (Cappelli et al., 1997; Cappelli, 1999). Until the 1980s, US companies experienced virtually no foreign competition, and the demand for their products was easily predictable even for a five-year time span. The rapid changes in the business environment and the onset of foreign competition hindered corporations from producing long-term business plans. Since long-term business planning served as the foundation for workforce planning, succession planning, and internal career development, these activities were also eliminated or their importance decreased. In addition, the rapid changes in the economic environment made some of the existing skill sets of employees rapidly obsolete, and demanded the acquisition of these skills from the outside labor market, or the outsourcing of these activities, rather than the development of the new skills inside organizations. To accommodate the changes in the business environment, companies increasingly resorted to downsizing and restructuring their activities, which eliminated layers of management. Furthermore, innovations in management practices, such as employee empowerment and employee participation in decision-making and advancements in information technology, decreased the need for the decision and control functions of middle management and created flatter organizational hierarchies. This work reorganization increased the demand of skills at lower levels in the organization. Specifically, more and new types of skills were required to succeed in these high involvement jobs.

12.2.2 The 'New' Employment Model

The new socioeconomic environment brought about four major changes in the ways in which organizations acquired and developed human capital:

The first change concerns the *decrease in the importance of internal talent development*. Until the late 1980s, virtually every company of any size carried out sophisticated workforce planning, and succession planning for the management and executive ranks (Cappelli, 2008). Since the 1990s, however, companies have gradually abandoned the systematic approach to managing talent. The approach of IBM to human capital development aptly illustrates this trend. Between 1985 and 1993, IBM pushed 250,000 employees out of the company, breaking their lifetime employment tradition, and hired 100,000 new ones, many of them experienced hires at the management and executive level. Both development opportunities and relocations became less pervasive (Cappelli, 2008). As of today, the majority of organizations have no systematic approach to developing talent: the Society for Human Resource Management annual succession planning survey in 2006 found that only 29 percent of the companies surveyed had a formal succession plan, and that 42 percent of the organizations had no plan at all (Society of Human Resource Management, 2006a).

The second change concerns the *increase in outside hiring*—the rise in the percentage of employees who join organizations with an already existing skill set instead of taking entry-level positions. A recent survey by CareerXroads, a staffing strategy firm, found that about two-thirds of the job vacancies of their respondents (organizations with 5,000 employees or more) were filled by outside hires (CareerXroads, 2007). One interesting proxy for the growth of outside hiring is the fact that the revenues from corporate recruiting firms that perform outside searches for companies *tripled* during the mid-1990s. The 'employment services industry' that manages this outside labor market employed 3.6 million people in the US in

2004, and had revenues that exceeded $100 billion. This industry includes temporary help, professional employer organizations (which take on the legal obligations of an employer but not their day-to-day management), and employment placement agencies of various kinds (Staffing Industry Analysts, 2004).

Another important trend in outside hiring is that firms increasingly go to the external labor market to hire top executives and chief executive officers. Murphy and Zábojnik (2004) report that while the percentage of outside successors was 15 percent in the United States in the 1970s, it steadily increased to 26.5 percent by the 1990s. At the same time, the percentage of apprentice CEOs—those CEOs who served as second-in-command under the outgoing CEO—decreased by half in the decade between 1995 and 2005 globally (Lucier et al., 2006). The sharpest decrease in the percentage of apprentice CEOs took place in Europe, where the percentage of such CEOs fell from 67 percent in 1995 to 22 percent in 2005. The increase in outside CEOs also highlights the inability of firms to forecast the type of skills and abilities that they need in the future. Rather than betting on the skills that they may need and developing their high-potentials inside the organization, an increasing percentage of them choose to hire the skill set on demand, from the outside labor market.

Outside hiring of top executives is particularly important for issues of human capital development because the new leaders often bring with them their own team of managers, blocking succession to all the executive roles and undercutting the development programs whose goal was to fill those executive positions. Outside hiring of executives also shifts the attention of the managers and executives to networks of potential employers outside the firm as they get the message that the way to get ahead involves changing employers.

The increasing reliance of employers on *alternative work arrangements—part-time employment, temporary help, and contract work*—represents the third consequence of the socioeconomic changes. As of 2005, about 11 percent of the US workforce was on alternative employment arrangements—working either as independent contractors, on-call workers who are called on to work as needed, and workers provided by temporary help agencies or contract firms. Table 12.1 shows the distribution of employees with contingent arrangements in various occupational categories. Perhaps not surprisingly, production and transportation employees are more likely to have temporary rather than traditional arrangements. Employees in natural resources, construction-related, and maintenance occupations are more likely to be temporary workers or independent contractors or be 'loaned' to corporations by contract firms. What is more interesting is that the proportion of managerial and professional employees who enjoyed the most employment protection in the traditional 'build' model is greater among independent contractors and workers provided by contract firms than among workers with traditional arrangements. Overall, these trends reveal that corporations intend to obtain the skill sets that they need by acquiring them from the external labor market in the form of short-term

Table 12.1. US Employed Workers with Alternative and Traditional Work Arrangements by Occupation, 2005 (% distribution)

	Independent contractors	On-call workers	Temp. help agency workers	Workers provided by contract firms	Workers with traditional arrangements
Management, professional, and related	39.9	35.6	20.3	39.6	35.0
Service	13.7	22.1	15.6	26.2	15.5
Sales and office	20.5	12.6	26.9	7.2	26.6
Natural resources, construction, and maintenance	19.7	16.9	7.1	21.8	9.4
Production, transportation, and material moving	6.1	12.7	30.1	5.2	13.5

Source: US Bureau of Labor Statistics, 2005.

arrangements, and they increasingly develop a transaction-based (rather than a long-term) relationship with those who provide these skills.

In Europe, 14 percent of the workforce of the EU27 is on temporary contracts. Spain, Portugal, and Poland employ the greatest percentage of temporary workers (32 percent of the Spanish workforce is under such contracts), while this type of arrangement is rare in Ireland (2.5 percent), Romania (1.8 percent), and Lithuania (3.7 percent) (Romans and Hardarson, 2007). The high figure in Spain is mainly due to a change in the employment legislation in 1984, aimed at reducing unemployment (which was about 20 percent). Specifically, the reform affected fixed-term contracts and liberalized the use of temporary contracts that until that date could only be used for non-regular productive activities such as the tourist industry. The new Employment Protection Legislation allowed employers to use temporary contracts also for regular activities, and these fixed-term contracts entailed much lower dismissal costs than regular permanent contracts. Under the new legislation, employers moved towards hiring employees under non-permanent contracts, and there was a huge increase in the use of these temporary employees (Dolado *et al.*, 2002).

The fourth major change in the way organizations obtain human capital concerns the necessity for organizations to counterbalance the *decreasing attachment of employees* to organizations and to place major efforts into retaining their most valuable workers. Of employees in the US 2.7 percent change employers each month (Fallick and Fleishman, 2002), which gives an annual turnover rate of about 32 percent. As a comparison, companies in the private sector in the UK experience an annual turnover rate of 22.6 percent (Chartered Institute of Personnel and Development, 2007), lower but still high in absolute terms (Auer *et al.*, 2005). What is more intriguing, however, is the extremely high percentage of those employees who constantly look for employment opportunities at other employers. Of currently employed individuals in the US, 72 percent are searching for opportunities with a different employer. While the majority post résumés online and browse job openings, they are still undecided about leaving their employer. However, 31 percent of the currently employed workforce searches for jobs with the intention of changing organizations (Society of Human Resource Management, 2006b).

Decreasing attachment to employers is not restricted to lower-level employees. In fact, executives are also likely to search for opportunities with another employer. A study on the behavior of executives in the financial services industry examined how many of the executives would be willing to take up the invitation from an executive search firm to become a candidate for a position elsewhere. The executives learnt relatively little about the potential position before responding, so their answer reflects their attachment to their current organization. Table 12.2 shows the percentage of executives who were willing to become a candidate in the search done by the search firm at the various hierarchical levels: 52 percent of the executives were willing to begin the process of becoming a candidate and leaving their current

Table 12.2. Percentage of Executives Willing to Consider Becoming a Candidate for Position at Another Employer

In positions	N	%
CEO	112	55.2
EVP	44	64.7
SVP	196	54.1
VP	97	46.8
Other	117	49.8
Total	566	52.0

Source: Cappelli and Hamori, 2006.

organization, and the willingness actually increased among individuals who were higher in the hierarchy (Cappelli and Hamori, 2006).

Furthermore, most employees consider changing employers for a minor and short-term improvement. A national probability survey of employees conducted in the US in 2003, at the time of a slack job market, asked what would be required in terms of compensation to induce employees to leave their current job and take an equivalent position elsewhere. Even in 2003, large proportions of employees were willing to leave for small amounts of additional compensation. Especially noteworthy was their short-term orientation: a $1,000 bonus today would move as many employees to a new job as would a potential salary increase of $6,000 in five years (Ledford and Lucy, 2003); 50 percent of employees would move for a one-time bonus opportunity of $5,000, while 75 percent of employees would move for a bonus opportunity of $10,000.

Not surprisingly, the percentage of organizations that experience retention difficulties is huge. For example, 78 percent of UK employers surveyed by the CIPD in 2007 indicated that they had retention problems. More strikingly, the number had increased from 69 percent in just one year. Firms are becoming increasingly aware of these retention problems Attracting and retaining key staff were by far the most important priorities for a sample of top executives surveyed by Accenture in 2005. Issues related to human capital came ahead of research and development, financial systems, supply chain management, production improvement, or risk management (Accenture, 2005).

12.2.3 Differences across Organizations

The trends described above reveal a general increase in the reliance of firms on the external market to acquire the skills they need and a decrease in their internal development mechanisms. However, firms present variation in terms of their use of human capital practices. The few existing studies that look at the firm-level predictors of hiring and talent management practices find that this variation across firms is explained by the differences in the type of human capital required by companies.

Lepak and Snell (2002) propose that firms use four different strategies to manage their employees depending on the *strategic value* and *uniqueness* of their human capital. The strategic value of human capital signifies its potential to improve the efficiency and effectiveness of the firm, exploit market opportunities, and neutralize potential threats. The uniqueness of human capital represents the degree to which it is firm-specific; that is, not readily available in the labor market and not easily duplicated by other firms. The four different employment strategies ('employment modes') are shown in Figure 12.1.

When human capital is both unique and valuable (Quadrant 1 in Figure 12.1) it is most likely to be viewed as core to the firm, and it serves as the knowledge base around which firms build their strategies. Accordingly, employment practices will focus on the internal development of competencies and on the establishment of long-term relationships with the core employees. The ways in which organizations obtain human capital will also be distinctive from the other quadrants: since firms create jobs in which long-term learning is important and they empower employees to make independent decisions, selection criteria should focus on aptitude rather than achievement and include the ability to adapt to change, work independently, and show flexibility and learning agility. Another important selection criterion is fit with the values and culture of the organization, since firms want to develop long-term relationships with their employees.

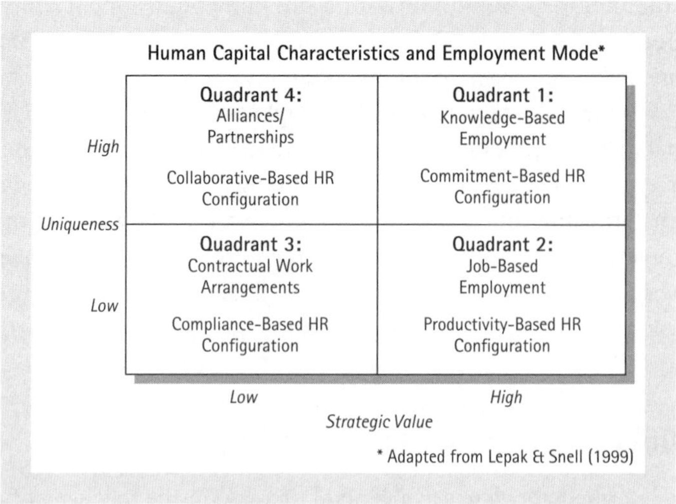

Human Capital Characteristics and Employment Mode*

High	**Quadrant 4:** Alliances/ Partnerships Collaborative-Based HR Configuration	**Quadrant 1:** Knowledge-Based Employment Commitment-Based HR Configuration
Uniqueness		
Low	**Quadrant 3:** Contractual Work Arrangements Compliance-Based HR Configuration	**Quadrant 2:** Job-Based Employment Productivity-Based HR Configuration
	Low	*High*

Strategic Value

* Adapted from Lepak & Snell (1999)

Figure 12.1. Human Capital Characteristics and Employment Modes (Lepak and Snell, 2002: 520)

Firms are more likely to acquire employees whose human capital has strategic value, but limited uniqueness (Quadrant 2) instead of developing them. The selection practices that constitute the most important piece of the employment strategy focus on job-specific skills and previous job performance. The human capital in Quadrant 3 is neither unique nor valuable to firms, and may be most effectively managed in short-term contractual arrangements. Finally, firms manage the human capital that is unique but of great strategic importance to their organization (Quadrant 4) in the form of alliances or partnerships in which both parties contribute to an outcome, share information, and maintain trust.

Using a survey of 148 firms, Lepak and Snell (2002) found that firms indeed employ strategies that best suit the type of capital in Quadrants 2, 3, and 4. With respect to Quadrant 1, the authors found, however, that firms do not follow this ideal type to manage their valuable and unique human capital. Rather, they use a mixture of employment practices that apply to all four quadrants, with the exception of subcontracting.

12.2.4 The Increasing Importance of Human Capital?

The socioeconomic changes of the 1980s substantially changed the ways in which firms acquire and manage their human capital. An important question that emerges is whether these changes have also increased the perceived importance of human capital in corporations. Fieldwork in more than twenty companies by Bartlett and Ghoshal (2002) shows that most firms pay only marginal attention to human capital issues. In the late 1980s the strategic imperatives which until then focused on creating defensible product-market positions by identifying which businesses to grow or divest, gave way to a strategic direction that emphasized the internal development of resources, competencies, and capabilities. But since the competency-based strategies are heavily dependent on human capital, many companies recognized that they have to build their strategy on a human capital foundation. Despite this shift in strategic direction, however, many firms today use tools that are more adequate for a strategy based on identifying defensible product-markets rather than for one based on human capital. Bartlett and Ghoshal argue that the adequate management mode would be one that focuses on the redistribution of wealth to employees, nurtures individual expertise and initiative, and leverages it through cross-unit knowledge-sharing. Many companies, however, still have human resource management systems that have a deeply embedded bias towards financial assets. Except for companies such as GE, Microsoft, or McKinsey, which devote enormous resources to recruitment and have a rigorous selection process that actively involves their middle management, most companies have not converted recruitment and selection into a strategic task. In order to fill a position opening, for example, which Bartlett and Ghoshal label a two-million-dollar decision, given the salary and the tenure of the newly hired employee with the organization, most employers resort to placing an advertisement and then choosing a finalist from three or four mediocre applicants.

12.3 HUMAN CAPITAL ACQUISITION: AN OVERVIEW OF CURRENT TRENDS

The following section presents an overview of the most commonly used recruitment sources, and highlights the major global trends in human capital acquisition over the past decade. Figure 12.2 shows the sources that US organizations with more than 5,000 employees used for obtaining talent in 2006 (CareerXroads, 2006). The highest percentage (over one-third of the positions) are filled from the pool of the current employees of the organization, via internal transfers and promotions. Although internal movement is still the main source of new hires, external hires now fill two-thirds of the open positions—a major change since the 1980s when very little non-entry-level hiring was done from the outside (CareerXroads, 2006).

Employee referrals represent the most important source of external hires. Referrals solicit workers for their recommendations regarding the people they know who may make good co-workers. The popularity of referrals is due to the fact that they are the most inexpensive source of applicants and generate the highest-quality

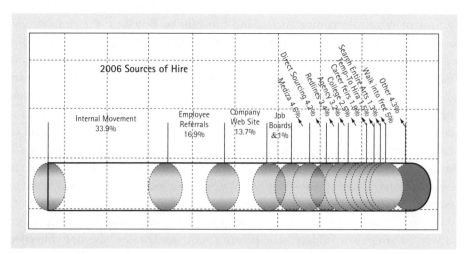

Figure 12.2. Percentage of New Hires from Various Recruitment Sources in Large US Organizations in 2006 (source: CareerXroads)

applicants. Of staffing professionals surveyed by a non-profit association of employ-ers, 88 percent said that referrals bring above average-quality candidates (Cober and Brown, 2006).

The second largest source for external hires in the United States is the Internet: 21 percent of the external hires came through the company website (the 'careers' seg-ment of corporate web pages) and 12 percent through job boards in 2006. The Internet as a recruitment source experienced a great evolution in the previous dec-ade. In a 1996 survey of HRM professionals (Terpstra, 1996), Internet-based recruit-ment tools were not even included in the list of nine recruitment sources from which the survey respondents could choose. The three highest-ranked resources in the survey were employee referrals, college recruiting, and executive search firms. As of 1996, even the most Internet-savvy job-seekers preferred company brochures over corporate web pages that in general 'lacked useful information' (King, 1996). The late 1990s saw the rapid rise of electronic recruitment in the US. Between 1997 and 1998, for example, the number of companies using the Internet for recruitment grew by 353 percent (Alter, 1998). In the first years, recruitment professionals remained frustrated by the Internet's lack of personal contact and the large quantity of unqualified candidates generated by this source. As of 1999, only 10 percent of external hires came through Internet resources—a figure that increased by 3.5 times by 2006 (Anonymous, 2000).

The use of the Internet as a recruitment method is not only a US phenomenon. However, the adoption in other countries took place at a much slower pace, and it has only recently started to represent a fundamental recruiting tool. For example, in the UK, until 2004, internal recruitment, agencies, and newspaper advertising rep-resented the main recruitment sources, while only a minority of employers used their own careers website and job boards (Anonymous, 2004). It was only in 2006 that local newspaper advertisements and corporate websites tied with respect to the percentage of employers using these sources (CIPD, 2007).

Printed advertisements make up 7 percent of external hires. Interestingly, they show a slightly growing trend since 2001—probably due to the fact that many of the large job boards such as Monster or CareerBuilder use a combined print and Internet pres-ence. The significance of printed advertisements, however, decreases as the income of job-seekers grows. They represent one of the worst recruiting options both in terms of cost effectiveness and the quality of hires generated (Cober and Brown, 2006). Between the 1950s and early 1990s, newspaper advertisements represented the major source of hires, besides internal recruitment, employee referrals, college campuses, and private employment agencies, and have experienced significant decline over the past fifty years (see for example, Carr and Dufty 1957; Kusel, 1988).

Finally, although only 3 percent of the applicants come from agencies, agencies including executive search firms represent the major source for positions of Vice-President level and above. A 2003 survey by the International Association of Professional Recruiters showed that 54 percent of the positions with an annual salary level over $150,000 were filled with the help of executive search firms (IACPR, 2003). The increasing rate of career moves across organizations will make the role of search firms even more important in the coming years.

From among the recruitment sources above, employee referral has been found to be the most effective recruitment source both in academic (Zottoli and Wanous, 2000) as well as in survey-based sources (Cober and Brown, 2006). The effectiveness of a recruitment source, however, depends on the type of employee group (blue-collar, white-collar, managerial) and the type of effectiveness criteria applied (rate of applicant turnover after entry to the organization, performance on the job, satisfaction of the hiring manager, cost effectiveness, and so on). In the case of professional hires, for example, employee referrals and networking were found to be the most effective recruitment sources, followed by corporate recruiters' cold-calling candidates on the phone and placing advertisements on job boards such as monster.com (GLR, 2004).

In light of the socioeconomic changes described we believe that two emerging trends are especially relevant to explain how companies recruit their human capital. One trend is the growing importance of search firms as a supplier of management talent. The second concerns the appearance and increasing adoption of Internet recruiting sources. In the sections that follow we introduce these two recruitment sources in detail. We focus on the ways in which they have altered the human capital acquisition processes of organizations, and present the main academic work carried out in these two areas.

12.4 EXECUTIVE SEARCH

12.4.1 The Executive Search Landscape: Retained and Contingency Search Firms

The birth of the executive search industry dates to the late 1940s. The economic boom that followed the Second World War created a serious talent shortfall in the United States. Employers responded to this shortfall by raiding their competitors for talent. One consequence of this interest in poaching talent by corporations was the rise of the modern executive search industry. The demand for executive search firms began to increase rapidly, starting from the late 1980s, when the pressure on corporations to improve financial performance and respond more quickly to changing markets led to more radical changes in business strategies. These changes, in turn, forced companies to look for managerial talent, with different skill sets and experiences, outside their organization. Besides the increase in hiring chief executive officers from the outside, executive search firms were increasingly charged with hiring for other positions in the executive ranks. Their activities expanded to lower levels, as each of the functional areas in organizations started to consider outside hires as the avenue for making abrupt organizational changes.

Search firms fall into two major types: contingency and retained search firms. Contingency search firms make up about 85 percent of all recruiters, handle about 90 percent of the search assignments (Finlay and Coverdill, 2002), and typically place candidates for middle and lower managerial positions. They are paid a fee by organizations only if they successfully place a candidate. For this reason they prefer to work on a large number of openings simultaneously, and want to produce as many applicants in front of the client organization as possible. After they learn the basic facts of a vacancy, they use their large database of candidates to look for potential matches and send information on the applicants to their client firms in the hopes that the candidate will be interviewed.

At the executive level, most of the recruitment is carried out by retained search firms. Unlike contingency search firms, retained search firms work under an exclusive contract with the client organization and are paid a fee (a retainer) even if they do not secure a placement. Since retained search firms do not have the incentive to fill a

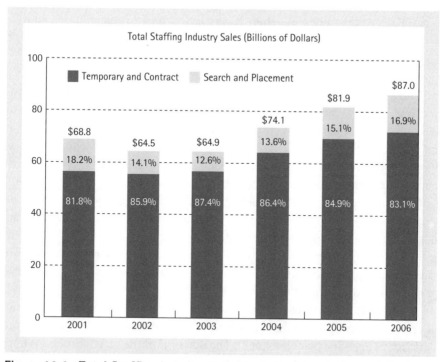

Figure 12.3. Total Staffing Industry Sales, Including Temporary and Contract, and Search and Placement (Berchem, 2007)

Source: American Staffing Association, Employment and Sales Survey, and Staffing Industry Analysts Inc.

vacancy just by any candidate who matches the job specification, they often serve as management consultants on the assignments. They help clients understand the type of person that the position requires, and identify the best match for a position. Retained executive search firms include large, multioffice multinational search firms which cover several functional areas and industries. Or they may be small, boutique search firms that specialize in a single job function or industry.

The total revenues of the executive search industry are very hard to estimate because of the large number of small, privately held companies. Hunt Scanlon consultants—an online data provider and industry consultant to the executive recruiting and human capital industries—estimates that the largest twenty-five US retained search firms had a combined revenue of $1.506 billion in 2006 (Hunt Scanlon, 2007). According to other estimates of the American Staffing Association, executive search firms represent a part of the staffing industry's Search and Placement segment that had revenues of $14.7 billion in 2006. Figure 12.3 shows the revenues of the staffing industry between 2001 and 2006.

12.4.2 Research on Executive Search Firms

Search firms play an increasingly important role as intermediaries in the executive labor market. At the same time, there is very little academic research that addresses their role, the ways in which they help organizations obtain human capital, and the ways in which they change the human capital pool of organizations.

Academic papers credit two major roles to search firms: expert and intermediary. Search firms take on an expert role because of their superior capabilities to understand and manage the increasing complexity involved in hiring (Ammons and Glass, 1988), their information advantages over clients (Britton and Ball, 1999) and their greater efficiency in the search process (Finlay and Coverdill, 2002). In an ethnographic study of contingency recruiters, Finlay and Coverdill (2002) show that compared to human resource management professionals, search firms are more adept at searching for and then cultivating networks with candidates, since they specialize in narrow segments of the labor market, keep a file of candidates for subsequent searches, and are not influenced by the organizational interests of the hiring organization. Khurana (2002) adds that search firms constitute an objective third party and signal to shareholders that the organization has devoted resources and is committed to hiring the new CEO.

In the important intermediary role that search firms play between organizations and applicants, search consultants function as 'impresarios' to the hiring process (Clark, 1995; Clark and Salaman, 1998). The outcome of the search process is highly dependent on the quality of the interaction between the client and the consultant. Successful search consultants concentrate on the management of the client and candidate relationship, provide backstage support to this interaction, and even manipulate this interaction in order to create a favorable impression of their service. Similarly, Khurana (2002) points out that consultants act as a buffer between the hiring organization and the candidates by emphasizing their shared interests, ensuring confidentiality, and resolving substantive issues such as compensation between the parties.

The issue that is probably most relevant to human resource management professionals and hiring organizations concerns the ways in which search firms affect the quality of the human capital pool of organizations. Interestingly, all the existing empirical evidence points to the ways in which search firms restrict the type of human capital that organizations may access. By relying on the services of search consultants at the managerial and executive levels, hiring organizations create a 'closed ecosystem of top-tier executives' (Khurana, 2002) who are similar to each other based on their personal and demographic attributes. These executives all come from employers with above-average financial performance and a reputation or status higher than that of the hiring organization. Status-related judgments are most commonly obtained from the rankings of corporations produced by *Fortune* magazine or *Business Week*. The executive's actual performance matters less for the hiring decision. The result is a pool of executives who resemble each other based on their previous work history.

Further, 'chemistry': an employer's sense of comfort and trust in an employee plays a major role in the selection of candidates for upper level positions. In external CEO searches, search consultants mention 'chemistry, articulation and stature' as some of the most desirable CEO characteristics, and prefer candidates whom they consider to possess these attributes. By relying on 'chemistry', however, organizations end up devaluing candidates based on their age, appearance, gender, and race, and create an employee population that is alike in personal attributes (Khurana, 2002).

The analysis of a search target dataset of one of the top five global retained executive search firms reported in Hamori (2004) confirms the conclusions above. The search firm consults the target database when it launches a search assignment and needs to identify the executives who should be contacted for a job opening. For each executive who is included in the database, the database lists the executive's current and previous employers, as well as the job function, industry segment, and tenure of the executive in a particular role. A look at the list of current employers reveals the differences between the profile of the 'desirable' and that of the 'average' executive. The executives' current employers that are included in the database are disproportionately large-sized (the 'average' organization is in the top 5 percent of its industry segment on the basis of sales). Over a third of the employers are included in the Fortune 500, *Fortune*'s most admired companies, and Forbes 500 lists. The data reveal that executives who are employed by publicly traded, large-sized, and highly reputable organizations have a greater chance of being contacted for a search opening.

Arguably, some of the most important issues in connection with search firms—those related to their impact on the human capital pool of organizations—have not been researched. Many questions need to be analyzed and answered in quantitative analyses of large-scale samples. Do search firms facilitate employer changes and therefore increase the rate of voluntary turnover? Do search firms increase the overall compensation level of executives in various industry segments because they facilitate employer changes that come with greater salary increases than moves inside employers? How do search firms impact the knowledge flows and knowledge transfer in industries? In particular, do they facilitate knowledge flows from the most reputable organizations to more resource-stricken organizations? Data that can answer these research questions are not publicly available and, due to their confidential nature, are hard to obtain from private organizations. Data access poses the most serious problem to further empirical research in this area.

12.5 ONLINE RECRUITING

12.5.1 The Role of Online Recruiting in Human Capital Acquisition

Online recruiting presents the latest development in the way in which organizations obtain human capital. The demand for online recruiting was induced by the use of the Internet and the increase in the personal career-related information that is available on the World Wide Web. Online recruiting brought three important innovations to the ways in which organizations obtain human capital. Each of the innovations is connected to the ability of online recruiting to offer vast amounts of information cheaply (Cappelli, 2001).

The first innovation concerns the employer side and refers to the possibility of identifying a large number of candidates at a much lower cost than traditional recruiting means. Of especial relevance is the fact that online searching facilitated finding high-quality 'passive' candidates who were employed by an organization and were not necessarily looking to move, and identifying them cheaply.

Companies have creatively used the Internet to identify passive candidates. According to a 2007 survey by the Society of Human Resource Management (2007), the most popular online sources to identify passive candidates included viewing membership directories for associations and trade groups, scanning social networking sites, mining blogs and discussion groups, and techniques known as 'flipping' (using a search engine to find candidates who link themselves to web pages), 'peeling back' (peeling back an organization's website to reveal employee contact information), and 'X-raying' (using a search command to locate employee information on non-public web pages). A considerable portion—22 percent of the responding organizations—used 'flipping', and 14 percent of the organizations resorted to 'peeling' competitors' web pages (SHRM, 2007).

Since social networking sites and online communities (such as linkedin or xing. com) are a recent phenomenon and are predicted to grow in importance, they merit more detailed discussion. These sites leverage their membership and offer recruiting services to companies. Xing.com, for example, matches job openings posted in the network with the profile of its members. Sites such as Blue Chip Expert further increase their offering to corporations by maintaining an exclusive membership. Individuals can only join Bluechipexpert.com if they are referred by a member. In fact, it is impossible to enter the site without an 'invitation code'. As a result, the site prides itself on the high quality of its members, the majority of whom have graduate degrees and positions at the director level and above. Another form of online community is represented by sites such as the German e-fellows. net, which preselects high-quality students between the ages of 18 and 30, based on their academic excellence, professional experience such as internships, international experience, and extracurricular interests, and then targets its members with the job openings and recruiting events of its partner organizations. By becoming a partner organization of e-fellows.net, hiring companies benefit by building up future contact with high-quality professionals who are just about to start their professional career.

Access to a vast pool of candidates makes it easier to find the right type of human capital. The negative side of this, however, is that companies may experience difficulties in retaining their employees, as other competitors are also likely to poach employees. Even if employees do not consider leaving, receiving information on job opportunities may reduce the commitment that they have to their current job, since having more job choices reduces commitment.

The second innovation is related to the employee side and concerns the substantial increase of detailed information available to individuals about potential employers and job opportunities. For example, organizations such as Vault or Wetfeet offer information about the upsides and downsides of working for a certain employer, salary levels, or even the type of questions that are asked in job interviews. Other sites such as 'salarysource' offer customized data on compensation by type of occupation and job location. A related development is that online recruiting made recruiting more like marketing. Companies explicitly attempt to tie positive company images into hiring and build a human resources brand by linking their recruiting advertisements to their product advertisements (similar colors and style) so that applicants immediately recognize the company (Cappelli, 2001).

Recruitment blogs represent the latest entry in this area. Blogs are a good tool for employment branding and outreach, because they are interactive and provide job seekers with a good impression of the company's work environment. Blogs are most commonly written by corporate recruiters, and offer recruiters' personal thoughts and opinions about the corporation and its recruiting process (Hasson, 2007).

The increased access to information about outside offers breaks the monopoly of information at employers' hands, and has increased the bargaining power of employees, resulting in higher salaries. The shift in power from firms to employees means that companies may now have to pay more to retain or attract human capital. Furthermore, companies are likely to suffer retention problems. In effect, since employees can now find jobs faster and track a wider array of openings that improves matches between their skills and interests and the requirements of the corporation, they are faster to change corporations. One implication is that employers need to be more active in eliminating the issues that may induce employees to consider leaving, because once employees start to search for jobs, corporations will not have time to respond.

The third innovation concerns the emergence of web screening mechanisms that allow for cheaper and more effective matching processes between employers and employees. Because online recruitment generates many applicants, sorting among them is challenging. Traditional methods of sorting, such as human resource professionals reviewing résumés, are prohibitively expensive, given that the number of applications generated is often much larger than via printed advertisements. Companies have reacted to this problem by introducing creative methods to screen individuals online. The most common solutions include companies asking simple screening questions of applicants, or applicant tracking systems that allow the effective searching, filtering, and routing of applications through automated processes. Other companies go even further by using psychometric instruments that evaluate the suitability of individuals for relevant jobs, or use computer games that reveal information about the interests and abilities of job candidates. Still other websites change the way in which information is organized, and instead of asking for résumés they require job-seekers to complete applications that organize the information in a way that suits the particular employer (Cappelli, 2001). Due to these new screening mechanisms, companies may be able to find the human capital they need and end up with even better matches, even though the larger pool may include more potential misfits with the company.

12.5.2 The Academic Research on Online Recruiting

Although there has been a remarkable growth in the use of the Internet for recruiting purposes, academic research on the topic of online recruiting is still scarce. In particular, much more research is needed to fully understand the effects of this new form of recruiting on the ways companies acquire and develop their human capital. As discussed before, different forces may be taking place with respect to how online recruiting affects the type of human capital acquired, and the effects could actually go in different directions. Some empirical literature has started to develop to address these types of question.

Several papers have analyzed whether individuals who use online recruiting sources are different from those who search through more traditional sources. The literature has found mixed evidence with respect to differences in demographic characteristics. Specifically, when looking at the effects of age and race, some papers have found that older and minority individuals are less likely to use online search, while other papers have failed to find so (for a review see Hogler et al., 1998; Anderson, 2003). Looking at the Current Population Survey data, Stevenson (2006) finds that it is in the access to Internet sources that these demographic characteristics make a difference. When the sample is restricted only to the group that has access to the Internet, there are no important demographic differences in the use of online recruiting. An implication of this finding is that companies that use only online recruiting to attract candidates may run into difficulties in satisfying legal and diversity issues. Other individual characteristics that have been related to the effort spent on online recruiting are individual preferences such as wide geographical location and Internet fluency (Bauer et al., 2006).

A related finding is that companies may attract different types of human capital depending on the type of online recruiting source which they use. A study of large banks in the US found that banks using websites attracted a pool of candidates different from those using job lists (Pearce and Tuten, 2001). Specifically, the pool of applicants from organizational websites were experienced applicants, and applicants with little or no experience but with relevant skills. College students made up the applicant pool at most web-based job sites. The authors also found that the quality fit of applicants varied with respect to the method used. Companies wanting to recruit a particular type of human capital should beware of the effects of the different recruitment sources.

Another important finding of the literature is that individuals find more jobs when using online recruiting than when using traditional sources, which is consistent with a cheaper access to information (Van Rooy et al., 2003). The generation of a large pool of applicants, however, may also generate a large number of applicants who are not a good fit for organizations. Some researchers have proposed that companies can actually ameliorate this problem by using specific features in their web designs to generate different levels of attraction among individuals (Cober et al., 2004a, 2004b). For example, the provision of customized feedback about the fit with the company has been shown to increase attraction to the organization (Dineen et al., 2002, 2007).

A related issue is that not all recruitment sources have the same effectiveness in generating attraction towards the organization. Studies have found that different individual as well as website characteristics are important determinants of organizational attraction and positive intentions toward the organization. Examples of individual characteristics are personal information privacy concerns, which are negatively related, and familiarity with computers, which is positively related (Feldman and Klaas, 2002). Examples of website characteristics include features such as aesthetics and customized information, which are positively related (Dineen et al., 2007), the orientation of the website, whether recruiting, screening, or dual purpose, with recruiting positively related (Williamson *et al.*, 2003), and the amount of job and organizational information provided on the web, which is positively related although this information does not substitute for pre-existent information (Allen *et al.*, 2007).

The question of whether using online recruiting generates better or worse matches is largely underexplored, however. Some indirect evidence supporting that it improves matches is provided by Stevenson (2003, 2006). She found an increase in employment to employment flows resulting from higher state-level Internet penetration—particularly for those with college degrees indicating a better match. Workers who are online are more likely to change jobs than those who are not online and, similarly, workers online are more likely to change jobs within the same firm.

In summary, although online recruiting may have important implications in the ways in which companies attract and develop their human capital, the literature analyzing these effects is scarce. Some evidence has been found supporting the fact that companies may attract different pools of human capital, that it increases information available to employees (shift of information), and that it may lead to better matches. However, much work is needed to know some of the important consequences. Does this better match result in higher salaries? Does this higher amount of information result in higher salaries or faster increase of salaries within the organization? Do these lower costs result in worse matches? Are individuals hired through online recruitment sources more likely to leave the organization? These are all extremely important questions that need to be addressed by future research.

12.6 Conclusions

A generation ago, large employers secured talent almost exclusively through entry-level jobs, typically hiring school-leavers. All other vacancies in the organization were filled from within through often elaborate internal promotion processes. Since the 1980s the process has changed quite radically, with even the largest and oldest employers drawing much more of their talent from the outside labor market. The reasons for this shift have mainly to do with the uncertainty of business demands, which are driven by much more competitive and changeable markets. With demand being much less certain, employers find it much more difficult to develop candidates internally, because doing so requires predictability: ensuring that investments will pay off requires knowing for sure that they will be needed. As employers moved to lateral hiring of experienced workers, it created retention problems for the other employers whose workers were leaving. Retention challenges further eroded the internal model.

What we see now is a very different landscape in which the acquisition of talent has become the most important activity and internal development is more of a sideline. New arrangements and institutions have developed to facilitate outside hiring—the most important of which are brokers and agents of various kinds, from search firms to online recruiting to temp and employee leasing agencies.

The important questions for research have a way of following the important questions for practice. Given that trend, we should expect that the research agenda for people interested in the topics in this volume will begin to shift as well, paying much greater attention to markets and the role which they play in shaping employment arrangements, as well as determining who obtains which jobs.

More specifically, an agenda for future research should focus on the shift toward more market-driven employment relationships. The arguments above make a case for understanding the new institutions and arrangements that form the intermediaries between individuals and employers. Beyond that, many of the most important questions in the broad study of work and employment remain, but the explanations for them are different now.

- Employee selection has long been the mainstay of personnel psychologists but has largely been ignored by other fields. Understanding the factors that predict successful hires is now enormously more important because employers do so much more hiring and at all levels of jobs.
- Understanding career decisions has already become a more important topic as the challenge of managing careers becomes much more difficult and has shifted from being the responsibility of the employer to that of the employee. Similarly, the factors that shape careers shift from focusing on the attributes of the employer/organization to those associated with markets.
- Traditional topics such as employee attitudes and turnover decisions also need a new focus as the factors that drive them shift from being largely internal to the firm to forces in the market-place and beyond.

The developments in the workplace outlined above create new challenges that call into question the received paradigm of employee behavior as a largely within-the-organization phenomenon. But such developments also create considerable opportunities for researchers to carry out important new work and build their own careers in the process.

REFERENCES

Accenture (2005) 'Executive Issues'. URL: http://www.accenture.com/NR/rdonlyres/8356E61F-92E0-4C90-8E4F-2A222E32204F/0/ideas_inno_exec_issues.pdf (accessed Sept. 2007).
ALLEN, D. G., MAHTO, R. V., and OTONDO, R. F. (2007). 'Web-Based Recruitment: Effects of Information, Organizational Brand, and Attitudes toward a Web Site on Applicant Attraction', *Journal of Applied Psychology*, 92(6): 1696–1708.
ALTER, A. E. (1998). 'Online Recruiting Soars, But Effectiveness Unclear', *Computerworld*, 32(18): 81.

AMMONS, D. N., and GLASS, J. J. (1988). 'Headhunters in Local Government: Use of Executive Search Firms in Managerial Selection', *Public Administration Review*, 48(3): 687–93.

ANDERSON, N. (2003). 'Applicant and Recruiter Reactions to New Technology in Selection: A Critical Review and Agenda for Future Research', *International Journal of Selection and Assessment*, 11(2–3): 121–36.

Anonymous (2000). 'More Pros and Cons to Internet Recruiting', *HR Focus*, 77(5): 8.

——(2004). 'Recruitment in the UK: Electronic Over Traditional Methods?', *Personnel Today* (7 Sept.): 4.

AUER, P., BERG, J., and COULIBALY, I. (2005). 'Is a Stable Workforce Good for Productivity?', *International Labour Review*, 144(3): 319–43.

BARTLETT, C. A., and GHOSHAL, S. (2002). 'Building Competitive Advantage through People', *MIT Sloan Management Review* (Winter): 34–41.

BAUER, T. N., TRUXILLO, D. M., TUCKER, J. S., WEATHERS, V., BERTOLINO, M., ERDOGAN, B., and CAMPION, M. A. (2006). 'Selection in the Information Age: The Impact of Privacy Concerns and Computer Experience on Applicant Reactions', *Journal of Management*, 32(5): 601–21.

BRITTON L. C., and BALL, D. F. (1999). 'Trust versus Opportunism: Striking the Balance in Executive Search', *Service Industries Journal*, 19(2): 132–49.

CAPPELLI, P. (1999). *The New Deal at Work* (Boston: Harvard Business School Press).

——(2001). 'Making the Most of Online Recruiting', *Harvard Business Review*, 79(3): 139–46.

—— (2008). *Talent on Demand: Managing Talent in an Age of Uncertainty* (Boston: Harvard Business School Press).

——and HAMORI, M. (2006). *Executive Loyalty and Job Search* (Philadelphia: Wharton School Working Paper, Center for Human Resources).

—— BASSI, L., KATZ, H., KNOKE, D., OSTERMAN, P., and USEEM, M. (1997). *Change at Work* (New York and Oxford: Oxford University Press).

CareerXroads (2007). '6th Annual Sources of Hire Survey'. URL: http://www.careerxroads. com/news/SourcesOfHire06.pdf (accessed Oct. 2007).

CARR, C. E., and DUFTY, N. F. (1957). 'Recruitment in an Australian Labor Market', *Industrial and Labor Relations Review*, 10(4): 579–87.

Chartered Institute of Personnel and Development (2007). 'Recruitment, Retention and Turnover: Annual Survey Report'. URL: http://www.cipd.co.uk/subjects/recruitmen/general/_recruitretnt.htm (accessed Sept. 2007).

CLARK, T. (1995). *Managing Consultants: Consultancy as the Management of Impressions* (Buckingham: Open University Press).

—— and SALAMAN, G. (1998). 'Creating the "Right" Impression: Towards a Dramaturgy of Management Consultancy', *Service Industries Journal*, 18(1): 18–38.

COBER, R., and BROWN, D. (2006). '2006 DirectEmployers Association Recruiting Trends Survey'. URL: http://www.jobcentral.com/DEsurvey.pdf (accessed Sept. 2007).

————KEEPING, L. M., and LEVY, P. E. (2004a). 'Recruitment on the Net: How do Organizational Web Site Characteristics Influence Applicant Attraction?', *Journal of Management*, 30(5): 623–46.

————and LEVY, P. E. (2004b). 'Form, Content and Function: An Evaluative Methodology for Corporate Employment Web Sites', *Human Resource Management*, 43(2–3): 201–18.

DINEEN, B. R., ASH, S. R., and NOE, R. A. (2002). 'A Web of Applicant Attraction: Person–Organization Fit in the Context of Web-Based Recruitment', *Journal of Applied Psychology*, 87(4): 723–34.

——NOE, R. A., and WANG, C. (2004) 'Perceived Fairness of Web-Based Applicant Screening Procedures: Weighing the Rules of Justice and the Role of Individual Differences', *Human Resource Management*, 43(2–3): 127–45.

——LING, J., ASH, S. R., and DEL VECCHIO, D. (2007). 'Aesthetic Properties and Message Customization: Navigating the Dark Side of Web Recruitment', *Journal of Applied Psychology*, 92(2): 356–72.

DOERINGER, P., and PIORE, M. (1971). *Internal Labor Markets and Manpower Analysis* (Lexington, Mass.: Heath Lexington Books).

DOLADO, J. J., GARCIA-SERRANO, C., and JIMENO J. F. (2002). 'Drawing Lessons from the Boom of Temporary Jobs in Spain', *Economic Journal*, 112: 270–95.

FALLICK, B. C., and FLEISHMAN, C. A. (2002). *Employer-to-Employer Flows in the US Labor Market.* (Washington, DC: Federal Reserve Board Working Paper.)

FELDMAN, D. C., and KLAAS, B. S. (2002). 'Internet Job Hunting: A Field Study of Applicant Experiences with On-Line Recruiting', *Human Resource Management*, 41(2): 175–92.

FINLAY, W., and COVERDILL, J. E. (2002). *Headhunters: Matchmaking in the Labor Market* (Ithaca, NY: ILR Press, Cornell University).

GLR Recruitment Trends Survey (2004). URL: http://www.glresources.com (accessed Aug. 2007).

HAMORI, M. (2004). 'Executive Search and Selection with Mediation: The Role of Search Firms in Executive Succession', dissertation, University of Pennsylvania, Philadelphia.

HASSON, J. (2007). 'Blogging for Talent', *HR Magazine*, 52(10). URL: http://www.shrm.org/hrmagazine/articles/1007/1007sr-hasson.asp (accessed Nov. 2007).

HOGLER, R. L., HENLE, C., and BEMUS, C. (1998). 'Internet Recruiting and Employment Discrimination: A Legal Perspective', *Human Resource Management Review*, 8(2): 149–65.

HUNT SCANLON (2007). 'US Recruiting Business up 10 percent from 2006'. URL: http://www.huntscanlon.com/pdf/ESR_March07_rankings.pdf (accessed Sept. 2007).

International Association of Corporate and Professional Recruiters (2003) 'IACPR 2003 Survey'. URL: http://www.iacpr.org (accessed May 2004).

KERR, A. (1954). 'The Balkanization of Labor Markets', in E. Wight Bakke, L. Palmer, Charles A. Myers, Dale Yoder, and Clark Kerr (eds.), *Labor Mobility and Economic Opportunity* (Cambridge, Mass.: MIT Press), 92–111.

KHURANA, R. (2002). *Searching for a Corporate Savior: The Irrational Quest for Charismatic CEOs* (Princeton: Princeton University Press).

KING, J. (1996). 'Corporate Web Sites Given an Incomplete', *Computerworld*, 30(47): 24.

KUSEL, J. (1988). 'Trends in the Job Market', *Internal Auditor*, 45(2): 27.

LEDFORD, G., and LUCY, M. (2003). 'The Rewards of Work: The Employment Deal in a Changing Economy'. URL: http://www.sibson.com/publications/ROW.pdf (accessed Oct. 2007).

LEPAK, D. P., and SNELL, S. A. (2002). 'Examining the Human Resource Architecture: The Relationships among Human Capital, Employment, and Human Resource Configurations', *Journal of Management*, 28(4): 517–43.

LUCIER, C., KOCOUREK, P., and HABBEL, R. (2006). 'CEO Succession 2005: The Crest of the Wave', *Strategy+business* (Summer). URL: http://www.strategy-business.com/press/article/06210 (accessed Nov. 2007).

MURPHY, K. J., and ZÁBOJNIK, J. (2004). *Managerial Capital and the Market for CEOs* (Los Angeles, Calif.: Marshall School of Business, University of Southern California).

PEARCE, C. G., and TUTEN, T. L. (2001). 'Internet Recruiting in the Banking Industry', *Business Communication Quarterly*, 64(1): 9–18.

ROMANS, F., and HARDARSON, O. (2007). 'Labour Market Latest Trends', 1st quarter 2007 data, Eurostat. URL: http://epp.eurostat.ec.europa.eu/cache/ITY_OFFPUB/KS-QA-07-016/EN/KS-QA-07-016-EN.PDF (accessed Sept. 2007).

SLICHTER, S., HEALY, J., and LIVERNASH R. (1960). *The Impact of Collective Bargaining on Management* (Washington, DC: Brookings Institution).

Society of Human Resource Management (2006a) '2006 Succession Planning'. URL: http://www.shrm.org/hrresources/surveys_published/2006%20Succession%20Planning%20Survey%20Report.pdf (accessed Oct. 2007).

——(2006b). 'US Job Retention'. URL: http://www.shrm.org/hrresources/surveys_published/2006%20U.S.%20Job%20Retention%20Poll%20Findings.pdf (accessed Oct. 2007).

——(2007). 'Advances in e-Recruiting: Leveraging the Jobs Domain'. URL: http://www.shrm.org/hrresources/surveys_published/2007%20Advances%20in%20E-Recruiting%20Leveraging%20the%20.Jobs%20Domain%20Survey%20Report.pdf (accessed Oct. 2007).

Staffing Industry Analysts (2004). 'Staffing Industry Report'. URL: http://www.staffingindustry.com/issues/sireport (accessed May 2004).

STEVENSON, B. (2003). *The Internet, Job Search and Worker Mobility* (National Bureau of Economic Research Working Paper 13886; URL: www.nber.org/papers/w13886.pdf).

——(2006). *The Impact of the Internet on Worker Flows* (Working Paper, Wharton School of the University of Pennsylvania; URL (accessed May 2010): www.kellogg.northwestern.edu/mgmtstrategy/deptinfo/seminars/stevenson041107.pdf).

TERPSTRA, D. E. (1996). 'The Search for Effective Methods', *HR Focus*, 73(5): 16–17.

VAN ROOY, D. L., ALONSO, A., and FAIRCHILD, Z. (2003). 'In with the New, Out with the Old: Has the Technological Revolution Eliminated the Traditional Job Search Process?', *International Journal of Selection and Assessment*, 11(2–3): 170–4.

WILLIAMSON, I. O., LEPAK, D. P., and KING, J. (2003). 'The Effect of Company Recruitment Web Site Orientation on Individuals' Perceptions of Organizational Attractiveness', *Journal of Vocational Behavior*, 63: 242–63.

ZOTTOLI, A. A., and WANOUS, J. P. (2000). 'Recruitment Source Research: Current Status and Future Directions', *Human Resource Management Review*, 10(4): 353–82.

CHAPTER 13

···

ALIGNING HUMAN CAPITAL WITH ORGANIZATIONAL NEEDS

···

DAVID P. LEPAK

RIKI TAKEUCHI

JUANI SWART

13.1 INTRODUCTION

···

This chapter focuses on the alignment between human capital and organizational needs. Human capital, which is generally defined as the knowledge, skills, and experience of employees (Bontis, 1998; Davenport, 1999; Pennings *et al.*, 1998; Walker, 2002; Zucker *et al.*, 1998), is viewed as a key resource for all organizations. According to Pennings *et al.* (1998: 426), 'professionals endowed with a high level of human capital are more likely to deliver consistent and high-quality services'. Similarly, Snell and Dean (1992) suggested that human capital adds value to firms because of the potential for enhanced productivity that is realized through higher knowledge and skills among employees. We therefore define human capital as the value-generating potential of employee knowledge, skills, and abilities (Kang *et al.*, 2007).

Hitt *et al.* (2001) examined the relationship between human capital and return on sales, and found a positive curvilinear association between the two. In a study of the

Egyptian software industry, Seleim *et al.* (2007) found a significant and positive relationship between the number of superstar developers in firms (an average of four times the performance of their colleagues) and firm performance, as well as the number of star developers (an average of twice the performance of their colleagues) and firm performance. These results provide support for the idea that the quality and volume of human capital within a firm is important for performance. In other words, the higher the level of knowledge, skills, and abilities of employees, the more potential impact human capital has on performance.

While these studies clearly demonstrate that a firm's human capital can have important and meaningful implications for performance, it is important to recognize that there is considerable variability in the type and level of human capital among a firm's entire workforce. Based on this logic, several researchers have suggested that it might be more appropriate to adopt a differentiated view of a firm's human capital to better understand who drives value and how best to manage their workforce.

Arguments for differentiating how different groups of human capital are managed is grounded in the logic that not all employees make equivalent strategic contributions to competitive success. As a result, the nature of the employment arrangement and associated HR system designs should differentiate core versus non-core employees (Delery and Shaw, 2001) or between A players, B players, and C players (Huselid *et al.*, 2005). Boxall (1998: 268) suggested that firms differentiate their core employees who are 'responsible for valuable innovations or for successful imitations' from an outer group of more peripheral employees who are instrumental in maintaining process efficiencies and capacity.

Lepak and Snell (1999) suggested that by considering two dimensions—strategic value and uniqueness—we can conceptualize a matrix of four distinct groups of human capital, each of which is associated with a different form of employment as well as a different human resource (HR) system. According to their arguments, *strategic value* reflects the extent to which the human capital of employees helps firms improve efficiency and/or effectiveness, exploit market opportunities, and/or neutralize potential threats. *Uniqueness* refers to the extent to which knowledge and skills are specialized (not widely held, developed expertise) or firm-specific (for example, Williamson, 1975) as opposed to generic human capital that is widely available and/or transferable to other companies (Becker, 1962).

On the one hand, with high strategic value and uniqueness, core knowledge workers are most likely to contribute directly to a firm's core competencies on the basis of what they know and how they use their knowledge (Purcell *et al.*, 2009; Snell *et al.*, 1999). Thus, firms are encouraged to invest in these employees via the use of commitment-based HR systems (for example, Lepak and Snell, 2002) that focus on the development of employee competencies, employee empowerment, and encouraging employee participation in decision-making and discretion on the job. On the other hand, 'internal partners' (traditional, job-based employees: Lepak and Snell, 1999; Kang *et al.*, 2007) are also necessary (or compulsory) for the firm because

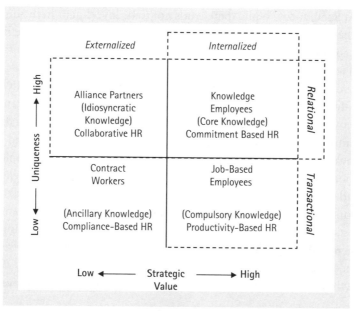

Figure 13.1. HR Architectural Perspective (adapted from Lepak and Snell, 1999, 2002; Snell *et al.*, 1999)

they are important for value creation, although this form of human capital is not unique and is readily available in the market. To manage this group of human capital, organizations adopt a more traditional job-based orientation focused on immediate performance (Lepak and Snell, 2002). Managers are likely to rely more on a productivity-based HR configuration that focuses on standardized jobs, and on selecting people from the external labor market who can contribute immediately (see Tsui *et al.*, 1995).

While the previous two employment modes are internalized within firms, as the strategic value of human capital diminishes, there is no strong incentive to internalize employment. Lepak and Snell (2002) found that firms are most likely to use contract workers for tasks that are limited in strategic value and uniqueness. Managing these contract workers tends to involve a transactional logic with a focus on short-term productivity and compliance with present rules, regulations, and procedures. Finally, some individuals make contributions that are unique but of limited strategic value. As their role is not central to value creation, companies may search externally for these workers. However, given the uniqueness of their contributions, these individuals have human capital that is not easy to find in the market, or they must possess skills that are firm-specific in their application. The cultivation of this firm specificity often takes time to develop. To manage these external 'alliance partners' firms may create long-term partnerships to preserve continuity over time, ensure trust among partners, and engender reciprocity and collaboration

(Lepak and Snell, 2002). While there tends not to be investment in the human capital itself, there is substantial investment in the relationship with these individuals through a collaborative HR configuration characterized by group incentives, cross-functional teams, and the like.

Lepak and Snell (2002) demonstrated that companies use different HR systems to manage different employee groups, depending on their strategic value and uniqueness. Moreover, each group of human capital tended to be managed via distinct HR systems. Similarly, in a study of 375 companies in Spain, Gonzalez and Tacorante (2004) showed that more than 70 percent of the companies in their sample relied on all four modes of employment, 27 percent used three of the four employment modes, and 2 percent used only two employment modes. Like Lepak and Snell (2002), Gonzalez and Tacorante (2004) also found consistent differences in the human resource management (HRM) practices used for each employee group. Looking across these studies, the evidence suggests that firms do utilize contract work to meet fairly generic needs or access a widely available skill set, while at the same time they take steps to ensure they identify and retain core employees.

13.2 LINKING HUMAN CAPITAL WITH PERFORMANCE

The implicit logic of the HR architecture and other models of a differentiated workforce is based on the importance of aligning human capital with company strategic goals. Strategic value, by definition, implies alignment with company goals. Employees are only rated as strategically valuable if they are instrumental in helping companies to capitalize on opportunities or to minimize threats in the environment (Lepak and Snell, 1999). In this regard, the notion of alignment between human capital and strategy is embedded within the architectural perspective. At the same time, however, an architectural perspective suffers from several limitations.

First, it focuses on factors that influence the development of a firm's HR architecture without explicit discussion of the performance implications of a differentiated approach to employing and managing people. If we recognize that firms rely on various employment arrangements with their employees (Osterman, 1987; Rousseau 1995; Tsui et al., 1995), a fundamental issue is whether they should be managed the same or differentially. Ultimately, the criteria we should use for this test depends on various performance indicators that are of interest. Second, the original HR architectural model is static in nature and does not explicitly consider how organizations maintain fit in the face of changes over time or in various contexts. In the remainder of this chapter we focus explicitly on these two issues.

13.2.1 Performance Implications

The logic of adopting a differentiating approach to human capital in general, and the HR architecture in particular, is based on the implicit notion that proper alignment of human capital with the appropriate employment modes and company needs will be positively associated with performance. Yet while this implicit assumption is completely plausible, researchers have not fully investigated the performance benefits associated with these approaches. In particular, there are two issues worthy of future investigation that are needed to better understand how the adoption of a differentiated approach to human capital impacts relevant outcomes.

First, we need to separate the basic decision to employ people differently (internal, contract, partner) from how people are managed in these different employment modes. Both issues are likely to have implications for performance. For example, Delery and Shaw (2001) suggest that high-performance HR systems may be most important for a firm's strategic core workforce. Baron *et al.* (1986), Osterman (1987), and Pinfield and Berner (1994) noted that different internal labor markets exist within firms. Osterman (1987) suggested that technological change, reduced supply of an appropriate labor force, and sharply rising wages contribute to the creation of different employment subsystems within firms. It is also essential to establish a fit between these two separate decisions; that is, between the contractual arrangements and the subsequent HR systems that are used to employ the particular set of human capital. While researchers acknowledge that variability exists in how human capital is employed as well as the use of HR systems within firms for different groups of human capital, we do not know whether these actions are beneficial or harmful for organizations.

Second, we need to acknowledge that a differentiated approach to employment and managing employees may be positively related to some performance outcomes and negatively related to others. For example, differentiation may enable firms to realize labor cost efficiencies while potentially compromising other potential dimen-

Table 13.1. Future Research Topics on Performance/Outcomes for the HR Architecture

	Organization Level	Individual Level
Employment mode use	Cost savings Flexibility	Job security / career prospects Target of commitment
How people are managed	Skill flexibility	Balanced /unbalanced investments
	Targeted HR systems	Perceived organizational support Equity and fairness

sions of performance. An additional vantage point is that we need to consider the impact of these decisions on both individual level microperformance outcomes and how these translate into organizational level macroperformance outcomes.

If we consider these two issues simultaneously we can see at least four key areas of research related to level of analysis and issue of focus. As shown in Table 13.1, the first key area is research on the organizational implications related to employment mode use. The second area relates to organizational level implications regarding how people in those employment modes are managed. Third, research is needed that examines individual outcomes related to employment mode use. Finally, research is needed that explores the individual level outcomes related to how people are managed.

13.2.2 Organizational Performance and Employment Mode Use

At the organizational level of analysis there is a variety of potential benefits from an increased reliance on external labor in place of, or in combination with, internal workers. There are two primary types of benefit that may potentially be associated with the use of different employment modes for human capital: cost reduction or containment, and increased flexibility (Lepak and Snell, 2007; Matusik and Hill, 1998).

Cost Savings

From a cost perspective, the use of external employment for human capital is argued to allow firms to realize cost savings from several avenues. First, companies only pay for human capital when it is used. Rather than employ an accountant full-time, for example, companies may contract for accounting services from a variety of professional service organizations. Even if the average hourly rate for these services is higher, labor costs savings materialize by only paying for the services when used, rather than for an entire year.

There may also be cost savings associated with specialization by external labor suppliers. Because these parties focus on a particular skill set or contribution, they are able to deploy their talents across a variety of organizations, effectively creating economies of scale for their services. In contrast, within a single organization, maintaining a particular group of human capital may be prohibitively expensive to employ full-time, in comparison with market rates. If a consulting company provides services for twenty companies, their overhead costs are likely to be much lower per employee than a company that only has a handful of employees performing similar tasks.

Finally, relying on external labor may also allow firms to realize a decrease in the administrative or bureaucratic overhead associated with managing full-time employees (Pfeffer and Baron, 1988). Advocates of outsourcing have long argued that a key saving for organizations relates to personnel expenses such as benefits and training. Moreover, when a third party is involved in providing external services, they may take on the responsibilities of identifying and hiring qualified individuals, managing the performance evaluation process for those individuals, and providing those individuals with their total compensation packages. Client organizations simply pay the relevant fee for these services.

Despite these espoused benefits, research is needed that investigates whether or not these savings materialize. For one, there may be labor cost savings as well as bureaucratic cost savings, but at the same time, additional costs may be incurred related to coordinating among providers and coordinating work with a revolving workforce. Moreover, to say that training is not necessary is not likely to be completely accurate. Even when external labor is employed, if they are integrated into a firm's workforce, there are aspects of training and performance management that must be carried out. External workers probably have to be trained in the rules, regulations, and procedures for how work is carried out. And if external labor is sought to increase access to specialized skills, efforts must be taken to transfer that knowledge to employees within the firm (Kang *et al.*, 2007). Though speculative, these issues suggest that there may be trade-offs between strict labor cost savings and personnel expenses associated with coordination and knowledge-sharing. Research is needed that directly addresses how the use of different employment arrangements for human capital impacts these different cost metrics.

Flexibility Increase

Beyond potential costs savings, an additional reason for engaging in differentiation of employment is the potential to achieve increased flexibility. More to the point, there are several forms of flexibility associated with the use of externalization and internalization of employment. *Numeric* flexibility refers to the ability to adjust how many individuals are used to perform tasks and activities. The primary method for achieving this type of flexibility is through the use of external labor as a means to influence the number and type of human capital. Similarly, Lepak and Snell (2007) suggested firms may benefit from *knowledge access flexibility*—the ability to gain access to important knowledge resources without the commitment of long-term employment. Closely related is what Nesheim *et al.* (2007: 251) refer to as *qualitative flexibility* or 'the ability to assess, create, and implement new knowledge and to change tasks and activities according to changes in the market, the strategy of the firm, and relevant technology'.

Beyond how and where to deploy employees, an additional form of flexibility is *functional flexibility*. At the individual level this form of flexibility refers to the ability of individuals to perform a variety of tasks, which we label 'skill flexibility'. At the organizational level, functional flexibility refers to the ability of organizations to deploy individuals to perform a variety of tasks and activities. At this level the coordination and integration of the various knowledge sets across a variety of tasks become important; hence we refer to this as coordination flexibility. Conceptually, functional flexibility may be a function more of how employees are managed than of the use of different employment modes, and we therefore discuss this flexibility benefit in the next section.

Existing research provides some support for these flexibility perspectives. For example, Lepak *et al.* (2003) found that a more extensive reliance on core knowledge employees and/or short-term contract workers was positively associated with ROA and market-to-book value, while an increased reliance on non-core job-based employees and external alliance partners was associated with diminished firm performance. Moreover, the combined use of knowledge work and contract employees displayed the highest levels of performance. These results suggest that the benefits of both functional and numerical flexibility were enhanced when knowledge workers were used in conjunction with contract workers. At the same time, however, the combined use of alliances and traditional employment minimizes the benefits of flexibility and, as a result, was negatively associated with firm performance. These findings indicate that there are multiple ways to improve performance via the use of knowledge workers as well as contract workers, due to the realization of different types of organizational flexibility. These findings support arguments made by researchers such as Baron *et al.* (1986), Davis-Blake and Uzzi (1993), Lepak and Snell (1999), Matusik and Hill (1998), and Pinfield and Berner (1994), in that firms might benefit from the simultaneous use of both external and internal employment modes.

What is less well known is how different combinations of employment modes are associated with various types of performance metrics. For example, if the metric is customer service or innovation, does a greater use of core knowledge work or contract work prove more beneficial? Conceptual arguments regarding numerical and functional flexibility can be made, but empirical investigation is necessary. Similarly, while job-based employment and alliances were negatively related to financial performance metrics, are they positively related to other metrics such as productivity or morale? From a knowledge-access or a qualitative flexibility perspective, greater reliance on external human capital in the form of ongoing alliance partnerships might be more beneficial to gain access to a wide network of know-how necessary for organizational innovation. For example, Nesheim *et al.* (2007) found a positive relationship between innovation strategy and consulting firms and between a price strategy and the use of temporary help agencies. Moreover, they found that managers see different benefits from different sources of external labor. The acquisition of special competences was viewed as the major benefit of using consulting firms, while acquisition of special competencies was negatively associated with temporary help agencies.

The term 'performance' is broad and encompasses a variety of fundamentally different performance metrics. Research is needed to further examine how different

employment arrangements facilitate or hinder the achievement of these. We anticipate that certain employment modes are particularly beneficial for some performance
metrics and detrimental for others. The challenge is to identify those relationships.

13.2.3 Organizational Performance and Employment Mode Management

While researchers have examined how the use of different employment modes
relates to relevant measures of organizational performance, we know less about its
impact on individual performance. Two potentially important perspectives for
understanding this relationship are the achievment of functional or skill flexibility
and architectural alignment via targeted HR systems.

Skill Flexibility

According to Tsui *et al.* (1995) and Wright and Snell (1998), firms may realize performance benefits to the extent that their internal workforce is able and willing to
perform a wide variety of tasks and responsibilities. This ability reflects the extent
to which organizations have resource flexibility at an organizational level; that is, an
ability of organizations to deploy individuals to perform a variety of tasks and
activities. Lepak *et al.* (2003) found that a greater reliance on core knowledge workers was associated with higher firm performance. A key argument in their study was
that these performance benefits materialized due to heightened levels of skill flexibility among core employees. What is missing from that study is an assessment of
how these people were managed. Simply allocating or informing people that they
are core is not likely to translate into enhanced organizational performance.
Companies must align the HR system for these workers to ensure that they have the
skills, motivation, and opportunity to display skill flexibility. Unfortunately, strategic HRM researchers have not paid attention to this particular point.

Researchers have argued that high-performance work systems and commitment-
oriented HR systems might be positively related to aspects of resource flexibility (discretion, organizational citizenship behaviors, and teamwork). For example, Kim and
Gong (2009) found that group-based pay led to higher levels of organizational citizenship behaviors (OCBs), which facilitate the sharing of tacit knowledge among core
employees. OCBs and tacit knowledge, in turn, enhance firm performance. The question that remains, however, is whether these are the best systems to realize this? Or is
there some other HR system that is better configured to achieve skill flexibility among
a firm's core workforce? For example, skill flexibility probably requires employees to
be provided with broad job responsibilities and discretion, and to be involved in
self-managed teams. Moreover, these employees need to be motivated to perform a
variety of tasks, some of which may go beyond the scope of their immediate job.

What performance management, compensation, and incentive plans are best positioned to accomplish this? This is not to say that a commitment HR system is not appropriate, but research is needed that examines the combinations of different practices that are associated with the highest levels of skill flexibility.

A related question concerns which outcomes are likely to be influenced by skill flexibility. Logically, firms would be able to realize increased efficiencies in the use of their human capital, as fewer people would conceivably be able to perform a wider range of tasks. Related, skill flexibility might serve as a moderator—moderating the negative implications associated with absenteeism and turnover, as employees could cover for vacant positions until companies are at full staff. But does skill flexibility lead to greater innovation, customer service, or quality? It might, but researchers have not identified the various outcomes associated with skill flexibility.

While skill flexibility may be primarily associated with the core workforce, it is important to recognize that all individuals who work in the interest of an organization may impact important performance outcomes. Considering this potential, it is useful to think about how all groups of employees are managed, not just the core. Underlying this perspective is the importance of adopting a targeted approach to HR systems.

Targeted HR systems

Strategic HRM researchers have tended to focus on the use of HR systems for an entire workforce, or for a particular group of a workforce. Indeed, the strategic HRM literature is littered with references to the benefits of 'high-performance work systems' (Huselid, 1995). However, rather than focusing on the performance benefits related to the use of a single HR system across an entire workforce, it may be useful to examine the use of HR systems for specific groups of human capital with consideration of their respective contributions for company success.

Extending this logic, the metrics we choose to assess HR system effectiveness might have to be more fine-grained. For example, focusing on financial or market-based metrics may not reflect employee performance related to sales growth or customer satisfaction. There may be a strong relationship between HR system use for certain groups of human capital with more narrow performance metrics than with organization-wide metrics that are influenced by a variety of factors, many of which may have nothing to do with how specific groups are managed. For example, would a commitment-based HR system targeting sales be more strongly related to sales for salespeople than ROA for an entire company? Targeting the HR system toward specific contributions, and then assessing its impact on those contributions, relative to general organizational performance metrics, might provide great insights into the relative contribution of different HR systems on various performance metrics. Research is needed to ascertain whether the use of high investment (or other HR configurations) for all employees or a differentiation approach to different groups of human capital is more beneficial for various company performance metrics.

Related, much of the strategic HRM literature examining the HR architecture and other models of differential approaches to human capital tends to focus on the performance of core employees. Yet, while not all employees may be of equal strategic importance (Stewart, 1997), all employees have the potential to impact a firm's bottom line—either positively or negatively. Certainly it is important to understand how the management of core employees relates to key performance indices. But it is conceivable that how these other groups of workers are managed might be even more important for firm performance. This may be particularly relevant when core workers represent a small portion of a firm's workforce (Delery, 1998), or when a firm uses a variety of employee groups simultaneously. When the core is relatively small, the opportunity for other workers to influence performance is likely to increase as they represent a greater proportion of the firm's workforce. By extension, it may be the case that the impact of HRM practices on performance depends on the employee group of focus. Moreover, if a larger portion of a firm's workforce is employed in a job-based employment, as found by Lepak and Snell (2002) and Gonzalez and Tacorante (2004), then it seems logical that this group of workers would have the greatest opportunity to impact firm performance.

While researchers have clearly demonstrated a fairly strong link between certain types of high-investment or high-commitment HR systems and performance, when we view the relative contributions of different groups of human capital, research is needed to examine the relative impact of management of different groups on firm performance. Failure to do so may overstate the impact of certain HR systems on core workers, and understate the potential contributions of how other, non-core, employees are managed.

13.2.4 Individual Performance and Employment Mode Use

In the previous section we explored the potential relationships between employment mode use and organizational performance metrics. We focused on the potential benefits of flexibility and cost savings. At the individual level of analysis there are also potential implications for various potential employee performance metrics associated with the use of various employment arrangements. We focus on metrics associated with job security/career prospects and the target of individuals' commitment.

Job security/career prospects

One of the most obvious implications for employees related to a differentiated approach to deploying human capital relates to the notion of job security and career prospects. Viewing the four primary employment modes in the HR architecture, it is logical that core knowledge-based employees would experience the greatest levels of security and career prospects. The human capital which they possess is directly instrumental to the short- and long-term viability of their organization's success. As a result, organizations have an incentive to provide these individuals with job security and career prospects to retain their contributions (Lepak and Snell, 1999). At the same time, individuals in other employment modes may have vastly different perceptions of their security and potential long-term career prospects based on how they are employed. For example, job-based employees are not likely to realize a similar commitment from their employer. Since the human capital they possess is replaceable, there is disincentive for companies to take steps to ensure the long-term employment and development of specific individuals (see Becker, 1964; Williamson, 1975). As a result, individuals with transferable and replaceable human capital are less likely to realize extensive job security and career prospects within a single organization.

Considering external human capital, their job security and career prospects with a client organization are negligible. They may, however, have varying degrees of security and career prospects depending on their host organization. For example, in a consulting organization, consultants may be viewed as core for the consulting business and receive extensive commitments for long-term employment. In contrast, individuals who are self-employed or who work for temporary agencies may experience varying degrees of security and career prospects. We would anticipate that this would depend, in part, on the nature of their human capital. External workers with human capital that is not widely available in the labor market, or human capital that is highly specialized in some manner, who are in significant demand, may be able to obtain extensive opportunities to deploy their talents across a variety of organizations. In contrast, external workers with general human capital (widely available) are likely to experience much less security with both a host provider (temporary agency) and the client organization.

One area of research that is needed is to understand how employees in different arrangements experience job security and career prospects, and what impact this has on their attitudes and behavior. It may be the case that it depends on the personal preference or level of risk aversion of individuals. Some individuals may have a stronger preference for variety in the tasks, and clients they work for, relative to their need for job security. Building on this logic, it is conceivable that some individuals are better fit than others for different employment arrangements. Individuals with specialized talents may be quite satisfied with working as an external service provider, knowing that the market for this skill is strong. In contrast, someone with generalized human capital may worry if they have to depend on the market to sell their skills.

Target of commitment

The topic of commitment has garnered considerable attention in the HR literature. Researchers have demonstrated that commitment is positively associated with a variety of important individual behavioral and performance outcomes (Judge *et al.*, 2001; Mathieu and Zajac, 1990). A high-trust, high-commitment work environment, which is based on a *quid pro quo* arrangement of providing high job security in exchange for an engaged and productive workforce, can enhance organizational performance (Osterman et al., 2001). Committed employees may be more willing to learn new skills, to share their knowledge and offer ideas and suggestions, and to care about quality and productivity (Osterman, 2000).

Viewing commitment from an employment mode use perspective may provide some interesting insights into how a differentiated approach to employing human capital may impact individuals. For example, is commitment always desired? While there are certainly benefits of employee commitment, it is conceivable that situations exist where companies do not want employees to be loyal or committed, because that may contradict the needs of a dynamic and complex environment, which calls for more adaptability and innovation by companies. By extension, is commitment equally desired from all individuals? Are there other individual attitudes that are more desired for different groups?

Should commitment be expected for each group? One view of this question may focus on whether or not it is reasonable to expect individuals in different employment arrangements to display equal levels of commitment to an organization. A different view of this question asks whether or not it is even fair to expect commitment from all groups of employees. While commitment in general is important, when the focus is on various employment arrangements, an important question to consider is the target of commitment, and the implications for potentially different targets of commitment on other relevant individual and organizational outcomes.

For example, because core knowledge workers possess valuable and unique human capital, we can envision that this is a group from whom organizations would desire high levels of commitment. The more these employees perceive that they are viewed as assets by their employers and that their organization maintains a long-term commitment to them, the more they are likely to be willing to give back to their employers in the form of commitment to the organization (Eisenberger et al., 1990). Let us consider the other employment modes. Job-based employees possess valuable competencies but lack the uniqueness of core knowledge workers. Given the nature of their human capital, they may be viewed as careerists. Rousseau (1995) and Rousseau and Wade-Benzoni (1994) suggested that careerists may be more committed to their own career rather than seek or receive lifelong employment within a single organization. Given the nature of their human capital, they are able to market their talents in a variety of organizations. While this does not preclude them from being committed to any particular organization, it does raise the prospect that their level of commitment toward their organization, as well as the focus of their commitment—toward their own career versus toward their organization—may differ from core employees.

The target of individual commitment for external workers may also differ. From the client organization perspective, these individuals are viewed as contributors to their organization's operations. But from the external employee's perspective they are simultaneously involved in relationships with multiple parties. They may work for a third-party provider, a consulting organization, or be self-employed. In these scenarios, where do their commitments lie? Consider consultants. While consultants have a professional obligation to perform their duties for their client organizations, is it more likely that the personal commitment is focused on their consulting organization for whom they work, or for their own company if self-employed? If so, is it reasonable to expect commitment from these employees? Should commitment even be a relevant outcome for these individuals, or should some other metric such as task performance be more important?

Research is needed to examine how the use of different employment modes impacts individual attitudes and potential resultant behaviors. For example, it is possible that the simultaneous use of multiple employment modes may result in some interactional outcomes for individuals. Consider a project team. If a team is comprised of core employees, job-based employees, and external partners, is each team-member equally committed to the company? If not, how does it affect the team's performance? If people interact with others of different employment modes, does that influence one another's attitudes and behavior, perhaps due to issues related with justice? It is conceivable that non-core employees may be envious or jealous of their core employee team-mates; or external workers may be resentful that internal employees have job security while both are working on a common project. Though speculative, these issues highlight several important avenues for future research to better understand how employment mode use might impact individual outcomes.

13.2.5 Individual Performance and Management of Employment Modes

Beyond how they are employed, individuals in different employment arrangements are also exposed to various HR practices that may further influence their attitude and behavior. From an architectural perspective there are several issues that may be of particular importance: (un)balanced investments, perceived organizational support, and equity/justice concerns.

Balanced and unbalanced investments

Drawing from social exchange theories, Tsui et al. (1997) examined the exchange relationship between employees and employers from the employer perspective. They categorized exchange relationships as either balanced (when employers and employees perceive similar expectations and obligations regarding the nature of their exchange) or unbalanced (when differences exist regarding the obligations that are expected from each other) in terms of the investments provided to employees relative to their expected contribution. In an empirical investigation they found that a high balance approach and an overinvestment approach were associated with higher levels of core job performance and more favorable attitudes. Similarly, Shore and Berksdale (2000) examined the consequences of balanced or unbalanced exchange and found that employees categorized in a mutually high balanced relationship (high obligations toward the organization and perceived high obligations on the employer's part) had lower intention to quit, and higher perceived organizational support (POS), career prospects in the firm, and affective commitment than employees in underobligations.

Although Tsui et al. (1997) and Shore and Berksdale (2000) focused on permanent employees, the logic may apply to other employment arrangements as well. For instance, contract workers may be in a balanced relationship where low investments and contributions are expected. However, organizations may invest more in these contract workers or expect more contributions from them (unbalanced relationship). If workers employed in different arrangements are managed via different HR systems (Lepak and Snell, 1999), what are the implications for individual performance?

Companies may 'overinvest' in job-based employees, providing greater exposure to commitment-oriented HR systems than expected in the terms of their employment as well as their psychological contracts. In these cases, would we expect individual performance to increase? Do they work harder or faster? Do they justify the investments? Alternatively, companies may 'underinvest' in employees, providing less exposure to certain HR practices than expected in the terms of their employment arrangement. In these cases, do employees withhold effort to reflect their perceptions of their lack of investment? For external employees, do they maintain discretion in how they respond to balanced or unbalanced investments? Or do they simply focus on the task at hand? Research is needed that explicitly examines how the employment mode in which people are being managed influences their reactions to over- and underinvestments and balanced investments.

Perceived organizational support

Wayne et al. (1997) found that developmental HR practices are positively related to perceived organizational support. POS, in turn, has been found to be positively associated with affective organizational commitment and constructive suggestions (Eisenberger et al., 1990) and OCBs (Wayne et al., 1997). In addition, POS is negatively associated with absenteeism (Eisenberger et al., 1990) and turnover intentions (Guzzo et al., 1994).

From an architectural perspective, the question that needs to be examined is as follows. If employees in different employment arrangements are exposed to different levels of developmental HR practices, or HR practices that demonstrate a concern for the long-term well being of employees, what is their reaction? Even if the degree/level of HR system exposure is technically appropriate for their value added and degree of uniqueness, it is conceivable that their perceptions of POS might not reflect that rationale. More to the point, even if individuals understand they are not core, and how they are managed is a reflection of that, it does not mean that non-core employees or external individuals do not react to how they are managed. Furthermore, these reactions are likely to have an impact on organizational performance.

It is conceivable, for instance, that individuals in alliances, contract work, or job-based employment may feel a low level of POS, even if they are being managed in a manner that is aligned with their role with the company. In these circumstances, what is the impact on performance? If the employee perceives low organizational support, and even if the organization do not believe that employees should receive high support, they may display the general patterns associated with lower percep-tions of organizational support: lower OCBs, higher absenteeism, and greater turn-over. Alternatively, if organizations invest in employees beyond what is expected (overinvest), do the benefits of increased POS offset the costs required to achieve the higher POS?

Equity and fairness

People with variations in human capital, and different levels of value and unique-ness, must often interact to realize strategic priorities. Certain employees are hired to perform a relatively standardized job, while others are sought for what they know and for their potential (Lepak and Snell, 2007). At the outset, these different groups of employees are likely to have different assumptions and expectations of their employment relationship. In situations where employees who are treated dif-ferently work together, factors that may emerge in importance are concerns about justice and equity.

These equity comparisons may be magnified when people in different employ-ment modes work interdependently (Boxall, 1998; Rubery et al., 2004). For example, employee groups that receive lower levels of investment, though possibly justified in terms of their potential strategic contributions, may experience inequity and dis-play less than desired attitudes and behaviors due to their exposure to other employ-ees who receive higher levels of investment. At the same time, treating all employees equally might involve overinvesting in non-critical employees and underinvesting in critical employees. While such an approach may alleviate equity concerns among non-core employees, it may not be cost effective. Although slight increases in indi-vidual performance may occur, the cost of obtaining this increase in performance may be offset by the additional costs. As a result, an overinvestment HR configura-tion for employees may not materialize in an added effect on firm performance. Moreover, failure to differentiate between core and non-core employees may cause core employees to feel undervalued, thereby resulting in negative attitudes and behavior.

Beyond concerns of equity among employees, it is possible that there may be additional equity concerns stemming from potential differences between managers and employees in the perceived value added and uniqueness of employees' human capital. Liao *et al.* (2009) demonstrated that managers and employees perceive differences in the use of HR practices to manage employees. Extending this logic, it is possible that from their respective vantage points of their value and uniqueness, managers and employees may have different assumptions of how employees should be managed. For example, an employee may be managed via a productivity HR system appropriate for high value and low uniqueness. If the employee perceives that they make more unique contributions, their reactions to the HR system investments may be negative. The employees might believe they deserve to be managed via a different HR systems (a high-commitment HR system) compared to management's assessment of their role within the organization.

It is also possible that there are equity perceptions among employees in a single employment mode regarding how they are managed. Four categories of employment are admittedly broad. Rather than having either high or low value or uniqueness, employees are likely to span a continuum. For example, two employees may be in a job-based employment arrangement (high value, low uniqueness) but employee A has medium value added and employee B has high value added. If both employees are managed via the same productivity HR system, it is conceivable that employee B will feel undervalued relative to employee A.

Researchers have established that perceptions of equity and justice are important determinants of employee attitudes and behaviors. Yet, the potential trade-offs of a differentiated approach to employing and managing human capital have not been empirically investigated. While these approaches may enable firms to make efficient use of their limited resources by targeting groups of human capital that have the most potential to drive company success, there may be side-effects that adversely impact the efficiency gains in terms of diminished commitment, satisfaction, and motivation due to equity perceptions. Research is needed that explicitly examines the implications for individuals—positive and negative—associated with these approaches.

13.3 A Dynamic Perspective

Beyond exploring the individual and organizational performance implications of adopting an architectural perspective, it is important to consider the notion of alignment of human capital and organizational needs from a temporal perspective and in a social context, and explore different ways that employees may add value.

13.3.1 A Temporal View of Human Capital

One important criticism of existing research on the HR architecture and other differentiating approaches to employing and managing human capital is that they are static. Human capital value is mainly conceptualized within one time dimension. That is, if we define human capital as the value-generating potential of employee knowledge, skills, and abilities (Kang *et al.*, 2007) then the most frequently used approach to human capital management would be to align current human capital (knowledge, skills, and abilities) with current firm strategies and needs.

However, the value of human capital also lies in its ability to create competitive advantage, which by implication has a future dimension. Human capital has both a current and a future value. Given this notion, we need to think of how we can manage current human capital to create future value for the firm. Here the question 'which skills, knowledge sets and capabilities will ensure future success?' becomes important. Likewise, the development of firm-specific and/or valuable capital in time 1 may be less advantageous at time 2 if industry and market demand change. This future alignment perspective brings into focus the notion of *human capital renewal* as it relates to organizational learning.

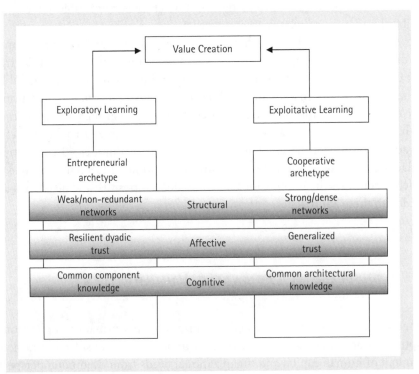

Figure 13.2. Relational Components of Organizational Learning (Kang *et al.*, 2007)

Previous research (Crossan *et al.*, 1999; March, 1991) indicates that the renewal of human capital comprises both the refinement of existing knowledge and skills (exploitation) and the development of new and/or alternative skill sets (exploration) which enable a firm to reconfigure its competitive strategy. The ability of the firm to renew its human capital can be regarded as a dynamic capability (Blyler and Coff, 2003) that requires consideration of two factors: (*a*) the configuration of human capital for renewal, and (*b*) how firms manage human capital renewal.

While human capital may be viewed from a variety of perspectives, Kang *et al.* (2007) focus on the notion that a firm's human capital varies according to the breadth (or variety) of knowledge or expertise which its employees possess. This variety of human capital can be broadly classified as generalist and specialist (Becker, 1962, 1964). From a renewal perspective, the breadth of individual knowledge or expertise has significant effects on their ability to search for and interpret new knowledge (Kang *et al.*, 2007). Furthermore, individuals who possess a broad range of expertise tend to develop more flexible mental models, which are less entrenched in a particular perspective and can be adjusted across alternative situations and problems (Bunderson and Sutcliffe, 2002; Walsh, 1988). This broad range of expertise facilitates the recombination of new knowledge across a broad range of knowledge domains (Wright and Snell, 1998). The breadth of human capital could therefore play an important role in facilitating the process of alternative skill development or exploration.

Likewise, Henderson and Clark (1990) found that the breadth of human capital, defined as common architectural knowledge, provides a cognitive mechanism to transfer complicated knowledge and experiences. Thus, it facilitates the efforts of individuals to integrate their own knowledge with other group members, which in turn supports exploratory renewal processes. However, firms often rely on specialist skills and knowledge, or valuable and unique human capital, which enables them to differentiate their services and products from their competitors. This reliance on firm-specific and occupation-specific human capital may favor the process of knowledge refinement (exploitation). For example, an accountancy partnership would rely on the experience of its tax specialists to continue to refine their knowledge in order to develop more innovative and unique tax solutions that will differentiate them from the other firms in the same competitive space.

This process of the refinement of existing human capital and the exploration of renewed human capital presents several HR challenges. Firms may be more inclined to attract and develop core knowledge workers (core human capital) and use high-commitment HR practices aligned with this group of employees' needs to provide an advantage at time 1. The challenge, however, is that firms need to develop not only the depth of experience which will pay off in time 1, but also to attract and develop human capital which may provide a bridge for exploratory learning (March, 1991) and a possible competitive advantage in time 2. These sets of human capital (specialized for time 1 advantage and generalized at time 1 for time 2 advantage) need to be managed with diverse sets of HR practices.

The challenge essentially rests with the question of which is more important—today or tomorrow? From an architectural perspective, how do organizations differentiate today's star (core) from tomorrow's star who might not yet be delivering? If both are treated as core there could be equity concerns—particularly for those who view themselves as adding more to the firm's competitive advantage. Alternatively, failure to invest significantly in people who might be core in the future runs the risk of diminishing the organizational pipeline of future competitiveness. A somewhat related question that has not been addressed in the literature is how organizations manage human capital that has diminished in its value-creating potential. One tactic would be to try to renew it through investments. Another tactic might be to reclassify these employees as non-core. In these situations, what is the outcome? How would employees react to being 'downgraded' in importance?

An alternative situation exists if we focus on the notion of change in human capital over time. As noted above, firms may certainly conscientiously invest in human capital to increase its value-creating potential. But it is important to recognize that other changes may happen as well. For example, Lepak and Snell (1999) suggested that there is a natural tendency for human capital decay on both the dimensions of uniqueness and value. It is also conceivable that generic human capital may, over time, evolve into incorporating firm-specific aspects learnt through experiences in a particular organization. This would result in increased depth to complement what was viewed as breadth. Alternatively, through participating in different training experiences, educational opportunities, and simply observing and working with others, the breadth of an individual's skills may increase over time. In this context, someone with firm-specific competencies may retain those talents but complement them with a broader array of general human capital. Given this potential, is it fair to categorize someone as either generic human capital or firm-specific, or could they simultaneously have elements of both?

There are no clear answers to these questions. Yet these are questions that have practical significance in organizations. Research is needed to understand how firms balance current and future human capital contributions through employment mode use and HR systems.

13.3.2 Human Capital in a Social Context

In addition to consideration of temporal dynamics regarding human capital, it is also important to recognize the context of human capital. While researchers have demonstrated that the level and/or type of human capital may be positively related to important performance metrics, the nature of this relationship may depend on the context in which it is employed. In particular, the degree of social capital may enhance or diminish the ability of individuals to leverage their talents in organizations (see Chapters 2 and 16 of this volume).

While an architectural perspective reflects how firms structure and manage their portfolio of human capital, it does not directly address how to promote knowledge flow within and across different employment modes. In an attempt to overcome this limitation, Kang *et al.* (2007) suggested that success in creating customer value requires that firms are successful in both exploitative and exploratory innovation based on employee knowledge. Because different employee groups within the HR architecture possess different levels and types of human capital, leveraging their full potential requires that organizations design HR systems so as to encourage entrepreneurial activity among employees for exploratory innovation, as well as cooperative activity among employees to exploit and extend existing knowledge for competitive advantage.

Existing evidence provides some support for the importance of attending to both human and social capital. Subramaniam and Youndt (2005), for example, found that human and social capital interacted positively to influence radical innovative capability. This finding suggests that human capital provides the most value for innovative capabilities when employee knowledge is shared among employees. Related to this, Collins and Clark (2003) explored the relationships among network-building HRM practices, internal and external social networks of top management teams, and firm sales growth and stock growth. Their results provide support for a mediating effect of top managers' social networks. As these findings suggest, human capital is most valuable when paired with appropriate social capital.

In addition, it is important to consider the context of human capital. Human capital exists within a social context, as individuals rarely work in isolation. Rather, companies configure tasks and jobs in a manner that is intended to benefit from synergies of talent across individuals. But with a focus on the social context of human capital, how does the nature of support and quality of human capital in the immediate social context of an employee impact their contributions? Is someone who is an exceptional talent likely to perform at a higher or lower level when paired with marginal human capital? What happens if that talent is exceptional? While social capital is a key component to understanding the flow of knowledge within and across organizations, the immediate social context of individuals may also impact employee attitudes and behavior.

13.3.3 What it Means to Add Value

Another dynamic aspect of human capital is that there are different ways to add value. For example, one can conceive of employees as being *direct* contributors to competitive advantage. Other employees may be viewed as *enablers*. Their personal contributions are not directly valuable but their indirect contributions may be critical. We can conceive of these roles as providing key supporting roles that enable other employees—even core employees—to successfully perform their jobs. A third form of value added may be *connectors*—individuals who bridge disparate pools of human capital and are instrumental in facilitating the exchange of knowledge throughout the organization.

To date, the literature has focused predominantly on the first category—direct contributors—as the primary group of human capital that drives competitive success. We would argue, however, that without enablers and connectors, direct contributors are not likely to generate consistent value over time. These alternative forms of value contributions are key to organizations, particularly in light of the growing trends toward a differentiated workforce. Yet researchers have not examined how the form of value contributions influences performance metrics. For example, it might be the case that connectors are particularly important in dynamic environments in which knowledge is dispersed through industry. By serving as a catalyst for identifying and linking external knowledge, the effectiveness of connectors may be of upmost importance for firm creativity and innovation. Extending this logic, research is needed that examines the different types of value contribution as well as when the different forms of value contribution are more or less instrumental in achieving important outcomes.

13.4 CONCLUSION

In conclusion, we consider three aspects which will be important in future considerations of the alignment of human capital with organizational needs. The first relates to the *boundaries of the firm*, which in turn dictates the needs of the firm. Increasingly, the boundaries of the firm are blurred as knowledge is shared and learning created at the network level. As Lepak and Snell (2007: 211) note, 'the knowledge that companies rely on for competitive success not only resides in the minds of their employees but also in the minds of contractors, consultants and other external workers with whom they collaborate'. Given these trends, it is important to examine how employees are managed within networks. That is, could core knowledge workers reside within a network but outside the boundaries of the firm? Expressed differently, can groups of consultants, software engineers, or research scientists be seen to hold valuable and unique knowledge? Given the dynamic renewal processes within the firm, these employees may not be managed within the firm—that is, directly employed. This would extend the HR architecture model and would challenge the strategic freedom at the firm level.

The second issue for future consideration is directly related to the reasoning behind the HR architecture model and its link to performance. Here we have referred to the *HR-value-chain* which relies on the implementation of appropriate HR practices, which differ according to the human capital segments, to generate employee attitudes, which in turn generate organizational performance (Purcell *et al.*, 2009). However, as the boundaries of the firm are blurred the benefit of the attitude–performance chain is less clear. For example, if account executives in a marketing agency work closely with the client in a cross-boundary team, then commitment toward the client may be stronger than toward the firm. The discretionary behavior and the performance benefits that result from this may therefore not favor the employing organization. Indeed, it may favor the client at the cost of the firm. The multiplicity of the HR-value-chain therefore holds further implications for the alignment of human capital with organizational needs.

Finally, we need to acknowledge that in the process of managing human capital there is a strong influence of *human agency*. That is to say, core knowledge workers will hold clear commitment to their profession (Alvesson and Empson, 2006; Alvesson and Willmott, 2002) and may not be willing to engage in extra-role behaviors nor align their efforts with organizational needs if they perceive that these may cut across their professional identity. Several accounts of accountancy consultancies and investment banks have been recorded to illustrate these tensions between organizational needs and professional identity. It is therefore important to consider the multiplicity of commitment/identification when aligning the management of human capital with the perceived organizational need.

In this chapter we have considered the performance implications for organizational decisions regarding the use of different employment, how individuals in these employment arrangements are managed, how human capital contributes over time, and the social context in which human capital is deployed. Our objective was to go beyond existing thinking in the management of human capital and to identify potential avenues for future research to further our understanding of how to leverage human capital for both individual and organizational interests.

REFERENCES

ALVESSON, M., and EMPSON, L. (2006). *The Construction of Organizational Identity* (Lund: Lund Institute of Economic research; Working paper series, 2006/3).

—— and WILLMOTT, H. (2002). 'Identity Regulation as Organizational Control: Producing the Appropriate Individual', *Journal of Management Studies*, 39(5): 619–44.

BARON, J. N., DAVIS-BLAKE, A., and BIELBY, W. T. (1986). 'The Structure of Opportunity: How Promotion Ladders Vary within and among Organizations', *Administrative Science Quarterly*, 31(2): 248–73.

BECKER, G. S. (1962). 'Investment in Human Capital', *Journal of Political Economy*, 70(S5): 9–49.

—— (1964). *Human Capital* (New York: Columbia University Press).

BLYLER, M., and COFF, R. (2003). 'Dynamic Capabilities, Social Capital and Rent Appropriation: Ties that Split Pies', *Strategic Management Journal*, 24(7): 677–86.

Bontis, N. (1998). 'Intellectual Capital: An Exploratory Study that Develops Measures and Models', *Management Decision*, 36(2): 63–76.

Boxall, P. (1998). 'Achieving Competitive Advantage through Human Resource Strategy: Towards a Theory of Industry Dynamics', *Human Resource Management Review*, 8(3): 265–88.

Bunderson, J. S., and Sutcliffe, K. M. (2002). 'Comparing Alternative Conceptualizations of Functional Diversity in Management Teams: Process and Performance Effects', *Academy of Management Journal*, 45(5): 875–93.

Collins, C. J., and Clark, K. D. (2003). 'Strategic Human Resources Practices, Top Management Team Social Networks, and Firm Performance: The Role of HR Practices in Creating Organizational Competitive Advantage', *Academy of Management Journal*, 46(6): 740–52.

Crossan, M. M., Lane, H. W., and White, R. E. (1999). 'An Organizational Learning Framework: From Intuition to Institution', *Academy of Management Review*, 24(3): 522–32.

Davenport, T. (1999). *Human Capital* (San Francisco: Jossey-Bass).

Davis-Blake, A., and Uzzi, B. (1993). 'Determinants of Employment Externalization: A Study of Temporary Workers and Independent Contractors', *Administrative Science Quarterly*, 38(2): 195–223.

Delery, J. E. (1998). 'Issues of Fit in Strategic Human Resource Management: Implications for Research', *Human Resource Management Review*, 8(3): 289–309.

—— and Shaw, J. D. (2001). 'The Strategic Management of People in Work Organizations: Review, Synthesis, and Extension', in G. Ferris (ed.), *Research in Personnel and Human Resource Management*, xx (Greenwich, Conn.: JAI Press), 165–97.

Eisenberger, R., Fasolo, P., and Davis-LaMastro, V. (1990). 'Perceived Organizational Support and Employee Diligence, Commitment, and Innovation', *Journal of Applied Psychology*, 75(1): 51–9.

Gonzalez, S. M., and Tacorante, D. V. (2004). 'A New Approach to the Best Practices Debate: Are Best Practices Applied to All Employees in the Same Way?', *International Journal of Human Resource Management*, 15(1): 56–75.

Guzzo, R. A., Noonan, K. A., and Elron, E. (1994). 'Expatriate Managers and the Psychological Contract', *Journal of Applied Psychology*, 79(4): 617–26.

Henderson, R. M., and Clark, K. B. (1990). 'Architectural Innovation: The Reconfiguration of Existing Product Technologies and the Failure of Established Firms', *Administrative Science Quarterly*, 35(1): 9–30.

Hitt, M. A., Bierman, L., Shimizu, K., and Kochhar, R. (2001). 'Direct and Moderating Effects of Human Capital on Strategy and Performance in Professional Firms: A Resource-Based Perspective', *Academy of Management Journal*, 44(1): 13–28.

Huselid, M. A. (1995). 'The Impact of Human Resource Management Practices on Turnover, Productivity, and Corporate Financial Performance', *Academy of Management Journal*, 38(3): 635–72.

—— Becker, B. E., and Beatty, D. (2005). *The Workforce Scorecard: Managing and Measuring Human Capital to Drive Strategy Execution* (Boston: Harvard Business School Press).

Judge, T. A., Thoresen, C. J., Bono, J. E., and Patton, G. K. (2001). 'The Job Satisfaction-Job Performance Relationship: A Qualitative and Quantitative Review', *Psychological Bulletin*, 127(3): 376–407.

KANG, S. C., MORRIS, S., and SNELL, S. (2007). 'Relational Archetypes, Organizational Learning and Value Creation: Extending the Human Resource Architecture', *Academy of Management Review*, 32(1): 236–57.

KIM, H., and GONG, Y. (2009). 'The Roles of Tacit Knowledge and OCB in the Relationship between Group-Based Pay and Firm Performance', *Human Resource Management Journal*, 19(2): 120–39

LEPAK, D. P., and SNELL, S. A. (1999). 'The Human Resource Architecture: Toward a Theory of Human Capital Allocation and Development'. *Academy of Management Review*, 24(1): 31–48.

—— and —— (2002). 'Examining the Human Resource Architecture: The Relationships among Human Capital, Employment, and Human Resource Configurations', *Journal of Management*, 28(4): 517–43.

—— and —— (2007). 'Employment Sub-Systems and Changing Forms of Employment', in P. Boxall, J. Purcell, and P. Wright (eds.), *The Oxford Handbook of Human Resource Management* (Oxford: Oxford University Press), 210–30.

—— TAKEUCHI, R., and SNELL, S. A. (2003). 'Employment Flexibility and Firm Performance: Examining the Interaction Effects of Employment Mode, Environmental Dynamism, and Technological Intensity', *Journal of Management*, 29(5): 681–703.

LIAO, H., TOYA, K., LEPAK, D. P., and HONG, Y. (2009). 'Do they See Eye to Eye? Management and Employee Perspectives of High-Performance Work Systems and Influence Processes on Service Quality', *Journal of Applied Psychology*, 94(2): 371–91.

MARCH, J. G. (1991). 'Exploration and Exploitation in Organizational Learning', *Organization Science*, 2(1): 71–87.

MATHIEU, J. E., and ZAJAC, D. M. (1990). 'A Review and Meta-Analysis of the Antecedents, Correlates, and Consequences of Organizational Commitment', *Psychological Bulletin*, 108(2): 171–94.

MATUSIK, S. F., and HILL, C. W. L. (1998). 'The Utilization of Contingent Work, Knowledge Creation, and Competitive Advantage', *Academy of Management Review*, 23(4): 680–97.

NESHEIM, T., OLSEN, K. M., and KALLEBERG, A. L. (2007). 'Externalizing the Core: Firms' Use of Employment Intermediaries in the Information and Communication Technology Industries', *Human Resource Management*, 46(2): 247–64.

OSTERMAN, P. (2000). 'Work Reorganization in an Era of Restructuring: Trends in Diffusion and Effects on Employee Welfare', *Industrial and Labor Relations Review*, 53(2): 179–96.

—— (1987). 'Choice of Employment Systems in Internal Labor Markets', *Industrial Relations*, 26(1): 48–63.

—— KOCHAN, R., LOCKE, R., and PIORE, M. (2001). *Working in America: A Blueprint for the New Labor Market* (Cambridge, Mass.: MIT Press).

PENNINGS, J. M., LEE, K., and VAN WITTELOOSTUIJN, A. (1998). 'Human Capital, Social Capital and Firm Dissolution', *Academy of Management Journal*, 41(4): 425–40.

PFEFFER, J., and BARON, J. (1988). 'Taking the Workers Back Out: Recent Trends in the Structuring of Employment', in B. M. Staw and L. L. Cummings (eds.), *Research in Organizational Behavior*, x (Greenwich, Conn.: JAI Press), 257–303.

PINFIELD, L. T., and BERNER, M. F. (1994). 'Employment Systems: Toward a Coherent Conceptualization of Internal Labor Markets', in G. R. Ferris (ed.), *Research in Personnel and Human Resources Management*, xii (Greenwich, Conn.: JAI Press), 41–78.

PURCELL, J., KINNIE, N., SWART, J., RAYTON, B., and HUTCHINSON, S. (2009). *People Management and Performance* (New York: Routledge).

ROUSSEAU, D. M. (1995). *Psychological Contracts in Organizations: Understanding Written and Unwritten Agreements* (Thousand Oaks, Calif.: Sage).

—— and WADE-BENZONI, J. M. (1994). 'The Contracts of Individuals and Organizations', in L. L. Cummings and B. M. Staw (eds.), *Research in Organizational Behavior*, xx (Greenwich, Conn.: JAI Press), 1–43.

RUBERY, J., CARROLL, M., COOKE, F. L., GRUGULIS, I., and EARNSHAW, J. (2004). 'Human Resource Management and the Permeable Organization: The Case of the Multi-Client Call Centre', *Journal of Management Studies*, 41(7): 1199–1222.

SELEIM, A., ASHOUR, A., and BONTIS, N. (2007). 'Human Capital and Organizational Performance: A Study of Egyptian Software Companies', *Management Decision*, 45(4): 789–801.

SHORE, L. M., and BARKSDALE, K. (2000). 'Examining Degree of Balance and Level of Obligation in the Employment Relationship: A Social Exchange Approach', *Journal of Organizational Behavior, 19* (S1): 731–44.

SNELL, S. A., and DEAN, J. W., JR. (1992). 'Integrated Manufacturing and Human Resource Management: A Human Capital Perspective', *Academy of Management Journal*, 35(3): 467–504.

—— LEPAK, D. P., and YOUNDT, M. A. (1999). 'Managing the Architecture of Intellectual Capital: Implications for Strategic Human Resource Management', in P. Wright, L. Dyer, J. Boudreau, and G. Milkovich (eds.), *Research in Personnel and Human Resource Management: Strategic HRM in the Twenty-First Century*, suppl. 4 (Greenwich, Conn.: JAI Press), 159–74.

SUBRAMANIAM, M., and YOUNDT, M. A. (2005). 'The Influence of Intellectual Capital on the Types of Innovative Capabilities', *Academy of Management Journal*, 48(3): 450–63.

STEWART, T. (1997). *Intellectual Capital* (New York: Doubleday-Currency).

TSUI, A. S., PEARCE, J. L., PORTER, L. W., and HITE, J. P. (1995). 'Choice of Employee-Organization Relationship: Influence of External and Internal Organizational Factors', in G. R. Ferris (ed.), *Research in Personnel and Human Resources Management*, xiii (Greenwich, Conn.: JAI Press), 117–51.

——PEARCE, J. L., PORTER, L. W., and TRIPOLI, A. M. (1997). 'Alternative Approaches to the Employee–Organization Relationship: Does Investment in Employees Pay Off?', *Academy of Management Journal*, 40(5): 1089–1121.

WALSH, J. P. (1988). 'Selectivity and Selective Perception: An Investigation of Managers' Belief Structures and Information Processing', *Academy of Management Journal*, 31(4): 873–96.

WAYNE, S. J., SHORE, L. M., and LIDEN, R. C. (1997). 'Perceived Organizational Support and Leader-Member Exchange: A Social Exchange Perspective', *Academy of Management Journal*, 40(1): 82–111.

WALKER, W. W. (2002). 'Human Capital: Beyond HR?', *Human Resource Planning*, 24(2): 4–5.

WILLIAMSON, O. E. (1975). *Markets and Hierarchies* (New York: Free Press).

WRIGHT, P. M., and SNELL, S. A. (1998). 'Toward a Unifying Framework for Exploring Fit and Flexibility in Strategic Human Resource Management', *Academy of Management Review*, 23(4): 756–72.

ZUCKER, L. G., DARBY, M. R., and BREWER, M. B. (1998). 'Intellectual Human Capital and the Birth of U.S. Biotechnology Enterprises', *American Economic Review*, 88(1): 290–306.

CHAPTER 14

....

MAXIMIZING VALUE FROM HUMAN CAPITAL

....

RUSSELL COFF

14.1 INTRODUCTION

....

The resource-based view focuses on sustainable competitive advantages that stem from valuable, rare, and inimitable resources (Barney, 1991; Penrose, 1959; Wernerfelt, 1984). Following this, prescriptive advice has tended to revolve around identifying and acquiring key resources. Thus, Barney (1991: 110) noted that 'physical technology, whether it takes the form of machine tools or robotics in factories or complex information management systems, is by itself typically imitable'. Human capital refers to knowledge that people gain through education, training, and experience. Thus, it can be relatively hard to imitate due to scarcity, specialization, and tacit knowledge (Hatch and Dyer, 2004; Lado and Wilson, 1994; Lippman and Rumelt, 1982). Many assume that firms that have such resources will necessarily outperform their rivals (Peteraf, 1993; Reed and DeFillippi, 1990). The prescription for firms, then, is that substantial investments in hiring, training, and learning may result in handsome gains.

This chapter departs from this tradition in the literature by exploring first why human capital might *not* lead to a competitive advantage, and second, why a human-capital-based advantage might *not* lead to superior profitability or returns for investors. For example, merely having unusually knowledgeable employees does not mean that a sustainable advantage exists. Such assets are hard to imitate because they are difficult to understand, evaluate, and observe (Barney, 1991; Peteraf, 1993). Given that tacit or complex knowledge is hard to convey, how can management organize and leverage such employees to attain an advantage (Kor and Leblebici, 2005; Penrose, 1959)? Tacitness may be 'desirable' because it is hard to imitate, but as a result, firms face serious management challenges. This is one reason why work has begun to focus on the problems of organizing and motivating people in this context (Gottschalg and Zollo, 2007; Osterloh and Frey, 2000; Wang and Barney, 2006).

Furthermore, even if the firm is successful in organizing human capital to generate rent, this is no guarantee that it will maximize shareholder value. It is perhaps not surprising to find that the nature of the resources that drive rent generation also influence the patterns of how the rent will be distributed (Coff, 1999). For example, at the height of its success, Microsoft warned its investors and employees that, 'as partners, they are also rivals who compete for the same spoils' (Lowenstein, 1997: C1). This rivalry raises a broader question. When a firm has a competitive advantage, how much rent will be appropriated by employees? This is important because appropriated rent may be unobservable in performance measures (for example, wage and benefits expenses are deducted before determining profitability). Thus the question of how to maximize value from human capital cannot be addressed without specifying for whom value will be maximized. Indeed, most of the human capital literature explicitly addresses returns to human capital that employees realize—not firms or their shareholders (Becker, 1993; Schonberg, 2007).

Unfortunately, while early resource-based theory extolled the benefits of human assets, it did not examine how the related management dilemmas and rent appropriation patterns may hinder or obscure the link to organizational performance. Human capital represents a significant strategic opportunity according to the resource-based view, but this potential cannot be realized without addressing the inherent challenges associated with such assets. Accordingly, the first part of this chapter draws on the strategy literature to examine how attributes that make human assets hard to imitate also lead to management dilemmas. I then draw on a variety of literature to describe coping strategies that may help to mitigate the problems. Finally, I turn to the problem of rent appropriation to examine when rent will be apparent in measures of firm performance.

14.2 WHY HUMAN CAPITAL MAY NOT LEAD TO A COMPETITIVE ADVANTAGE

Although human capital appears promising as a source of competitive advantage, it should be clear at the outset that not all human capital offers this promise. As Barney (1991) notes, strategic assets must first be valuable. The human capital literature focuses on education as an investment good and so, in one sense, value might be defined as whether the investment pays off. In other words, to what extent does the value of the human capital exceed the direct and opportunity cost of obtaining it? However, this definition addresses value to individuals, not value in an organizational or strategic context.

Here, I define value in terms of competitive advantage; that is, it refers to the role that human capital plays in either lowering economic costs[1] or elevating customers' willingness to pay (Porter, 1996). In this sense, value refers primarily to an enhanced ability to compete against rivals in the market-place for customers. Of course, this value could not be a source of performance differentials if rivals could offer the same value proposition. Accordingly, valuable resources alone cannot result in competitive advantage unless the resources are also rare such that there is not competitive parity. It is not hard to imagine that individuals' knowledge and experience may lower costs or attract customers either directly or indirectly. For example, customers may be aware of specific individuals and directly attracted by their reputations, or they may only be aware of the end result (such as a reputation for delivering a superior product or service).

Such advantages might be short-lived unless accompanied by isolating mechanisms—factors that hinder rivals' attempts to gain access to the valuable resources and capabilities. For example, attributes such as asset specificity, social complexity, and causal ambiguity make resources hard to imitate and/or trade, thereby allowing for a more sustained advantage. Firm-specific human assets are tailored for use in one context. A firm that relies on such knowledge may attain high returns because there is no competitive market to bid up wages (Klein *et al.*, 1978). Socially complex resources are hard to replicate, since they are embedded in complex social systems (Barney, 1991). Finally, causally ambiguous assets are hard to imitate because the link between the resource and performance is not understood (Lippman and Rumelt, 1982). Human capital may represent a causally ambiguous asset, since many social and cognitive processes are not well understood (by employees, management, or researchers).

14.3 HUMAN CAPITAL AS A SOURCE OF MANAGEMENT DILEMMAS

While these 'desirable' attributes may make human assets hard to imitate, they also cause dilemmas that may make a competitive advantage elusive. Most likely, all human assets are associated with both turnover and information problems. However, the relative seriousness of information versus turnover dilemmas varies with the type of human assets.

14.3.1 Asset Specificity, Turnover, and Hiring Dilemmas

Firm-specific human assets refer to special skills, knowledge, or personal relation-ships that are only applicable within a given firm. In contrast, general skills, such as knowledge of chemistry, law, or medicine, might be valuable in a variety of firms or industries. While human assets are typically harder to manage than tangible assets, general and specific human assets produce different dilemmas.

General human assets and the threat of turnover

Unlike tangible assets, firms cannot own employees, who are free to quit at will. This risk of turnover is a problem, since the firm may lose its most critical assets if they are dissatisfied, underpaid, or unmotivated. In many cases rivals actively raid trou-bled firms to hire away their best talent (Groysberg *et al.*, 2008).

The threat of turnover is relatively more serious for general human assets. Human capital theory assumes that general skills are 'traded' in competitive labor markets (Becker, 1993). Thus, other firms should bid up wages so that the profits flow to the workers rather than to stockholders. However, if firms are able to control turnover they may still be able to achieve an advantage. This threat of turnover is so serious that some believe that general skills cannot be a source of advantage. Following Becker's (1993) reasoning, Dittman *et al.* (1976) argue that human assets must have firm-specific skills. Thus, the strategy literature often considers specificity to be a requirement for strategic assets (Amit and Schoemaker, 1993). However, general human assets can be the source of advantage if they are rare, if they have no strategic substitutes, and if the firm can retain them over time. For example, Castanias and Helfat (1991, 1992) argue that a general human asset, such as an exceptional CEO whose skills could be applied in a variety of contexts, can be a source of advantage due to its rarity. As we shall see, retention may come at a cost which in turn reduces rent available for other stakeholders. Of course, this is only a general asset to the extent that it is not embedded in firm-specific systems.

External social complexity as a general asset

External social complexity refers to boundary-spanning networks with stakeholders such as customers or suppliers. Boundary-spanners furnish information that helps firms innovate and respond to dynamic environments (Tushman, 1977). Presumably, some have more valuable external networks than others, and can be a source of competitive advantage.

While boundary-spanning networks pose some of the information dilemmas associated with teams, the skills may be especially valuable to competitors. Thus, such skills are relatively general and pose a risk of turnover not normally connected with internal networks. The many examples of professional firms raiding their rivals' human assets illustrate how a firm can be affected when it loses human assets and their customer networks. Such external networks tend to make people more cosmopolitan and thus more aware of outside opportunities (Bartol, 1979; Kerr et al., 1977).

Firm-specific learning as second-order general human capital

A paradox arises from the fact that firms often seek people who, once hired, will be adept at learning firm-specific knowledge and routines. In this case, ironically, the best labor market signal may be whether individuals have been able to acquire firm-specific skills at another firm. Here, the most observable indicator may be their tenure at another firm known to produce proprietary knowledge. The employee's actual knowledge may not be valuable in another firm. However, his or her second-order ability to acquire new firm-specific knowledge may be extremely valuable. The irony, then, is that while the knowledge itself is not valuable to other firms, the individuals are mobile as though the knowledge were more general in nature as other employers seek this second-order ability to acquire new firm-specific knowledge. Accordingly, turnover may be more of a threat for firm-specific human assets than is normally presumed.

Firm-specific human assets, causal ambiguity, and social complexity

Nevertheless, idiosyncratic skills should reduce turnover to the extent that they are not directly in demand (unlike the exceptional CEO whose more general skills are applicable across businesses). However, by its very nature, specificity leads to additional management dilemmas arising from causal ambiguity and social complexity. That is, firm-specific human assets have idiosyncratic knowledge that may be hard for rivals to understand. If so, such assets are causally ambiguous. Similarly, firm-specific skills often involve tacit knowledge of interpersonal relationships or corporate culture. Since these are elements of social complexity, firm-specific human assets present the same dilemmas that arise from causal ambiguity and social complexity. These issues are examined below.

14.3.2 Internal Social Complexity, Causal Ambiguity, and Information Dilemmas

Internal social complexity and causal ambiguity both lead to serious information dilemmas. Internal social complexity poses the classic dilemmas inherent in team production. Alchian and Demsetz (1972) note that team production is challenging, since individual contributions are unobservable. They argue that the information problems are more hazardous in markets and that hierarchies are therefore more efficient at governing teams. However, while hierarchies may be more efficient for team production, asymmetric information poses governance dilemmas for firms as well.

From a different perspective we can see that social complexity is linked to social capital. That is, to the extent that an advantage is driven by an underlying social structure, one would need to understand how social capital allows for the creation of intellectual capital. Nahapiet and Ghoshal (1998) discuss three dimensions of social capital that help us to understand how such social structures can create value (see also Chapter 2 above). At the core is a notion that there are knowledge asymmetries within the social structure such that it may be unclear exactly where critical knowledge can be found—especially for those outside the social system.

Thus, from both an economic and sociological perspective, complex social structures can be a source of causal ambiguity which, in turn, can be a source of a sustainable advantage (Lippman and Rumelt, 1982). While this certainly creates information asymmetries with rivals, it also means that the favored firm may have limited information about its own operations. In fact, if the favored firm had complete information, the knowledge might be diffused to competitors through predatory hiring (Barney, 1991). Lippman and Rumelt (1982: 421) even refer to the favored firm as 'lucky' to underscore this point.

Accordingly, both social complexity and causal ambiguity are associated with information dilemmas. Specifically, firms must learn to cope with the problems of adverse selection, moral hazard, and bounded rationality in decision-making. These issues are more carefully reviewed in Chapters 6 and 7 above, and are summarized briefly here.

Adverse selection/hiring

Adverse selection is caused by asymmetric information in the labor market. Specialized or tacit knowledge is not observable and may lead to a 'market for lemons' problem (Akerlof, 1970). This means that the labor market would harbor a disproportionate number of low-quality workers. This occurs if employers offer lower wages to hedge their risk of hiring a 'lemon'. High-quality workers might then be reluctant to change jobs—perpetuating the problem.

Causal ambiguity can further exacerbate this problem. Applicants may misrepresent themselves by taking credit for the success of their former employers. Causal ambiguity will thwart efforts to verify such claims. Similarly, political candidates are notorious for taking credit for positive events that were beyond their control. Employers may then discount information that cannot be verified, and offer even lower starting wages.

Moral hazard/motivation

Moral hazard refers to shirking, motivation problems, or even the subversion that can occur in team production when individual contributions are difficult to observe. While these problems are the focus of principal–agency theory (Jensen and Meckling, 1976), the motivation literature also documents reduced effort in some team settings (Kidwell and Bennett, 1993). When individual contributions are intertwined, employees may be uncertain about whether their effort will impact performance (such as expectancy). In addition, the firm cannot easily provide performance-based rewards (such as instrumentality). If both expectancy and instrumentality are low, it will be difficult to motivate employees (Vroom, 1964).

Causal ambiguity also paves the way for problems of moral hazard. People often take credit for successes and assign external attributions for failures when it is difficult to observe causality. Attribution theory refers to this as the 'self-serving bias' (Ross, 1977). Since causality cannot be established, organizations may inadvertently reward or punish employees for events that are beyond their control or influence (Kerr, 1975, 1995).

Bounded rationality/poor decisions

Finally, even in the absence of opportunism, asymmetric information is a hazard for decision-makers. Since managers are boundedly rational, they may not know to ask for required information, and employees may not know what to provide (Simon, 1976). While this lack of information can lead to serious errors in decision-making, the problem is not driven by opportunism.

Causal ambiguity is especially hazardous in this respect. Not only do managers lack information required to make decisions; in extreme cases the information may not be readily available from any source (Mosakowski, 1997). For example, in the knowledge literature there is a great deal of focus on the production and transfer of tacit knowledge (Levin and Cross, 2004; Polanyi, 1966). Implicit in this discussion is the notion that managers may have less knowledge than those they oversee. This presents serious organization and motivation dilemmas, as managers may not be able to effectively deploy the firm's knowledge assets (Gottschalg and Zollo, 2007; Osterloh and Frey, 2000). Ouchi (1980) suggests that such extreme uncertainty can cause hierarchies, as a transaction governance mechanism, to break down—indeed the extent of this problem should not be underestimated.

In sum, adverse selection, moral hazard, and bounded rationality may be formidable challenges when human assets are socially complex or causally ambiguous. While hierarchies may be more efficient than markets, they also fail under conditions of asymmetric information (Grossman and Hart, 1986; Ouchi, 1980). Thus in order to generate a sustainable advantage, firms must either find ways to obtain scarce information or learn to cope in the absence of information.

14.4 SOME POSSIBLE COPING STRATEGIES

It is safe to say that these management dilemmas make it less likely that superior human capital will lead to a competitive advantage. Firms (and managers) must acquire, organize, and motivate employees under substantial information asymmetries. It is under these conditions that both markets and hierarchies may be prone to failure (Ouchi, 1980). This does not mean that human capital cannot lead to a competitive advantage; merely that complementary management capabilities must also be present (such as the ability to resolve these management challenges).

While there cannot be a 'rule for riches' that fully codifies exactly how these dilemmas may be resolved, this chapter does offer some insight into how firms might cope with these dilemmas. Since human assets are typically associated with turnover and/or information dilemmas, the overarching proposition is that firms must develop coping mechanisms in order to achieve an advantage. For example, without effective turnover management, human assets may exit and any advantage will be lost. Similarly, firms must be able to cope with the information problems, else they will not be able to organize, coordinate, and motivate their human assets.

Coff (1997) identifies four types of coping strategy to address these dilemmas: (1) retention strategies; (2) rent-sharing strategies; (3) organizational design strategies; and (4) information strategies. Retention strategies reduce turnover by binding employees to the firm. In contrast, rent-sharing strategies allocate a portion of the rent to reduce turnover and provide incentives to motivate effort. Organizational design strategies involve manipulating the firm's governance, structure, and culture to cope with dilemmas. Finally, information strategies entail obtaining and analyzing unique sources of information to gain an information advantage.

These coping strategies derive largely from the organizational behavior and human resource management literature, and are not particularly new in that sense. However, the extant literature has generally not linked these solutions specifically to attributes of strategic assets. This may contribute to some inconclusive or anomalous findings. For example, research on participation in decision-making has produced mixed results (Cotton et al., 1988; Wagner and Gooding, 1987)—perhaps because little of the work was conducted in human-capital-intensive contexts. Below, I briefly explore retention, organizational design, and information strategies. Rent sharing will be examined later in the context of rent appropriation.

14.4.1 Retention Strategies

Turnover control is a key component of strategy whenever there are human assets (Huselid, 1995). Since the strategy literature draws our attention to rent generation and distribution, retention strategies specifically refer to policies that promote retention, loyalty, and effort without allocating the rent. In other words, while firms could simply pay people enough for them to stay (Weiss, 1990), this allocates rent and is considered a rent-sharing strategy.

Drawing from the turnover literature, we find that a person's propensity to change jobs depends on perceptions of the current job relative to alternatives (Mobley, 1982; Rusbult *et al.*, 1988). Thus, firms may decrease turnover either by raising perceptions of the current job or by lowering the perceptions of alternatives. Perceptions can be influenced by managing the non-financial aspects of job satisfaction and by investing in firm-specific skills.

Perceptions of the current job and non-financial facets of satisfaction

Job satisfaction is featured prominently in the turnover literature as a trigger to prompt search behavior (Hom *et al.*, 1992; Lee *et al.*, 1996). This underscores the fact that mere retention understates what is required—a sustainable advantage demands employees who are loyal and committed as well.

The job satisfaction literature is particularly helpful, since pay is one of many facets of satisfaction (Rice *et al.*, 1991). For example, the Job Descriptive Index measures five dimensions: (1) pay; (2) supervision; (3) co-workers; (4) promotion; and (5) the work itself (Jung *et al.*, 1986). There is evidence that non-financial facets can substitute for wages (Greenberg and Ornstein, 1983). Mobley (1982: 127) wrote about these trade-offs: 'An organization that puts all its emphasis on one facet (such as pay, considerate supervision, job content, or working conditions, etc.) may be disappointed. Alternatively, the employer who cannot adequately satisfy one value may be able to partially compensate by enhancing the attainment of other values.'

The four non-financial facets offer significant opportunities to retain employees while preserving rent for other stakeholders. First, firms can improve satisfaction with supervision by training and selecting people to provide learning opportunities, promote employee participation, provide recognition, and to be fair. Second, satisfaction with co-workers can be increased by managing group demography and social activities to create a team-based work environment (O'Reilly *et al.*, 1989). As people develop strong relationships within the firm, they are less likely to leave (Shaw *et al.*, 2005; Yperen and Hagedoorn, 2003). Third, firms can enhance satisfaction with promotion by structuring career paths so that assignments are offered as rewards. This is a consistently important facet across populations but especially those with substantial human capital (Rice *et al.*, 1991; Scarpello and Campbell, 1983). The last dimension, the work itself, is particularly important to professionals who often seek autonomy and input (Raelin, 1991)—something that may be inexpensive to provide.

In sum, since employees' value non-financial dimensions of satisfaction, these facets can substitute for wages. Indeed, some have studied the extent to which attempts to motivate individuals extrinsically (wages, and so on) can crowd out natural intrinsic motivation (Frey, 1993, 2002; Murdock, 2002). Since these intrinsic facets are valuable to employees, but relatively cheap to maintain (once in place), they may serve as important components of a sustainable advantage.

Perceptions of alternative jobs and firm-specificity

Firms have a less direct influence on employees' perceptions of alternative jobs. However, since firm-specificity may limit worker mobility, firms can influence these perceptions by offering firm-specific compensation or implementing more firm-specific routines so that comparable jobs are hard to find.

'Firm-specific compensation' refers to remuneration such as interpersonal relationships, challenging work, and advancement opportunities that are unique to, and embedded in, a given firm. For example, the intrinsic components of job satisfaction discussed earlier may limit mobility even for those with general human capital, since other firms cannot readily duplicate them. While the human capital literature suggests that workers will not undertake firm-specific investments without added wages (Becker, 1993), firm-specific compensation requires no such inducements. Ultimately, rivals must offer pay increases to lure workers away and to compensate them for the loss in 'psychic' income. For example, brokerage firms have raided rivals by offering large signing bonuses which might reimburse brokers for the loss in firm-specific remuneration.

Another way to reduce mobility is to actively introduce firm-specific knowledge. This would promote retention to the extent that the knowledge would be less transferable to rivals. If this knowledge has no intrinsic positive utility (such as the dimensions of job satisfaction), it is best analyzed in the traditional investment framework, rather than in a compensation framework above. Human capital theory suggests that the cost and benefits from such training will be shared (Becker, 1993). However, if the firm gains an advantage as a result, the remaining rent may be substantial. Wang and Barney (2006) discuss settings and processes by which employees are likely to invest in firm-specific skills. This is also a key topic of Chapter 8 above.

In sum, firms may be able to retain human assets without directly allocating rent. Such retention strategies involve managing job satisfaction and creating firm-specific knowledge and routines. From a strategic standpoint, rivals might be able to imitate these strategies. For example, they might be able to create a supportive environment or firm-specific routines. Even so, this may leave substantial switching costs imposed on employees as they adjust to the new relationships and culture in a different firm.

14.4.2 Organizational Design Strategies

Organizational design strategies involve managing or influencing elements of the structure and culture to align individual goals with those of the organization in the absence of information. Within the domain of design strategies there are three types of mechanisms that might be distinguished: shared governance, organic structure, and culture. Each of these in turn may help the firm cope with both the threat of turnover and the hazards of asymmetric information.

Shared governance can help limit turnover and cope with information dilemmas. It is similar to participation in decision-making; however, much of the research in that area examines interventions at the lower levels, such as quality circles or individual goal setting (Wagner and Gooding, 1987). Shared governance focuses on more strategic higher-level issues.

We have already suggested how shared governance might help manage turnover to the extent that employees are more satisfied. This may also be one reason why professional organizations, such as law firms, involve employees in decision-making, particularly with respect to professional norms (Abbott, 1981; Raelin, 1991).

In addition to reducing turnover, shared governance can help managers make decisions when there is asymmetric information. The availability of information is one of the primary situational factors in Vroom and Yetton's (1973) normative model of participation in decision-making. Participation plays a fundamental role in higher-level strategic decisions where 'grass-roots' strategy-making reveals insights from those most integrally involved in the firm's core activities (Mintzberg and Waters, 1985). Asymmetric information and uncertainty demand that those with critical human capital be involved in 'crafting' the strategy for the company as a whole.

Organic structure

Mechanistic structures have clearly specified routines and authority (Burns and Stalker, 1961). However, such systems may break down if there is asymmetric information (Ouchi, 1980). The alternative is a more organic or flexible structure. Organic structures are flatter, with more lateral and face-to-face communication. Tasks and roles also tend to be loosely defined. Expressed differently, organic structures are designed to accommodate social complexity in that they are less oriented toward formal hierarchical relationships.

Corporate culture and clan control

Culture refers to common values, beliefs, and norms held within a firm. A strong culture is one that is widely shared in the organization (Schein, 1996). Like the other design strategies, a strong culture may help a firm cope with both the threat of turnover and information dilemmas. In the case of turnover, once employees are acculturated, it may be very hard for them to find a match at rival firms. Thus, firms with strong or 'high commitment' cultures tend to experience lower turnover rates (Arthur, 1994).

Culture is also important for coping with information dilemmas. Ouchi (1980) suggests that a strong culture (such as clan control) may substitute for other types of control that do not function well under conditions of asymmetric information. That is, employees may choose to adhere to the firm's informal norms and not act opportunistically even if the firm cannot monitor them.

Therefore, organizational design strategies in the form of shared governance, organic structures, and culture management may help firms to address both turnover and information dilemmas. This may help explain why design strategies are featured in many of the 'emergent' organizational forms that have been highlighted for their ability to generate advantages in human-capital-intensive contexts (ambidextrous, networked, boundaryless, virtual, upside down, and so on).

14.4.3 Information Strategies

As discussed, asymmetric information can lead to agency problems, and even in the absence of opportunism, poor decisions. If a firm can obtain scarce information, this in itself may be an important source of competitive advantage (Barney, 1986). Firms must seek distinct types of information to mitigate the problems of moral hazard and adverse selection.

Information sources to cope with moral hazard

Firms may seek information about current workers' effort through supervisory monitoring, peer and subordinate feedback, or external information sources. Agency theory suggests monitoring as a common way of mitigating the risk of moral hazard. However, this can be very costly when there are large knowledge asymmetries (as human capital intensity often implies), and ineffective, especially if it lowers morale.

Peer and subordinate feedback is an alternative form of monitoring that may bridge information asymmetries more effectively. Firms often collect such information as part of management development efforts. Managers then use these multiple perspectives to improve their skills (Smith, 1986). Some firms also use peer and subordinate evaluations as part of the formal appraisal system. Pritchard *et al.* (1988) found that in a team production context, group feedback may improve performance substantially. A group may be able to disentangle differences in performance and effort that a manager cannot observe.

External information sources for evaluating employees

Firms may also seek external information from customers, external peers, or suppliers to evaluate employees. In the case of professionals, the external network of peers can help the firm evaluate performance. Zucker (1991) describes how universities often lack expertise in specific fields to evaluate academic excellence. Consequently, they use external networks to mitigate asymmetric information. Similarly, Henderson and Cockburn (1994) found that pharmaceutical companies rely on external recognition, in the form of publications, to reward top performers.

Information sources to cope with adverse selection

Firms must attract high-quality employees amidst imperfect information about their skills and abilities. They often rely on crude signals, such as educational level, even though wide variations in productivity remain (Delfgaauw and Dur, 2007; Spence, 1973). Accordingly, adverse selection might keep high performers out of the labor market; in the absence of strong signals, it will be hard for people to demonstrate their exceptional human capital (Akerlof, 1970). Thus, the ability to identify human assets using incomplete information may be quite central to competitive advantage.

This mastery may take the form of a competency in gathering and interpreting labor market signals. This is the driving force behind strategic factor market theory (Barney, 1986; Makadok and Barney, 2001). For example, as knowledge about productivity has increasing strategic value, employment information from rivals takes on strategic significance (Waldman, 1990). In his book *Moneyball*, Michael Lewis (2004) describes how Oakland Athletics used a different set of signals from that of their rivals, and so were able to identify good baseball players whom other teams ignored, and acquire them at a much lower price. Chapter 12 provides additional discussion of hiring dilemmas associated with human capital.

Many of the coping strategies discussed above have long been prescribed as sources of advantage (Likert, 1961; Pfeffer, 1998). Nevertheless, they are not an easy path to competitive advantage. First, firms are notoriously ineffective at implementing the strategies. Second, the strategies are rarely discussed in terms of resolving specific dilemmas linked to human capital intensity. As such, firms may attempt to apply the coping strategies indiscriminately.

14.5 WHY A HUMAN-CAPITAL-BASED ADVANTAGE MAY NOT CREATE SHAREHOLDER VALUE

Suppose that management has beaten the odds and is successful in acquiring, motivating, and organizing human capital to generate an advantage. Does this mean that the value will be apparent in measures of firm performance and thereby flow to shareholders? The answer is that it depends on how the value is distributed—the rent appropriation regime.

Up to this point I have tried to steer clear of how human capital affects the rent appropriation process—though it should be apparent that financial and ownership incentives may discourage turnover and motivate employees by aligning incentives. One important way to address the management dilemmas inherent in knowledge-based assets is to offer powerful incentives to key stakeholders. I separate incentives because they are part of the process by which human capital appropriates the rent from a competitive advantage (such as 'rent-sharing' strategies)—the topic to which I now turn.

14.5.1 Rent Appropriation and Firm Performance

It is fair to say that managers and employees are active participants in negotiating wages and setting incentives. Much has been made of executives who influence the pay-setting process to garner compensation that sometimes exceeds what some consider is reasonable (Combs and Skill, 2003; Zajac and Westphal, 1994). However, valuable employees at all levels seek compensation commensurate with their contributions. If they believe they have played an important role in rent generation, it is likely that they will seek a portion of the rent—perhaps even more than their fair share (Chacar and Coff, 2000; Groysberg et al., 2008).

In general, successful employee rent appropriation activities will reduce the rent available for shareholders and, accordingly, measures of firm performance. However, the reader should not construe this to mean that a firm with a competitive advantage could perform poorly. Rather, it would generate at least average returns for all stakeholders and above-average returns for some stakeholders (Coff, 1999). Furthermore, the firms would have access to valuable, inimitable capabilities which rivals lack.

However, the firm might not generate super-normal returns based on traditional measures of organizational performance. For example, profit is the residual calculated after employees have been paid (among other things). Since pay includes rent that employees have appropriated, profit may reflect primarily the rent that shareholders are able to appropriate. Because profit confounds rent generation with rent appropriation, it can be a poor indicator of total rent in the nexus. Indeed, most performance measures focus on the residual that accrues to shareholders, and ignores other rent. How, then, can we identify the total rent, and who will appropriate it?

While it is clear that the rent will flow to the firm's stakeholders (including investors), few have studied how the gains from a resource-based advantage are distributed (notable exceptions are Amit and Schoemaker, 1993; Collis and Montgomery, 1995). Even where appropriability is explored, it is presented as uncorrelated with the factors that make resources hard to imitate. Here, I treat appropriability as tightly linked to the knowledge-based assets that drive a sustainable competitive advantage. It is endogenous to theories of rent generation.

The resource-based view can become a significant tool for predicting firm performance if it simultaneously explores how rent is generated and how it is appropriated. In the following sections I apply a bargaining-power model to predict rent appropriation in the context of a resource-based advantage.

14.5.2 Human Capital and Bargaining Power

Several determinants of bargaining power are adapted from the negotiation and bargaining-power literature (Hinings *et al.*, 1974; Marburger, 1994; Pfeffer and Moore, 1980; Porter, 1985). Specifically, bargaining power is highest when stakeholders (1) are capable of acting in a unified manner, (2) have access to key information, (3) have a very high replacement cost to the firm, and (4) face low costs if they move to another firm.

Human capital may or may not enable stakeholders to negotiate as a block. However, it does grant access to essential knowledge that may increase the cost to the firm should they exit. In many cases, human capital enhances labor market mobility either because it is a valuable signal for other employers (Berg, 2003; Spence, 1973) or because it is coupled with social capital that may enhance external opportunities (Coleman, 1988; Granovetter, 1973). Indeed, even firm-specific human capital can enhance external mobility if employers value it as a signal of willingness to make future investments in firm-specific skills. For example, firm-sponsored training does increase wages offered by other firms in future jobs (Booth and Bryan, 2005).

Bargaining power is especially enhanced to the extent that human capital is visible, and helps to make it clear who are the most critical contributors. Barney (1991) indicates that when key players are known, rivals will pay handsomely to hire them away—the threat of which forces firms to share rent with key individuals. The implicit assumption is that if key individuals are not known (for example, high causal ambiguity), they cannot appropriate rent and it will be observable in firm performance and flow to residual claimants (such as shareholders). There are certainly numerous examples, both in sports and business, where superstars are well known and command substantial salary premiums (Groysberg *et al.*, 2008).

Indeed, the most common assumption in traditional economic models is that wages are set equal to the marginal revenue product (Dittman *et al.*, 1976). In other words, individuals are paid according to their contribution. If their knowledge is especially valuable, that would command a higher wage.

However, in some circumstances, where causal ambiguity is more prevalent, the specific contributions that individuals make cannot be easily traced to rent generation. It is important to note that while human capital may be associated with causal ambiguity, this does not create a bargaining power vacuum. That is, causal ambiguity does not imply that more rent will go unclaimed and thus accrue to shareholders (Blyler and Coff, 2003).

Ambiguity increases the self-serving bias (Dahl and Ransom, 1999)—the tendency to take credit for successes when causality is unclear (Bettman and Weitz, 1983; Zaccaro *et al.*, 1987). Equally important, many of their claims on the rent may seem legitimate, since they would be hard to disprove. Here, individuals may believe that high levels of compensation are justified and earned (Louie *et al.*, 2000). Even the investing public found self-serving attributions in corporate annual reports convincing; stock prices improved following letters to shareholders with self-serving attributions (Staw *et al.*, 1983).

That said, not all claims may be viewed as equally legitimate. If credit allocation is difficult, then the 'fair' allocation of compensation may also be hard. Boundedly rational decision-makers may seek signals that allow them to satisfice or approximate fair solutions (Cyert and March, 1992; Simon, 1976). Human capital may provide such a signal, since it would appear plausible that a given individual is essential even if the direct evidence is ambiguous.

This is especially true when compared to the claims of investors who are much more tenuously connected to the firm's success, since their contribution tends to be much more fungible (Mahoney, 2008). Furthermore, investors typically have limited means to participate in the allocation of rent within the firm. A board of directors' compensation committee can handle only the highest-level decisions, and even here we see that managers typically have a great deal of influence.

14.5.3 When is Rent Most Likely to be Observable in Firm Performance?

From the preceding discussion it should be apparent that the very processes that allow a firm to generate rent also suggest that little of the rent will flow to shareholders. The implication is that competitive advantages are like icebergs. The bulk of the rent lies below the water line and cannot be observed in traditional performance measures. Yet those measures remain important outcomes for a variety of reasons. As such, it is critical to adapt and augment the theory of competitive advantage so that we can more accurately predict performance.

A broad conclusion of this discussion is that competitive advantages will tend to impact observable performance when employees and other active stakeholders have limited bargaining power. For example, the preceding discussion would indicate that increasing investments in firm-specific skills or providing firm-specific compensation might accomplish this to a degree. It would tend to hold key stakeholders in place while limiting their ability to appropriate rent.

A related (and complementary) approach would be to minimize the role of individuals by routinizing tasks. In this way individuals may be relatively replaceable and thus unable to appropriate substantial rent. To the extent that routines are robust to the loss of some individuals, this would tend to limit their bargaining power.

While such steps may reduce the bargaining power of some individuals, it is unclear that they will make the advantage more transparent in measures of firm performance. This is because there will always be key individuals who must manage the creation of routines and who are essential for the competitive advantage to persist. Furthermore, as a general rule, top managers will have better information than will shareholders. As such, even if lower-level employees are not in a position to appropriate rent, it is unclear whether top managers will pass the rent on to shareholders.

In the end, it probably depends more on whether governance mechanisms grant shareholders bargaining power in terms of strong information and direct influence. This will be most apparent in situations where ownership is concentrated and large blockholders are active in the decision-making process. Absent this, it seems likely that few other stakeholders would be in a position to assess the value that is created but remains hidden below the water-line.

However, having said this, if large blocks are held by insiders or suppliers, they may have alternative means to appropriate rent (such as through compensation, perquisites, or other transactions). These modes may have the advantage of reducing the portion of the rent captured by external stakeholders including the government if they are classified as expenses (such as minimizing the tax liability). For example, in family owned firms, family members may work in the company and draw on other forms of payment which may obviate the need to produce accounting profits that are visible to, and auditable by, external stakeholders. Accordingly, rent may be most observable when large blocks are held by external investors who have no other means of appropriating rent than directly through their ownership stake.

14.6 CONCLUDING THOUGHTS

We are left with a bit of a conundrum. Competitive advantages will continue to require substantial investments in intangible rent-generating assets. Theories of competitive advantage emphasize how such resources are the source of asymmetries experienced by disadvantaged rivals. However, resources of this type are also likely to favor some stakeholders over others. First, managers seeking to organize and motivate strategic assets face serious challenges. If they cannot resolve these dilemmas it will not be possible to generate rent; the mere presence of valuable resources is a necessary but not sufficient condition.

Even if managers are successful in creating rent-generating capabilities, this does not assure that they will be represented in measures of firm performance. That is, such assets would still engender powerful information asymmetries between shareholders and managers. Stakeholders who are closer to the rent-generation process are likely to have better information and will inevitably be in a strong position to appropriate value. Even if managers structure transactions (routinize, and so on) to limit bargaining power, this only enhances their ability to appropriate rent. It does not assure that the rent will accrue to shareholders.

All of this suggests that the observable impact of competitive advantages in measures of firm performance may be understated by a considerable margin. Furthermore, it underscores the need to both empirically and theoretically explore how theories of competitive advantage may actually be linked with firm performance.

NOTE

1. Note that economic costs differ from accounting costs. If employees appropriate rent, this may increase accounting costs and lower accounting profits. However, it does not alter economic costs—merely the distribution of rent. Thus employees would receive more compensation than the minimum required to hold them in place.

REFERENCES

ABBOTT, A. (1981). 'Status and Status Strain in the Professions', *American Journal of Sociology*, 86(4): 819–35.

AKERLOF, G. A. (1970). 'The Market for "Lemons": Qualitative Uncertainty and the Market Mechanism', *Quarterly Journal of Economics*, 84: 488–500.

ALCHIAN, A. A., and DEMSETZ, H. (1972). 'Production, Information Costs, and Economic Organization', *American Economic Review*, 62: 777–95.

AMIT, R., and SCHOEMAKER, P. J. H. (1993). 'Strategic Assets and Organizational Rent', *Strategic Management Journal*, 14(1): 33–46.

ARTHUR, J. B. (1994). 'Effects of Human Resource Systems on Manufacturing Performance and Turnover', *Academy of Management Journal*, 37(3): 670–87.

BARNEY, J. B. (1986). 'Strategic Factor Markets: Expectations, Luck, and Business Strategy', *Management Science*, 32(10): 1231–41.

——(1991). 'Firm Resources and Sustained Competitive Advantage', *Journal of Management*, 17(1): 99–120.

BARTOL, K. M. (1979). 'Professionalism as a Predictor of Organizational Commitment, Role Stress, and Turnover: A Multidimensional Approach', *Academy of Management Journal*, 22(4): 815–21.

BECKER, G. S. (1993). *Human Capital: A Theoretical and Empirical Analysis, with Special Reference to Education* (3rd edn. Chicago: University of Chicago Press).

BERG, I. (2003). *Education and Jobs: The Great Training Robbery* (New York: Percheron Press; orig. publ. 1970).

BETTMAN, J. R., and WEITZ, B. A. (1983). 'Attributions in the Board Room: Causal Reasoning in Corporate Annual Reports', . *Administrative Science Quarterly*, 28(2): 165–83.

BLYLER, M., and COFF, R. W. (2003). 'Dynamic Capabilities, Social Capital, and Rent Appropriation: Ties that Split Pies', *Strategic Management Journal*, 24(7): 677–86.

BOOTH, A. L., and BRYAN, M. L. (2005). 'Testing Some Predictions of Human Capital Theory: New Training Evidence from Britain', *Review of Economics and Statistics*, 87(2): 391.

BURNS, T., and STALKER, G. M. (1961). *The Management of Innovation* (London: Tavistock Publications).

CASTANIAS, R. P., and HELFAT, C. E. (1991). 'Managerial Resources and Rents', *Journal of Management*, 17(1): 155–71.

—— and —— (1992). 'Managerial and Windfall Rents in the Market for Corporate Control', *Journal of Economic Behavior and Organization*, 18(2): 153–84.

CHACAR, A., and COFF, R. (2000). 'Deconstructing a Knowledge-Based Advantage: Rent Generation, Rent Appropriation and "Performance" in Investment Banking', in M. Hitt, R. Bresser, D. Heuskel, C. Nettesheim, and R. Nixon (eds.), *Winning Strategies in a Deconstructing World* (New York: John Wiley & Sons).

COFF, R. W. (1997). 'Human Assets and Management Dilemmas: Coping with Hazards on the Road to Resource-Based Theory', *Academy of Management Review*, 22(2): 374–402.

—— (1999). 'When Competitive Advantage Doesn't Lead to Performance: The Resource-Based View and Stakeholder Bargaining Power', *Organization Science*, 10(2): 119–33.

COLEMAN, J. S. (1988). 'Social Capital in the Creation of Human Capital', *American Journal of Sociology*, 94(S): 95–120.

COLLIS, D. J., and MONTGOMERY, C. A. (1995). 'Competing on Resources: Strategy in the 1990s', *Harvard Business Review*, 73(4): 118–28.

COMBS, J. G., and SKILL, M. S. (2003). 'Managerialist and Human Capital Explanation for Key Executive Pay Premiums: A Contingency Perspective', *Academy of Management Journal*, 46(1): 63.

COTTON, J. L., VOLLRATH, D. A., FROGGATT, K. L., and LENGNICK, H. (1988). 'Employee Participation: Diverse Forms and Different Outcomes', *Academy of Management Review*, 13(1): 8–22.

CYERT, R. M., and MARCH, J. G. (1992). *A Behavioral Theory of the Firm* (2nd edn. Cambridge, Mass.: Blackwell; orig. publ. 1963).

DAHL, G. B., and RANSOM, M. R. (1999). 'Does Where you Stand Depend on Where you Sit? Tithing Donations and Self-Serving Beliefs', *American Economic Review*, 89(4): 703–27.

DELFGAAUW, J., and DUR, R. (2007). 'Signaling and Screening of Workers Motivation', *Journal of Economic Behavior and Organization*, 62(4): 605.

DITTMAN, D., JURIS, H., and REVSINE, L. (1976). 'On the Existence of Unrecorded Human Assets: An Economic Perspective', *Journal of Accounting Research* (Spring): 49–55.

FREY, B. S. (1993). 'Motivation as a Limit to Pricing', *Journal of Economic Psychology*, 14(4): 635.

—— (2002). 'Creativity, Government and the Arts', *De Economist*, 150(4): 363.

GOTTSCHALG, O., and ZOLLO, M. (2007). 'Interest Alignment and Competitive Advantage', *Academy of Management Review*, 32(2): 418–37.

GRANOVETTER, M. S. (1973). 'The Strength of Weak Ties', *American Journal of Sociology*, 78(6): 1360–80.

GREENBERG, J., and ORNSTEIN, S. (1983). 'High Status Job Title as Compensation for Underpayment: A Test of Equity Theory', *Journal of Applied Psychology*, 68(2): 285–97.

GROSSMAN, S. J., and HART, O. D. (1986). 'The Costs and Benefits of Ownership: A Theory of Vertical and Lateral Integration', *Journal of Political Economy*, 94(4): 691–719.

GROYSBERG, B., LEE, L.-E., and NANDA, A. (2008). 'Can they Take it with them? The Portability of Star Knowledge Workers' Performance', *Management Science*, 54(7): 1213.

HATCH, N. W., and DYER, J. H. (2004). 'Human Capital and Learning as a Source of Sustainable Competitive Advantage', *Strategic Management Journal*, 25(12): 1155.

HENDERSON, R., and COCKBURN, I. (1994). 'Measuring Competence? Exploring Firm Effects in Pharmaceutical Research', *Strategic Management Journal*, 15 (special issue): 63–84.

HININGS, C. R., HICKSON, D. J., PENNINGS, J. M., and SCHNECK, R. E. (1974). 'Structural Conditions of Intraorganizational Power', *Administrative Science Quarterly*, 19(1): 22–44.

HOM, P. W., CARANIKAS-WALKER, F., PRUSSIA, G. E., and GRIFFETH, R. W. (1992). 'A Meta-Analytical Structural Equations Analysis of a Model of Employee Turnover', *Journal of Applied Psychology*, 77(6): 890–909.

HUSELID, M. A. (1995). 'The Impact of Human Resource Management Practices on Turnover, Productivity, and Corporate Financial Performance', *Academy of Management Journal*, 38(3): 635–72.

JENSEN, M., and MECKLING, W. H. (1976). 'Theory of the Firm: Managerial Behavior Agency Costs and Ownership Structure', *Journal of Financial Economics*, 3: 305–60.

JUNG, K. G., DALESSIO, A., and JOHNSON, S. M. (1986). 'Stability of the Factor Structure of the Job Descriptive Index', *Academy of Management Journal*, 29(3): 609–16.

KERR, S. (1975). 'On the Folly of Rewarding A, While Hoping for B', *Academy of Management Journal*, 18(4): 769–84.

——(1995). 'On the Folly of Rewarding A, While Hoping for B', *Academy of Management Executive*, 9(1): 7–15.

——VON GLINOW, M., and SCHRIESHEIM, J. (1977). 'Issues in the Study of Professionals in Organizations: The Case of Scientists and Engineers', *Organizational Behavior and Human Performance*, 18: 329–45.

KIDWELL, R. E., and BENNETT, N. (1993). 'Employee Propensity to withhold Effort: A Conceptual Model to Intersect Three Avenues of Research', *Academy of Management Review*, 18(2): 429–56.

KLEIN, B., CRAWFORD, R. G., and ALCHIAN, A. A. (1978). 'Vertical Integration, Appropriable Rents and the Competitive Contracting Process', *Journal of Law and Economics*, 21: 297–326.

KOR, Y. Y., and LEBLEBICI, H. (2005). 'How do Interdependencies among Human-Capital Deployment, Development, and Diversification Strategies Affect Firms' Financial Performance?', *Strategic Management Journal*, 26(10): 967.

LADO, A. A., and WILSON, M. C. (1994). 'Human Resource Systems and Sustained Competitive Advantage: A Competency-Based Perspective', *Academy of Management Review*, 19(4): 699–727.

LEE, T., MITCHELL, T. R., WISE, L., and FIREMAN, S. (1996). 'An Unfolding Model of Voluntary Turnover', *Academy of Management Journal*, 39(1): 5–36.

LEVIN, D. Z., and CROSS, R. (2004). 'The Strength of Weak Ties you can Trust: The Mediating Role of Trust in Effective Knowledge Transfer', *Management Science*, 50(11): 1477.

LEWIS, M. (2004). *Moneyball: The Art of Winning an Unfair Game* (New York: W. W. Norton & Co.).

LIKERT, R. (1961). *New Patterns of Management* (New York: McGraw-Hill).

LIPPMAN, S. A., and RUMELT, R. P. (1982). 'Uncertain Imitability: An Analysis of Interfirm Differences in Efficiency Under Competition', *Bell Journal of Economics*, 13(2): 418–38.

LOUIE, T. A., CURREN, M. T., and HARICH, K. R. (2000). ' "I Knew we would Win": Hindsight Bias for Favorable and Unfavorable Team Decision Outcomes', *Journal of Applied Psychology*, 85(2): 264–72.

LOWENSTEIN, R. (1997). 'Microsoft and its Two Constituencies', *Wall Street Journal* (4 Dec.): C10.

MAHONEY, J. T. (2008). *Towards a Stakeholder Theory of Strategic Management* (Champaign and Urbana, Ill.: University of Illinois).

MAKADOK, R., and BARNEY, J. B. (2001). 'Strategic Factor Market Intelligence: An Application of Information Economics to Strategy Formulation and Competitor Intelligence', *Management Science*, 47(12): 1621–39.

MARBURGER, D. R. (1994). 'Bargaining Power and the Structure of Salaries in Major League Baseball', *Managerial and Decision Economics*, 15(5): 433–42.

MINTZBERG, H., and WATERS, J. A. (1985). 'Of Strategies, Deliberate and Emergent', *Strategic Management Journal*, 6(3): 257–72.

MOBLEY, W. H. (1982). *Employee Turnover: Causes Consequences, and Control* (Reading, Mass.: Addison-Wesley).

MOSAKOWSKI, E. (1997). 'Strategy Making under Causal Ambiguity: Conceptual Issues and Empirical Evidence', *Organization Science*, 8(4): 414–42.

MURDOCK, K. (2002). 'Intrinsic Motivation and Optimal Incentive Contracts', *Rand Journal of Economics*, 33(4): 650.

NAHAPIET, J., and GHOSHAL, S. (1998). 'Social Capital, Intellectual Capital, and the Organizational Advantage', *Academy of Management Review*, 23(2): 242–66.

O'REILLY, C. A. I., CALDWELL, D. F., and BARNETT, W. P. (1989). 'Work Group Demography, Social Integration, and Turnover', *Administrative Science Quarterly*, 34(1): 21–37.

OSTERLOH, M., and FREY, B. S. (2000). 'Motivation, Knowledge Transfer, and Organizational Forms', *Organization Science*, 11(5): 538–50.

OUCHI, W. (1980). 'Markets, Bureaucracies, and Clans', *Administrative Science Quarterly*, 25: 129–41.

PENROSE, E. T. (1959). *The Theory of the Growth of the Firm* (Oxford: Basil Blackwell).

PETERAF, M. A. (1993). 'The Cornerstones of Competitive Advantage: A Resource-based View', *Strategic Management Journal*, 14(3): 179–91.

PFEFFER, J. (1998). *The Human Equation: Building Profits by Putting People First* (Boston: Harvard University Press).

——and MOORE, W. L. (1980). 'Power in University Budgeting: A Replication and Extension', *Administrative Science Quarterly*, 25(3): 387–406.

POLANYI, M. (1966). *The Tacit Dimension* (New York: Anchor Day Books).

PORTER, M. E. (1985). *Competitive Advantage: Creating and Sustaining Superior Performance* (New York: Free Press).

——(1996). 'What is Strategy?', *Harvard Business Review*, 74(6): 61–78.

PRITCHARD, R. D., JONES, S. D., ROTH, P. L., STUEBING, K. K., and EKEBERG, S. E. (1988). 'Effects of Group Feedback, Goal Setting, and Incentives on Organizational Productivity', *Journal of Applied Psychology*, 73(2): 337–58.

RAELIN, J. A. (1991). *The Clash of Cultures: Managers Managing Professionals* (Boston: Harvard Business School Press).

REED, R., and DEFILLIPPI, R. J. (1990). 'Causal Ambiguity, Barriers to Imitation, and Sustainable Competitive Advantage', *Academy of Management Review*, 15(1): 88–102.

RICE, R. W., GENTILE, D. A., and MCFARLIN, D. B. (1991). 'Facet Importance and Job Satisfaction', *Journal of Applied Psychology*, 76(1): 31–9.

ROSS, L. (1977). 'The Intuitive Psychologist and his Shortcomings: Distortions in the Attribution Process', in L. BERKOWITZ (ed.), *Advances in Experimental Social Psychology* (New York: Academic Press), 174–214.

RUSBULT, C. E., FARRELL, D., ROGERS, G., and MAINOUS, A. G. I. (1988). 'Impact of Exchange Variables on Exit, Voice, Loyalty and Neglect: An Integrative Model of Responses to Declining Job Satisfaction', *Academy of Management Journal*, 31(3): 599–627.

SCARPELLO, V., and CAMPBELL, J. P. (1983). 'Job Satisfaction: Are All the Parts There?', *Personnel Psychology*, 36(3): 577–600.

SCHEIN, E. H. (1996). *Organizational Culture and Leadership* (2nd edn. San Francisco: Jossey-Bass).

SCHONBERG, U. (2007). 'Wage Growth Due to Human Capital Accumulation and Job Search: A Comparison between the United States and Germany', *Industrial and Labor Relations Review*, 60(4): 562.

SHAW, J. D., DUFFY, M. K., JOHNSON, J. L., and LOCKHART, D. E. (2005). 'Turnover, Social Capital Losses, and Performance', *Academy of Management Journal*, 48(4): 594.

SIMON, H. A. (1976). *Administrative Behavior* (3rd edn. New York: Free Press).

SMITH, D. E. (1986). 'Training Programs for Performance Appraisal: A Review', *Academy of Management Review*, 11(1): 22–40.

SPENCE, M. A. (1973). 'Job Market Signaling', *Quarterly Journal of Economics*, 87(3): 355–74.

STAW, B., MCKECHNIE, P. I., and PUFFER, S. M. (1983). 'The Justification of Organizational Performance', *Administrative Science Quarterly*, 28(4): 582–600.

TUSHMAN, M. L. (1977). 'Special Boundary Roles in the Innovation Process', *Administrative Science Quarterly*, 22(4): 587–605.

VROOM, V. H. (1964). *Work and Motivation* (New York: Wiley).

——and YETTON, P. W. (1973). *Leadership and Decision-Making* (Pittsburgh: University of Pittsburgh Press).

WAGNER, J. A. I., and GOODING, R. Z. (1987). 'Shared Influence and Organizational Behavior: A Meta-Analysis of Situational Variables Expected to Moderate Participation-Outcome Relationships', *Academy of Management Journal*, 30(3): 524–41.

WALDMAN, M. (1990). 'Up-or-Out Contracts: A Signaling Perspective', *Journal of Labor Economics*, 8(2): 230–50.

WANG, H. C., and BARNEY, J. B. (2006). 'Employee Incentives to Make Firm-Specific Investments: Implications for Resource-Based Theories of Corporate Diversification', *Academy of Management Review*, 31(2): 466–78.

WEISS, A. (1990). *Efficiency Wages: Models of Unemployment, Layoffs, and Wage Dispersion* (Princeton: Princeton University Press).

WERNERFELT, B. (1984). 'A Resource-Based View of the Firm', *Strategic Management Journal*, 5(2): 171–80.

YPEREN, N. W. V., and HAGEDOORN, M. (2003). 'Do High Job Demands Increase Intrinsic Motivation or Fatigue or Both? The Role of Job Control and Job Social Support', *Academy of Management Journal*, 46(3): 339.

ZACCARO, S. J., PETERSON, C., and WALKER, S. (1987). 'Self-Serving Attributions for Individual and Group Performance', *Social Psychology Quarterly*, 50(3): 257–63.

ZAJAC, E., and WESTPHAL, J. (1994). 'The Costs and Benefits of Managerial Incentives and Monitoring in Large U.S. Corporations: When is More Not Better?', *Strategic Management Journal*, 15(S2): 121–42.

ZUCKER, L. (1991). 'Markets for Bureaucratic Authority and Control: Information Quality in Professions and Services', in S. BARLEY and P. TOLBERT (eds.), *Research in the Sociology of Organizations: Organizations and the Professions* (Greenwich, Conn.: JAI Press).

CHAPTER 15

....

ACCOUNTING FOR HUMAN CAPITAL AND ORGANIZATIONAL EFFECTIVENESS

....

ROBIN KRAMAR

VIJAYA MURTHY

JAMES GUTHRIE

15.1 INTRODUCTION

....

In modern times, developed nations have seen a distinguishable movement in terms of the important economic activities that constitute gross domestic product (GDP). Today, these nations are far less reliant upon either traditional primary (resource-based) commodities or even secondary (low value-added) commodities, such as manufactured goods. In these economies, the emphasis is on service activities and intangible-based outputs (Petty and Guthrie, 2000). Moreover, with the rise of economies driven by knowledge, information, and changing patterns of interpersonal activities, intellectual capital is of greater importance.

The growth of the knowledge economy and the realization of the importance of understanding intellectual and human capital have been reflected in the accounting literature (Barth *et al.*, 2001; Boedker *et al.*, 2005). Frameworks to account for intellectual capital that contain human capital measures have been developed, including the

Balanced Scorecard (Kaplan *et al.*, 1992) and the Intangible Asset Monitor (Sveiby, 1997). In addition, frameworks known as extended performance reports—which include measures such as workforce demographics, workforce competency profiles, and numbers of staff enrolled in training, leadership, and education courses—provide another way of accounting for human capital (SKE, 2005; GRI, 2006; Boedker *et al.*, 2007).

The development of the knowledge-based economy requires management to approach its resources from a different perspective, especially with respect to human capital. Human capital has been shown to contribute to an organization's performance and competitive advantage, and therefore to provide evidence of future organizational value and sustainability (for instance, Barney and Wright, 1998; Becker *et al.*, 2001; Dunphy and Griffiths, 1998; Pfeffer and O'Reilly, 2000). However, research indicates that managerial awareness of the importance of human capital is still low, although there has been a shift from the traditional perception of work environments as cost centers towards a situation where the knowledge and skills of employees are considered as key elements of an organization (Roslender, 2008).

In the future, organizations may depend more heavily on the human dimension, and therefore it is likely that human capital and its management, measurement and reporting will be critical to the success of all public or private organizations. Accounting for human capital has developed over the last forty-five years from a focus on cost and investment in individuals and education (Becker, 1965) to a broader approach (Roslender, 2008). Such an approach involves accounting for knowledge, information, culture, values, skills, links to the community, practices to improve the environment, and customer service (Morgan, 2006).

This chapter is structured as follows. The next section sets the background and context by providing the definition of human capital and discussing the various attempts made by researchers and scholars to account for human capital. The third section discusses the several challenges faced by scholars and practitioners in their attempt to account for human capital. Section 4 discusses contemporary frameworks that attempt to overcome these challenges. The fifth section provides a discussion that draws together the threads of the argument, and the final section summarizes the key points, identifying implications for research and practice and possible future direction.

15.2 Understanding Human Capital: Definition and History

There are several concepts central to this chapter. A broad, overarching concept is intellectual capital. The resources of organizations can be considered in terms of tangible physical resources such as financial resources, plant, and equipment. But organizational resources also include intellectual capital (such as brands, reputation, copyright, culture, organizational processes, and relationships with customers).

The term 'intellectual capital' has been used to represent knowledge resources (Guthrie and Kramar, 2004; Baron and Armstrong, 2007). Intellectual capital refers specifically to flows of knowledge available to the organization. This knowledge can involve explicit knowledge, which is written down or verbalized, and tacit knowledge, which is based on intuition, emotion and belief (Nonaka, 1991). Intellectual capital has been categorised using a tripartite framework (Petty and Guthrie, 2000; Ricceri and Guthrie, 2008). These categories include human capital, relational capital, and organizational capital. Human capital usually refers to employee capability, knowledge, innovation, adaptability, experience, and education.

Relational/relationship capital captures relationships with external parties such as customers, suppliers, company reputation and brands, distribution channels, licensing agreements, and franchising agreements. Organizational capital can be regarded as value arising from internal structures represented in intellectual property and infrastructure assets (Guthrie and Kramar, 2004).

Human Capital Accounting was defined by the American Accounting Association (1973) as 'the process of identifying and measuring data about human resources and communicating this information to the interested parties'. While human capital accounting in the initial years was based on placing a value for people in the balance sheet, more recently, human capital accounting is no longer seen to be about financial statements (Gröjer and Johanson, 1998; Verma and Dewe, 2008). Although there is no precise agreement on the concept of human capital, researchers claim that a broad approach needs to be adopted (Bassi and McMurrer, 2005; Berkowitz, 2001). For instance, Roslender and Dyson (1992) suggest that human capital accounting needs to take the approach of accounting for strategic positioning that highlights the competitive advantage of human capital and organizational effectiveness. This is because senior management is increasingly recognizing the worth of its human capital, and the accountancy profession is faced with the challenge of providing some form of accounting information on human capital.

The purpose of this section is to briefly outline the development of human capital accounting since the 1960s, focusing on authors, concepts and key themes. Table 15.1 highlights various frameworks developed since that time. It is noted that there are six main stages in the development of human capital accounting.

The significance of human capital (labor) was recognized in the eighteenth century by Adam Smith, who included labor as one of the factors of production used in the creation of goods and services that contributed to the wealth of nations (Smith, 1776). In the early twentieth century Paton (1922) called for the recognition of personnel as important 'assets' of a successful organization.

As indicated in Table 15.1, we start with the 1960s, in which the first attempts were made to account for the 'human element' in the form of Human Asset Accounting (Becker, 1965; Hekimian and Jones, 1967; Hermanson, 1964; Johnson, 1960; Likert,

Table 15.1. Contemporary Developments of Human Capital Accounting

Proponents	Concept	Focus	Themes
Schultz (1961) Johnson (1960) Becker (1965) Hermanson (1964) Hekimian and Jones (1967) Likert (1967)	Form of capital to be included as a balance-sheet item	Financial accounting External reporting only. Projecting human resources in monetary terms.	Human asset accounting
Brummet et al. (1968) Flamholtz (1971, 1974) Lev and Swartz (1971) Fadel (1977) Scarpello and Theeke (1989)	Information on human resources required for management decisions	Financial and management accounting. Development of theories and models. Internal reporting purposes. Projecting human resources in monetary terms.	Human resource accounting
Johanson and Mabon (1998) Gröjer and Johanson (1998a, 1998b)	Human resources cost/benefit analysis based on utility analysis	Interdisciplinary perspective (labor economics, social democratic philosophy) to human resource accounting. Monetary measurement of human factor. Management accounting focus.	Human resource costing and accounting
Roslender and Dyson (1992)	Accounting for human capital worth positioned parallel to strategic management accounting. Move from hard financial numbers.	Call to transcend distinctions between financial and management accounting. Introduction of soft accounting information. Quantitative non-monetary measurement. Interdisciplinary approach (management studies and sociological perspectives).	Human worth accounting

(continued)

Table 15.1. Continued

Proponents	Concept	Focus	Themes
Sveiby (1998) Edvinsson (1997) Bontis et al. (1999) Kaplan and Norton (1992) Andriensson and Tiessen (2000) Lev (2001) Mouritsen et al. (2001)	Human capital as an intangible knowl-edge asset. Different frameworks developed to measure intellectual capital.	Contemporary accounting involving off-balance-sheet values to measure relationship among people, ideas and knowledge. People seen as 'revenue creators' and not as 'cost'. Reports produced both for internal management and external reporting. Recommend the use of narratives in human capital accounting. Move from quantitative measures to qualitative and narrative measures.	Human competences (as a part of intellectual capital statements).
SKE (2005) GRI (2006)	'Best practices' tools and guidelines to address the needs of organizations requiring contemporary measurement systems. Frameworks for reporting on economic, environmental and social performance.	Qualitative and subjective account for both internal and external reporting. Recognition of the challenge to create a consistent report and measurement metrics. Use of performance indicators.	Human capital accounting (embedded in social accounting)

1967; Schultz, 1961). These researchers pointed out the need for recognizing the skills and knowledge of human beings as a form of capital that generated the productive superiority of advanced countries (Schultz 1961; Johnson 1960). These pioneer studies focused on ideas to include human capital in the balance sheet by assigning quantitative financial numbers to human resources.

The second stage was Human Resource Accounting, when accountants realized that they had traditionally treated outlays for human resources as 'expenses' and not as 'assets' (Brummet et al., 1968). In the 1970s, researchers were involved in developing human resource accounting theories and models, such as human asset multiplier theory (Giles and Robinson, 1972), normative model for human resource valuation (Flamholtz, 1971), and economic theory (Lev and Schwartz, 1971). Flamholtz (1972) considered the need for non-monetary accounting information to determine the value of people (economic, social, and psychological) and their interrelationships in a formal organization, and developed a model called the theory of human resource value that formed a preliminary framework for understanding the nature and determinants of a person's value to the organization.

Scarpello and Theeke (1989) highlighted the limited focus of Flamholtz's engagement with the measurement issues based on cost and value models and projecting human resources in monetary terms. The ensuing debate led researchers of human resource accounting to move towards non-monetary measures for internal management purposes. Throughout the 1980s, interest in accounting for people declined, but it never disappeared (Sackmann et al., 1989; Scarpello and Theeke, 1989). Human resource accounting was primarily viewed as a tool for decision-making that helped management to plan and control human resources effectively and efficiently (Boudreau, 1983; Cascio and Ramos, 1986; Gul, 1984; Harrell, 1980; Hunter and Schmidt, 1982; Ogan, 1988).

The third stage dates from the early 1990s when researchers in Sweden developed the area of 'Human Resource Costing and Accounting', but its impact was restricted to Scandinavian countries. The Swedish researchers formed the Institute of Personnel Economics in 1988 to research in the area of human resource accounting (Johanson and Mabon, 1998) under the term 'human resource costing and accounting' (HRCA).

A fourth stage developed in the early 1990s, when Roslender and Dyson (1992) revived the interest in accounting for people, giving it a new name: 'Human Worth Accounting'. They recommended the use of soft accounting information rather than hard financial numbers. They argued that in the past, research had been focused on the measurement aspects of cost and value rather than on the management of human capital.

The fifth stage in human capital accounting was developed by Sveiby (1997), who advocated the use of non-financial measures in conjunction with financial measures in accounting for intangibles and human capital. His emphasis was on Human Competences. Sveiby developed the Intangible Asset Monitor—a framework that could be adopted and used as a tool for organizational learning rather than as a new management control system (Sveiby, 1998). The flexibility of the Intangible Asset Monitor allowed it to be tailor-made to fit the implementing organization (Bontis et al., 1999).

In this period, Swedish organizations were dominating the field of accounting for human capital (as a part of intellectual capital), and published several intellectual capital statements as supplements to their external annual reports. Some examples are the Intangible Asset Monitor published by Celemi, and the Intellectual Capital Index published by Skandia. Many more tools for managing knowledge and intangibles, such as the Balanced Scorecard (Kaplan and Norton, 1992), Value Chain Scoreboard (Lev, 2001), The Value Explorer (Andriensson and Tiessen, 2000), to name a few, were developed in the 1990s and widely tested and refined by researchers.

Although this decade witnessed improvements in accounting for human capital, the argument around the nature and measurement of human resources persisted. Bontis et al. (1999), for instance, considered human resource accounting as a storehouse of tools available to the management for managing intangibles. Cascio (1998) moved from the narrow definition of human resource accounting and argued that human resources should be measured in terms of their strategic management potential, utilizing both financial and non-financial measures.

In the sixth stage, Human Capital Accounting is linked with social accounting. In Australia, the Society for Knowledge Economics (SKE) published *The Australian Guiding Principles to Extended Performance Management*. The SKE recognized the drawbacks of traditional financial accounting and introduced an 'extended performance account' in an attempt to 'make visible' knowledge-intensive resources. It is a one-page account, which provides a summary of the value and performance of the organization's knowledge-intensive resources (including human capital) and activities relating to its strategic objectives. It was acknowledged that, given the value-laden and qualitative nature of (intangible) human resources, it is a challenge to create consistent reporting and measurement metrics (DISR, 2001; Mouritsen, 2007; SKE, 2005).

In the Netherlands the Global Reporting Initiative (GRI) was developed, consisting of a multi-stakeholder network from different countries, with the aim of creating and continuously improving 'sustainability reporting'. The Sustainability Reporting Framework thus developed provides guidelines for organizations disclosing economic, environmental, and social information (GRI, 2006). The guidelines include standard disclosures made up of non-financial performance indicators, and other disclosure items on human capital such as total number and rate of employee turnover by age, gender, and region, workforce represented in formal joint management–worker health and safety committees, rate of injury, occupational disease, lost days, absenteeism, education, training, counselling, risk-control programs to assist employees, their families, or community, percentage of employees receiving regular performance and career development reviews, and the ratio of basic salary of men and women employees by category (GRI, 2006).

There is little doubt that accounting for human capital has been considered important for the past four decades. But concentrating on the reduction of costs has been the foremost measure of human resources performance, and has resulted in human capital being managed as a commodity rather than as a strategic asset. Managing a workforce effectively is an underlying source of 'value creation' that increases shareholder value by differentiating the organization from its primary competitors (Becker and Huselid, 2003). This is recognized in the emerging work on human capital analysis which provides frameworks for demonstrating the value of qualitative data to security analysts (Royal and O'Donnell, 2005; O'Donnell *et al.*, 2009). Therefore, contemporary human capital accounting should focus on measuring human resources' strategic performance, and not limit itself to non-strategic measures such as cost reduction or benefits of hire as a percentage of revenue.

In summary, the more contemporary frameworks gave a 'new' perspective to human capital accounting, pointing towards moving beyond financial numbers in the balance sheet. They highlight the importance of incorporating qualitative measures using narratives and non-financial indicators. While there is ongoing debate about accounting for human capital and the techniques that should be used, academics and practitioners agree that accounting for human capital allows for the growth and development of people and contributes to organizations' growth (Verma and Dewe, 2008).

15.3 HUMAN CAPITAL CHALLENGES

In order for management to confront the issues of managing intellectual capital—and particularly human capital—the first challenge that managers must recognize is the identification of the factors that are critical for sustainable competitive advantage and which contribute to the current and future value creation of an organization. The Resource-Based View (RBV) of the firm (Penrose, 1959) focuses on the way organizations can combine clusters of tangible and intangible resources, such as human and technical resources, in a unique way, and build sustainable, competitive performance (Barney, 1991; Boxall and Purcell, 2003: 72).

A second challenge for organizations is in facing the risk of having insufficient intellectual capital and human capital both now and in the future. Changing population and workforce demographics in developed economies and the rapid expansion of economies such as China and India are contributing to a shortage of skilled people in many knowledge economies (SKE, 2005). Therefore, a major challenge for many organizations is, and will continue to be, having sufficient talented people with the necessary capabilities for the organization to be effective.

A third challenge is that in accounting practice, employees are treated as a cost and are therefore managed so that costs are minimized. In recent decades, large organizations have claimed that human resource practices are used to attract, develop, motivate, and retain people as a way of achieving organizational strategy and to therefore ensure that sufficient people are available to perform the activities required by the organization. Although the academic literature on human resource management claims that employees are an asset which create future value (Beer et al., 1984; Dyer and Singh, 1998; De Cieri and Kramar, 2008), they are still treated as an expense. This is shown to have a negative impact on organizational performance, particularly when downsizing or mergers take place.

A fourth challenge is the development of individual competencies that could be suitably aligned to organizational objectives. The management of human capital, with a view to leveraging the skills of employees to create value to the organization, is important in a knowledge-based world. Unlike physical, financial, intellectual, and other property over which an organization has rights of ownership, its ability to create value through the skills and commitment of its people depends upon the quality of its relationship with them. Competent human capital management would strengthen those relationships so as to support the organization's strategies by focusing on the impact of intrinsic factors such as motivation and retention, skills development and organizational culture among others (Kingsmill, 2003). Physical health and psychological well-being play a crucial role in an individual's capability to be efficient and innovative, and are intermediate steps on the pathway to an organization's profitability (Nielsen et al., 2007).

Finally, it has still not been empirically proven that there is a causal link between human capital accounting to human resource practices and organizational performance. Research in a variety of industries has demonstrated that 'bundles' of human resource practices contribute to an organization's financial success (Becker and Huselid, 1999; Delery and Doty, 1996; Foong and Yorston, 2003; Huselid et al., 1997). These 'bundles' of human resource practices include empowerment practices (such as decision-making, decentralization, harmonization of status, rotation, and internal flexibility), remuneration practices, training practices, competency development, and practices related to sharing and circulating information (Barraud-Didier and Guerrero, 2002). These human resource practices have been shown to build unique cultures, which encourage flexibility, discretionary effort, and trust (Pfeffer and O'Reilly, 2000; Dunphy and Griffiths, 1998; Ricceri, 2008). But since there is little empirical evidence to establish that human capital accounting could help in the development of these bundles, there is a lack of enthusiasm among practitioners to adopt the existing human capital accounting frameworks.

Overarching the challenges outlined in this section is a major challenge, as traditional accounting has a profound bias towards tangible assets. Traditional accounting's narrow focus towards financial numbers and short-sighted cost reductions compromises the future competitiveness and survival of organizations (Miller,

1999). The means to overcome this shortcoming is the development of a reporting framework that will manage and measure human capital competences. Several frameworks which attempt this are outlined in the next section.

15.4 HUMAN RESOURCE FRAMEWORKS

Human resource frameworks have been developed in an attempt to provide insights into human capital. These include competency frameworks, benchmarking studies, human capital management systems, and surveys such as engagement surveys. These frameworks capture information about the attributes of employees, human resource practices, and employee attitudes. The information captured in these frameworks provides information about the extent to which the employees are able to, and enabled by organizational practices to, contribute to an organization's effectiveness. Several of these will now be discussed in detail.

First, competency frameworks are a way of capturing the particular types of attributes possessed by employees. A competency is an underlying characteristic of a person which produces effective or superior performance in a role. Competencies are usually considered in terms of two categories: generic competencies and technical competencies. Generic competencies apply in a general context, such as an organization, an occupation, or a wide range of jobs. An example of the generic competencies identified in a competency framework for managers includes:

- intellectual competence which involves a strategic perspective, analytical power, commercial judgment, and planning ability;
- interpersonal competence which includes persuasiveness, managing employees, assertiveness and decisiveness, communication skills, and interpersonal sensitivity;
- achievement orientation which includes personal drive, impact, initiative, and organizing capability; and
- adaptability, which includes flexibility and resilience.

Technical competencies are more specific and refer to those attributes, or skills and abilities, required to perform a particular role, such as human resources manager. Included among the technical competencies required by a human resources manager are knowledge of legislation, such as occupational safety and health, knowledge of providers of human resource services, and an ability to identify human resource issues that impact on the business. Competencies are therefore a form of human capital necessary for the organization to attain competitive advantage. Competency frameworks have the potential to provide organizations with information about the stock of competencies which they possess. These frameworks can be applied when recruiting, selecting, and assessing employees' performance.

Second, benchmarking studies provide a way of accounting for aspects of human capital which contributes to organizational capital. Extensive research by large consulting companies reveals similar links. Watson Wyatt, through its Human Capital Index, Accenture's Human Capital Development Framework, Mercer's Business Impact Modelling, and Hewitt's The People Practices Inventory used as part of their Best Employer awards, indicate a link between particular human resource practices and company success. Organizations are able to benchmark the human resource practices they use against the human resource practices identified by researchers and consulting companies as a way of determining the extent to which they have captured processes.

Third, Human Capital Management Systems focus on the processes of managing and developing human capital to improve organizational performance. Human Capital Management systems can use metrics to measure human capital. This enables the value of the human capital attributes to be not only measured but to be used as an input into the management of organizations.

Baron and Armstrong (2007) propose a three-phase model of human capital management. The first phase focuses on identifying the drivers or needs of the business. The second phase requires development of a human capital management process that involves measuring, reporting, and assessing the significance of the measurements of human capital drivers such as retention and motivation, leadership and succession planning, remuneration and fair employment practices, and size and composition of the workforce. The third phase uses the assessment as a way of developing an action plan to refine the human capital business drivers. Therefore, a human capital management system is another way of measuring the value of human capital.

The fourth framework to be reviewed is surveys, which provide another method of measuring human capital. Employers have been using surveys for many years to assess employee attitudes, employee engagement, and organizational culture and climate. The surveys are believed to provide a check on the 'health' of the organization; that is, research suggests that there is a correlation between employee characteristics such as employee satisfaction and organizational performance. Surveys of employee engagement measure an employee's emotional commitment to an organization, and this commitment is reflected in employee pride, discretionary effort, productivity, and retention. Organizations with high employee engagement are also favored as places to work. Consequently, the results of engagement surveys are a way of measuring particular aspects of human capital. A high employee engagement score represents a positive measure of human capital.

Rust et al. (1996) claimed that improving employee satisfaction is instrumental in decreasing employee turnover, and suggested that it is critical for contemporary organizations to measure employee satisfaction. This gives rise to the need to address issues such as people's motivation, competencies, and personal development needs (such as career development aspirations, work–life balance, physical and mental health, and work-ability). The complexity of accounting for human capital increases substantially, since such intangibles cannot be objectively measured (Johanson *et al.*, 2007: 22).

There is emerging evidence that reporting on particular human resource systems can provide information about the drivers of the intangible value of organizations. For instance, recruitment systems can be indicators of growth, training and development systems indicators of renewal, and career and succession planning indicators of stability. These systems of human resource practices can then also be regarded as part of the human capital of the organization and can be accounted for in a qualitative way (O'Donnell *et al.*, 2009).

15.5 Discussion

In a knowledge society, people are the dominant creators of wealth, and the survival/success of the organization depends on the efficiency of their knowledge workforce. In an era that is witnessing scarcity of talented employees, an organization can be successful only by managing its existing human capital to deliver greater productivity and organizational effectiveness. Employees are not treated any more as 'labor' but as 'stock of capital'. As Drucker (2002) points out, what is decisive in performance of capital is not what it costs, but the productivity of the capital. Therefore, it is important for organizations to focus on the productivity of their capital—human capital.

To enable management to concentrate on the productivity of their human capital, accounting for human capital must take an alternative approach with a broad focus. The existing financial accounting statements identify human capital as a 'stock' of expenses. This does not bring out the value of the employees nor does it explain their attributes such as skills, competencies, experience, education, motivation, commitment, or the relationship existing between the employee and the organization. Contemporary accounting for human capital that includes non-financial indicators and narratives may therefore be adopted to assist management to face the challenge of developing, communicating, monitoring, and evaluating the organization's human capital effectiveness.

Therefore, the pivotal argument of this chapter is the need for different ways to strategically account for human capital by focusing on the differentiation tactics and developing alternatives to traditional accounting. To manage knowledge-based resources—in particular, human capital—the 'value' of human capital needs to be conceptualized by alternative models to traditional (financial) accounting. It should be noted that quantitative measures could never picture the interrelations of organizational developments and performance of employees, but can form the starting point for management debate (Litschka *et al.*, 2006). Non-financial indicators, on the other hand, would assist in defining, measuring, and evaluating the initiatives taken by management. The narratives would perform the role of linking the initiatives to the knowledge resources and show the types of knowledge resources that would be required to enhance human capital productivity and thus create value for the organization. A combination of non-financial indicators and narratives would thus be a way forward in human capital accounting for contemporary organizations.

15.6 SUMMARY

To summarize, in today's economy human resource development is too important for firms to ignore or to leave to someone else. The quality and productivity of a firm's human resources are fundamental to its competitive advantage and its ability to move beyond competing solely on the basis of natural resources (Crocombe *et al.*, 1991). For organizations to be successful, it is important that their human capital is recognized as a key source of competitive advantage, and their human capital functions should be managed effectively. The human capital management functions are aided by accounting for human capital. Human capital accounting should therefore be considered as a further development in accounting to achieve competitive advantage; in other words, accounting for strategic positioning (Roslender and Dyson, 1992).

Accounting for human capital has been developing for over four decades and is divided into six stages: human asset accounting, human resource accounting, human resource costing and accounting, human worth accounting, human competences as a part of intellectual capital accounting, and human capital accounting. The developments in human capital accounting have brought researchers and practitioners to a consensus that accounting for human capital is important and necessary, but it has seldom been translated into practice. This is because human capital poses many challenges that make it difficult to account for.

In an attempt to combat the various human capital challenges, different human capital frameworks have been developed and tested by academics and practitioners. These include competency frameworks, benchmarking studies, human capital management systems, and engagement surveys. These frameworks have been able to provide only partial solutions. Therefore, it is suggested that accounting for human capital should encompass financial and non-financial indicators and also use narratives in order to bring out the value of human capital.

This chapter has several implications for practice and research. First, recent developments suggest linking human capital accounting to social accounting, and new forms of accounts, such as 'extended performance accounts' and 'global reporting initiatives', have been developed (Guthrie et al., 2007; Yongvanich and Guthrie, 2006). In the future, studies could be conducted to empirically test the use of these new forms of accounts and the use of qualitative and narrative measures suggested by these new developments. Further studies should be conducted to test the effect of these measures in the success of an organization's performance and organizational effectiveness.

Second, though there is evidence that managing human capital is a key to organizational effectiveness, there is a dearth of research showing the link between human capital management and human capital accounting and how these could lead to successful organizational performance. Empirical research could be conducted to determine causal links between human capital management and human capital accounting. Further studies could be conducted to test the association between human capital accounting and organizational effectiveness.

REFERENCES

AMERICAN ACCOUNTING ASSOCIATION (1973). 'Report of the Committee on Human Resource Accounting', *Accounting Review*, 48: 169–185 (suppl.).

ANDRIENSSON, D., and Tiessen. (2000). *Weightless Wealth: Find your Real Value in a Future of Intangible Assets*. London: Pearson Education.

BARNEY, J. (1991) 'Firm Resources and Sustained Competitive Advantage', *Journal of Management*, 17(1): 99–120.

——and WRIGHT, P. M. (1998). 'On Becoming a Strategic Partner: The Role of Human Resources in Gaining Competitive Advantage', *Human Resource Management*, 37(1): 31–46.

BASSI, L., and McMURRER, D. (2005). 'What to Do when People are your Most Important Asset', *Handbook of Business Strategy*, 6(1): 219–24.

BARON, A. and ARMSTRONG, M. (2007). *Human Capital Management: Achieving Added Value through People* (London: Kogan Page).

BARTH, M. E., KASZNIK, R., and McNICHOLS, M. F. (2001). 'Analyst Coverage and Intangible Assets', *Journal of Accounting Research*, 39(1): 1–34.

BARRAUD-DIDIER, V., and GUERRERO, S. (2002). 'Impact of Social Innovations on French Companies' Performance: A Study of High-Involvement Practices', *Measuring Business Excellence*, 6(2): 42–8.

BECKER, B. E., and HUSELID, M. A. (1999). 'Overview: Strategic Human Resource Management in Five Leading Firms', *Human Resource Management*, 38(4): 287–301.

BECKER, G. S. (1965). *Human Capital* (2nd edn. New York: Columbia University Press).

——and HUSELID, M. A. (2003). 'Measuring HR?' (cover story), *HR Magazine*, 48(12): 56–61.

—— ——and ULRICH, D. (2001). *The HR Scorecard* (Cambridge, Mass.: Harvard Business School Press).

BEER, M., SPECTOR, B., LAWRENCE, P., QUINN MILLS, D., and WALTON, R. (1984). *Managing Human Assets* (New York: Free Press).

BERKOWITZ, S. J. (2001). 'Measuring and Reporting Human Capital', *Journal of Government Financial Management*, 50(3): 12.

BOEDKER, C., GUTHRIE, J., and CUGANESAN, S. (2005). 'An Integrated Framework for Visualising Intellectual Capital', *Journal of Intellectual Capital*, 6(4): 510–27.

——— BINNEY, D. and GUTHRIE, J. (2007). *New Pathways to Prosperity: International Trends and Developments in Extended Performance Management, Measurement and Reporting* (Sydney: Society for Knowledge Economics).

BONTIS, N., DRAGONETTI, N. A., JACOBSEN, K., and ROOS, G. (1999). 'The Knowledge Toolbox: A Review of the Tools Available to Measure and Manage Intangible Resources', *European Management Journal*, 17(4): 391–402.

BOUDREAU, J. W. (1983). 'Effects of Employee Flows on Utility Analysis of Human Resource Productivity Improvements Program', *Journal of Applied Psychology*, 68: 396–406.

BOXALL, P., and PURCELL, J. (2003). *Strategy and Human Resource Management* (Basingstoke: Palgrave Macmillan).

BRUMMET, L. R., FLAMHOLTZ, E., and PYLE, W. C. (1968). 'Human Resource Measurement: A Challenge for Accountants', *Accounting Review*, 43(2): 217–24.

CASCIO, W. F. (1998). 'The Future World of Work: Implications for Human Resources Costing and Accounting', *Journal of Human Resource Costing and Accounting*, 3(2): 9–19.

———and RAMOS, R. A. (1986). 'Development and Application of a New Method for Assessing Job Performance in Behavioural/Economic Terms', *Journal of Applied Psychology*, 71: 20–8.

CROCOMBE, G. T., ENRIGHT, M. J., and PORTER, M. E. (1991). *Upgrading New Zealand's Competitive Advantage* (Auckland: Oxford University Press).

DE CIERI, H., and KRAMAR, R. (2008). *Human Resource Management in Australia* (Sydney: McGraw-Hill).

DELERY, J., and DOTY, D. H. (1996). 'Modes of Theorizing in Strategic Human Resource Management: Tests of Universalistic, Contingency, and Configurational Performance Predictions', *Academy of Management Journal*, 39(4): 802–35.

DISR (2001). *Invisible Value: The Case for Measuring and Reporting Intellectual Capital* (Canberra: Department of Industry, Science and Resources).

DRUCKER, P. (2002). 'They're Not Employees, They're People', *Harvard Business Review*, 80(2): 70–7.

DUNPHY, D., and GRIFFITHS, A. (1998). *The Sustainable Corporation: Organisational Renewal in Australia* (Sydney: Allen & Unwin).

DYER, J. H., and SINGH, H. (1998). 'The Relational View: Co-operative Strategy and Sources of Interorganizational Competitive Advantage', *Academy of Management Review*, 23(4): 660–79.

FLAMHOLTZ, E. (1971). 'A Model for Human Resource Valuation: A Stochastic Process with Service Rewards', *Accounting Review*, 46(2): 253–67.

——— (1972). 'On the Use of the Economic Concept of Human Capital in Financial Statements: A Comment', *Accounting Review*, 47(1): 148–52.

FOONG, K., and YORSTON, R. (2003). 'Human Capital Measurement and Reporting: A British Perspective'. URL: http://www.berr.gov.uk/files/file38840.pdf (accessed Feb. 2008).

GILES, W. J., and ROBINSON, D. F. (1972). *Human Asset Accounting* (London: Institute of Personnel Management and Institute of Cost and Management Accountants).

GRI (2006). *Sustainability Reporting Guidelines* (Amsterdam: Global Reporting Initiative).

GRI G3 Guidelines. (2006). *Sustainability Reporting Guidelines* (Amsterdam: Global Reporting Initiative).

GRÖJER, J.-E., and JOHANSON, U. (1998a). 'Current Development in Human Resource Costing and Accounting: Reality Present, Researchers Absent?', *Accounting, Auditing and Accountability Journal*, 11: 495–506.

GUL, F. A. (1984). 'An Empirical Study of the Usefulness of Human Resources Turnover Costs in Australian Accounting Firms', *Accounting, Organisations and Society*, 9(3/4): 233–9.

GUTHRIE, J., and KRAMAR, R. (2004). 'Measuring and Managing Human Capital', in *Australian Master Human Resources Guide: For HR and Line Managers* (3rd edn. Sydney: CCH), 315–34.

GUTHRIE, J., CUGANESAN, S., and WARD, L. (2007). 'Extended Performance Reporting: Evaluating Corporate Social Responsibility and Intellectual Capital management', *Issues in Social and Environmental Accounting*, 1(1): 1–25.

HARRELL, A. M. (1980). 'Comparing the Impact of Monetary and Nonmonetary Human Asset Measures on Executive Decision-Making', *Accounting, Organisations and Society*, 5(4): 393–400.

HEKIMIAN, J., and JONES, C. H. (1967). 'Put People in your Balance Sheet', *Harvard Business Review*, 45(1): 105–13.

HERMANSON, R. H. (1964). *Accounting for Human Assets* (East Lansing, Mich.: Bureau of Business and Economic Research, Graduate School of Business Administration, Michigan State University).

HUNTER, J. E., and SCHMIDT, F. L. (1982). 'Fitting People to Jobs: The Impact of Personnel Selection on National Productivity', in M. D. Dunnette and E. A. Fleischman (eds.), *Human Capability Assessment* (Hillsdale, NJ: Erlbaum), 223–72.

HUSELID, M. A., JACKSON, S., and SCHULER, R. (1997). 'Technical and Strategic Human Resource Management Effectiveness as Determinants to Firm Performance', *Academy of Management Journal*, 40(1): 171–88.

JOHANSON, U., and MABON, H. (1998). 'The Personnel Economics Institute After Ten Years: What have we Achieved and Where are we Going to', *Journal of Human Resource Costing and Accounting*, 3(2): 65–76.

——AHONEN, G., and ROSELENDER, R. (2007). 'What this Book is About and Not About', in U. Johanson, G. Ahonen and R. Roselender (eds.), *Work Health and Management Control* (Stockholm: Thomson Fakta).

JOHNSON, H. G. (1960). 'The Political Economy of Opulence', *Canadian Journal of Economics and Political Science*, 26(4): 552–64.

KAPLAN, R. S., and NORTON, D. P. (1992). 'The Balanced Scorecard: Measures that Drive Performance', *Harvard Business Review*, 70(1): 71–9.

KINGSMILL, D. (2003). *Accounting for People Report* (London: Secretary of State for Trade and Industry).

LEV, B. (2001). *Intangibles: Management, Measurement and Reporting* (Washington, DC: Brooking Institution Press).

——and SCHWARTZ, A. (1971). 'On the Use of the Economic Concept of Human Capital in Financial Statements', *Accounting Review*, 46(1): 103–13.

LIKERT, R. (1967). *The Human Organisation: Its Management and Value* (New York: McGraw-Hill Book Co.).

LITSCHKA, M., MARKOM, A., and SCHUNDER, S. (2006). 'Measuring and Analysing Intellectual Assets: An Integrative Approach', *Journal of Intellectual Capital*, 7(2): 160–73.

MILLER, P. (1999). 'Governing the Enterprise: The Hidden Face of Accounting', in T. Porter and D. Ross (eds.), *The Cambridge History of Science*, vii. *Modern Social and Behavioural Science* (Cambridge: Cambridge University Press).

MORGAN, D. (2006). 'It's Not All Profits', *Sydney Morning Herald* (12th Apr.).

MOURITSEN, J. (2007). 'Intellectual Capital and the Choices towards the Future', in C. Charminade and B. Catasus (eds.), *Intellectual Capital Revisited: Paradoxes in the Knowledge-Based Organization* (Cheltenham: Edward Elgar), 166–88.

NIELSEN, C., HUSSI, T., SCHUNDER-TATZBER, S., ROSLENDER, R., and AHONEN, G. (2007). 'The Interrelations between Health and Intellectual Capital', in U. Johanson, G. Ahonen and R. Roselender (eds.), *Work Health and Management Control* (Stockholm: Thomson Fakta).

NONAKA, I. (1991). 'The Knowledge Creating Company', *Harvard Business Review* 69(3) (Nov.–Dec.): 96–104.

O'DONNELL, L., KRAMAR, R., and CADIZ DYBALL, M. (2009). 'Human Capital Reporting: Should it be Industry Specific?', *Asia Pacific Journal of Human Resources*, 47(3) (Dec.): 358–73.

OGAN, P. (1988). 'Assessing the Impact of Human Resource Accounting Information on Managerial Decisions: A Field Experiment', *Personnel Review* (Mar.): 29–35.

PATON, W. A. (1922). *Accounting Theory* (New York: Ronald Press).

PENROSE, E. (1959). *Theory of the Growth of the Firm* (Oxford: Blackwell).

PETTY, R., and GUTHRIE, J. (2000). 'Intellectual Capital Literature Review: Measurement, Reporting and Management', *Journal of Intellectual Capital*, 1(2): 155–76.

PFEFFER, J., and O'REILLY, C. A. (2000). *Hidden Value: How Great Companies Achieve Extraordinary Results with Ordinary People* (Boston: Harvard University Press).

RICCERI, F. (2008). *Intellectual Capital and Knowledge Management* (Abindgon: Routledge).

——and GUTHRIE, J. (2009). 'Critical Analysis of International KR Guidelines for Knowledge Intensive Organisations', in D. Jemielniak and L. Kozminski (eds.), *Handbook on Research on Knowledge Intensive Resources* (Hershey, Pa.: IGI Global), 375–92.

ROSLENDER, R. (2008). 'Editorial', *Journal of Human Resource Costing and Accounting*, 12(2): 68–9.

——and DYSON, J. R. (1992). 'Accounting for the Worth of Employees: A New Look at an Old Problem', *British Accounting Review*, 24(4): 311–29.

ROYAL, C., and O'DONNELL, L. (2005). 'Embedding Human Capital Analysis in the Investment Process: A Human Resources Challenge', *Asia Pacific*, 43(1): 117–36.

RUST, R. T., STEWART, C. L., MILLER, H., and PIELACK, D. (1996). 'The Satisfaction and Retention of Frontline Employees: A Customer Satisfaction Measurement Approach', *International Journal of Service Industry Management*, 7(5): 62–80.

SACKMANN, S. A., FLAMHOLTZ, E., and BULLEN, M. L. (1989). 'Human Resource Accounting: A State-of-the-Art Review', *Journal of Accounting Literature*, 8: 235–64.

SCARPELLO, V., and THEEKE, H. A. (1989). 'Human Resource Accounting: A Measured Critique', *Journal of Accounting Literature*, 8: 265.

SCHULTZ, T. W. (1961). 'Investment in Human Capital', *American Economic Review*, 51(1): 1–17.

SKE (2005). *Australian Guiding Principles on Extended Performance Management* (Melbourne: GAP Congress on Knowledge Capital, Parliament House).

SMITH, A. (1776). *An Inquiry into the Nature and Causes of the Wealth of Nations*. URL: http://www.econlib.org/LIBRARY/Smith/smWN.html (accessed Apr. 2007).

SVEIBY, K. E. (1997). *The New Organisational Wealth: Managing and Measuring Knowledge-Based Assets* (San Francisco: Berrett-Koehler).

——(1998). 'Measuring Intangibles and intellectual Capital: An Emerging First Standard'. http://www.sveiby.com/portals/0/articles/emergingstandard.html (accessed Apr. 2007).

VERMA, S., and DEWE, P. (2008). 'Valuing Human Resources: Perceptions and Practices in UK Organisation', *Journal of Human Resource Costing and Accounting*, 12(2): 102–23.

YONGVANICH, K., and GUTHRIE, J. (2006). 'An Extended Performance Reporting Framework for Social and Environmental Accounting', *Business Strategy and the Environment*, 15(5): 309–21.

PART IV

HUMAN CAPITAL INTERDEPENDENCIES

CHAPTER 16

....

INTERDEPENDENCIES BETWEEN PEOPLE IN ORGANIZATIONS

....

ROBERT M. GRANT

JAMES C. HAYTON

16.1 INTRODUCTION

....

In this chapter we examine interdependencies among people in organizations as a critical aspect of human capital that organizations must leverage. Our primary focus is organizations that serve some economic purpose; that is, they use human capital in order to produce goods or services that are then supplied to outside individuals and organizations. From the viewpoint of the organization, human capital is the totality of human potential available to it. While the issue of alignment of individuals and groups with the organizational objectives is important for the appropriability of human capital, the agency-problem is the focus of Chapter 14 of this volume. In the current chapter we take the perspective suggested by Lin (2001), that human capital is closely bound up with social capital, and that the benefits that organizations are able to appropriate from human capital are equally dependent on their ability to encourage the functional interdependence of individuals. From this perspective, human capital is more than simply the aggregation of individuals' skills and knowledge. It must also take account of the complementarities among individuals' abilities which allow individuals to perform beyond their perceived limits and permit human skills to be integrated into organizational capabilities (see

Chapter 18). Therefore, in the present chapter we address the issue of interdependency between people, which is fundamental to their productivity within an organizational context.

To examine the interdependencies between individuals within organizations we begin by addressing the fundamental organizational challenge. Organizations permit multiple individuals, each with different skills and knowledge, to combine their efforts. But to exploit the benefits of division of labor, organizations must find ways of integrating individual efforts, which requires overcoming the problems of *cooperation* and *coordination*. The capacity of an organization to successfully integrate the efforts of its members depends upon two major factors. First is the collaboration potential of the individual organizational members, which depends upon their relations with others both inside and outside the organization, and the capacity of individuals to create, maintain, and utilize those relationships. Second, it depends upon the capacity of the organization to foster cooperation and coordination through appropriate structures and management practices. As we shall see, investigating interdependency among organizational members raises issues that are at the core of management theory and management practice. These issues have attracted the attention of several streams of management and organizational literature.

Our goal in this chapter is to identify the critical issues concerning the nature of interdependency between people within organizations, to review the key areas of literature that address these issues, and to establish some degree of synthesis that allows us to recognize the extent of current knowledge and the priorities for future research.

16.2 The Challenge of Organizing

To explore interdependencies between people, we must first identify the nature of organization. If 'organizations are assemblages of interacting human beings' (March and Simon, 1958: 4), we need to clarify the purpose of these interactions. We have established that our concern is with *economic organizations*—organizations that exist to produce some good or service supplied to people outside of the organization. This would include business firms; not-for-profit organizations such as homeless shelters, famine relief charities, art galleries; and most public-sector organizations such as the police, army, judicial system. It would exclude most amateur sports teams, clubs formed by enthusiasts, and most religious organizations. But why does productive activity require organizations as opposed to 'individuals acting or working alone' (Child, 2005: 6). The reason is to exploit the efficiency advantages of specialization ('division of labor') while providing for the integration of separate but complementary efforts.

The fundamental source of efficiency in production is *specialization*—especially the *division of labor* into separate tasks. In this sense each task represents a modular element of a production process. The organization of production processes into tasks therefore defines the number of boundaries across which individual inputs must be coordinated: between individuals; between individuals and the technologies they must use; and between people and the production processes themselves. The classic statement on the gains from specialization is Adam Smith's description of pin manufacture:

One man draws out the wire, another straightens it, a third cuts it, a fourth points it, a fifth grinds it at the top for receiving the head; to make the head requires two or three distinct operations; to put it on is a peculiar business, to whiten the pins is another; it is even a trade by itself to put them into the papers. (Smith, 1910: 5)

Smith's pin-makers produced about 4,800 pins per person each day. 'But if they had all wrought separately and independently, and without any of them having been educated to this peculiar business, they certainly could not each have made 20, perhaps not one pin, in a day.' Applying these same principles, Henry Ford achieved huge productivity gains by installing moving assembly lines and assigning individuals to highly specific production tasks. Between the end of 1912 and early 1914, the time taken to assemble a Model T fell from 106 hours to just over six hours. More generally, the difference in human productivity between modern industrial society and primitive subsistence society is the result of the efficiency gains from individuals specializing, coupled with the development of formal and informal structures, processes, and systems that facilitate their coordination.

Specialization therefore comes at a cost. The more a production process is divided between different specialists and across different technologies, the greater is the challenge—and the costs—of coordination. These costs of coordination depend upon the extent and type of decision-making and adjustment among organizational members. In turn, the extent and types of decision-making and adjustment are determined by the extent of environmental complexity and volatility. Organizations that operate in fairly stable environment are likely to maximize efficiency with high levels of specialization. Under stable conditions it is possible to predict and plan for environmental contingencies and program activities using standard procedures. When exceptions do occur, these are more likely to be resolved using programmed decision-making. For example, during the 1950s and 1960s General Motors experienced a technologically and economically stable market environment with limited competitive pressure. The result was an organization that operated successfully with high levels of horizontal and vertical specialization.

In contrast, when environments are dynamic and complex, extensive planning becomes ineffective. The range of contingencies becomes too great, and there is a greater need for non-programmed decision-making in response to the numerous exceptions. Under such conditions coordination costs increase due to the need for more intensive communication and the use of mutual adjustment and *ad hoc* rather than planned coordination mechanisms. For example, Google operates within a dynamic environment, and although it is a very a large organization (17,000 employees at the end of 2007), levels of job specialization tend to be low, and much coordination is achieved through the reciprocal interactions among individuals working in autonomous teams.

Integrating the efforts of multiple individuals presents two problems. The *cooperation* problem arises because individuals each have their own personal goals: integration requires that the interests of organizational members be aligned with those of the organization. Even without conflicting goals, there is still the problem of *coordination*: everyone in the organization may wish to achieve the same goal, but organizational members have to find ways of synchronizing their individual efforts.

The emphasis of the literature has been on the problems of cooperation. Organizational sociology has emphasized problems of goal alignment and intra-organizational conflict. Political science approaches to organizational theory have been concerned with the sources and exercise of power within organizations, and the means by which individuals and groups mold organizational outcomes to their own ends. The organizational economics literature has been preoccupied with agency issues: conflict between the goals of owners and those of managers and other employees. In the economics literature the issues of cooperation and issues of coordination have been distinguished within the context of game theory.

The distinction between cooperation and coordination has been explained as follows:

In a cooperation game [e.g. prisoners' dilemma] the payoff space of the game is such that at the efficient equilibrium any player has an incentive to change his behavior, given other players' behavior…A coordination game is a game in which the payoff space is such that, at the equilibrium point(s), not only does no player have any incentive to (unilaterally) change his behavior (given the behavior of other players), but no player wishes any other player to (unilaterally) change his strategy as well. (Foss, 2001: 358)

The critical issue in coordination games is not the incentive to reach a Pareto equilibrium but the mechanics for doing so.

Camerer and Knez (1996) identify 'convergent expectations' as the essential condition for coordination. Puranam (2007) defines coordination as:

the harmonious combination of agents or functions towards the production of a result… Common use of the term 'coordination' may often conflate it with cooperation, or with one of the mechanisms by which coordination is achieved (e.g. planning, joint decision-making, communication). I find it helpful to think about coordination as a process that creates reliable beliefs about the likely actions of others; actions are coordinated when there is reciprocal predictability of action among interdependent individuals.

If the central issues for this chapter are the interdependencies between individuals within organizations, what light does the literature shed upon this topic?

16.3 Managing Interdependencies within Organizations

16.3.1 Types of Interdependence

If interdependence is a fundamental feature of work within organizations, the nature and characteristics of that interdependence are critically important to organization design. The dominant framework for the analysis of interdependency is that provided by James Thompson (1967).

Thompson identified three basic types of interdependency between individuals created by the nature of the tasks they perform. These three types of interdependency provide the basis for understanding issues of coordination within organizations, and are a primary consideration in designing organizational structures. In increasing levels of interdependence the three types are:

1. *Pooled task interdependence.* Under pooled interdependence each individual operates independently but is linked by a common process technology and common inputs. Examples of pooled task interdependence include a telephone sales department and a university's teaching faculty. Because each individual can operate with a high degree of independence from co-workers, coordination needs are minimal. Alignment can be achieved through rules and standard operating procedures.

2. *Sequential task interdependence* exists where the output of one individual (or unit) is the input to another. Coordination requirements are greater than in the case of pooled interdependence, typically requiring planning and the scheduling of activities. The classic example of sequential task interdependence is the assembly line production system.

3. *Reciprocal task interdependence* involves individuals (or units) working together simultaneously to perform the task. The actions of each individual needs to be harmonized with those of others requiring a continuous flow of information between those involved units throughout the execution of the task. This flow of information allows the individuals involved to mutually adjust their activities. An acrobatic team, a jazz combo, and a new product development team are examples of reciprocal interdependence.

Thompson postulated that each type of interdependence required a different coordination mechanism. While pooled interdependence required only *standardization*, sequential interdependence required *planning*, and reciprocal dependence required *mutual adjustment*. As the task environment becomes increasingly dynamic and complex, there is a move from formal to informal coordination. For example, in the complex and dynamic task environment of cross-functional innovation processes, coordination depends largely on mutual adjustment through informal organizational networks rather than along formal lines of authority (Faraj and Sproull, 2000). Thompson also established intensity of interdependence as the basic criterion for organizing hierarchy. Thus, at the first (bottom) level of organizational hierarchy, tasks characterized by reciprocal interdependence should be grouped together. After that, sequential interdependence should be the subsequent criterion for identifying organizational groupings.

The informal coordination of people receives the most attention because it is the most complex relative to standardization and planning, and also because of its significance as a means of coordination in an increasingly uncertain world. Coordination by mutual adjustment also implies the individual differences in traits and competencies, the structures of social relations (social networks), and organizational culture and climate can be expected to have a significant influence on interdependencies between people. These are themes we return to shortly.

Mintzberg (1979) extended Thompson's analysis of interdependency. In particular, he disaggregated the types of standardization through which pooled interdependence could be coordinated into three: standardization by process, standardization by outputs, and standardization by skills. More importantly, he linked each of his five mechanisms for coordination to five organizational archetypes—forming the basis for his 'structure in fives' framework (Mintzberg, 1983). Table 16.1 shows the correspondence between coordination mechanisms and organizational archetypes.

Although satisfyingly symmetric—especially Mintzberg's one-to-one correspondence between five types of interdependence, five modes of coordination, and five organizational archetypes ('structure in fives')—there is a lack of empirical

Table 16.1. Interdependence as the Basis for Analyzing Coordination and Organization Design

Thompson's types of interdependence	Thompson's coordination mechanisms	Mintzberg's organizational archetypes
Pooled	Coordination by standardization	Machine bureaucracy
	(Mintzberg's three-way elaboration by work processes, outputs, by skills)	Divisionalized form Professional bureaucracy
Sequential	Coordination by plan (Mintzberg: direct supervision)	Simple structure
Reciprocal	Coordination by mutual adjustment	Adhocracy

Source: Thompson, 1967; Mintzberg, 1979.

verification for the categories and the relationships. Since the work of Thompson, Mintzberg, and others, the study of interdependency and coordination has progressed primarily within the fields of information systems, computer science, and systems science. For example, Tolksdorf (2002) identifies a number of key features of systems that determine the nature of interdependency and types of coordination required. These include:

- the distinction amongst interactors, non-interactors, and the management of relations;
- the degree of coupling between interactors;
- the degree of autonomy of interactors;
- the degree of stability of interactors;
- the stability of relations.

Malone and his colleagues at the MIT Center for Coordination Science have approached interdependency from an empirical rather than a conceptual standpoint. Through creating a database of organizational processes and their characteristics, they have identified three principal types of dependency within processes (see Table 16.2).

Although they are diverse in their approaches to explaining the mechanisms for organizational coordination, each implies that the interaction requirements vary according to the resources, processes, and goals of production technologies. At a fundamental level, the demands of organizational processes constrain options for formal and informal structure, including the need for social and human capital (Nadler and Tushman, 1997).

Table 16.2. Malone's Analysis of Interdependence and Coordination

Types of interdependence	Examples of coordination mechanisms
Fit: different activities combine to produce a single outcome	Boeing's total simulation vs. Microsoft's daily build
Flow: output of one activity input for another	
prerequisite (right time)	Make to order vs. make to inventory ('pull' vs. 'push'). Place orders using 'economic order quantity'. 'Just In Time' (kanban system). Detailed advance planning.
accessibility (right place)	Ship by various transportation modes or make at point of use
usability (right thing)	Use standards or ask individual users (e.g. by having customer agree to purchase and/or by using participatory design)
Sharing: different activities use the same resource	'First come, first serve', priority order, budgets, managerial decision, market-like bidding

Source: Malone *et al.*, 1999.

A limitation of the approaches reviewed so far is that they limit themselves to one aspect of interdependence—the task. In addition to considerations of task characteristics, Tjosvold (1986) argues for consideration of roles, rewards, individual characteristics, culture/values/climate, and power in order to fully understand the nature of interdependencies in organizations. He proposes a framework that links task and rewards, goals and expectations, justice and social exchange, and values and attitudes in a complex, dynamically interacting whole, which describes the true nature of interpersonal interdependence in organizations. Weaving all of these factors together are the underlying social dynamics of cooperation (positive interdependence), competition (negative interdependence), and neutrality (independence) drawn from Deutsch (1949, 1973, 1980).

Deutsch's theory proposes that interactions among individuals are a result of the perceived interdependence (positive or negative) of goals. Naturally, an important factor influencing the perceived interdependence of goals at work is the nature of the task and its inherent interdependencies. Therefore, high levels of positive independence may be perceived by a line worker whose inputs are dependent on the outputs of workers further up the line. In contrast, high levels of negative interdependence may be perceived by sales persons sharing a territory. Goal *independence* is likely to be perceived (or rather, there will be an absence of perceptions of *interdependence*) by employees working in different lines of the same factory. More significantly, the key insight that is derived from application of Deutsch's approach is that perceived goal interdependence and the result of that interdependence are influenced by a number of other important social psychological factors including social norms and values of the individuals concerned, and the need to maintain harmony and justice in social exchanges.

The structural characteristics of tasks, as analyzed by Thompson and others, create the possibilities for shared or overlapping responsibilities. The extent of overlap is an important factor influencing the perception of shared (or conflicting) goals. In addition, the extent to which organizational controls on performance, such as monitoring, and rewards increase attention to the overlapping responsibilities will strengthen the perception of interdependence. Employees respond to these structural features with increased cooperation or competition, leading to specific patterns of interaction. The patterns of interaction will then influence evaluations of the social exchange for fairness and equity, and also produce some cognitive and affective attitudinal response towards the interaction. This in turn will also influence the nature of future interaction patterns (see Figure 16.1).

The framework developed by Tjosvold (1986) is far more complete than earlier work on interdependence, in terms of considering the influence of structure, culture, social-psychological and psychological factors. It provides a useful way of organizing the diverse influences into a coherent framework, as depicted in Figure 16.1. In the remainder of this chapter we will examine what the literature says about

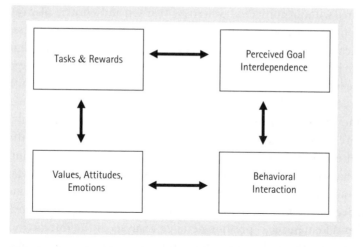

Figure 16.1. The Structural, Social, and Psychological Factors
Influencing Interdependence (adapted from Tjosvold, 1986)

the effects of organizational structures and processes, as well as social and personal factors that influence the interdependence of people in organizations.

16.3.2 Organizational Processes as the Foundation of Organization Structure

One of the key implications of the study of interdependency within organization is the recognition that the basic unit of organization design is the process (Nadler and Tushman, 1997). An organizational process is a 'sequence of goal-oriented actions' (Crowston and Osborn, 1998: 5). It is through these sequences of actions that specific organizational tasks are achieved. The organizational process approach identifies the basic elements of organization not as people but as individual actions. One difference is that organizational members are typically involved in multiple processes and one process may require the coordinated actions of multiple individuals. The analysis of organizational processes (often called 'business processes') has taken place largely within the fields of operations management and process engineering where the emphasis has been on the mapping of processes as a prerequisite to process redesign (Jeston and Nellis, 2006).

The neglect of organizational processes within mainstream organizational research may be partly due to the fact that studies of organizational evolution and organizational learning have emphasized the role of *organizational routines* as the principal mechanisms through which individuals interact within organizations. Organizational routines are 'repetitive patterns of activity' that are 'ordinarily accomplished without conscious awareness' (Nelson and Winter, 1982: 15). Although organizational routines are essentially the same as organizational processes, because of the tendency to emphasize the automatic nature of routines, research has focused on the ways in which routines develop and are replicated rather than upon the specifics of the interpersonal interactions through which routines are performed.

Recently, however, organizational routines and organizational processes have received increasing attention from organizational scholars—primarily as a result of the desire to investigate the basis and microstructures of organizational capabilities. For example, in studying the learning through which companies develop their internationalization capabilities, Bingham and Eisenhardt (2005) focus on the processes through which internationalization takes place. In analyzing the performance of organizational tasks, Pentland and colleagues (Pentland, 1992; Pentland and Reuter, 1994) provide detailed analysis of the interactions between individual employees and seek to model these using the principles of grammatical analysis.

The tendency has been to regard the nature and intensity of the interdependencies between people within organizations as determined primarily by the requirements of the technologies that are deployed in organizational processes. 'Socio-technical' analysis focused upon the importance of adapting the social system of an organization or work unit to the technology being deployed. In their classic study of the introduction of a new coal-mining technology, Trist and Bamforth (1951) found that the failure to anticipate the impact of a new organization design on the types of interactions required by the new technology resulted in deteriorating productivity. However, the need for the organizational design to take account of the impact of technology on human interactions implies that interdependencies are not wholly exogenously determined. The design of processes and organizational units can have a major impact on the extent and form of interdependency. For example, concurrent engineering turns sequential interdependence (in Thompson's terminology) into reciprocal interdependence. Similarly, modular, loosely coupled designs can substantially reduce the degree of interdependence experienced by organizational units (Orton and Weick, 1990; Langlois, 2002).

While relatively sparse, the literature on interdependence that takes a structural approach has a history of increasing degrees of refinement starting from the socio-technical systems perspective, further developed by Thompson in his model of task interdependence, and then formally integrated into views of organizational coordination by processes (Malone et al., 1999) and routines (Pentland and Reuter, 1994). Inevitably, this work leads to a consideration of the role of human actors in coordinated action, and Tjosvold's (1986) work, building on Deutsch, provides a compelling view that accommodates task, culture, and cognition, as well as social psychological factors. We take Tjosvold's cue, and in the next section examine how culture, climate, and social capital concepts relate to interdependence in organizations. We then turn to individual-level considerations.

16.3.3 Organizational Culture as a Coordinating Device

Interest in the role of culture in facilitating coordination within organizations can be traced to the influence of several popular and influential management books during the early 1980s. Organizational culture refers to the coherent pattern of beliefs and values that represent effective solutions to major problems faced by the organization internally and externally (for example, Dyer, 1986; Schein, 1985). The members of the organization, as a group, share the experience of facing and solving organizational challenges and learning about effective and ineffective solutions. As a result, organizational members develop a shared view of how the world works, including basic assumptions of cause and effect relations in the internal and external organizational environment. Effective solutions are repeated, leading to the reinforcement of beliefs and norms regarding appropriate behaviours and actions (Schein, 1985).

Peters and Waterman's *In Search of Excellence* (1982) famously emphasized the role of culture in the sustained success of America's 'excellent companies', where 'loose–tight' structures with fewer formal rules and structure were complemented (or replaced) by strong, clear organizational cultures to guide behavior. Contemporaneously, Ouchi (1981) and Pascale and Athos (1982) turned to cultural factors in explaining the remarkable global success of a number of Japanese companies. Ouchi's 'theory Z' is of particular interest because it developed a theory of coordination and cooperation that established culture as the basis for a 'clan' mode of governance that is distinct from both hierarchy and the market mechanism (Ouchi, 1980). Meanwhile, Deal and Kennedy (1982) focused most directly on the role of culture as a central theme of corporate life and a key determinant of firm performance. While organizational scholars have long been interested in the role of anthropological aspects of organizations, the key development during the 1980s was in viewing organizational culture less as emergent phenomenon and more as a resource that was potentially manageable (Barney, 1986).

Organizational culture has tended to become a catch-all term referring to a range of phenomena that relate to patterns of beliefs, values, behaviors, and symbols. Schein describes organizational culture as:

A pattern of shared basic assumptions that the group learned as it solved its problems of external adaptation and internal integration, that has worked well enough to be considered valid and, therefore, to be taught to new members as the correct way to perceive, think, and feel in relation to those problems. (Schein, 1985: 12)

However, he also makes clear that while shared basic assumptions form the core of organizational culture, it is institutionalized through other important organizational phenomena, including values and behavioral norms and, more observably, through patterns of behavior and organizational symbols and artifacts. Some indication of the breadth of the concept is provided by the range of definitions used. Thus, O'Reilly and Chatman (1996: 160) focus on values and norms rather than assumptions: they define organizational culture as 'a system of shared values (that define what is important) and norms that define appropriate attitudes and behaviors for organizational members (how to feel and behave)'.

Specifying what organizational culture comprises is a vital first stage in converting it from a broad-based organizational resource that acts as a general catalyst of cooperation and coordination, into a clearly defined construct whose characteristics have a well-specified (and empirically verifiable) impact on organizational behavior. The next stage is to articulate the mechanisms through which culture influences organizational performance. Søorensen (2002) points to three major influences. First, a strong culture—in the sense of unanimity over values—improves goal alignment between the organization and its members, hence avoiding goal conflict within organizations. Indeed, an organizational culture may be regarded as an informal mechanism for social control—a low-cost mechanism for avoiding the agency problems that bedevil cooperation within organizations (O'Reilly and Chatman, 1996). Second, by increasing identity between the organization and its members, culture can increase motivation among organizational members, resulting in greater effort on behalf of the organization (O'Reilly, 1989). Finally, and most relevant to our examination of interaction between people, culture can play a key role in enhancing coordination between organization members. To the extent that the essence of coordination is consistent with expectations among organizational members about the behavior of others (Tjosvold, 1986), then common cognitive frameworks, behavioral norms, and patterns of behavior can be exceptionally important in facilitating the smooth operation of organizational routines as well as permitting spontaneous mutual adjustment in novel situations (Cremer, 1993).

Most empirical studies have not attempted to disentangle the mechanisms through which culture impacts performance, but have simply postulated that strength of organizational culture positively impacts performance—primarily because shared values are conducive to shared goals. Empirical support for the relationship between strength of culture and firm performance is offered by Denison (1990), Kotter and Heskett (1992), and Gordon and DiTomaso (1992). However, the recent literature offers a nuanced view of the impact of culture on performance.

Naïve arguments about the beneficial role of organizational culture presume that culture is fairly homogeneous within an organization. In fact, within a single organization, different operating units and functions may develop different organizational cultures (Sackmann, 1992). There may also be vertical distinctions: the culture of the boardroom may be different from that of the factory floor. Vertical cultural differences reflect the values and norms of different socioeconomic classes. This is due, in part, to the fact that organizational cultures emerge within open systems: they are influenced by the cultures of nations, socioeconomic groupings, ethnicity, and professions. Internal differentiation of organizations is also a source of cultural differentiation (Lawrence and Lorsch, 1969): due to differences in occupational norms, languages, subunit goals, and time frames, the culture of the R&D lab will differ from that of the sales department.

Culture may also represent a formidable barrier to organizational adaptation and change. Values and norms tend to be deeply embedded. Therefore, strategic and organizational changes that are inconsistent with them will tend to be rebuffed. A common occurrence in organizations is a new CEO's strategic vision and program for organizational renewal foundering upon a deeply embedded system of values. Reconciling organizational flexibility with the continuity of culture is best achieved where the culture is formed by broad values capable of accommodating a range of strategies. Collins and Porras (1994) suggest that a few timeless core values can facilitate rather than constrain adaptation to external change, with the result that many of the companies that they studied were able to achieve outstanding long-term success.

The identity and sense of belonging that a strong organizational culture confers may undermine rather than facilitate superior performance. John Weeks' (2004) study of a British retail bank identifies a culture founded upon complaining, where the common weight of internal skepticism and criticism provided a near-insurmountable barrier to almost any initiative or innovation. The implication is that, in order to recognize the influence of culture on the interactions between people within organizations, it is essential that we go beyond simplistic generic notions of culture as a 'glue', or possibly a lubricant, and identify in precise terms the assumptions, values, and norms of the organization and then explore their implications for how individuals interact with one another. Such criticisms of the culture literature—that it fails to address more directly the impact of culture on coordination—may miss the point. Arguably, the culture literature has been more concerned with the evolution of organizational social systems over time. In contrast, researchers focusing on the construct of organizational climate have tended to be interested in the impact of the organization's social system on individuals and groups (Denison, 1996). Therefore, we turn to the climate literature to examine what may be learnt about informal coordinating mechanisms.

16.3.4 Organizational Climates for Coordination

The climate literature may prove more appropriate for explaining interdependencies between people because this research stream has 'placed greater emphasis on organizational members' perceptions of "observable" practices and procedures that are closer to the "surface" of organizational life' (Denison, 1996: 622). Conceptualizations of culture examine deep structures and systems of symbolism which, although influential on behavior, may not be evident to either organizational leadership or membership. In contrast, climate focuses on aspects of the social environment that are perceived by participants and also subject to organizational control. Thus, while climate studies attempt to capture behavioral regularities at the organizational level, culture studies seek an explanation for why these behavioral regularities emerge (for example, Patterson *et al.*, 2005; Schneider, 2000; Svyantek and Bott, 2004).

Although climate and culture may actually observe the same underlying phenomena (Denison, 1996), they do so with different metaphysical assumptions and theoretical framework, and therefore the climate literature may reveal understandings regarding interdependence and coordination that are not found in the culture literature. Culture studies frequently involve rich, ethnographic explorations that develop in great depth interpretations of underlying meanings and assumptions (Denison, 1996). In contrast, the generally positivist epistemological stance of climate research is compatible with the imposition of functional climate categories that relate directly to organizational needs such as service, safety, innovation, learning, cooperation and quality (for example, Anderson and West, 1998; Murphy *et al.*, 1996; Schneider *et al.*, 1996; Smith *et al.*, 2005; West, 1990). Because the focus is not on the definition or interpretation of intersubjective experiences, climate studies generally start from the outcome of interest, and work backwards, attempting to define and detect patterns of behavior that are consistent with these outcomes.

The more positivistic orientation toward the phenomenon of organizational climate may also yield answers that speak more readily to the problem of what drives interdependencies between people in organizations (for example, Hitt and Morgan, 1977). The various proposed multidimensional conceptualizations of organizational climate certainly suggest that, at a global level, the construct will be influential on interpersonal coordination. For example, Campbell *et al.* (1970) identified four dimensions that are clearly linked to the problem of coordination: individual autonomy; structure; reward orientation; and consideration, warmth, and support. Similarly, James and his colleagues identify the four dimensions: role stress; job challenge and autonomy; leadership support; and work group cooperation, friendliness, and warmth (James and James, 1989; James and McIntyre, 1996; James and Sells, 1981). In an early contribution, Litwin and Stringer (1968) define nine climate dimensions: conflict, identity, responsibility, reward, risk, standards, structure, support, and warmth. Several of these dimensions of the social climate are relevant to the perception of shared goals and the possibility for, and reaction to, social interactions (Tjosvold, 1986).

There is empirical evidence of the impact of different dimensions of organizational climate on coordination. For example, in a study conducted in a military context, Griffin and Mathieu (1997) provide evidence that the dimensions of communications flow, motivation, and human resource planning and utilization of the climate measure 'Survey of Organizations' were influential upon measures of coordination in the work group. Smith *et al.* (2005) provide evidence that climate for teamwork and risk-taking support organizational learning and innovation by encouraging the sharing and combination of knowledge.

What is emerging in the literature on organizational climate is evidence that individual willingness and ability to coordinate is, at least in part, influenced by the perceived characteristics of the organizational environment. While there are many possible dimensions of the organizational climate, the majority of them appear to have some implications for coordination. This may be through their influence on ability to coordinate (leader support, role stress, training), willingness to coordinate (such as rewards climate, friendliness, warmth, supportiveness, cooperation), or opportunity to coordinate (such as climate for autonomy, teamwork). Therefore, one way in which climate may be influential on interpersonal coordination is through the familiar 'ability, motivation, opportunity framework' that is frequently employed in studies of how human resource management practices can be understood to impact behavior and organizational performance (Locke and Latham, 1990).

While clear and compelling, the ability, motivation, opportunity explanation on its own lacks depth in its ability to account for climate's influence. It must be supplemented by more specific accounts of how each element is influenced by climate, and in turn influences coordination. For example, ability to coordinate is enhanced by the presence of specific climate features that create skills required for the sharing and combination of knowledge (for example, Smith *et al.*, 2005). The influence of organizational climate for autonomy versus teamwork may influence the social structure of the organization in terms of patterns of interaction, which in turn promotes informal coordination (for example, Nahapiet and Ghoshal, 1998). Finally, motivation to coordinate may be influenced in part by the quality of social exchange within the organization, which is influenced by such features as supportive leadership and supervision (for example, Rhoades and Eisenberger, 2002). However, these are only partial explanations. The literature has not, so far, attempted a broader integration of how features of the organizational climate can impact coordination. The answer to this question would certainly need to consider the construct of social capital (Nahapiet and Ghoshal, 1998), to which we turn next.

16.4 SOCIAL CAPITAL

Within the social science literature—especially economics, sociology, and public administration—social capital has emerged as one of the most important concepts in the analysis of social relations. It has also been influential within the field of management and organizational studies. Most significantly it has been viewed as a key complement of human capital.

16.4.1 Social Capital and Social Networks

Social capital refers to the value of social relationships. Adler and Kwon (2002: 17) describe it as 'the goodwill that is engendered by the fabric of social relations and that can be mobilized to facilitate action'. The predominant approach views social capital as owned by individuals: 'Social capital describes circumstances in which individuals can use membership in groups and networks to secure benefits' (Sobel, 2002: 139). Given that social capital is founded upon social relations, social network analysis is a valuable tool for analyzing and evaluating social capital (Burt, 2000). A number of studies show how the social capital derived from a network of relationships can be appropriated by individuals. For example, social capital can assist in finding a job and gaining better pay (Belliveau et al., 1996; Podolny and Baron, 1997).

The extent of the benefit from networks of relations is likely to depend upon the structure of these networks. There are two competing arguments for how network structure creates social capital. Coleman points to the reciprocity and reinforcement of trust engendered by closed networks with dense relationships between network members (Coleman, 1988). Such networks promote coordination by creating disincentives for opportunistic behavior. In dense networks, opportunism is more likely to be detected and effectively sanctioned. Conversely, Burt (1992) argues that a sparse network offers benefits to network members who can access information in parts of the network that are not closely connected to other parts of the network—'bridging structural holes'. The ability to act as a 'broker' or 'gatekeeper' in a network is a key source of benefit from social capital. The coordination benefits here arise from the broker's role of 'network integrator' which brings together otherwise unconnected and therefore uncoordinated actors. Granovetter's research on weak ties offers some clarity for this explanation. Granovetter (1983) argues that in terms of deriving benefits from network relationships, weak ties (associated with acquaintance rather than close friendship) are typically of greater tangible value, and they achieve this value by helping coordinate job-seekers and employers market. In an organizational setting we expect both forms of social capital to be supportive of coordination.

16.4.2 Social Capital as a Public Good

The contradictory conclusions derived by Coleman and Burt concerning the network configurations that maximize social capital are also reflected in their different conceptions of who owns the social capital. While Burt views social capital as owned by individuals, Coleman views it as a collective good—a property of the network. This view of social capital as a public good—the collective value of goodwill within a social network—is also endorsed by Fukuyama (1997), who defines social capital as 'the existence of a certain set of informal values or norms shared among members of a group that permit cooperation among them'.

In his study of the decline of social participation in America, *Bowling Alone*, Robert Putnam (1995) identifies the decline in community involvement as a decline in social capital with devastating effects on social and individual welfare. These adverse effects include declining educational attainment, poorer health, less charity, and weakened democratic processes. Therefore, social capital has influence at the network or social system level. However, its importance cannot be limited to this level of analysis. Binding collective and individual notions of social capital is the recognition that social capital can also be appropriated by individuals seeking to advance their own social and economic interests. Indeed, social capital can play a key role in the creation of human capital. Social capital facilitates the transmission of human capital both within families (from parents to children) and within society more broadly (Coleman, 1988).

16.4.3 Social Capital within Organizations

Social capital has provided a useful umbrella concept for linking economic ideas of value with sociological concepts of community, reciprocity, and social relationships. But what about organizations? To what extent is social capital a useful concept for analyzing the interdependencies between people in the workplace? Much of the research into social capital at the organizational level treats organizations as the unit of analysis and examines network relations between them. Thus, social capital derived from network relations assists firms in finding capital (Uzzi, 1999). Similarly, within interfirm networks, the presence of social capital can offer considerable benefits in terms of encouraging knowledge transfer (Powell *et al.*, 1996), facilitating collaboration within supplier networks, and supporting open innovation communities (Fleming and Waguespack 2007).

More interesting from the viewpoint of managing interdependencies between people in organization are the implications of social capital for interactions between organizational members. Nahapiet and Ghoshal (1998: 245) locate social capital at the heart of their attempt to develop a theory of the firm that is independent of arguments about transactional efficiency. The essence of the firm, in their view, is its network of social relations (primarily weak ties) which give the firm an advantage over markets in building 'intellectual capital'—which comprises acquired knowledge, skills, and capabilities that enable persons to act in new ways. The presence of social capital facilitates knowledge exchange and provides the foundation for knowledge combination. In their analysis of how social capital contributes to the creation of intellectual capital they identify three dimensions of social capital within the firm:

- the structural dimension, which comprises the network ties and network configuration;
- the cognitive dimension, which comprises shared codes, language, and narratives;
- the relational dimension, which includes trust, social norms, obligations, and identification.

These approaches to intraorganizational social capital focus attention on the structure of relations between organizational members and the cognitive, social, and institutional characteristics of the organization. Since these factors are the building blocks of organizational capability, social capital offers considerable insight into the nature and content of interaction between people within organizations. The paradox is that in the course of such analysis, social capital as a distinct concept tends to disappear. Once social capital is identified as the outcome of a network of social relations, it is the structure and character of these relations that are the primary focus of interest. Understanding interdependencies between people within organizations, and how such interdependencies result in an organization's distinctive capabilities, is not assisted substantially by the umbrella of social capital itself.

The danger is twofold: first, social capital is such a multifaceted concept that it lacks precise meaning; second, it becomes a catch-all term for assembling a number of loosely connected concepts that relate to the social relationships. As one researcher has observed: 'social capital [has] taken a circus-tent quality: all things positive and social are piled beneath it' (De Souza Briggs, 1998: 178). Not only is social capital a broad and ill-defined concept; it has been augmented by a number of related concepts including cultural capital, institutional capital, relational capital, and structural capital. Baron and Hannan (1994) complain of 'a plethora of capitals' in the social capital literature.

For the purposes of understanding the implications of interactions between people for human capital within an organizational context, social capital offers only limited insight. Social capital is an outcome of social relations—but our concern is the form and determinants of these relations rather than their outcome. Therefore, network structure and position, whose value is described in terms of social capital, are themselves the constructs of interest—along with the content of social exchanges—from the perspective of explaining coordination. Although social capital can help to explain investments in human capital and the deployment of human capital to create value, from the point of view of the organization, social capital is likely to cloak rather than illuminate the ways in which human interactions create value for individuals, organizations, and society. Our challenge is to investigate more precisely the individual and the organizational factors that contribute to the integration of human effort. We now turn to the individual-level factors that have been hypothesized to influence coordination.

16.5 INTERPERSONAL COMPETENCIES: INDIVIDUAL DIFFERENCES IN KNOWLEDGE, SKILLS, ABILITIES, AND TRAITS

In common with other concepts that originated in one field of knowledge and were then transferred to another, the application of the term 'capital' to human beings imposes constraints which derive from its original associations with physical capital:

machinery, equipment, computers, and office buildings. Thus, human capital tends to be viewed as having similar characteristics to physical capital: it is the result of investment and, so long as it is utilized and maintained effectively, then it can offer similar output in different firms (Solow, 1999).

Human beings are different. Not only does their humanity make them heterogeneous and idiosyncratic, but their productive value is not simply an outcome of investment in education and training, and their productivity depends upon complex individual and social factors. If we begin with the individual characteristics that determine an individual's work performance, we are faced with an array of factors that extend well beyond the education and training that was the focus of the early human capital researchers. Much of the early research into job performance emphasized work design—notably, the scientific management school associated with Frederick Taylor (1911). Subsequent research by what became known as the 'human relations school' shifted attention to the social environment of work (Mayo, 1945). Over the same period, the field of industrial/organizational psychology led to a broader view of the determinants of job performance, which includes individual differences in knowledge, skills, abilities, and also traits, attitudes, and emotions. Perhaps the most inclusive statement of individual differences as a determinant of job performance is found in the competency-based approach (for example, McClelland, 1973).

The contrast between the competency approach and that traditionally taken by researchers into human capital is a focus that extends to a broader range of human characteristics than those resulting from education and training (Hayton and McEvoy, 2006; Hayton and Kelley, 2006; Spencer and Spencer, 1993). Central to competency-based understandings of human capital is a focus on empirical inquiry driven by the simple question: what determines job performance? In *Testing for Competence rather than for Intelligence*, McClelland (1973) outlined an approach to individual work performance that was based not on intelligence, education, or training, but on exhibited behaviors driven by human motivations. These competencies include complex combinations of traits, knowledge, and skills (Hayton and McEvoy, 2006; Spencer and Spencer, 1993). Therefore, competencies involve not only the capacity but also the willingness to perform specific behaviors. These competencies were found to be more valid predictors of performance than scores from traditional intelligence or aptitude tests. The key element of McClelland's approach was in probing the behavioral characteristics that distinguished superior performers within a particular job category from average performers. Rather than focus upon the task elements of jobs, McClelland was 'interested in the characteristics of the people who did a job well' (Spencer *et al.*, 1994: 4).

Over time, empirical applications of competency modeling discovered a remarkable consistency in the competencies associated with superior job performance that appeared to vary little between industries or type of occupation. In their work with the McBer consulting firm, McClelland and Berlew distilled 360 behavioral indicators into 21 competencies which accounted for between 80 and 98 percent of the performance differentials associated with superior performers in different job categories. These competencies were further clustered into six categories (Spencer *et al.*, 1994). The competency clusters are seen as reflecting the intrinsic motivations that serve as their foundations. Table 16.3 lists the six categories and their component competencies.

It is apparent from the definitions in Table 16.3 that many of the competencies in this framework may be supportive for coordination of people in organizations. However, the framework suffers from two limitations. First, the focus of many of the competencies is extremely trait-like (such as flexibility, confidence, achievement oriented, self-control, stress resistance) placing greater emphasis on personality characteristics rather than combinations of knowledge, skills, and traits. As a result, sometimes the competency approach does not extend our understanding of organizational behavior beyond that achieved by purely personality-based explanations. Second, the framework does not explicitly address *how* coordination may be influenced by some or all of these competencies. However, this perspective does imply that combinations

Table 16.3. Competency Clusters

Cluster	Competencies
Achievement cluster	Achievement orientation Concern for quality and order Initiative
Helping/service cluster	Interpersonal understanding Customer-service orientation
Influence cluster	Impact and influence Organizational awareness Relationship building (networking)
Managerial cluster	Developing others Directiveness Teamwork and cooperation Team leadership
Cognitive thinking/problem-solving cluster	Analytical thinking Conceptual thinking Technical expertise Information seeking
Personal effectiveness cluster	Self-control; stress resistance Self-confidence Flexibility Organizational commitment; 'business-mindedness'

Source: Spencer *et al.*, 1994.

of individual differences should be significant for influencing the perception of shared goals, the motivation to interact, and ability to satisfy individual needs through interpersonal interaction. Furthermore, several ensuing studies have demonstrated specific relationships of this kind (for example, Ellis et al., 2005; Hayton and Kelley, 2006; Reagans, Argote and Brooks, 2005). Ellis *et al.* (2005) demonstrate that training in team-oriented knowledge and skills has a positive influence on planning and task coordination, collaborative problem-solving, and communication.

Organizational capabilities are also influenced by aggregate human capital characteristics such as diversity of experience, functional background or education, and shared experience working together (Hayton, 2005; Reagans *et al.*, 2005). Diversity in experience brings a greater range of cognitive resources, but also presents a greater challenge for coordination (Hayton, 2005; Hayton and Zahra, 2005). Interpersonal coordination is supported by shared experience because it enhances the capacity for individual members to leverage the collective knowledge of the group, and to better coordinate action (for example, Reagans *et al.*, 2005).

16.5.1 Emotional Intelligence

During the 1990s the competencies identified were reinterpreted in the light of contemporary research into the nature and types of intelligence. In many respects this work was a reaction against the Western propensity to identify intelligence with rationality. As Stanley Greenspan observed:

Ever since the ancient Greeks, philosophers have elevated the rational side of the mind above the emotional and seen the two as separate. Intelligence, in this view, is necessary to govern and restrain the base passions. This concept has been profoundly influential in Western thought; indeed it has shaped some of our most basic institutions and beliefs....Because of this dichotomy, our culture has an immense, longstanding intellectual and institutional investment in the notion that reason and emotion are separate and irreconcilable and that, in a civilized society, rationality must prevail. (1997: 2)

The notion that intelligence extends beyond an individual's cognitive capacity resonates with management thinkers. In a *Harvard Business Review* article, Katz (1974) explored the 'Skills of an Effective Administrator'. He identified three categories of skills needed for effectiveness: (*a*) conceptual skill—the ability to see the enterprise as a whole and understand its interrelationships within the industry, the society, and the world environment; (*b*) technical skill—proficiency in a specific kind of activity, methods, processes, procedures, or techniques; and (*c*) human skill—the ability to work effectively as a group member and to build a cooperative effort within the team.

These 'human skills' linked closely with Gardner's notions of *intrapersonal* and *interpersonal intelligence*. *Intrapersonal intelligence* is the ability to understand one's own feelings and emotions; *interpersonal intelligence* is the ability to understand other people, what motivates them, their intentions, and, potentially, to act upon this knowledge (Gardner, 1983: 239). Subsequent work by Salovey and Mayer (1990) combined these two concepts and used the term 'emotional intelligence' to refer to 'the ability to monitor one's own and other's feelings and emotions, to discriminate among them, and to use this information to guide one's thinking and action'. They identified five components of emotional intelligence:

(1)   self-awareness: observing self and recognizing a feeling as it happens;

(2)   managing emotions: handling feelings appropriately; realizing what is behind a feeling; finding ways to handle fears, anxieties, anger, and sadness;

(3)   motivating oneself: emotional self-control, channeling emotions in the service of a goal, delaying gratification and stifling impulses;

(4)   empathy: sensitivity to other's feelings, concerns, and perspective; appreciating differences in how people feel about things; and

(5)   handling relationships: managing emotions in others; social competency and social skills. (Salovey and Mayer, 1990: 189)

As well as popularizing the concept of emotional intelligence, Daniel Goleman's key contribution was in linking emotional intelligence to the competency clusters identified by McClelland's competency analysis. He identified four key areas of competency that contributed to emotional intelligence and argued for competency-based testing to augment traditional aptitude tests as a more comprehensive predictor of an individual's capability (Goleman, 1995):

(1)   self-awareness: recognizing own emotions and their effects, knowing one's strengths and limits, and a sureness about one's self-worth and capabilities;

(2)   self-regulation: managing disruptive emotions and impulses, maintaining standards of honesty/integrity, taking responsibility for personal performance, flexibility in handling change, and being comfortable with and open to new ideas and new information;

(3)   self-motivation: striving to improve or meet a standard of excellence, aligning with the goals of the group or organization, readiness to act on opportunities, and persistence in pursuing goals despite obstacles or setbacks;

(4)   social awareness: sensing other's feelings and perspective and taking an active interest in their concerns, anticipating/recognizing/meeting customer's needs, sensing what others need in order to develop, cultivating opportunities through diverse people, and reading a group's emotional currents and power relationships.

Goleman's (1998) claim that emotional intelligence is the best predictor of success in the workplace is supported by other studies (for example Bradberry and Greaves, 2005). However, the concept has been attacked as being so broad as to be useless (Locke, 2005) and having weak predictive validity (Landy, 2005). What seems indisputable, however, is that across a very wide range of different job types, and particularly for managerial work, the capacity to interact constructively with others is critical to job performance, and that these competencies depend heavily on individuals' abilities to understand and respond to both their own emotions and those of others. Across a wide range of different occupations and across a variety of different types of organization, superior job performance tends to be associated with generic competencies that extend beyond job-specific skills and know-how. These generic competencies combine conceptual and analytic competences (associated with IQ), motivational factors, and competences related to the capacity for personal and interpersonal relations (emotional intelligence).

This review suggests a number of individual difference variables that are associated with ability and willingness to form, and effectively maintain, social relations. Research in competencies identifies a number of potential characteristics of individuals, including initiative, relationship-building, information-seeking, and influence that are associated with if, and how well, individuals are able to coordinate with others. Emotional intelligence research provides a stronger theoretical explanation, grounded in abilities for awareness and regulation of one's own emotional states as well as sensitivity to those of others. The fact that emotional intelligence is supportive of general workplace success is further encouraging in that this is an important individual characteristic that precedes effective interpersonal coordination.

16.6 CONCLUSION

The emphasis of the human capital literature has been on the skills and know-how of individuals—especially upon those skills and expertise developed through investments in education and training. Yet as far as productive activities are concerned, the creation of goods and services occurs primarily within organizations we call 'firms'. The dominant feature of production by firms is that individuals cooperate with one another and coordinate their efforts in order to achieve levels of creativity and productivity that could not be attained by individuals acting alone. Hence, to understand human creativity and productivity, the study of human capital must be complemented by the study of how human beings interact with one another within organizations.

The literature we have reviewed points to interactions between individuals within organizations being influenced by three sets of factors: the characteristics of the individuals, the characteristics of the organizations within which they interact, and the characteristics of the work they do. Let us briefly review our findings on each of these.

16.6.1 Individuals' Attributes (Competencies)

Applications of psychology to individuals' work performance have resulted in the identification of personal characteristics associated with superior job performance. Applications of competency modeling to a wide variety of different occupations across a range of organizations have identified a several attributes that consistently characterize high performers. These include *achievement motivation, self-awareness, social awareness*, and *self-regulation*—a set of factors that have been grouped under the term 'emotional intelligence'. An interesting feature of this research is that these components of emotional intelligence together account for more of the variability in performance between individuals doing the same job than traditional determinants of human capital such as education, training, and on-the-job experience.

16.6.2 Organizational Characteristics (Social Capital, Organizational Culture, and Climate)

The literature on the organizational influences on individuals' cooperation and coordination has coalesced around three closely related concepts: *social capital, organizational culture*, and *climate*—each of which, we have argued, offers limited insight into the characteristics of interdependence. Despite its extensive influence, social capital tells us little about different organizations' capacity for coordinated effort—part of the problem being ambiguity over whether social capital is an individual or a collective asset. To the extent that social capital is formed through social relationships, we suggest that the study of social networks rather, than the study of social capital is likely to be more productive to understanding the organizational and interorganizational cooperation and performance. Likewise, 'organizational culture' is very much a catch-all term that comprises a number of anthropological influences on cognition and behavior within firms and non-profit entities. Indeed, despite their derivation from different disciplinary traditions, the two overlap considerably. Thus, the OECD defined social capital as comprising key elements of organizational culture: 'networks together with shared norms, values and understandings that facilitate cooperation within or among groups' (Cote and Healy, 2001: 41). However, the conceptualization and empirical operationalization of the two differs. Organizational culture tends to be viewed in terms of multiple, idiosyncratic attributes, while social capital is viewed either as a univariate construct of which organizations have either more or less, or as comprised of a few generic and measurable characteristics (such as participation, trust, and interaction). As a result, the components of culture—notable values and behavioral norms—offer a considerable potential for both explaining and predicting patterns of interaction between individuals within organizations.

Somewhere between the idiosyncratic nature of organizational culture and the notion of social capital we find the concept of organizational climate. The climate perspective takes a more functional view, which categorizes objective drivers and patterns of interaction. This approach has facilitated the identification of organizational characteristics that promote productive interactions among employees (such as cooperation and learning) and with other stakeholders (such as orientation to quality, safety, and service). The integration of climate explanations with individual and structural explanations for interdependence offers a challenging new avenue for further exploration.

16.6.3 Characteristics of Work (Interdependency)

The idea that the nature of work fundamentally determines the way in which individuals interact with one another has been a central theme of organizational analysis since advent of sociotechnical systems thinking at the beginning of the 1950, and was further developed by Thompson in his analysis of different types of interdependency. Subsequent development of interdependency with the context of coordination between individuals has been taken up by researchers into organizational processes (Malone et al., 1999) and routines (Pentland and Reuter, 1994). This work leads us into the structural dimensions of human interactions: ultimately, organizations can only be productive if they group individuals and structure their interactions to meet the coordination requirements of the work. A more complete statement of interdependence is found in the work of Tjosvold (1986), which considers task, culture, cognition, and social psychological factors. This perspective would readily integrate with the work previously reviewed and may provide a useful foundation for a more complete, multileveled exploration of interdependencies between people in organizations.

A significant implication of this review is that human capital does not reside solely or exclusively with the individual, the organization, or the social context. It is created and leveraged in the nexus of these three conceptual domains. Certainly within the context of economic organizations, the organizational task environment and associated processes are important drivers of *how* individual and collective knowledge and skills can be leveraged to create economic value. However, the extent of integration across individuals and between individuals and processes will also be subject to (*a*) individual competencies for interaction, and (*b*) collective norms and values for interaction. Therefore, the locus of human capital and the targets for relevant investments will necessarily be on each of these elements rather than one.

Thus far we have looked only at these different components of, and perspectives on, the interactions between individuals within organizations. Ultimately our interest is in the ability of organizations to effectively translate individuals' efforts into organizational effectivity. This takes us into the realm of organizational capability, which is the subject of Chapter 18.

REFERENCES

ADLER, P. S., and KWON, S. W. (2002). 'Social Capital: Prospects for a New Concept', *Academy of Management Review*, 27: 17–40.

ANDERSON, N., and WEST, M. (1998). 'Measuring Climate for Work Group Innovation: Development and Validation of the Team Climate Inventory', *Journal of Organizational Behaviour*, 19: 235–58.

BARNEY, J. B. (1986). 'Organizational Culture: Can it be a Source of Sustained Competitive Advantage?', *Academy of Management Review*, 11(3): 656–65.

BARON, J., and HANNAN, M. (1994). 'The Impact of Economics on Contemporary Sociology', *Journal of Economic Literature*, 32: 1111–46.

BELLIVEAU, M. A., O'REILLY, C. A., III, and WADE, J. B. (1996). 'Social Capital at the Top: Effects of Social Similarity and Status on CEO Compensation', *Academy of Management Journal*, 39: 1568–93.

BINGHAM, C. B. and EISENHARDT, K. M. (2005). *Learning from Heterogeneous Experience: The Internationalization of Entrepreneurial Firms*. Working Paper, Stanford, Calif.: Stanford University.

BRADBERRY, T., and GREAVES, J. (2005). 'Heartless Bosses', *Harvard Business Review*, 83 (Dec.): 24–36.

BURT, R. S. (1992). *Structural Holes: The Social Structure of Competition* (Cambridge, Mass.: Harvard University Press).

——(2000). 'The Network Structure of Social Capital', in B. M. Staw and R. I. Sutton (eds.), *Research in Organizational Behavior* (Amsterdam: Elsevier Science JAI), 345–423.

CAMPBELL, J. P., DUNNETTE, M. D., LAWLER, K. E., and WEICK, K. E. (1970). *Managerial Behavior, Performance, and Effectiveness* (New York: McGraw-Hill).

CAMERER, C., and KNEZ, M. (1996). 'Coordination, Organizational Boundaries and Fads in Business Practices', *Industrial and Corporate Change*, 5(1): 89–112.

CHILD, J. (2005). *Organization* (Oxford: Blackwell).

COTE, S., and HEALY, T. (2001). *The Well-Being of Nations: The Role of Human and Social Capital* (Paris: Organization for Economic Co-operation and Development).

COLEMAN, J. S. (1988). 'Social Capital in the Creation of Human Capital', *American Journal of Sociology*, 94 (suppl.): S95–S120.

COLLINS, J. C., and PORRAS, J. I. (1994). *Built to Last: Successful Habits of Visionary Companies* (New York: HarperBusiness).

CREMER, J. (1993). 'Corporate Culture and Shared Knowledge', *Industrial and Corporate Change*, 2: 351–86.

CROWSTON, K., and OSBORN, C. (1998). *A Coordination Theory Approach to Process Description and Redesign* (Center for Coordination Science, WP 204; Cambridge, Mass.: MIT).

DEAL, T. E., and KENNEDY, A. A. (1982). *Corporate Cultures: The Rites and Rituals of Corporate Life* (Reading, Mass.: Addison-Wesley Publishing Co.).

DENISON, D. R. (1990). *Corporate Culture and Organizational Effectiveness* (New York: Wiley).

—— (1996). 'What is the Difference between Organizational Culture and Organizational Climate? A Native's Point of View on a Decade of Paradigm Wars', *Academy of Management Review*, 21(3): 619–54.

DE SOUZA BRIGGS, X. (1998). 'Brown Kids in White Suburbs: Housing Mobility and the Many Faces of Social Capital', *Housing Policy Debate*, 9(1): 171–221.

DEUTSCH, M. (1949). 'A Theory of Cooperation and Competition', *Human Relations*, 2(2): 129–52.

—— (1973). *The Resolution of Conflict* (New Haven, Conn.: Yale University Press).

—— (1980). 'Fifty Years of Conflict', in L. Festinger (ed.), *Retrospections on Social Psychology* (New York: Oxford University Press), 46–77.

DYER, W. G. (1986). *Cultural Change in Family Firms: Anticipating and Managing Business and Family Transitions* (San Francisco: Jossey-Bass).

ELLIS, A. P. J., BELL, B. S., PLOYHART, R. E., HOLLENBECK, J. R., and ILGEN, D. R. (2005). 'An Evaluation of Generic Teamwork Skills Training with Action Teams: Effects on Cognitive and Skill-Based Outcomes', *Personnel Psychology*, 58(3): 641–72.

FARAJ, S., and SPROULL, L. (2000). 'Coordinating Expertise in Software Development Teams', *Management Science*, 46: 1554–68.

FLEMING, L., and WAGUESPACK, D. M. (2007). 'Brokerage, Boundary Spanning, and Leadership in Open Innovation Communities', *Organization Science*, 18: 165–80.

FOSS, N. (2001). 'Leadership, Beliefs and Coordination: An Explorative Discussion', *Industrial and Corporate Change*, 10(2): 357–88.

FUKUYAMA, F. (1997). 'Social Capital and the Modern Capitalist Economy: Creating a High Trust Workplace', *Stern Business Magazine*, 4(1): 4–17.

GARDNER, H. (1983). *Frames of Mind* (New York: Basic Books).

GOLEMAN, D. (1995). *Emotional Intelligence* (New York: Bantam).

—— (1998). *Working with Emotional Intelligence* (New York: Bantam).

GORDON, G. G., and DITOMASO, N. (1992). 'Predicting Corporate Performance from Organizational Culture', *Journal of Management Studies*, 29: 783–99.

GRANOVETTER, M. (1983). 'The Strength of Weak Ties: A Network Theory Revisited', *Sociological Theory*, 1: 201–33.

GREENSPAN, S. I. (1997). *The Growth of the Mind and the Endangered Origins of Intelligence* (Reading, Mass.: Merloyd Lawrence).

GRIFFIN, M. A., and MATHIEU, J. E. (1997). 'Modeling Organizational Processes across Hierarchical Levels: Climate, Leadership, and Group Process in Work Groups', *Journal of Organizational Behavior*, 18: 731–44.

HAYTON, J. C. (2005). 'Competing in the New Economy: The Effect of Intellectual Capital on Corporate Entrepreneurship in High-Technology New Ventures', *R&D Management*, 35(2): 137–55.

—— and KELLEY, D. J. (2006). 'A Competency-Based Framework for Promoting Corporate Entrepreneurship', *Human Resource Management*, 45(3): 407–27.

—— and McEVOY, G. M. (2006). 'Guest Editors' Note: Special Issue: Developing and Assessing Professional and Managerial Competence', *Human Resource Management*, 45(3): 291–4.

—— and ZAHRA, S. A. (2005). 'Venture Team Human Capital and Absorptive Capacity in High Technology New Ventures', *International Journal of Technology Management*, 31(3–4): 256–74.

HITT, M. A., and MORGAN, C. P. (1977). 'Organizational Climate as a Predictor of Organizational Practices', *Psychological Reports* 40(3/2): 1191–9.

JAMES, L. A., and JAMES, L. R. (1989). 'Integrating Work Environment Perceptions: Explorations into the Measurement of Meaning', *Journal of Applied Psychology*, 74: 739–51.

JAMES, L. R., and MCINTYRE, M. D. (1996). 'Perceptions of Organizational Climate', in K. Murphy (ed.), *Individual Differences and Behavior in Organizations* (San Francisco: Jossey-Bass), 416–50.

——and SELLS, S. B. (1981). 'Psychological Climate: Theoretical Perspectives and Empirical Research', in D. MAGNUSSON (ed.), *Toward a Psychology of Situation: An Interactional Perspective* (Hillsdale, NJ: Erlbaum), 275–450.

JESTON, J., and NELLIS, J. (2006). *Business Process Management: Practical Guidelines to Successful Implementations* (Oxford: Elsevier).

KATZ, R. L. (1974). 'Skills of an Effective Adminstrator', *Harvard Business Review* (Sept.–Oct.): 90–102.

KOTTER, J. P., and HESKETT, J. L. (1992). *Corporate Culture and Performance* (New York: Free Press).

LANDY, F. J. (2005). 'Some Historical and Scientific Issues Related to Research on Emotional Intelligence', *Journal of Organizational Behavior*, 26: 411–24.

LANGLOIS, R. N. (2002). 'Modularity in Technology and Organization', *Journal of Economic Behavior and Organization*, 49: 19–37.

LAWRENCE, P. R., and LORSCH, J. W. (1969). *Organization and Environment* (Boston: Harvard Business School Press).

LIN, N. (2001). *Social Capital: A Theory of Social Structure* (Cambridge: Cambridge University Press).

LITWIN, G. H., and STRINGER, R. A., JR. (1968). *Motivation and Organizational Climate* (Boston: Harvard University Press).

LOCKE, E. A. (2005). 'Why Emotional Intelligence is an Invalid Concept', *Journal of Organizational Behavior*, 26: 425–31.

——and LATHAM, G. P. (1990). *A Theory of Goal-Setting and Task Performance* (Englewood Cliffs, NJ: Prentice-Hall).

MCCLELLAND, D. C. (1973). 'Testing for Competence rather than for "Intelligence"', *American Psychologist*, 28: 1–14.

MALONE, T. W., CROWSTON, K., LEE, J., and PENTLAND, B. (1999). 'Tools for Inventing Organizations: Toward a Handbook of Organizational Processes', *Management Science*, 45: 425–43.

MARCH, J. G., and SIMON H. A. (1958). *Organizations* (New York: John Wiley & Sons).

MAYO, E. (1945). *The Social Problems of an Industrial Civilization* (Boston: Graduate School of Business Administration, Harvard University).

MINTZBERG, H. (1979). *The Structuring of Organizations* (Englewood Cliffs, NJ: Prentice Hall).

——(1983). *Structure in Fives: Designing Effective Organizations* (Englewood Cliffs, NJ: Prentice Hall).

MURPHY, L. R., GERSHON, R. M., and DEJOY, D. (1996). 'Stress and Occupational Exposure to HIV/AIDS', in C. L. Cooper (ed.), *Handbook of Stress Medicine* (Boca Raton, Fla.: CRC Press), 176–90.

NADLER, D., and TUSHMAN, M. (1997). *Competing by Design: The Power of Organizational Architecture* (Oxford: Oxford University Press).

Nahapiet, J., and Ghoshal, S. (1998). 'Social Capital, Intellectual Capital, and the Organizational Advantage', *Academy of Management Review*, 23: 242–66.

Nelson, R. R., and Winter, S. G. (1982). *An Evolutionary Theory of Economic Change* (Cambridge, Mass.: Belknap Press of Harvard University Press).

O'Reilly, C. A. (1989). 'Corporations, Culture and Commitment: Motivation and Social Control in Organizations', *California Management Review*, 31(4): 9–25.

——and J. A. Chatman (1996). 'Culture as Social Control: Corporations, Culture and Commitment', in B. M. Staw and L. L. Cummings (eds.), *Research in Organizational Behavior* (Greenwich, Conn.: JAI Press), xviii. 157–200.

Orton, J. D., and Weick, K. E. (1990). 'Loosely Coupled Systems: A Reconceptualization', *Academy of Management Review*, 15: 203–23.

Ouchi, W. G. (1980). 'Markets, Bureaucracies, and Clans', *Administrative Science Quarterly*, 25: 129–41.

——(1981). *Theory Z: How American Business Can Meet the Japanese Challenge* (Reading, Mass.: Addison-Wesley Publishing Co.).

Pascale, R., and Athos, A. (1982). *The Art of Japanese Management: Applications for American Executives* (New York: Simon & Schuster).

Patterson, M. G., West, M. A., Shackleton, V. J., Dawson, J. F., Lawthom, R., Maitlis, S., Robinson, D. L., and Wallace, A. M. (2005). 'Validating the Organizational Climate Measure: Links to Managerial Practices, Productivity and Innovation', *Journal of Organizational Behavior*, 26(4): 379–408.

Pentland, B. T. (1992). 'Organizing Moves in Software Support Hot Lines', *Administrative Science Quarterly*, 37(4): 527–48.

——and Reuter, H. H. (1994). 'Organizational Routines as Grammars of Action', *Administrative Science Quarterly*, 39(3): 484–510.

Peters, T., and Waterman, R. (1982). *In Search of Excellence* (New York: Harper & Row).

Podolny, J. M., and Baron, J. N. (1997). 'Resources and Relationships: Social Networks and Mobility in the Workplace', *American Sociological Review*, 62: 673–93.

Powell, W. W., Koput, K. W., and Smith-Doerr, L. (1996). 'Interorganizational Collaboration and the Locus of Innovation: Networks of Learning in Biotechnology', *Administrative Science Quarterly*, 41: 116–45.

Puranam, P. (2007). Personal webpage: Research. URL: http://faculty.london.edu/ppuranam/Research.htm (accessed Jan. 2008).

Putnarn, R. (1995). 'Bowling Alone: America's Declining Social Capital', *Journal of Democracy*, 6: 65–78.

Reagans, R., Argote, L., and Brooks, D. (2005). 'Individual Experience and Experience Working Together: Predicting Learning Rates from Knowing Who Knows What and Knowing How to Work Together', *Management Science*, 51(6): 869–81.

Rhoades, L., and Eisenberger, R. (2002). 'Perceived Organizational Support: A Review of the Literature', *Journal of Applied Psychology*, 87: 698–714.

Sackmann, S. A. (1992). 'Culture and Subcultures: An Analysis of Organizational Knowledge', *Administrative Science Quarterly*, 37: 140–61.

Salovey, P., and Mayer, J. D. (1990). 'Emotional Intelligence', *Imagination, Cognition and Personality*, 9(3): 185–211.

Schein, E. H. (1985). *Organizational Culture and Leadership: A Dynamic View* (San Francisco: Jossey-Bass).

SCHNEIDER, B. (2000). 'The Psychological Life of Organizations', in N. M. Ashkanasy, C. Wilderom, and M. F. Peterson (eds.), *Handbook of Organizational Culture and Climate* (Thousand Oaks, Calif.: Sage).

——BRIEF, A. P., and GUZZO, R. A. (1996). 'Creating a Climate and Culture for Sustainable Organizational Change', *Organizational Dynamics*, 24(4): 7–19.

SMITH, A. (1910). *The Wealth of Nations* (London: Dent).

SMITH, K., COLLINS, C., and CLARK, K. (2005). 'Existing Knowledge, Knowledge Creation Capability, and the Rate of New Product Introduction in High-Technology Firms', *Academy of Management Journal*, 48: 346–57.

SOBEL, J. (2002). 'Can we Trust Social Capital?', *Journal of Economic Literature*, 40(1): 139–54.

SOLOW, R. M. (1999). 'Notes on Social Capital and Economic Performance', in P. Dasgupta and I. Serageldin (eds.), *Social Capital: A Multifaceted Perspective* (Washington, DC: World Bank), 6–10.

SØRENSEN, J. B. (2002). 'The Strength of Corporate Culture and the Reliability of Firm Performance', *Administrative Science Quarterly*, 47: 70–91.

SPENCER, L. M., JR., and SPENCER, S. M. (1993). *Competence at Work* (New York: John Wiley & Sons).

——McCLELLAND, D. C., and SPENCER, S. M. (1994). *Competency Assessment Methods: History and State of the Art* (Boston: Hay McBer Research Press).

SVYANTEK, D. J., and BOTT, J. P. (2004). 'Organizational Culture and Organizational Climate Measures: An Integrative Review', in J. C. Thomas (ed.), *Comprehensive Handbook of Psychological Assessment: Industrial and Organizational Assessment* (Hoboken, NJ: John Wiley), iv. 507–24.

TAYLOR, F. W. (1911). *The Principles of Scientific Management* (New York: Harper Bros.).

THOMPSON, J. D. (1967). *Organizations in Action: Social Science Bases of Administrative Theory* (New Brunswick, NJ: Transaction Publishers).

TJOSVOLD, D. (1986). 'The Dynamics of Interdependence in Organizations', *Human Relations*, 39: 517–40.

TOLKSDORF, R. (2002). 'Models of Coordination and Web-Based Systems', in Dan C. Marinescu and Craig Lee (eds.), *Process Coordination and Ubiquitous Computing* (Boca Raton, Fla.: CRC Press), 27–48.

TRIST, E., and BAMFORTH, K. (1951). 'Some Social and Psychological Consequences of the Longwall Method of Coal Getting', *Human Relations*, 4: 3–38.

UZZI, B. (1999). 'Embeddedness in the Making of Financial Capital: How Social Relations and Networks Benefit Firms Seeking Financing', *American Sociological Review*, 64: 481–505.

WEEKS, J. (2004). *Unpopular Culture: The Ritual of Complaint at a British Bank* (Chicago: University of Chicago Press).

WEST, M. A. (1990). 'The Social Psychology of Innovation in Groups', in M. A. West and J. L. Farr (eds.), *Innovation and Creativity at Work: Psychological and Organizational Strategies* (Chichester: John Wiley & Sons), 309–33.

CHAPTER 17

UNDERSTANDING INTERDEPENDENCIES BETWEEN HUMAN CAPITAL AND STRUCTURAL CAPITAL

SOME DIRECTIONS FROM KANTIAN PRAGMATISM

DAVID O'DONNELL

17.1 INTRODUCTION

Within the field of intellectual capital (IC), the distinctions between its human capital, structural capital, and relationship capital dimensions (and variants of this people/internal/external taxonomy) are essentially, and acknowledged by most to be, heuristic. These distinctions provided progressive management over the past twenty years with an initial means of coping with the increasingly intangible and immaterial nature of economic activity in the late-modernist knowledge economy and society. Pioneering managerial practitioners such as Leif Edvinsson (1997; Edvinsson and Malone, 1997), and Karl-Erik Sveiby (1997) led the way; academics and other key institutional actors followed. The main emphasis in this *first wave* of activity, understandably enough from the managerial perspectives of performance management, performance measurement, and reporting, was on the analysis, design, development, implementation, and continuous (re)evaluation of a set of appropriate indicators within each of the three dimensions, measurements over time, and construction of intellectual capital statements. Many firms now produce intellectual capital statements as a supplement to their annual financial reports, providing useful information to stockholders, capital markets, customers or clients, potential investors, partners or employees, and other stakeholders. These taxonomies are deemed to be most useful to management through monitoring changes in indicators over time and making appropriate managerial interventions within a conventional performance management mindset.

The purpose of this chapter is to address and begin to explore interdependencies between human capital and structural capital. With others in this part of the volume, the focus is explicitly intraorganizational. But how? The various taxonomies that have emerged, notwithstanding their perceived pragmatic usefulness to managerial practice, and both internal and external reporting, are mainly descriptive, static, and linear. They are not dynamic. From the outset, this suggests a number of observations and challenges to certain assumptions. Initial academic research, following the institutionalization of a taxonomic approach in the late 1990s, which is critically if briefly discussed below, largely followed the modernist natural science analysis of variance model. Human, structural, and relationship dimensions of intellectual capital were operationalized as independent variables with various measures of firm performance constituting the dependent variable. It is worth noting at this stage that within this empirical–analytical paradigm, no difference is permitted between the natural, social, and psychological sciences; human capital and structural capital are both deemed to be mere categories of the real, such as apples and oranges, and their interaction is presumed to be unproblematic. This presumption is unequivocally challenged here.

Notwithstanding reasonably significant research effort within this neopositivist world-view over the past twenty years, no consensus has emerged on definitions or construct operationalizations of the dimensions of intellectual capital, or indeed of the broader concept itself which remains fuzzily somehow related to, and often viewed as equivalent to, that other elusive concept, *intangibles*. Sveiby (2007), for example, has identified at least thirty-four different methods/models of measuring and reporting on intellectual capital. The limits of the *static* modernist natural science model in this complex field are now increasingly recognized, as it quite simply does not allow us to gain any theoretically substantive understanding of the *dynamics* of the production and co-production of these interacting forms of capital within the firm.

This begs the key question addressed in this chapter: how might one begin to better theoretically understand, and gain some empirical access to, the dynamic interdependencies between human capital and structural capital in an intraorganizational context? Human capital, building on the seminal work of Becker (1964) and Schultz (1961), has been reasonably well if not overtheorized over the past half century or so from the macroeconomic neoclassical perspective. Conceptualizations of human capital as a dynamic heterogeneous organizational level construct, however, remain undertheorized (see Chapters 5 and 7). Moreover, structural capital remains seriously undertheorized, and problematic, in terms of its inclusion within intellectual capital discourse, notwithstanding significant prior, if highly contentious, theorizations of social structure within the philosophy of science, and the agency–structure debate in social theory. This is challenging. The focus in this chapter is explicitly on enhancing our understanding, as distinct from prediction, control, measurement, or reporting. Such interdependency is not now to be assumed or taken for granted. If such interdependency exists, what is the nature of such interdependency, and how does one address or research such interdependency in terms of theory, ontology, and methodology? The nature of such interdependency, the degrees of independence, and how research should be conducted, are all highly contentious issues discussed here.

In broad terms, this chapter may be viewed both as a response to Spender's (1996) call for greater effort on developing a more dynamic knowledge-based theory of the firm, and as a critique of solely one-sided, non-dynamic, reductionist, determinist, or neopositivist approaches to addressing these key relationships. Within the field of intellectual capital, and building on a decade or so of personally grappling with these concepts in collaboration with colleagues, this chapter may also be viewed as an attempt to contribute to the *second wave* (O'Donnell. 2004a; Mouritsen and Larsen, 2005; Spender, 2006) of research on intellectual capital which seeks a more theoretically grounded understanding of the dynamics of the production and co-production of these interacting forms of capital. The discussion presented in this chapter in order to begin to address this dynamic interdependency, if in part, is inclusive of, but goes beyond, many mainstream conceptualizations of formal organization, dominant in organization theory since Weber. This may be viewed as an attempt to incorporate Tsoukas's call for incorporating 'greater complexity' and 'theoretical sophistication' in organization theory by focusing on *organization* in late-modern knowledge economies, which may enable us to get a clearer picture of the 'dynamic processes through which organization emerges' (2003: 609–10; 2005).

From the perspective of the ordinary everyday life-as-lived of employees and managers in time and place, human capital demands that one take the wonderful complexity of human agency, human (inter)action, and language into account; structural capital points in the direction of identifying relevant enabling and con-straining social structures within the firm. To access the dynamic interdependencies between these two phenomena of interest demands that one obtain some grasp on an approach to intraorganizational reality that is sophisticated enough to guide research. People create capital, and people create intellectual capital. Acknowledging the various artifacts, tools, and technologies available to assist this process of creation, they create it in discussions with other people. Language is the primary human tool. Hence, the firm is viewed in this chapter as a social community that specializes in the creation, maintenance, development, and leveraging of the competitive advantage inherent in the asset specificity/ambiguity of its dynamic processes of knowing relative to other firms in similar sectors.

It is argued here that Kantian pragmatism provides a sufficiently rich relationist/realist world-view wherein guidance may be found on how to begin to address these dynamic interdependencies in an intraorganizational context. I do not pretend to provide any definitive naïve solutions here; I simply sketch the broad outlines of how one particular approach to organizational reality may assist us in future research in enhancing our understanding of the complexities involved. Methodologically, this relationist/realist approach demands inclusion of *both* the internal interpretive perspectives of participants within the firm *and* the external perspectives of an observer in any substantive analysis. Kantian pragmatism, following the *mature* work of Jürgen Habermas (1984, 1987*a*, 1987*b*, 1990, 1993, 1996, 2003), transcends the divisions between interests and norms, between instrumental action, normative action, and subjective experiences; communication, action, and representation are deemed equiprimordial from this perspective. The two key conceptualizations appropriated from *The Theory of Communicative Action* (Habermas, 1984, 1987*a*) to begin to address this dynamic interdependency, if in part, between intra-organizational structural capital and human capital are *organizational lifeworld* (Figure 17.1) and *communicative action*, its correlate, respectively. This theory 'regards the dialectic of knowing and not knowing as embedded within the dialectic of successful and unsuccessful mutual understanding' (Habermas 1987*b*: 314). I can now plausibly locate human capital within the philosophical and social theoretical space of an organizational lifeworld, and begin to think about and map out some possible interdependencies.

The remainder of this chapter is as follows. In the next section I provide a brief, if somewhat critical, recent history of the emergence of the intellectual capital concept and how a largely taxonomic approach, and forms of neopositivist research, became institutionalized. The broad outlines of four approaches to addressing the agency–structure debate in social theory—namely, reductionist, determinist, conflationist, and relationist/realist—are very briefly discussed to set the scene for providing a skeletal outline of a Kantian pragmatist approach, which is relationist/realist, in the following section. This is the kernel of the future-oriented approach to intellectual capital research advocated here to overcome the limits of both extant taxonomies and neopositivist worldviews. The conclusion reached is that future research from a Kantian pragmatist perspective has the potential to substantively enhance our understanding in this complex field.

17.2 EMERGENCE OF CONCEPTS AND THE ROAD NOT TAKEN

The concept of intellectual capital is essentially a product of the 1990s. It is useful here to provide an initial brief review on how this concept emerged, on the 'conceptual-theoretic apparatus' (Keenoy, 2009: 464) deployed, and particularly how key actors and institutions legitimized a largely reductionist and static taxonomic approach which influenced both research funding from bodies such as the OECD and the European Commission, and neopositivist approaches, with some exceptions, to such research. The limits of both are now increasingly apparent, and it is probable, following Ghoshal (2005), that anything that is written on possible interdependencies between human capital and structural capital may have little if any correlation with temporal reality and intraorganizational working life-as-lived unless we can somehow transcend theses limits. It follows that some engagement with the agency–structure debate in social theory and the philosophy of science is unavoidable, and necessitates identifying, justifying, and taking an explicit position within this debate.

The future direction suggested in this chapter is Kantian pragmatism. This draws on the broad traditions of continental European interpretative philosophy since Kant (thinkers such as Gadamer, 1992/1960; Heidegger, 1990/1927; Husserl, 1970; Schütz, 1967; Wittgenstein, 2001/1953), and American pragmatism (Dewey, 1998; Mead, 1932; Peirce, 1905). It also includes the more recent synthesis and further development of both following the *linguistic turn*, including aspects of analytic philosophy related to representation and objectivity, and is best illustrated in the works of Karl-Otto Apel (1987, 1998), Hilary Putnam (1990), and Jürgen Habermas (2003: for a concise overview, see Fultner, 2003). The influence of Habermas is perhaps best known in work from critical theory and critical management studies perspectives (Adler *et al.*, 2007; Alvesson *et al.*, 2009; O'Donnell, 2007; Scherer, 2009), but the focus here is solely on the potential of his mature work to enhance our understanding of the focal interdependencies between human capital and structural capital in future research.

17.3 ON THE ARCHAEOLOGY, EMERGENCE, AND INSTITUTIONALIZATION OF INTELLECTUAL CAPITAL

In 1991 Leif Edvinsson initiated and led a project team of accountants and finance specialists to develop a new 'accounting taxonomy' with the purpose of presenting the dimensions of intellectual capital in Skandia, a large Scandinavian insurance and financial services firm. They reached the conclusion that key success factors in an intangibles and knowledge-driven economy could be grouped into four distinct areas of focus (financial, customer, process, renewal and development), and one common area of focus: human capital. Within each, key indicators could be identified and these indicators used to measure performance. This resulted in the document *Visualizing Intellectual Capital* being distributed to Skandia's stockholders at the May 1995 annual general meeting, as a supplement to Skandia's 1994 Annual Report. News of this innovation spread rapidly, and Edvinsson, the world's first director of intellectual capital, was contacted within months by representatives of hundreds of other firms who wished to learn from, and follow, this initiative (see Edvinsson, 1997; Edvinsson and Malone, 1997).

Conferences on intellectual capital began to appear worldwide, including a Securities and Exchange Commission (SEC) symposium on intangibles in Washington in 1996, and a number of OECD and European Commission conferences followed. The first World Congress on Intellectual Capital was held in Canada in 1998, and the *Journal of Intellectual Capital* was launched in 2000, amongst other developments (see Blair and Wallman, 2001; Danish Ministry of Science, Technology and Innovation 2003; European Commission, 2003; MERITUM 2002). What Edvinsson and his colleagues had achieved was to place intellectual capital in close proximity to, if *not on*, the balance sheet for the first time. The greatest benefit arises from discussions of goals, strategies, indicators, and so on, related to these taxonomies; the narratives and the numbers are inseparable because they constitute each other (Mouritsen, 2004; Mouritsen *et al.*, 2001). Conversely, where inappropriate indicators are selected, probably due to incomplete understanding of the processes involved, the productive potential of the firm may be damaged (Leitner and O'Donnell, 2007). That said, the concept of intellectual capital, notwithstanding increasing and significant business management and academic attention, remains elusive and contested. I do not provide any essentialist definition here, but since I first presented a paper on this topic, with the purpose of 'making darkness visible' (O'Donnell 1999), I continue to simply view this phenomenon as a complex dynamic process of situated collective knowing within the firm that is capable of being leveraged into economic and social value (O'Donnell, 2004*a*).

Note that an understanding of the centrality of intangibles, including goodwill, is not new, and Hayek's (1948/1945) work on the role of knowledge in economic activity, notwithstanding personal reservations on his ideology, remains influential and very relevant. (See Lewin, Chapter 5, who presents key insights from 'Austrian economics' in arguing that 'the knowledge of *many people* is combined in capital goods; capital development is a process of *social* interaction, not a matter of individuals working autonomously'.) Intangible assets, as distinct from the dynamics of their original production, include copyrights, patents, trademarks, goodwill, customer databases, know-how, and others (Bounfour, 2008; European Commission, 2003). Stefano Zambon, in his introduction to a comprehensive literature review in this area, including the various taxonomies and measurement systems in use, cites the following from a well-known institutional economist: 'The substantial foundation of the industrial corporation is its immaterial assets', and it is 'commonly believed that the value creation process of the "modern corporation" as well as of economic systems are largely founded on, and fostered by, intangibles' (European Commission, 2003: p. iii). This could very well have been written yesterday; but in fact, it was written more than a hundred years ago by Thorstein Veblen (1904).

It is worthwhile here to briefly revisit the emergence and institutionalization of intellectual capital concepts in the course of the 1990s. In an insightful and personal *insider* account, Ulf Johanson outlines how the 'archaeology' of intellectual capital concepts starts with a battle between the concepts of human resource accounting (HRA) and intellectual capital, initiated during the 1996 OECD conference in Helsinki (Johanson and Henningsson, 2007). This meeting represents a seminal moment in the battle of ideas in this area. Johanson's account provides a useful point of departure for anyone wishing to gain an understanding of the concept of intellectual capital, its perceived dimensions of structural capital and human capital, their relation to the broader concept of intangibles, their contested nature (Gallie, 1956), and the influence of institutional power and key actors (academic, governmental, business) in socially constructing, legitimizing, and disseminating such concepts, and associated research methodologies. By the time of the 1999 OECD conference in Amsterdam, the agenda had been set, and the battle between financial and non-financial reporting had concluded. Non-mandatory reporting through narrative supplements to annual reports, as in Skandia's seminal supplement, was the direction proposed, and it has since been the dominant approach to addressing intellectual capital (Andriessen, 2007; Bontis, 1998; Bounfour, 2008; Chaminade and Catasús, 2007; Marr and Chatzkel, 2004). Those who argued for an extension of traditional accounting (including Johanson, Baruch Lev (see Lev, 2001, 2003), and European Union Commissioner Edith Cresson, who argued strongly for the inclusion of intangibles in firm's financial statements and for treating both employee training investment and capital investment on an equal basis) had lost out. The influential prediction by Steven Wallman, US SEC Commissioner, that in ten years these intellectual capital measures would be the most watched numbers, and that financial accounts would take a back seat, has evidently not come to pass by the time of writing this chapter. This battle of ideas is far from over, and almost certainly needs to be revisited if the field of intellectual capital is to progress beyond the limits of heuristic taxonomies and the natural science model.

To make a contested concept intelligible one needs to map its complex connections to the range of other concepts to which it is related—which can be termed 'cluster concepts' (Connolly, 1993). Johanson and Henningsson (2007) cogently suggest that the concept of intangibles and its relations to human resource accounting (HRA: Flamholtz, 1985) and human resource costing and accounting (HRCA: see Gröjer and Johanson, 1996; Johanson *et al.*, 1998; Chapter 15), the taxonomy of the balanced scorecard (BSC: Kaplan and Norton, 1992, 1996), and intellectual capital, form a cluster concept.

From the academic literature, the following provides an illustrative, but certainly not exhaustive, listing of other 'concepts' available at the time for inclusion in this cluster concept. Karl-Erik Sveiby was, and remains, heavily influenced by his reading of Michael Polanyi (1958, 1966)—particularly the concept of *tacit knowing* on which he based his doctoral dissertation presented at Stockholm university in 1994, as he applied his prior business experience and thinking (Sveiby and Risling 1986), leading to the development of the Intangible Assets Monitor™ (Sveiby, 1997). By far the most influential appropriation of Polanyi's ideas, albeit contested (see Gourlay, 2004; Tsoukas, 2005), in the academic fields of knowledge management and intellectual capital, is Ikujiro Nonaka's (1994; Nonaka and Takeuchi, 1995; Chapter 18) 'dynamic theory of organizational knowledge creation' and the now well-known SECI-Model, published in *Organization Science*, which has become the most cited work in both these fields (Serenko and Bontis, 2004).

Other than those noted above, key influences that one may reasonably link to this 'cluster concept' in the battle of ideas in this area in the mid- to late 1990s include Edith Penrose's (1959) seminal theory of firm growth; the resource-based view (RBV) of the firm (Barney, 1991; see Chapters 8 and 10 above); Arthur's (1994) work on increasing returns and path dependence; Hall's (1992) seminal paper on the strategic analysis of intangible resources; Granovetter's (1985) influential work on 'embeddedness'; Itami and Roehl's (1987) focus on invisible assets; Stewart's (1991) *Fortune* article on intellectual capital 'becoming America's most valuable asset' and Davenport and Prusak's (1998) book on 'working knowledge'; the special issue of the *Strategic Management Journal* edited by Spender and Grant (1996) on 'knowledge and the firm'; Nahapiet and Ghoshal's (1998) paper linking social capital to intellectual capital; Kogut and Zander's work (1992, 1993) on 'knowledge of the firm'; Brown and Duguid's (1991) paper on organizational learning and communities of practice; Teese *et al.'s* (1997) conceptualization of 'dynamic capabilities'; the increasing influence of work following Bourdieu's (1984) extension of the concept of capital and Giddens' (1984) structuration theory in 'practice-oriented' academic research; and Weick and Roberts's (1993) influential paper on 'collective mind' in *Administrative Science Quarterly*. While certainly by no means exhaustive, these examples illustrate the range of ideas available in the late 1990s to participants at these defining conferences.

Returning to the Helsinki meeting in 1996, Johanson gave the first presentation following the opening address by Pertti Sorsa, Secretary General of Finland's Ministry of Labor. He was followed by Leif Edvinsson who, noting the increasing gap between book value and market value in many firms, gave a robust presentation on his success with the Skandia Navigator™. Johanson's speech drew on the Swedish experience with human resource costing and accounting (HRCA) over the previous fifteen years. One of his conclusions was that 'a discussion of objectivity with respect to HRCA's possibilities of representing reality is meaningless because it is the subjective interpretation of different phenomena that governs the individual's behavior' (Johanson and Henningsson, 2007: 8).

By the time of the 1999 OECD conference in Amsterdam, when the key decisions were made, Johanson's key insight, which could perhaps have provided impetus for debate on a more dynamic conceptualization of possible interdependencies between human capital and structural capital, had largely disappeared from the agenda. The proceedings from the Helsinki Conference (OECD, 1997) include the following illustrative statement: 'No one imagines that this supreme intangible, so protean and so slippery, can be accommodated within existing accounting practice' (Johanson and Henningsson, 2007: 9). The outcome was essentially *reductionist*, and a very impoverished conception of human agency, dominant in mainstream accounting, finance, and economic disciplines, prevailed (see Chapter 7). As noted above, there was a range of sophisticated intellectual tools available within the broad cluster concept that could have been applied in the mid- to late 1990s to gain a more sophisticated conceptualization of this 'supreme' if somewhat 'slippery' intangible! Solely reductionist or determinist approaches, however, are incapable of providing insights into the focal dynamic interdependency addressed in this chapter.

17.4 Returning to the Agency–Structure Debate and the Fork in the Road Not Taken

A voluminous literature exists on the contested nature of the agency–structure debate (Reed, 2003; Seidman and Alexander, 2001; Turner, 1991; Winch, 1958; Winship and Rosen, 1988). On human agency, the key to gaining some grasp of its 'dynamic possibilities', according to Emirbayer and Mische (1998: 964), is to 'view it as composed of variable and changing orientations within the flow of time. Only then will it be clear how the structural environments of action are both dynamically sustained by and also altered through human agency, by actors capable of formulating projects for the future and realizing them, even if only in small part, and with unforeseen outcomes, in the present.' This initial view of agency as a 'temporally embedded process of social engagement' complements a Kantian pragmatist relationist/realist approach and suggests a move beyond methodological individualism towards communicative action in the following section. For reasons of space and parsimony of exposition I draw heavily here on Reed's (2003) concise discussion of four main approaches in social theory: reductionist, determinist, conflationist, and relationist/realist.

Reductionism, or forms of behaviorist individualism, attempts to resolve ontological, methodological, and analytical complexity through a strategy of extreme simplification. Structure is reduced to a merely 'residual analytical category' referring to the aggregated consequences of individual behavior. The atomized and decontextualized human being is viewed as an independent center striving to maximize her/his personal utility functions. This ontology refuses to recognize the 'subjective interpretation' of various phenomena governing individual behavior noted by Johanson (above). In *determinist* and purely structuralist accounts, human agency becomes essentially 'powerless in the face of structural causality'. Structural Marxism, structuralism, and much of post-structuralism provide the exemplars here within an eclectic gathering of social scientists. Structure is 'regarded as an independent, *sui generis* entity, completely unaffected by agency, individual or collective' (Reed, 2003: 294). Whereas social structure disappears in reductionist approaches, agency disappears as an 'ontological reality in its own right' in determinist approaches; it can 'only be fleetingly glimpsed as a residual element or trace left over from the inexorable operation of structural forces' (ibid. 297). Neither reductionist nor determinist approaches are capable of guiding an understanding of the complex and dynamic interdependencies addressed in this chapter.

The *conflationist* approach, influenced by the work of Bourdieu (1984) and Giddens (1984), is much more promising in terms of our focus on understanding. It opposes both reductionist and determinist approaches in insisting on the 'mutual and equal co-determination' of agency and social structure. Here we meet the emphasis on practices, routines, scripts, and so on, in recent academic literature. Agency and structure are deemed 'ontologically inseparable and mutually constitutive' in that they refer to 'active constituting processes or practices' and 'constraining and enabling conditions' that are viewed as of equal causal significance in accounting for social action or agency and the structural forms or relations generated' (Reed, 2003: 297–8). Conflationists, however, tend to 'ontologically and analytically collapse structure into agency' (ibid., 298).

Relationist/realist approaches, such as those from Kantian pragmatism that I advocate in this chapter, 'hold firm' to the ontological and analytical separability of agency and structure. These are viewed as 'distinct and separable strata of social reality pertaining to different powers and capacities such as institutionalized constraints and enablements (structure) as opposed to collective articulation and mobilization of shared interests (agency)' (Reed, 2003: 303). It then follows, according to Reed (2003), that the 'dynamic interplay' between agency and structure provides the 'explanatory key' to how we access the 'temporal and relational complexities of the agency–structure dilemma'. This dynamic interplay and the 'distinctive sets of causal powers that they necessarily entail' must be disentangled and then reconstructed before the dynamics and trajectory of 'organizing in any particular situation can be identified with any degree of confidence' (2003: 303). Relationist/realist approaches to this debate, from a Kantian pragmatist world-view, can deal with the 'double constitution of agency and structure' (301) in that creative agency within the firm and the constraining/enabling social structures of an organizational lifeworld are equally recognized as constitutive features of social and intraorganizational life. The broad contours of how this might be addressed, drawing on the substantive, and real, Habermasian concepts of *organizational lifeworld* and *communicative action*, are outlined in the following section.

17.5 ORGANIZATIONAL LIFEWORLD AND COMMUNICATIVE ACTION

People live, think, speak, and act *in* the world (Heidegger, 1990/1927), *in* time (Bergson, 2001/1889; Mead, 1932; Emirbayer and Mische, 1998: 969), and they are *situated* within their own local lifeworlds or organizational lifeworlds. Such lifeworlds are sustained and regenerated through communicative action (Habermas, 1984, 1987a). As noted in the introduction, the firm is viewed here as a *social* community specialized in the creation, development, maintenance, and leveraging of its dynamic processes of knowing relative to other firms in similar sectors. The intraorganizational context of the firm is essentially local and contextual, and human capital may be located within its lifeworld. Acknowledging the influence of Polanyi's (1958, 1966) *phenomenological* work in diverse fields, particularly in the knowledge management and intellectual capital fields, I argue here on the merits of taking an alternative, more *language-analytic*, route into philosophical and social theoretical space within which the dynamic interdependencies between human capital and structural capital may be substantively addressed so as to enhance our understanding of the complexities involved. The two volumes of *The Theory of Communicative Action* (Habermas, 1984, 1987a) run to over 1,000 pages of philosophical and social theoretical discourse. All I attempt to do here is provide a skeletal outline of the core concepts appropriated from this theory to address the focal interdependencies, if in part, and in the process point in the direction of, and encourage further research from, the relationist/realist perspective of Kantian pragmatism. The reader is referred to Thomas McCarthy's (1984) translator's introduction for an excellent synopsis of this major twentieth-century work. I alternate here between discussions of theory and method and suggest some implications for management where I deem it appropriate. This is largely future-oriented, hence there is little explicit empirical evidence available from this perspective.

17.6 CONTOURS OF AN ORGANIZATIONAL LIFEWORLD

Adopting the demanding perspective of Kantian pragmatism advocated here requires an explicit shift in focus from individual action and methodological individualism to human interaction, from the monological to the dialogical, and from the now exhausted philosophy of consciousness to the philosophy of language and speech-act theory. The conceptualization of *lifeworld*, which includes developments of the work of Husserl (1970), Schütz (1967) in particular, and Parsons (1968), and its correlate *communicative action*, is appropriated from Habermas (1984, 1987*a*). In agreement with Turner (1991), these conceptualizations provide analytical depth to the discussion of *organizational lifeworld* (Figure 17.1), which follows. This directs us toward a deeper conceptualization of the *social* aspects of structural capital, if not to other phenomena in extant intellectual capital approaches deemed to form part of structural capital, such as databases, intellectual property, technology, ICT systems (see Te'eni, 2001; Chapter 20 below), and so on. Lifeworlds only exist in a 'uniquely pre-reflexive form of background assumptions, background receptivities, or background relations' (Honneth *et al.*, 1981: 16) and this allows us to now recognize the existence of the collective background knowing of an organizational lifeworld as an alternative to more individualistic approaches to tacit knowing, such as Polanyi's (O'Donnell 2004*b*).

The focus here is social, collective, and communicatively rational as distinct from non-social, individual, and instrumentally rational (Table 17.1), which I discuss below. Acknowledging that all firms are knowledge-intensive, I tend to speak of 'knowing' and 'knowing-intensive firms' to emphasize the dynamic nature of the communicative relation between people. Habermas refers to culture, society, and personality development as the three structural components of a lifeworld. In terms of an organizational lifeworld I refer to community, as distinct from society, and 'selves development' to emphasize the interactionist and collective focus on human capital. Communicative action is the form of agency adopted here, and it refers to:

the interaction of at least two subjects capable of speech and action who establish interpersonal relations (whether by verbal or extra-verbal means). The actors seek to reach an understanding about the action situation and their plans of action in order to coordinate their actions by way of agreement. (Habermas, 1984: 86)

Set within the broad philosophy of Kantian pragmatism, this approach is sophisticated enough to substantively engage with 'the complex interplay between agency and structure', viewed as the 'fundamental dynamic that shapes the institutional context' (Reed, 2003: 306) noted earlier—the institutional context in this case being the intraorganizational lifeworld of the firm. I fully concur with Reed's assertion that:

we cannot begin to do this if we continue to believe that we can reduce and/or collapse the distinctive ontological and analytical domains to which these two concepts refer. Only by separating and interrelating the distinctive realities to which these concepts refer can we develop approaches to the study of organizations and organizing that properly attend to the *endemic tensions between social action and social structure* as they work their way through in our everyday and institutional lives. (2003: 306; emphasis added)

With these strategic moves into the space of Kantian pragmatism, we can now reconceptualize the firm in a more dynamic fashion from a coherent relationist/realist

Reproduction Processes	Structural Components of an Organizational Lifeworld			Dimensions of Evaluation
	Culture	Community	Selves Development	
Cultural Reproduction	Interpretative schemata fit for consensus: valid processes of knowing [loss of meaning]	Legitimations [withdrawal of legitimation]	Behavior patterns effective in learning & development [crisis in orientation & development]	Rationality of Knowledge
Social Integration	Obligations [unsettling of collective identity]	Legitimately ordered interpersonal relations [anomie]	Social memberships and ownership [alienation]	Solidarity of Members
Socialization	Interpretative accomplishments [rupture of tradition]	Motivations for actions that conform to norms [withdrawal of motivation]	Interpretative capabilities and personal identities [psycho-pathologies]	Personal Responsibility

Figure 17.1. Contours of an Organizational Lifeworld

Source: Adapted from Habermas (1987*a*: 142–3).

framework. The point of departure is the communicative relation *between* people (human capital in action; social action; communicative action; agency) as this provides the key empirical assess point in terms of 'speech acts' (Searle, 1969), discussed in more detail below, to each of the nine segments of an organizational lifeworld noted in Figure 17.1. The communicative relations (human capital in interaction) within each segment are dynamically interdependent with the cultural, social/community, and developmental/psychological social structures within the firm, and with their associated reproduction processes of cultural reproduction, social integration, and socialization (*social* structural capital); finally, the dimensions of rationality of knowledge, solidarity of members, and personal responsibility provide pointers to evaluation.

At first glance this appears to be somewhat overly complex; but it is essentially a scientifically justifiable map of how employees and/or managers may communicate, argue various points of view, make distinctions, make judgments, draw on experiences, and reach decisions on both day-to-day activities and the problematic situations which are the usual stuff of organization. In terms of empirical research, the 'quality' of discourse within such firms, 'insofar as it is measured by the procedural properties of its process of generation, is an empirical variable' (Habermas, 1996: 362). The main implication for management is to avoid seriously damaging the quality of communicative relations, as this will result in negative consequences (such as alienation, loss of motivation, unsettling of collective identity, and others in parentheses in Figure 17.1), leading to suboptimal linguistic processing of available expertise, and impoverished or suboptimal solutions to problematic situations.

Not all activity within the firm demands communicative action, but the increasing complexity of economic life in many areas demands collaborative effort, and collaboration points in the direction of linguistic competence. The logic or rationality of formal organization is largely instrumental; instrumental rationality, however, does not encompass the totality of human forms of rationality, of action, or of interaction. Before addressing the key linguistic validity claims within the communicative relation, the point of empirical access to the 'quality of discourse', a very brief explanation of the distinctions between forms of human action and their associated rationalities (Table 17.1) is necessary here—particularly the distinction between instrumental rationality and communicative rationality. These distinctions are central to understanding the properties of the communicative relation, its ontology, and the validity basis of speech-acts related to the objective, social, and subjective worlds. Without this understanding one cannot conduct plausible empirical research with a point of departure in the communicative relation, or present or defend any reasonably plausible findings.

Table 17.1. Types of Action

Action Situation	Action Orientation	
	Oriented to success	*Oriented to reaching understanding*
Non-social	instrumental action	—
Social	strategic action	communicative action

Source: Habermas (1984: 285).

Action oriented to success or efficacy is the usual idea of rationality dominant in organization theory and microeconomics. This can be further divided into instrumental action and strategic action. In contrast, communicative action is oriented to reaching intersubjective understanding (*Verständigung*), and this form of rationality is communicative. Such agentic orientations allow us to identify three broad action types:

We call an action oriented to success *instrumental* when we consider it under the aspect of following technical rules of action and assess the efficiency of an intervention into a complex of circumstances and events. We call an action oriented to success *strategic* when we consider it under the aspect of following rules of rational choice and assess the efficacy of influencing the decisions of a rational opponent. Instrumental actions can be connected with and subordinated to social interactions of a different type; for example, as the "task elements" of social roles; strategic actions are social actions by themselves. By contrast, I shall speak of *communicative* action whenever the actions of the agents involved are coordinated not through egocentric calculations of success but through acts of reaching understanding. In communicative action participants are not primarily oriented to their own individual successes; they pursue their individual goals under the condition that they can harmonise their plans of action on the basis of common situation definitions. In this respect the negotiation of definitions of the situation is an essential element of the interpretive accomplishments required for communicative action. (Habermas, 1984: 285; emphasis in original)

These distinctions of action types, action orientations, and rationalities beg the key methodological question of how to go about identifying and distinguishing between them.

Social actions can be distinguished according to whether the participants adopt either a success-oriented attitude or one oriented to reaching understanding. And under suitable conditions, these attitudes should be identifiable on the basis of the intuitive knowledge of the participants themselves. (Habermas, 1984: 286)

This 'intuitive knowledge of the participants themselves' suggests some parallels with Johanson's assertion at the 1996 conference in Helsinki (noted above) on accessing meaning, and the subjective interpretations governing behavior; meaning is *not* available to the external observer. As will hopefully become somewhat clearer in the following discussion, Kantian pragmatism can address this 'subjectivity', and it can also include sociality/intersubjectivity, and objectivity. Methodologically, this relationist/realist approach demands that one include both the internal perspectives of participants within the firm *and* the external perspectives of an observer. In this way one can transcend the divisions between interests and norms, between instrumental action, normative action, and subjective experiences.

Organizational lifeworlds are held together, develop, change, and regenerate through the set of ongoing communicative relations within them. The point of departure in addressing, researching, or indeed managing any organizational lifeworld, from the language-analytic perspective presented here, is the communicative relation between two people—the set of symmetric and reciprocal relations presupposed in communicative action; and this relation is grounded in 'an explication of the rational potential built into the validity basis of speech' (Habermas, 1987b: 314). We can now reasonably conceive of *organizational* lifeworlds as 'culturally transmitted and linguistically organized stock(s) of interpretative patterns' (Habermas, 1987a: 124), and these stocks of interpretative patterns will influence the processual flows of knowing through communicative relations within the firm. Whatever the stock of individual human capital, as conventionally conceived, that members of a firm bring with them to the office or the factory floor each morning, it is the quality of the flows of knowing between these members, the quality of conversations, and full and frank argumentative discussions on addressing problematic situations or organizational goals, that is decisive from the perspective of employees, managers, and board directors.

17.7 COMMUNICATIVE ACTION

Now I turn attention to briefly describing the procedural properties and ontological richness of the Habermasian communicative relation—the relation between two people who wish to engage in substantive discussion about reaching an agreed understanding on how to act in the usual problematic situations which are the stuff of everyday working life-as-lived in any real firm. Human capital demands a context; without a context human capital is simply an abstraction. This is the decisive and defining moment in this chapter as the communicative relation is the point of departure that allows us to substantively conceptualize the dynamic interdependencies between human capital and structural capital in the context of an intraorganizational lifeworld.

At the microlevel, communicative action is a two-way dynamic process between *One* and *Other* which incorporates *three* clearly identifiable validity claims related to the objective, social, and subjective worlds. Facts, norms, and subjective experiences are all recognized here. When at least two people communicate with each other within an organizational lifeworld, face-to-face speech-acts, body-language, e-mail, or other means of communication, each utterance or speech-act that *One* makes can be explicitly or implicitly accepted or challenged/rejected by *Other* on a very simple 'Yes' or 'No' basis. *One* is perceived by *Other* as making a claim to validity with each speech-act, and *Other* may accept, challenge, seek further evidence, or reject such claims. Assuming the general claim to linguistic comprehensibility—that is, 'I understand what you are saying'—the corresponding validity claims of propositional truth/efficacy related to the objective world of facts and/or states-of-affairs, normative rightness related to the social world around here in any organizational lifeworld, and authenticity/genuineness/sincerity related to the subjective world are all ontologically available—this latter claim often addressed silently or internally by *Other*. All speech acts, however implicitly, make these three claims, although one may be emphasized more than the other two in any particular situation. Claims in this instance are not settled by recourse to the power of managerial or hierarchical authority, but by providing reasons for or against such claims in the mutual give-and-take of this form of rational argumentative discourse (O'Donnell, 2004a, 2009).

Returning to the contours of an organizational lifeworld (Figure 17.1), one can now begin to think about, and carry out research on, the dynamic interdependencies between communicative action (human capital in interaction with the validity claims within speech acts as the empirical points of reference) and organizational lifeworld structures and processes (structural capital) in each of the nine segments of any organizational lifeworld within the firm. Dalvir Samra-Frederick (2000, 2004) provides an excellent example of how to conduct in-depth ethnographic research based on these validity claims in her study of a board of directors and senior management team 'in-action' in a manufacturing firm. This form of research is not for the faint-hearted, or those seeking a 'quick hit' in academic journals: monthly board meeting were attended for over a year, and fieldwork included conversations, observations, work-shadowing, interviews, and audio and video recordings of 'naturally occurring events'. Her findings, based on analysis of a daunting volume of data over following years, illustrate how the skilled nature of the board's interactive routines and behavioral dynamics could be made more transparent (Samra-Fredericks, 2000) and how 'power effects' are constituted through linguistic interactions (Samra-Fredericks, 2004).

Some further implications for management may now be suggested. Communicative action is central to the healthy functioning of organizational lifeworlds and the general well-being of its members: under the functional aspect of reaching understanding it transmits and renews cultural knowledge; under the aspect of coordinating action it is central to social integration and the establishment of group solidarity within the firm; and the process of socialization may be linked to issues related to employee motivation, interpretive capabilities, and the development and formation of personal identities, and others (as in Figure 17.1). The implication for management here is to recognize and come to understand that communicative action is a fragile process, and when this process is impeded or endangered, the quality of communication, general well-being, and emergent creative capacity may suffer (see also Chapter 25 below). If one accepts this plausible argument, it follows that anything which negatively influences the ability to raise such validity claims within the set of communicative relations will severely impair, or perhaps even destroy, the healthy functioning of particular knowing-communities within the firm, with implications for knowledge creation, knowledge-sharing, learning, problem-solving, innovation, and creativity (O'Donnell, 2004a; O'Donnell et al., 2003a, 2003b).

This procedural architecture of the communicative relation, the core building block for all of Habermas's mature work, can be shown to be universally valid in a specific or particular sense, and this is sufficient to satisfy the scientific requirements of 'objectivity' (Habermas, 1984: 137) in a post-foundationalist manner. Its key characteristics in the context of the intraorganizational lifeworld of the firm may now be summarized as follows: (i) the three ontological world-relations of organizational members and the corresponding concepts of the objective, social, and subjective worlds; (ii) the corresponding validity claims within the communicative relation to the objective, social, and subjective worlds of propositional truth/efficacy, normative rightness, and authenticity/sincerity, respectively—note that the general claim to comprehensibility may be assumed in most cases but is not to be taken for granted; (iii) the concept of a rationally motivated agreement based on the intersubjective recognition of criticizable validity claims in time and context; and (iv) the concept of reaching understanding as the cooperative negotiation of common definitions of the situation. I must emphasize the key fact that *only* the *procedural properties* of the communicative relation associated with these three validity claims are deemed to be *universal*; content and specifics are always contextual (O'Donnell, 2004a, 2009). It is worth noting here that Kantian pragmatists insist on maintaining some connection to the universal, particularly in terms of post-metaphysical moral discourse (Apel, 1987, 1998; Habermas, 1990, 1993, 2003; Putnam, 1990; for a concise overview, see Cronin, 1993), and in the areas of democracy and law (Habermas, 1996).

This organizational lifeworld, which always remains *at the back* of actors in communication or collaboration, provides a particular context of relevance within which human agency, and human capital, is *always already situated*, and it cannot be transcended. Even within the modern reflexivity of organizing where existing traditions and institutional norms are regularly challenged, employees cannot step completely out of their organizational lifeworlds, nor can they objectify them in a supreme act of reflection (McCarthy, 1984), and neither can managers or researchers. This organizational lifeworld, however, does have a transcendental character in that it functions as a condition of possibility for communicative action, as an intersubjectively shared background of mutual intelligibility that *first* makes the communicative relation possible; hence its centrality to gaining an understanding of creative human agency in increasingly knowing-intensive firms (O'Donnell, 2004b).

17.8 Returning to Methodology

This organizational lifeworld approach—grounded in its correlate, the communicative relation—appears to be best suited to interpretive case study, ethnographic or co-creation research (Henriksen *et al.*, 2004; O'Donnell and Henriksen, 2002; Samra-Fredericks, 2000, 2004), and from the perspective of a performative research participant, virtual or real (O'Donnell 2004a). Following Habermas (1987a), this runs the risk of an 'hermeneutic idealism' by conceptualizing the complexity of an organizational lifeworld from the sole perspective of the intuitive knowledge or self-understanding of its members, and remaining 'blind to causes, connections and consequences that lie beyond the horizon of everyday practice'. This transition, according to Habermas, from one problem area to the other of this *disjecta membra* is tied to a 'change of methodological attitude and conceptual apparatus' in that 'functional integration' only comes into view when the organizational lifeworld is objectified as a 'boundary-maintaining system' (see McCarthy, 1984: pp. xxviii–xxix). From such an observer perspective, however, relevant phenomena are

described in a language that objectivistically disregards actors' self-understanding. This language neither seeks nor gains an entry into the intuitive knowledge of participants. Under the artificially defamiliarizing gaze of the system observer who conceives [herself/himself] as a system in an environment, or that of the ethnologist who approaches even [her/his] own native practices and language games as an uninitiated stranger, every context of social life crystallizes into a hermeneutically inaccessible second nature, about which counter-intuitive knowledge is gathered as it is in the natural sciences. (Habermas, 1996: 48)

The usefulness of natural science methodologies, where appropriate, is certainly not dismissed here. With this ontological transition a researcher must also take on the perspective of an observer which Kantian pragmatism demands. This allows many techniques and methods from analytical and systems approaches to be employed, if not their associated philosophies of science, in this particular approach to accessing the dynamic interdependencies between human capital and structural capital. It also provides space for reconstructing and incorporating much complementary empirical research from conflationist work by theorists of practice and those who focus on sensemaking in organizational life. Kantian pragmatism, albeit relationist/realist, may reconstruct certain empirical evidence from conflationist approaches arising from theoretical overlaps with pragmatism, phenomenology, and the role of habit, routines, and scripts in shaping social interaction within the firm (for example, Nicolini *et al.*, 2003; Orlikowski, 1992; Weick and Roberts, 1993); and some insights from both reductionist and determinist approaches where deemed appropriate. There is no need for paradigm wars on method here, but an understanding of reductionist, determinist, and conflationist approaches is a prerequisite to learning from them, and reconstructing their findings from a more relationist/realist perspective where deemed appropriate and possible (see Arbnor and Bjerke, 1997; O'Donnell, 2004a).

17.9 Concluding Comments

In this chapter I addressed the challenging question of how one might begin to better theoretically understand, and gain some empirical access to, the dynamic interdependencies between human capital and structural capital in an intraorganizational context. The guiding approach to addressing this question is explicitly to enhance understanding of the complexities involved, as distinct from prediction, control, measurement, or reporting. The firm is viewed as a social community specialized in the creation, maintenance, development, and leveraging of the competitive advantage inherent in the asset specificity/ambiguity of its dynamic processes of knowing relative to other firms in similar sectors. The various first-wave indicator-based taxonomies that have emerged, notwithstanding their pragmatic usefulness in raising awareness, in focusing attention in managerial practice, and in both internal and external reporting, are mainly descriptive, static, and linear. Further, the limits of the natural science empirical—analytical model in this complex field were noted as this model does not allow us to gain any theoretically substantive understanding of the dynamics of the production and co-production of these interacting forms of capital. To access the dynamic interdependencies between these two phenomena of interest I argue that we move beyond both reductionist and determinist approaches in social theory on the agency–structure debate as both are incapable of substantively addressing the question; the strength of conflationist/practice approaches were briefly noted, but again these do not really allow us to get at the focal dynamic interdependencies.

I have argued that Kantian pragmatism provides a sufficiently sophisticated relationist/realist worldview wherein guidance may be found on how to address the dynamic interdependencies between human capital and structural capital, and guide future empirical research. The two key concepts of *organizational lifeworld*, and its correlate, *communicative action*, were appropriated here from *The Theory of Communicative Action* (Habermas, 1984, 1987a) to address this dynamic interdependency, if in part, between intraorganizational structural capital and human capital, respectively. I have sketched the broad outlines of this approach in terms of theory and method, and in the process pointed to an indicative range of dynamic interdependencies between communicative action (human capital as dynamically located within the communicative relation between at least two people) and the social structures and regenerative processes (structural capital) of an organizational lifeworld. Kantian pragmatism allows us to defend the *mutual irreducibility and equiprimordiality* of objectivity, intersubjectivity, and subjectivity (Habermas, 2003). The corresponding validity claims within the communicative relation, and the constraints under which they stand, are substantive and real social phenomena open to future empirical investigations from participant, virtual participant, and observer perspectives.

Acknowledgements

I am grateful to Alan Burton-Jones and J.-C. Spender for insightful and very constructive suggestions as this chapter emerged. The usual disclaimer applies.

References

ADLER, P. S., FORBES, L. C., and WILLMOTT, H. (2007). 'Critical Management Studies', *Academy of Management Annals*, 1(1): 119–79.

ALVESSON, M., BRIDGMAN, T., and WILLMOTT, H., eds (2009). *The Oxford Handbook of Critical Management Studies* (Oxford: Oxford University Press).

ANDRIESSEN, D. (2007). 'Designing and Testing an OD Intervention; Reporting Intellectual Capital to Develop Organizations', *Journal of Applied Behavioral Science*, 43: 89–107.

APEL, K.-O. (1987). 'The Problem of Philosophical Foundations in Light of a Transcendental Pragmatics of Language', in K. Barnes, J. Bohnmann, and T. McCarthy (eds), *After Philosophy: End or Transformation?* (Cambridge, Mass.: MIT Press), 250–90.

—— (1998). 'The Cartesian Paradigm of First Philosophy: A Critical Appreciation from the Perspective of Another (The Next?) Paradigm', *International Journal of Philosophical Studies*, 6(1): 1–16.

ARBNOR, I., and BJERKE, B. (1997). *Methodology for Creating Business Knowledge* (2nd edn. London: Sage).

ARTHUR, W. B. (1994). *Increasing Returns and Path Dependence in the Economy* (Ann Arbor: University of Michigan Press).

BARNEY, J. (1991). 'Firm Resources and Sustained Competitive Advantage', *Journal of Management*, 17: 99–120.

BECKER, G. S. (1964). *Human Capital* (1st edn. New York: Columbia University Press, for the National Bureau of Economic Research).

BERGSON, H. L. (2001/1889). *Time and Free Will*, tr. F. L. Pogson (New York: Dover).

BLAIR, M., and WALLMAN, S. (2001). *Unseen Wealth: Report from the Brookings Taskforce on Intangibles* (Washington, DC: Brookings Institution).

BOUNFOUR, A., eds (2008). *Organizational Capital* (London: Routledge).

BONTIS, N. (1998). 'Intellectual Capital: An Exploratory Study that Develops Measures and Models', *Management Decision*, 36(2): 63–76.

BOURDIEU, P. (1984). *Distinction: A Social Critique of the Judgement of Taste* (London: Routledge).

BROWN, J., and DUGUID, P. (1991). 'Organizational Learning and Communities of Practice: Toward a Unified View of Working, Learning, and Innovation', *Organization Science*, 2: 40–57.

CHAMINADE, C., and CATASÚS, B., eds (2007). *Intellectual Capital Revisited: Paradoxes in the Knowledge Intensive Organization* (Cheltenham and Northampton, Mass.: Edward Elgar).

CONNOLLY, W. E. (1993). *The Terms of Political Discourse* (Oxford: Blackwell).

Danish Ministry of Science, Technology and Innovation (2003). *Intellectual Capital Statements: The New Guidelines* (Copenhagen: Danish Ministry of Science, Technology and Innovation).

CRONIN, C. (1993). 'Translator's Introduction', in J. Habermas, *Justification and Application* (Cambridge, Mass.: MIT Press), pp. xi–xxxi.

DAVENPORT, T. H., and PRUSAK, L. (1998). *Working Knowledge: How Organizations Manage What They Know* (Cambridge, Mass.: Harvard Business School Press).

DEWEY, J. (1998). *The Essential Dewey*, ed. L. Hickman and T. M. Alexander (2 vols. Bloomington, Ind.: Indiana University Press).

EDVINSSON, L. (1997). 'Developing Intellectual Capital at Skandia', *Long Range Planning*, 30(3): 366–73.

EDVINSSON, L. and MALONE, M. S. (1997). *Intellectual Capital* (London: Piatkus).

EMIRBAYER, M., and MISCHE, A. (1998). 'What is Agency?', *American Journal of Sociology*, 103(4): 962–1023.

European Commission (2003). *Study on the Measurement of Intangible Assets and Associated Reporting Practices* (Brussels: European Commission, DG Enterprise). URL: http://ec.europa.eu/internal_market/services/docs/brs/competitiveness/2003-study-intangassets-full_en.pdf (accessed Nov. 2009.

FLAMHOLTZ, E. (1985). *Human Resource Accounting* (San Francisco: Jossey-Bass).

FULTNER, B. (2003). 'Translator's Introduction', in J. Habermas, *Truth and Justification* (Cambridge, Mass.: MIT Press), pp. vii–xxii.

GADAMER, H.-G. (1992/1960). *Truth and Method* (2nd rev. edn. New York: Crossroad Publishing).

GALLIE, W. B. (1956). 'Essentially Contested Concepts', *Proceedings of the Aristotelian Society*, 66: 167–98.

GHOSHAL, S. (2005). 'Bad Management Theories are Destroying Good Management Practices', *Academy of Management Learning and Education*, 4(1): 75–91.

GIDDENS, A. (1984). *The Constitution of Society* (Berkeley, Calif.: University of California Press).

GOURLAY, S. (2004). 'Knowing as Semiosis: Steps towards a Reconceptualization of Tacit Knowledge', in H. Tsoukas and N. Mylonopoulos (eds.), *Organizations as Knowledge Systems* (Basingstoke: Palgrave Macmillan), 86–105.

GRANOVETTER, M. (1985). 'Economic Action and Social Structure: The Problem of Embeddedness', *American Journal of Sociology*, 91: 481–510.

GRÖJER, J.-E., and JOHANSON, U. (1996). *Human Resource Costing and Accounting* (Los Angeles, Calif.: Jossey-Bass).

HABERMAS, J. (1984). *The Theory of Communicative Action*, i. *Reason and the Rationalization of Society*, tr. T. McCarthy (Cambridge: Polity).

——(1987a). *The Theory of Communicative Action*, ii. *The Critique of Functionalist Reason*, tr. T. McCarthy (Cambridge: Polity).

——(1987b). *The Philosophical Discourse of Modernity* (Cambridge: Polity).

——(1990). *Moral Consciousness and Communicative Action* (Cambridge, Mass.: MIT Press).

——(1993). *Justification and Application* (Cambridge, Mass.: MIT Press).

——(1996). *Between Facts and Norms* (Cambridge: Polity).

——(2003). *Truth and Justification* (Cambridge, Mass.: MIT Press).

HALL, R. (1992). 'The Strategic Analysis of Intangible Resources', *Strategic Management Journal*, 13(2): 135–44.

HAYEK, F. A. (1948/1945). 'The Use of Knowledge in Society', in F. A. Hayek, *Individualism and Economic Order* (Chicago and London: University of Chicago Press), 77–91; 1st publ. in *American Economic Review*, 35(4): 519–30, 1945).

HEIDEGGER, M. (1990/1927). *Being and Time*, tr. J. Macquarrie and E. Robinson (Oxford: Basil Blackwell).

HENRIKSEN, L. B., NØRREKLIT, L., JØRGENSEN, K. M., CHRISTENSEN, J. B., and O'DONNELL, D. (2004). *Dimensions of Change: Conceptualising Reality in Organisational Research* (Copenhagen: Copenhagen Business School Press).

HONNETH, A., KNÖDLER-BUNTE, E., and WIDMANN, A. (1981). 'The Dialectics of Rationalization: An Interview with Jürgen Habermas', *Telos*, 49: 5–31.

Husserl, E. (1970). *Logical Investigations*, tr. J. N. Findlay (2 vols. London and New York: Routledge and Kegan Paul/Humanities Press).

Itami, H., and Roehl, T. W. (1987). *Mobilizing Invisible Assets* (Cambridge, Mass.: Harvard University Press).

Johanson, U., and Henningsson, J. (2007). 'The Archaeology of Intellectual Capital: A Battle between Concepts', in C. Chaminade and B. Catasús (eds.), *Intellectual Capital Revisited: Paradoxes in the Knowledge Intensive Organization* (Cheltenham and Northampton, Mass.: Edward Elgar), 8–30.

——Eklöv, G., Holmgren, M., and Mårtensson, M. (1998). *Human Resource Costing and Accounting versus the Balanced Scorecard: A Literature Survey of Experiences with the Concepts* (Paris: OECD).

Kaplan, R. S., and Norton, D. P. (1992). 'The Balanced Scorecard: Measures that Drive Performance', *Harvard Business Review*, 70(1): 71–9.

——and——(1996). 'Using the Balanced Scorecard as a Strategic Management System', *Harvard Business Review*, 74(1): 75–85.

Keenoy, T. (2009). 'Human Resource Management', in M. Alvesson, T. Bridgman, and H. Willmott (eds.), *The Oxford Handbook of Critical Management Studies* (Oxford: Oxford University Press), 454–72.

Kogut, B., and Zander, U. (1992). 'Knowledge of the Firm, Combinative Capabilities and the Replication of Technology', *Organization Science*, 3: 383–97.

——and——(1993). 'Knowledge of the Firm and the Evolutionary Theory of the Multinational Corporation', *Journal of International Business Studies*, 24: 625–45.

Leitner, K.-H., and O'Donnell, D. (2007). 'Conceptualizing IC Management in R&D Organizations: Future Scenarios from the Complexity Theory Perspective', in C. Chaminade and B. Catasús (eds.), *Intellectual Capital Revisited: Paradoxes in the Knowledge Intensive Organization* (Cheltenham and Northampton, Mass.: Edward Elgar), 78–99.

Lev, B. (2001). *Intangibles: Management, Measurement, and Reporting* (Washington, DC: Brookings Institution).

——(2003). 'Remarks on the Measurement, Valuation, and Reporting of Intangible Assets', *Economic Policy Review*, 9(3): 17–22.

McCarthy, T. (1984). 'Translator's Introduction', in J. Habermas, *The Theory of Communicative Action*, i. *Reason and the Rationalization of Society* (Cambridge: Polity), pp. vii–xxxix.

Marr, B., and Chatzkel, J. (2004). 'Intellectual Capital at the Crossroads: Managing, Measuring and Reporting of IC', *Journal of Intellectual Capital*, 5(2): 224–9.

Mead, G. H. (1932). *The Philosophy of the Present* (Chicago: University of Chicago Press).

MERITUM (2002). *Guidelines for Managing and Reporting on Intangibles*. European Project Report, ed. L. Cãnibano, P. Sanchez, M. Garcia-Ayuso, and C. Chaminade (Madrid: Fundación Airtel Móvil).

Mouritsen, J. (2004). 'Measuring and Intervening: How do we Theorise Intellectual Capital Management?', *Journal of Intellectual Capital*, 5(2): 257–67.

——and Larsen, H. T. (2005). 'The 2nd Wave of Knowledge Management: Re-centering Knowledge Management through Intellectual Capital Information', *Management Accounting Research*, 16(3): 371–94.

——Larsen, H. T., and Bukh, P. N. D. (2001). 'Intellectual Capital and the "Capable Firm": Narrating, Visualizing and Numbering for Managing Knowledge', *Accounting, Organizations and Society*, 26(7–8): 735–62.

NAHAPIET, J., and GHOSHAL, S. (1998). 'Social Capital, Intellectual Capital, and the Organizational Advantage', *Academy of Management Review*, 23: 242–66.

NICOLINI, D., GHERARDI, S., and YANOW, D., eds (2003). *Knowing in Organizations: A Practice-Based Approach* (Armonk, NY: M. E. Sharpe).

NONAKA, I. (1994). 'A Dynamic Theory of Organizational Knowledge Creation', *Organization Science*, 5(1): 14–37.

——and TAKEUCHI, H. (1995). *The Knowledge-Creating Company* (New York: Oxford University Press).

O'DONNELL, D. (1999). 'Intellectual Capital Creation: Making Darkness Visible', unpublished paper presented at the Centre for Labour Market Studies, University of Leicester, 27 Nov.

——(2004a). 'Theory and Method on Intellectual Capital Creation: Addressing Communicative Action through Relative Methodics', *Journal of Intellectual Capital*, 5(2): 294–311.

——(2004b). 'On Background Knowledge: Mapping the Limits of Tacit Knowing', in A. Neely, M. Kennerly, and A. Walters (eds.), *Proceedings of PMA2004: Performance Measurement and Management. Public and Private*, Edinburgh International Conference Centre, 28–30 July (Cranfield, UK: Cranfield University School of Management).

——(2007). 'On Critical Theory in a Truth-Less World', *Advances in Developing Human Resources*, 9(1): 111–19.

——(2009). 'Communicative Action (Habermas)', in A. J. Mills, G. Durepos, and E. Weibe (eds.), *Encyclopedia of Case Study Research* (Thousand Oaks, Calif.: Sage).

—— and HENRIKSEN, L. B. (2002). 'Philosophical Foundations for a Critical Evaluation of the Social Impact of ICT', *Journal of Information Technology*, 17(2): 89–99.

—— O'REGAN, P., COATES, B., KENNEDY, T., KEARY, B., and BERKERY, G. (2003a). 'Human Interaction: The Critical Source of Intangible Value', *Journal of Intellectual Capital*, 4(1): 82–99.

——PORTER, G., McGUIRE, D., GARAVAN, T. N., HEFFERNAN, M., and CLEARY, P. (2003b). 'Creating Intellectual Capital: A Habermasian Community of Practice (CoP) Introduction', *Journal of European Industrial Training*, 27(2): 80–7.

OECD (Organization for Economic Cooperation and Development) (1997). *Enterprise Value in the Knowledge Economy* (Proceedings of the Helsinki Conference 1996) (Boston: OECD and Ernst & Young).

ORLIKOWSKI, W. J. (1992). 'The Duality of Technology: Rethinking the Concept of Technology in Organizations', *Organization Science*, 3(3): 398–427.

PARSONS, T. (1968). *The Structure of Social Action* (2 vols. New York: Free Press).

PEIRCE, C. S. (1905). 'What Pragmatism is', *The Monist*, 15(2): 161–81.

PENROSE, E. (1959). *The Theory of the Growth of the Firm* (Oxford: Basil Blackwell).

POLANYI, M. (1958). *Personal Knowledge* (1st edn. Chicago: University of Chicago Press; corrected edn. London: Routledge & Kegan Paul, 1962).

——(1966). *The Tacit Dimension* (London: Routledge & Kegan Paul).

PUTNAM, H. (1990). *Realism with a Human Face* (Cambridge, Mass.: Harvard University Press).

REED, M. (2003). 'The Agency Structure Dilemma in Organization Theory: Open Doors and Brick Walls', in H. Tsoukas and C. Knudsen (eds.), *The Oxford Handbook of Organization Theory: Meta-Theoretical Perspectives* (Oxford: Oxford University Press), 289–309.

SAMRA-FREDERICKS, D. (2000). 'An Analysis of the Behavioural Dynamics of Corporate Governance: A Talk-Based Ethnography of a UK Manufacturing "Board in Action"', *Corporate Governance: An International Review*, 8(4): 311–26.

——(2004). 'Strategic Practice, "Discourse" and the *Everyday* Interactional Constitution of "Power Effects"', *Organization*, 12(6): 803–41.

SCHERER, A. G. (2009). 'Critical Theory and its Contribution to Critical Management Studies', in M. Alvesson, T. Bridgman, and H. Willmott (eds.), *The Oxford Handbook of Critical Management Studies* (Oxford: Oxford University Press), 29–51.

SCHULTZ, T. W. (1961). 'Investment in Human Capital', *American Economic Review*, 51: 1–17.

SCHÜTZ, A. (1967). *The Phenomenology of the Social World* (Evanston, Ill: Northwestern University Press).

SEARLE, J. (1969). *Speech Acts* (Cambridge: Cambridge University Press).

SEIDMAN, S., and ALEXANDER, J. C. (2001). *The New Social Theory Reader* (London and New York: Routledge).

SERENKO, A., and BONTIS, N. (2004). 'Meta-review of Knowledge Management and Intellectual Capital Literature: Citation Impact and Research Productivity Rankings', *Knowledge and Process Management*, 11(3): 185–98.

SPENDER, J.-C. (1996). 'Making Knowledge the Basis of a Dynamic Theory of the Firm', *Strategic Management Journal*, 17(2): S45–S62.

——(2006). 'Method, Philosophy, and Empirics in KM and IC', *Journal of Intellectual Capital*, 7(1): 12–28.

——and GRANT, R. M., eds (1996). 'Knowledge and the Firm', special issue, *Strategic Management Journal*, 17(2).

STEWART, T. A. (1991). 'Brain-Power: How Intellectual Capital is Becoming America's Most Valuable Asset', *Fortune* (3 June): 44–60.

SVEIBY, K.-E. (1997). *The New Organizational Wealth: Managing and Measuring Knowledge Based Assets* (San Francisco: Berrett-Koehler).

——(2007). *Measuring Models for Intangible Assets*. URL: http://www.sveiby.com/articles/IntangibleMethods.htm (accessed Nov. 2009).

——and RISLING, A. (1986). *Kunskapsforetaget* (The Know-How Company) (Malmö, Sweden: Liber).

TE'ENI, D. (2001). 'Review: A Cognitive-Affective Model of Organizational Communication for Designing IT', *MISQ (Management Information Systems Quarterly)*, 25(2): 251–312.

TEESE, D. J., PISANO, G., and SHUEN, A. (1997). 'Dynamic Capabilities and Strategic Management', *Strategic Management Journal*, 18(7): 509–33.

TSOUKAS, H. (2003). 'New Times, Fresh Challenges: Reflections on the Past and Future of Organization Theory', in H. Tsoukas and C. Knudsen (eds.), *The Oxford Handbook of Organization Theory: Meta-Theoretical Perspectives* (Oxford: Oxford University Press), 607–22.

——(2005). *Complex Knowledge* (Oxford: Oxford University Press).

TURNER, J. H. (1991). *The Structure of Sociological Theory* (5th edn. Belmont, Calif.: Wadsworth Publishing Co.).

VEBLEN, T. (2005/1904). *The Theory of Business Enterprise* (New York: Cosimo; 1st publ. New York: Charles Scribner).

WEICK, K., and ROBERTS, K. (1993). 'Collective Mind in Organizations: Heedful Interrelating on Flight Decks', *Administrative Science Quarterly*, 38: 357–81.

WINCH, P. (1958). *The Idea of a Social Science and its Relation to Philosophy* (London: Routledge & Kegan Paul).

WINSHIP, C., and ROSEN, S. (1988). 'Introduction: Sociological and Economic Approaches to the Analysis of Social Structure', *American Journal of Sociology*, 94: S1–S16.

WITTGENSTEIN, L. (2001/1953). *Philosophical Investigations* (3rd edn. Oxford: Blackwell).

CHAPTER 18

....

THE DISTRIBUTED AND DYNAMIC DIMENSIONS OF HUMAN CAPITAL

....

IKUJIRO NONAKA

RYOKO TOYAMA

VESA PELTOKORPI

18.1 INTRODUCTION

....

The development and utilization of human capital has been described in several complementary ways. While labor economists emphasize the financial returns to formal education and training (such as Becker, 1964; Schultz, 1961), transaction economists explain the management of human capital through employment contracts (for example, Williamson, 1985). In the resource-based view of the firm (for example, Barney, 1991; Peteraf, 1993; Wernerfelt, 1984), human capital is a source of sustainable competitive advantage because tacit knowledge and the related social complexities are hard to transfer and imitate. It has consequently become a widely held premise that the effective management of human capital, not physical capital, is the ultimate determinant of organizational performance.

While the above perspectives have contributed to our knowledge of what human capital is, and how it contributes to the competitive advantage of the firm, there has been little discussion about the development and utilization of human capital. We thus describe in this chapter how the distributed dynamic dimensions of human capital are developed and utilized in knowledge-creating companies. We perceive human capital as the most important resource for a firm, and argue that a firm's sustainable competitive advantage came from its ability to create knowledge in a changing environment. Because knowledge is created by people in their interactions with each other and the environment (Nonaka, 1994; Nonaka and Takeuchi, 1995; Nonaka *et al.*, 2008), it is important to understand the nature of human beings in order to keep creating knowledge and make knowledge a sustainable competitive advantage of the firm. Compared to other resources, human capital is different because humans are subjective, interrelated beings who make value judgments. We build on the philosophical concept of phronesis (practical wisdom) to describe the development and utilization of distributed, dynamic human capital.

The rest of this chapter is organized in a following way. The following section provides a review of human capital literature. In the third section, the characteristics of human agents are discussed drawing from interpretative philosophy. The next sections describe the development and utilization of distributed, interconnected human capital through phronesis.

18.2 HUMAN CAPITAL LITERATURE

The concept of human capital has been described in several complementary ways in academic literature. In the early works (such as Becker, 1964; Schultz, 1961), the concept was not about knowledge, abilities, and skills, but about investment in and financial returns to formal education and training. Considering all workers identical (Becker, 1964: 301), human capital could be measured in terms of investment costs and the higher income streams presumed to be derived from them. While useful for measurement purposes, these early works overlook the degree to which methods of organization can facilitate organizational learning and knowledge creation because 'the growth in capital depends on investments in new technologies, basic research and human capital' (Becker, 1964: 311). By also neglecting experience and informal on-the-job training, these works have not taken into account factors crucial to informal skill acquisition, insight, and innovation. Some of these issues are addressed in intellectual capital literature consisting of human, structural, and relational capital (Edvinsson and Sullivan, 1996).

Building on Gary Becker and other labor market economists, Williamson (1985) has offered a transaction cost economic (TCE)-based argument in which the services of specific human capital are organized through employment contracts.

Market transactions and internal production in TCE literature are described as alternatives; there are costs associated with managing employees through market arrangements (transaction costs) versus hierarchical arrangements (bureaucratic costs). Transaction costs in terms of specificity and separability apply to the movement of labor between organizations (Williamson, 1985). In order to retain human capital high on specificity and non-separability, organizations use various types of incentives and contacts. Despite providing the most comprehensive treatment of the organizational ramifications of human capital in economics, the treatment of human capital, like any other asset in TCE, has been heavily criticized by management scholars (such as Kogut and Zander, 1992; Ghoshal and Moran, 1996).

In the resource-based view (RBV) of the firm, valuable and unique human capital has been described as contributing to competitive advantage due to its inimitability based on its intangible, firm-specific, and socially complex nature (for example, Barney, 1991; Barney and Wright, 1998; Peteraf, 1993; Wernerfelt, 1984). In contrast to physical assets, human resources take the form of collectively performed tacit routines, which are difficult to replicate and thus enable the firm possessing these resources to sustain higher levels of profit. The development of human capital is normally instigated by managers, and the contributing processes have been conceptualized as dynamic capabilities (Teece et al., 1997). The dynamic capability perspective suggests that intangible assets, including the skills, knowledge, and abilities of employees, can be reconfigured into routines that enable the firm to renew, augment, adapt, and create capabilities responsive to the ambiguous and unpredictable forces of the business environment. Drawing from the RBV, human resource management research has been focused on the influence of human capital—employees' collective knowledge, skills, and abilities—and the impact of that management on firm level performance (for example, Huselid, 1995).

While each perspective discussed above offers a different lens for understanding what human capital is and how it contributes to the sustainable competitive advantage of the firm, little has been discussed about the processes that enable organizations to develop and utilize their human capital. There are several reasons to explain the lack of literature on this matter. First, human agents are described as objective entities without intuitions, dreams, and intentionality. However, in knowledge-creating organizations, human agents should be seen as the existence who are in the state of becoming, rather than being. They are constantly changing their intentions toward their dreams. Second, since organizations are frequently conceptualized as mechanisms for utilizing human capital based on the positivist philosophy of science, little is known about the processes explaining the creation of knowledge and skills of human capital. Due to the increasing recognition of human capital as the main resource of sustainable competitive advantage, we need to reconsider the conceptualization of human agents and their interactions in organizations.

18.3 Human Capital Interdependencies as Distributed Phronesis

Descriptions of organizational knowledge creation necessitate a movement from the positivist explanations in which organizations exist as information-processing machines towards conceptualizations of organizations as dynamic, organic entities. In the following sections we discuss the nature of human agents and describe the distributed, dynamic dimensions of human capital in organizations building on the philosophical concept of phronesis.

18.3.1 Human Agents

Human capital has often been described as aggregated phenomenon composed of skills, knowledge, and abilities (SKAs) of individual actors (for example, Becker, 1964; Edvinsson and Sullivan, 1996). The focus has been on what individual actors possess rather than their thoughts, feelings, intentionality, and what they apply in action (Peltokorpi, 2008). In these perspectives, the variances in SKAs are considered 'noise' to be overcome to run the machine efficiently. While mass-production assembly-line systems typical of the Ford factory have been the foundation of modern capitalism, they are, in fact, systems trying to produce standardized products with the same level of quality regardless of the varying degrees of capability of labor. Information systems are developed in such a way that the information transmitted conveys the same meaning regardless of the sender or recipient. Bureaucracy defines authority and responsibility in a clear chain of command to ensure uniform operation, even though the people occupying these positions have varying levels of ability.

In contrast to these information process-based conceptualizations, we argue that human agents need to be allowed to have idiosyncratic properties, because these very differences, which management theories have tried to weed out, are necessary to the creation of new knowledge. The traditional Greek definition of knowledge as 'justified true belief' suggests further that knowledge is something that is objective, absolute, and context-free (Nonaka, 1994). However, the positivist perspectives of knowledge as a 'truth' existing independent of us and beyond our experience, and at the same time waiting to be discovered by us, draw our attention away from the essential meaning of knowledge. Instead, equating information with knowledge we should focus on 'belief' as the starting point to an understanding of knowledge, because it is belief that is the source of all knowledge, and it is human beings who hold and justify such belief. For example, quoting St Augustine, Polanyi (1969) stressed the importance of belief to understanding knowledge: 'Unless ye believe, ye shall not understand.'

Knowledge cannot exist without human subjectivities and the contexts that surround human beings, because 'truth' differs according to who we are and from where we view it (Nonaka, 1994). Knowledge is information that is meaningful, and as John Dewey (1916) observed, meaning is not a fixed quality associated with a specific event, but is the variety of possible ways in which the event may influence our future activities and shared understanding. It is human subjectivity that interprets the significance of information. In other words, knowledge requires value judgment to be knowledge. New meaning is created and leads to the creation of new value because subjective viewpoints differ from person to person, depending on the context. We thus need management theories that tackle head-on the issue of differences in individual subjectivity, such as how we view the world and what we value, rather than theories that treat human beings as replaceable parts of an organization and attempts to weed out human subjectivity as 'noise' in the 'machine'.

It should, however, be noted that a subjective belief by itself cannot be knowledge. Knowledge is created by people in their interactions with each other and the environment. It is a process in which the individual's thoughts are justified through social interaction with others and the environment to become objective 'truth'. Justification of belief through social interaction is necessary because the meaning derived from a phenomenon varies with each individual. New knowledge is born of the multiple perspectives of human interaction. Through this multiple perspective one is able to see various aspects of a phenomenon in different contexts that, viewed together, approach an understanding of the essence or truth of the whole phenomenon in each. The knowledge-creating process has thus been conceptualized as a social process of validating truth (Nonaka, 1994). In order to develop a more comprehensive understanding of knowledge, we have to focus on the process in which humans are interrelated. In the substance thinking of conventional economic theory where the person is conceptualized as *homo economicus*, individual relationships are defined in contracts for satisfying people's desires only in terms of possession and consumption of goods and accumulation of wealth. There is no community, only individuals who exist apart from others. A contract-based view of external relationships cannot grasp the social process of knowledge creation.

As stated earlier, knowledge is created from one's belief, and for a belief to become knowledge it has to be justified as truth. Michael Polanyi (1958) has argued that knowledge has to be judged in terms of its significance. Knowledge emerges in a series of value judgments. Such value judgment depends on how we perceive truth, goodness, and beauty. In other words, it depends on our aesthetic sense. Aesthetic sense is necessary not only for judging the knowledge that is being created, but also for determining what kind of knowledge to create. We create knowledge according to our values and ideals. Firms differ from each other because they envision different futures and strive to realize them (Nonaka and Toyama, 2007).

A firm's new opportunities, development of human capital, new markets, new technologies, or new business models are all based on its vision of the future, and it is the values, ideals, and aesthetic sense of the organizational members that determine this vision. In other words, the ontology of the firm, which defines 'how the organization should exist in the world', first sets the firm's vision of the future and then defines the firm's existence, the knowledge it creates, and eventually, the environment in which it operates.

18.3.2 Phronesis: The Practical Ability to Make Value Judgments

In a constantly changing environment, the practical ability to make value judgments in each particular situation in relationship with others is necessary to create a sustainable competitive advantage (Nonaka *et al.*, 2008). This ability was described by Aristotle as an essential habit of mind that grasps the truth. It is the intellectual virtue he called 'phronesis'—often translated as prudence, practical wisdom, and practical rationality (Birmingham, 2004).

In the *Nicomachean Ethics*, Aristotle distinguishes between three types of knowledge: *episteme*, *techne*, and *phronesis*. *Episteme* is universal truth, corresponding to the universal validity principle in the practice of modern science. *Techne* is know-how or practical skill required to be able to create. *Phronesis* is an intellectual virtue: the ability to determine and undertake the best action in a specific situation to serve the common good. The ethical component makes phronesis the highest intellectual virtue, beyond the other two (Nyberg, 2008). Phronesis is not the 'right' way of doing things, but the ethically good action which a practical wise person would take to achieve common good.

In firms, phronesis can be understood as the ability to understand and realize what is considered 'good' by individual customers in specific times and situations in the forms of products or service. For a firm to create revenue it has to offer a product or service that is considered valuable enough for customers to pay its price. Phronesis is necessary, since it is the knowledge of what a 'good' product is (value judgment) and how to make such a product (realize the value judgment). Neither *techne* nor *episteme* can answer the question of what a good product is. 'Good' is a subjective value, and cannot be a universal truth since it continuously changes depending on the context, or who perceives that goodness.

In leadership, phronesis is manifested in the capacity to choose the appropriate goals and to successfully devise means to reach them (Halverson, 2004). Phronetic leaders use their sense of the details to 'see' or 'feel' the problems of their organizations as solvable within local constraints and develop successful plans to address the problems identified. In decision-making, phronetic leaders must be able to synthesize contextual knowledge, accumulated through experience, with universal knowledge gained through training.

While phronesis has traditionally been considered the property of individuals, scholars have recently proposed that leaders, through ethical visions and distributed leadership, are able to create collective phronesis in organizations that guide practices and allow employees to combine general knowledge with the particular knowledge of concrete situations (Halverson, 2004; Nonaka and Toyama, 2005, 2007; Nonaka and Peltokorpi, 2006; Nonaka *et al.*, 2008; Roos, 2006; Statler and Roos, 2007).

18.3.3 The Abilities that Constitute Phronesis

What exactly is phronesis, then, in the context of a knowledge-creating company? We propose that it consists of the following six abilities: (1) The ability to make a judgment on 'goodness'; (2) the ability to share contexts with others to create the shared space of knowledge, *ba*; (3) the ability to grasp the essence of particular situations/things; (4) the ability to express and communicate the essence; (5) the ability to use necessary political means well to realize concepts for the common good; and (6) the ability to foster phronesis in others. These six abilities explain the development and utilization of distributed, dynamic human capital in knowledge-creating companies.

The ability to judge goodness

This is the ability to practice one's moral discernment of what is 'good', and enact that judgment on a practical level according to the particular situation. Knowledge created in an organization depends upon the values of truth, goodness, and beauty possessed by organizational members. Without a solid, philosophical foundation for their values, an individual cannot make a judgment on what is good, and a company is unable to produce value based on such judgment.

Since phronesis is the ability to judge goodness for the *common* good, one has to have a higher point of view to be able to see what is good for the whole. It is this kind of value of the common good that gives a firm an absolute value to pursue that it is a goal in itself, rather than a means to enhance profit.

The ability to share contexts with others to create ba

Ba—which roughly means 'place' in Japanese—is a shared context in motion, where knowledge is shared, created, and put to use. At *ba*, individual, subjective views are understood and shared so that one can see oneself in relation to others and accept others' views and values to create new knowledge. To participate in a *ba* is to become involved and to transcend one's own limited perspective. Husserl (1995) called such a state 'intersubjectivity'.

Therefore, one must have the ability to empathize—to put oneself in the position of the other and to understand their feelings to function effectively in *ba*. It is an imaginative capacity to understand and empathize with others and to elicit empathy in return. In pragmatism, Mead (1934) observed that efficient social interaction was predicated on an individual's capacity to anticipate how others would respond to her behavior.

The ability to share emotion is not just about understanding others' emotions but being able to communicate one's own emotions. A phronetic leader must also have the ability to engage in and cultivate sharing among participants in *ba*. For that, social capital such as care, love, trust, and a sense of security, has to be cultivated to form *ba* (von Krogh *et al.*, 2000).

As knowledge is created in dynamic interaction with the environment, managing the knowledge-creating process requires the ability to foster and manage those interactions according to the situation. It is the responsibility of the leadership to mobilize knowledge that is distributed throughout and across the organization. To do so, knowledge leaders must be able to connect various *ba* both inside and outside the organization. This can be done through the formation of small world networks (Watts, 2003).

The ability to grasp the essence of particular situations and things

This is the ability to quickly sense the essential meaning of the particular experience. Since phronesis is 'a form of reasoning and knowledge that involves a distinctive mediation between the universal and the particular' (Bernstein, 1983: 146), one has to see what lies behind each particular phenomenon and grasp the universal essence of it. To do this, one has to be able to see at both the micro and the macro levels simultaneously. Like the saying, 'God is in the detail', the kind of consciousness that enables one to sense truth in individual details is the starting point of creativity. Also, scholars influenced by phenomenology have argued that small questions can lead to big answers. A keen sensitivity to daily change and the ability to see the implications of that change in the bigger picture are essential attributes of phronesis.

The ability to express and communicate the essence

This is the ability to articulate and conceptualize subjective, intuitive ideas in clear language, link these 'micro' concepts to a macro context, and convincingly communicate them to others. As stated earlier, phronesis requires more than just practical knowledge of a particular situation. It requires the ability to contemplate and grasp a universal 'truth' from the particular in order to determine the best way to act for the common good. Hence, it requires continuous interaction between subjective insight and objective knowledge to identify the optimal way to behave.

The ability to use any necessary means well to realize concepts for the common good

This is the ability to bring people together and spur them to action, combining and synthesizing everyone's knowledge and efforts to achieve the common good. For that, phronetic leaders must choose and utilize the means suitable to each particular situation, including Machiavellian means, where shrewdness and determination can help to achieve 'the good' result (Badaracco, 1997).

Phronetic leaders exercise political judgment by understanding others' emotions in verbal and non-verbal communication, and by giving careful consideration to the timing of their interaction with others (Steinberger, 1993). Since knowledge is a source of power and fragile, mobilizing organizational members' knowledge requires leaders to exercise their political power to energize the emotional and spiritual resources of the organization, based on personal magnetism, consideration of others' viewpoints, and a sense of timing.

A sense of balance to avoid extremes and to act with moderation to resolve contradiction is also important in making political judgments. The reality of management is that it is dynamic and full of confusion and contradiction. In a knowledge-creating organization, contradictions are not obstacles to overcome but are sources of new knowledge. Political power is the ability to understand the contradictions in human nature and to harmonize them in a timely fashion as each situation arises. In short, phronetic leaders need to think in the way of 'both and', not 'either or'.

The ability to foster phronesis in others

This is the ability to foster and transfer the phronetic capabilities of individuals in the organization among others. Fostering phronesis enables the firm to cultivate the critical, next generation of employees. Leadership in a knowledge-creating company is not about fixed administrative control, but a flexible and *distributed* leadership, where the leader is determined by the context. Distributed phronesis will ensure that an organization has the resilience (Hamel and Valikangas, 2003) to respond flexibly and creatively to any situation to pursue its own good. By cultivating practical wisdom in an organization, people can develop the 'everyday strategic preparedness' needed to deal with a complex and uncertain world (Roos, 2006; Statler and Roos, 2007).

18.4 FOSTERING COLLECTIVE PHRONESIS

How can an organization foster distributed phronesis? We propose the following conditions:

(1) Make the organizational members think the essence of good in their daily activities.
(2) Create *ba* to experience actuality.
(3) Create the organizational routine of pursing the essence.
(4) Foster the ability to practice the practical syllogism.
(5) Create opportunities for peak experience.
(6) Provide phronetic examples.
(7) Provide aesthetic and cultural experience.
(8) Create the evaluation and reward system to foster knowledge creation and sharing.

Make the organizational members think the essence of good in their daily activities

Since phronesis requires the judgment on good, an organization has to foster the value system or philosophy on which each organizational member makes such judgments. It would be most effectively fostered by constantly asking the question 'what is good?' in carrying out their daily activities. At Honda, employees are constantly asked 'what do *you* think?' because it is believed that the Honda's value is created based on each individual's values or philosophy, which cannot be given by others. Its management principle, *Respect for the Individual*, acknowledges that every human being is different, and these differences are an important source of the values which Honda creates.

However, it does not mean that the goodness they pursue is something that is good only for each individual. To judge goodness for the *common* good, one has to be able to see what is good for the whole, even though that view stems from his or her own values and desires. At Honda, each employee has to strive to achieve Honda's fundamental belief, *The Three Joys*, through his or her work. These are: the joy of buying, the joy of selling, and the joy of creating. In the efforts to create something that gives them joy to create, based on their own values and at the same time, something that those who sell the product and those who buy the product can enjoy, the ability to judge and realize what is good for both the individuals and the society will be fostered. In its philosophy handbook that is given to each employee, Honda states: 'We believe that sincerely responding to the changing demands of the world through The Three Joys will provide joy to society and make Honda a company that society recognizes and wants to exist.' Here, serving for common good is clearly connected to the survival of the company.

Mitsui and Co. Ltd—one of the largest trading companies in Japan—created several *ba* to think and discuss about 'Yoi-Shigoto' (good-quality work) throughout the company. After a series of incidents concerning its compliancy, Mitsui implemented a company-wide program called 'YOI-SHIGOTO! Our Origins, Your Future'. Workshops and seminars for all management and staff were held globally to re-examine their ideals and aspirations. Shouei Utsuda, the President who implemented the program, held a series of 'circle meetings' to discuss Yoi-Shigoto. Once or twice a month he held a meeting with around ten employees during lunch or after work to intensely discuss their aspirations or the vision to reform Mitsui's business. As a result, he met about 2,000 employees in 117 meetings.

In these meetings and workshops, questions such as 'What is the Yoi-Shigoto that we should be doing?' and 'Is the work I am doing now Yoi-Shigoto?' were asked so that each employee was required to think of goodness in relation to his or her own work. Again, it should be 'good' not only for each individual or the company, but for society. Utsuda says: 'Good quality work means two things. One is whether it does something good for the society, and creates good value for Mitsui. The other is whether it really worth doing, considering you would spend valuable time of your life doing that particular work.' While carrying out their work, Mitsui employees are required to ask themselves constantly such questions as: 'Does our work really create new value and benefit society?'; 'Can we always be proud of its processes and quality?' In their efforts to answer these questions, Mitsui employees could develop the ability to judge goodness.

Eisai, a Japanese pharmaceutical company, created a vision of 'human health care' (*hhc*). Under *hhc* vision its mission is defined as: 'We give first thought to patients and their families, and to increasing the benefits health care provides.' It sounds rather simple and ordinary—nothing but a statement of customer satisfaction. However, it can create contradictions for a pharmaceutical company. Since doctors and pharmacists are their direct customers, it is easy for a pharmaceutical company to lose sight of its end user: patients. A profitable drug for doctors and the company is not necessarily beneficial to the patients who take it. The *hhc* vision clearly states that patients and their families should come first, and therefore makes Eisai employees at all levels think deeply about what really is good for patients and their families and what they can do as a pharmaceutical company to deliver this. To connect the ideal of *hhc* to the actual daily work and realize the vision, Eisai forms *hhc* projects in which cross-functional teams discuss and work on what they could really do to increase the benefit to patients and their families. Among the projects, examples of commendable activities in Japan and abroad are announced once a year and receive an award from the President.

Create ba *to experience actuality*

Since phronesis is the ability to make decisions and act in particular situations, it is necessary for one to read the situation correctly. For that, one has to put oneself in actuality, experience it with five senses, and grasp it correctly. Unlike the word 'reality', which refers to an existing substance or object that could be observed, the word 'actuality' refers to a situation in progress that can only be grasped by those committed to and dwelling in the actual situated experience (Kimura, 1994). Actuality is the origin of knowledge creation, since the most committed of experiences comes closest to truth. By indwelling in the situation and empathizing with others, one can transcend one's limited perspective to create new knowledge. For example, Seven-Eleven Japan relies on on-the-job training rather than a well-defined manual to train its employees, since the situation each store faces is different, and the written manual cannot teach how to deal with the actuality which changes every day. To grasp the actuality correctly, employees of Seven-Eleven Japan are told: 'Don't think *for* the customers, think *as* a customer.' By seeing things from the customers' viewpoint one can overcome fixed notions about the convenience store business and derive innovative solutions to meet the needs and wants of the customers. Honda also emphasizes the importance of direct experience with its three *gen* principle: going to *genba* or actual place; knowing *genbutsu* or the actual elements and situation; and *genjitsusuteki* or being realistic.

Eisai created several training programs to let its employees see the actuality of the patients and their families. This training included hospital ward training, volunteer work at a care home, or elderly movement simulation, in which trainees wear special gears to simulate the eyesight and movement of older people. By experiencing the actual situation of patients for themselves and observing how they were using medicines, employees could start to understand patient's points of view, their needs, and their feelings. Through the experience, employees gained a new perspective and a deeper understanding of the meaning of their own work. Researchers who had been pursuing development of the most effective drug treatments started with a new question, such as: 'What can I do to raise the quality of life of the patients?' Instead of seeing a drug as chemical substance, they saw their work as a part of care for the patients in which emotions such as the joy or fear of the patients and their families play an important part. Based on such perspectives and understanding, innovations such as rapidly disintegrating tablets or transferable labels for injection were made.

Create the organizational routine of pursing the essence

Contemplation in action means that one has to see things in a larger context rather than seeing them in isolation from each other. For that, one needs the ability to grasp the universal essence that lies behind each particular phenomenon. Such ability can be fostered through the routine of asking relentlessly what the essence is. For example, Taiichi Ohno, the 'father' of the Toyota Production System, repeatedly emphasized the importance of pursuing the essence by saying: 'Root cause rather than source: root cause lies hidden beyond the source.' And he had the routine of asking 'why' five times, in order to determine the root cause.

Foster the ability to practice the practical syllogism

Phronesis is the ability to choose the best action to achieve the objective. Since the 'best' depends on situation, we choose an action that satisfies both the objective and the situation rather than following a given principle deductively. In practical syllogism one begins with intention to decide what action to take, and takes action that satisfies both the objective and the situation. While logical syllogism judges whether the proposition is true, practical syllogism judges whether the action can be justified. Here one chooses the 'best' action as an hypothesis rather than the absolute truth. The hypothesis will be corrected if necessary to close the gap between the outcome of the action and the objective. Hence, practical syllogism can promote the relentless pursuit of perfection toward the ideal.

To foster the ability to create hypotheses, practicing the method of abduction is effective. Abduction is a method of reasoning which freely combines the vertical logic of deduction with the horizontal, analogous reasoning of induction to achieve the objective through hypothesis building and testing (Josephson and Josephson, 1994).

Create opportunities for peak experience

Phronesis is also fostered through life experiences as a human being—not just in the workplace but in every aspect of life. Especially important is a peak experience; that is, the experience of having faced great challenges, adversity, or failure. Through the experience of being tested to the limit of one's ability, one can transcend oneself and grow.

An organization can create such peak experiences by giving its employees tough challenges. For example, Honda has a system called the Large Project Leader (LPL), which provides opportunities for individuals to gain the experience necessary to cultivate leadership. An LPL is assigned to each project and is responsible for coordinating the activities of the team and overseeing the progress of the whole project. The position not only requires management skill, but imagination and a sense to choose appropriate action beyond one's field of expertise. Since an LPL does not have power over personnel, he cannot influence the promotion or salary level of project members or even choose the individual members of the project. An LPL has to lead a team not by power legitimated by organizational hierarchy, but by the personal power and magnetism to attract people with his vision, commitment, integrity, energy, and expertise.

Provide phronetic examples

The phronetic way of thinking and acting can be learnt only through practice. Therefore, it is important for an organization to provide living 'exemplars' of phronetic leadership at different levels of the organization, who can show the phronetic way of thinking and acting in their daily works. As Dobson (1999: 133) states, ethics is something that is learnt through observation of others' behavior. People learn to act with phronesis by interacting with others and by observing others' behavior in practice. At Honda, Souichiro Honda, the founder, is still the dominant exemplar. Takeo Fukui, the former President of Honda, remarked: 'Every worker should be Soichiro Honda. It is important for Honda to create many Soichiro Hondas.' However, it does not mean that Honda workers should imitate Soichiro Honda's action. The situations they face today are very different from the one that Soichiro faced when he was alive. Rather, it means that each worker has to ask 'if I were Soichiro, what would I do?' when a judgment call has to be made.

Another way to foster phronesis is through apprenticeship. In the traditional connotation of apprenticeship, phronesis is acquired from a master/student or mentor/mentee relationship, in which experiences, contexts, and time are shared. In apprenticeship, knowledge is acquired through learning *kata*. Roughly meaning a pattern or way of doing things, *kata* is a traditional Japanese code of knowledge which describes the practice of perceiving essence in order to act in a way that is appropriate to the context. It is the distilled essence of a program of behavior that is the ideal of master practitioners (Saito, 2001).

Kata is different from a routine in the sense that it contains a continuous self-renewal process. Continuous self-renewal is achieved by incorporating a high-quality feedback function that helps to notify and modify the differences between predicted outcomes and reality (Feldman, 2000). *Kata* functions with a high degree of freedom to make continuous modifications based on real-time feedback from the situation as it unfolds. It is learnt through the three stages of *Shu* (learn), *Ha* (break) and *Ri* (create). In *Shu*, one learns by following the instruction of a teacher—imitating the teacher's practice repeatedly to master the teacher's values and techniques as one's own. In the next stage, *Ha*, the practitioner attempts to revise the teacher's *kata*, using his own creative influence. In the final stage, *Ri*, the practitioner leaves the teacher and works to develop his own *kata*. It is a continuous tacit process of self-renewal, motivated by the pursuit of truth, goodness, and beauty.

Provide aesthetic and cultural experience

According to Aristotle, phronesis is the character embodied in a good man. To foster goodness one needs experiences as a human being in every aspect of life. Especially important are aesthetic experiences and a culture of philosophy, history, literature, and the arts, which foster insights into historical and social situations. Drucker (2004: 15) has argued that: 'Management is what tradition used to call a liberal art—liberal because it deals with the fundamentals of knowledge, self- knowledge, wisdom, and leadership; art because it deals with practice and application.'

Since knowledge is created by humans in relationship it is important for phronetic leaders to see things and situations in context, and construct a larger relationship that transcends the existing one to envision a unique future. This requires rich imagination (phantasia; see Noel, 1999)—especially historical imagination. Experiencing a wide diversity of contexts and going through a broad variety of pseudo-experiences by reading novels or going to the theater can also foster the ability to see relationships between things, people, and events in an imaginative way.

Create the evaluation and reward system to foster knowledge creation and sharing

For knowledge to be created and shared, organizational members have to be highly motivated and committed to the goals. Research into the motivating factors behind knowledge creation suggests the importance of intrinsic motivation such as personal aspiration and achievement (Osterloh and Frey, 1997). An extrinsic motivator such as money does not necessarily encourage externalization of tacit knowledge in highly valued employees. In fact, in the worst case, extrinsic motivation might 'crowd out' (Osterloh and Frey, 1997) intrinsic motivation and subsequently stall the SECI (socialization, externalization, combination, and internalization) engine.

Therefore, it is necessary for an organization to provide conditions for individuals to sustain intrinsic motivation, such as high-quality learning experiences, a mentoring and coaching *ba*, and a multidimensional incentive system that encourages the creation and sharing of knowledge.

For example, Mitsui and Co. Ltd. introduced a new personnel appraisal standard based on Competency Development Standards for the assessment of individual employees in 2006. The standards include such items as whether one has acted on the company's mission and values. It also introduced an organizational performance evaluation system that shifts the weight of evaluations more toward qualitative objectives. Compared to the old evaluation system that was based only on quantitative objectives, the new system was based on 80 percent qualitative and 20 percent quantitative. Before the reform, Mitsui employees had tended to be concerned only about their own short-term performance. Total optimization and long-term investments—such as building a good relationship with customers—were neglected, and knowledge-sharing and creation were hindered. The new system gradually changed the employees to think and act for total optimization, and the relationships within and across the organization were vastly improved.

In 2009, Mitsui introduced the 'Leadership Values', which states the values on which leaders of Mitsui have to act to achieve Yoi-Shigoto. It consists of five elements:

- Toku: Act with integrity and humility and energize others through personal magnetism. Have depth in character, while acting with dignity and a cultivated mind. Be virtuous and humble with a sense of awe.
- Inspire People: Show strong commitment to the development and motivation of others. Lead by example and provide opportunities for others to see a broader perspective and develop a keener sense of responsibility.

- Create '*ba*': Create an environment within which team members can build mutual trust, share tacit knowledge, and continuously and jointly develop knowledge in order to achieve a sustainable competitive advantage.
- Lead Change for Evolution: Grasp the essence of changing conditions and initiate a new wave of change. Create new values with the spirit of challenge and entrepreneurship.
- Commit to our Future: Be fully committed to one's personal mission with passion, courage, and perseverance, even in the face of adversity. Foresee and mitigate risks at all time.

18.5 CONCLUSION

This chapter has built on the philosophical concept of phronesis to discuss the development and management of distributed, dynamic dimensions of human capital in knowledge-creating organizations. Instead of understanding human capital development as simple investment in, and financial returns to, formal education and training (Becker, 1964) or employment contracts (Williamson, 1985), phronesis allows attention to be given to contextual and value-laden knowledge.

We have argued that a firm's sustainable competitive advantage ultimately depends on the kind of value it can continue to produce. Value is not created by combining and processing information or logically analyzing environments. Rather, it arises from the human's ability to subjectively interpret environments, and above all, from phronesis; that is, the ability to pursue an absolute value determined by a company's unique vision of 'goodness' and applying it contextually to suit the specific situation. It is knowledge that embraces idealistic pragmatism to pursue both universal ideal and particular reality simultaneously toward perfection. When one relentlessly pursues excellence as a way of life, one's knowledge becomes wisdom. Management of firms in the knowledge economy needs to be based on such wisdom.

Management of a knowledge-creating company and the related development and utilization of distributed human capital is not the sole domain of elite entrepreneurs, but is an emergent, distributed, phronetic process. The goal of distributed leadership is to ensure needed overlaps in values, norms, thinking, and practices. The building of collective phronesis that synthesizes environment, organization, and the human agent is at the heart of knowledge-based management. Companies that have established organizational *phronesis* are tenacious, and are able to respond actively to any kind of environmental change because they are engaged in the sustainable practice of turning knowledge into wisdom, aimed at actualizing the corporate vision in real time.

References
BADARACCO, J. L. (1997). *Defining Moments: When Managers Must Choose between Right and Right* (Boston: Harvard Business School Press).

BARNEY, J. B. (1991). 'Firm Resources and Sustained Competitive Advantage', *Journal of Management*, 17: 99–120.

——and WRIGHT, P. M. (1998). 'On Becoming a Strategic Partner: The Role of Human Resources in Gaining Competitive Advantage', *Human Resource Management*, 37(1): 31–46.

BECKER, G. S. (1964). *Human Capital* (Chicago: University of Chicago Press).

BERNSTEIN, R. J. (1983). *Beyond Objectivism and Relativism: Science, Hermeneutics, and Praxis* (Philadelphia: University of Pennsylvania Press).

BIRMINGHAM, C. (2004). 'Phronesis: A Model for Pedagogical Reflection', *Journal of Teacher Education*, 55(4): 313–24.

DEWEY, J. (1916). *Democracy and Education: An Introduction to the Philosophy of Education* (New York: Free Press).

DOBSON, J. (1999). *The Art of Management and the Aesthetic Manager: The Coming Way of Business* (Westport, Conn.: Quorum Books).

DRUCKER, P. F. (2004). *The Daily Drucker* (New York: HarperCollins).

EDVINSSON, L., and SULLIVAN, P. (1996). 'Developing Model for Managing Intellectual Capital', *European Management Journal*, 14(4): 356–64.

FELDMAN, M. S. (2000). 'Organizational Routines as a Source of Continuous Change', *Organization Science*, 11(6): 611–29.

GHOSHAL, S., and MORAN, P. (1996). 'Bad for Practice: A Critique of the Transaction Cost Theory', *Academy of Management Review*, 21(1): 13–47.

HALVERSON, R. (2004). 'Accessing, Documenting and Communicating Practical Wisdom: The *Phronesis* of School Leadership Practice', *American Journal of Education*, 111(1): 90–121.

HAMEL, G., and VALIKANGAS, L. (2003). '*The Quest for Resilience*', *Harvard Business Review* (Sept.): 52–63.

HUSELID, M. A. (1995). 'The Impact of Human Resource Management Practices on Turnover, Productivity, and Corporate Financial Performance', *Academy of Management Journal*, 38: 635–72.

HUSERL, E. (1995). *Cartesian Meditations: An Introduction to Phenomenology*, tr. D. Cairns (Dordrecht: Kluwer).

JOSEPHSON, J. R., and JOSEPHSON, S. G. (1994). *Abductive Inference: Computation, Philosophy, Technology* (Cambridge: Cambridge University Press).

KIMURA, B. (1994). *Kokuro no Byouri wo Kangaeru* (Thoughts on Pathology of the Mind) (Tokyo: Iwanami Shoten).

KOGUT, B., and ZANDER, U. (1992). 'Knowledge of the Firm, Combinative Capabilities and the Replication of Technology', *Organization Science*, 3(3): 383–97.

MEAD, G. H. (1934). *Mind, Self and Society* (Chicago: University of Chicago Press).

NOEL, J. (1999). 'Phronesis and Phantasia: Teaching with Wisdom and Imagination', *Journal of Philosophy of Education*, 33(2): 277–86.

NONAKA, I. (1994). 'A Dynamic Theory of Organizational Knowledge Creation', *Organization Science*, 5(1): 14–37.

——and PELTOKORPI, V. (2006). 'Visionary Knowledge Management: The Case of Eisai Transformation', *International Journal of Learning and Intellectual Capital*, 3(2): 109–29.

——and TAKEUCHI, H. (1995). *The Knowledge-Creating Company* (New York: Oxford University Press).

——and TOYAMA, R. (2005). 'Phronesis Toshite No Senryaku' (Strategy-as-Phronesis), *Hitotsubashi Business Review*, 53(3): 88–103.

—— and —— (2007). 'Strategic Management as Distributed Practical Wisdom (Phronesis)', *Industrial Corporate Change*, 16(3): 371–94.

——TOYAMA, R., and HIRATA, T. (2008). *Managing Flow: A Process Theory of the Knowledge-Based Firm* (New York: Palgrave).

NYBERG, D. (2008). 'The Morality of Everyday Activities: Not the Right, But the Good Thing to Do', *Journal of Business Ethnics*, 81: 587–98.

OSTERLOH, M., and FREY, B. (1997). *Managing Motivation: Crowding Effects in the Theory of the Firm* (Diskussionsbeitrag, 31; Zürich: Institut für betriebswirtschaftliche. Forschung).

PELTOKORPI, V. (2008). 'Synthesizing the paradox of Organizational Routine Flexibility and Stability: A Processual View', *International Journal of Technology Management*, 41(1–2): 7–21.

PETERAF, M. A. (1993). 'The Cornerstones of Competitive Advantage: A Resource-Based View', *Strategic Management Journal*, 14: 170–81.

POLANYI, M. (1958). *Personal Knowledge: Towards a Post-Critical Philosophy* (Chicago: University of Chicago Press).

POLANYI, M. (1969). *Knowing and Being*, ed. Marjorie Grene (Chicago: University of Chicago Press).

ROOS, J. (2006). *Thinking from Within: A Hands-On Strategy Practice* (Basingstoke: Palgrave Macmillan).

SAITO, T. (2001). *Dekiru Hito Ha Doko Ga Chigau Noka* (What Makes Effective People Different) (Tokyo: Chikuma Shobo).

SCHULTZ, T. W. (1961). 'Investment in Human Capital', *American Economic Review*, 51: 1–17.

STATLER, M., and ROOS. J. (2007). *Everyday Strategic Preparedness: The Role of Practical Wisdom in Organizations* (Basingstoke: Palgrave Macmillan).

STEINBERGER, P. J. (1993). *The Concept of Political Judgment* (Chicago: Chicago University Press).

TEECE, D. J., PISANO, G., and SHUEN, A. (1997). 'Dynamic Capabilities and Strategic Management', *Strategic Management Journal*, 18(7): 509–33.

VON KROGH, G., ICHIJO, K., and NONAKA, I. (2000). *Enabling Knowledge Creation: How to Unlock the Mystery of Tacit Knowledge and Release the Power of Innovation* (New York: Oxford University Press).

WATTS, D. J. (2003). *Six Degrees: The Science of a Connected Age* (New York: W. W. Norton).

WERNERFELT, B. (1984). 'A Resource-Based View of the Firm', *Strategic Management Journal*, 5(2): 171–80.

WILLIAMSON, O. (1985). *The Economic Institutions of Capitalism: Firms, Markets, Relational Contracting* (New York: Free Press).

CHAPTER 19

....

HUMAN CAPITAL AND THE ORGANIZATION– ACCOMMODATION RELATIONSHIP

....

JACQUELINE C. VISCHER

19.1 INTRODUCTION

....

Human capital comprises the skills, knowledge, and capabilities of the workforce of a firm, as well as the organizational arrangements and networks of relationships that enable employees to be innovative and productive. As pointed out in Chapter 1 of this volume, the notion that the stock of productive knowledge and skills possessed by people are a form of 'capital' that can be acquired and enhanced by various kinds of investments has proved to be an evocative and powerful way to frame discussions and analyses of what kinds of investment make organizations more productive. In this chapter we look at one factor among the diverse influences on human capital in organizations: the physical environment in which people work.

The 'work environment' is an important concept that typically includes employee–employer relations and HR policies, corporate values, job design, and organizational structure, as well as informal networks and work patterns. Environment also includes accommodation: the buildings, locations, interior space layouts, office space, furniture, and equipment, including information and communications technology (ICT), that employees occupy and use to perform work. An often neglected dimension of the employee experience, an organization's accommodation and decisions about workspace bear on the investment a company makes in its human capital and consequently in employee performance and competitive advantage (Holtham, 2003). The workspace employees occupy has an effect on—but is not the only determinant of—how well they work, how much they work, and how they feel about their work. The accommodation that an organization selects both defines its organizational environment and is a key factor facilitating or hindering human activities. Accommodation supplies workspace—an important mediating influence on the relationship of the organization to its human capital.

The concept of an organization's environment has several overlapping meanings. These include the social context: employee interactions, social support networks, social norms and expectations within and among groups, as well as amount and type of socialization. The social and cultural norms that guide employee behavior and relationships are both transmitted and mediated by space and spatial decisions. For example, are senior executives accommodated in open plan offices that communicate their availability and approachability to employees, or do they occupy remote private offices that communicate their superior status, and are only reachable by scaling long and possibly intimidating hallways?

Environment also includes corporate culture; that is, the way the company is structured and managed, patterns of employer–employee relationships, styles of decision-making (more hierarchical versus more autonomous), managing the flow of information, and staff behavioral expectations, as well as norms and types of individual and group behavior. The space which an organization occupies is an important communicator of organizational culture and values; it has a symbolic function, such as larger and more private individual space allocation typically marking an employee's advancement through the company. Hierarchy is expressed through spatial divisions and distinctions: spatial features can reinforce issues of privacy and confidentiality, just as flatter and more open organizations favor open-plan workspace that facilitates communication. Its choice of workspace concept or type indicates whether a company's HR policies support 'coordination' or 'cooperation' as preferred mechanisms for the integration of organizational knowledge (Grant, 1996).

Environment also incorporates the virtual environment: the information and communications technology that is available and used, the times and ways in which it is used and by whom, constraints on its use and effectiveness, as well as relationships created through its use. ICT tools employees use for their tasks and in their relationships complement the spaces they occupy to become determining factors in how learning occurs, how knowledge is acquired and shared, and how production decisions are made. For example, one of the effects of globalization is that project teams rely increasingly on remotely located members, some of who may work for other companies and occupy other time-zones (Langhoff, 2006). In addition to physical resources, such as co-locating team members' desks and assigning them a project room, teams need network access that lets geographically distributed members meet in real time to share notes, documents, and drawings.

In this chapter, the environment being examined is physical: the type, features, and location of the buildings that are occupied, and the interior spaces—or work-space—within which work is performed. The chapter examines ways in which the physical environment has a direct effect on human performance and organizational processes. The design, configuration, and features of its workspace affect how well and how much a company benefits from 'the acquired and useful abilities of all the inhabitants or members of the society'—its human capital. There are three key ways in which space affects people in organizations: space as an *organizational resource*, linking accommodation decisions with corporate business objectives (Fischer, 1997; Guillen, 1997); space as a *tool for work*, providing needed support for employees' daily tasks (Leaman and Bordass, 2001; Vischer, 1996); and space as it frames organizational interactions and social network formation, a mediating influence on the creation and operation of *intraorganizational relationships* (Kampschroer and Heerwagen, 2005; Stephenson, 1998).

Corporate decision-makers frequently underestimate the value of space as a resource in which to invest, owing to the prevalence of the view that sees accommodation as a cost to the organization. This has resulted in common workspace features such as the standardization of workstations and furniture, efforts to reduce 'footprint' and increase density, and a 'value engineering' approach to construction projects that does not address the human aspect and can have the effect of eliminating anything new and humanizing about workspace design. Employers tend to demand proof that there is a payoff from investing in high-quality workspace before they look into an alternative to the least-cost options. The payoff in terms of image or corporate branding though building design and architectural features is well-established—consider how Frank Gehry's design of the Bilbao Museum has affected museum design and attendance worldwide. And the payoff from 'green building' certification is becoming increasingly clear. But a payoff defined in terms of more effective use of human capital, such as employee and knowledge retention, more employee learning and commitment, new knowledge creation and sharing, and improved performance outcomes, is slow to be accepted by corporate decision-makers in spite of the increasing amount of persuasive research.

This chapter reviews the current state of our knowledge under the following headings: first, the ways in which an organization's choice and design of its physical environment affects the success of corporate business practices, especially in combination with HR policies and procedures; second, the role of space in the social contract and its influence on the employer–employee relationship; and third, how workspace affects human learning, task performance, and knowledge creation and communication.

19.2 THE ORGANIZATION–ACCOMMODATION RELATIONSHIP

Space is a resource to the organization. How can it derive value from this resource? Space is itself a fuzzy term. Most commonly, space is defined by the building or buildings in which employees work, and in this chapter we use the term 'workspace' for this meaning of space. Workspace can be thought of as a set of concentric circles, at the centre of which, the individual worker occupies his or her workstation or office. Each individual workplace is connected by walls or circulation to others, and these in turn to hallways and elevators that lead to other workgroups. Eventually, workspace extends beyond the building. Workspace exists at all these scales because workers' behavior and therefore effectiveness is influenced not only by the size, style, comfort/convenience, and location of individual space, but also by the circulation paths they walk along, the meeting-rooms they sit in, the cafeteria and coffee station they stop at, and the time it takes them to access support spaces such as copier rooms, stairs or elevators, and parking. Moreover, space is increasingly defined virtually. Some employees work at home, or from airports, hotels, or their cars. Some start-up companies think it is no longer necessary to occupy space at all; instead they supply workers with laptops and cellphones and keep them on the road.

For decision-makers, the contextual space in which their company's building is located also has meaning. Companies choose locations that facilitate access to a trained labor pool, for example, or to suppliers, or to transportation. There are examples of socially responsible companies opting to build in deteriorating neighborhoods to increase land values and provide jobs for the community.[1] How a company defines and thinks about its space can be summed up in its organization–accommodation (O–A) relationship; that is, that unique configuration of land, buildings, interiors (workspace) and information technology that each company defines for itself, according to its views of itself and of its workers, dynamically and over time.

The idea that an organization has a relationship with its accommodation that, like all relationships, ebbs and flows and changes over time, is not new but is relatively unexamined (Vischer, 1996; O'Mara, 1999). This contrasts with the employee–organization relationship, which has received considerable attention and in which companies are encouraged to invest (Tsui et al., 1997). The traditional view of space as a cost to the organization—a view that originates with and is endorsed by the real-estate industry—considers investment in property acquisition and divestment terms rather than in human capital terms. Trends such as the rise of the networked organization and the knowledge economy (see Chapter 2) have affected the O–A relationship as well as corporate views of human capital. The move toward 'hotelling' or temporarily occupied offices and meeting-rooms was hailed a few years ago by large accounting and management consulting firms. Designing workspace for hotelling rather than permanent occupancy reflected the economic fact that the more professional and technical employees were out of the office, the more they were in clients' offices and therefore increasing their billable time. By taking away their desks, these employers believed people would spend less time 'catching up on paperwork' or other unbillable activities in the home office, and more time with their clients. To facilitate this transition, companies such as Accenture provided extensive concierge services to help people who spent their weekdays on the road with such prosaic matters as taking their car to the garage for repair, dropping off and picking up dry cleaning, acquiring tickets for theatre and sports events, and reserving specific spaces—a desk, an office, a meeting-room—for when they would be back in the building. A less deluxe model of the hotelling concept has been widely applied to corporate sales teams. IBM realized up to 30 percent reduction in real-estate costs in North America by providing a limited number of small, shared workstations for its sales teams, on the grounds that they need to be outside the building more than inside it to carry out their work.

Seen from the company's perspective, hotelling and other non-territorial workspace options, such as 'hot desking', would seem to present a reasonable balance between cost reduction and better returns on the human capital investment.[2] While hotelling accommodation is comfortable and supportive, access to it is limited. These limits on accessing workspace define ways in which workers can make the company more profitable, but not necessarily the ways in which they can communicate and collaborate to learn and increase knowledge. Thus the decisions an organization makes about its accommodation need to find a balance similar to that which is sought in other organizational systems, between 'exploration'—space that provides opportunities for new behavior—and 'exploitation'—space that facilitates existing ways of doing things (March, 1991).

In most companies, however, the conventional organization–accommodation relationship is not balanced. It is more reactive and retrospective than it is innovative and embracing of change. It is reactive in that companies typically change their accommodation not to embrace new ideas and processes, but to solve problems of numbers—of too much or too little space. It is retrospective in that decisions about new space are most commonly based on what already exists in the firm, and result in reproducing workspace concepts that are already known and familiar. This approach serves the need for exploitation better than the need for exploration, and may therefore limit innovative thinking and the creation of new knowledge.

Relatively few organizations take advantage of the opportunity offered by an accommodation change or move to rethink the relationship between workspace and human capital and to seek improvements, although lowering costs as the single most important objective a company has for its accommodation is slowly being replaced by more diverse and organization-related goals (Ouye and Serino, 2004). These include better customer relations, improving worker productivity, generating opportunities for tacit learning and mentoring, and growing and consolidating community and culture. To facilitate a shift towards defining accommodation in terms of how well it attains these human capital-related objectives, it is useful to think of four basic categories or states that characterize the O–A relationship. Each has a key influence on the social contract and on the employer–employee relationship. These categories are 'poor', 'neutral', 'positive', and 'active' (Vischer, 2005). Where workspace hinders work— perhaps people are too crowded, or they have to move too often, or noise distractions hinder concentration—the relationship is *poor*, adding no value and even detracting from business activities and worker efficiency. This can impair customer relations and over time increase employee turnover, and the loss of organization-specific skills and knowledge. A move or other workspace change provides an opportunity to improve business processes and solve problems. The relationship can become *neutral*—less adverse to worker activities—and it can become *positive*, supporting people's tasks and improving their ability to perform them. A positive O–A relationship means accommodation that supports information exchange, helps build trust, and enables collaboration—all goals of strategic human resources and essential to increase competitive advantage (Lepak and Snell, 1999). Ideally, an organization has an *active* relationship to its accommodation, in which accommodation is viewed as a resource and workspace as a tool, and the organization has O–A strategies in place to derive maximum value from its facilities.

Making accommodation decisions explicit and purposeful is one way to initiate a process that makes the O–A relationship more active. Strategies for involving and engaging workers in planning their own workspace help ensure that both their explicit knowledge (what they do) and their tacit knowledge (how they do it) are applied to workspace decision-making (Dewulf and Van Meel, 2003; Gann and White, 2003; Lennertz and Lutzenhiser, 2006). Increasing employee empowerment in relation to the buildings and space they occupy by providing information and offering opportunities to participate in decisions helps knowledge dissemination, increases commitment, and improves work performance (Lawler *et al.*, 1995).

19.3 From Social to Socio-Spatial Contract

Like ICT, accommodation is an important investment for a firm, and the workspace it provides is a strategic tool for implementing HR policies and philosophies. Companies increasingly believe that a dynamic and supportive workspace plays an active part in making a business successful. Google, Muzak, Capital One, and Macquarie Bank are well-known examples of companies that have invested in high-quality and innovative buildings. They recognize that workspace is a powerful mechanism in the relationship between employees and the organization, symbolizing mutual commitment and assuring both sides that each worker has 'a place' and that some degree of territorial control can be negotiated. It is this implicit deal between employee and employer that gives workspace its symbolic power.

To understand fully the power of workspace symbolism, we need to analyze the implicit terms of the employer–employee agreement known as the sociospatial contract (Vischer, 2005). This contract—rarely made explicit and unlikely to be acknowledged unless violated—includes space as a key component of the deal that both sides make when an employee joins a company. Although space is not typically part of the HR function of fitting people to tasks and jobs, there is an implicit promise that physical space—along with pay, training, supervision, and other forms of compensation—is offered to employees in exchange for their time, energy, skills, knowledge, and commitment. In view of the importance of combining 'core', 'traditional', 'alliance', and 'contract' workers for optimal organizational performance, the way their time–space is structured, equipped, and provided is likely to be a key influence on the effectiveness of the combination selected (Lepak *et al.*, 2003).

The most critical of the unexamined assumptions on which the socio-spatial contract is based are territoriality, environmental control, and job performance. Territoriality is a basic human behavioral trait, and people at work occupy, decorate, and defend the space which they have been assigned individually, as well as space they consider to be their group or team territory (Becker, 1981; Brown, 1987; Vischer, 2005). Typically, the contemporary open-plan office concept encourages territorial expression in at least two ways. First, the forest of cubicle partitions that greets visitors to almost any modern office building floor in North America is characterized by its standardization and homogeneity. Its lack of distinctive features fails to support wayfinding and orientation, and sends employees a message from employers that 'you are all the same to us'. This very sameness inspires people to personalize, expand, or make other individual changes to indicate their uniqueness that the environment seems to deny. Second, the symbolism of the individual office, desk, or workstation is a powerful and deeply rooted symbol of the individual's and the organization's mutual rights, responsibilities, expectations, and commitment. Without 'my desk', however modest and ill-defined, I do not have a clear role and place in the organization. In laying claim to 'a space I can call my own', I maintain my individuality and the uniqueness of my contribution. The socio-spatial contract provides at least one small space in the building where the individual user is 'in charge', and some companies supply individual environmental controls (task lights, task air, heater and fan, white noise controls) to give each worker control over her environmental comfort (Aronoff and Kaplan, 1995).

The combined effect of their needs for territory and environmental control often causes workers to resist workspace change, although managing workspace change to increase efficiencies, generate process improvements, and make better use of human capital is an important aspect of an organization's ability both to adapt to and to create change (see Chapter 18). Companies experimenting with non-territorial approaches, such as shared desks or 'hot desking', mobile or remote offic-ing, and various forms of telecommuting and telework, find that their employees' first response is resistance to workspace redesign and renovation. Features of the physical environment in which work is done communicate the importance of the work, and therefore the importance of the role and rank of those who are doing it. They also sustain one's sense of self as defined by job, self-image, and role (Fischer et al., 2004). Workspace change risks violating the terms of the sociospatial contract by threatening employees' expectations, and thereby challenging the implicit accom-modation promise. This is one reason why emotional upheavals and employee resistance have accompanied workspace change in many companies. In order for workspace change to be successful, employees need to be empowered to participate in decision-making. Studies show that the more people are informed and engaged in workspace change, the more accepting they are of both the process and the out-come, and the more effective and successful the new work environment that they occupy (Becker and Kelley, 2004; Davenport and Bruce, 2002).

The spatial aspect of the social contract has many facets. As well as the employer committing to providing workers with the tools necessary to perform the job, the work environment also operates at symbolic and semiotic levels. The presence or absence of walls or partitions around individual offices, and the height of those partitions, are a key indicator of social status, as are proximity to windows to the outside, and proximity to management offices. In more traditional companies, meticulous attention is paid to status indicators such as number of visitors' chairs, art on the walls, and chrome accessories, to ensure that employee promotions are rewarded by environmental recognition of seniority (Vickers, 1999). Companies less concerned with maintaining a hierarchical structure honor the spatial part of the social contract by providing services and amenities that go beyond what employ-ees need for their work. These might include fitness facilities, dry-cleaning services, and a choice of places to eat, as well as the concierge-type services mentioned previ-ously that are offered in environments favoring 'hotelling'.

Modern workspace design trends are weakening the traditional symbolism of the individual office. The emphasis on projects and teamwork mean that more space is needed for shared and group work. The flattening of organizational hierarchies means fewer size and other distinctions among spaces at different levels and ranks. Companies—Hypertherm, HP, Sun Microsystems, and others—are embracing space standards based on functional and task needs rather than on rank. A participatory space planning process not only gives employees the chance to voice their opinions and preferences, but also enables the organization to draw on and use their knowledge—especially the tacit knowledge of how they perform their tasks—to provide the best fitting workspace. However, as we know, companies today operate in a rapidly changing business and economic environment, and need to be proactive toward their constantly changing circumstances. As a result, the challenge of defining the right workspace is also a challenge of balancing 'fit' and 'flexibility', much as these must be balanced in strategic human resources (Wright and Snell, 1998). A responsive HR system fits the strategic needs of the firm but also enables a flexible response to changing strategic requirements over time. Similarly, the optimal workspace meets users' needs at one point in time in order to 'fit'—to support, enable and enhance—how people work. It is also readily adaptable (flexible) to changes such as team reconfigurations and moves, mergers with newly acquired companies, and unanticipated facilities expansion or shrinkage. Both concepts are essential for organizational effectiveness. Workspace that successfully balances fit and flexibility contributes to competitive advantage, and how a company defines this balance for itself depends largely on the competitive environment in which it operates.

For many firms over the past decade—telecommunications companies, for example—the challenge has been shifting from the fit of a stable and predictable competitive environment to the flexibility needed in a dynamic and unpredictable competitive environment (Vischer, 1995, 1999). As workspace is defined more flexibly, thought can be given to a better fit between human capital characteristics, strategic HR practices (job design, staffing, training, remuneration), contractual terms, and workspace concept. Contractual terms may include making the sociospatial contract explicit—letting future employees know not only what kind of space they will occupy, but also organizational rules and expectations regarding acceptable uses of the space that they have been allocated. Examples of implicit cultural rules include whether or not advancement to more senior positions is accompanied by larger and more enclosed (private) space, which communal spaces are shared by which staff members in the organization, and how supplementary and support spaces for tasks not performed inside individual offices or workstations are made available and accessed. Typically, most space-related rules and expectations are unstated, and learning them is one of the ways new employees gain knowledge of the organizational culture. However, making them explicit as part of the hiring process is one way to speed up employee acceptance into the culture and thereby help them make optimum use of workspace resources sooner, thus reducing the time between investing in new space and the human capital return on that investment.

As Chapter 11 of this volume points out, companies invest differently in different employee sub-groups, depending on their value to the organization. The next section looks at how workspace investment decisions are made as a function of type of employee, technological environment, and kinds of services. A better understanding not just of how an employee works, of her skills and knowledge and what she has to contribute, and the tools, training, and support she requires to be effective, but also of the most suitable space-time framework for her to perform opens new horizons in organizational use of human capital. This understanding is part of the process of defining an optimal balance between fit and flexibility for work environments that are moving beyond standardization to a more customized approach, and designing workspace to fit the human capital characteristics of the organization.

19.4 THE ENVIRONMENTAL PSYCHOLOGY OF WORKSPACE

Detailed knowledge of user–environment interaction and how workspace features affect human behavior is needed to negotiate the sociospatial contract and to understand and improve the organization–accommodation relationship. The space–time environment that accommodation provides structures the relationship between value and time that is basic to human capital (see Chapter 3).

Some interest in the physical environment for work—mostly in factory settings—is evident in research published earlier in the twentieth century, such as the Hawthorne studies of the effects of changed lighting conditions in the 1930s, Herzberg's analysis of factors influencing worker motivation in the 1940s and 1950s, and Barnard's advice to factory managers in the 1960s (Barnard, 1964; Herzberg, 1966; Roethlisberger and Dixon, 1939). Systematic studies of what has come to be called the environmental psychology of workspace began in the 1980s. One of the first studies compared workers' assessment of, and responses to, office buildings that they occupied before and after a major move (Brill et al., 1984). Based on the dominant paradigms of environmental psychology, this study and those that followed looked at how positively workers felt about the buildings in which they worked—whether they felt they were 'productive', how many health-related symptoms they reported, and whether or not they were satisfied with the work environment.

Substantial knowledge has since accumulated on how people work in different physical settings and how they interact with workspace. Research results indicate that the environment has a powerful effect on human performance at work, and can positively or negatively affect human output, including creativity and ideas generation, communication and knowledge-sharing, and individual and group problem-solving.

The concept of *ba* or *place* is gaining currency in part because it combines physical, virtual, and mental space to signify 'a shared space for emerging relationships' (Nonaka and Konno, 1998: 40). A recent analysis of space use in organizations concluded that accommodation must provide not only space, but also the time, attention from leaders, and opportunities for relationship-building to facilitate the creation of new knowledge (Nenonen, 2004). The author proposes a list of ten environmental attributes needed for high-quality *ba*—space for knowledge creation and sharing— that includes balancing open areas for connection with 'cocoon' space to facilitate new ideas, a sense of 'purpose' and 'intention', and ensuring that 'dialogue' and 'high quality conversations' are encouraged (Nenonen, 2004: 236). The 'topos' or physical space that is a critical component of *ba* is formed through a balance among physical, social, and virtual work environments, and quality of place is an important factor shaping the quality of knowledge (Nonaka *et al.*, 2001).

The design research orientation of the environmental psychology of workspace has been slow to shift its paradigm away from users' workspace preferences and toward human capital priorities. For example, studies of whether workers are satisfied with an open-plan configuration in various office environments demonstrate that they are mostly dissatisfied. This is usually attributed to lack of privacy, too much noise, or insufficient storage (Hedge, 1986; McCoy and Evans, 2005; Mital *et al.*, 1992). By limiting the outcome measured to individual satisfaction, little new insight has been gained about exactly how people's work is affected by open office conditions, whether new knowledge is slower or faster to be generated, how formal and informal networks of communication are affected, or if open plan affects rates of employee turnover—all factors influencing human capital and investment in it.

We are learning more about how workers' perceptions of the quality of place is shaped by ambient environmental conditions such as lighting, acoustics, ventilation, and temperature, as well as by configuration of physical features and dimensions of spatial layout (Vischer, 2008*b*). Analysis of ambient environmental conditions in indoor work environments enable regulating bodies to determine ideal standards for *physical* comfort relative to ventilation and thermal comfort, indoor air quality, and illumination conditions and light levels (ASHRAE, 2007; NIOSH, 1991; IESNA, 1999). These standards are routinely applied to workspace environmental design. Analysis of ambient conditions has also generated a better understanding of *functional* comfort; that is, how well the physical environment supports employees' tasks and activities. The notion of functional comfort provides a direct link between the environmental psychology of workspace and the value and uniqueness of human capital. An environment designed to provide functional comfort ranges from meeting the practical requirements of daily tasks—such as the right lighting and ergonomic furniture for working on the computer—to facilitating the tasks and activities needed for better customer relations, generating opportunities for tacit learning and mentoring, and growing and consolidating community and culture. Whereas functionally comfortable workspace improves employee performance and thereby organizational productivity, a functionally uncomfortable workspace reduces workers' effectiveness and can even be considered a cause of stress at work (Vischer, 2007a). Companies whose employees struggle to hear on the telephone in noisy settings, squint at their computer screens to deal with glare, and whose shoulders ache or who get headaches if they do not leave the building during the day, are wasting their human capital on overcoming environmental barriers —capital that should be invested in their work. Environmental conditions in offices can range from comfortable (supportive of employees' tasks) to uncomfortable (stress-generating), regardless of whether they are 'liked' (Vischer, 2007b).

Users providing feedback on their functional comfort also assess key ergonomic features such as furniture configuration and floor layout. Distances to meeting-rooms, printers and copiers, time to climb stairs or take the elevator, proximity and accessibility of co-workers and collaborators, as well as access to file storage for both individuals and teams, number and dimensions of work-surfaces, and wall or partition height, are all influential factors affecting worker productivity (Brill and Weideman, 2001; Hatch, 1987; Sullivan, 1990; Vischer, 1989). Furniture and spatial layout influence not only the performance of individual workers, but also of teams (Heerwagen et al., 2004). A recent study of functional comfort in the Canadian offices of a large pharmaceutical corporation revealed that providing highly paid professional employees with large private offices did not compensate for the lack of meeting-rooms and collaborative spaces of varying sizes and functions (Vischer and Prasow, in press). Team leaders and members spent their workdays not only in back-to-back meetings, but also in covering large distances to move from one meeting-room to the next. A poor fit between workspace design and how people work is costly, no matter the quality of the space provided. Feedback from employees on what works and what does not can lead to changes that result in a better fit between workspace design and employees' use of their tacit and explicit knowledge.

It is a simple matter to expand the concept of functional comfort to include Nenonen's conditions for creating ba. In human capital terms, it is not only people's tasks and daily activities that are important, but also their knowledge, their skills, their creativity, and their connections with co-workers. The importance of well-designed collaborative workspace is growing as companies rely more on project teams than on individual work, and on collaboration though both formal and informal networks, for generating new ideas and sharing new knowledge. While 'quality of place' is affected by ambient environmental conditions and aspects of furniture and layout, knowledge creation and sharing are most directly affected by the configuration of interactive and collaborative space. Shared and interactive workspace provides opportunities for the four stages of the SECI knowledge-generating cycle: socialization, externalization, combination, and internalization (Von Krogh et al., 2000). The topos that might be said to correspond to ba is located by and large in shared group space, rather than in the features of individual workspace that have traditionally been important for the sociospatial contract.

19.5 IMPROVING ACCOMMODATION TO INCREASE KNOWLEDGE CREATION

The SECI sequence promotes the conversion of tacit to explicit knowledge and therefore the creation of knowledge in an organization. Whereas studies of users in workspace have tended to focus on individual space and individual perceptions of environmental conditions, the four behavioral or activity categories of the SECI sequence take place primarily in physically or virtually shared space. *Socialization* is focused on the individual, but involves sharing experience with another and is therefore not only an isolated activity but also requires interaction; *externalization* requires the articulation of tacit knowledge largely through the use of dialogue that others can understand and use, and therefore requires a 'place' in which to occur; *combination* results in the appearance of new knowledge that transcends the group in which it has arisen—who perhaps occupy shared workspace—and is diffused throughout the organization because physical and virtual opportunities are there for it to do so; and *internalization* requires learning by doing, training, and exercises—activities that mostly take place with others in places designed for that purpose. Although some of these activities are also solitary—for example, where reflection is required, or testing—most depend on contact and connecting, for which spatial opportunities are key. Consequently, shared and group workspace in offices and other work environments need to be designed with a view to enhancing the SECI sequence.

Collaboration is a general term for a range of group activities. It can mean two people together, or four, or fourteen. From a space–time viewpoint it can mean anything from a quick question, taking less than a minute to answer, to several hours in a meeting, to a weeks-long project with a dedicated team. Co-workers who need to work together collaborate using communications technology when they are not in the same space or close by, and in these situations the quality of ICT determines how effectively team members interact, cooperate and make decisions when connecting remotely (Joroff and Bergman, 2007). People working on individual tasks—that is, whose work is not team-based—also need to communicate with colleagues to receive and impart information. Waiting to meet in conference rooms that have to be reserved in advance is not an effective way to create or to transfer new knowledge. Recent trends in workspace design, such as reducing the dimensions of individual workstations and offices and providing a more varied and accessible array of communal workspaces, reflect the increasing importance of generating and sharing knowledge in organizations.

The social dimensions of collaboration have been categorized, variously, as 'awareness'—knowing what is happening around one, while not necessarily being involved in actions and events—'brief interaction'—rapid and momentary personal and work-related exchanges—and 'collaboration'—two or more people working together over time to produce a joint outcome (Heerwagen *et al.*, 2004). The matrix in Table 19.1 can be used to focus on the implications that each of these has for designing workspace to support SECI.

Table 19.1. Workspace Design Considerations to Respond to SECI

	Socialization	Externalization	Combination	Internalization
Awareness	Open office teamspace concept	Shared space and meeting-rooms	Information on screens and displays	Open office teamspace concept
Brief interaction	Co-located teams	Informal and formal places to meet	Information exchanged while crossing paths, meeting, getting coffee	Team shared spaces
Collaboration	Communications tools	Project and war-rooms	Shared group facilities	Training rooms and workrooms

As the table shows, some companies provide a range of spaces for collaborative work, from 'war rooms', where members of project teams occupy the same space to 'collaborate' for the duration of a project to a series of just-in-time workrooms, useful for 'brief interaction', where two or three people sit on a first-come, first-served basis, conveniently located for easy access and no reservations needed. Various forms of team workspace cluster team members' desks around a worktable or file cabinets or display surfaces to ensure that team members are 'aware' of new information by overhearing what others say, and to provide centrally located space to facilitate socialization, externalization, and combination. Informal spaces designed to be attractive and convenient for unscheduled meetings and impromptu collaborative work sessions are furnished with mobile worktables and whiteboards, network access, and café-type tables and chairs clustered near windows or coffee counters. Formal meeting (conference) rooms range from boardroom-style—deep carpets, upholstered chairs, and dark wood—to a minimalist-style workroom providing network access and file sharing, and enabling connections to remote team members.

Collaborative spaces do not encourage use for knowledge creation and sharing activities when

- they are in an inconvenient or inappropriate location;
- if employees are embarrassed by their informal and 'non-work' appearance; and
- when there are not enough of them and they are unavailable.

Principles for ensuring the effective design of group workspace include keeping group size relatively small (four to eight people), ensuring control over environmental conditions such as lighting, ventilation, and temperature, and protecting users from unwanted distractions (Leaman, 2003). Well-designed group workspace and spatial layouts that encourage contact and communication facilitate socialization and externalization. Combination activities also need robust and accessible communications technology (virtual workspace). Internalization depends on all of these as well as on a corporate culture that encourages training, mentoring, continuous learning, and the like. Human capital value—the accumulated knowledge and skills that employees apply to improving processes, increasing efficiencies, and providing more and better benefits to customers—and uniqueness—the degree of specialization and specificity of knowledge and skills to the organization—are affected by HR architecture (Morris et al., 2005). Human capital value and uniqueness are also affected by workspace architecture. The distinction between entrepreneurial activities that generate new knowledge—exploration—and cooperative activities that 'involve the refining and recombining of existing knowledge in new ways' (ibid. 20)—exploitation—implies that the same standardized approach to workspace may not work for all companies, nor for all departments in one firm. Companies such as 3M and Ideo Product Design favor entrepreneurial activities that culminate in new ideas and new processes, rapid development decisions, and a short time to market. The sociospatial contract offered to these employees is not based on individual territorial identity so much as on team opportunities. Ideo's space in Burlington, Massachusetts, has the chaotic appearance of work-surfaces cluttered with objects and gadgets, polished concrete floors on which desks can be pushed around, a circular ramp leading up to meeting-rooms with whiteboards on all four walls, interior windows that look into the labs and fabrication workrooms for prototyping, and a large airy coffee bar with café tables and seating. There are almost no walls or doors. At one stage, team leaders thought they should have offices, and a wood framework for enclosed individual offices was constructed, and then left unfinished—a symbolic nod to irrelevant corporate management practices!

For employees working in firms whose activities require cooperation and integration to support the exploitation of existing knowledge, the pharmaceutical company that favored comfortable private offices for everyone rather than an abundance of places to meet offers a cautionary tale. The sociospatial contract was apparently respected in that employees had large private offices with walls and doors, but the situation yielded an uncomfortable ambiguity: lacking opportunities for teamwork and collaboration, the space was not supporting them or the value and uniqueness of their knowledge. The effect was an underperforming organization handicapped by a negative O–A relationship. As the company embarked on a renovation and upgrade of its space, negotiations were initiated with employees to convert them to a belief in teamspace and eventually to giving up their walls, doors, and heavy dark status-symbol furniture in order to communicate and collaborate more effectively.

For knowledge application as well as knowledge creation, workspace provides opportunities for a supportive and enabling physical environment. If taken advantage with, these opportunities can ensure that value is added; but if they are ignored, the organization–accommodation relationship may remain neutral or even become negative, adversely affecting knowledge stocks and the performance of human capital.

19.6 CONCLUSIONS

To facilitate workspace change, design criteria and building performance guidelines exist to ensure that new work environments support individual tasks, facilitate group processes, and contribute to organizational effectiveness (Preiser and Vischer, 2004). Many of these guidelines address design outcomes, such as the right lighting for individual tasks, control over accessibility (privacy) in group settings, and flexible furniture configurations that can be adapted as work changes. The criteria identified as necessary for 'high quality *ba*' offer a different approach to identifying guidelines to aid and improve workspace design (Nenonen, 2004). In identifying *ba* as a desirable design outcome, these guidelines go above and beyond directives for improving physical workspace to incorporate ideas about how workspace performs, how people use it, and what intangible qualities it might have. By invoking design guidelines oriented to creating topos for *ba*, accommodation can be explicitly designed to enhance knowledge creation rather than being based on more conventional rationales for accommodation decisions—either reducing occupancy costs or worker dissatisfaction, or both. As Nenonen's ten qualities are not limited to physical space but also consider virtual space as well as social and relationship space—the emotional/spiritual dimensions of organizational culture—they enable the complexity and interactivity of the user–space relationship to be incorporated into workspace design. This kind of 'design guideline' goes beyond the dualistic concept of environment that artificially distinguishes between built space and the behavior of people occupying it. Guidelines that promote workspace for knowledge creation and sharing assume that the people occupying space and the way they perceive and interact with space is part of the definition of space. While it is tempting to focus on how people are affected by features of the environment in which they work—a one-way relationship—in reality the relationship is equally affected by what people do in and with their space, as well as the experience of interacting with it.

This belief is at the core of the concept of the organization–accommodation relationship. As we achieve a better understanding of the interactive effects of users and space, more accommodation decisions are made in the light of this mutually adaptive relationship. If accommodation's goal is to enable knowledge creation and application, workspace that supports HR objectives emerges as a more comprehensive design objective. Thus HR—as well as facilities—architecture need to be designed, hopefully in concert, to ensure that the right type of employee is hired, that opportunities exist for training and other activities that increase knowledge, and that new knowledge is applied and integrated among the firm's internal work-groups and departments. The organization–accommodation framework is available to place facilities decisions along with HR as essential considerations in enhancing the value and uniqueness of human capital.

In understanding the mechanics of the O–A relationship, space is a powerful if unrecognized element in the social contract. As many have pointed out (see Chapter 25), modern trends toward a global, knowledge-driven economy with a diverse workforce and increasing employee mobility mean that the terms of the social contract are changing, and that they will need to be based on more trust and belief in mutually beneficial outcomes than has historically been the case. What does this mean for the sociospatial contract?

It means, *first*, that feedback and engagement of workers in devising their own space must be activated to ensure that both their implicit and tacit knowledge are applied to workspace design processes. This is a departure from the usual space planning process in which managers make selections from limited choices offered by facilities staff and design teams. The resulting environment is imposed on workers, and they have to adapt to it. In the future, using an approach based on human capital considerations, they will have a chance—indeed they will need—to be involved in participatory design. *Second*, it means that workspace will function less as a reward for promotion through the company and more as a functional and supportive tool for work. Employees will seek out space—physical and virtual—that supports their work and has an enhancing effect on their performance. If space is planned as a tool, changes that are presently considered anomalies may seem obvious—such as administrative assistants having larger offices than their bosses because they store files and information, and because managers are often away and their offices are empty. *Third*, it means that workspace design will focus increasingly on group and shared space and opportunities for communication, collaboration, and networking. Valuing knowledge means ensuring that it is produced and actively used, as well as ensuring that it stays inside the organization and accumulates. This requires a balance between comfortable individualized space for people to perform solitary and thinking tasks, and a range of attractive and functional collaborative and communicative opportunities. *Fourth*, it means that not just conventional space but ICT and other tools must be integrated to facilitate 'distributed working' and dispersed teams as people collaborate with colleagues in other parts of the world (Harrison *et al.*, 2004). *Finally*, it means that companies will identify the type of human capital in which they want to invest, and will make accommodation decisions both to recruit and to retain the kind of employee mix that suits the management of knowledge in the organization. An emphasis on exploration for producing new knowledge may not yield the same workspace concept as an emphasis on exploitation of existing knowledge or as a balance between the two. Moreover, an optimal fit between employee characteristics, HR architecture, and workspace is likely to be time-limited, meaning that some degree of flexibility must be built into any workspace concept because of the changing circumstances of modern business.

Studies of the environmental psychology of workspace aimed at identifying the various ways in which people are affected by and interact with their physical environment at work provide evidence that people not only have instrumental relationships with their milieu—environment as a tool for work—but also experience their workspace as a powerful cultural and emotional symbol (Vischer, 2008*a*). To date, measurement of workers' functional comfort has been oriented to forging a link between the environment's effects on worker performance and the overall productivity of the organization. Linking functional comfort to the concerns of human capital researchers expands the theoretical framework to include studies that examine how effectively occupants' knowledge is acquired, used, transferred, and integrated in the context of the space provided to attain improved company performance and competitive advantage. The desirability of *ba* and the space-dependent aspects of SECI offers an important new paradigm for measuring dimensions of the organization–accommodation relationship and the effectiveness of workspace in the future.

In summary, the workspace provided by a company's accommodation is a critical element in effective use of and access to its own human capital. Space structures the relationship between value and time that is basic to fulfilling the human capital potential. The puzzle remains as to why it is taking businesses so long to see the value of investing in workspace and to evaluate their investment in terms other than returns on real-estate assets. The first call for managers to pay attention to 'an underutilised resource' came in the early 1980s (Seiler, 1984). More than twenty years later, the same call is still being issued (Morgan and Anthony, 2008). And although some companies appear to be paying attention, perhaps recognizing that by designing innovative and high-quality workspace they are investing in their human capital, studies designed to follow up not only on the quality of 'fit' of innovative workspace concepts but also on how 'flexible' they are as the organization's needs change over time, have yet to be published. As a mediator of key organizational activities such as information flow, social contact, and reinforcement of corporate values, the occupied environment needs to be recognized for the underutilized asset that it is. Greater attention to the organization–accommodation relationship, making the sociospatial contract explicit, and designing space to support workers' collaboration and communication as well as their individual tasks, are all needed to derive maximum value from an organization's human capital.

NOTES

1. An early example was the (then) NMB Bank which relocated to south-east Amsterdam in the 1980s (see Vischer and Mees, 1991). In the 1990s the CDPQ (Caisse de dépôt et placement du Québec) building was built in and designed to revitalize the Quartier International in Montreal, Quebec. More recently, Australia's Macquarie Bank built a new flagship building in the docklands area of Melbourne.

2. 'Hot desking' applies to environments in which employees do not go to a fixed location every day, but instead may choose from a variety of work settings within the building, depending on what is appropriate for the tasks on which they are working.

REFERENCES

ARONOFF, S., and KAPLAN, A. (1995). *Total Workplace Performance: Rethinking the Office Environment* (Ottawa: WDL Publications).

ASHRAE (2007) *Standard 62.1-2007 Ventiliation for Acceptable Indoor Air Quality* (Atlanta, Ga.: Association for Heating, Refrigeration and Air Conditioning Engineers).

BARNARD, C. I. (1964). *The Functions of the Executive* (Cambridge, Mass.: Harvard University Press).

BECKER, F. D. (1981). *Workspace: Creating Environments in Organizations* (New York: Praeger).

——and KELLEY, T. (2004). *Offices at Work: Uncommon Workspace Strategies that Add Value and Improve Performance* (San Francisco: Jossey-Bass).

——and STEELE, F. (1994). *Workplace by Design: Mapping the High Performance Workscape* (San Francisco: Jossey-Bass).

BRILL, M., and WEIDEMAN, S. (2001). *Disproving Widespread Myths about Workplace Design* (Jasper, Ind: Kimball International).

——MARGULIS, S. T., KONAR, E., and BOSTI in association with Westinghouse Furniture Systems (1984). *Using Office Design to Increase Productivity*, i–ii. Buffalo, NY: Workplace Design and Productivity, Inc.

BROWN, B. B. (1987). 'Territoriality', in D. STOKOLS and I. ALTMAN (eds.), *Handbook of Environmental Psychology* (New York: J. Wiley & Sons), ch. 13.

DAVENPORT, E., and BRUCE, I. (2002). 'Innovation, Knowledge Management and the Use of Space: Questioning Assumptions about Non-Traditional Office Work', *Journal of Information Science* 28(3) (June): 225–30.

DEWULF, G., and VAN MEEL, J. (2003). 'Democracy in Design?', in R. Best, C. Langston, and G. de Valence (eds.), *Workplace Strategies and Facilities Management: Building in Value* (London: Butterworth-Heineman), 281–91.

FISCHER, G. N. (1997). *Individuals and Environment: A Psychosocial Approach to Workspace* (New York: Walter de Gruyter).

——TARQUINIO, C., and VISCHER, J. C. (2004). 'Effects of the Self-Schema on Perception of Space at Work', *Journal of Environmental Psychology*, 24(1): 131–40.

GANN, D., and WHITE, J. (2003). 'Design Quality: Its Measurement and Management in the Built Environment', *Building Research and Information*, 31(5): 314–17.

GRANT, R. M. (1996). 'Toward a Knowledge-Based Theory of the Firm', *Strategic Management Journal*, 17 (winter special issue): 109–22.

GUILLÉN, MAURO F. (2006). *The Taylorized Beauty of the Mechanical: Scientific Management and the Rise of Modernist Architecture* (Princeton: Princeton University Press).

HARRISON, A., WHEELER, P., and WHITEHEAD, C. (2004). *The Distributed Workplace* (London: Spon Press).

HATCH, M. (1987). 'Physical Barriers, Task Characteristics, and Interaction Activity in Research and Development Firms', *Administrative Science Quarterly*, 32(3): 387–99.

HEDGE, A. (1986). 'Open versus Enclosed Workspace: The Impact of Design on Employee Reactions to their Offices', in J. D. WINEMAN (ed.), *Behavioural Issues in Office Design* (New York: Van Nostrand Reinhold), 139–76.

HEERWAGEN, J., KAMPSCHROER, K., POWELL, K., and LOFTNESS, V. (2004). 'Collaborative Knowledge Work Environments', *Building Research and Information*, 32(6): 510–28.

HERZBERG, F. (1966). *Work and the Nature of Man* (New York: World Publishing Co.).

HOLTHAM, C. (2003). 'Knowledge and Space: Why the Most Important Technology in Knowledge Management is Physical Space', paper presented at Knowledge and Innovation Workshop: 'Creating Physical and Virtual Knowledge Spaces—New Opportunities for Knowledge Management', Coventry, Sept.

IESNA (Illumination Engineering Society of North America) (1999). *RP-1-04 American National Standard Practice for Office Lighting* (New York: IES).

JOROFF, M., and BERGMAN, M. (2007). *Strategies for Capturing Business in Integrated Workplace and Real Estate Project Markets* (Helsinki: Tekes).

KAMPSCHROER, K., and HEERWAGEN, J. (2005). 'The Strategic Workplace: Development and Evaluation', *Building Research and Information*, 33(4): 326–37.

LANGHOFF, J. (2006). *An Overview of Remote Virtual Teams and Productivity*, New Ways of Working URL: www.newwow.net (accessed June 2008).

LAWLER, E. E., MOHRMAN, S. A., and LEDFORD, G. E. (1995). *Creating High Performance Organizations: Practices and Results of Employee Involvement and Total Quality Management in Fortune 1000 Companies* (Boston: Harvard Business School Press).

LEAMAN, A. (2003). 'Productivity Improvement', in R. Best, C. Langston, and G. de Valence (eds.), *Workplace Strategies and Facilities Management* (Oxford: Butterworth-Heinemann), ch. 19.

——and BORDASS, W. (2001). 'Assessing Building Performance in Use: The Probe Occupant Surveys and their Implications', *Building Research and Information*, 29(2): 129–43.

LENNERTZ, B., and LUTZENHISER, A. (2006). *The Charrette Handbook: The Essential Guide for Accelerated Collaborative Community Planning* (Washington, DC: APA Planners Press, American Planning Association).

LEPAK, D. P., and SNELL, S. A. (1999). 'The Human Resource Architecture: Towards a Theory of Human Capital Allocation and Development', *Academy of Management Review*, 24(1): 31–48.

——TAKEUCHI, R., and SNELL, S. A. (2003). 'Employment Flexibility and Firm Performance: Examining the Interaction Effects of Employment Mode, Environment Dynamism, and Technological Intensity', *Journal of Management*, 29: 681–703.

McCoy, J. M., and EVANS, G. W. (2005). 'Physical Work Environment', in J. Barling, E. K. Kelloway, and M. R. Frone (eds.), *Handbook of Work Stress* (Thousand Oaks, Calif.: Sage), 219–45.

MARCH, J. G. (1991). 'Exploration and Exploitation in Organizational Learning', *Organization Science*, 2: 71–87.

MITAL, A., McGLOTHLIN, J. D., and FAARD, H. F. (1992). 'Noise in Multiple Workstation Open-Plan Computer Rooms: Measurements and Annoyance', *Journal of Human Ergology*, 21: 69–82.

MORGAN, A., and ANTHONY, S. (2008). 'Creating a High Performance Workspace: A Review of Issues and Opportunities', *Journal of Corporate Real Estate*, 10(1): 27–39.

MORRIS, S., SNELL, S. A., and LEPAK, D. (2005). 'An Architectural Approach to Managing Knowledge Stocks and Flows: Implications for Reinventing the HR Function' (CAHRS series; Ithaca, NY: Cornell University). URL: http://www.ilr.cornell.edu/depts/cahrs (accessed Oct. 2007).

NENONEN, S. (2004). 'Analysing the Intangible Benefits of Workspace', *Facilities*, 9/10: 233–9.

NIOSH (National Institute for Occupational Health and Safety) (1991). *Building Air Quality: A Guide for Building Owners and Facility Managers* (Washington, DC: EPA/NIOSH).

NONAKA, I., and KONNO, N. (1998) 'The Concept of "Ba": Building a Foundation for Knowledge Creation', *California Management Review*, 40(3) (spring): 40–54.

——SCHAMER, O., and TOYAMA, R. (2001). *Building Ba to Enhance Knowledge Creation and Innovation at Large Firms*. URL: www.dialogonleadership.org.

O'MARA, M. A. (1999). *Strategy and Place: Marketing Corporate Real Estate and Facilities for Competitive Advantage* (New York: Free Press).

OUYE, J., and SERINO, M. (2004). 'Human Capital and Why Place Matters', paper presented at the Northern California Human Resources Assn Conference, Sept.

PREISER, W. F. E., and VISCHER, J. C., eds. (2004). *Assessing Building Performance* (Oxford: Elsevier Science Publishing).

ROETHLISBERGER, F. J., and DIXON, W. J. (1939). *Management and the Worker.*(Cambridge, Mass.: Harvard University Press).

SEILER, J. A. (1984). 'Architecture at Work', *Harvard Business Review* (Sept.–Oct.): 111–20.

STEPHENSON, K. (1998). 'What Knowledge Tears Apart, Networks Make Whole', *Internal Communication Focus*, 36. URL: www.netform.com/html/icf.pdf (accessed Jan. 2007).

SULLIVAN, C. (1990). 'Employee Comfort, Satisfaction and Productivity: Recent Efforts at Aetna', in P. SOUTER, G. H. DURNOFF, and J. B. SMITH (eds.), *Promoting Health and Productivity in the Computerized Office* (London: Taylor & Francis).

TSUI, A. S., PEARCE, J. L., PORTER, L. W., and TRIPOLI, A. M. (1997). 'Alternative Approaches to the Employee–Organization Relationship: Does Investment in Employees Pay Off?', *Academy of Management Journal*, 40(5): 1089–1121.

VICKERS, M. (1999). 'No More Ivory Towers', *Today's Facility Manager* (Sept.): 1.

VISCHER, J. C. (1989). *Environmental Quality in Offices* (New York: Van Nostrand Reinhold).

——(1995). 'Strategic Workplace Planning', *Sloan Management Review*, 37(1) (fall): 33–42.

VISCHER, J. C. (1996). *Workspace Strategies: Environment as a Tool for Work* (New York: Chapman & Hall).

——(1999). 'Case Study: Can This Open Space Work?', *Harvard Business Review* (May–June): 28–40.

——(2005) *Space Meets Status: Designing Workplace Performance* (London: Taylor & Francis/Routledge).

——(2007a). 'The Effects of the Physical Environment on Job Performance: Towards a Model of Workspace Stress', *Stress and Health*, 23(3) (Aug.): 175–84.

——(2007b). 'The Concept of Workplace Performance and its Value to Managers', *California Management Review* (winter): 62–79.

——(2008a). 'Towards a User-Centred Theory of the Built Environment', *Building Research and Information*, 36(3) 231–40.

——(2008b). 'Towards an Environmental Psychology of Workspace: How People are Affected by Environments for Work', *Architectural Science Review*, 51(2): 97–108.

——and MEES, W. C. (1991). 'Organic Design in the Netherlands: Case Study of an Innovative Office Building', in W. F. E. Preiser and J. C. Vischer (eds.), *Design Intervention: Towards a More Humane Architecture* (New York: Van Nostrand Reinhold), ch. 15.

——and PRASOW, S. D. (in press). *Designing Workplace Performance Now and for the Future* (Toronto: Teknion Furniture Systems).

VON KROGH, G, ICHIJO, K., and NONAKA, I. (2000). *Enabling Knowledge Creation: How to Unlock the Mystery of Tacit Knowledge and Release the Power of Innovation* (Oxford: Oxford University Press).

WRIGHT, P. M., and SNELL, S. A. (1998). 'Toward a Unifying Framework for Exploring Fit and Flexibility in Strategic Human Resource Management', *Academy of Management Review*, 23(4): 756–72.

....

CHAPTER 20

INTERDEPENDENCIES BETWEEN PEOPLE AND INFORMATION SYSTEMS IN ORGANIZATIONS

....

ALAN BURTON-JONES
ANDREW BURTON-JONES

20.1 INTRODUCTION

....

Organizations are multilevel systems composed of interconnected and interdependent elements that must work together to be effective (Kozlowski and Klein, 2000). Two essential and increasingly important elements are people and information systems (ISs)—both forms of intangible capital: resources that organizations invest in with expectations of returns. Despite the interconnectedness of these human and technological assets there has been very little research on the nature of their interdependencies and how these dependencies affect their functioning and complementarity (Wade and Hulland, 2004). In this chapter we discuss how a better understanding of the dynamics of interdependencies between people and information systems can help researchers study organizations and help organizations improve the interoperation of their human and technological assets, thus returns on investments in them.

We begin by reviewing the concept of capital and its application to people—human capital—and information systems—information systems capital. Next we survey past literature on interdependencies and recent literature relating to interdependencies between people and information systems. Based on our analysis we propose an agenda for future research aiming to conceptualize interdependencies between people and information systems in a richer fashion. We conclude with an analysis of the implications for research and practice.

20.2 APPLYING THE NOTION OF CAPITAL TO PEOPLE AND INFORMATION SYSTEMS (ISs)

To apply the notion of capital to people and information systems (ISs), we need to understand the nature of each entity and the extent to which each one exhibits features of capital. The lay person's understanding of the nature of people is sufficient for our discussion at this stage, but the lay person's understanding of the nature of ISs may vary. As a result, we briefly clarify the nature of ISs before we examine the extent to which people and ISs can be called 'capital'.

In the IS academic discipline, there is no single agreed-upon definition of an IS (Orlikowski and Iacono, 2001). One approach is to think of the IS as a stand-alone tool, such as a sales system that can be used to produce sales reports. Another approach is to think of the IS as a combination of technology and people. For example: (*a*) infrastructure (hardware, networks, and operating systems), (*b*) applications that use infrastructure (such as sales reporting systems), (*c*) technical skills (involved in programming or maintaining systems), and (*d*) managerial skills (involved in managing projects to develop systems) (Melville *et al.*, 2004). A third perspective, which we adopt in this chapter, pays particular attention to what makes ISs unique as a resource. According to this view, the primary characteristic of an IS is that it serves to represent some other system in the world. Weber (2004: p. viii) writes:

Representation [is] the essence of all information systems. The *raison d'être* for information systems [is] that they track states of and state changes in other systems. By observing the behavior of an information system, we obviate the need to observe the behavior of the system it represents...For example, with an order-entry information system, we track states of and state changes in customers, which means that we do not have to consult with each customer individually to determine the goods or services they wish to purchase.

According to this view, businesses invest in ISs because having computerized representations is useful. It is useful because it can *informate* the business, enabling workers to make better decisions, and because it allows a business to *automate* tasks involving representations, enabling tasks to be accomplished more quickly (Zuboff, 1988). Drawing on this research, therefore, we adopt the view that (1) an IS is an artifact that provides representations of some domains in the world, and (2) the development and use of an IS depends on both technologies (infrastructure and applications) and people (developers, suppliers, managers, support staff, and users) (Melville *et al.*, 2004).

Given this view of ISs, what 'capital-like' features do people and ISs share and in what respects do they differ as forms of capital? Answers to these questions should help us to understand essential similarities and differences between human and IS capital and provide a context and rationale for discussing their interdependencies. Key features of capital described in past research relate to investment, structure, time, depletion, knowledge, labor, ownership, social processes, complementarity, fungibility, returns, and measurability. In Table 20.1 we briefly review the extent to which each of these features is present in human capital and IS capital.

Overall, our analysis in Table 20.1 suggests that people and ISs exhibit many features of capital. This is intuitive because people and ISs have often been referred to in past research as types of capital. The notion of human capital, for example, has been studied by economists for many years (Schultz, 1961; Mincer, 1958; Becker, 1962; Laroche *et al.*, 1999). This and subsequent research led to the identification of many important aspects of human capital such as the value of firm-specific skills (Becker, 1962), rare and unique skills (Burton-Jones, 1999; Lepak and Snell, 1999), and high-level generic skills (Drucker, 1966; Reich, 1991). ISs are also often considered a type of capital. One common view is that ISs are a type of 'intellectual capital'—typically classified into human capital, social capital, and structural or organizational capital, with ISs being a type of structural or organizational capital (Brooking, 1996; Sveiby, 1997).

Table 20.1 does highlight, however, that human and IS capital have characteristics that distinguish them from other types of capital. In particular, the value of both depends heavily on personal knowledge. Consequently, ownership and fungibility cannot be achieved fully, returns are difficult to measure, and value can amplify rather than deteriorate with use over time. Moreover, the value of human capital and IS capital are clearly interdependent. To perform their work, most people in organizations have to use ISs. Likewise, ISs cannot be created and used without skilled people. As a result, attempts to study, measure, or manage human capital in isolation from ISs is unlikely to succeed, just as attempts to study, measure, or manage IS capital in isolation from IS designers and users is unlikely to succeed. Accounting for the interdependencies between IS capital and human capital thus appears to require a holistic approach. How to design such an approach is the challenge we seek to address in this chapter.

Table 20.1. Mapping of Features of Capital to Human Capital and IS Capital

Features of capital	Mapping to human capital	Mapping to IS capital
Investment	People and organizations regularly invest in human capital via expenditures on education and health (Schultz, 1961).	Surveys suggest that US businesses spend about 50% of their capital expenditure on IT (Gurbaxani et al., 2003; Meeker et al., 2007).
Structure	Organizations can choose different ways of structuring the way they obtain human capital; for example, via insourcing or outsourcing.	Organizations often choose different ways of structuring the way they obtain IS capital for example, via insourcing or outsourcing.
Time	Investments in human capital often yield future returns and can even be made without opportunity costs; for example, on-the-job learning (Ben-Porath, 1967).	Investments in ISs are made over time and it takes time to generate returns from them (Barua et al., 1995; Weill, 1992; Soh and Markus, 1995).
Depletion	Human capital deteriorates with ageing but usage can often amplify its value, e.g. through learning (Mincer, 1958)	The physical aspects of ISs deteriorate with age, but the conceptual aspects can be used indefinitely and their value can amplify with use (Romer, 1993).
Knowledge	Human capital is essentially constituted in the knowledge and other attributes of the human knower (Becker 1962).	The core of an IS is the representation that it provides of a domain, a product of human knowledge (Brooks, 1995).
Labor	Human capital depends on labor because it is embodied in people.	ISs cannot be created and used without labor.
Ownership	Human capital cannot be owned because people cannot be owned.	Some aspects of ISs can be owned (such as via licenses) but ownership of data is more challenging (Coombs et al.)
Social processes	Social processes influence human capital because people construct their knowledge socially (Berger and Luckman, 1967)	Social processes heavily influence the development and use of ISs (DeSanctis and Poole, 1994; Orlikowski, 2000).

Complementarity	Human capital is developed and its value amplified by its interaction with other forms of capital such as social and structural capital (Ch. 2, above).	Economic studies have shown that firms need to make complementary investments to get positive returns from ISs (Brynjolfsson, 2003).
Fungibility	Human capital is not fungible because all human beings are unique.	Fungibility is a property of some aspects of an IS such as hardware and some software, but not data.
Returns	Human capital offers a stream of returns and employers and workers often vary in their ability to appropriate these returns (Becker, 1962; Ben-Porath, 1967).	ISs offer the potential for returns and businesses, their workers, and customers may vary in their ability to appropriate them (Orlikowski, 1991; Hitt and Brynjolfsson, 1996).
Measurability	Because human capital depends on human knowledge, it is transient and difficult to observe and measure, other than in action (Blackler, 1995).	The value of hardware and some software is often measurable, but measurability is a difficult challenge for firm-specific data and software.

20.3 THE NATURE OF INTERDEPENDENCIES

To understand how the interdependencies between human capital and IS capital might be conceptualized and studied it is useful to review the nature of interdependencies in general. Three types of interdependency are particularly relevant for our analysis: interdependencies among *people*, among *tasks*, and among *resources*;. see Figure 20.1.

Of these three types of interdependence, *interdependencies among people* have received the greatest attention in the literature. Early research on interdependencies among people was conducted by Deutsch (1949) and Thibaut and Kelley (1959) when they extended Lewin's (1951) work on field theory. Their research showed that the way that people think, feel, and act at any given time is affected greatly by the manner in which those people depend on others (such as colleagues, competitors, friends, and partners). These ideas have had an ongoing impact in social psychology (Rusbult and Van Lange, 2008), education (Johnson, 2003), and organizational studies (Tjosvold, 1986). In organizational studies, for instance, researchers have often focused on interdependencies among employees and their work units (Victor and Blackburn, 1987). Because of the work-oriented nature of organizations, however, a recurring theme in organizational studies has been that interdependencies among people often also involve interdependencies among *tasks* and *resources* (Pennings, 1973; Victor and Blackburn, 1987).

The most well-known typology of *interdependencies among tasks* (and the dominant framework of interdependencies in organizational science) was provided by

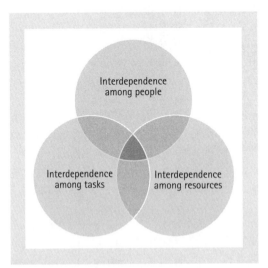

**Figure 20.1. Interdependencies among People,
Tasks, and Resources**

Thompson (1967). He identified three types of interdependency reflected in tasks involving people. In order of increasing levels of interdependency, these are: pooled, sequential, and reciprocal. In pooled interdependence, an organization depends on the performance of multiple tasks but each task may occur independently, such as in sales firms that depend on multiple salespeople who operate quite independently. In a sequential interdependence, tasks occur in sequence with the output of one serving as input to another, such as in manufacturing production lines. In reciprocal interdependence, tasks are reciprocally and dynamically dependent on each other, such as in the tasks performed by a medical team in an emergency room.

Thompson's ideas have been extended by many researchers. Nonetheless, an enduring idea in his work is that when interdependencies exist among tasks, an organization will need coordination mechanisms to deal with them. Furthermore, each type of interdependence requires a different coordination mechanism: pooled interdependence requires standardization and rule conformance, sequential interdependence requires planning and scheduling, and reciprocal dependence requires mutual adjustment and feedback.

Subsequent research on coordination led to the realization that interdependence among tasks often also involves *interdependence among resources* (Malone and Crowston, 1994; Victor and Blackburn, 1987). For example, Crowston (1997) proposed that organizational processes often involve three types of dependency: (1) task–task (when tasks share an input or output, or when the output of one task is the input of another), (2) task–resource (when a task requires a resource), and (3) resource–resource (when one resource requires another resource). Likewise, Malone *et al.* (1999) suggested that three types of dependency often arise in organizations due to the way that resources relate to tasks: (1) flow (when a task produces a resource used by another task), (2) sharing (when multiple tasks require one resource), and (3) fit (when multiple tasks must be performed to produce a resource). While often useful in practice to distinguish people from other resources, as shown in Figure 20.1, resources may also be referred to generically Malone and Crowston (1994: 92), for example, note that a resource can include 'money, storage space or an actor's time'.

These typologies are useful for our analysis because ISs can be studied in terms of tasks (the tasks involved in developing, maintaining, and using them) or in terms of a resource (the resource provided by the IS). As a result, these typologies enable us to describe the possible types of interdependency that can exist among people, tasks, and systems. Specifically, interdependencies can exist among people (people–people), tasks (tasks–tasks), systems (system–system), and among any combination (people–task, people–system, task–system, or people–task–system). Given the focus of our chapter on interdependencies among people and systems, we are especially interested in interdependencies within and among people and systems. Such interdependencies will often occur, of course, in the performance of tasks.

20.4 A REVIEW OF RECENT RESEARCH ON INTERDEPENDENCIES BETWEEN HC AND ISC

To examine how interdependencies have been examined recently, we developed a model to describe the ways in which such interdependencies may be realized. Figure 20.2 distinguishes between two types of resource—people and systems—and two types of activity and associated tasks: functional support activities and primary activities. Functional support activities refer to all the tasks performed to procure, develop, and maintain resources. We use the term 'functional' because the groups in organizations that perform these support activities are typically located in discrete organizational functions such as HR departments for human resources and IS departments for IS resources. Work tasks are the primary value activities (Porter, 1985) *for which* people and systems are procured, developed, and maintained, such as buying and selling products and services and executing an organization's strategy. Outputs from these work tasks, by reducing costs or increasing margins, add to organizational value—the pool of rents available for reinvestment or distribution to stakeholders. Organizational effectiveness derives from the organizational value or rents that are appropriated by the organization and used to improve capabilities, performance and returns to shareholders (see Chapter 14 above). Figure 20.2 also depicts four types of dependency involving resources and functions: IS–people; people–IS support; IS–people support; people support–IS support.

Among the more obvious dependencies that can be deduced from this framework is that people and ISs depend on each other because people depend on ISs to perform tasks and ISs require people to use them. Similarly, people depend on IS support—if only because they require training by IS support to use systems. ISs in turn depend on people support because people must be hired that have the requisite skills to use the ISs. Dependencies between people support and IS support include the need to maintain fit between support practices involving people and IS procurement, development, and maintenance, in order that people can use the IS and that the IS can be effectively used by people. Overall, the figure illustrates many examples of the types of dependency that we noted above among people, systems, and different types of task, including functional support tasks and work tasks.

To understand the extent to which researchers have studied interdependencies like those in Figure 20.2, we hired a graduate student with an M.Sc. in information systems and coursework in organizational studies to review all research articles published in 2008 in two organizational science journals and two IS journals. In both cases, one journal was chosen to reflect the leading research in that field (*Academy of Management Journal* and *MIS Quarterly*) and another major journal was included that specializes in more European, interpretive research (*Organizational Studies* and *Information Systems Journal*) because such research is sometimes

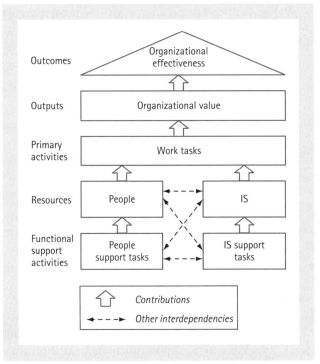

Figure 20.2. Interdependencies among HR Support, Task Performance, and IS Support Activities

underrepresented in leading North American journals. The coder was asked to read each article in the sample and identify those that examined interdependencies between people and systems, whether in the context of work tasks or functional support tasks (HR or IS support) (as per Figure 20.2). To provide additional assurance that articles were not missed, the coder also searched electronically across all articles in the sample for terms related to interdependencies.

Table 20.2 summarizes the results. As the table shows, few articles were found in the IS journals, and no articles were found in the organizational science journals. We therefore added one more year of organizational science journals (2007), but only one new article was found. The lack of examination of interdependencies among people and systems in organizational science was surprising given the importance of this issue in practice, but it confirms Orlikowski and Scott's (2008) recent observation that organizational scientists rarely examine IS-related issues.

After identifying the ten articles in Table 20.2, the coder then read each article and classified the way in which interdependencies were studied according to a coding scheme which we created. The coding scheme required the coder to first identify terms used to study interdependencies, whether or not the term 'interdependency' was used in an article. Second, the coder classified the nature of interdependencies studied

Table 20.2. Recent Studies of Interdependencies in Organizational Science and Information Systems

Journal	Year	Issues	Articles	Articles examining interdependencies
MISQ	2008	4	32	5
ISJ	2008	6	26	4
AMJ	2008	6	55	0
	2007	6	58	0
OS	2008	12	50	0
	2007	12	65	1

MISQ = MIS Quarterly; ISJ = Information Systems Journal; AMJ = Academy of Management Journal; OS = Organization Studies. Interdependencies examined included those between IS activities and work tasks and/or between IS activities and HR support activities.

according to the types identified in past research (Crowston, 1997; Malone and Crowston, 1994; Malone *et al.*, 1999; Thompson, 1967). Third, drawing on Figure 20.2, the coder specified whether the article examined interdependencies among IS support functions and work tasks, HR and IS support functions, or all three (IS support activities, HR support activities, and work tasks). Fourth, the coder distinguished between simple and composite interdependencies where simple interdependencies are *between* elements (such as between ISs and tasks) and complex interdependencies are *both within and between* elements (such as within different elements of ISs or tasks *and* between ISs and tasks). Finally, the coder classified the level of analysis at which the interdependency was studied (individual, group, or organization).

Table 20.3 summarizes the results of the coding. To some extent, the table suggests that interdependencies have been viewed in a wide variety of ways because researchers have used many concepts to study interdependencies and have examined interdependencies at various levels of analysis (individual, group, and organizational levels). However, the table also indicates that researchers have conceptualized interdependencies in fairly simple ways that do not account for the full range of interdependencies in organizations. Specifically, *they have generally conceptualized interdependencies in terms of how multiple people rely on an IS to perform their tasks* (task–resource, sharing, pooled, IS–tasks, simple/composite). Although our analysis is limited to just four journals and a limited time period, it illustrates how rarely and simply researchers have studied interdependencies between people and ISs in organizations.

Table 20.3 indicates that researchers could study interdependencies between people and systems in many more ways than they have studied them in the past. Given the importance of interdependencies in organizations, this would seem to be a significant opportunity for future research. Our review indicates that research is

Table 20.3. How Interdependencies were Studied in the Ten Articles (from Table 20.2)

	Concepts used to study interdependencies	Rely on, cause, enable, match, share, exhibit synchronicity/continuity
	Crowston	Task–Resource (10 articles), Task–Task (1 article)
	Malone	Sharing (4 articles), Fit (1 article), NA (6 articles)
	Thompson	Pooled (4 articles), Reciprocal (1 article), NA (6 articles)
Nature of interdependencies studied	Tasks	IS–Tasks (10 articles)
	Simple/composite	Simple (IS–Tasks) (8 articles), Composite (IS–Tasks) (2 articles)
	Level of analysis	Individual (4 articles), Group (1 article), Organization (5 articles)

Notes: The numbers in each line may add to more than 10 because an article may study interdependencies in more than one way. Crowston = task–task, task–resource, resource–resource; Malone = fit, flow, sharing; Thompson = pooled, sequential, reciprocal; Tasks = IS–Tasks, IS–HR, IS–HR–Tasks. NA = cannot be coded: if a paper does not delineate sets of activities or tasks.

particularly needed to examine (1) interdependencies among resources, (2) interdependencies that involve temporal elements such as flow, (3) sequential and reciprocal interdependencies, (4) interdependencies among IS and HR functions, and (5) composite interdependencies. In the next section we provide an illustration of how some of these opportunities might be tackled.

20.4 Enhancing our Perspective of People–IS Interdependencies: Illustrations

Researchers could take an inductive or deductive approach to research on interdependencies. In this section we illustrate how researchers could carry out such studies by providing an example of each approach: an inductive examination of interdependencies among resources, and a deductive analysis of interdependencies among support functions, resources, and work tasks as they contribute toward organizational outcomes.

20.4.1 Example A: Inductive Approach

An inductive approach begins with data rather than theory. The aim is to use data to discover phenomena rather than to prove or disprove a particular theory. In this case we draw upon an empirical study conducted in a large inner-city hotel. The aim of the study was to measure the influence of three resources on hotel performance: the hotel workforce (people), hotel information systems and processes (IS), and the hotel brand standard. The hotel workforce comprised all management and staff working for the hotel, including full-time employees, part-time and temporary staff, and contractors. The hotel IS comprised the computer hardware, software, and communications infrastructure and applications used by the hotel workforce. The brand standard comprised the set of standard operating procedures and methods prescribed for use by the workforce by the hotel's head office.

To determine the extent to which each of these resources influenced performance and depended on each other, data were collected and analyzed using the method of causal mapping. Both qualitative and quantitative causal maps were created using concepts and techniques proven in prior studies and described in the relevant literature (Eden *et al.*, 1992; Clarkson and Hodgkinson, 2005; Abernathy *et al.*, 2005).

Expert consultative panels comprising the managers of the major hotel functions were established to oversee the causal mapping process. Overall, twenty-five elements were identified that influenced hotel performance. Causal relationships were then identified among these elements and collectively on hotel performance and the causal influence in each case was quantified in percentage terms. Elements were divided into three major groups: external environmental elements, internal elements, and outcome elements.

1. *External environmental elements* comprised elements largely outside the hotel's sphere of influence, such as physical location, competitors, and head-office policies.

2. *Internal elements* comprised elements largely within the hotel's sphere of influence. These elements were further subdivided into two types:
   - *hotel resources*, comprised of intellectual resources (hotel workforce, IS, and hotel brand standard), and physical and financial resources (property and amenities and purchasing power);
   - *management activities*, comprised management of hotel operations, hotel infrastructure, hotel supply chain, and hotel pricing.

3. *Outcome elements* comprised key performance indicators such as guest volume, guest yield, costs, revenues, market share, gross profit contribution, guest satisfaction, guest loyalty, and employee turnover.

Detailed causal maps were created to reflect the contributions of each of these elements to hotel performance (for full details, see Burton-Jones, 2007). The causal maps showed that although many of these elements contributed to hotel performance, few did so in isolation. Most elements depended on other elements for their effects. The investigation was therefore expanded to investigate the nature of the interdependencies involved. In order to keep the exercise manageable it was decided to focus solely on identifying and measuring interdependencies between the hotel's major intellectual resources: the hotel workforce, the hotel ISs, and the hotel brand standard. No attempt was made in this study to identify or measure interdependencies between resources and support functions.

To identify the extent to which patterns of interdependencies varied, six contexts were identified, each context representing an important hotel function or outcome element in which the hotel workforce, hotel IS, and hotel brand standard were all considered by senior management to play an important role: (1) operations management, (2) infrastructure management, (3) supply chain management, (4) pricing, (5) guest satisfaction, and (6) guest volume.

A semi-structured questionnaire was used to identify and measure the extent of interdependencies between workforce (people), IS, and brand standard in each of these contexts. Interdependencies were quantified by asking informants to estimate the extent in percentage terms to which the hotel workforce, IS, and the brand standard were distinguished from each other in their individual effects on performance. Each of the six members of the expert management panel was interviewed separately to obtain their individual impressions of interdependencies, and the results were correlated and averaged.

Table 20.4 shows the results averaged across all six causal contexts—the figure in each cell representing the percentage dependency of one element on another in their effects. Interdependencies between IS and the brand standard were not assessed as they were outside the scope of the study. Net dependency refers to the balance of dependency in each case; for example, the figure in row C is the difference between rows A and B.

As Table 20.4 shows, interdependencies between the workforce and IS and the workforce and the brand standard in their influence on hotel performance were both high. In the case of workforce–IS dependencies, the dependency was also quite symmetric. The higher estimates of workforce–IS dependencies may have been due to IS use being more readily observable than use of the brand standard, as IS use typically involved a greater range of stylized activities and use of artifacts

Table 20.4. Summary of Interdependencies between Intellectual Resources (%)

A. Dependency of Workforce on IS	80.9
B. Dependency of IS on Workforce	91
C. Net Dependency (IS on Workforce)	10.1
E. Dependency of Workforce on Brand Standard	45
F. Dependency of Brand Standard on Workforce	71.4
G. Net Dependency (Brand Standard on Workforce)	26.4

(hardware and software), whereas the latter frequently involved only mental reference to a set of policies or procedures. Alternatively, it may simply reflect the high level of reliance on IT systems experienced in the hotel.

Findings from example

Whereas previous studies have tended to focus on task–resource or task–task interdependencies (as shown in Table 20.3), this inductive analysis demonstrates the existence of strong resource–resource interdependencies. Moreover, rather than just studying one-way dependencies by people and systems (as in the case of people who use systems), this study explored and measured the strength of dependencies in both directions. The study also identified and measured interdependencies in a range of operational contexts, and included an analysis of three resources that are each typically the domain of a different academic discipline (people studied in organizational science, systems studied in information systems, and brand standards studied in marketing). In addition to adding to the literature on resource–resource interdependencies, therefore, this inductive study suggests that discipline-centric theoretical models that posit an independent effect of people, brands, or systems on organizational effectiveness may be incomplete and possibly misleading.

20.4.2 Example B: Deductive Approach

Deductive approaches begin with theory. In this example we use existing theories to develop a model to explain how functional support tasks affect the provision of resources that are used to perform work tasks that influence organizational effectiveness. In the context of this model we then explain the interdependencies that exist among the different elements along the causal chain to organizational effectiveness. Figure 20.3 shows the theoretical model.

The theoretical model draws on contingency theory (Donaldson, 2001), knowledge-based theory of the firm (Grant, 1996; Spender, 1996), and theories associated with human capital (Becker, 1964) and strategic human resource management (Lepak and Snell, 1999, 2002). The underlying idea is that organizations must obtain resources (such as people and systems) that fit their strategy (needs), structure (such as their contracts), and processes (such as work practices). Organizations that are able to achieve greater degrees of fit are more likely to be able to generate value from resources (such as via employee contributions; Bandura, 1977; Stajkovic and Luthans, 1998) and appropriate value from these resources (Coff, 1999; Blyler and Coff, 2003; Chapter 14 above) and, thereby, perform more effectively.

The model has four high-level constructs, with each construct formed by its dimensions (Law et al., 1998). In the following subsections we describe the

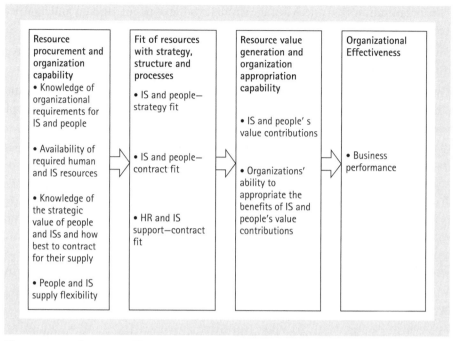

Figure 20.3. Resource Fit and Dependency Model

dimensions of each construct and the dependencies that we expect between systems and people within each construct.

Resource procurement and organization capability

(a) Dimensions

The model includes four dimensions that we propose drive the capability of an organization to procure the resources (whether people or systems) it needs. These four dimensions were selected based on previous research into the importance of IT-business alignment (Chan and Reich, 2007), knowledge congruence (Grant, 1996) and strategic flexibility (Sanchez, 1995; Volberda, 1998) to achieve strategic and operational fit.

Drawing on this prior work, we suggest that, at any point in time, the ability of an organization to achieve fit depends on the constraints that the organization faces. The model incorporates three dimensions to reflect such constraints:

- the organization's knowledge of the human and IS resources it needs to meet its strategic objectives;
- the availability of required human and IS resources in internal or external markets; and

- the organization's knowledge of the strategic value of people and ISs and how best to contract for their supply.

Having fit at a point in time, however, is not enough. Maintaining fit of resources over time requires an additional dimension:

- resource supply flexibility—the ability of the organization to adapt its people and IS supply practices to new demands, and the ability of the organization's people and ISs to adapt or be adapted to new demands.

As Figure 20.3 shows, we propose that these four factors collectively drive the level of fit that an organization can achieve and sustain.

(b) Dependencies among people and systems

Each of the dimensions noted above involves dependencies among people and ISs. For example:

- Knowledge of resource requirements may depend on knowledge of which ISs are required and the IS knowledge people need to have.
- Availability of people and IS resources may depend on the availability of people with requisite IS knowledge.
- Knowledge of the strategic value of resources may depend on estimates of people's IS knowledge and estimates of IS's value to people.
- Human resource supply flexibility may depend on people's knowledge of IS. The extent to which people management practices can be reconfigured to adapt to new demands may depend on the flexibility of ISs.

Resource relationships with strategy, structure, and process

(a) Dimensions

The model uses an alignment or 'fit' perspective (Wright and Snell, 1998; Lepak and Snell, 1999; Birkinshaw *et al.*, 2002; Chapter 13 above) that emphasizes the reduction of strategic knowledge and process gaps to improve organizational effectiveness (Zack, 1999; Rosemann and Chan, 2000). Drawing on this literature, we propose that this fit consists of three dimensions:

- IS–strategy and people–strategy fit: fit of people/human knowledge and ISs with organizations' strategic requirements (Zack, 1999);
- IS–contract and people–contract fit: fit of people and ISs with the organization's supply contracts in terms of the match of contractual modes and relationships to the value of the human resources (Lepak and Snell, 1999) and IS resources being supplied;
- HR support–and IS support–contract fit: fit of HR support activities (Lepak and Snell, 1999) and IS support activities with the characteristics of organizations' people (Lepak and Snell, 2002) and IS supply contracts.

(b) Dependencies among people and systems

Each of these dimensions involves dependencies among people and ISs. For example:

- People–strategy fit may depend on people's knowledge of IS. For example, for ISs to fit the strategy, they must be used in a way that is consistent with it, which requires having the right people with the right knowledge to use the ISs.
- People–contract fit and IS–contract fit may overlap as well as influence each other. Poor contracts with internal or external IS suppliers (for example, lacking appropriate financial incentives or quality controls) may lead to supply of poor ISs. Likewise, because people are needed to achieve and maintain IS–contract fit, if an organization lacks people–contract fit this will constrain its ability to maximize IS–contract fit.
- HR support practices depend on IS support practices. Because HR support practices are supported by ISs, achieving HR support–contract fit depends on having IS support–contract fit, because without the right contracts with the right IS suppliers, HR support practices cannot function appropriately.

Resource value generation and organization appropriation capability

(a) Dimensions

Because organizations have limited property rights over human knowledge, people's willingness to contribute what they know is critical to organizational value creation (Burton-Jones, 1999; Scarbrough, 1999; Hislop, 2003). Individuals contribute what they know through their continuance, attendance, organizational citizenship behavior, and task performance (Allen and Meyer, 1990; Tsui *et al.*, 1997; Van Dyne *et al.*, 1994; Kelloway and Barling, 2000; Organ and Ryan, 1995). Organizations can generate and appropriate value from human knowledge by using it to create rent-generating products and services or strategic assets that they can control (Amit and Schoemaker, 1993). Organizations can generate and appropriate value from IS by designing or buying in ISs with the required capabilities and having the policies and procedures in place to enable them to appropriate value from both the ISs and the people involved in their supply and use.

To account for the effect of fit on organizational effectiveness, therefore, the model posits an intervening process involving two dimensions:

- IS and people's value contributions; and
- organizations' ability to appropriate the benefits of IS and people's contributions.

(b) Dependencies among people and systems

Each of these dimensions involves dependencies among people and ISs. For example:

- People's contribution of what they know may depend in practice on their having access to appropriate ISs. For example, deficiencies in ISs can inhibit information-sharing in organizations (Te'eni, 2001).
- IS suppliers' contribution of ISs may depend on knowing what to supply to meet organizational needs or access to people with that knowledge.
- Because all job functions require knowledge to perform them and most involve use of ISs, appropriating value from job performance must depend on appropriating value from knowledge applied in using ISs.

Organizational effectiveness

The final construct in the model is organizational effectiveness. As the model shows, organizational performance will increase if organizations can obtain greater contributions from their resources and if they can appropriate more of the benefits from these contributions. We have already shown that dependencies exist among ISs and people at each stage leading up to organizational effectiveness: the procurement of resources, the fit of resources, and the performance of work tasks with resources. As a result, organizational effectiveness will depend heavily on the way these interdependencies are managed.

Findings from example

The proposed model illustrates the richness and complexity of dependencies that can exist between people and IS resources and support functions in organizations— some degree of dependency being apparent at every stage and in all components of the model.

Patterns of interdependent relationships were observed both within and between stages in the model. For example, in the fit stage of the model, the ability to achieve HR support–contract fit depends on having IS support–contact fit, but the model also shows that both types of contract fit are dependent on the organization's prior ability, reflected in the first stage of the model, to procure the right people and the right ISs and to do so using the right contracts.

The model provides explicit examples of reciprocal dependencies. For example, people support activities depend on IS support activities and vice versa. Pooled interdependencies, while not explicitly represented, are implied. For example, people need ISs to perform their tasks, and ISs, to be effective, need people to use them. Sequential interdependencies are similarly implied. For example, people's use of IS to (say) search a database for suitable job candidates typically involves sequential human–IS interaction, in which the output of one step becomes the input for the next.

While the implications of the dependencies discussed here would need to be empirically tested, the findings from our theoretical analysis are consistent with prior research that highlights the importance of understanding the interplay between human, IS, and other forms of intellectual capital in organizations (Wade and Hulland, 2004; Youndt *et al.*, 2004).

20.5 CONCLUSION

Organizations are systems composed of interconnected and interdependent elements of which two critical elements are people and information systems. People and ISs may also be regarded as forms of capital: resources in which organizations invest by way of procurement, use, and development, and from which they expect returns through improved organizational capabilities and performance.

In this chapter we have sought to demonstrate how a better understanding of the nature and dynamics of interdependencies between people and IS can help organizations optimize their interconnections and thereby improve returns on investments in them.

At least three major implications flow from our findings:

1. When human capital is studied (by researchers) or managed (by practitioners), they must account for the effects of IS capital, because otherwise their attribution of cause–effect relationships on, for example, organizational performance or the development of organizational capabilities, may be spurious.

Our empirical study, while limited in scope, suggests that there are strong interdependencies between people and IS in their effects on organizational performance. These findings and our theoretical model both imply that models that seek to show how to use human capital to improve organizational performance need to incorporate not only people but IS and to model not only resource fit but resource interdependency.

Development of organizational capabilities has been closely linked to workers' willingness to contribute their knowledge and organizations' ability to appropriate and retain the benefits of individuals' contributions (Liebeskind, 1996; Spender, 1996; Nahapiet and Goshal, 1998). Prior research has shown that organizational policies and procedures are required for appropriation (Coff, 2003; Chapter 14 above). Our analysis suggests that such appropriation mechanisms will also depend highly on an organization's IS, because the way that people acquire, use, and transfer what they know is increasingly reliant on IS.

From an accounting perspective (see Chapter 15 above) there has been a dearth of research into the links between human capital accounting and human capital management, and between human capital accounting and organizational effectiveness. Our findings suggest that to attempt to account for the effects of people or IS on performance without explicitly including IS–people dependencies is likely to be at best suboptimal and at worst misleading.

2. Because of the close interdependencies between human and IS capital, researchers and practitioners should attend to the management of these interdependencies. At present people/HR support and IS support are separate functions within organizations. Closer coordination of these functions may improve organizational returns on investments in people and IS.

From a strategic perspective, closer ordination between IS support and people support functions would appear useful at each stage of the supply chain depicted in our theoretical model, from resource procurement through fit, to maximizing value and organizational effectiveness.

Thompson notes that where interdependence is reciprocal, coordination requires positioning the functions involved tangential to one another, in a common group (Thompson, 1967). It is evident from our theoretical model that activities such as planning future workforce requirements and planning future IS requirements are activities that are likely to benefit from cross-functional, team-based approaches. Similar benefits would appear likely to flow from closer coordination of HR and IS activities within and across all stages in our model. The evident need for greater coordination of HR and IS support activities suggest that organizations may need to develop strategies for overcoming structural, disciplinary, and cultural barriers between the relevant functions.

As noted at the outset of this chapter, the core of the IS discipline and its main purpose in organizations is to provide representations of what is known so as to inform people and help automate task performance. The validity and relevance of such representations and how they are subsequently used is pivotal to the success of both IS and people investments. Research and development into creating better (more accurate and relevant) representations has been surprisingly limited to date, and has been largely conducted by IS specialists as part of systems analysis and design (for example, Weber, 1997). Given that such representations depend fundamentally on knowledge elicitation and abstraction and that much human knowledge is uncertain and tacit, an interdisciplinary approach involving IS and HR perspectives may be beneficial.

Research and development into ways to optimize IS usage has also been limited, and largely conducted to date by IS researchers. The popular technology acceptance model (TAM) (Bagozzi *et al.*, 1992) conceptualizes an individual's decision to use an IS as cognition but his/her actual usage as behavior. Recent advances in cognitive research indicate that this model and others like it are out of date and that IS usage should be studied as cognitive behavior (Burton-Jones and Straub, 2006). These findings suggest that a fusion of technological and humanistic perspectives would be beneficial.

3. We have shown that people and IS are strongly interdependent within organizations. We have also shown that both may be dependent on other forms of intellectual capital. These findings suggest that researchers and practitioners should be cautious about taking a reductionist perspective in relation to capital

in organizations, and may obtain more value from seeing it in a systemic and dynamic fashion.

As noted in the Introduction, human capital is essentially constituted in the knowledge and other attributes of the human knower (Becker, 1962). The core of an IS—the representation that it provides of a domain—is a product of human knowledge (Brooks, 1995). Given that knowledge is essentially a human resource, then human capital, IS capital, and other forms of intellectual capital are ultimately dependent on, and reducible to, the human knower. Thus, all forms of intellectual capital (human, social, and structural) are arguably human 'knowledge capital' (see also Chapter 5 above). Even so, the human knower increasingly depends on the instruments of his knowing—in particular, IS.

The preceding arguments indicate that investments in both human and IS capital may be viewed as investments in knowledge, which suggests the need for a unified approach to managing them. An obstacle to achieving such an approach is that organizations have suffered to date from having two divergent perspectives of knowledge: knowledge as an abstract, symbolic representation, and knowledge as embodied in the human knower—the former supported by the IS function, and the latter supported by the HR/people management function.

Functionally separating the management of knowledge representations from the management of human embodied knowledge clearly has some merits but also significant limitations, due to the strong interdependencies between these two types of knowledge capital. A unified approach to managing both forms of capital implies new strategies and structures as indicated earlier, plus, importantly, a shift in beliefs, not just about what constitutes knowledge in organizations but more practically about the relationships between people, IS, and knowledge in action. We endorse Blackler's (1995) call to focus on the process of knowing rather than the abstract concept of knowledge, and for an activity-based approach to conceptualizing knowing in organizations. Organizations that can overcome the cultural and functional barriers involved should reap the benefits through improved returns on their human and IS capital.

REFERENCES

ABERNETHY, M. A., HORNE, M., LILLIS, A. M., MALINA, M. A., and SELTO, F. H. (2005). 'A Multi-Method Approach to Building Performance Causal Maps from Expert Knowledge'. URL: http://leeds-faculty.colorado.edu/selto/Building%20causal%20performance%20 maps.pdf (accessed Jan. 2009).

ALLEN, N. J., and MEYER, J. P. (1990). 'The Measurement and Antecedents of Affective, Continuance and Normative Commitment to the Organization', *Journal of Occupational Psychology*, 63: 1–18.

AMIT, R., and SCHOEMAKER, P. J. H. (1993). 'Strategic Assets and Organizational Rent', *Strategic Management Journal*, 14: 33–46.

BAGOZZI, R. P., DAVIS, F. D., and WARSHAW, P. R. (1992). 'Development and Test of a Theory of Technological Learning and Usage', *Human Relations*, 45(7): 660–86.

BANDURA, A. (1977). 'Self-Efficacy: Toward a Unifying Theory of Behavior Change', *Psychological Review*, 84: 191–215.

BECKER, G. S. (1962). 'Investments in Human Capital: A Theoretical Analysis', *Journal of Political Economy*, 70(5) (Oct.): 9–49.

——(1964). *Human Capital: A Theoretical and Empirical Analysis, with Special Reference to Education* (3rd edn. 1993; Chicago: University of Chicago Press).

BIRKINSHAW, J., NOBEL, R., and RIDDERSTRALE, J. (2002). 'Knowledge as a Contingency Variable: Do the Characteristics of Knowledge Predict Organizational Structure?', *Organization Science*, 13(2): 274–89.

BLACKLER, F. (1995). 'Knowledge, Knowledge Work and Organizations: An Overview and Interpretation', *Organization Studies*, 16(6): 1021–46.

BLYLER, M., and COFF, R. (2003). 'Dynamic Capabilities, Social Capital, and Rent Appropriation: Ties that Split Pies', *Strategic Management Journal*, 24(7): 677–86.

BROOKING, A. (1996). *Intellectual Capital* (London: Thomson Business Press).

BROOKS, F. P. (1995). *The Mythical Man-Month* (Anniversary edn. Reading, Mass.: Addison-Wesley).

BRYNJOLFSSON, E. (2003). 'The IT Productivity Gap', *Optimize Magazine* (July), 21.

BURTON-JONES, A. (1999). *Knowledge Capitalism: Business, Work, and Learning in the New Economy* (Oxford: Oxford University Press).

——(2007). 'A Comparative Case Study of Knowledge Supply and Organizational Effectiveness', unpublished doctoral dissertation, University of Canberra.

——and STRAUB, D. W. (2006). 'Reconceptualizing System Usage: An Approach and Empirical Test', *Information Systems Research*, 17(3): 228–46.

CHAN, Y., and REICH, B. H. (2007). 'IT Alignment: What have we Learned?', *Journal of Information Technology*, 22(4) (Dec.): 297–315.

CLARKSON, G. P., and HODGKINSON, G. P. (2005). 'Introducing Cognizer™: A Comprehensive Computer Package for the Elicitation and Analysis of Cause Maps', *Organizational Research Methods*, 8(3): 317–41.

COFF, R. W. (1999). 'When Competitive Advantage Doesn't Lead to Performance: The Resource-Based View and Stakeholder Bargaining Power', *Organization Science*, 10(2): 113–19.

——(2003). 'The Emergent Knowledge-Based Theory of Competitive Advantage: An Evolutionary Approach to Integrating Economics and Management', *Managerial and Decision Economics*, 24(4): 245–51.

CROWSTON, K. (1997). 'A Coordination Theory Approach to Organizational Process Design', *Organization Science*, 8(2) (Mar.–Apr.): 157–75.

DEUTSCH, M. (1949). 'A Theory of Cooperation and Competition', *Human Relations*, 2: 129–52.

DONALDSON, L. (2001) *The Contingency Theory of Organization* (Thousand Oaks, Calif.: Sage).

DRUCKER, P. F. (1966). *The Effective Executive* (New York: Harper Collins).

EDEN, C., ACKERMAN, F., and CROPPER, S. (1992). 'The Analysis of Cause Maps', *Journal of Management Studies*, 29(3): 309–24.

GRANT, R. M. (1996). 'Toward a Knowledge-Based Theory of the Firm', *Strategic Management Journal*, 17: 109–22.

HISLOP, D. (2003). 'Linking Human Resource Management and Knowledge Management via Commitment: A Review and Research Agenda', *Employee Relations*, 25(2): 188–202.

JOHNSON, D. W. (2003). 'Social Interdependence: Interrelationships among Theory, Research, and Practice', *American Psychologist* (Nov.): 934–45.

KELLOWAY, E. K., and BARLING, J. (2000). 'Knowledge Work as Organizational Behavior', *International Journal of Management Reviews*, 2(3): 287–304.

KOZLOWSKI, S. W. J., and KLEIN, K. J. (2000). 'A Multilevel Approach to Theory and Research in Organizations', in K. J. KLEIN and S. W. J. KOZLOWSKI (eds.), *Multilevel Theory, Research, and Methods in Organizations*, (San Francisco: Jossey-Bass), 3–90.

LAROCHE, M., MERETTE, M., and RUGGERI, G. C. (1999). 'On the Concept and Dimensions of Human Capital in a Knowledge-Based Economy Context', *Canadian Public Policy*, 25(1): 87–100.

LAW, K. S., WONG, C.-S., and MOBLEY, W. H. (1998). 'Toward a Taxonomy of Multidimensional Constructs', *Academy of Management Review*, 23(4) (Oct.): 741–55.

LIEBESKIND, J. P. (1996). 'Knowledge, Strategy, and the Theory of the Firm', *Strategic Management Journal*, 17: 93–107.

LEPAK, D. P., and SNELL, S. A. (1999). 'The Human Resource Architecture: Toward a Theory of Human Capital Allocation and Development', *Academy of Management Review*, 24(1) (Jan.): 31–48.

——— (2002). 'Examining the Human Resource Architecture: The Relationships among Human Capital, Employment and Human Resource Configurations', *Journal of Management*, 28(4): 517–43.

LEWIN, K. (1951). *Field Theory in Social Science: Selected Theoretical Papers*, ed. D. Cartwright (New York: Harper & Row).

MALONE, T. W., and CROWSTON, K. (1994). 'The Interdisciplinary Study of Coordination', *ACM Computing Surveys*, 26(1): 87–119.

——CROWSTON, K., LEE, J., PENTLAND, B., DELLAROCAS, C., WYNER, G., QUIMBY, J., OSBORNE, C., BERNSTEIN, A., HERMAN, G., KLEIN, M., and O'DONNELL, E. (1999). 'Tools for Inventing Organizations: Toward a Handbook of Organizational Processes', *Management Science*, 45(3): 425–43.

MELVILLE, N., KRAEMER, K., and GURBAXANI, V. (2004). 'Information Technology and Organizational Performance: An Integrative Model of IT Business Value', *MIS Quarterly*, 28(2): 283–322.

MINCER, J. (1958). 'Investment in Human Capital and Personal Income Distribution', *Journal of Political Economy*, 66(4) (Aug.): 281–302.

NAHAPIET, J., and GHOSHAL, S. (1998). 'Social Capital, Intellectual Capital, and the Organizational Advantage', *Academy of Management Review*, 23(2): 242–66.

ORGAN, D. W., and RYAN, K. (1995). 'A Meta-Analytic Review of Attitudinal and Dispositional Predictors of Organizational Citizenship Behavior', *Personnel Psychology*, 48: 775–802.

ORLIKOWSKI, W. J., and IACONO, C. S. (2001). 'Desperately Seeking the "IT" in IT Research: A Call to Theorizing the IT Artifact', *Information Systems Research*, 12(2): 121–34.

—— and SCOTT, S. V. (2008). 'Sociomateriality: Challenging the Separation of Technology, Work and Organization', *Academy of Management Annals*, 2(1): 433–74.

PENNINGS, J. (1973). 'The Relevance of the Structural-Contingency Model for Organizational Effectiveness', *Administrative Science Quarterly*, 20: 393–410.

PORTER, M. (1985). *Competitive Advantage* (New York: Free Press).

REICH, R. (1991). *The Work of Nations: Preparing Ourselves for 21st-Century Capitalism* (London: Simon & Schuster).

ROSEMANN, M., and CHAN, R. (2000). 'Structuring and Modeling Knowledge in the Context of Enterprise Resource Planning', *4th Pacific Asia Conference on Information Systems* (Hong Kong: Publishing Technology Center, Hong Kong University of Science and Technology), 623–40.

RUSBULT, C. E., and VAN LANGE, P. A. M. (2008). 'Why we Need Interdependence Theory', *Social and Personality Psychology Compass*, 2(5): 2049–70.

SANCHEZ, R. (1995). 'Strategic Flexibility in Product Competition', *Strategic Management Journal*, 16: 135–9.

SCARBROUGH, H. (1999). 'Knowledge as Work: Conflicts in the Management of Knowledge Workers', *Technology Analysis and Strategic Management*, 11(1): 5–16.

SCHULTZ, T. W. (1961). 'Investment in Human Capital', *American Economic Review*, 51(1): 1–17.

SPENDER, J.-C. (1996). 'Making Knowledge the Basis of a Dynamic Theory of the Firm', *Strategic Management Journal*, 17: 45–62.

STAJKOVIC, A., and LUTHANS, F. (1998). 'Self-Efficacy and Work-Related Performance: A Meta-Analysis', *Psychological Bulletin*, 124: 240–61.

SVEIBY, K. E. (1997). *The New Organizational Wealth: Managing and Measuring Knowledge-Based Assets* (San Francisco: Berrett-Koehler).

TE'ENI, D. (2001). 'A Cognitive-Affective Model of Organizational Communication for Designing IT', *MIS Quarterly*, 25(2) (June): 251–312.

THIBAUT, J., and KELLEY, H. H. (1959). *The Social Psychology of Groups* (New York: Wiley).

THOMPSON, J. D. (1967). *Organizations in Action* (New York: McGraw-Hill).

TJOSVOLD, D. (1986). 'The Dynamics of Interdependence in Organizations', *Human Relations*, 39: 517–40.

TSUI, A. S., PEARCE, J. L., PORTER, L. W., and TRIPOLI, A. M. (1997). 'Alternative Approaches to the Employee–Organization Relationship: Does Investment in Employees Pay Off?', *Academy of Management Journal*, 40(5): 1089–1121.

VAN DYNE, L., GRAHAM, J. W., and DIENESCH, R. M. (1994). 'Organizational Citizenship Behavior: Construct Redefinition, Measurement, and Validation', *Academy of Management Journal*, 37(3): 765–802.

VICTOR, B., and BLACKBURN, R. S. (1987). 'Interdependence: An Alternative Conceptualization', *Academy of Management Review*, 12(3): 486–98.

VOLBERDA, H. W. (1998). *Building the Flexible Firm: How to Remain Competitive* (Oxford: Oxford University Press).

WADE, M., and HULLAND, J. (2004). 'The Resource-Based View and Information Systems Research: Review, Extension, and Suggestions for Future Research', *MIS Quarterly*, 28(1): 107–42.

WEBER, R. (1997). *Ontological Foundations of Information Systems* (Melbourne: Coopers & Lybrand and Accounting Association of Australia and New Zealand).

——(2004). 'Editor's Comments: Still Desperately Seeking the IT Artifact', *MIS Quarterly*, 27(2): pp. iii–xi.

WRIGHT, P. M., and SNELL, S. A. (1998). 'Toward a Unifying Framework for Exploring Fit and Flexibility in Strategic Human Resource Management', *Academy of Management Review*, 23: 756–72.

YOUNDT, M. A., SUBRAMANIAM, M., and SNELL, S. A. (2004). 'Intellectual Capital Profiles: An Examination of Investments and Returns', *Journal of Management Studies*, 41(2): 335–61.

ZACK, M. H. (1999). 'Developing a Knowledge Strategy', *California Management Review*, 41(3): 125–44.

ZUBOFF, S. (1988). *In the Age of the Smart Machine: The Future of Work and Power* (New York: Basic Books).

PART V

HUMAN CAPITAL IN THE FUTURE ECONOMY

CHAPTER 21

HUMAN CAPITAL, CAPABILITIES, AND THE FIRM

LITERATI, NUMERATI, AND ENTREPRENEURS IN THE TWENTY-FIRST-CENTURY ENTERPRISE

DAVID J. TEECE

21.1 INTRODUCTION

The business enterprise is the engine of innovation in the global economy, and human capital provides the parts of that engine. In the main, businesses in advanced economies finance and develop new products and processes and bring them to market. Such firms are increasingly multinational in the geographic scope of their activities—not just in their sales, but also in their sourcing of raw materials, components, subsystems, and today even in the components of innovation itself. Firms also heavily rely on building and leveraging human capital, at home and abroad.

The return that human capital receives is wages, fees, bonuses, and other forms of compensation. Indeed, human capital—which can be quantified by calculating the present value of future compensation—is the largest 'asset' class in the economy;

and for the overall economy, compensation is the largest component of corporate expenses.

According to Alfred Marshall, 'the most valuable of all capital is that invested in human beings' (1898: 647). The general notion that through education and training people could become the functional equivalent of a capital asset is a very old idea in economics, traceable back before Marshall to at least Adam Smith, who noted that 'a man educated at the expense of much labour and time, may be compared to one of those expensive machines' (Smith, 1801: 102).

However, I suggest an extension of Marshall's proposition. It is contended that a nation's educational institutions and the capabilities of the business enterprise, undergirded by the (deep) skills of the 'literati', 'numerati', and entrepreneurial managers, are critical to the supply of human capital and to the maintenance of high wages/compensation, as well as to the income of the nation-state(s) in which the enterprise operates. Expressed differently, for employees to achieve high compensation, the nation must have well-functioning national and regional 'systems of innovation' (including educational institutions and laws). Prosperity requires that the business ecosystems of the nation-state must support enterprises that can develop and deploy human capital astutely. In short, the productivity of the workforce and the value of the human capital that a nation possesses depends very much on certain organizational capabilities of businesses (what I will call dynamic capabilities), on a set of supporting institutions at the national and regional level, and also on society's social capital. An abundant supply of human capital will not by itself guarantee national prosperity.

In this chapter, the roles in economic development of both human capital and certain types of firm-level organizational capital are examined together.[1] Given the importance of supporting institutions and laws, it is reasoned that enterprise-level success in a competitive global economy depends upon the ability of the enterprise, led by entrepreneurial management, to sense/develop and seize opportunities on a continuous basis. The firm's entrepreneurial, administrative, and transformational capabilities—which I call dynamic capabilities—undergird its capacity to build and sustain competitive advantage. Maintaining these capabilities in turn requires the business enterprise to recruit, organize, motivate, and deploy highly talented literati and numerati. The basic thesis here is that organizational capabilities (along with social capital) and the institutional and legal fabric of society are needed to enable human capital—including the literati and numerati[2]—to generate prosperity and economic progress.

21.2 KNOW-HOW, HUMAN RESOURCES, AND ECONOMIC DEVELOPMENT

It has long been recognized by some that economic prosperity rests upon knowledge and its use. As Simon Kuznets noted almost half a century ago, 'the increase in the stock of useful knowledge and the extension of its application are the essence of modern economic growth' (Kuznets, 1966). Enlightened economic historians have emphasized the role of technology, management, organization, and institutions in economic development (see for example, Rosenberg and Birdsell, 1986; also, Teece, 1981c). The importance of entrepreneurship and management has also received some weight from business historians. However, these factors are often neglected in more mainstream analyses of economic growth.

One class of explanations is simply that policy and strategy analysts have for far too long worn intellectual blinders. Theories of economic growth that stressed the important role of the capital stock (Kaldor, 1957; Hicks, 1965) and natural resources received unwarranted extended play in textbooks and policy pronouncements. These theories did not recognize the importance of innovation and knowledge transfer. Innovation and knowledge transfer were relegated to a backwater in mainstream economics as well as in the other social sciences.[3] Today the importance of innovation and knowledge management is being established and disseminated to a wider audience—not through the work of mainstream economists, but through the efforts of insightful interdisciplinary protagonists such as Clayton Christensen, Giovanni Dosi, Gary Hamel, Connie Helfat, Rebecca Henderson, Richard Nelson, Ikujiro Nonaka, Hirotaka Takeuchi, and Sidney Winter.

A second class of factors is that the literati, the numerati, and entrepreneurs have become more important to the functioning of advanced economies than in recent years. The greater the importance of intangible assets to competitive advantage, the greater the premium afforded to entrepreneurial capacities, both individual and organizational. It is now well recognized that entrepreneurial insight and capacity which are needed to build and direct the organizations that are necessary to harness the skills of the literati and numerati.

Schumpeter observed that entrepreneurs are instrumental in bringing about new combinations in the economy, often resulting in creative destruction. Creative destruction is the result of bringing new products and processes into the market, to the great benefit of the consumer. This process drives the economic system out of equilibrium. However, the out-of-equilibrium circumstance presents opportunities to those who can help drive the market back toward equilibrium. This is sometimes referred to as Kirznerian entrepreneurship.[4] It is no less important as a source of profits (and potential losses) than Schumpeterian creative destruction.

The hallmark of the entrepreneur is an ability to see opportunities that are unseen by others, and then act on them. Business entrepreneurs frequently create new enterprises to address new opportunities. Entrepreneurs build new enterprises, as incumbent organizations are often not hospitable to new product and process concepts. Along the way, entrepreneurs create opportunities for the literati and numerati. Sometimes they are themselves 'members' of the literati and numerati.

The entrepreneur is today well recognized as important to the evolving behavior of firms, and in many treatments is 'assigned a heavy responsibility for the vitality of the free enterprise society' (Baumol, 1993: 2). At the same time, however, the entrepreneur has 'virtually disappeared from the theoretical literature' in economics (p.3). This chapter and other writings by this author (for example, Teece, 2007a, 2007b) try to remedy this deficiency by building entrepreneurship into a capability-based theory of the firm (and through the theory of the firm into the economics literature itself).

A third class of factors relates to structural changes that have occurred in the economies of advanced developed countries. These structural changes have served to modify the nature of what is strategic, and have highlighted the importance of knowledge and its management. They are addressed below.

In today's open economy, with widespread outsourcing and offshoring, entrepreneurial capacities are even more important than they were historically. That is because there is now a premium on sensing developments early and responding quickly. Traditional management must either become more entrepreneurial, or embrace and support the entrepreneurs that exist within their own organizations. Ideally they should do both. This is rarely easy, because established firms also need to produce and sell products currently in the market. This innate tension is rarely resolved satisfactorily, and leads to endless opportunities for new firms to enter the market, to create new markets, and to grow—usually at the expense of the incumbents.

While human capital and entrepreneurship are important to economic development, the mere existence of large numbers of trained literati and numerati will not produce good organizational outcomes. What the literati and numerati work on and how they work together is as important as their individual skill.[5] This is the 'strategic' aspect. The manner in which individuals (routinely) work together defines in part the organization's capabilities. Organizational capabilities, along with technological capabilities (and intellectual property), in turn define an organization's intangible assets.

In any organization, the command that top management has over resources is considerable, and decisions (or the lack thereof) of the top management team are likely to have great consequences for enterprise performance. This may show up quickly in some enterprises (such as professional services, where keeping top talent is important to the business and the loss of top talent is manifested quickly in deteriorated financial performance), or perhaps slowly, where the enterprise has fixed investments in place or a significant new product development pipeline.

To some extent the existence of organizational routines that define how people work together makes particular individual skills a little more fungible. Practiced organizational routines have the effect of blunting the power that any individual has to withdraw their services and damage the enterprise. When individual employees depart, it is less likely to harm an enterprise with an already established set of procedures and a practiced panoply of relevant routines. The organization can rehire and anticipate reasonable continuity of its business.

In short, it is trite to claim that organizations depend upon people. At one level it is indisputable, but to say no more is to give excessive credence to a naïve human capital thesis.[6] Human capital is not particularly valuable unless employed cooperatively and deployed astutely. If management performs its combinatorial and entrepreneurial functions well, the value associated with achieving useful coordination and cooperation can be considerable and cannot all be captured by individual employees.

It is not the purpose of this chapter to comprehensively survey human resource/ human capital management issues.[7] Rather, the purpose is to indicate the types of human resource and other management practices more likely to be consistent with establishing and maintaining competitive advantage.

21.3 THE ROLE OF TOP TALENT

21.3.1 The Non-Uniform Distribution of Human Performance

Whether one is focusing on creating value or capturing it, in recent decades the numerati and literati (expert talent) and entrepreneurs have become more important to the creation and management of technology in the global economy (Reich, 2002; Albert and Bradley, 1997). Society has always had a non-uniform distribution in productive talents, with some individuals and groups being more skilled and committed than others. Every organization has a good chance of attracting/ recruiting a percentage of top talent, but retaining them is another matter. Barriers to the interorganizational transfer of personnel have been lowered in most Western countries (and also between countries) by greater labor mobility, the relative decline of corporate pension plans, the weakening of strong corporate cultures, and the erosion of loyalty toward employers. Visa programs of some countries also allow at least limited transfer of highly skilled individuals. The movement of skilled personnel internationally has increased, and the competition for top talent has been amplified. Accordingly, greater attention needs to be placed on understanding how best to manage the literati and the numerati. That is the subject of this section.

As a starting point, one must recognize that individual productivity in science and engineering is quite skewed. This was first observed by Alfred Lotka (1926) in a study of the authorship of articles in nineteenth-century physics journals. Lotka found that approximately 6 percent of publishing scientists produced half of all papers.[8] Lotka's results are reasonably robust, and they have been shown to hold for many disciplines in many different time periods. 'Winner-take-all' effects in science may be one factor at work here, along with differences in the underlying distribution of human talent.

While not important to the analysis here, the non-uniform distribution of performance does not represent differences in intelligence amongst groups. Studies by Nisbett (2009) of high-performing groups in the USA—Jews, Chinese Americans, and West Indian Blacks—provide overwhelming evidence that what is distinctive about these three groups is not innate advantage but hard work, and respect for learning. According to Nisbett, Jews and Chinese people have a particularly strong respect for scholarship. Intact families were also an important predictor of success with respect to West Indian Blacks. At the group level, these results indicate that success depends less on intellectual endowment than on persistence and environment. As Nisbett explains, 'there is much that we can do to increase [our] intelligence and academic achievement' (2009: 198).[9]

Other studies confirm that the most productive and eminent scientists are strongly motivated. Almost all have good stamina in the sense that they work hard in the pursuit of long-run goals.[10] Eminent scientists and engineers also have high intelligence and a broad knowledge base, and enjoy professional autonomy, but are nevertheless willing to collaborate when they perceive that collaboration will yield benefits.

Because of increased specialization and a corresponding need to integrate individual capabilities, teams have become increasingly important to science and engineering. However, the non-uniform distribution of expert talent means that teaming amongst experts will not look quite the same as teaming on the shop floor.

The innovation process places a premium on the talents of the literati, numerati, and engineers. The economic significance of the literati and the numerati has become greater as markets expand and as traditional bases of competitive advantage become undermined. The growing importance of knowledge and rapid changes in the business environment mean that specialized talent and organizational capabilities are becoming more important (Albert and Bradley, 1997: 4). The outsourcing of components and low-end services to lower-cost locations has also worked to the benefit of skilled workers (Feenstra and Hanson, 1999) in the advanced economies of the USA, Western Europe, and Japan.

Indeed Reich (2002: 107) and many others have observed that talented and ambitious people can earn more today, relative to the median wage, than could talented and ambitious people in the industrial era. Larger and more open or 'contestable' markets are the reasons why dispersion in earnings has increased. The higher rewards which top talent can command stem from the value which now seems to flow from creative, analytical, and 'rainmaking' abilities of leading professionals. In particular, the skill to help solve complex problems, to help make critical decisions or resolve complex disputes, help win business, and help design and develop new products and services, commands high value.

It is not just research scientists, engineers, designers, athletes, movie stars, musicians, and film producers who can earn high rewards. So too do other types of professionals and consultants such as lawyers, financial analysts, investment advisers, fund managers, turnaround specialists, and even former government officials and economists.

Competition for high-end talent is also increasingly global as many highly talented individuals have mobility. In the USA, immigrants have always been significant in the scientific and engineering workforce. In recent years the foreign-born have also played a significant role in entrepreneurship. A survey by Duke University and the University of California shows that one quarter of newly founded engineering technology firms in the USA in the decade 1995–2005 had at least one foreign-born founder. In Silicon Valley, the numbers constituted more than 50 percent. Competition for this talent comes first when they apply to graduate schools, and secondly when they graduate and consider opportunities at home or in their host country, or possibly elsewhere (Kirkegaard, 2007).

21.3.2 Literati, Numerati, and Entrepreneurs

There are three categories of human resources that are discussed in this chapter: the literati, the numerati, and entrepreneurial managers. The first two are closely related. The literati and the numerati are the highly educated 'classes'. They represent expert talent. The literati tend to have both undergraduate and usually graduate education in arts and sciences, economics, business, or law. The numerati are likewise highly educated, but usually have capabilities in mathematics or statistics, information systems, computer science, engineering, or accounting and finance. They might also be software programmers. Both groups have specialized skills. Both groups synthesize and analyze, but the former tend to be more specialized at synthesis and the communication of ideas. The latter excel at analysis, especially of large data sets. Both groups of expert talent are important to today's knowledge economies. Both groups earn top quartile salaries. Members are educated at institutions of higher learning—although sometimes at trade schools.

Managing the literati and numerati involves special opportunities and challenges. According to one study (Chambers et al., 1998) 75 percent of executives believed that they had insufficient talent in the ranks of their top leaders. Traditional hierarchical approaches (as discussed in section 21.6.1 below) are less likely to succeed than more accommodating systems. Also, research shows (Sturman and Trevor, 2001) that those with the most training, education, and ability are the most likely to quit if dissatisfied.

The third category is entrepreneurial managers. As Baumol and Strom (2007: 233) note: 'A close look at the extraordinary economic growth of the last two centuries, however, suggests that the market mechanism does not do its work without the input of individual actors—the entrepreneurs who bring cutting edge innovation to market'. Indeed, in fast-paced, globally competitive environments, consumer needs, technological opportunities, and competitor activity are constantly in a state of flux. Opportunities open up for both newcomers and incumbents, putting the profit streams of incumbent enterprises at risk. As discussed in Teece *et al.* (1997), the path ahead for some emerging marketplace trajectories is easily recognized. In microelectronics this might include miniaturization, greater chip density, and compression and digitization in information and communication technology. However, most emerging trajectories are hard to discern. For instance, when will 3D flat screen technology emerge? Will it be first on small panels, or on large-panel public display monitors? Sensing (and shaping) new opportunities are very much a scanning, learning, creative, and interpretive activity at which, by definition, entrepreneurs excel. Investment in research and related activities is usually a necessary complement to this activity.

The success of the enterprise depends importantly not only on the performance of entrepreneurial managers in sensing opportunities, but also on their capacity to seize opportunities, and to reconfigure a business so that it fits its evolving environment. Opportunities are detected by the enterprise because of two classes of factor. First, as stressed by Kirzner (1973), entrepreneurs can have differential access to existing information, or they can discern patterns and trends not evident to others. Kirzner stressed how the entrepreneurial function recognizes any disequilibrium and takes advantage of it. The Kirznerian view is that entrepreneurship is the mechanism by which the economy moves back toward equilibrium. On the other hand, Schumpeter (1934) stressed upsetting the equilibrium through the introduction of innovation. As Baumol (2005: 3) notes: 'The job of Schumpeter's entrepreneur is to destroy all equilibria, while Kirzner's works to restore them'. These are some of the mechanisms underlying continuous industrial evolution and change. Equilibrium is rarely if ever achieved (Shane, 2003: 20). Both forces are relevant in today's economy.

When opportunities are first glimpsed, entrepreneurs and managers must figure out how to interpret new events and developments, which technologies to pursue, and which market segments to target. They must assess how technologies will evolve, and how and when competitors, suppliers, and customers will respond. Competitors may or may not see the opportunity, and even if they do they may calibrate it differently. Their actions, along with those of customers, suppliers, standard-setting bodies, and governments can also change the nature of the opportunity and the manner in which competition will unfold.

The literature on entrepreneurship emphasizes that opportunity discovery and creation can originate from the cognitive and creative ('right brain') capacities of the individual(s). However, discovery can also be grounded in organizational processes, such as continuous research and development activity, scanning externally for new technologies, and co-development activities with alliance partners.

The ability to create and/or sense opportunities is clearly not uniformly distributed amongst individuals or enterprises. Opportunity creation and/or discovery by individuals require both access to information and the ability to recognize, sense, and shape developments. The ability to recognize opportunities depends in part on the individual's capabilities and extant knowledge (or the knowledge and learning capacities of the organization to which the individual belongs) particularly about user needs in relationship to existing as well as novel solutions. This requires specific knowledge, creative activity, the ability to understand user/customer decision-making, and practical wisdom (Nonaka and Toyama, 2007). It involves interpreting information in whatever form it appears—a chart, a picture, a conversation at a trade show, news of scientific and technological breakthrough, or the anxiety expressed by a frustrated customer. One must accumulate and then filter information from professional and social contacts to create a conjecture or a hypothesis about the likely evolution of technologies, customer needs, and marketplace responses. This task involves scanning and monitoring internal and external technological developments and assessing customer needs, expressed and latent. It involves learning, interpretation, and creative activity.[11] It is a key dimension of entrepreneurship.

As discussed in more detail below, entrepreneurship involves not only the discovery/creation and evaluation, but also capturing value from discoveries. Neither the identification nor even the creation of opportunities results spontaneously in exploitation (capturing value). Indeed, many inventions go unexploited for extended periods. The pioneer may not turn out to be the winner (Teece, 1986, 2006).

The value capture side of entrepreneurship requires the design and implementation of new business models. Correctly establishing the basic elements of the business model is a critical part of the innovation process (Teece, 1986, 2010). As an executive in the music business noted: 'Entrepreneurs are also realizing they need to spend as much energy on their business model as they do on technological innovation.'[12] There is always risk involved, whether the opportunity is developed (created), or discovered.[13] The risk is amplified when imitation (and/or piracy) is easy.

It is also possible to distinguish the function of the entrepreneur from the function of the ordinary manager. The ordinary manager is the individual who oversees the continuing efficiency of established processes. Managers see to it that inputs/resources are not wasted, that schedules are met and contracts honored, that pricing decisions are properly made, that receivables are collected, and that the business model is constantly tuned. Fulfilling the basic business operations in a static environment is relatively easy. In economic language, this type of management involves endeavoring to maximize profits against a known set of constraints.

In today's global economy with rapid change, the challenge is harder. The hallmark of good managers in this context is that they must also be entrepreneurial, although a great entrepreneur need not be particularly adept at operations—but of course they do need to be supported by a strong operations team.

Nurturing entrepreneurship and an entrepreneurial culture raises both governmental (nation-state) level issues as well as firm-level issues. In societies where there is a reasonable supply of intrinsically entrepreneurial individuals, the issue collapses to how to motivate/reward such individuals, how to deepen and channel their expertise, how to focus them on socially productive activity, how to provide supporting institutions such as venture capital and intellectual property protection, and how to morph the functions of the entrepreneur and the manager in the organizational settings of larger enterprises. Although it is not analyzed here, the nation-state's culture and reward structure is important (see Scotchmer, 2004). Nevertheless, the focus in this chapter is on firm-level rewards and structures to support firm-level innovation.

It is also important to note that entrepreneurial activity is not always socially productive. As Baumol notes: 'The entrepreneur may even lead a parasitic existence that is actually damaging to the economy' (1990: 894). For instance, the entrepreneur can seek government handouts, improper risk absorption, or improper spoils from litigation. How the entrepreneur acts will be a function of the reward structure in the economy. It is clearly important for society to design the rules to encourage productive entrepreneurship and thwart unproductive entrepreneurship. The same principle holds inside the corporation. Internal rewards must be set to reward productive entrepreneurship and discourage unproductive activity.

21.4 Dynamic Capabilities

21.4.1 General

With few exceptions, the work on human capital has not differentiated much between the functions of managers, entrepreneurs, and experts. This chapter focuses primarily on these relatively neglected categories. This section links human capital and organizational capital.

Developments in recent decades, including improvements in information technology and the liberalization of markets, have given consumers more choices. In order to compete better, firms have had to place as much attention on innovation as on optimizing 'production'. In today's world, the supply-side-driven logic of the industrial era no longer works. New products need to be marketed, and customers cannot be taken for granted, even when a firm offers a superior product. Innovation itself requires changes to management structures and systems. What are often needed are decentralized structures and self-managed teams, united by commitment to an overall strategic vision. These can form the backbone of a firm's organizational capital.

Dynamic capabilities have become the shorthand by which many understand the processes whereby, in fast-paced global environments, firms organize to develop sought-after new products and processes. The chapter also reviews the nature of the individual skills (human capital) along with the organizational capabilities necessary for firms to maintain dynamic capabilities. Attention is given to the mechanisms and structures that help retain, attract, motivate, and utilize critical talent. Special attention is given to mechanisms for achieving value-enhancing coordination amongst highly skilled literati and numerati. The goal is to understand how the enterprise competes in a global economy of ubiquitous complexity, overlapping invention, and deep co-specialization of assets.

Complexity and Multi-Inventions

In order to innovate, business firms must develop and combine numerous inventions, many of which may be developed—and contain intellectual property, owned by others. Such combinations are a technological consequence of greater complexity, particularly in industries where innovation is cumulative. I have referred to this elsewhere as systemic innovation (Teece, 2000), or the multi-invention (Somaya and Teece, 2007) phenomenon. It creates the need to combine very large numbers of intellectual property components and patented inventions in a single product (Teece, 1998). For example, large software programs may require the combination of thousands of pieces of copyrighted (and possibly patent-protected) code. In electronics, technological innovation is highly cumulative, and innovators often will wish to build on not only their own but also their competitors' past innovative activity. Intellectual property rights may be implicated. In biotechnology, innovators must often assemble large portfolios of patented genetic information, research tools, and other inventions to bring new medical solutions to fruition.

The multi-invention context in which new product development frequently takes place imposes special demands on management. As described elsewhere by Teece (1981a), the markets for know-how and intellectual property are riddled with imperfections and inefficiencies possibly requiring internalization (and managerial action) by the enterprise. This is the very essence of what firms do in today's economy.

Co-specialization

When design/production involves a complex system, co-specialization often results. With co-specialization, the parties are likely to be in a situation of mutual dependence as they may not be able to readily redeploy their assets to alternative uses.

Specialization and co-specialization enable business units around the globe to focus on what they do best. There is benefit to the provider as well as the customer from such specialization and co-specialization. The multi-invention phenomenon just discussed is a major cause of co-specialization. Co-specialization requires alert management, and may lead to common ownership.

To make the global system of vertical specialization and co-specialization work, there is a need (indeed an enhanced need) to develop the right assets and combine the various elements of the value chain in the right way at the right time so as to develop a 'solution' that customers value. The supply-driven logic of the industrial era does not hold in today's knowledge-based economy. There is no longer just the need for management and organization to provide an integration function to link production flows end-to-end. Rather, the need is to orchestrate a medley of activities located in organizational units without common ownership, often operating in disparate locations.

Dynamic capabilities define a firm's capacity to create and utilize (orchestrate) the system of global specialization and co-specialization.[14] This often requires extending, modifying, or if necessary completely revamping what the enterprise is doing so as to maintain a good fit with the environment (the ecosystem). Sometimes the ecosystem must itself be shaped or reshaped to support the development and deployment of new technology. These capabilities include the managerial and organizational capacity associated with first sensing opportunities, then seizing them, and then transforming again as the situation requires (Teece, 2007a). Entrepreneurial management is a critical factor undergirding dynamic capabilities.

Critical issues for the manager of the multinational enterprise exist around how innovation should be managed. Where should research and development be done, organizationally and geographically? Should it be done internally or collaboratively with external partners? As explained in Teece (1986), the goal should be to own/control only the difficult-to-replicate aspects—the bottleneck asset.[15] In a world where products require multiple inventions, complex management issues arise. It is not a good decision guide to simply perform internally the highest value-added activities—although it is often the case that the difficult-to-imitate aspects end up commanding higher prices, and hence providing high value added. Teece (1986, 2006) provides more rigorous guidance than an *ex post* assessment of value added is able to yield.

In addition to owning and controlling (managing) the bottleneck assets, it is also essential for a profit-seeking enterprise to provide the orchestration function—to function as the 'systems integrator'. Elsewhere (Teece, 2007a) I have explained that systems integration capabilities help undergird dynamic capabilities.

21.4.2 Human Resource Architecture

How can the (strategic) management of human resources, along with human resource management practices, support dynamic capabilities, and thereby assist in building and maintaining competitive advantage?[16] Becker and Huselid (2006: 899) note that the most pressing theoretical challenge facing the strategic management of human resources is an articulation of the 'black box' that describes the logic between the firm's human resources architecture and its subsequent performance. The dynamic capabilities framework provides this logic.

Dynamic capabilities are those attributes of the business enterprise that enable it to orchestrate assets and organizational units, while remaining relevant to the market and other aspects of the business environment. In contrast, a firm's basic operational capabilities can enable it to perform properly the activities that it set out to perform, without considering the issue of whether the enterprise is setting out to make the right product and address the right market segment.

As noted, a consequence of globalization and the opening up of markets is that competitive advantage increasingly depends on two classes of asset. The first are those unique skills/assets/resources/components that are in scarce supply. The literati and numerati are in this category. A second class of asset consists of the dynamic capabilities needed to deploy human capital astutely.

The very nature of capabilities/knowledge is that much of it is tacit.[17] It does not travel well; it is difficult to transfer absent the transfer of skilled and experienced personnel. Hence it is often (though not always) difficult to replicate. This provides a certain amount of natural protection to an organization's dynamic capabilities.

In short, it is not human capital *per se* that underpins competitive advantage. Rather, it is human capital associated with relevant idiosyncratic skills and organizational capital—particularly tacit organizational knowledge and dynamic capabilities—that creates the possibility of building a quasi-sustainable competitive advantage at the level of the firm.

Another way of stating this is to say that the natural way to think about assessing the value of human capital at the enterprise level is to ask whether the constellation of talent employed by the enterprise is (1) relevant to contemporary and future customer needs and business environment, (2) unique and difficult to replicate,[18] and (3) enveloped into productive organizational routines. If all three conditions are met, the firm's human resources are likely to become valuable. The first two points are obvious, although often forgotten. There is simply no point in having good people assigned to the wrong activities. This is consistent with the Strategic Human Management Resources literature (see section 21.5 below).

A framework is needed to synthesize the various elements discussed above. This is what is attempted with 'dynamic capabilities' (Teece *et al.*, 1997; Teece 2007*a*). Dynamic capabilities can be categorized as to whether they assist value creation or value capture.

21.4.3 Creating and Capturing Value

The first observation, elaborating the distinctions made in section 21.2 above, is that the stock of human capital readily available to the firm (its employees and affiliates) cannot meaningfully be thought of as a dynamic capability. Dynamic capabilities are organizational-level capabilities that transcend individual capabilities. Of course, individual leaders/entrepreneurs may play a key role in shaping dynamic capabilities. However, an organization's capability does not stem from mere presence on the payroll of talented individuals; rather, it derives from ways in which employees interact and work together in productive combinations.

A second observation is that the manner in which human resources need to be managed is task-specific. The three clusters of capabilities identified in the dynamic capabilities framework—sensing, seizing, and transforming—require somewhat different human resource management practices. Moreover, sensing, seizing, and transforming are not necessarily sequential. In high-performing enterprises, they take place simultaneously, especially if it is a multidivisional/multiproduct enterprise. In an enterprise with dynamic capabilities, selecting

	Sensing	Seizing	Transforming
Creating Value	• spotting opportunities • identifying opportunities for research and development • conceptualizing new customer needs and new business models	• investment discipline • commitment to research and development • building competencies • achieving new combinations	• achieving recombinations
Capturing Value	• positioning for first mover and other advantages • determining desirable entry timing	• intellectual property qualification and enforcement • implementing business models • leveraging complementary assets • investment or co-investment in 'production' facilities	• managing threats • honing the business model • developing new complements

Figure 21.1. Activities Conducted to Create and Capture Value (Organized by Clusters of Dynamic Capabilities)

the relevant human resource management practices and procedures is itself likely to be demanding.

To greatly simplify the analysis even further, dynamic capabilities can be regrouped into two essential elements: creating value and capturing value (see Figure 21.1). There is variation in the relative importance of the different activities associated with sensing, seizing, and transforming varies.

Creating and capturing value are analytically separable functions, each requiring somewhat different human resource management skills, suggesting that a certain amount of variety should be permitted and expected in human resource management practices. What is needed to support value creation activities is not quite what is needed to support value capture activities. What follow are some brief high-level remarks on the human resource management implications of each.[19]

Creating value

Sensing involves identifying and calibrating trends in the business environment, the technology, and the activities of competitors, complementors, and governmental entities. As a capability it requires entrepreneurial activity and foresight. From a human resource perspective, the issue becomes how one builds and manages an enterprise so as to give it the best chance of developing robust sensing and creative capabilities.

The first and most obvious step for an established enterprise is to select (hire) individuals with the requisite skills, and to develop and retain such individuals inside the enterprise. Hiring needs to focus not only on relevant knowledge, experience, and aptitude, but also on creative and entrepreneurial skills.

One must recognize at the outset that there is a wide variety of factors—some societal, some organizational—that impact the amount of creative and entrepreneurial talent in the economy or in an organization. Kirzner (1979) and Shane (2005) analyze entrepreneurship as a process of discovering opportunities. While this is one component of entrepreneurship, as already noted, entrepreneurship is not just a search for opportunities. It is also the proactive creation of them (through research and development), the accurate assessment of them, the avoidance of unnecessary risk, and the mobilization of resources to address opportunities and manage risk.

Sensing an opportunity merely paves the way to deploy resources on further creative and/or combinatorial activity. Creative activity is necessary to produce new products or artistic media (such as a Broadway performance). Creativity is a difficult process to 'manage', as it cannot be forced. Creative people pursuing creative activity may need some direction, but they cannot be micromanaged. As Gil and Spiller (2007: 244) note: 'High-level creative activity can only be fostered; it cannot be coerced'. This is as true for research and development activity as it is for the arts.

However, because it is difficult to monitor and measure the output of creative individuals, there are also hazards for an enterprise involved in financing creative activity. Gil and Spiller refer to one class of these as 'dynamic hazards'. The creative individual can potentially have good ideas/breakthroughs and leave the organization where these ideas were developed in order to commercialize them in a context where it may not be necessary to share the rewards with the capital provider. Gil and Spiller point out that these are 'transaction hazards quite different from the standard transaction cost framework' (2007: 245). The fundamental organizational 'problem' associated with managing creative activity stems from the nature of creative work: high uncertainty and informational asymmetries (Caves, 2000). The problem is not completely solved by internal organization, as is the case with many types of high transaction cost situations (Coase, 1937; Williamson, 1975, 1985; Tadelis, 2007). Instead, it is better managed inside the firm, particularly if the entrepreneur is not rewarded until market success of the innovation has occurred.

In principle, then, one might imagine that a market economy would allow individuals and organizations to specialize in one of three necessary capabilities: (1) identification and assessment of an opportunity (sensing), (2) mobilization of resources to address an opportunity and to capture value from doing so (seizing) and (3) continued renewal (transforming). However, the market for opportunities is riddled with inefficiencies and high transaction costs, and 'dynamic hazards'. As a consequence, many entrepreneurs are forced to bundle sensing, seizing, and transforming activities (create an enterprise to perform all three). The market is 'imperfect', due both to problems of conveying the merits of ideas and also because of opportunism.[20]

Opportunism complicates the situation and can lead to the 'lemons' problem identified by Akerlof (1970). In general, entrepreneurs will be reluctant to 'sell' or simply licence ideas they believe are undervalued. Buyers are also aware that enterprises have incentives to overstate the magnitude of the opportunity. Since a 'meeting of the minds' between 'seller' and 'buyer' is difficult, the market does not work well, and transactions tend to become internalized. Entrepreneurs will find it necessary and beneficial to set up firms and develop all three capabilities. Working with capital providers, entrepreneurs often end up with a share of equity in the enterprise in exchange for contributed insights/discoveries.[21]

Besides just spotting opportunities and internalizing them, a complementary strategy is to pursue an 'open innovation'[22] model (Chesbrough, 2006) whereby the business enterprise seeks to identify new technologies externally and to transfer them to the firm. Open innovation involves many of the same 'dynamic hazards' identified above. However, it is a desirable practice because, as the global sources of invention and innovation become dispersed, it is necessary to tap into new sources of ideas. It is simply impossible to invent everything internally.

Capturing value

Companies that rely too heavily on creativity but do not possess other relevant capabilities will not perform well commercially. In particular, creativity without good execution and without a strategy for capturing value is unlikely to produce commercial success for the innovator. Commercial success requires purposeful goal-oriented action. It also requires commercial discipline. Indeed, to develop and implement effective strategies to capture value generally requires some understanding of how difficult-to-replicate competitive advantage is built and protected. Relevant skills include an understanding of competitive strategy and intellectual property management. Whereas creativity will involve the selection and recombination of ideas and artifacts (technologies), capturing value will probably involve the development of strategies, processes, and intellectual property able to help establish and maintain a leadership position in a market. It is also likely to require the heavy commitment of resources to bring the product to market.

Over the past two decades our understanding of value capture from innovation and the link to firm strategy has expanded dramatically. A stream of research stressed the importance of the architecture of the enterprise (especially the boundaries of its ownership and its control of complementary assets) in effecting the identity of the winners and losers when new technologies are commercialized. Along with enterprise capabilities and structure, the role of supporting institutions and public policy has also been highlighted (see for example, Nelson, 1993).

The body of work that explains the links between strategy and innovation has come to be known as the Profiting from Innovation framework,[23] which insists that 'aspects of economic organization, business strategy, technology and innovation must all be understood' if one wants to understand market outcomes when new technologies are commercialized (Chesbrough et al., 2006). We will not restate the framework here, except in summary form. It has recently been the topic of a special issue of *Research Policy* (35(8), October 2006). The Profiting from Innovation framework has also been extended to consider how the appropriability regime (the protection afforded the innovator by intellectual property and by barriers to imitation) and the architecture of the industry—previously treated as exogenous—can be usefully shaped by managerial decisions (Pisano and Teece, 2007).

The Profiting from Innovation literature addresses a puzzle that had not been well explained in the previous literature. Why is it that highly creative pioneering firms often fail to capture the economic returns from innovation? The original framework (Teece, 1986) cites several examples (for example, EMI in CAT scanners, Bowmar in calculators), and the phenomenon does indeed endure. The first-generation PC manufacturers all but disappeared from the scene (and even IBM, while not a first-mover in PCs, exited the business in 2005 by selling its PC business to a Chinese company, Lenovo). Xerox (PARC) and Apple invented the graphical user interface, but Microsoft Windows dominates the PC market with a follow-on graphical user interface. Apple also invented the PDA (the bricklike Newton) but for years Palm was the dominant player (at least until convergence of mobile telephony and computing led to 'smart phones'). Netscape invented the browser, but Microsoft captured more of the market. Apple's iPod was not the first MP3 player, but it has a commanding position in the category today. Merck was a pioneer in cholesterol-lowering drugs (Zocor), but Pfizer, a late entrant, secured a superior market position with Lipitor. Excite and Lycos were the first real web search engines, but they lost out to Yahoo. And Yahoo then lost out to Google.

At first glance it is tempting to say that these examples reflect the result of Schumpeterian gales of creative destruction where winners are constantly challenged and overturned by entrants. Indeed, entrants with potentially disruptive innovations[24] are almost always waiting in the wings. However, one should note that there is ample variance in the phenomenon. There are many cases where first or early movers captured and sustained significant competitive advantage over time. Genentech was a pioneer in using biotechnology to discover and develop drugs, and thirty years later was the second largest biotechnology firm (and, the most productive in its use of research and development dollars) right up to its acquisition by Hoffmann-La Roche in 2009. Intel helped pioneer the microprocessor and still has a leading market position more than thirty years later. Dell pioneered a new distribution system for personal computers and, despite recent challenges and many would-be imitators, has remained one of the top three PC vendors since the launch of its website in 1996. Toyota's much studied 'Toyota Production System' provided the auto maker with a source of competitive advantage for decades, despite numerous and sustained attempts at imitation, with the company finally becoming the world's biggest car manufacturer in 2008.

The Profiting from Innovation framework provides an explanation as to why some highly creative innovators profit from innovation while others lose out, and why it is not inevitable that the pioneers will lose. Ralph Waldo Emerson is said to have pointed out more than 150 years ago: 'Build a better mousetrap and the world will beat a path to your door.' Emerson might have been partially right within the supply-driven logic of the industrial era; but the adage is not correct in the consumer-empowered knowledge economy era. One of several factors neglected by Emerson was that a better mousetrap will invite reverse engineering by would-be imitators. And, predictably, suppliers and those offering complementary products will also try to get a piece of the action if they can.

The conundrum that managers must confront is at least twofold. First, creative activity frequently does not yield value on a stand-alone basis. To provide value to the users almost every innovation requires complementary products, technologies, and services. Hardware requires software (and vice versa); operating systems require applications (and vice versa); digital music players require digital music and ways of distributing digital music (and vice versa); mobile phones need mobile phone networks (and vice versa); web browsers and web search engines require web content (and vice versa); airlines require airports (and vice versa). In short, the technology which results from creative activity must be embedded in a system to yield value to the end user/consumer. Value capture becomes more difficult if other entities control other required elements.

Secondly, the delivery of product/process innovation requires the employment not just of complements but of many inputs/components up and down the vertical chain of production. Hence, when the inventor/innovator is not already in control of the necessary inputs/components, the economic muscle of the inventor/innovator will be considerably compromised by whatever economic muscle is possessed by owners of required inputs/components.

The unavoidable implication is that unless the inventor/innovator enjoys strong natural protection against imitation and/or strong intellectual property protection (which collectively describe its 'appropriability' regime) or unless the complements and other inputs are available in competitive supply, then the providers of complements and other inputs will force the innovator to yield a large portion (possibly the greater portion) of the fruits of innovation to them. If the technology does not have strong natural barriers to imitation, then owning patents and trade secrets or having technology which is hard to copy are important tools for fighting back.

Perhaps the single greatest contribution of the Profiting from Innovation framework is that it highlights that commercial success requires creative activity to be complemented by a carefully thought through business model that defines the appropriability mechanisms. The business model should help distinguish the critical complementary technologies and/or bottleneck asset(s) in the value chain. These may then need to be secured. Otherwise the owner of the bottleneck, not the innovator, will be in a position to extract much of the value generated by the innovation—whether or not the owner(s) of the bottleneck directly contributed to funding the creative activity that produced the innovation. The prediction of the framework is that the profits generated by a successful technological innovation go either to the owners of the underlying invention (if protected by strong intellectual property or other natural barriers to imitation), or to the owners of complementary technologies and/or assets (including other components of the value chain).

An obvious implication is that the firm's endowment of literati and numerati, no matter how talented and creative, does not guarantee that the organization will either create or capture value from innovation. In the absence of quality entrepreneurial managers, excellent performance by literati and numerati is likely to be in vain. Nor will world-beating human resource practices lead to success unless the matrix of factors identified by the Profiting from Innovation framework is also favorable to the innovating enterprise.

The received wisdom from Profiting from Innovation is that management's task is at least to ensure that the enterprise secures the intellectual property protection available to it and makes the right decisions with respect to building/buying the critical co-specialized complementary technologies and/or assets. Timing is of course always a critical element, as the nature of the bottleneck may change due to innovation elsewhere in the system and in other market dynamics.

21.5 STRATEGIC HUMAN RESOURCE MANAGEMENT AND ORGANIZATIONAL CAPITAL

In the midst of the often harsh conditions of the Industrial Revolution, the nineteenth-century English mill owner Robert Owen (1813) recognized the benefits to be had from investing in people and demonstrating care for employees. The field of human resource management has subsequently developed to reflect some understanding of how to manage human resources.

Human capital is now commonly thought of as part of the intellectual capital or intangible assets of the firm. (For a review of the intellectual capital literature, see Marr, 2005.) Indeed, studies unpacking intellectual capital (see for example, Ahonen, 2008) typically divide it into (*a*) human capital and (*b*) all other intangibles (such as intellectual property, relationship capital, brand value, reputational capital). The problem is that many of these categories are overlapping.[25] Without crisp definitions and boundaries, quantification of these categories is not possible.

It is not clear that human resources management properly recognizes strategic considerations important to confronting more intense levels of national and global competition, and the importance of special skills (especially expert and entrepreneurial skills) to the economic performance of the firm and the nation-state. Today's highly competitive business environments require that firms excel at innovation (both technological and/or in business methods/models) in order to survive and prosper. As outlined above, this in turn requires that the enterprise attract, train, and retain sufficient literati and numerati—almost certainly requiring compensation differentials and new organizational forms. Until recently this was not the purview of the field of human resources. Indeed, the notion that the literati, numerati, and entrepreneurial managers are especially critical to today's firms and the firms of the future—and require special rewards—is not emphasized in the mainstream human resources literature. However, it is at least implicitly recognized by the emerging field of Strategic Human Resource Management (SHRM), which explores the role that human resources play in undergirding business strategy.

The resources and capabilities literature in the field of strategic management is the cornerstone of SHRM. The resources/capabilities frameworks emphasize the importance of the internal factors that impact competitive advantage. (Michael Porter's well-known 'Five Forces' framework to explain the foundations of competitive advantages remains silent as to any connection between firm-level attributes and enterprise performance.[26]) However, the resources/capabilities perspectives do not lead to the conclusion that the quality and management of people (human) resources impact performance monotonically. Rather, it is implicitly recognized in the SHRM literature that other value-relevant, difficult-to-imitate intangible assets are also essential to creating and sustaining competitive advantage.

The growing recognition that the business environment is global and that intangible assets are important to competitive advantage (for example, Teece, 2000) has triggered the development of SHRM. The strategic management of human resources is necessary because human resource management must be aligned with business strategy. SHRM requires a firm's leadership not only to articulate human resource philosophies and policies, but also to execute programs to make philosophies and policies meaningful and relevant to the competitive environment. The basic idea is that human resource policies cannot be disconnected from the strategic needs of the organization. Human resource management must support the firm's efforts to develop and sustain competitive advantage.

Analytically, one might think about SHRM in the following terms. Firm performance over time in the context of industries experiencing rapid technological change is a function of (*a*) the stock (and changes to the stock) (amount plus quality) of human capital the firm has under contract, (*b*) the degree to which that stock is unique and non-replicable by competitors,[27] (*c*) the relevance of that stock to the opportunities and challenges the firm faces, (*d*) the (unique) human resources practices employed to manage the human resources and keep employees and affiliates committed and motivated, (*e*) the panoply of complementary assets the firm has assembled, (*f*) the appropriability regime (especially how hard it is for the firm to capture value from innovation through the use of the tools of intellectual property), and (*g*) the skill with which management has directed the available/accessible resources inside and outside the firm.

The impact of human resources practices on performance is likely to be mediated by other factors too. It is important to realize that one should not expect to observe a simple relationship between human resource practices and performance.

It is also reasonably well recognized that the stock of human capital is related to the individual competence of employees. It includes their knowledge, skills, experiences, and abilities. When orchestrated collectively in an organizational context, human capital can be shaped into organizational capabilities which manifest themselves in what might be thought of as organizational capital. Both forms of capital underlie the enterprise's financial performance, but disaggregating them is very difficult. Notwithstanding these difficulties, Becker, Huselid, and Ulrich (2001) introduced the human resources scorecard to link strategy and performance. Becker *et al.* argue that it is important to causally link people and their activities to strategic objectives to better understand how human capital creates value. Pfeffer (1997) counsels caution, pointing out that 'the measurement pitfalls are indeed treacherous'.

However, what the SHRM theme has highlighted is the reality that having access to excellent human resources/capital is necessary but not sufficient to create and sustain competitive advantage. Indeed, achieving best practices in human resource management will not achieve much of anything in terms of competitive advantage unless this resource is strategically managed. For instance, an enterprise that is highly creative and entrepreneurial with unique human resource management systems but which fails to consider the appropriability challenge (how to capture value from innovation) will not be successful. Hence human resource analysis and business strategy must be joined if one is to have a framework capable of guiding management towards building and sustaining competitive advantage, or informing policy-makers with respect to how the skill base of the economy will affect the performance of firms.

21.6 'Organizing and Managing' the Literati/Numerati

21.6.1 Cooperation, Teams, and Management

Horizontal interaction among diverse groups is almost always required to solve complex problems. Project work associated with developing new products and processes requires cooperation/collaboration amongst the literati, the numerati, and entrepreneurs.

With respect to the literati and numerati, strongly authoritative management aimed at forcing people to collaborate is anathema. Management must have a light touch, otherwise cooperative efforts will be suppressed and creativity will be compromised. Also, difficult and granular technical trade-offs and judgments of the literati and numerati with respect to problem-solving can rarely be second-guessed by management.

Accordingly, management usually needs to be decentralized/distributed. Traditional notions of management which rely heavily on authority and hierarchy and decisions driven from the center are unlikely to work well.

Self-organized cooperative activity is frequently observed in science projects and in creative engineering projects. Richard Nelson studied the development of the transistor at Bell Labs, and noted (1962: 569) that:

the type of interaction we have noted in the transistor project requires that individuals be free to help each other as they see fit. If all allocation decisions were made by a centrally situated executive, the changing allocation of research effort called for as perceived alternatives and knowledge change would place an impossible information processing and decision making burden on top management. Clearly the research scientists must be given a great deal of freedom...

Nelson likewise notes that teamwork in a creative context is likely to differ from traditional contexts. The development of the transistor did involve teamwork. But here is how Nelson describes what teamwork meant (pp. 578, 579):

It meant interaction and mutual stimulation and help…But several people outside the team also interacted in an important way…teamwork…did not mean a closely directed project…The project was marked by flexibility—by the ability to shift directions and by the rather rapid focusing of attention by several people on problems and phenomena unearthed by others.

…The informality of the decision structure played a very important role in permitting speedy cooperative response to changing ideas and knowledge. Thus the transistor was a team invention, but not in the sense of the team which has grown fashionable in recent years.

Fifty years later, the same lessons—particularly the importance of decentralization and flexibility—are being relearnt. John Chambers, CEO of US network equipment company Cisco, remarked: 'In 2001, we were like most high-tech companies—all decisions came to the top 10 people in the company, and we drove things back down from there' (quoted in McGirt, 2008).

Cisco now has a more decentralized and collaborative management system, with a network of councils and boards entrusted and empowered to launch new businesses, and incentives to encourage executives to work together. Chambers claims that 'these boards and councils have been able to innovate with tremendous speed. Fifteen minutes and one week to get a [business] plan that used to take six months' (ibid.).

According to McGirt, Cisco is now 'a distributed idea engine where leadership emerges organically, unfettered by a central command' (ibid.). One motivating factor is the complexity associated with the proliferation of what Chambers calls 'market adjacencies'—twenty-six areas not relevant to the company's revenues today but likely to become so three to four years down the road. Reward structures have changed too—executives are now compensated by how well the 'collective of businesses' performs, not their own individual product line. In short Cisco has rejected its old command and control culture—there is now a pool of talent that can lead working groups.

Apparently, what actually exists at Cisco today is a hybrid model of innovation. Most efforts are led from below (decentralized or distributed); some are led from the center. Chambers puts the ratio at 70/30 (ibid.).

The point here is a simple one: in fast-paced complex environments where there is heterogeneity in customer needs and the focus is on technological innovation, it is simply impossible to achieve the necessary flexibility and responsiveness with a command and control organizational structure. Moreover, with a highly talented workforce, excessive centralization can shut down local initiatives.

Managers of innovative enterprises must learn to lead without the authority that comes from a position in an organizational chart or the 'C' designation in their title. This imposes new challenges for some companies and some individuals, but it is the way of the future in such contexts. It has also been one of the ways of the past. The challenge is to connect individual initiatives to the overall corporate strategy without building an expensive and initiative-sapping hierarchy.

As noted, skilled individuals are especially critical to business success. This is because highly skilled individuals are scarce, and profitable technological innovation depends on many factors, including their availability and their creative and productive engagement within the enterprise. This should lead one to a focus on the study of professional intellect—but with few exceptions, it has not. As James B. Quinn *et al.* (1996: 71) note:

This oversight is especially surprising because professional intellect creates most of the value in the new economy. Its benefits are immediately visible in the large service industries, such as software, health care, financial services, communications, and consulting. But in manufacturing industries as well, professionals generate the preponderance of value—through activities like research and development...

Quinn *et al.* may underemphasize the importance of organizational capital. Nevertheless, their thesis is in broad agreement with the one advanced here.

Managing professionals, especially high-level expert professionals, requires rejection of traditional heavy-handed hierarchical structures that may work in more stable industries. Indeed, congruent with the analysis here, Quinn *et al.* go so far as to say that it is often necessary to invert the traditional hierarchy in order to create the organizational structures that successful professionals will accept. This is consistent with Teece (2003). With an inverted hierarchy, the job of the manager is to provide support structure. Management's role is to create incentive alignment and to expedite resources and remove barriers standing in the way of professionals doing their work,[28] so long as that work is consistent with the organization's goals. Of course, strong accountability is still required from the literati and the numerati. Autonomy and accountability go hand in hand.

Fortunately, the commonest purpose for hierarchy—to delegate tasks to 'workers'—is simply not needed for many types of expert professional work. Truly top talent tends to be substantially self-motivated and self-guided. Top talent is also likely to be functionally elitist, at least to some small degree (though one corollary is that they will be reluctant to accept authority from managers who are not, or have not been, respected professionals themselves in the recent past). According to Quinn *et al.*, this is 'why most professional firms operate as partnerships and not as hierarchies' (1996: 72).

While inverted organizations are desirable for high-end professional service firms, the apparent absence of formal authority may be traumatic for some traditional line managers; and without accountability achieved through linking performance and rewards, the empowerment of professionals can be problematic. According to Quinn *et al.*: 'A classic example is the rapid decline of People's Express, which consciously inverted its organization and enjoyed highly empowered and motivated point people but lacked the systems or the computer infrastructures to enable them to adapt as the organization grew' (1996: 77). People's Express did not employ many literati and numerati; nevertheless, the observation is instructive.

In short, when innovative firms employ many highly skilled individuals, they have to create organizations of colleagues and associates.[29] Compensation differentials must also be established. The modern knowledge-based organization cannot organize with traditional boss/subordinates dichotomies. The nature of the tasks and the talents requires a relatively flat organizational structure, with distributed leadership and self-organizing teams, but differentiated compensation. Of course, to make a distributed leadership model work, every member must act as a responsible decision-maker within their professional domain, and there must also be strong leadership in the top management team; and as already noted, incentive alignment is a prerequisite.

Implemented properly, the distributed leadership approach is not an abdication of managerial responsibility. It is just the opposite. The executive leadership team should be responsible to the board and to shareholders, as well as to employees and other constituents. Any 'power' that individual leaders have should stems from professional and personal respect gained through professional success and through creating and maintaining an open, honest, and transparent culture.

Moreover, even though creative activities need to be organized in a distributed/decentralized way, there are always mundane activities that should not be managed in this way. The accounting, finance, and treasury functions are obvious examples. Also, there may well be certain functions that require tight integration because the project/technology spans multiple lines of business, or because there are very significant sales benefits to be achieved from a coordinated approach. The management of intellectual property, such as patents, may be one such activity. The more fundamental/generic the firm's patents, the more a centralized approach will be required. Hence, pioneering companies may well need to split off certain technical as well as intellectual property functions and manage them more centrally, and possibly more hierarchically.

The thesis advanced here is that today the competitive advantage of the enterprise is rooted both in the stock (resource) of literati and numerati which it can access,[30] along with what were earlier labeled as 'dynamic capabilities', which in turn depend upon entrepreneurial talent and the structure and values of the organization in which that talent is embedded. Hence, competitive advantage by no means depends on human capital alone. Organizational capital, and in particular dynamic capabilities, also matter.

21.6.2 Intrinsic Talent, Contextual Talent, and Teams

To function productively, both the literati and the numerati must learn to work cooperatively in teams. However, teams can be non-traditional. Teams can change with each project. It is desirable to keep project teams small, but intense and intimate. Teams need not emphasize consensus and compromise; rather, the aim should

Table 21.1. Key Differences between Traditional Teams and Virtuoso Teams

Team Characteristics	Traditional Teams	Virtuoso Teams
Membership	Members chosen based on who has available time.	Members chosen based on expertise.
Culture	Collective	Collective and individual.
Focus	Tight project management. Time and budget more important than content.	Ideas, understanding, and breakthrough thinking emphasized.
Clients	Mundane	Sophisticated
Intensity	High/medium	High
Stakes	Low/medium	High

Source: Drawn from Fischer and Boynton, 2005.

be to achieve excellence while giving some degree of rein to individualism. Certain especially creative and exceptionally talented individuals can be given special recognition. Hence, team-building with experts is different from everyday team-building because of the need to engage their creativity. Such teams have been called 'virtuoso teams' (Fischer and Boynton, 2005). Table 21.1 summarizes some of the differences between traditional teams and virtuoso teams.

Teaming amongst the literati and numerati ('experts') is different from teaming amongst shop floor talent. The team arrangements and dynamics in a research laboratory are likely to be different from those on an assembly line or on a bucket line. In the expert context, pay differentials ought not be an issue, so long as they are capability/performance-based. With expert teams, the identity of the team leader/captain is likely to be of considerable importance. For all to succeed there must be mutual respect between and amongst experts and leaders.

A key feature of expert (literati/numerati-based) teams is that they are likely to be quite fluid. Indeed, not everything is appropriately organized in teams. Rather, groups need to form, accomplish their work, and disband or move onto other project teams.

The nature of the requirements for expert-led teams is likely to be somewhat different from the common emphasis on building team harmony and vision. Indeed, there is a great deal about conventional or traditional teams that involves hidden and unnecessary costs. When team requirements are too heavy, decision cycles lengthen, expenses mount, and the organization adopts an inward focus.

Expressed differently, one cannot simply assume that 'more is better' when it comes to collaboration. Consensus and participatory leadership is not always a good thing, particularly when the issues are complex and there is considerable asymmetry in the distribution of talents on the team. The right voices need to be heard. Forced teaming often leads to excessive consensus-building, slow decision-making, and the wasting of time and money. Unproductive collaboration can sometimes be more dangerous than missed opportunities for collaboration.

In assessing individual talent and the merits of teaming, it is also necessary to distinguish between intrinsic talent and contextual talent. Intrinsic talent is talent which commands full value on a stand-alone basis. In the professional services context, for instance, this might represent the business the professional can source based on their own wits and capabilities—independent of the brand or platform on which they stand.

Contextual talent reflects the value that the talent can generate in a particular organizational context. This could be, in theory, lower or higher than the individual intrinsic value. Contextual talent depends on how the individual benefits from the other complementary assets (individual as well as infrastructure and brand) that the organization provides. Contextual value may be very large, especially in circumstances where teams must be employed to complete the job, and when the firm's infrastructure and staffing play important support roles. Needless to say, the recruitment of top talent can be fraught with hazards, as performance on one platform need not be a good indicator of performance on another. This is why the recruitment of top talent must be performed by experienced professionals who are themselves able to make good assessments, and are in turn made accountable for their decisions.

To summarize, the literati and numerati are unlikely to be productive and satisfied in a traditional hierarchical organization, being compensated in traditional ways, and having compensation put at risk for events beyond their control. Dynamically competitive enterprises must understand the contextual value of talent, and must develop new ways of compensating exceptional talent, and a (new) way of organizing the daily business so as to enable the highest quality of service to be provided. Table 21.2 tabulates some of the ways in which traditional firms are likely to be different from dynamically competitive firms.

21.6.3 Incentives

The discussion has so far been bereft of a critical dimension: incentives. There is a large amount of literature in economics on incentive design. Getting incentives right is fundamental. Suffice to note that there is ample evidence that pay for performance is associated with higher performance at both the individual (Jenkins *et al.*, 1998) and organizational levels (Gerhart, 2000).

This is too broad a topic to address here. However, there is interesting new theoretical literature using the principal–agent framework that shows how persuasion and authority can be either substitutes or complements. An important finding is that principals will rely more on persuasion (without authority) when agents have strong

Table 21.2. Contrasting Views of the Business Enterprise

Organizational Characteristics	Industrial Model	Knowledge Model (for Literati and Numerati)
Hierarchy	Deep	Shallow
Leadership	Centralized	Distributed
Work	Segmented	Collaborative
People	Cost	Asset
Basis of control	Authority	Influence and example
Assumptions about individuals	Opportunistic	Honorable
Financial incentives	Base salary plus discretionary bonus salary	Metrics-based compensation; limited management discretion

pay-for-performance incentives and when the potential value of a project is high. Incentives and confidence in the project work multiplicatively (Van den Steen, 2009).

21.7 CONCLUSION

The modern corporation began with the advent of the railroad and the telegraph. It was not at first highly integrated with respect to research and development. It relied in part on contract research to develop new products and processes. Towards the end of the nineteenth century and the beginning of the twentieth, the modern corporation became vertically integrated, and research and development laboratories were brought inhouse. The era of the large integrated enterprise with internal research and development dominated American, European, and even Japanese companies through much of the twentieth century.

The twenty-first century has seen a partial return to a more open/offshore and often outsourced model for innovation, at least in most industries. This trend is well developed, though its natural limits have yet to be reached. No matter where those limits are, management is still left with the problem of how to manage and integrate the output of highly skilled 'individuals' (literati and numerati) across countries, time zones, and organizational boundaries. Management involves not only motivating talent and ensuring that the job is accomplished. There is also a strategic component: what tasks to assign, what priorities to set, what resources to use, and where to acquire them. To respond to these challenges, enterprises need to develop their dynamic capabilities and deploy them on a global basis.

One would hope that the theory of the firm would provide some assistance when one contemplates the enterprise of the future. Unfortunately, whether one uses the lens of transaction costs (for example, Coase, 1937; Williamson, 1975), ownership perspectives (such as Hart and Moore, 1990), incentive perspectives (for example, Holmstrom and Milgrom, 1994), or other 'modern' theories of the firm, nicely summarized and illustrated by Roberts (2004), the theories seem inadequate, especially with respect to the neglect of innovation. Perspectives from international business (for example, Dunning, 1998, 2000; Teece, 1981*b*) show some connection to the modern firm emerging and orchestrating global knowledge networks designed to produce new goods and services.

The phenomenon observed and sketched here, admittedly faintly, is consistent with knowledge-based theories of the firm that have emerged outside the boundaries of mainstream economics. One can only hope that mainstream economics recognizes that it must reconceptualize the theory of the firm if it wants to combine both relevance and rigor. At the moment it has neither.

This chapter has explained the importance of organizational capabilities and the management of talented individuals—the literati, numerati, and entrepreneurs—to the performance of the business firm, and secondarily to the nation-state. The treatment stresses how management and entrepreneurship impacts the value of human resources and human capital. Globalization is placing a premium on dynamic capabilities—which include the ability not just to sense, seize, and transform, but especially to integrate global resources and systems to address opportunities and to meet the needs of customers at home and abroad.

Acknowledgment

I would like to thank Greg Linden, Christos Pitelis, Miguel Palacios, and Gary Pisano for useful comments and insights.

Notes

1. While social capital is mentioned and is recognized as being important, it is not the focus of attention here. For a quick introduction, see Abramovitz, 1986; Coleman, 1988.
2. These terms are defined in the next section.
3. Notwithstanding the above, a small cadre of dedicated economists has long emphasized the role of technological innovation in economic development, often with few accolades. I am referring to the important work of Chris Freeman, Giovanni Dosi, Simon Kuznets, Edwin Mansfield, David Mowery, Richard Nelson, Nate Rosenberg, Sidney Winter, and

others. Mainstream economic theorists (such as Romer, 1986) and mainstream strategic management researchers have now discovered the importance of knowledge, human capital, and organizational capabilities.

4. Based on the ideas of 'Austrian Economics'; most notably those of Israel Kirzner (1973).

5. Managers are always faced with two deep conundrums. Are we doing things right, and are we doing the right things? Clearly, one needs to do both.

6. The naïve thesis asserts that people are an organization's most important asset. This is of course true at one level, but if people are not incentivized, motivated, and managed then an organization will not perform well.

7. At a very general level, two major strands can be identified in modern human resource management. (1) Scientific management, advanced in the early 1900s by F. W. Taylor (1856–1915), focused on precise analytical schemes to select and reward individuals. The focus was on motivating and controlling individuals to improve their productivity. In the main, however, scientific management aimed to adapt worker to task. Taylorism was based on the strict division of labor: managers commanded and workers carried out orders. (2) In contrast, the human relations school veered toward adapting the tasks to the worker. The primary thrust of the human relations school owed much to the Australian Elton Mayo (1880–1949), who downplayed the single-minded focus of Taylor on technical skills and highlighted the importance of leadership and group decision-making.

8. Of course, most scientists do not work in the corporate sector. In the USA, academia is responsible for about 70% of academic research measured by publications, and the remainder is distributed more or less evenly amongst industry, government, and not for profits (calculated from data from 1995 to 2005 in National Science Board, 2008: appendix table 5–36).

9. The social policy implications are clear: the best weapon against poverty is not transfer payments; rather, it is strong families, societal values, and education.

10. Fox, 1983: 287. Empirical studies of scientists and engineers suggest that high performers are absorbed and involved, and strongly identify with their work. They also have a preoccupation with ideas, not people. Early in their lives they show autonomy, independence, and self-sufficiency. They are self-motivated. To maintain their productivity, they do not generally require other people to approve of their work.

11. While certain individuals in the enterprise may have the necessary cognitive and creative skills, the more desirable approach is to embed scanning, interpretative, and creative processes inside the enterprise itself. The enterprise will be vulnerable if the sensing, creative, and learning functions are left to the cognitive traits of a few individuals. Organizational processes can be put in place inside the enterprise to garner new technical information, tap developments in exogenous science, monitor customer needs and competitor activity, and shape new product and process opportunities.

12. Michael Nash, Executive Vice President for digital music at Warner Brothers, quoted in the global edition of the New York Times (28 May 2009): 17.

13. Discovery-based theories of entrepreneurship lead one to ask about how change in the business environment creates opportunities; while creative approaches ask how entrepreneurs create opportunities (Alvarez and Barney, 2007). Both types of entrepreneurship exist in the economy.

14. Despite growing literature on dynamic capabilities, the concept remains relatively unanalyzed. However, the concept signals that something of importance is being recognized.

It is now necessary to unpack the concept to discover the components of dynamic capabilities and how they undergird value creation and capture. See Coleman (1988) for an analogous statement with respect to research on social capital.

15. In distribution, this involved what in the marketing literature is sometimes referred to as becoming the 'channel captain'.

16. Raymond Miles (2007) notes that US scholars were amongst the early leaders in studying and describing effective managerial and organizational approaches to knowledge creation, sharing, and utilization. However, practice in the field has fallen short of the theory outlined in the textbooks. Miles goes on to give a remarkably good overview of basic management issues.

17. Difficulty in replication implies difficulty in imitation, which in turn means that certain forms of know-how—and in particular tacit know-how—can form a basis of competitive advantage. Put simply, if one's competitors cannot imitate or otherwise replicate the basis of competitive advantage, economic profits will not be eroded as quickly as otherwise.

18. The second point recognizes that profits will quickly be competed away in most environments unless there are isolating mechanisms at work. The skills employed must not be ubiquitously available, and the routines within which talented people are enveloped must be scarce.

19. The human resource management literature tends to want to bring uniformity to human resource management practices across the organization. The rationale for this is that (1) employees will judge the system as unfair if disparities in compensation open up, and (2) it is more complex to manage an organization if there is variety in human resource management systems and practices. The latter observation may be true; but variety may be unavoidable because building different capabilities requires different systems, and organizations/enterprises usually need to be ambidextrous to create and capture value.

20. Arrow, 1974. Here is a quote from a board-level business document available to the author. The company at issue was an electronics company that had developed multilayer (3D) displays and was also developing games for the gaming industry. Referring to the development of games for a supplier of gaming equipment, the CEO noted that 'their motivation may be to get a game with our best techniques and know-how so they can see them and use them in the future and not accept games from us in the future. So there is a lingering question of whether we will get a second game accepted!' (13 April 2009 document).

21. This implies a theory of the firm based on internalizing market failures associated with 'selling' opportunities. Such firms may subsequently integrate backwards into manufacturing for classical vertical integration reasons (Williamson, 1975, 1985). However, their core activity remains in orchestrating the various elements of the value chain (Teece, 2007a, 2007b, 2007c).

22. Open innovation does not necessarily mean that property rights are not sought, protected, and respected.

23. The core paper is Teece (1986). The intellectual origins of the framework can be traced to Williamson (1975) for his work on contracting, to Abernathy and Utterback (1978) for their work on the innovation lifecycle, to economic historians such as Nathan Rosenberg (1982) and Alfred Chandler (1977) for their work on complementary technologies, to Nelson and Winter (1982) for their work on the nature of knowledge, and to Schumpeter

(1934). See Winter (2006) for a review of intellectual origins. Recent additions include Pisano and Teece (2007). The above discussion draws, in part, on Pisano and Teece.
24. There is extensive literature on the role of new entrants in dislodging established firms. See for example, Anderson and Tushman, 1990; Clark, 1985; Henderson and Clark, 1990; Christensen, 1997.
25. The 'dynamic capabilities' framework (Teece, 2007a) makes this clear.
26. See Porter (1980). Porter represents received wisdom for many practitioners of competitive analysis.
27. Inasmuch as the literati and numerati are not ubiquitous, it is these categories which warrant special attention.
28. This does not mean that accountability is forgotten. Far from it.
29. The W. L. Gore Co., inventor of Gore-Tex, is a well known case of an innovative organization which has abandoned all hierarchical designations. Everyone, including the *de facto* chief executive officer, is an 'associate' (Hamel and Breen, 2007).
30. Pricing and productivity clearly matter too.

References

ABERNATHY, W. J., and UTTERBACK, J. M. (1978). 'Patterns of Industrial Innovation', *Technology Review*, 80(7): 40–7.
ABRAMOVITZ, M. (1986). 'Catching Up, Forging Ahead, and Falling Behind', *Journal of Economic History*, 46(2): 385–406.
AHONEN, G., ed. (2008). *Inspired by Knowledge in Organisations* (Helsinki: Hanken School of Economics).
AKERLOF, G. A. (1970). 'The Market for Lemons', *Quarterly Journal of Economics*, 84(3): 488–500.
ALBERT, S., and BRADLEY, K. (1997). *Managing Knowledge Experts, Experts, Agencies and Organizations* (Cambridge: Cambridge University Press).
ALVAREZ, S., and BARNEY, J. (2007). 'Opportunities, Organizations, and Entrepreneurship', *Strategic Entrepreneurship Journal*, 2(3): 171–3.
ANDERSON, P., and TUSHMAN, M. L. (1990). 'Technological Discontinuities and Dominant Design', *Administrative Science Quarterly*, 35(4): 604–33.
ARROW, K. J. (1974). *The Limits of Organization* (New York: W. W. Norton & Co.).
BAUMOL, W. J. (1990). 'Entrepreneurship: Productive, Unproductive, and Destructive', *Journal of Political Economy*, 98(5): 893–921.
——(1993). *Entrepreneurship, Management, and the Structure of Payoffs* (Cambridge, Mass.: MIT Press).
——(2005). *Entrepreneurship and Invention: Toward Their Microeconomic Value Theory* (Related Publication 05–38; Washington, DC: AEI–Brooking Joint Center for Regulatory Studies).
——and STROM, R. J. (2007). 'Entrepreneurship and Economic Growth', *Strategic Entrepreneurship Journal*, 1(3–4): 233–7.
BECKER, B. E., and HUSELID, M. A. (2006). 'Strategic Human Resources Management: Where do we Go from Here?', *Journal of Management*, 32(6): 898–925.

——Huselid, M. A., and Ulrich, D. (2001). *HR Scorecard: Linking People, Strategy, and Performance* (Boston: Harvard Business School Press).

Caves, R. E. (2000). *Creative Industries: Contracts between Art and Commerce* (Boston: Harvard University Press).

Chambers, E. G., Foulton, M., Handfield-Jones, H., Hankin, S. M., and Michaels, E. G. III (1998) 'The War for Talent', *McKinsey Quarterly*, 1998(3): 44–57.

Chandler, A. D., Jr. (1977) *The Visible Hand: The Managerial Revolution in American Business* (Cambridge, Mass.: Belknap Press).

Chesbrough, H. (2006). *Open Business Models* (Boston: Harvard Business School Press).

——Birkinshaw, J., and Teubal, M. (2006). 'Introduction to the Research Policy 20th Anniversary Special Issue of the Publication of "Profiting from Innovation" by David J. Teece', *Research Policy*, 35(8): 1091–9.

Christensen, C. M. (1997). *The Innovator's Dilemma* (Boston: Harvard Business School Press).

Clark, K. B. (1985). 'The Interaction of Design Hierarchies and Market Concepts in Technological Evolution', *Research Policy*, 14(5): 235–51.

Coase, R. A. (1937). 'The Nature of the Firm', *Economica*, 4(16): 386–405.

Coleman, J. S. (1988). 'Social Capital in the Creation of Human Capital', *American Journal of Sociology*, 94(s1): S95–S120.

Dunning, J. H. (1988). 'The Eclectic Paradigm of International Production: A Restatement and Some Possible Extensions', *Journal of International Business Studies*, 19(1): 1–31.

——(2000). 'The Eclectic Paradigm as an Envelope for Economic and Business Theories of MNE Activity', *International Business Review*, 9(2): 163–90.

Feenstra, R. C., and Hanson, G. H. (1999). 'The Impact of Outsourcing and High-Technology Capital on Wages: Estimates for the United States, 1979–1990', *Quarterly Journal of Economics*, 114(3): 907–40.

Fischer, B., and Boynton, A. (2005). 'Virtuoso Teams', *Harvard Business Review*, 83(7): 116–23.

Fox, M. F. (1983). 'Publication Productivity among Scientists: A Critical Review', *Social Studies of Science*, 13(2): 285–305.

Gerhart, B. (2000). 'Compensation, Strategy, and Organizational Performance', in S. L. Rynes and B. Gerhart (eds.), *Compensation in Organizations* (San Francisco: Jossey-Bass), 151–94.

Gil, R., and Spiller, P. T. (2007). 'The Organizational Dimensions of Creativity: Motion Picture Production', *California Management Review*, 50(1): 243–60.

Hamel, G., and Breen, B. (2007). *The Future of Management* (Boston: Harvard Business School Press).

Hart, O., and Moore, J. (1990). 'Property Rights and the Nature of the Firm', *Journal of Political Economy*, 98(6): 1119–58.

Henderson, R. M., and Clark, K. B. (1990). 'Architectural Innovation: The Reconfiguration of Existing Product Technologies and the Failure of Established Firms', *Administrative Science Quarterly*, 35(1): 9–30.

Hicks, J. R. (1965). *Capital and Growth* (New York: Oxford University Press).

Holmström, B., and Milgrom, P. (1994). 'The Firm as an Incentive System', *American Economic Review*, 84(4): 972–91.

JENKINS, G. D., JR., MITRA, A., GUPTA, N., and SHAW, J. D. (1998). 'Are Financial Incentives Related to Performance? A Meta-Analytic Review of Empirical Research', *Journal of Applied Psychology*, 83(5): 777–87.

KALDOR, N. (1957). 'A Model of Economic Growth', *Economic Journal*, 67(268): 591–624.

KIRKEGAARD, J. F. (2007). *The Accelerating Decline in America's High-Skilled Workforce: Implications for Immigration Policy* (Washington, DC: Peterson Institute for International Economics).

KIRZNER, I. (1973). *Competition and Entrepreneurship* (Chicago: University of Chicago Press).

——(1979). *Perception, Opportunity and Profit: Studies in the Theory of Entrepreneurship* (Chicago: University of Chicago Press).

KUZNETS, S. (1966). *Modern Economic Growth* (New Haven: Yale University Press).

LOTKA, A. J. (1926). 'The Frequency Distribution of Scientific Productivity', *Journal of the Washington Academy of Sciences*, 16(12): 317–23.

McGIRT, E. (2008). 'Revolution in San Jose', *Fast Company*, 131: 90–3.

MARR, B., ed. (2005). *Perspectives on Intellectual Capital* (Oxford: Elsevier Butterworth-Heinemann).

MARSHALL, A. (1898). *Principles of Economics* (4th edn. London: Macmillan & Co.).

MILES, R. E. (2007). 'Innovation and Leadership Values', *California Management Review*, 50(1): 192–201.

National Science Board (2008). *Science and Engineering Indicators 2008* (Arlington, Va.: National Science Foundation).

NELSON, R. (1962). 'The Link between Science and Invention: The Case of the Transistor', in National Bureau of Economic Research, *The Rate and Direction of Inventive Activity* (Princeton: Princeton University Press).

——(ed.) (1993). *National Systems of Innovation* (New York: Oxford University Press).

——and WINTER, S. G. (1982). *An Evolutionary Theory of Economic Change* (Cambridge, Mass.: Harvard University Press).

NISBETT, R. E. (2009). *Intelligence and How to Get it: Why Schools and Cultures Count* (New York: Norton).

NONAKA, I., and TOYAMA, R. (2007). 'Strategy as Distributed Practical Wisdom (Phronesis)', *Industrial and Corporate Change*, 16(3): 371–94.

OWEN, R. (1813). *A New View of Society, or Essays on the Principle of the Formation of the Human Character* (London: Dent).

PFEFFER, J. (1997). 'Pitfalls on the Road to Measurement: The Dangerous Liaison of Human Resources with the Ideas of Accounting and Finance', *Human Resource Management*, 36(3): 357–65.

PISANO, G., and TEECE, D. J. (2007). 'How to Capture Value from Innovation: Shaping Intellectual Property and Industry Architecture', *California Management Review*, 50(1): 278–96.

PORTER, M. (1980). *Competitive Strategy: Techniques for Analyzing Industries and Competitors* (New York: Free Press).

QUINN, J. B., ANDERSON, P., and FINKELSTEIN, S. (1996). 'Managing Professional Intellect: Making the Most of the Best', *Harvard Business Review* (Mar.–Apr.), 71–80.

REICH, R. (2002). *The Future of Success: Working and Living in the New Economy* (New York: Vintage Books).

ROBERTS, J. (2004). *The Modern Firm* (Oxford: Oxford University Press).

ROMER, P. M. (1986). 'Increasing Returns and Long-Run Growth', *Journal of Political Economy*, 94(5): 1002–37.

ROSENBERG, N. (1982). *Inside the Black Box: Technology and Economics* (New York: Cambridge University Press).

——and BIRDSELL, L. E. (1986). *How the West Grew Rich* (New York: Basic Books).

SCHUMPETER, J. (1934). *The Theory of Economic Development* (Boston: Harvard University Press).

SCOTCHMER, S. (2004). *Innovation and Incentives* (Cambridge, Mass.: MIT Press).

SHANE, S. A. (2003). *A General Theory of Entrepreneurship: The Individual–Opportunity Nexus* (Northampton, Mass.: Edward Elgar Publishing).

——(2005). *Finding Fertile Ground: Identifying Extraordinary Opportunities for New Ventures* (Upper Saddle River, NJ: Wharton School Publishing).

SMITH, A. (1801). *An Inquiry into the Nature and Causes of the Wealth of Nations* (6th edn. Dublin: Gilbert & Hodges).

SOMAYA, D., and TEECE, D. J. (2007). 'Patents, Licensing and Entrepreneurship: Effectuating Innovation in Multi-Invention Contexts', in E. Sheshinki, R. J. Strom, and W. J. Baumol (eds.), *Entrepreneurship, Innovation, and the Growth of Free-Market Economies* (Princeton: Princeton University Press).

STURMAN, M. C., and TREVOR, C. O. (2001). 'The Implications of Linking the Dynamic Performance and Turnover Literature', *Journal of Applied Psychology*, 86(4): 684–96.

TADELIS, S. (2007). 'The Innovative Organization: Creating Value through Outsourcing', *California Management Review*, 50(1): 261–77.

TEECE, D. J. (1981a). 'The Market for Know-How and the Efficient International Transfer of Technology', *Annals of the Academy of Political and Social Science*, 458(1): 81–96.

——(1981b). 'The Multinational Enterprise: Market Failure and Market Power Considerations', *Sloan Management Review*, 22(3): 3–18.

——(1981c). 'Technology Transfer and R&D Activities of Multinational Firms: Some Theory and Evidence', in R. G. Hawkins and A. J. Prasad (eds.), *Technology Transfer and Economic Development* (Greenwich, Conn.: JAI Press), 39–74.

——(1986). 'Profiting from Technological Innovation', *Research Policy*, 15(6): 285–305.

——(1998). 'Capturing Value from Knowledge Assets: The New Economy, Markets for Know-How, and Intangible Assets', *California Management Review*, 40(3): 55–79.

——(2000). *Managing Intellectual Capital: Organizational, Strategic, and Policy Dimensions* (Oxford: Oxford University Press).

——(2003). 'Expert Talent and the Design of (Professional Services) Firms', *Industrial and Corporate Change*, 12(4): 895–916.

——(2006). 'Reflections on Profiting from Innovation', *Research Policy*, 35(8): 1131–46.

——(2007a). 'Explicating Dynamic Capabilities: The Nature and Microfoundations of (Sustainable) Enterprise Performance', *Strategic Management Journal*, 28(13): 1319–50.

——(2007b). 'The Role of Managers, Entrepreneurs and the Literati in Enterprise Performance and Economic Growth', *International Journal of Technological Learning, Innovation and Development*, 1(1): 43–64.

——(2007c), 'Managers, Markets, and Dynamic Capabilities', in C. Helfat, S. Finkelstein, W. Mitchell, M. Peteraf, H. Singh, D. J. Teece, and S. Winter (eds.), *Dynamic Capabilities: Understanding Strategic Change In Organizations* (Oxford: Blackwell), 19–29.

TEECE, D. J. (2010). 'Business Models, Business Strategy and Innovation', *Long Range Planning*, 43(2–3): 172–94.

——PISANO, G., and SHUEN, A. (1997). 'Dynamic Capabilities and Strategic Management', *Strategic Management Journal*, 18(7): 509–33.

VAN DEN STEEN, E. (2009). 'Authority versus Persuasion', *American Economic Review: Papers and Proceedings*, 99(2): 448–53.

WILLIAMSON O. E. (1975). *Markets and Hierarchies* (New York: Free Press).

——(1985). *The Economic Institutions of Capitalism* (New York: Free Press).

WINTER, S. (2006). 'The Logic of Appropriability: From Schumpeter to Arrow to Teece', *Research Policy*, 35(8): 1100–6.

CHAPTER 22

LOOKING TO THE FUTURE

BRINGING ORGANIZATIONS DEEPER INTO HUMAN CAPITAL THEORY

PETER D. SHERER

22.1 INTRODUCTION

In industries as diverse as corporate law (Koegel, 1953) and semiconductors (Brittain and Freeman, 1980; Saxenian, 1994), human capital is transferred across organizations through the interfirm movement of talent. Organizational research suggests that the interfirm movement of talent has effects on individual performance (for example, Allison and Long, 1990), firm founding and population (across-organization) dynamics (Brittain and Freeman, 1980; Hannan and Freeman, 1989; Saxenian, 1994), and firm survival and innovativeness (for example, Beckman, 2006; Phillips, 2002; Rao and Drazin, 2002). Perhaps surprisingly, much of the organizational research does not tie back to the human capital theory developed by Gary Becker (1964) in his classic work, *Human Capital*. This state of affairs is unfortunate. Organizational research on the interfirm movement of talent can add to and benefit from Becker's theory of human capital. This chapter takes the view that integration of these types of literature will lead to a fuller understanding of human capital and the value it offers firms and industries. As such, the chapter looks to the future with the idea of bringing organizations deeper into human capital theory.

The chapter begins by examining how human capital is transferred across organizations in a population, by looking at the case of US corporate law firms. The case reveals that in the early 1900s, firm-specific human capital was transferred among what came to be a number of the most prominent New York City law firms through the inter-firm movement of lawyers (Koegel, 1953). The case further reveals that in the last twenty or so years, corporate law firms have competed fiercely for specialized partners with highly valued general human capital (Gilson and Mnookin, 1989; Hillman, 1999), often with the aim of building practice groups and multi-practice teams around them (Sherer, 2008).

The case of corporate law firms highlights how Becker's (1964) critical distinction between firm-specific and general human capital is at the heart of the missing role for organizations in human capital theory. Becker took an outcome-based view to distinguish between firm-specific and general human capital by comparing the value that individual human capital had when it was moved from the organization providing it, to an alternative organization. By definition, general human capital had equal value in both firms; while firm-specific had higher value in the organization providing it. This view allowed for a market imperfection in the higher value of firm-specific human capital, but it did not suggest a role for the receiving organization in the transfer of human capital, nor did it see any significant value in doing so. If it had, it would have suggested general human capital might not relocate so easily, or that it might have more value in another firm, or that firm-specific human capital might be replicated from one firm to another and possibly provide equal if not greater value in the alternative firm. These possibilities suggest revisiting the general and firm-specific distinction to allow for the possibility that both forms of human capital have potentially greater, equal, or lesser value in alternative organizations.

These points suggest that organizations have an influence via their capabilities to transfer in outside human capital (Cohen and Levinthal, 1990). As such, I propose two organizational processes that arise in the transfer of human capital in inter-firm movements. *Relocation* occurs when general human capital is transferred from one firm to another. *Replication* occurs when firm-specific human capital is transferred from one firm to another. These two proposed processes serve as an organizing framework to review organizational research on the interfirm movement of talent from business strategy (for example, Almeida and Kogut, 1999; Huckman and Pisano, 2006), strategic HRM (for example, Groysberg *et al.*, 2008), organizational sociology (for example, Allison and Long, 1990; Burton *et al.*, 2002; Phillips, 2002), and institutional theory (Kraatz and Moore, 2002). Both relocation and replication lead to a range of findings, suggesting the missing role for organizations in the transfer of human capital.

The organizational processes do not occur in isolation, however, as the actions of individual firms have implications for population dynamics. As such, three proposed population processes are explored. *Diffusion* arises when firm-specific human capital spreads across organizations and becomes general human capital in a population. *Specification* arises when general human capital becomes fragmented such that its use becomes firm-specific in a population. *Drift* arises when firm-specific human capital becomes fragmented such that it has multiple versions in a population. These processes have not been studied much, but are important in their own right and are critical for understanding how population dynamics interact with firm actions (Oliver, 1997).

By bringing organizations deeper into human capital theory, the chapter argues for a more complete yet less elegant view of Becker's theory of human capital. This perspective can also serve as a bridge to theory and research on organizational learning and innovation, knowledge transfers, industry evolution, and ultimately firm competitive advantage. Finally, while the chapter focuses on the interfirm movement of talent, it suggests other mechanisms involving human capital transfers that need to be examined—particularly M&As, firm alliances, and intrafirm job movements.

22.2 THE TRANSFER OF HUMAN CAPITAL IN CORPORATE LAW FIRMS

In the late 1800s, corporate law firms in New York City and other major US centers operated with a few partners and with individuals in apprenticeship to become lawyers (Sherer, 2009). Walter Carter developed an approach to the development of human capital in law firms that was a significant change from the past practice of apprenticeship. It involved procuring talented lawyers from elite law schools, developing them, and then moving most of them out after several years. Robert Swaine (1946: 3), a leading partner at the prestigious law firm of Cravath, Swaine, and Moore, stated about Carter:

It was Carter's practice to seek, annually, one or more of the best graduates of the leading schools, principally Columbia, and train them through a clerkship of several years. They then left him for their own practice or other connections.... He kept moving through his office a current of brilliant, ambitious young lawyers, many of whom later became outstanding leaders at the bar.

The lawyers who practiced at the Carter law office read like a 'who's who' of law, and had a profound influence on the way in which law and its management were conducted in the twentieth century. Koegel (1953) provides a genealogy in appendix VII of his book that identifies the Carter law office's influence on many of the most prestigious New York City law firms. Of particular note, Paul Cravath became the lead partner at Cravath, Swaine and Moore, and developed the Cravath System—the standard management practice in corporate law firms for much of the twentieth century

(Galanter and Palay, 1991; Gilson and Mnookin, 1989; Koegel, 1953; Sherer and Lee, 2002; Swaine 1946, 1948).

The human capital of the Carter firm was transferred across law firms and became the general human capital for many top corporate law firms. This scenario is by no means extraordinary. Brittain and Freeman (1980) and Saxenian (1994) detail how Fairchild, similar to Clark's law firm, had a genealogical effect on the semiconductor industry in Silicon Valley. Brittain and Freeman (1980: 308) note that 'the leading development group during the sixties and early seventies was at Fairchild Semiconductor. From 1960 to 1978, twenty-three of the sixty-four newly founded semiconductor manufacturing firms were direct offshoots of Fairchild'. Saxenian (1994: 31) likewise states: 'During the 1960s it seemed as if every engineer in Silicon Valley had worked there.... Many of the region's entrepreneurs and managers still speak of Fairchild as an important training ground and applaud the education they received at "Fairchild University."' Saxenian (1994: 31) further notes: 'To this day, a poster of the Fairchild family tree, showing the corporate genealogy of the scores of Fairchild spin-offs, hangs on the walls of many Silicon Valley firms.'

More generally, population ecology models posit that the movement of human capital is central to organizational founding in the early years of an industry (Brittain and Hannan, 1980; Hannan and Freeman, 1989). Hannan and Freeman (1989: 132) argue that job movements are essential for growth in young industries because 'existing organizations are the only training grounds for knowledgeable organization builders'. Brittain and Freeman (1980: 332) state: 'When individuals start new organizations...such individuals will seek models to imitate...Such models are found in the individual's own experience and in the experience of his or her colleagues.' Similarly, Rao and Drazin (2002: 495) argue: 'Managers hired from large [and older] organizations enable [young] firms to acquire not only visibility, but also access to the routines of competitors.'

The above arguments address the interfirm movement of talent and the transfer of human capital in the context of young industries or young organizations. Additionally, older and larger organizations also access the human capital of other organizations through the interfirm movement of talent (Cappelli, 2000; Gardner, 2005; Sherer, 2008). In corporate law firms, the acquisition of lateral (from another firm) partners is now part of the way most major law firms operate (Braverman, 2001; Hillman, 1999; Sherer, 2008). Gilson and Mnookin (1989) argue that lateral partners have deep specialties and expertise that reflect general human capital, in contrast to the generalist partners of the past whose expertise reflected firm-specific human capital tied to a firm's clients.

Firms acquire lateral partners to develop new practice areas, to do so quickly, and to renew and deepen existing practice areas (Sherer, 2008). In many instances the acquiring firm is seeking to gain more than just the specific talents of a lateral partner. Firms leverage lateral partners by building practice groups or multi-practice teams around them. These efforts at leveraging often fail because they require acquiring firms to be highly adept at the selection and integration of outsiders.

What happened in corporate law firms and Silicon Valley and what appeared in theoretical arguments in population ecology were not sufficiently addressed in Becker's theory of human capital. A more complete theory would address the processes by which human capital is transferred across organizations and what firms gain or lose through human capital transfers. To address these issues, though, first requires going back to the firm-specific/general human capital distinction in human capital theory and seeing what is transferred and determining what is valued.

22.3 THE FIRM-SPECIFIC/GENERAL HUMAN CAPITAL DISTINCTION

Gary Becker's (1964) *Human Capital* was critically important in conceiving of investments in human capital as akin to other investments by individuals or firms. Becker showed how investments in human capital equated with other financial investment decisions in capital markets, and had major implications for understanding employee and firm investments in human capital and for determining is individual productivity and wages. For the purposes of this chapter, Becker's important point is his distinction between firm-specific versus general human capital in the context of on-the-job training.[1] Becker made this distinction in the context of specifying what an individual would receive for his/her general versus firm-specific human capital at the firm that provided the training versus at an alternative firm. The distinction raises critical questions about what is firm-specific versus general human capital, and what is the value of firm-specific versus general human capital.

22.3.1 What is Firm-Specific versus General Human Capital?

The basis of Becker's firm-specific/general distinction was the outcome generated by training when individuals moved from the organization providing it. Becker (1964: 11 and 12) specified: 'General training is useful in many firms besides those providing it.…"Perfectly general" training would be equally useful in many firms and marginal products would rise by exactly the same amount in all of them.' He (1964: 18) further specified: 'Training that increases productivity more in firms providing it will be called specific training. Completely specific training can be defined as training that has no effect on the productivity of trainees that would be useful to other firms.' In short, the key to Becker's distinction was the use or value that human capital had in the organization providing it versus in alternative organizations. General human capital had equal value in the firm providing it compared to other firms, while firm-specific human capital had its highest value in the specific firm providing it and lower value in other organizations.[2]

These distinctions were reflected in the expected wage outcomes for individuals with general and specific human capital in the event that they changed firms. Becker (1964: 24) stated: 'Rational firms pay generally trained employees the same wage and specifically trained employees a higher wage than they could get elsewhere.' What this means is that an employee with purely general human capital receives wages equal to those he/she could receive at alternative firms, while an employee with purely firm-specific human capital receives a higher wage at the firm which provided the skills than at alternative firms. These points are summarized as follows:

(1) General Human Capital: Firm-Wage = Alternative-Firm-Wage
(2) Firm-Specific Human Capital: Firm-Wage> Alternative-Firm-Wage

where Firm-Wage represents an individual's incumbent firm wage and Alternative-Firm-Wage represents a wage an individual receives at one or more other firms. Equations (1) and (2) show that an individual is paid equally for his/her general human capital, and is paid less for his firm-specific human capital when he/she moves to another firm.

Becker's distinction raises several points. The first is that it defines general and firm-specific human capital by their outcomes. By definition, Becker argued that what transfers is general, and what does not is firm-specific. As such, the distinction does not speak to the process by which general human capital and firm-specific human capital are acquired. In Becker's definitions this is not a point of difference, as both are provided in the organization. It is only the outcome of the transfer that matters in defining the form of human capital. Therefore, it is not entirely clear *a priori* what is firm-specific versus general human capital. In this light, the human capital that transferred from Carter's law firm or Fairchild would be treated as of equal value and hence general human capital, regardless of where or how it was developed.

Second, and following from this last point, the outcome-based nature of Becker's definitions have less than obvious implications at times. For example, when a firm can control the outward flow of generally valued information, through such mechanisms as covenants not to compete, or trade secret agreements (Hyde, 1998*a*, 1998*b*), then that human capital is defined as firm-specific. Or, if a firm can limit the information which other firms acquire regarding training that can be used more generally, then that training is considered to be firm-specific (Gilson and Mnookin, 1989). Indeed, as Becker (1964: 19) points out: 'Expenditures on acquiring knowledge of employee talents would be a specific investment if the knowledge could be kept from other firms, for then productivity would be raised more in the firms making the expenditures than elsewhere.' Taking an information economics perspective, Gilson and Mnookin (1989: 581) make such an argument in discussing the apprenticeship phase in law firms: 'If one looks only at the skills associates acquire during apprenticeship, they appear to be general human capital. It is the information asymmetry between the firm and alternative employers in evaluating the quality of the general human capital acquired that, in our analysis, transforms this general human capital into firm-specific human capital.'

The third reason is that firm-specific human capital and general human capital are assumed to be fixed temporally, but they can and do change form over time.[3] First, what is firm-specific at a point in time might be general human capital at a later point in time. For example, firm-specific human capital born of a technology started in one organization could prove to be generally useful at other organizations—if those firms find a way to make it useful. This might help to explain why organizations seek to recruit free agents from highly reputable firms with specific routines.[4] Second, what is general human capital at a point in time might become useful in only one or a few firms at a later point in time. For example, general human capital born of a technology that was used in many organizations could become less popular over time. This happens when an organization allows its IT system to age and when the human capital needed to make it operate becomes increasingly tied specifically to that organization.

Doeringer and Piore (1971) took a more institutional-based view of human capital in their work on internal labor markets that ultimately led to something of a different view of general and firm-specific human capital. Moving from training to the building block of skills and then up to jobs but using parallel language to Becker, Doeringer and Piore (1971: 14) stated: 'A completely specific skill is unique to a single job classification in a single enterprise; a completely general skill is requisite for every job in every enterprise.' Moving the level of analysis up to the job, Doeringer and Piore (1971: 15) stated: 'A completely specific job is one which utilizes only specific skills; a completely general job is one all of whose skills are general.'

Doeringer and Piore (1971) additionally took what I call a 'process-based view' of general and firm-specific skills by looking to how human capital was acquired. Becker saw on-the job training as integral to the development of both general and firm-specific human capital, but Doeringer and Piore (1971: 22) argued that on-the-job training was closely linked to the production of firm-specific human capital: 'As should be apparent from the preceding analysis, on-the-job training is closely related to skill specificity. Specificity tends to promote this type of training by reducing the number of people learning a particular skill at a given time. By precluding large-scale, standardized training, formal instruction is discouraged.' Doeringer and Piore (1971: 39) subsequently noted: 'Moreover, because skill specificity is often the result of elements of work which are difficult to codify in a formal training curriculum, on-the-job training may be the only way to transmit skills from one worker to another.'

The population ecologists Hannan and Freeman (1984) ostensibly adhered to Becker's notion of firm-specific skills, but they too offered something of an additional view (Hannan and Freeman, 1989: 132). They state that 'organization-specific skills (such as knowledge of specialized rules and tacit understandings)...have no value outside the organization' (Hannan and Freeman, 1984: 157), and also (1989: 131 and 132) state:

Knowledge about organizational strategies and structures is often available only to 'insiders'; that is, those already participating in such organizations. This is commonly the case when organizational functioning is shielded from public observation and when essential features of the organizational form have not been codified. In such situations, existing organizations are the only training grounds for knowledgeable organization builders.

In this view, firm-specific human capital is available only to insiders; while general human capital would be available without the requirement of being an insider—that is, to both insiders and outsiders. However, even though firm-specific human capital is most readily available to insiders, their human capital can be used in other organizations. That possibility is captured in Hannan and Freeman's point that existing organizations serve as 'training grounds'.

The point that firm-specific human capital is transferable is reflected in more recent work by Phillips (2002) and Beckman (2006). Phillips (2002: 476) states:

Whenever personnel leave one organization to found a new organization in the same population, there is a transfer of resources and routines. Not only does this imply that the offspring has some advantages over peers that lack parent organizations, but it suggests that the founding event poses a hazard to the parent: an offspring's founders leave with many *of the firm-specific skills* [my emphasis], insights, and resources (for example, customers, social capital, ties to external constituencies) that help sustain the parent.

Beckman (2006: 743) discusses the transfer of firm-specific knowledge that occurs when members of a founding team with shared human capital are reassembled in another organization.

The outcome-based view in Becker's theory of human capital looked to the outcome that human capital had at the firm providing it versus at alternative firms, to determine whether it was general or specific. This point was expressed in the expected wage levels of job holders in the incumbent firm and in an alternative firm. If we accept this view without any modifications, there is little if any role for organizations in the transfer of human capital. If we say that human capital has transferred, then it is by definition general human capital; but if we say that human capital has not transferred, then it is by definition firm-specific human capital. Moreover, general human capital transfers with equal value, while firm-specific human capital transfers only with lesser value. Doeringer and Piore's process-based view looked to whether human capital was acquired inside a firm as the means by which to define firm-specific human capital. However, taking this view to its boundary condition means that firm-specific human capital is limited to the firm in which it was originally developed, such as Carter's firm or Fairchild. Hannan and Freeman's (1989) distinction—that knowledge available to insiders constitutes firm-specific human capital while general human capital is knowledge available to both insiders and outsiders—is helpful in seeing that insiders have greater access to knowledge, but that human capital can still be transferred elsewhere. Phillips (2002) and Beckman (2006), more specifically, allow for equal if perhaps not greater transferability of firm-specific human capital.

We can overstate the differences here. These views often go hand-in-hand. Human capital acquired inside for which insiders have the most availability typically has the most value inside. But these views are not necessarily the same. What is developed inside an organization as firm-specific human capital might have as much or more value in an alternative organization at some later point in time. Likewise, general human capital might have more or less value in another organization than in the organization providing it.

These points suggest that it is important to recognize the immediate value of human capital to insiders versus outsiders, yet allow for human capital to be dynamic in its value to organizations. As such, we might say that general human capital is useful in many organizations at a point in time, while firm-specific human capital has its greatest immediate use at a point in time in one or a few organizations. That firm-specific human capital has immediate use in only one or a few organizations, and that general human capital has broader use, does not imply that this is fixed. The properties of human capital can change over time, and therefore firm-specific human capital can be useful in other organizations. Nonetheless, insiders will have greater access to firm-specific human capital than will outsiders, and general human capital can be more readily accessed across organizations.

22.3.2 What is the Value of Firm-Specific versus General Human Capital?

Becker's predictions on individual wages translated into expected values that human capital had for organizations. General human capital was expected to have equal use or value across organizations—no more, no less. Firm-specific human capital was expected to have its greatest value in the organization providing it, with no possibility of equal or greater value in other organizations. Becker's arguments on firm-specific human capital did not imply positive externalities for interfirm movement, as there were only negative outcomes for employees and for the firms providing the training.

Consider two possible scenarios that result in employees' human capital leading to higher value at another firm than at the current firm. One involves an employee who received general on-the-job training in an organization which was worth more at another organization. For example, consider the general human capital of a baseball player who received training in the minor leagues of a particular team (Ehrenberg and Smith, 1985). That training would be of potentially differential value to baseball teams based on their composition of talent (Ehrenberg and Smith, 1985), how they generated runs, and the layout of their ballparks. Babe Ruth, the heralded home-run hitter for the New York Yankees, truly came into his own after relocating to Yankee Stadium, with its short 'porch' in right field, made for a left-handed pull hitter just like him. In fact, the old Yankee Stadium was referred to as the 'House that Ruth built'. Had Babe Ruth stayed his whole career with the Boston Red Sox he might have remained a star pitcher who had been great for the times but who would not have been a superstar of all time as a home-run hitter.

The second scenario involves an individual who received firm-specific training at a firm known to have particularly strong firm-specific human capital as reflected in its organizational routines, such as Toyota. Ostensibly, at least, that individual's firm-specific human capital would be most valuable to Toyota, but the aim of the acquiring firm would be to replicate its routines. As such, that individual might provide even greater value at another firm as a result of his/her training in the Toyota 'way'.

These two scenarios mean that we can conceive of instances where individuals provide greater value by leaving their organization than would be predicted by human capital theory. While these scenarios are not meant to imply that this is the case a majority of the time, they raise the possibility there is greater value for individuals' human capital at times in an organization other than the one providing it.

These arguments on value are ultimately translated into a discussion of how firms gain competitive advantage from acquiring external assets (which presumably could be from 'purchasing' general or firm-specific human capital). Barney (1986) discussed two ways that firms could achieve such gains. One way, he argued, was through luck, but that was unreliable. The other way was to have superior insight, through having the skills and capabilities to better assess the value of assets external to an organization. Dierickx and Cool (1989) countered Barney by arguing that value did not come from such external assets and instead came from critical assets that are firm-specific, embedded in organizations, and not separable from the organization in which they resided. As such, they argued that firm-specific human capital provided distinct value to firms, but that the knowledge embedded in them were generally not transferable to other firms.[5]

Dierickx and Cool's (1989) view became something of the accepted wisdom, but there is more to the debate with Barney (1986). Arguments can be fashioned that general human capital as well as firm-specific human capital can contribute to what a firm needs to gain competitive advantage. The real issue is in determining when each provides such possibilities.

Discussions about how firms achieve competitive advantage through their human capital have centered on questions about the value and the rareness of firm-specific and general human capital. As Lepak and Snell (1999) in their human resource architecture point out, both firm-specific and general human capital can provide value. Lepak and Snell (1999: 35) note: 'Resources are valuable when they enable a firm to enact strategies that improve efficiency and effectiveness, exploit market opportunities, and/or neutralize potential threats'. Additionally, and importantly, they point out that value in the fuller sense of the term has to do with 'the ratio of strategic benefits to customers derived from skills relative to the costs incurred'.

Questions arise, however, about the significance of rarity in determining whether general human capital and firm-specific human capital are important for achieving competitive advantage. Doeringer and Piore's (1971) linkage of firm-specific skill acquisition to informal on-the-job training led to the view that firm-specific human capital is rare, and that by negation, general human capital is not rare. The notion that firm-specific human capital relates to rarity has carried over into the strategic HRM literature. Lepak and Snell's (1999: 35) human resource architecture provides the clearest statement of this view as they equate the two: 'the degree of uniqueness—or firm specificity—of human capital'.

But why firm-specific human capital is rare or unique *a priori* is not entirely clear, nor is it clear why general human capital is viewed as common.[6] Many individuals in a firm might have the same firm-specific skills. For example, many people might know how to use an IT system that is highly specific to a firm. And there are instances in which few individuals possess general skills, particularly at very high levels (Coff, 1997). Peteraf (1993: 187) concedes this point when she states that 'a brilliant, Nobel prize-winning scientist may be a unique resource'. Thus, in an absolute sense, it is quite possible that *both* general human capital and firm-specific human capital are rare.

More importantly, lost in this argument is that human capital is not an absolute but a relativistic concept (Zucker, 1988: 34) that exists in a market context. Hence, the focus should not be on rarity *per se* but on scarcity, which is a function of supply and demand in organizations. If firms find general human capital to be in greater demand than its supply, then that general human capital is (relatively) scarce. The same holds for firm-specific human capital.

Viewing human capital in relative terms leads to the argument that general human capital can at times be even scarcer than firm-specific human capital. General human capital is often in demand by a larger market of external organizations than firm-specific human capital; hence, it is likely to be scarcer. In contrast, demand for firm-specific human capital might be highly idiosyncratic, reflecting the needs of a single employer or a very few. Moreover, to the degree to which general human capital is tied to a standard practice, it is likely to lead to resource scarcities (Leblebici *et al.*, 1991; Sherer and Lee, 2002). For example, the MBA—a form of general human capital—is tied to the growth of the multidivisional firm and the need for business analysts. These points make it clear why organizations compete fiercely at times for the talents of those experts with general human capital. They might also help to explain why studies such as those of Cappelli (2004) find that employers are willing to pay for general human capital, even though human capital theory suggests otherwise.

In conclusion, both general and specific human capital can be useful and scarce. Their value has to do with what they contribute to an organization, while their scarcity has to do with their demand relative to supply. Human capital that is valued and scarce can contribute to a firm's achieving competitive advantage. This holds true for both general and firm-specific human capital.

22.3.3 Summary

As the above points suggest, Becker's outcome-based distinction between firm-specific and general human capital limits bringing organizations into human capital theory. Perhaps that is why much of the organizational research on the interfirm movement of talent does not directly connect to human capital theory. Opening up the firm-specific versus general human capital distinction to allow for a temporal component means that both general and firm-specific human capital might be transferred and have potential value to other organizations. The next section looks at the two proposed organizational processes for transferring human capital, and reviews literature on the range of effects of these processes.

22.4 ORGANIZATIONAL PROCESSES

Specifying the organizational processes by which human capital is transferred across organizations though the interfirm movement of talent is central to bringing organizations deeper into human capital theory. This section begins with the theoretical argument for the two proposed organizational processes. Then, relevant empirical literature on the interfirm movement of talent is reviewed that addresses these processes.

22.4.1 Theoretical Argument

Cohen and Levinthal's (1990) argument on absorptive capacities contributes to identifying the organizational processes by which firm-specific human capital and general human capital are transferred and potentially generate value across organizations. They argue that differences in organizations' capabilities to absorb outside knowledge reflect their varying levels of insight into selecting external individuals, integrating them, and appropriating their human capital. Given the differences between general and firm-specific human capital, organizations face different processes in transferring in general versus firm-specific human capital. The two proposed organizational processes for dealing with these transfers are shown in Figure 22.1.[7]

Relocation arises when general human capital is transferred from one organization to another organization (G_{L1} to G_{L2}, where G refers to general human capital and L refers to locations 1 and 2). Becker (1964) discussed such a mode of transfer as the means by which human capital readily moves from one organization to another. In his model, general human capital was perfectly transferable in the sense that there was no loss in transferring it from one organization to another. While the relocation of general human capital was frictionless, this also meant that the firm receiving the human capital did not receive any greater value. But there are times when the transfer of general human capital might lead to greater or lesser value, depending on the absorptive capacities of the receiving organization in taking in such outside human capital.

Replication arises when firm-specific human capital from one organization is transferred for use in another organization (F_{L1} to F_{L2}, where F refers to firm-specific human capital and L refers to locations 1 and 2). Replication is critical if organizations are to make use of firm-specific routines, practices, and the like from other organizations, and is particularly common when younger or troubled organizations seek to transfer the practices of highly successful firms (Brittain and Freeman, 1980: 308). Replication, however, typically involves an imperfect transfer of human capital that reflects differences between the organization in which the skills reside and the receiving organization (Dierickx and Cool, 1989). Moreover,

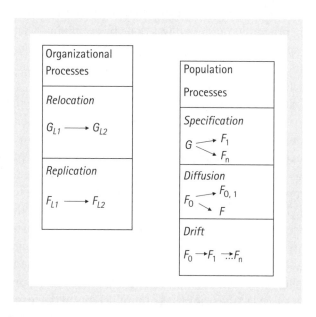

Figure 22.1. Organizational and Population Processes

mistakes occur in replication. Hannan and Freeman (1989: 58) state: 'Copying mistakes also occur routinely in ongoing organizations.' To minimize the imperfect transfer of firm-specific human capital, organizations might seek to replicate the total system of another organization by hiring an entire team of individuals from another firm or by merging with or acquiring an organization (Beckman, 2006; Groysberg and Abrahams, 2006; Sherer, 2008).

As the discussion suggests, both general and firm-specific human capital vary in the value which they bring to another organization. An organization needs to have significant insight into which firm-specific human capital to replicate, and what it has to do to use such human capital. General human capital might bring more or less value than it had at another organization. This suggests that we need to focus on the possible range of effects for acquiring general and human capital through the processes of relocation and replication.

22.4.2 Findings

Before proceeding to studies which have examined the interfirm movement of talent, some cautions are in order. First, while an effort was made to conduct an extensive review of the relevant literature, the review is not necessarily exhaustive. Quite possibly, studies have been overlooked, given the diversity of subfields studying the interfirm movement of talent. The point of this literature review, though, is not to determine mean effects but to demonstrate the range of possible effects. Second, a larger caution might be that most studies did not specifically identify what form of human capital was being transferred. Determination of whether general or firm-specific human capital was being primarily transferred was done by examining what appeared to be transferred, the specific sample, and the context of the study. While in some studies this was less clear cut, omission of the studies with the most ambiguity did not change the range of effects.

As Table 22.1 shows, relocation has been addressed in three studies. The earliest studies were carried out by the sociologists Paul Allison and his colleagues (Allison and Long, 1987, 1990; Allison et al., 1982; Long, 1978). They examined the effects on scientists' productivity of changing to more or less prestigious departments in different universities.[8] Since a scientist's knowledge is regarded as general human capital, a scientist's productivity was not expected to differ according to the prestige of the department. To the contrary, Allison and Long (1990) found that job changers who went to more prestigious departments than their current departments increased their productivity as reflected in the number of publications and citations. This did not happen all at once, as there was a decline in publications immediately following the job change that went on for few years, followed by a steady upward increase in productivity that exceeded the prior level of productivity at the former department. The effect on citations, a proxy for quality, to a more prestigious department was a

Table 22.1. Performance Effects for Relocation and Replication Processes

Study	Relocation	Key Effects
Allison and Long (1990)	Scientists	Positive (negative) individual performance effects to more (less) prestigious universities
Groysberg et al. (2008)	Investment analysts	Negative or no individual performance effects
Boeker (1997)	Top managers	Firm diversification
Study	**Replication**	**Key Effects**
Huckman and Pisano (2006)	Cardiac surgeons	Lack of transfer of firm-specific human capital
Rao and Drazin (2002)	Stock portfolio managers	Product innovation
Burton et al. (2002)	Founding team members	Product innovation and external financing
Kratz and Moore (2002)	Outside college top administrators	Adoption of professional programs
Phillips (2002)	Founding law firm partners	Increased survival for newly founded law firms
Beckman (2006)	Founding team members	Incremental innovation
Almeida and Kogut (1999)	Engineers	Transfer limited spatially
Song et al. (2006)	Engineers	Transfer limited by firm's extant stock of HC

relatively steady, upward slope with no discontinuity after the job change. Allison and Long attributed the upward productivity effects to facilities (such as laboratories, and the quality of graduate students) as opposed to social structure factors such as intellectual stimulation and motivation of colleagues ('team effects'). For job changers who moved to departments which were less prestigious than their current departments, these movers showed sustained lower performance after their job changes. Thus, the results show that the general human capital of individuals—their training in graduate school and subsequent professional on-the-job training—had different effects in more and less prestigious departments at different universities.

Groysberg et al. (2008) examined whether star security analysts' general human capital was transferable across organizations. As Groysberg et al. (2008: 1215) note, star performance is typically equated with general human capital: 'In knowledge work, star performance has traditionally been attributed to general human capital, or the skills, characteristics, and competencies of the individual performer...' They found: (1) the movement of stars, in general, led to a reduced likelihood of a star analyst being subsequently ranked; (2) star analysts who moved to banks of lower prestige were less likely to be ranked among the top five analysts; (3) star analysts who went to banks of comparable prestige were less likely in the first two years to be ranked among the top five analysts but subsequently there was no significant negative effect; and (4) star analysts who moved to a better firm saw no gain or loss in their likelihood of being ranked among the top five analysts. They additionally found that stars who moved with their team did not suffer a significant negative effect (but there was not a significant, positive effect). Thus, Groysberg *et al.* found negative effects and no effects, but no positive effects for moving. The result might be specific to stars in that they might have achieved a high level of success because they found the 'equilibrium context' in which they shine best. However, the more general model suggests that relocation leads to stars shining not only less or no differently, but also brighter.

Boeker (1997) examined the interfirm movement of top managers on firm diversification. The introduction of outside top managers resulted in greater diversification by firms into new product areas. This was especially true if top managers were from functional areas involving more general human capital, had more industry experience, and were higher in rank at the prior firm. And the less human capital the receiving firm had, the more likely it was to innovate. Thus, the study tells us that relocation led to entry into new product markets, but it does not reveal whether those firms that diversified were successful financially.

In summary, the three studies demonstrate that there is a range of effects for the relocation of general human capital. Allison and Long show that relocation leads to higher and lower performance effects in the receiving organization. Groysberg *et al.* show that relocation can lead to lower or no effects. Boeker shows that organizations utilize the general human capital of outsiders to enter into new product markets.

As Table 22.1 shows, eight studies have addressed replication and its performance effects. Huckman and Pisano (2006) examined cardiac surgeons who performed operations at two or more hospitals very close in time, in order to determine if individual performance varied by setting. The advantage of their methodology to studies in which there is a job switch is that positive or negative maturation effects due to ageing and tied to the time of movement can be ruled out. Huckman and Pisano (2006: 475) stated as the purpose of their study: 'The question we wish to explore is whether specific worker–firm combinations might yield higher performance than others. Why might a given worker's performance be better at one organization versus another...?' Using mortality rates of patients as the measure of performance, they found that experience or learning curves at one hospital did not transfer to other hospitals at which the surgeon performed cardiac operations. They conclude that familiarity among operating team members operates as a barrier to firm-specific human capital transferring across hospitals.[9] To assess their argument more fully, it would be valuable to determine whether intact teams transfer their firm-specific human capital across hospitals.

Rao and Drazin (2002) examined the effects of the interfirm movement of stock portfolio managers on product innovation in mutual fund families. They found that mutual fund families were more likely to introduce product innovations, defined as offering new mutual funds, when the externally hired portfolio manager came from: (1) a short-term and high-performing (hot-hand) fund; (2) a larger fund; and (3) an older-aged fund. Their findings suggest that the more firm-specific the manager's skills—as reflected in size of fund and age of firm—the greater the likelihood of innovation. Rao and Drazin (2002) also found that the receiving firm was likely to be small and younger, and therefore not constrained by its limited stock of firm-specific capital.

Burton *et al.* (2002) examined how the reputational status of founding team members influenced innovativeness in Silicon Valley startups. They showed that having founding team members from a firm regarded as highly entrepreneurial—what they refer to as 'entrepreneurial prominence'—led to more product innovation and greater likelihood of gaining external financing. Their findings are consistent with Rao and Drazin (2002) in the effects for reputation, and highlight the value of human capital from an individual's prior firm in firm innovation. The findings are important in suggesting future research to separate out the effects due to: (1) the general versus firm-specific human capital that founding members brought to the startup, (2) the pure reputational effects of having founding team members from prominent firms, and (3) the presumably larger network and hence greater social capital of founding team members from those prominent firms.

Phillips (2002) examined the interfirm movement of law partners among Silicon Valley law firms on the failure rates of both the departing and receiving firms. Phillips found that the movement of a named partner increased the probability of failure of the parent organization. The finding suggests that departing partners actually take with them—not simply transfer—the firm-specific resources and routines of the parent company. Phillips also found that the movement of named partners increased the probability of success of the newly founded law firm, and that regular partners generally had the same effect. His findings for a genealogical effect suggest that firm-specific human capital is transmitted from firm to firm. These findings call for a greater understanding of the firm-specific routines and resources that partners take with them to their new firms, and what their former firms lose.

Beckman (2006) examined how the composition of founding teams influences startup firms' innovation strategy. He determined that founding teams with individuals from the same firm engaged in an innovation strategy of exploitation (incremental innovation). Presumably, that exploitation tied back to the firm-specific strategy employed by the founding teams' prior organization. If that is the case, the results suggest that firm-specific human capital from the departing organization is more readily transferable when it is embodied in teams. In this regard, Groysberg and Abrahams (2006) found that professional service firms are more likely to succeed when they hire teams of professionals from other organizations in what are called 'lift outs', and Sherer (2008) argues that larger-scale acquisition of talent from the same target organization has potentially stronger and positive effects.

Kraatz and Moore (2002) examined the effects of hiring outside new presidents on the adoption of professional programs in liberal arts colleges. They found that hiring outside college presidents from schools in which there were professional programs, and especially if those programs had been recently adopted, increased the probability of adopting professional programs. Kraatz and Moore (2002: 124) note: 'The migration of a leader from one organization to another creates a relatively high-capacity conduit between the organizations and may thus promote the transfer of reliable and fine-grained information, which is often necessary for social learning.' Kraatz and Moore do not identify whether the information is firm-specific or general human capital, but its fine-grained nature presumably makes it more likely to be the former than the latter.

Almeida and Kogut (1999) examined the interfirm movement of design engineers on localized knowledge externalities. They assessed knowledge externalities through examining a patent for citations to prior patents in the same region. Almeida and Kogut (1999: 908) argue: 'the knowledge held by design engineers has a tacit quality and that these same engineers are mobile among firms *within* the spatial boundaries of a region'. They found that this tacit knowledge, what is viewed here as firm-specific human capital, only 'travels' in a localized area. As such, Almeida and Kogut's (1999) findings suggest the boundaries for firm-specific human capital do not end at the door of the firm in which these engineers work, but are circumscribed by localized areas in which they think and operate alike.

Song *et al.* (2006: 357) examined the effects of the interfirm mobility of engineers on the sourcing of knowledge, which they defined as 'the number of citations each hiring firm patent makes to any patent from the mobile engineer's previous firm'. Their findings suggested that the likelihood that a firm's patent made reference to a patent from the prior firm of a job changer increased when the new firm was not on a strong path, when the mobile engineers' technical expertise matches the hiring firm's technical expertise; and when the mobile engineers' expertise lies outside of the core technology of the new firm. Thus, the existing firm-specific human capital of a firm acts as a constraint on what firm-specific human capital is transferred in.

In sum, these eight studies suggest the transfer of firm-specific human capital through replication has a range of effects. Rao and Drazin, Burton *et al.*, Beckman, and Phillips suggest positive transfers of firm-specific human capital. Beckman also shows that firms can do more to insure the transfer of firm specific human capital. Huckman and Pisano provide the strongest evidence for the lack of transferability of firm-specific human capital. Almeida and Kogut suggest localized limits to the transfer of firm-specific human capital, but these exceed the boundaries of the firm. Song *et al.* show the existing firm-specific human capital of a firm acts as a constraint on the transfer in of outside firm-specific human capital.

Summary

Organizational research on the interfirm movement of talent makes important headway in establishing the range of effects for the movement of general and firm-specific human capital. However, the next step for this literature is to address more fully the value of such transfers and the potential effects of such transfers on firm competitive advantage (Barney, 1991). An individual who moves to another organization might be more productive, and a firm that benefits from the acquisition of top managers might be more innovative, but in neither case are we assured that the firms achieve value or gain a competitive advantage. As Lepak and Snell (1999) suggest, the acquisition of talent might be more costly than its benefits. Moreover, other firms might take similar actions. Therefore, it is critical to go the next step in assessing the competitive potential of such moves for organizations. A part of addressing these concerns comes from identifying the population level processes that are operating.

22.5 POPULATION PROCESSES

Organizational processes in the transfer of general and firm-specific human capital ultimately feed into population processes. Three population-level processes are proposed in this section, and are shown in Figure 22.1. Built into these population-level processes is the notion that human capital can change forms, as reflected in how isomorphic or fragmented human capital becomes over time.

Diffusion arises when the same or similar firm-specific human capital is spread to other organizations and operates as general capital in that it has use in many organizations. As shown in Figure 22.1, firm-specific human capital from an originating firm (F_0) is diffused across organizations ($F_{0,1}...F_{0,n}$) to the point at which it becomes general to a population.[10] Brittain and Freeman (1980: 337) argue that high levels of mobility among firms in young industries lead to 'a great deal of structural similarity among related firms'. Diffusion occurs when the replication of the firm-specific human capital from an originating organization to other organizations is largely complete. Kraatz and Moore's (2002) findings on the adoption of professional programs show how firm-specific human capital spreads across organizations.

Specification arises when general human capital is fragmented such that it becomes firm-specific to the organizations in an industry. As shown in Figure 22.1, general human capital (G) fragments into firm-specific capital at a first firm (F_1), and at other organizations ($...F_n$). Specification arises when the relocation process is incomplete or varied in some manner. It might arise because of the division of roles among firms in a maturing industry (Hannan and Freeman, 1977, 1989), isolating mechanisms that firms develop so that only they can access human capital (Rumelt, 1984, 1987), or the life-cycle of organizations and technologies.

Drift refers to the process by which firm-specific human capital changes over time such that there are many different versions of it. As shown in Figure 22.1, firm-specific human capital of an originating firm (F_O), fragments into multiple versions ($F_1 ... F_n$), specific to different organizations. The key means by which drift occurs is through the incompleteness of replication and recombination (Hannan and Freeman, 1989; Nelson and Winter, 1982). Organizations also might tailor or customize firm-specific human capital and create isolating mechanisms to reduce the transfer of such human capital. Drift leads to erosion or accentuation of elements of firm-specific human capital. It can be functional, simply accidental, or dysfunctional for organizations.

These three population-level processes arise because the activity of individual organizations ultimately has collective effects. When firm-specific human capital is more completely replicated across a population it begins to take on the property of general human capital, which itself can also lose its generality over time through the incompleteness of relocation. Finally, the fragmentation of firm-specific human capital that arises through the incompleteness of replication can result in many different versions of it.

These population processes are as important to study as the organizational processes. However, much less attention has been given to population processes. Clearly, more research is needed on these and other potential population processes. As Oliver (1997) suggests, the interactions of organizational and population processes hold particular promise for understanding how firms achieve competitive advantage.

22.6 Conclusion

Organizational research on the interfirm movement of talent allows us to see that human capital transfers of general and firm-specific human capital through the organizational processes of relocation and replication lead to positive, negative, and no firm performance effects. These organizational processes feed into the population-level processes of specification, diffusion, and drift. We should be particularly concerned with the interaction of the organizational processes with the population processes, as they have the potential to help uncover how industries evolve and how organizations achieve competitive advantage.

The underlying argument in this chapter—that organizations matter to human capital theory—suggests a research agenda. It first requires that we leverage what we know about the organizational processes, particularly from the findings on the interfirm mobility of talent, and integrate them into human capital theory. We should be particularly open to theoretical possibilities that can reconcile differences in the literature and provide new insights. We should also expect to discover more about organizational processes—particularly those pertaining to firms gaining competitive advantage through general and firm-specific human capital. Finally, we should move to expand our understanding of population processes, in the search for understanding industry evolution and firm competitive advantage.

We should also study other important mechanisms by which human capital is transferred through organizational processes. Organizations engage in numerous internal movements through rotations and promotions that serve as vehicles for intra-organizational knowledge transfers. As Szulanski and his colleagues (for example, Szulanski 1996; Szulanski *et al.*, 2004) show in their work on intraorganizational knowledge transfers, even then the transfer of human capital is anything but perfect. M&As are also particularly important to study. The difficulty of replicating firm-specific human capital suggests it may take M&As and other large-scale transfers to do so successfully. Additionally, in M&As we see the blending of firm-specific human capital from different firms, which raises important questions on how (or how not) to achieve value.

Gary Becker's almost perfect human capital market and resultant brilliant theory is admittedly quite a bit less elegant once we bring organizations deeper into it. But we see that organizations truly matter—theoretically, descriptively, and practically speaking. It is to that less elegant yet richer future to which we can look forward.

Acknowledgments

Special thanks are extended to Peter Cappelli, Huseyin Leblebici, Janice Molloy, Scott Rankin, and the editors, for their valuable comments.

Notes

1. Becker (1964: 27 and 28) noted that the distinction between general and specific human capital extended beyond firms to that of industry, occupation, and even to country: 'Some training may be useful not in most firms nor in a single firm, but in a set of firms defined by product, type of work, or geographical location. For example, carpentry training would raise productivity primarily in the construction industry, and French legal training would not be very useful in the United States.' The application of the distinction to other levels of analysis does not, however, obviate the questions that arise. For example, does industry-specific human capital always have less value when an individual moves to another industry, or can it have equal or greater value in another industry?
2. The general/firm-specific distinction is a theoretical dichotomy for what empirically is on a continuum. Individuals often have a combination of the two (Ehrenberg and Smith, 1985). Becker (1964: 18) focused on pure forms, but he was well aware of this point:

'Much of on-the-job training is neither completely specific nor completely general'. Thus, it can be difficult to distinguish empirically between the two.

3. Lazear (2003: 13 and 14) touches on this point in his discussion of how the thickness (where the availability of jobs and the ease of search are both high) of labor markets affects human capital: 'The definition of firm-specific human capital is actually endogenous. As market thickness increases, investments that would otherwise by viewed as firm specific become more general...[A]s market thickness increases, the chances of finding a firm that uses skills [in like fashion] of those at the initial firm improve. It is in this sense that the definition of specific capital is endogenous.'

4. In this regard, Gardner's (2005) work on interfirm competition for human resources is intriguing. Gardner (2005: 255) assessed the transferability of employees' human capital in part by the following question: 'How much of the knowledge and skills that employees learn on this job at your company could be used in a similar job at a typical company in the software industry? In particular, we're interested in the knowledge and skills they learn beyond what they knew before joining the company.' Although it might be argued that these questions refer solely to general skills, Gardner's focus on skills acquired after the individual came to the firm suggests a significant firm-specific component.

5. Lazear (2003: 1) argues the other extreme by suggesting that firm-specific human capital has, at best, modest use: 'When searching for examples of firm-specific human capital, many of us fall back on the same clichéd examples. "Knowing how to find the restrooms," "learning who does what at the firm and to whom to go to get something done," "learning to use equipment or methods that are completely idiosyncratic," are ones that come to mind. *The problem is that it is difficult to generate convincing examples where the firm-specific component approaches the importance of the general component* [my emphasis]. If we think of our own jobs as academics, there is surely some value to knowing the specifics of the university at which we are employed, but does that capital come close to the amount of general economic knowledge that we have acquired...? The answers is [sic] almost certainly no, and that is true for virtually every job that one considers.'

6. Lepak and Snell (1999: 36) capture that state of the literature by equating general human capital with skills 'generic and available to multiple firms'.

7. The organizational processes bear similarity to Nonaka's (1991) modes for transferring tacit and explicit knowledge. The term 'relocation' appears in Brown's (1981: 27) classic work on innovation diffusion, but is used more specifically in this chapter. For Brown, relocation refers to the diffusion that arises when an individual in a population moves locations from $_t$ to $_{t+1}$. Brown does not address whether this movement involves general or firm-specific human capital.

8. Allison and Long (1987) found that the majority of movements were to less prestigious departments.

9. While a cardiac surgeon's performance reflects his/her general human capital (professional training) and firm-specific human capital, general human capital is arguably the larger source of performance (Lazear, 2003). Without it, an individual cannot even go into the operating room to perform the surgery. In this regard, Huckman and Pisano (2006: 476) note the extensive general training of cardiac surgeons: 'They are highly trained, typically receiving up to seven years of residency and fellowship following their four years of medical school.'

10. F_0 refers to firm-specific human capital from originating ($_0$) firm; $F_{0,1}$ to $F_{0,n}$ refers to that same firm-specific capital in organizations 1 through n.

REFERENCES

ALLISON, P. D., and LONG, J. S. (1987). 'Interuniversity Mobility of Academic Scientists', *American Sociological Review*, 52(5): 643–52.

—— —— (1990). 'Departmental Effects on Scientific Productivity', *American Sociological Review*, 55(4): 469–78.

—— ——and KRAUZE, T. K. (1982). 'Cumulative Advantage and Inequality in Science', *American Sociological Review*, 47(5): 615–25.

ALMEIDA, P., and KOGUT, B. (1999). 'The Localization of Knowledge and the Mobility of Engineers in Regional Networks', *Management Science*, 45(7): 905–17.

BARNEY, J. (1986). 'Strategic Factor Markets: Expectations, Luck and Business Strategy', *Management Science*, 32(10): 1231–41.

—— (1991). 'Firm Resources and Sustained Competitive Advantage', *Journal of Management*, 17(1): 99–120.

BECKER, G. S. (1964). *Human Capital* (New York: National Bureau of Economic Research).

BECKMAN, C. M. (2006). 'The Influence of Founding Team Company Affiliations on Firm Behavior', *Academy of Management Journal*, 49(4): 741–58.

BOEKER, W. (1997). 'Executive Migration and Strategic Change: The Effect of Top Manager Movement on Product Market Entry', *Administrative Science Quarterly*, 42(2): 213–36.

BRAVERMAN, P. (2001). 'In Motion: Lateral Moves by Attorneys in Top 200 US Law Firms', *American Lawyer* (Feb.): 88–90 and 93.

BRITTAIN, J. W., and FREEMAN, J. H. (1980). 'Organizational Proliferation and Density Dependence Selection', in J. R. Kimberly and R. H. Miles (eds.), *The Organization Life Cycle* (San Francisco: Jossey-Bass), 291–338.

BROWN, L. A. (1981). *Innovation Diffusion: A New Perspective* (London and New York: Methuen).

BURTON, M. D., SORENSON, J. B., and BECKMAN, C. M. (2002). 'Coming from Good Stock: Career Histories and New Venture Formation', in M. Lounsbury and M. Ventresca (eds.), *Research in the Sociology of Organizations* (Oxford: Elsevier Science, JAI Press), xix. 229–62.

CAPPELLI, P. (2000). 'A Market-Driven Approach to Retaining Talent', *Harvard Business Review*, 78(1): 103–11.

—— (2004). 'Why do Firms Pay for College?', *Journal of Econometrics*, 121(1–2): 213–41.

COFF, R. (1997). 'Human Assets and Management Dilemmas: Coping with Hazards on the Road to Resource-Based Theory', *Academy of Management Review*, 22(2): 374–402.

COHEN, W. M., and LEVINTHAL, D. A. (1990). 'Absorptive Capacity: A New Perspective on Learning and Innovation', *Administrative Science Quarterly*, 35(1): 128–52.

DIERICKX, I., and COOL, K. (1989). 'Asset Stock Accumulation and Sustainability of Competitive Advantage', *Management Science*, 35(12): 1504–13.

DOERINGER, P. B., and PIORE, M. J. (1971). *Internal Labor Markets and Manpower Analysis* (Lexington, Mass.: Heath, Dore).

EHRENBERG, R. G., and SMITH, R. S. (1985). *Modern Labor Economics: Theory and Public Policy* (Glenview, Ill.: Scott, Foresman, & Co.).

GALANTER, M., and PALAY, T. (1991). *Tournament of Lawyers* (Chicago: University of Chicago Press).

GARDNER, T. M. (2005). 'Interfirm Competition for Human Resources: Evidence from the Software Industry', *Academy of Management Journal*, 48(2): 237–56.

GILSON, R. J., and MNOOKIN, R. H. (1989). 'Coming of Age in a Corporate Law Firm: The Economics of Associate Career Patterns', *Stanford Law Review*, 41: 567–95.

GROYSBERG, B., and ABRAHAMS, R. (2006). 'Lift Outs', *Harvard Business Review*, 84(12): 133–40.

GROYSBERG, B., LEE, L., and NANDA, A. (2008). 'Can they Take it with them? The Portability of Star Knowledge Workers' Performance', *Management Science*, 54(7): 1213–30.

HANNAN, M. T., and FREEMAN, J. H. (1977). 'The Population Ecology of Organizations', *American Journal of Sociology*, 82(5): 929–64.

——— (1984). 'Structural Inertia and Organizational Change', *American Sociological Review*, 49(2): 149–64.

——— (1989). *Organizational Ecology* (Cambridge, Mass.: Harvard University Press).

HILLMAN, R. W. (1999). *Hillman on Lawyer Mobility: The Law and Ethics of Partner Withdrawals and Law Firm Breakups* (2nd edn. New York: Aspen Law and Business).

HUCKMAN, R. S., and PISANO, G. P. (2006). 'The Firm Specificity of Individual Performance: Evidence from Cardiac Surgery', *Management Science*, 52(4): 473–88.

HYDE, A. (1998a). 'The Wealth of Shared Information: Silicon Valley's High-Velocity Labor Market, Endogenous Growth, and the Law of Trade Secrets'. URL: http:andromeda. rutgers.edu/~hyde/WEALTH.htm (accessed May 2008).

——— (1998b). 'How Silicon Valley Effectively Abolished Trade Secrets'. URL: http:andromeda. rutgers.edu/~hyde/WEALTH3.htm (accessed May 2008).

KOEGEL, O. E. (1953). *Walter S. Carter: Collector of Young Masters or the Progenitor of Many Law Firms* (New York: Round Table Press).

KRAATZ, M. S., and MOORE, J. H. (2002). 'Executive Migration and Institutional Change', *Academy of Management Journal*, 45(1): 120–43.

LAZEAR, E. P. (2003). *Firm-Specific Human Capital: A Skill-Weights Approach* (NBER Working Paper, 9679; Cambridge, Mass.: NBER; May).

LEBLEBICI, H., SALANCIK, G., COPAY, A., and KING, T. (1991). 'Institutional Change and the Transformation of Interorganizational Fields: An Organizational History of the U.S. Radio Broadcasting Industry', *Administrative Science Quarterly*, 36(3): 333–63.

LEPAK, D. P., and SNELL, S. A. (1999). 'The Human Resource Architecture: Toward a Theory of Human Capital Allocation and Development', *Academy of Management Review*, 24(1): 31–48.

LONG, J. S. (1978). 'Productivity and Academic Position in the Scientific Career', *American Sociological Review*, 43(6): 880–908.

NELSON, R. R., and WINTER, S. (1982). *An Evolutionary Theory of Economic Change* (Cambridge, Mass.: Belknap Press).

NONAKA, I. (1991). 'The Knowledge-Creating Company', *Harvard Business Review*, 69 (Nov.–Dec.): 96–104.

OLIVER, C. (1997). 'Sustainable Competitive Advantage: Combining Institutional and Resource-Based Views', *Strategic Management Journal*, 18(9): 697–713.

PETERAF, M. (1993). 'The Cornerstone of Competitive Advantage: The Resource-Based View', *Strategic Management Journal*, 14(3): 179–91.

PHILLIPS, D. J. (2002). 'A Genealogical Approach to Organizational Life Chances: The Parent–Progeny Transfer among Silicon Valley Law Firms, 1946–1996', *Administrative Science Quarterly*, 47(3): 474–506.

Rao, H., and Drazin, R. (2002). 'Overcoming Resource Constraints on Product Innovation by Recruiting Talent from Rivals: A Study of the Mutual Fund Industry, 1986–94', *Academy of Management Journal*, 45(3): 491–507.

Rumelt, R. P. (1984). 'Towards a Strategic Theory of the Firm', in R. B. Lamb (ed.), *Competitive Strategic Management* (Englewood Cliffs, NJ: Prentice-Hall), 566–70.

——(1987). 'Theory, Strategy, and Entrepreneurship', in D. Teece (ed.), *The Competitive Challenge: Strategies for Industrial Innovation and Renewal* (Cambridge, Mass.: Ballinger), 137–59.

Saxenian, A. (1994). *Regional Advantage: Culture and Competition in Silicon Valley* (Cambridge, Mass.: Harvard University Press).

Sherer, P. D. (2008). 'The Changed World of Large Law Firms and Their Lawyers: An Opportune Context for Organizational Researchers', in P. Cappelli (ed.), *Understanding Employment in the 21st Century* (Cambridge: Cambridge University Press), 179–222.

Sherer, P. D. (2009). 'The Rise and Development of Large US Corporate Law Firms', paper at the Annual Meeting of the Academy of Management, Chicago, Aug.

——and Lee, K. (2002). 'Institutional Change in Large Law Firms: A Resource Dependency and Institutional Perspective', *Academy of Management Journal*, 45(1): 102–19.

Song, J., Almeida, P., and Wu, G. (2003). 'Learning-by-Hiring: When is Mobility More Likely to Facilitate Interfirm Knowledge Transfer?', *Management Science*, 49(4): 351–65.

Swaine, R. T. (1946). *The Cravath Firm and its Predecessors: 1819–1947* (New York: Ad Press), i.

——(1948). *The Cravath Firm and its Predecessors: 1819–1947* (New York: Ad Press), ii.

Szulanski, G. (1996). 'Exploring External Stickiness: Impediments to the Transfer of Best Practice within the Firm', *Strategic Management Journal*, 17 (winter special issue): 27–43.

——Cappetta, R., and Jensen, R. J. (2004). 'When and How Trustworthiness Matters: Knowledge Transfer and the Moderating Effect of Causal Ambiguity', *Organization Science*, 15(5): 600–13.

Zucker, L. G. (1988). 'Where do Institutional Patterns Come from? Organizations as Actors in Social Systems', in L. G. Zucker (ed.), *Institutional Patterns and Organizations: Culture and Persistence* (Cambridge, Mass.: Ballinger), 23–49.

CHAPTER 23

HUMAN CAPITAL FORMATION REGIMES

STATES, MARKETS, AND HUMAN CAPITAL IN AN ERA OF GLOBALIZATION

SEÁN Ó RIAIN

23.1 THE POLITICS OF HUMAN CAPITAL IN US AND JAPANESE INDUSTRY

In 1970 Bob Cole carried out a survey of auto workers in Detroit and Yokohama with a view to comparing work organization and employment histories among male workers in US and Japanese industry. Despite Japanese interest in Western management methods and Taylorist production, Cole found that Japanese workers participated more actively in workplace decisions (although typically at the prompting of management), had more employment security, stayed longer in their jobs, were able to develop career paths within blue-collar work, and saw a close alignment between their interests and those of the company (Cole, 1979).

By the late 1980s Cole was studying the spread of small-group activities across industry in the US, with comparisons to Japan and to Sweden (Cole, 1991). A mere fifteen years after Cole's initial study, team and small-group processes were widespread in US industry—including the auto industry that Cole had studied in the early 1970s. Under pressure from Japanese competition, prompted by an international movement for 'total quality management', and stimulated by Japanese auto company investment in the US, American auto firms were adopting Japanese work practices.

But if there was convergence on teamwork, significant national differences remained. Teams in Japan were important vehicles for management to mobilize the knowledge and effort of workers, whereas in Sweden teams became bastions of worker solidarity and team processes were used to safeguard worker autonomy from management. In contrast to these collectivist experiences, participation in teams in the US was seen as a way to build up the record and skills that could be the basis of individual career advancement, and calls for worker commitment were not balanced by commitments to employment security (Lincoln and Kalleberg, 1991). Team-based production has proven to be compatible with the hierarchical corporate employment relations of leading Japanese firms, with the workplace solidarity and worker autonomy of Swedish workplaces, and with the individualized careers of US firms (Cole, 1991). The kinds of skill involved in 'teamwork' varied considerably across the three countries.

The production strategies of auto firms were deeply shaped by the different kinds of work arrangements that were possible in each country. Even when a degree of 'convergence' occurred as auto makers concentrated on a new paradigm of team management and quality production, significant differences remained—in employment relations and the workplace bargain, but also in the character of teamwork itself and the kinds of skill required to work successfully within each production regime. Despite the relative similarity in the initial training required of workers and in the technology used in the work process, these differences proved durable across a period when convergence in work organization did not simply evolve but was actively pursued.

Indeed, the differences that did emerge in skills and technology were in large part consequences rather than causes of the different social and institutional arrangements in each national industry. In some cases the production technology itself was redesigned to facilitate different relations of production—including the famous Volvo assembly plant in Sweden that allowed workers to build large parts of the car as a group (Berggren, 1992), and the more limited redesign of subsupply systems in Japan (Womack *et al.*, 1990).

Crucially, the possibilities for organizing production in each country were shaped by the patterns of human capital formation. In both Japan and Sweden, employers made greater investments in training workers and were more concerned to elicit and use workers' knowledge about the work process itself (Cole, 1991). In each case, managers' ability to pursue certain production strategies were both enabled and constrained by the characteristics of the regime within which they operated.

What do we learn about 'human capital' from this brief tour through auto production in the US, Japan, and Sweden? We learn that the phrase 'human capital' is only partly appropriate. Even if it makes sense to think of human beings and their attributes as capital, those skills and attributes are only partly 'liquid' as 'capital' across different social contexts. The nature of skill and knowledge itself becomes partly context-dependent—whether that context is the factory, the nation, the sector, or another social world of production. We also find that production strategies are themselves tied up with the training structures and skill patterns of human capital formation regimes. Those regimes in turn are embedded in broader structures of the political economy, including industrial relations and the structure of welfare provision and social protection.

Putting these together, we find that firm production strategies are shaped by the broader institutional framework of capitalism in their regional or national context. Swedish social democracy makes worker solidarity in teams more likely, and is sustained by it. Japanese group-oriented cultural practices are both mobilized and reinforced in manager-controlled teams (Cole, 1979). But we also see that significant changes happen. Even within the relatively stable world of auto manufacturing, there were significant changes, including towards teamwork, and transnational influences often operated in directions which we might not have expected. In an era of more rapid sectoral and occupational change, we can expect even greater flux in human capital formation regimes, with important implications for managerial production strategies.

23.2 Contextualizing Human Capital

In an era when much has been said about the information economy, the knowledge society, the creative classes, and more, it has taken a surprisingly long time for studies of human capital to figure strongly in studies of states, markets, and economic growth and development. Similarly, studies of human capital have had relatively little to say about the institutional and political contexts of human capital formation and use, and they have largely been focused on the engagement between individual employees and employer organizations.

Economic studies of development have now firmly switched their analysis of capital accumulation from physical to human terms. The knowledge and skills of workers are increasingly seen as the critical factor in firm performance, productivity, and innovation. In particular, progressive management and public policy analysts focus on the formation and reward of human capital as central to a 'high road' model of firm, industry, and economic development. For example, intense debates regarding the merits of different national models of auto production raged among managers, trade unionists, and policy-makers in the 1980s and 1990s.

However, many studies of human capital and growth operate with an attenuated concept of human capital. Under the typical 'growth accounting' conceptualization, national economies contain 'stocks' of human capital, and skills themselves are located firmly within individuals and are largely portable across institutions and contexts. Important debates on the role of human capital policies in tackling inequality reveal the diversity of forms that human capital formation can take (Carneiro and Heckman, 2003). Many of the chapters in this volume analyze the complex interactions between human capital and other forms of capital, the organization of the firm, and elements of the organizational environment. However, once human capital enters the study of growth, this institutional complexity and insight into the situatedness of human capital is lost. One of the most telling attempts to extend the human capital framework in studies of economic development is that of Amartya Sen's 'capabilities' approach. Sen points out that the human capital framework is typically interested in the 'human qualities that can be employed as "capital" in production (the way that physical capital is)' (Sen, 1999: 293). However, for Sen this is only one element of development, as the expansion of human capital and human capabilities will also add directly to development by enhancing peoples' capabilities to live the lives they wish to lead. 'Human capital' captures only some of the human qualities relevant to development.

Most significantly for our purposes, Sen implies that the narrower conception of human capital, linked specifically to economic productivity, cannot be separated from the broader structures of particular human capital formation regimes that shape the character of labor itself. In order to understand human capital and economic production, we need to understand the changing forms and politics of labor, and the social formations and institutions that are associated with them. 'Human capital' therefore overstates the liquidity of this form of capital.

Peter Evans pushes Sen's framework still further (Evans, 2002). Evans argues that Sen remains wedded to a notion of capabilities as inhering in individuals, but that in practice any individual's ability to be productive, or to live the life they wish to lead, will depend significantly on their ability to act with others towards that goal. Human capabilities—and human capital—become collective and social, not only in their causes and consequences but in their very character. 'Teamwork skills' will be quite different in the Swedish and Japanese auto industries and, for example, valuing co-workers' perspectives over managers' may be a skill in Sweden, a deficit in Japan, and a matter of strategic self-interest in the USA. Lave and Wenger (1991) point out that entry into any trade depends upon the accumulation of certain skills and practices, and also upon the ability to be a successful member of the 'community of practice' within that trade. To be a carpenter—or indeed an economist or a sociologist—you must be able to culturally act like a carpenter, as well as to work with wood—or equations, field notes, concepts, and theories.

None of this is to say that there is no individual component to skill. However, what is clear is an emerging perspective that not only recognizes the growing importance of human capital in studies of capital accumulation, growth, and development, but goes beyond this to rethink the concept of human capital itself. Skills are themselves defined by social and institutional contexts (Ashton, 1999), and human capabilities not only give workers new human capital, but simultaneously change the character of labor and the social and political engagements of these workers. The individual, social, and institutional dimensions of human capital are interdependent.

A manager's concern will be not only with the technical skills required—although these will also vary across economies—but also with the capacity to work within the social worlds of production. As Ashton (1999) argues in a review of studies in the *Journal of Education and Work* in the 1990s:

> It is clear that we can no longer hope to understand the process of skill formation if we restrict our analysis to either the sociologists' traditional concern with the social construction of skills or the economists' use of the term to treat skill as an unproblematic attribute of the individual acquired through education or training. Here the big step forward is to conceptualise skill as a function of a broader set of social relations. (Ashton, 1999: 347)

The content of skills may depend on social relations and institutional contexts, but this does not mean that the meaning of skill is completely fluid, as discussions of the construction of skill sometimes suggest. In fact, the stability of social and institutional relations provides that same stability to skills as workers and managers develop shared understandings about work practices—even where there is conflict. Recent economic analysis of the firm places the specificity of human capital at the heart of what a firm is, with Rajan and Zingales (1998) defining the firm as where critical resources are brought into a complementary relationship with specialized human capital. In such a view, human capital is always tied into a broader set of relations and resources. The importance of the 'stabilizing' institutional context is such that it explains why it is so difficult to change human capital formation regimes or to transplant elements from one regime to another. Indeed, a vast amount of literature has explored the challenges of 'transplanting' Japanese production practices to the US auto industry (for example, Adler, 1992). To 'transplant' production strategies from one context to another typically requires not only restructuring workplace relations, but also changing broader institutional forces such as patterns of training, employment security, and more.

23.3 PRODUCTION STRATEGIES AND SKILL FORMATION REGIMES

As managers go about their daily work, they typically see themselves as responding to the technical and economic demands of their particular industry or sector. However, even within sectors our discussion of the auto industry shows that there are clear national differences in the kinds of production strategy that firms pursue.

Drawing on an EU-wide survey from 2000, Lorenz and Valeyre (2007) identify two new models of production across Europe, in addition to the more established 'Taylorist' assembly line control (without teams) and 'traditional' models of craft organization and/or direct managerial control. The 'learning' model is a relatively decentralized model where teams have a great deal of autonomy in controlling their own work and have strong employment security guarantees. The 'lean' model is a more hierarchical model which uses teams extensively but where managers more tightly regulate individual or group work pace, as well as offering fewer employment security guarantees.

These two models of team-based production have grown in importance, suggesting that there has been a significant overall shift towards the European and Japanese inspired models of production, even as employment security has come under threat, as global competition has increased, and as unions have been weakened. However, each of these approaches (and the others that the research documents) involves significant differences in human capital requirements and mobilization.

These models are linked to particular occupations (particularly professions and other skilled occupations) and to certain industries (predominantly high-tech and knowledge based). Both learning and lean models are associated with higher levels of training and employee representation than in the other models. Firms also often combine lean and learning approaches to HR and work organization, either by 'mixing' elements of the models or by applying them to different groups of workers within the firm (see Chapter 13 above).

However, there are also distinct national patterns. Even controlling for occupational, sectoral, and other effects, the 'learning model' predominates in the Scandinavian and continental European economies. The 'lean' model is more common in the liberal economies of the UK and Ireland, as well as in the Mediterranean economies (Lorenz and Valeyre, 2007). Evidence from the USA suggests that the 'lean' model predominates there also.

It is tempting to interpret these national differences in terms of whether countries emphasize general skills that are portable across workplaces and industries, or skills that are more specific to organizations or sectors (Iversen, 2005). The composition of skills clearly matters. German and Japanese workers typically had much deeper sets of industry-specific skills than their US counterparts, while workers in liberal economies tended to rely more heavily on general skills, enabling higher levels of mobility (Thelen, 2004). However, this may go too far in attributing institutional differences to skill composition when in fact institutional histories have a greater independent effect than this allows. O'Connell and Jungblut (2008) point out that while analysts rely heavily on the general–specific distinction, employers have much less respect for it, paying for both general and specific training. In addition, both employers and employees often find it difficult to say whether particular skills are general or specific.

There is a possibility here, with trends such as the commercialization of many professions, the international standardization of knowledge and standards, and the growth of transnational organizations and professional communities, that many 'specific skills' (such as knowledge of particular bodies of legal practice, or of laboratory techniques) are now increasingly general.[1] Furthermore, it may be increasingly important for workers to be able to possess a body of general skills that they can apply relatively quickly to quite specific sets of circumstances (such as the kinds of work that software engineers and craft workers carry out). The distinction remains tricky. For example, while craft workers are often seen as among those workers with the highest level of specific skills measured in terms of job titles or categories (see for example, Iversen, 2005), their skills are in practice highly portable across a wide range of manufacturing and construction industries—in many cases, much more so than the apparently more generally skilled professionals such as lawyers and accountants, whose skills are often confined to very specific areas of practice.

Within countries, there is evidence that even in the liberal USA with high levels of worker mobility, it is those firms that can attract highly skilled workers but then retain and develop them through long employee tenure that are the best placed competitively (Brown *et al.*, 2006). Similarly, data on literacy and educational outcomes suggest that German and Swedish workers are much more highly skilled in general terms than many comparable US workers—regardless of their level of specific skills (see for example, Pontusson, 2005). The question of whether skills are seen as general or specific—or more concretely, whether employers will hire in workers based on particular skill sets—may be as much an effect of institutionalized social bargains as the basis of them. The kinds of work being carried out and the skill mix of workers will probably affect HR practices—with, for example, workers with unique skills that are of high strategic value to the organization being managed through 'high commitment' models, while workers with less important and more easily available skills are managed through contract work and compliance-based HR (see Chapter 13 above). However, Bob Cole's research and the broader literature on work organization also suggest that HR management practices that value and reward workers will typically increase the strategic value of workers' contributions, relatively independent of the particular skills they possess or utilize on the job.

The mix of public and private spending on education at different levels also profoundly shapes the skill levels and distribution of skills among the workforce, even at the level of basic literacy (Pontusson, 2005). This is all the more important given that the decisive educational experiences over the life course are in childhood and adolescence, despite policy and scholarly focus on life-long and workplace learning (Carneiro and Heckman, 2007; Mueller and Jacob, 2008). While skill levels clearly enable and constrain different production strategies, a narrower distribution of skills should promote support for widespread upskilling, while a polarized skill distribution will encourage the most skilled to support more elitist approaches (Iversen and Stephens, 2008; Pontusson, 2005).

Industrial relations and other systems of regulating employment are also inter-dependent with human capital formation. In particular, coordinated industrial relations allow firms and workers to support worker participation and make invest-ments in skill acquisition that are much more difficult in more uncertain, less coordinated contexts (Iversen, 2005). Employment protection legislation—ease and cost of hiring and firing, and so on—is also clearly linked to production strate-gies. Lorenz and Valeyre (2007) find that the learning model of work organization is most prevalent in those countries with strongest employment protection, while the lean model is most prevalent in Ireland and the UK, with the weakest levels of protection. It also seems likely that the widespread decline in unionization levels is linked to the adoption of particular forms of production strategies, including 'lean' work organization.

Human capital formation regimes are a critical intervening mechanism between industrial relations and production strategies. Human capital formation patterns both enable and constrain managers' production strategies—despite the tendency to view all protections for workers as constraining on employers. In fact, analysts have long been interested in how certain economies were able to sustain higher levels of wages, welfare, and social protection while remaining competitive in export markets. In the 1980s the critical cases in this debate were Germany and Japan, both international manufacturing powerhouses that offered many employees benefits that were assumed in the USA and other liberal economies to be incompatible with economic competitiveness.

However, others showed that it was precisely these conditions that allowed German and Japanese firms to pursue different, 'high road' competitive strategies. Streeck (1991) pointed out that German firms could pursue a strategy of 'diversified quality production' because their workers were more skilled and more flexible in shifting between tasks and technologies. This in turn was linked to their job secu-rity, which lessened the risk of losing work due to technological or process changes, and to their higher levels of in-firm and apprenticeship-based training. Streeck (1991, 1997) argued that it was precisely the 'rigidities' in the formation and mobili-zation of human capital that acted as 'beneficial constraints' on German employers, both forcing employers to pursue high-quality, high-margin competitive strategies and enabling them to do so. The 'quality' of human capital—although essential—was only one element of the complex system that tied the interests of workers and firms together into an institutionalized set of production strategies.

The place of vocational education has attracted particular attention, given the success of the German system in developing specific skills that were able to support high-quality production. The significance of the German system was not only the development of particular skills but also the institutional foundations upon which it was built. Indeed, part of the significance of vocational education in Germany is that it is a platform, not only for skill formation, but for institution-building—a good in its own right. Kraak *et al.* point out that the German system rests upon the presence of firms pursuing high-quality production, intermediate institutions through which employers and unions can discuss wage setting and skills standards, a mix of cooperation and competition, and a pay structure that has a strong middle class that can afford to pay high rates of marginal tax to fund the system (2007: 49). These are conditions for the reproduction of the German 'dual system', but the vocational education system is a crucial mechanism through which these institutional arrangements are themselves reproduced and renegotiated.

Similarly, Dore (1986) argued that Japanese firms benefited from a set of historically constructed 'flexible rigidities' that generated enormously high levels of dependence upon and commitment to large employers on the part of Japanese workers, in the context of very high levels of employment security (and indeed relatively stable relations with suppliers and other firms). While the Japanese firms' production strategies were significantly more hierarchical than the German and Swedish models of quality production (Cole, 1991), the underlying connection between skills, work organization, and employment security was very similar. The debates of the 1980s around the pursuit of German and Japanese 'high road' models of work organization, compared to the 'low road' model adopted by the US or the 'low skill equilibrium' of the UK (Finegold and Soskice, 1988), were based on these fundamental arguments about skill levels and their institutional contexts.

Some analysts now suggest that given the fragmentation of industrial structures and national economies generated by global production networks, such 'national models' may have had their day as human capital has entered into global markets more fully. As unionization rates decline in almost all countries, this may also drive 'convergence'. The revival of the US and the export success of US high tech seemed to undermine the more ambitious claims for the supremacy of the high-security/high-skill models of production (Hall and Soskice, 2001). However, the evidence from Cole's research and from Lorenz and Valeyre's analysis shows that national differences and institutional effects remain significant—even on this new terrain. While the specific examples of Japanese and German manufacturing may appear less relevant, the basic point still stands: constraints may prove to be beneficial in encouraging upgrading, and institutional rigidities may enable production flexibilities. In fact, national institutional configurations are mediating the effects of trends such as deunionization, and well-institutionalized systems of social protection and investment have developed supports that are somewhat independent of the balance of workplace power that helped to form them.

Lorenz and Valeyre find, for example, that while the relative dominance of learning or lean models in a national economy does not appear to be tied to R&D intensity it is affected by the degree of employment protection, where high protection promotes the learning model. Despite the shift across different national models towards team production, linked to training, there remain significant differences in the degree of autonomy and security afforded to workers under each model and in the different national economies (Lorenz and Valeyre, 2007). These differences have significant social effects—research in the US shows the importance of autonomy and security as dimensions of worker satisfaction (Hodson, 2001)—but they also have significant economic effects. The prevalence of the learning model is also associated with higher levels of patent applications (a useful, although imperfect, proxy of innovative activity), representing a significant economic return (Lorenz and Valeyre, 2007).

23.4 SOCIAL PROTECTION AND THE POLITICS OF HUMAN CAPITAL

Production strategies, therefore, tie together human capital and skill formation with questions of work organization and competitive strategy. This is familiar territory for many managers who will come into contact with these institutions quite regularly. However, managers are less likely to see the relevance of the embedding of these human capital formation regimes within the broader politics of social protection and the welfare state.

Against Esping-Andersen's (1990) identification of the welfare state with 'decommodification' and protection from the market, Iversen (2005) argues that welfare states also represent systems of investment in the social foundations of the economy. As such, welfare spending may significantly benefit employers, and particularly those employers who are highly exposed to risks—despite their tendency to resist such spending, even when it is in their interests (Swenson, 1991, 2002; Mares, 2003). For Iversen and others, the form of social protection shapes workers' ability to accumulate particular kinds of skill, which in turn shapes firms' production strategies, as we have seen.

Huber and Stephens (2001) argue that welfare states (broadly conceived) form 'welfare production regimes', with crucial elements of the welfare state such as income replacement, education and training, public-sector employment, pensions, and childcare profoundly shaping both the human capital that workers bring to the firm and the contexts within which they make employment decisions and bargain with employers. Most recent work has concentrated on the role of the welfare state in providing social insurance against risks in the market—through welfare levels, replacement rates, pension coverage and levels, and so on (Iversen, 2005; Iversen and Stephens, 2008). Workers with specific skills—such as the German, Japanese, and Swedish manufacturing workers discussed above—are likely to have a greater interest in systems of social protection that buffer them against an industrial downturn, given the lack of alternative options elsewhere in the economy and the high costs of losing employment (Iversen, 2005). Of course, all workers have an interest in relatively high levels of social protection, although more highly skilled workers will be less willing to pay for them, given their own strong position in the market. There should, nonetheless, be a close tie between specific skill formation and social protection.

However, the connection between skill formation and social protection is somewhat more complex than this suggests—particularly given the blurred line between specific and general skills. This is further complicated when the position of women workers is considered: 'Specifically, whereas specific-skills regimes tend to reduce disparities among workers based on education and training, they tend to exacerbate disparities based on the gendered division of labor, in the realms of both paid work (Estévez-Abe, 2006) and household work (Iversen, 2005). General-skills countries, on the other hand, foster greater class disparities and weaker gender disparities' (McCall and Orloff, 2005: 162). This is largely because in specific skill production regimes there are high costs to labor turnover for the workers concerned, and women workers' work lives are typically characterized by high rates of turnover (due to other highly gendered family processes). The emphasis on risk and social protection in the recent research has neglected how the welfare state shapes human capital through its contribution to social reproduction. In the Scandinavian welfare states in particular, the state is heavily involved in the provision of public services in health and social services. While these services have less direct influence on skill acquisition, they significantly shape the mobilization of that human capital—particularly through shaping female labor force participation, and through influencing health and labor market inactivity (Esping-Andersen, 1999).

Shifts in the system of human capital formation will therefore have ramifications across the industrial and welfare systems. Changes in the structure of welfare states will shape the possibilities for creating and mobilizing human capital—whether that be through shaping women's labor force participation, worker investments in skills, managerial guarantees of employment security and social protection, or other factors.

23.5 THE POLITICS OF HUMAN CAPITAL FORMATION

Therefore, human capital formation regimes are not shaped simply by the demands of economic efficiency or institutional functionality but also by politics. The politics of capitalist economies are heavily shaped by the relationship between the socioeconomic demand for capital accumulation and the sociopolitical demand for legitimation of the mode of development (Offe, 1984; Scharpf, 1999). Human capital formation provides skills for accumulation and provides rank ordering for class (and other forms of) inequality and hierarchy. The process can also act to legitimize economic processes through socialization and through legitimizing and naturalizing particular patterns of hierarchy and inequality.

Studies in the new political economy of skill formation have pushed forward our understanding of the social interests and political struggles that shaped the institutionalization of different training systems. Thelen (2004) contrasts the training systems of Germany and Japan, with strong vocational systems and an emphasis on specific skills, with the training regimes of the US and UK where training is general and relatively weakly developed. The origins of these systems lie not in the functional demands of particular sectoral mixes within each economy, but in the resolution of the struggles between employers, skilled workers, and the state in each economy. Where artisans retained their power within the industrial system, craft and vocational training systems were strengthened, whereas they became the focus of class struggle and withered in the liberal economies where craft workers were drawn firmly into the ambit of managerial control and workplace hierarchy. Significant differences remain between Germany and Japan, however. Where German craft workers were able to retain a degree of autonomy which meant that their training system transferred to the industrial workplace, Japanese craft workers were incorporated into a new corporate-dominated system that nonetheless preserved their system of privilege (Thelen, 2004; Streeck and Thelen, 2005; Thelen and Kume, 1999; Dore, 1986). But if the origins of each training system lay in class and state politics, their long-term economic impact was significant, with each shaping the production strategies of each economy. The nineteenth-century struggles in the UK over artisan workers in the factory system were still played out in Soskice's 'low-skill equilibrium' in the 1980s and beyond (Finegold and Soskice, 1988). Any managerial, union, profession, or state effort to remake the training system will depend upon the outcome of similar struggles.

Nor is the politics of skill formation simply a matter of the historical origins of training systems. Iversen and Stephens (2008) observe three 'worlds of human capital formation', consisting of the various elements noted in the welfare production regimes but underpinned by different sets of class compromises and electoral politics. The power resources of labor (skilled and unskilled) and of capital matter in shaping skill formation. So too does electoral politics. Proportional representation systems favor the left and contribute to more egalitarian and more coordinated worlds of human capital formation, while majoritarian systems strengthen parties of the right and the liberal regimes that emphasize general skills and see higher levels of inequality. Party histories matter too. Christian democratic parties play a very particular role in mediating a vocational compromise between employers and labor through their emphasis on social compromises within different sectors of the economy. Particular managerial strategies for production and human capital formation will be more likely to succeed in different kinds of political systems.

Nor are managers and employers inevitably supportive of liberal regimes. Iversen and Stephens (2008) draw on welfare production regime theory to show that employers can develop an interest in maintaining any of the various skill formation regimes, as these regimes become enabling elements in their production strategies. As they note with regard to social democratic regimes:

> Social equality fosters high levels of human capital (both general and specific skills) especially at the bottom end of the skill distribution, which in turn reinforces social equality. The linkage between human capital and the welfare state is essential in understanding how countries with high levels of equality and redistribution have also been able to succeed economically. It also suggests why employers who rely on skilled workers sometimes, but certainly not always, support policies and institutions that are usually associated with the left. (Iversen and Stephens, 2008: 601–2)

Furthermore, this is not simply a question of political origins being reinforced by functional interdependencies. Iversen (2005) argues that workers develop interests in maintaining particular aspects of the human capital formation regimes as their skill profile is shaped by those same regimes. He argues that workers with specific skills will be more supportive of the welfare state as their demand for social protection will be higher. There is a link here between specific skills and the social insurance function of the welfare state that generates political support and legitimization for more generous welfare regimes. This version of the dynamic may be cast too narrowly. After all, there are problems with the conceptualization of specific skills, and welfare states do much more than provide social insurance. However, the central point that political 'feedback loops' exist that can reinforce human capital formation regimes is a critical one. This is only reinforced if we take a broader, more sociological position and note the variety of diverse interests which different classes and other social groups develop in systems of education and training. Given the central role of these systems in reproducing class inequalities, as avenues of mobility, and as institutions of broader social legitimization, struggles over education and training are likely to be intense and to profoundly shape human capital formation regimes. In the right social and political context, managers of highly skilled workers may find themselves supporting expansion of state spending on social protection and social reproduction, while their workers—particularly those with marketable and transferable skills—may find themselves inclined to oppose such measures.

From the historical origins of human capital formation regimes, to their current institutional and political conditions, to the interests and commitments of those incorporated within them, human capital formation is an intensely political process, constantly being negotiated between state, market, and labor. Local negotiations over new production strategies may be shaped by all of these various levels of institutional context.

23.6 COMPARATIVE POLITICAL ECONOMY AND HUMAN CAPITAL FORMATION REGIMES

We can summarize these various elements and the primary interactions among them. Figure 23.1 provides a schematic outline of the relations between production strategies, welfare production regimes, and the political dynamics of human capital formation regimes. These connections have been developed above, but it is worth noting that by incorporating human capital into the comparative political economy of states and markets, we open up the analysis of labor and capital themselves, their character and composition, and their identities and interests. For this reason, the chart notes that the dominant production strategies shape the kinds of firm that exist in the economy and that come to play a role in shaping the politics of human capital formation.

Furthermore, while labor has often entered comparative political economy as a largely undifferentiated category, a more sustained focus on human capital formation suggests that labor is both formed by, and exerts an influence upon, the politics of human capital. At the end of the day, labor enters this institutional

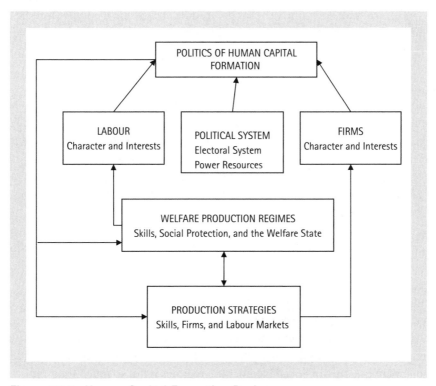

Figure 23.1. Human Capital Formation Regimes

politics not simply in search of skills and income but also to preserve and occasionally transform its own character and ways of working and living. These are powerful forces that generate interests in both continuity and change within human capital formation regimes. While this representation is highly schematic, it may allow different actors—managers, unionists, policy-makers, and others—to locate themselves within the typical structure of regimes and the dynamics that shape them.

This structure of embeddedness explains why it is so difficult to simply 'reform' training. For example, to reform US education and training would involve part reforming firms, the welfare state, and industrial relations, and would affect gender and class relations.

We can now briefly go on to apply the framework developed to the various kinds of human capital formation regimes. Here we explore in most detail the three regimes that Iversen and Stephens (2008) identify, building on Esping-Andersen's classic distinction among three worlds of welfare capitalism. Table 23.1 provides some key indicators of differences among Iversen and Stephens' three sets of regimes.

Liberal regimes (see Figure 23.2) are characterized by weak public spending on primary and pre-school education, despite strong evidence of high long-run returns to this investment even in liberal institutional contexts (Carneiro and Heckman, 2005). Government spending benefits the middle class while the upper middle class spends heavily on the private educational system, and particularly on higher education (Iversen and Stephens, 2008; Pontusson, 2005). There are widespread inequities in educational and literacy outcomes, with the level of literacy for the bottom quartile exceptionally low (Pontusson, 2005).

Liberal economies are typically, therefore, characterized by a 'skills problem' despite the presence of the prestigious US higher education system and a class of highly educated professionals. Similarly, while there are significant elements of knowledge-intensive production, company production strategies outside these clusters tend to pursue the 'low road', and workers work primarily under lean rather than learning work organizations, with relatively little employment protection.

The model becomes self-reinforcing through the resistance of the more highly skilled to paying taxes to support broader efforts at upskilling, and the weakness of the channels for acquiring skills and the incentives to invest in human capital for the less skilled. Indeed, the expansion of low-wage services appears to be linked to higher income inequality (Iversen, 2005), such that this may become a difficult pattern to break as wealthier families become increasingly dependent upon low-wage services for social reproduction needs.

Social Democratic regimes (see Figure 23.3) are characterized by strong public investment in social services of all kinds, including all levels of education. Indeed, the distinctive feature of Social Democratic regimes is not so much their redistributive tax system (which is less redistributive than Christian Democratic regimes) but

Table 23.1. Key Differences along Major Dimensions of Human Capital Formation Regimes

	Liberal	Social Democratic	Christian Democratic
Key cases	US, UK	Sweden, Denmark, Norway, Finland	Germany
Production Strategies			
Model of work organization	Lean	Learning	Learning
Knowledge intensity of Industry (R&D, patents, and so on)	Low (except for parts of US economy)	High	Medium
Welfare Production Regimes			
Education and Training Day care/pre-school spending	Low (extensive private spending)	High	Low
Primary and secondary	Medium	High	Medium
Higher education	Medium (extensive private spending)	Medium/high	Medium
Active labor market policy	Low	High	Low
Vocational	Low	High	High
Social Protection Income replacement	Low	High	High
Public spending on social programs	Low	High	High
Employment protection	Low	High	High
Coordination of Economy Union density	Low	High	Low
Collective bargaining coverage	Low	High	High
Macroeconomic coordination	Low	High	Medium/high
Political Conditions			
Electoral system	Majoritarian	PR	PR

(continued)

Table 23.1. Continued

	Liberal	Social Democratic	Christian Democratic
Historically dominant parties	Liberal	Social democratic	Christian democratic
Role of unions in national politics	Weak	Strong	Medium
Outcomes			
Employment growth in services in 1990s	High	Medium	Medium (but losses in manufacturing)
Literacy of lowest 20%	Low	High	High
Inequality in literacy levels	High	Low	Low
Wage inequality	High	Low	Medium

Source: Derived from Amable, 2004; Iversen and Stephens, 2008; Pontusson, 2005.

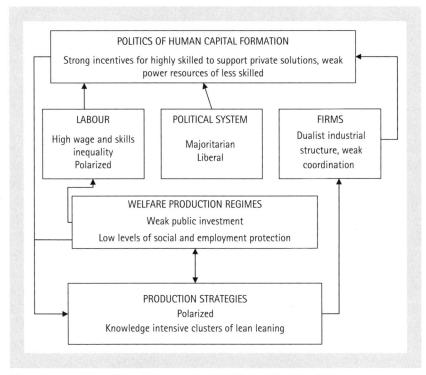

Figure 23.2. The Liberal Human Capital Formation Regime

their strong emphasis on extensive, egalitarian, and high-quality public services (Huber and Stephens, 2001; Pontusson, 2005). In addition, vocational education is strong, although more closely tied to the general education system than in Christian Democratic countries, fostering further cross-class solidarity. Active labor-market policies and extensive public childcare and family-friendly policies act together to promote high rates of labor-force participation, including among women.

This creates a labor force that is highly solidaristic in comparative terms, as there are few 'outsiders', households have ties to multiple occupations, wage and skills inequality is low, and economic sectors are not highly polarized. This in turn generates political support for the high-skill regime of human capital formation. As firms have little opportunity to pursue low-cost 'low road' production strategies, quality production for export and high-quality services dominate among firms. However, a degree of flexibility is provided for firms—through internal functional flexibility (Berggren, 1992) and through a structure of social protection that emphasizes income rather than employment protection. Strong public services and education and training provision both pressure firms into adopting 'high-road strategies' that can sustain the cost base of a highly educated, secure workforce, while at the same time providing the skills that can enable them to pursue such strategies successfully. The

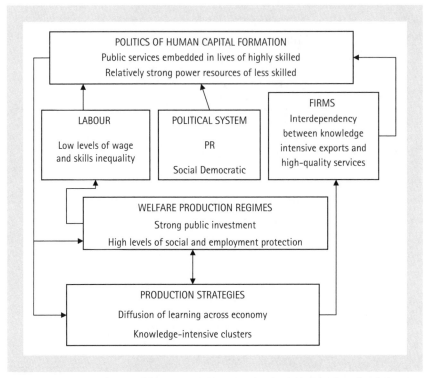

Figure 23.3. The Social Democratic Human Capital Formation Regime

economic benefits of the system are vital to its reproduction, as the investments involved are significant.

Christian Democratic regimes (see Figure 23.4) are also characterized by strong public investment, but labor force participation tends to be lower than in Social Democratic economies, with more emphasis on the male breadwinner model. A strong emphasis on vocational training to support high-quality production is central to the economic system, placing human capital formation at the center of the Christian Democratic system. In addition, these systems rely more heavily on income transfers through taxation and welfare to produce egalitarian outcomes (Pontusson, 2005), with the well-paid skilled manufacturing workers' ability to pay high marginal taxes from the middle of the income distribution central to this model (Iversen and Stephens, 2008). While there is relatively low mobility from the working to middle classes in Germany, those working classes' working conditions and income are significantly better than comparable workers elsewhere (Erikson and Goldthorpe, 2001). Those workers with high levels of specific skills are therefore central to the Christian Democratic economies, and their interest in strong systems of social and employment protection are central to the politics of a solidaristic welfare state.

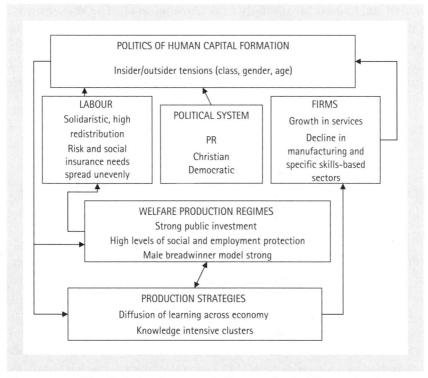

Figure 23.4. The Christian Democratic Human Capital Formation Regime

Nonetheless, Christian Democratic economies can produce stronger insider–outsider divisions than in Social Democratic regimes, generating potential coalitions that might support alternative models, and placing great economic and political emphasis on the skilled working class. This can generate intergenerational and gender tensions that may grow, given the substantial declines in manufacturing employment in the Christian Democratic economies (Pontusson, 2005).

While these three models are not the only forms of human capital formation regimes in contemporary capitalism, they capture many of the most important variations. The East Asian model is probably closest to the Christian Democratic model, with its emphasis on the specific training of a group of highly skilled workers, within a broader context that emphasizes relatively high degrees of educational attainment and a strong emphasis on the male breadwinner model. However, the leading employers (whether as stand-alone firms or as business groups) play a much more prominent role and exert more control over the work process (Cole, 1991) and over careers (Lincoln and Kalleberg, 1990). There are also variants of the Liberal model. While the Mediterranean regimes are also characterized by low-road production strategies and low levels of public investment, they are distinguished by a greater degree of familial and public social protections (albeit at a low level of funding).

Education and training are relatively weak (Amable, 2004). The 'wage-earner' welfare states of Australia and New Zealand are also cousins of the Liberal model. However, in these cases an historically stronger labor party and union movement has won greater protections for wage-earners, with many benefits that were historically universal becoming more closely linked to pay-related social insurance (Huber and Stephens, 2001).

23.7 CONTINUITY AND CHANGE IN HUMAN CAPITAL REGIMES

The analysis above suggests that human capital formation regimes are complex systems with powerful, mutually enabling and therefore self-reinforcing dynamics (Huber and Stephens, 2001). These regimes are both difficult to form and durable once formed, as they are embedded in their own institutional structures, are interlinked with other institutional and policy realms, and become built into workers' and firms' identities and interests. Some analyses within the new political economy of skill formation underestimate this by overemphasizing narrow interests based on skills and risk (for example, Iversen, 2005) and by underestimating the sociological dimensions of how workers become committed to these institutional systems (group formation, class and labor identity, status politics and attainment, institutional durability, embeddedness of skill in social relations, and others discussed above). The manager, labor leader, or state official seeking to implement training reform might be forgiven for feeling a little weary at the thought.

Nonetheless, such regimes do change over time, and despite their durability they face particularly demanding challenges at present. Changes in work, occupational structures, gender relations, global patterns of trade and business organization, and the growth of the service economy, all pose significant challenges and destabilize existing patterns of institutionalization within human capital formation regimes. Here it is important to avoid the assumption that liberal regimes are inherently better able to respond to changes or to assume that the only changes at work issue from the demands of global competitiveness. Most research suggests that while there are significant pressures, there continue to be significant institutional divergences (Thelen and van Wijnbergen, 2003; Huber and Stephens, 2001). Transformations in skill formation regimes will be mediated through existing institutions, and non-liberal institutions can deliver benefits to business despite the apparent constraining effects (Thelen, 2004; Streeck and Thelen, 2005). Politics will continue to play a central role.

Nonetheless, current structural transformations in the global economy are challenging existing human capital formation regimes. The service economy is challenging our understanding of human capital itself, while the feminization and internationalization of the labor force is providing new and different sources of human capital. In addition to profoundly affecting firms and education and training systems, these changes also challenge the coherence, effectiveness, and regulatory bite of national regimes. The rest of this section briefly examines the major developments along each of these key dimensions of human capital formation regimes.

23.7.1 New Forms of Human Capital: Service and Knowledge Economy

Echoing Peter Evans' argument about the collective dimensions of skills, Ashton has argued that there is a

serious possibility that human capital theory was very much a product of the Fordist techniques which dominated the productive system of the old western industrialized societies, especially those of the US and UK. There the use of narrow, tightly circumscribed job descriptions, a highly specialised division of labour and command and control hierarchies, led to the treatment of skill as an attribute of the individual which could be acquired through courses almost as an individual possession and then used in the workplace for which the individual received an appropriate return. Ashton suggests that 'the concept of collective intelligence may be more appropriate for the emergent high skills systems of the twenty first century' (1999: 348)

We have already seen that different national models of work organization emphasize teamwork and worker autonomy and self-organization to different degrees. However, we also see a secular shift toward such modes of work organization (Lorenz and Valeyre, 2007). Such systems of 'co-production' appear to be particularly closely tied to knowledge work (Benkler, 2006) and yet appear to be compatible with Liberal, Social Democratic, and Christian Democratic modes of social organization (Cole, 1991). It remains unclear how these models will reconstitute themselves to accommodate these changes in work.

Equally, the shift to a service economy suggests new challenges for human capital formation regimes. It has been suggested that new modes of working place greater emphasis on 'soft skills' associated with 'emotion work', although it must be remembered that the industrial era also (often brutally) inculcated new modes of thinking, feeling, and behavior in the factory regime that were quite alien until they became institutionalized and reproduced through the mass education system (Bowles and Gintis, 1976).

Occupational change is bringing a shift from craft to professionals as the key skilled class around which human capital formation regimes are built and institutionalized. Ironically, the new political economy of skill formation has been heavily influenced by the systems constructed for skilled workers in the industrial twentieth century at a time when that era is in decline. In fact, it could be argued that the literature in this area has not had enough to say regarding white-collar education and its varieties. The focus on skilled industrial workers covers a failure to examine the character of professional skills with sufficient care (Iversen, 2005). Furthermore, the comparative political economy of training has been much more developed than that of higher education, where efforts to shape the labor force are equally, and increasingly, significant. For example, in high technology, Ireland has pursued a sustained attempt to construct a new technical labor force, Taiwan has worked to Americanize its labor force, and US higher education plays a key role in the human capital formation of high-technology labor forces for a number of economies (Ó Riain, 2004). The potential tensions between the ethics of professionalism and commercialism are increasingly shaping the work lives of white-collar workers and their managers' production strategies—for example, how software developers think about their work and skills varies according to whether they see themselves as market-led contract workers or technical professionals (Barley and Kunda, 2004).

23.7.2 New Sources of Human Capital: Feminization of the Labor Force

These changes are also associated with shifts in the character of workers themselves. Systems initially built around the male breadwinner and the family wage will be particularly challenged by the feminization of human capital. Estevez-Abe (1999) argues that institutions that encourage male investment in specific skills exacerbate occupational sex segregation (see also McCall and Orloff, 2005). However, Charles (2005) finds that these skill-based differences are less significant than the emergence of new service occupations and persistent gender ideologies regarding gender-appropriate skills and activities in perpetuating sex segregation in the labor market. What difference the feminization of the labor force, and particularly the skilled labor force, will make to human capital formation regimes is difficult to predict precisely. However, there is likely to be a complex politics at work here, with women increasingly supportive of welfarist policies even as systems with high levels of social protection tend to strengthen gendered occupational segregation (McCall and Orloff, 2005; Iversen, 2005).

The rise of a class of female professionals, stretching across public (particularly) and private sectors, is likely to be one of the primary factors that will reshape national regimes. It may in particular raise a key tension in the current system of collaborative work and individualized careers (Benner, 2002). As Kochan notes (see Chapter 25 below), current organizational strategies rely heavily on the most expert workers. These workers face work situations that are rewarding and where there is ongoing learning and skill development, but also that are highly demanding (Green, 2003). This highly demanding regime is in a deep tension with the need Kochan identifies for work–life balance in order to release the skills of all (see also Fligstein and Sharone, 2002, for evidence from California). Different regimes will have different capacities to respond to these challenges.

23.7.3 Transnational Human Capital

In the longer term, the different national human capital formation regimes are likely to be significantly reconstituted by the increasing connections across those regimes. In this respect, international competitive pressures will be only one of the relevant factors. More significant in the long run is likely to be the interpenetration of different institutional complexes. The increasing collaboration among EU countries around educational and training qualifications is one example where the various systems may at least feed into a common template of educational awards and skills certifications. The increased integration of transnational firms and networks of firms promotes the diffusion of particular 'national models' to other settings (Ó Riain, 2004). Sectors such as information and communication technologies have seen the emergence of transnational production systems, with some common elements of work and human resource management across varying national institutional systems. It is worth noting the significant sectoral effects on work organization and skill formation found by Lorenz and Valeyre (2007), despite the significant national differences.

Transnational corporations are a major force in creating this momentum toward integration of different regimes—as in the example of Cole's research on Japanese production techniques. However, the relationship between local and global influences is complex. While NUMMI—Toyota's auto manufacturing joint venture with GM—imported Japanese techniques in detail into California (Adler, 1992), a variety of other Japanese companies in lower-wage sectors in California adopted the local norms of arbitrary control and poor employment security (Milkman, 1991). Equally, Swiss/Swedish company ABB's aspiration to be 'local worldwide' resulted in a much more complex system of work organization and employment than either 'local' or 'global' models—mixing solidaristic team-work in Sweden with lean work elsewhere, a network of Swedish managers with a policy of avoiding excessive Swedish influence, and local practices within a growing convergence of practices across the corporation (Belanger et al., 2000). States can also play an important role in promoting these connections with other regimes. As US high-tech firms in Ireland increasingly brought their work and employment practices with them, the Irish State helped develop the infrastructure of courses, professional associations, and research centers that would support the introduction of these work methods and employment practices (Ó Riain, 2007).

These institutional links—through networks and markets—are reinforced by migration flows and ties among workers, with the emergence of 'transnational technical communities' (Saxenian, 2006) as important elements of global production systems. Saxenian (2006) documents the significance of these connections between Silicon Valley, Taiwan, India, and other locations in promoting learning and industrial development in high tech. These informal structures of learning exist largely in the spaces between organizational hierarchies, but are no less powerful for that. However, they are also supported by the formal structures of human capital formation—as migration for higher education becomes a vital element in the mobility and networking process that forms such transnational technical communities (Saxenian, 2006). Zweig *et al.* (2004) find that there are now specifically transnational forms of human capital where the skill being valued cannot be separated from the knowledge and networks required to operate transnationally, even if the work is largely local. While human capital formation regimes are still heavily national there are now strong transnational ties that are likely to contribute to the reconstitution of those national regimes.

23.7.4 The End of 'National' Regimes of Human Capital Formation

The very notion of national regimes has of course become controversial in the face of economic globalization. Can these national institutional regimes continue to do the work of 'stabilizing' the meaning, supply, and use of human capital in the face of the changes discussed above? The economic globalization of recent decades appeared to spell a return to a world of 'pure' labor, where human capital was degraded through low-cost global competition. However, human capital is arguably more important than ever, as labor is a critical resource in the knowledge economy, is less mobile than other factors of production (particularly capital), and is one of the key elements of the 'innovative milieux' that are crucial to localized growth in a globalizing economy (Evans, 2007). In the face of the financial crisis and economic collapse of 2008, policy-makers have rediscovered human capital and innovation as the central planks of long-term growth. Thelen and van Wijnbergen (2003), for example, trace the complex effects of globalization on labor relations in Germany, suggesting that while long-run structural pressures may undermine unions, they are strengthened in the medium term by the heightened vulnerability to labor unrest of employers facing increased international competition. In this respect, the gains secured by labor under the German human capital formation regime may be increased.

In keeping with the feminization of human capital, Piore and Safford (2006) find that 'the New Deal industrial relations system ... has been replaced not by the market but by an employment rights regime, in which the rules of the workplace are imposed by law, judicial opinions, and administrative rulings, supplemented by mechanisms at the enterprise level that are responsive to the law but also are susceptible to employee pressures, both individual and collective' (2006: 299). Where class politics may have been marginalized by the liberalization of industrial relations, the workplace is increasingly shaped by the politics of race, ethnicity, gender, age, and other lines of division. Where unions may have been weakened, the role of the law in regulating human capital has been enhanced.

Although there are pressures towards the degradation of human capital through competition and threats of capital mobility, globalization has made human capital formation all the more crucial for states which increasingly see themselves as competitors with other states for exports and investment. Indeed, states are actively seeking to reshape their labor forces through education and training, making human capital formation regimes more central to national political economies (Reich, 1991; Ó Riain, 2004).

Furthermore, international institutions play an increasingly complex role. In Europe, the EU's 'Bologna process' is constructing new qualification standards and norms that will enhance mobility across countries within education and training. In addition, states are paying increased attention paid to other countries' systems, there are stronger interinstitutional ties among higher-education institutions, and intergovernmental organizations are playing increasingly important roles (for example, through the OECD skills strategy). In addition, human capital is increasingly formalized and codified through intellectual property laws—which themselves may restrict the further global development of human capital by favoring existing holders of intellectual property rights over innovators (Kurtz *et al.*, 2005). There is a great deal to be learnt about how these sectoral systems of production and national systems of human capital formation intersect in shaping skills and competitive outcomes.

23.8 CONCLUSION

Human capital formation is profoundly shaped by the mix of state, markets, and society in national political economies. In recent years we have begun to appreciate the more profound implications of this connection between human capital formation and political economy. The human capital formation process itself plays a central role in distinguishing differences between varieties of capitalism. National political economic regimes are more firmly institutionalized because the human capital formation process embeds the institutions within the interests and identities of workers themselves. Furthermore, we are challenged to rethink the nature of human capital itself. Rather than a property of individuals it is a property than can only be realized within social relations, making the realization of human capital (and the securing of its rewards) dependent upon the institutional and political context.

It is not surprising, therefore, to find a variety of historically specific, institution-alized systems of human capital formation associated with different varieties of capitalism. The effects of particular work techniques or specific sets of policies depend upon the institutional configurations within which they are located, enhanc-ing the effects of certain human capital initiatives but making them difficult to implement in a different institutional setting.

However, structural changes are challenging both the character of human cap-ital and the coherence of national institutional regimes. Increasingly, human capital formation regimes are being reconstituted on a different terrain—where the critical workers are often professionals and increasingly female, where work organization is based on teams but careers are individualized, and where firms, occupational communities, and policy actors are increasingly transnationally networked. Rather than seeing the demise of human capital formation regimes in the face of global marketization, we must ask what new kinds of regime will be formed, what new kinds of power resource will be developed and coalitions put in place to support those regimes, and what kinds of 'beneficial constraints' will be institutionalized that will lock firms into particular systems of human capital formation.

These institutional innovations and struggles will occur in a setting that is differ-ent from that when the industrial era regimes were built that sustained economies through the post-war Golden Age of Western capitalism and that are now under threat. Those regimes emerged largely on an institutional field that was poorly developed, with nascent public education systems, weak welfare state structures, and artisan-based structures of training. The new human capital formation regimes will be forged not only by classes and genders in a struggle with capital, not only by the new actors struggling with the new dilemmas that emerge from structural changes, but also on the institutional ground that is now firmly occupied by institu-tions that have been in place for many years. This will provide both additional con-straints and additional institutional capacities. The ability to mobilize them under new circumstances will be central to the success of efforts to develop new human capital formation regimes.

Note

1. I am indebted to Alan Burton-Jones for this insight.

REFERENCES

ADLER, P. S. (1992). 'The "Learning Bureaucracy": New United Motor Manufacturing Inc.', in B. M. Staw and L. L. Cummings (eds.), *Research on Industrial Behaviour* (Greenwich, Conn.: JAI Press), 111–94.

AMABLE, B. (2004). *The Diversity of Modern Capitalism* (Oxford: Oxford University Press).

ASHTON, D. (1999). 'The Skill Formation Process: A Paradigm Shift?' *Journal of Education and Work*, 12(3): 347–50.

BARLEY, S. R., and KUNDA, G. (2004). *Gurus, Hired Guns and Warm Bodies: Itinerant Experts in a Knowledge Economy* (Princeton: Princeton University Press).

BELANGER, J., BERGGREN, C., BJORKMAN, T., and KOHLER, C. (2000). *Being Local Worldwide: ABB and the Challenge of Global Management* (Ithaca, NY: Cornell University Press).

BENKLER, Y. (2006). *The Wealth of Networks* (New Haven: Yale University Press).

BENNER, C. (2002). *Work in the New Economy* (Oxford: Blackwell).

BERGGREN, C. (1992). *Alternatives to Lean Production: Work Organization in the Swedish Auto Industry* (Ithaca, NY: ILR Press).

BOWLES, S., and GINTIS, H. (1976). *Schooling in Capitalist America* (London: Routledge & Kegan Paul).

BROWN, C., HALTIWINGER, J., and LANE, J. (2006). *Economic Turbulence* (Chicago: University of Chicago Press).

CARNEIRO, P., and HECKMAN, J. J. (2003). 'Human Capital Policy', in J. J. Heckman, A. B. Krueger, and B. M. Friedman (eds.), *Inequality in America: What Role for Human Capital Policies?* (Cambridge, Mass.: MIT Press).

CHARLES, M. (2005). 'National Skill Regimes, Postindustrialism, and Sex Segregation', *Social Politics* 12: 289–316.

COLE, R. (1979). *Work, Mobility and Participation* (Berkeley, Calif.: University of California Press).

—— (1991). *Strategies for Learning: Small-Group Activities in American, Japanese, and Swedish Industry* (Berkeley, Calif.: University of California Press).

DORE, R. (1986). *Flexible Rigidities: Industrial Policy and Structural Adjustment in the Japanese Economy, 1970–1980* (Stanford, Calif.: Stanford University Press).

ERIKSON, R., and GOLDTHORPE, J. H. (1992). *The Constant Flux: A Study of Class Mobility in Industrial Societies* (Oxford: Clarendon Press).

ESPING-ANDERSEN, G. (1990). *The Three Worlds of Welfare Capitalism* (Princeton: Princeton University Press).

—— (1999). *Social Foundations of Postindustrial Economies* (Oxford: Oxford University Press).

ESTÉVEZ-ABE, M. (1999). *Multiple Logics of the Welfare State: Skills, Protection and Female Labor in Japan and Selected OECD Countries* (US–Japan Program Working Paper 99-02; Cambridge, Mass.: Harvard University).

—— (2006). 'Gendering the Varieties of Capitalism: A Study of Occupational Segregation by Sex in Advanced Industrial Societies', *World Politics*, 59(1): 142–75.

EVANS, P. B. (2002). 'Collective Capabilities, Culture, and Amartya Sen's Development as Freedom', *Studies in Comparative International Development*, 37(2): 54–60.

—— (2007). 'The Twenty First Century Developmental State', mimeo.

FINEGOLD, D., and SOSKICE, D. (1988). 'The Failure of Training in Britain: Analysis and Prescription', *Oxford Review of Economic Policy*, 4(3): 21–53.

FLIGSTEIN, N., and SHARONE, O. (2002). 'Work in the Postindustrial Economy in California', in R. Milkman (ed.), *The State of California Labor* (Berkeley, Calif.: University of California Press), 67–96.

GREEN, R. (2003). *Demanding Work* (Princeton: Princeton University Press).

HALL, P., and SOSKICE, D. (2001). *Varieties of Capitalism* (Oxford: Oxford University Press).

HODSON, R. (2001). *Dignity at Work* (Cambridge: Cambridge University Press).

HUBER, E., and STEPHENS, J. (2001). *Development and Crisis of the Welfare State: Parties and Policies in Global Markets* (Chicago: University of Chicago Press).

IVERSEN, T. (2005). *Capitalism, Democracy, and Welfare* (Cambridge: Cambridge University Press).

——and STEPHENS, J. (2008). 'Partisan Politics, the Welfare State, and Three Worlds of Human Capital Formation', *Comparative Political Studies*, 41(4–5): 600–37.

KURTZ, M., SCHRANK, A., and SHADLEN, K. (2005). 'The Political Economy of Intellectual Property Protection: The Case of Software', *International Studies Quarterly*, 49(1): 45–71.

KRAAK, A., LAUDER, H., BROWN, P., and ASHTON, D. (2007). *Debating High Skills and Joined-up Policy* (Cape Town: HSRC Press).

LAVE, J., and WENGER, E. (1991). *Situated Learning: Legitimate Peripheral Participation* (Cambridge: University of Cambridge Press).

LINCOLN, J. R., and KALLEBERG, A. L. (1990). *Culture, Control, and Commitment: A Study of Work. Organization and Work Attitudes in the United States and Japan* (Berkeley, Calif.: University of California Press).

LORENZ, E., and VALEYRE, A. (2007). 'Organizational Forms and Innovative Performance: A Comparison of the EU-15', in E. Lorenz and B. Lundvall (eds.), *How Europe's Economies Learn* (Oxford: Oxford University Press), 140–60.

McCALL, L., and ORLOFF, A. (2005). 'Introduction to Special Issue on "Gender, Class and Capitalism"', *Social Politics* (summer): 159–69.

MARES, I. (2003). *The Politics of Social Risk: Business and Welfare State Development* (Cambridge: Cambridge University Press).

MAYER, K. U., and SOLGA, H., eds. (2008). *Skill Formation: Interdisciplinary and Cross-National Perspectives* (Cambridge: Cambridge University Press).

MILKMAN, R. (1991). *Japan's California Factories* (Los Angeles: UCLA Institute of Industrial Relations; Monograph and Research Series, 55).

MUELLER, W., and JACOB, J. (2008). 'Qualifications and the Returns to Training across the Life Course', in K. U. Mayer and H. Solga (eds.), *Skill Formation: Interdisciplinary and Cross-National Perspectives* (Cambridge: Cambridge University Press), 126–72.

O'CONNELL, P., and JUNGBLUT, J.-M. (2008). 'What do we Know about Training at Work?', in K. U. Mayer and H. Solga (eds.), *Skill Formation: Interdisciplinary and Cross-National Perspectives* (Cambridge: Cambridge University Press), 109–25.

OFFE, C. (1984). *Contradictions of the Welfare State* (London: Hutchinson).

Ó RIAIN, S. (2004). *The Politics of High Tech Growth* (Cambridge: Cambridge University Press).

——(2007). 'Engineering Convergence: The Political Construction of Globalisation in Transnational High Tech Production Systems', American Sociological Association Annual Conference, New York.

PIORE, M., and SAFFORD, S. (2006). 'Changing Regimes of Workplace Governance, Shifting Axes of Social Mobilization, and the Challenge to Industrial Relations Theory', *Industrial Relations*, 45(3): 299–325.

Pontusson, J. (2005). *Inequality and Prosperity: Social Europe vs. Liberal America* (Ithaca, NY: Cornell University Press).

Rajan, R., and Zingales, L. (1998). 'Power in a Theory of the Firm', *Quarterly Journal of Economics*, 113(2): 387–432.

Reich, R. (1991). *The Work of Nations* (New York: Vintage Books).

Saxenian, A. (1999). *Silicon Valley's New Immigrant Entrepreneurs* (San Francisco: Public Policy Institute of California).

—— (2006). *The New Argonauts* (Cambridge, Mass.: Harvard University Press).

Scharpf, F. (1999). *Governing in Europe* (Oxford: Oxford University Press).

Sen, A. (1999). *Development as Freedom* (London: Anchor).

Streeck, W. (1991). 'On the Institutional Conditions of Diversified Quality Production', in Egon Matzner and Wolfgang Streeck (eds.), *Beyond Keynesianism* (Aldershot: Edward Elgar), 21–61.

—— (1997). 'Beneficial Constraints: On the Economic Limits of Rational Voluntarism', in J. R. Hollingsworth, J. Rogers, and Robert Boyer (eds.), *Contemporary Capitalism: The Embeddedness of Institutions* (Cambridge: Cambridge University Press), 197–219.

—— and Thelen, K., eds. (2005). *Beyond Continuity: Institutional Change in Advanced Political Economies* (Oxford: Oxford University Press).

Swenson, Peter (1991). 'Bringing Capital Back in, or Social Democracy Reconsidered: Employer Power, Cross-Class Alliances, and Centralization of Industrial Relations in Denmark and Sweden', *World Politics*, 43(4): 513–45.

—— (2002). *Employers against Markets* (Cambridge: Cambridge University Press).

Thelen, K. (2004). *How Institutions Evolve: The Political Economy of Skills in Germany, Britain, the United States and Japan* (Cambridge: Cambridge University Press).

—— and Kume, I. (1999). 'The Effects of Globalization on Labor Revisited: Lessons from Germany and Japan', *Politics and Society*, 27(4): 476–504.

—— and Wijnbergen, C. van (2003). 'The Paradox of Globalization: Labor Relations in Germany and Beyond', *Comparative Political Studies*, 36(8): 859–80.

Womack, J. P., Jones, D., and Roos, D. (1990). *The Machine that Changed the World: The Story of Lean Production* (New York: Rawson).

Zweig, D., Changgui, C., and Rosen, S. (2004). 'Globalisation and Transnational Human Capital: Overseas and Returnee Scholars to China', *China Quarterly*, 735–57.

CHAPTER 24

HUMAN CAPITAL IN DEVELOPING COUNTRIES

THE SIGNIFICANCE OF THE ASIAN EXPERIENCE

THOMAS CLARKE

24.1 INTRODUCTION

The World Bank placed the advance of knowledge at the center of world economic development in their influential annual report *Knowledge for Development* (1998). The emergence of economies based on the production, distribution and use of knowledge and information was charted by the OECD in their report *The Knowledge-Based Economy* (1996). The determinants of the success of enterprises, and of national economies as a whole, are ever more reliant upon their effectiveness in gathering and utilizing knowledge. The development and sharing of knowledge is so rapid in the new economy that the OECD suggests that innovation has developed from a linear model to a more complex relationship-based model. Instead of discovery and innovation proceeding along a fixed and linear sequence of phases, innovation is the result of numerous actions of many players involved in regional and national innovation systems. This has implications for the rapid emergence of global production networks of advanced technology.

The promise of the knowledge economy has attracted the interest of national governments around the world, not only in the advanced industrial countries, but also in the developing economies. In many developing countries aspirations toward a knowledge economy are confounded by an increasing digital divide. For other developing countries the prospects of making an early transition seem more realistic. A number of Asian countries now have national policies committed to developing as knowledge economies over the next decade, with specific investments in education and training, technological infrastructure, venture capital support, and research and development, including Singapore, Hong Kong, Malaysia, Korea, Taiwan, Thailand, India, and China. Excitement is generated by the apparent potential to leap through stages of industrial development from simple commodity production to high-value-added knowledge-based business. An additional incentive is the realization that it is likely that physical resources alone will not bring prosperity to developing countries. By employing their ingenuity to better effect, countries poor in material resources have regularly outperformed the resource-rich countries of the world (Maddison, 2000).

The challenge is to develop the human, social, and institutional capital necessary for competing in the knowledge economy. The Forum for the Future suggests a five-capitals model of human, social, finance, manufacturing, and natural capital (Porritt 2007). Here human capital is defined as people's health and well-being, knowledge, skills, and motivation, and social capital is defined as the institutions which sustain and develop human capital in partnership with others; for example, families, communities, businesses, unions, schools, and voluntary organizations, including the values and behavior that allow these social forms to operate. Human capital is one of these five interdependent forms of capital, and is not a separate, substitutable item in itself (it works with and complements other forms of capital: Porritt, 2007). Human and social capital become ever more critical as the knowledge economy progresses. Hoff and Stiglitz insist: 'Development is no longer seen primarily as a process of capital accumulation but rather as a process of organizational change' (2001: 389). The Asian Development Bank suggests a new paradigm for economic development: 'It is even envisaged that knowledge can eventually become a means of mass production—similar to manual labor in the industrial economy—once web-based information and communication technologies (ICTs) have reached worldwide penetration levels, allowing individuals to work and provide routine knowledge in a virtually networked (global) environment' (ADB, 2007: p. ix).

The rapid economic growth of the East Asian economies is often attributed to the sustained level of investment in human capital—particularly the enduring commitment to raising educational standards (Tilak, 2002). However, the development of human capital involves interplay between supportive institutions, endowments, and policies. In terms of the educational component of human and social advances, many developing countries have cultures that place a very high value on educational attainment (though in some cultures this commitment is heavily gender-biased—witness recent incidents of girls in Afghanistan being assaulted for going to school). Education is of central importance in many of the cultures of Asia.

For example, the desire for learning and the belief in personal development through education is more profound in Chinese culture than in the West. (Bejing taxi drivers will save hard for ten years to send their child to an overseas university.) The Chinese mode of learning has an ancient lineage and involves a classical approach to literature and science, but is often accompanied by a traditional pedagogy of rote learning of codified knowledge—an approach that will scarcely equip China for effective participation in a rapidly transforming global economy. Recognizing this, the Chinese government proposed a change in the mission of Chinese universities from 'the cultivation of knowledge' to the 'cultivation of talents and creativity' (Clarke, 1999). Yet the rhetoric of policy may not be matched by the rigor of practice in China. In contrast, India with a strong emphasis on mathematics and technical skills in its educational system, and the colonial legacy of the English language, appears better prepared for a knowledge-based economy.

However, for such an economically dynamic region it appears that comparatively little talent and creativity are exhibited in Asia Pacific industry. Young (1994) and Krugman (1994), who were early dissenters, dismissed Asia Pacific's economic growth as the result of a dramatic rise in the quantity of inputs to the economic system at an early stage of industrialization. Such gains from input-driven growth cannot continue indefinitely unless there are accompanying increases in efficiency. Asia Pacific growth can be attributed largely to a great mobilization of resources in export-oriented strategies, combined with a self-sacrificing level of personal savings. Lingle (1997: 85) argues:

East Asian economies have been following rather than leading the rest of the developed world, by relying upon ready access to Western technology and open markets. As the 'age of mass industrialization' passes, the competitive advantage of many East Asian economies will be challenged. Without producing their own domestic entrepreneurial talent and self-generated technological advance, these countries will continue to lag the developed economies in what could prove a perpetually dependent relationship.

Despite their obvious logic it is as well to remember that the same arguments were once applied to Japan, which did not stop a generation of highly innovative Japanese corporations introducing a series of radical new technologies into world markets—most notably Sony, which translated traditional skills for miniaturization into contemporary consumer electronics.

Once absolute poverty is escaped, however, the relentless pursuit of economic growth following the West might prove a singularly barren goal in a resource-constrained planet. As Evans (2007: 7) argues, development is not just about economic growth and consumption. It is about the capacity to make choices as one of the most important human capabilities: 'Processes of participation have to be understood as constitutive parts of the *ends* of development in themselves' (Sen, 1999: 291). More fundamental orientations and objectives are required than simply the incremental increase in GDP per capita that traditionally has been the critical indicator of economic growth.

Among all the recent contributions to development theory, the capability approach takes most seriously the universally accepted proposition that growth of GDP per capita is not an end in itself, but a proxy for improvements in human well-being, to be valued only insofar as it can be empirically connected to improved well-being. Sen argues that we should evaluate development in terms of 'the expansion of the "capabilities" of people to lead the kind of lives they value—and have reason to value.' Because it rejects reduction of developmental success to a single metric, the capability approach identifies 'public deliberation' as the only analytically defensible way of ordering capabilities and puts political institutions and civil society at the center of developmental goal-setting. (Evans, 2007: 7; Sen, 1999)

This chapter will examine the contested and controversial theories of growth, development, knowledge, and human capital, examining the process of human capital formation in developing economies. The trajectories of human and industrial capital development in the Asia Pacific region will be investigated as the most promising developing region in economic terms, posing the critical questions of whether this region will succeed in joining the advanced industrial countries in the knowledge economy, and whether other developing countries and regions of the world can follow the same path.

Despite the recent apparent success of investment in rapid industrialization in China, India, and South-East Asia, doubts remain whether this is a blueprint for advancing human capital and economic prosperity in the rest of the developing world. Globalization has intensified inequality *between* the advanced industrial world and the developing world, and has also compounded inequality *within* countries in both the developed and developing world, and the distribution of rewards and opportunities flowing from globalization are particularly unequal in developing countries.

Bairoch (1982) reminds us that in 1750 China and India produced almost 60 percent of the world's manufactured goods (Figure 24.1). With the industrial revolution in the West over the next century and a half the UK, US, Germany, and other European producers almost entirely displaced the indigenous producers of Asia. (As Marx tersely remarked in *Capital*, when the heavy artillery of the cheap prices of British machine-made commodities did not suffice, the heavy artillery did.) Though in the last two decades substantial tranches of manufacturing production have shifted to some of the poorer developing countries, the attraction of one dollar an hour labor—still the norm in India, Indonesia, China's inland provinces, Vietnam, and Pakistan—remains a significant factor. Simple commodity production and resource extraction has proved a hard road for the developing world. Gunter and Hoevan (2004: 3) indicate that while China and India's combined share of world gross domestic production increased from 4.4 percent in 1985 to 6 percent in 2002, the low-income countries, excluding India, experienced a reduction in their share of global GDP from 4.5 to 2 percent, and middle-income countries, excluding China, experienced a fall from 17.5 to 11.5 percent.

Meanwhile, the advanced industrial economies operating at the forefront of technology and the knowledge economy succeeded in increasing their share of global

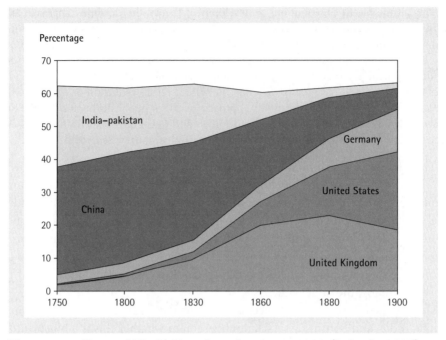

Figure 24.1. Share of World Manufacturing 1750–1900 (Bairoch, 1982)

Source: Bairoch

GDP from 73.6 to 80.5 percent in the same period. An insistent question asked in the developing world is how they might acquire the higher skills and technologies to secure entry to the social stability and economic prosperity apparently afforded by the knowledge economy. 'What kind of institutional arrangements will best enable societies to generate new skills, knowledge, and ideas, and the networks needed to diffuse and take advantage of them?' (Evans, 2007: 2).

24.2 THE EVOLUTION OF THEORIES OF GROWTH AND DEVELOPMENT

Theories of growth and economic and human development have proved among the most contested in economics. We can distinguish classical theories, linear stages of growth theory, patterns of structural change theory, international dependence theory (neocolonialist, dualist, Marxist, and others), and the neoclassical counter-revolution (supply-side, public choice theories).

The emphasis of classical economic theory, commencing with Adam Smith's (1776) concern for absolute advantage derived from unique factors of production (though Smith recognized the roles of education and skill formation in the production and growth processes, as well as assisting towards a more worthwhile life) and Ricardo's recognition of the comparative advantage that specialization may bring, was reinterpreted in the Heckscher, Ohlin, Samuelson (HES) theory, asserting that perfectly competitive markets, alongside free comparative-advantage-based trade, optimizes national and global resource allocation and competitiveness. These theoretical presuppositions, unthinkingly applied in the contemporary global context of dominant advanced industrial countries competing with economically weaker developing countries, have consigned many economies of Africa, South Asia, and South America to lives of endless struggle with asymmetric terms of trade. As Pitelis (2009: 5) states: 'The macroeconomic policy prescriptions deriving from the analytical foundations of the neoclassical perspective have been encapsulated in the various versions of the Washington and post-Washington-type policy advice to developing and transition economies (Shapiro and Taylor 1990). Their record has been at least questionable (Stiglitz 2001; Rodrik 2004; Dunning 2006).'

Confirming how a more interventionist stance has facilitated faster growth of different regions in the world, Krugman (1989, 1992) highlights how in the context of imperfect competition, increasing returns, spillover effects, and first-mover advantages, strategic trade policies to support particular sectors and firms may leverage advantage. Markets are less effective at identifying new possibilities for development and innovation than in signaling the profitability of activities that already exist (Scott-Kemmis, 2008: 63). Endogenous growth or new growth theory transcends the logic of development strategies based simply on the accumulation of physical capital, emphasizing the increasing returns to ideas as the key to growth (Sen, 1994; Romer, 1994; Easterly, 2001). Rates of return for investment in new knowledge are consistently higher than rates of return to physical capital, and investment in human capital is equally powerful (Helpman, 2004). New growth theory is complemented by institutional approaches that emphasize the importance of institutional development to long-run economic growth (Hoff and Stiglitz, 2001; Rodrik *et al.*, 2004; Acemoglu *et al.*, 2005).

Illustrative of a distinctive endogenous growth approach was the success of the Japanese economy in the period from the 1960s to the 1980s, with an emphasis on achieving market share through all forms of innovation including managerial, organizational, and human resources (Romer, 1986; Lucas, 1988), together with a focus on targeting strategic sectors (Krugman, 1987; Shapiro and Taylor, 1990). This fueled the debate on levels of research and development spending, links between government and industry funding and performance, and the important distinction between product and process innovation, which led to the recognition in the West of the importance of quality processes and ultimately onto learning and best practice.

Also the financial, technical, and social capital involved in the *keiretsu* networks was recognized as a contributor to competitiveness. Finally of significance was the Japanese emphasis on maintaining domestic competition, as in Porter's (1990) analysis of the importance of clusters of competing and collaborating producers. Porter (1990) is associated with the stress on the importance of the coexistence of important factor conditions, demand conditions, firm and sector strategy and rivalry, and related and supporting industries.

A further development is the systems of innovation approach, with the belief that innovation is best promoted not by competitive markets alone, but by systems-wide linkages involving markets, firms, governments, and social capital-promoting institutions (Pitelis, 2009: 12; Freeman, 1995). This constitutes a more holistic conception of the innovative process compared to the linear model of neoclassical theory (Table 24.1). In relation to the systems perspective on innovation as a basis for policy:

The argument is that government has a role to play in two areas. The first is provision of capabilities in areas where firms and markets may not be able to provide accessible support, such as basic R&D, marketing infrastructures, and training. The second lies in institutions and organizations that support the operations of the innovation system as a whole—education at all levels, IPR institutions, the finance system (especially with respect to venture capital), regulatory frameworks, and so on. (Georghiou *et al.*, 2003: 38).

Scott-Kemmis (2008) captures the increasing sense of the interdependence of successful economic systems:

The evolution of firms and industries involves systemic interdependence between technologies and organizations and institutions, interaction involving market and non-market relationships and the key drivers from increasing returns. Just as firms increasingly outsource elements of their production system, so they also increasingly outsource elements of their innovation systems. Just as there are many more options for business models so there are many more options for firms to develop their innovation systems, and again we see a great deal of exploration with knowledge-related relationships, (for example, through open innovation) the use of intermediaries, alliances, collaboration etc.

Finally there is the resource-based view of the firm, focusing on the firm's capabilities, and suggesting that in a more dynamic market economy firms position themselves in terms of their resources and capabilities, rather than on the products and services currently derived from their capabilities (Barney, 1991; Wernerfelt, 1984). The resource-based theory of the firm leads on logically to an emerging knowledge-based theory of the firm (Grant, 1996; Spender, 1996), which emphasizes the role of knowledge as the critical resource in organizations. As David Teece argues:

The decreased cost of information flow, increases in the number of markets (e.g. for intermediate products, and for various types of risk), the liberalization of product and labour markets in many parts of the world, and the deregulation of international financial flows

Table 24.1. Neoclassical and Systems of Innovation Growth Theories

	Neoclassical	Systems Innovation
Underlying assumptions	Equilibrium Perfect information	Non-equilibrium Asymmetric information
Focus	Allocation of resources for invention	Interactions innovation processes
Main policy	Science policy (research)	Innovation policy/systematic problems
Main rationale	Market failure	
Government intervenes to:	Provide public goods Mitigate externalities Reduce barriers to entry Eliminate inefficient market structures	Solve problems in the system or facilitate creation of new systems Induce changes in supporting structure for innovation: support creation and development of institutions, organizations, and networking Facilitate transition and avoid lock-in
Main strengths of innovation policies	Clarity and simplicity Long time series of science-based indicators	Context-specific Involvement of all policies related to innovation Holistic conception of the innovation process
Main weaknesses of innovation policies	Linear model of innovation Framework conditions not explicitly considered in the model (such as institutional framework) General policies	Difficult to implement in practice Lack of indicators for analysis of the IS and evaluation of IS policies

Source: Chaminade and Edquist, 2006; Doherty and Arnold, 2003.

is stripping away many traditional sources of competitive advantage and exposing a new fundamental core as the basis for wealth creation. That fundamental core is the development and astute deployment and utilization of intangible assets, of which knowledge, competence, and intellectual property are the most significant. (Teece 2000: 3)

Teece (2000) demonstrates how the flow of information, the expansion of markets, and the proliferation of alliances to access complementary assets is eroding traditional sources of competitive advantage. The special access to natural resources and skilled labor is gone. Scale and scope is of questionable value once physical assets or capacity can be rented on favorable terms. This leaves knowledge and competence, coupled with dynamic capabilities (the firm's entrepreneurial and strategic asset orchestration capabilities) as the foundations of competitive advantage.

The importance of human capital development becomes inescapable:

> The confluence of endogenous growth theory with institutional approaches to development and the capability approach jibe nicely with the shifting historical context. Together they suggest that 21st century development will depend on generating intangible assets (ideas, skills, and networks) rather than on stimulating investment in machinery and physical assets oriented to the production of tangible goods. This makes investment in human capabilities (which include what is traditionally known as 'human capital') more economically critical. At the same time, new development theories assume that economic growth depends on political institutions and the capacity to set collective goals. The capability approach sets out the political argument most firmly, arguing that only public interchange and open deliberation can effectively define development goals and elaborate the means for attaining them. (Evans, 2007: 2)

24.3 HUMAN CAPITAL THEORY

The realization of the criticality of human capital to economic growth and well-being has underlined the significance of investments in human capital formation, development, and sustenance: expenditure on education, health, and social services have become as essential as investment in physical capital (Bowman, 1969). With increasing returns to organizations from investment in human capital allowing specialization, economies with a larger stock of human capital will experience a faster rate of growth (Romer, 1990). There is growing agreement on the importance of skills as the engine of economic growth, but more debate on the significance of educational attainment for broad competencies supporting life-long learning, and more specific competencies, including the ability to use information and communication technologies, to solve problems and to work in teams (OECD, 2001: 100). In the OECD countries more than half of GDP is accounted for by knowledge-based industries, including the main producers of high-technology goods, high- and medium-technology manufacturing, and knowledge-intensive services such as finance, insurance, business, communication, and social services. This is manifest in the rising human capital levels of the population in OECD countries as measured in educational attainment, and in the increased demand for highly educated and highly skilled workers.

Presently the knowledge economy deploying the most advanced skills appears heavily concentrated in the established advanced industrial countries. According to the World Bank (2006: 4) the transition to the knowledge economy involves long-term investments in education, developing innovation capability, modernizing the information infrastructure, and having an economic environment conducive to market transactions. Four pillars supporting a knowledge economy are:

(1)   an *economic and institutional regime* providing for efficient mobilization and allocation of resources and able to stimulate creativity and incentives for development, dissemination, and use of knowledge;

(2)   *educated and skilled* workers who can continuously upgrade and adapt their skills to efficiently create and use knowledge;

(3)   an *effective innovation system* of firms, research centers, universities, consultancies, and other organizations that can promote the knowledge revolution, build networks globally, and assimilate and adapt knowledge to local needs;

(4)   an *information infrastructure* that can facilitate effective communication, dissemination, and processing of information and knowledge (World Bank, 2006: 4).

Though the countries of the developing world generally have large populations and a commitment to education and learning, for economic advance something more is needed than skills and abilities. Educated and trained people require an appropriate environment, with opportunities and incentives to utilize their acquired knowledge, but in many developing countries this is largely absent (Mizrahi, 2004). Foreign direct investment by multinational corporations often requires a skilled workforce, and in recent years such investment has moved toward relatively skill-intensive production and services, and less toward primary and resource-based manufacturing (OECD, 2003: 24). Multinational corporations may further enhance training and development opportunities. However, foreign direct investment is heavily skewed toward relatively few developing countries, and large tracts of the developing world are left largely to their own devices.

24.4 THE EDUCATIONAL INFRASTRUCTURE OF EAST ASIA

The central importance of the expansion of education for the human capital formation of the rapidly developing economies of East Asia has long been recognized. Somehow these countries compensated for a lack of physical resources by a sustained commitment to the development of human resources, essentially through the provision of an accessible and equitable mass educational system. This profound engagement in human capital development underpinned a series of social and economic advances including productivity growth in agriculture, rapid growth of manufacturing exports, declines in human fertility, increases in labor productivity, and high rates of domestic savings (Baker and Holsinger, 1996). However, the East Asian economies had demonstrated little improvement in educational advancement in the first half of the twentieth century when they were colonized (with the exception of Thailand, which was not a colony and introduced compulsory primary education in 1921). With independence following the Second World War the East Asian economies began a process of extensive educational expansion, commencing in Singapore in 1959 with investments in primary education, secondary education in 1965, and technical education by end of the 1970s (Goujon and Samir, 2006).

Not only did investment in education assist in promoting rapid economic growth, but education also proved an effective instrument for reducing income inequalities, promoting health, and enhancing social development. Allocating a sufficient proportion of national income to education is often considered difficult in developing countries until a significant level of economic growth occurs.

Generally it is argued that the higher level of the GNP per capita, the higher is investment in education, stressing the point that it is economic growth that helps education systems flourish. The East Asian experience shows that this is only partially true. For example, Korea at the time of its takeoff in the early 1960s lacked every factor that is normally associated with such

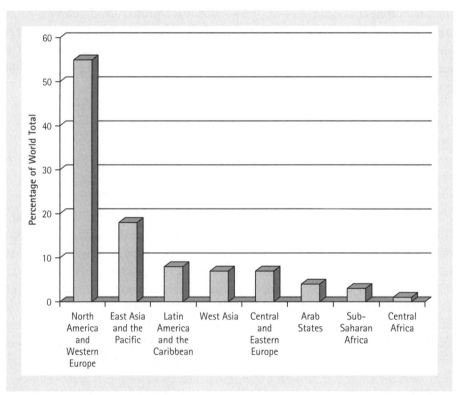

Figure 24.2. Global Distribution of Public Expenditure on Education by Region (compiled from UNESCO, 2007)

output, except for an educated and skilled labour force, which made all the difference for its growth in subsequent decades. (Tilak, 2002: 41)

Yet the UNESCO survey of global distribution of public expenditure on education suggests that it is primarily the East Asian region that has substantially pursued this route to economic and social development, with North America and Western Europe still accounting for more than half of world expenditure on education.

Generous investment in both primary and secondary education with a balanced pattern of investment of resources between different levels of education, together with legislation making nine years of education compulsory across the region, has resulted in unique levels of access and opportunity in East Asia compared to other developing economies. East Asian economies have also shown the benefits of investing in vocational and technical education. Finally the expansion of higher education in the East Asian economies has proved impressive in recent decades: 'While primary education serves as a threshold level of human capital development for economic growth, it is secondary and higher education (including investments in science and technology) that accelerates and sustains high economic growth' (Tilak, 2002: 42).

Japan forged the path for the other East Asian economies, becoming the world's most successful exporter of advanced consumer goods in the 1970s and 1980s, and promoted the rapid development of the other high-performing economies of East Asia. However, the small island nation of Singapore demonstrated an even more conscious and successful application of human capital formation as the key to economic growth. Experiencing economic problems and unemployment in the mid-1960s, they prepared a highly educated and skilled workforce and combined this with an aggressive policy of economic incentives, leading to successful industrialization involving many multinational electronic companies. Labor shortages resulted in a further major investment in technical and engineering skills and the expansion of higher education in the 1970s. Further acute labor shortages in manufacturing encouraged the government to restructure the economy into high-technology industries, providing support for knowledge skills, computer-related industries, and research and development in the 1980s. In the 1990s and beyond, the national strategy was to focus on knowledge-intensive industries, with research and innovation incentives and the establishment of elite medical, scientific, and university foundations.

Along the way all of the East Asian economies have had to deal with serious issues that at times have threatened to overwhelm their progress—for example, the differences in access to quality education between urban and rural areas, curriculum relevance and quality, and low-paid teachers. Recurrent efforts have been necessary in raising the quality of education, renewing the structure and curriculum, and expanding the scope of education (Goujon and Samir, 2006). At a deeper philosophical level there has always been the implication that the implicitly authoritarian regimes of East Asia have too much in common with the instrumental orientations of human capital approaches, rather than viewing education and human development as ends in themselves. However, more recent human resources strategies of employers in Singapore and some other East Asian countries have acknowledged the importance of the United Nations Global Compact, which recognizes human rights, labor rights, and the environment as important considerations in development. The East Asian financial crisis in 1997/8, and the global financial crisis of 2008, which both threatened the export-led model, were met by a stoical commitment to investing further in human capital, including education and health care, as the route to resilient economic growth (Ng, 2008; Tan, 2008; Liu *et al.*, 2010).

24.5 HUMAN CAPITAL FORMATION IN DEVELOPING COUNTRIES

Porter *et al.* (2007: 56) suggest that nations move through several stages in their economic development, each with enhanced capabilities (see Figure 24.3).

(1) *Factor driven*: Basic factor conditions, especially low-cost labor and natural resources, are critical for the production of simple commodities or products designed in more advanced countries. Technology is slowly assimilated, and companies compete on price in labor-intensive manufacturing and resource extraction in industries sensitive to world economic cycles, commodity prices, and exchange rate fluctuations.

(2) *Investment driven*: Efficiency in the production of more advanced but undifferentiated products, with investment in infrastructure, skill development, incentives for investment and productivity. Though the products are more sophisticated, both design and technology come from abroad, but with a growing capacity to use and improve the technology. More extended capabilities along the value chain, still susceptible to demand shocks but with greater resilience than countries depending on commodity cycles.

(3) *Innovation driven*: The ability to produce innovative products and services using advanced methods, with leading technology and supporting industries.

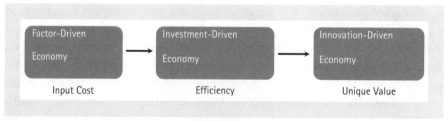

Figure 24.3. Stages of Competitive Development (Porter *et al.*, 2006)

Capability is based in specialist clusters of knowledge-based businesses, with supporting institutions and incentives encouraging an innovation-driven economy. Distinctive products and higher-level services offer greater protection from external economic shocks.

The hard path to growth which developing economies have traditionally followed begins with simple commodity production, as in assembly in the garment industry, following buyer's specifications, and using materials supplied by the buyer. The next stage up the value chain is for the producer to take on a wider range of manufacturing functions, including sourcing and logistics, and original equipment manufacture (OEM), with the buyer remaining responsible for design and marketing. With the following stage of original design manufacture (ODM) the producer carries out parts of the design process, and in the most advanced stages the buyer merely attaches his own brand to the product. Finally, reaching the top of the value chain with original brand manufacture (OBM) the producer designs, manufactures, and markets its own products under its own brand.

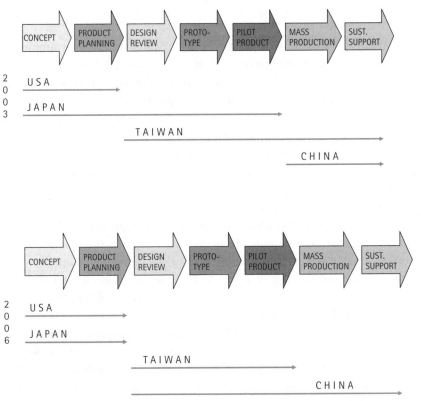

Figure 24.4. Location of Product Development for Notebook PCs

(Sources: Market Intelligence Center, Institute for the Information Industry, Taiwan, and company interviews)

This pathway to securing control of the value chain has to be patiently repeated with each new industry and technology that is entered. For example, in the product development of Notebook PCs by 2006, while concept design and product planning remained in the United States and Japan, and applied R&D and development of new platforms remained in Taiwan, product development for mature products and production engineering had shifted to China (an emerging reality recognized in the sale of IBM PCs to Lenovo of China in 2005). Dedrick and Kraemer (2005) argue that as China gains experience it will capture more of the production process, but it is unlikely to capture concept design and product planning for world markets, and unless its intellectual property protection is strengthened it will not become a center for advanced components, though it will begin to define products for the region (Figure 23.4).

24.6 TRAJECTORIES OF DEVELOPMENT IN THE ASIA PACIFIC

Though the Asia Pacific is widely regarded as the most successful example of economic and skill development, the route to rapid growth has not been without serious obstacles. The Asian economies learnt to their cost the limitations of attempting to compete in commodity markets, where overcapacity is continually driving down prices for semiconductors and other electronic components, the production of which had previously fueled their rapid economic growth. Recovering from the Asian financial crisis of 1997/8, the South-East Asian economies were reminded of the dependence of surviving as a contract manufacturer for US-based companies with the downturn in technology markets from 2000. Following the return of demand in 2003/4 that helped the fortunes of the East Asian economies to recover, the 2008 global financial crisis sharply ended the period of substantial growth of exports to the advanced industrial economies. In many sectors there is still a sense of dependence on technology and expertise from the advanced industrial countries.

Until the arrival of the new economy, to become an advanced economy involved treading a long and difficult path of industrial and structural transformation from labor-intensive industries (typified by textiles), to non-differentiated scale-driven industries (steel, basic chemicals, and heavy machinery), to differentiated assembly-based industries (automobiles, electric, electronic goods), and finally to the Schumpeterian R&D-intensive industries (specialty chips, biotechnology, and new materials) (Figure 24.5). This conceptualization of a stages-based process of industrialization is in line with growth as Joseph Schumpeter conceived, which envisaged a sequence of stages in each of which breakthrough innovations (new technologies) create a new dominant industry as the main engine of growth. Japan joined the Western industrial countries quickly in the first three stages early in the twentieth century, and more recently in the fourth stage. This prompted the East Asian countries to follow the Japanese model of growth: what the World Bank referred to as the East Asian Miracle was effectively this cultural borrowing of industrial technology (Ozawa *et al.*, 2001).

China's rapid export expansion threatens this flying geese pattern of economic development in East Asia. (The *flying geese* pattern was recognized by Akamatsu Kaname in the 1930s, and refers to the process by which countries move up the product and technology ladder as they develop, leaving the rungs they vacate to be occupied by the economies following in their flight.) In the 1990s the growth of China's exports to the United States came at the expense of the newly industrializing economies of East Asia, but were largely in product lines that the NIEs (Hong Kong, Republic of Korea, Singapore, and Taiwan) were abandoning, including footwear, clothing, toys, and household products. Meanwhile the ASEAN 4 (Indonesia, Malaysia, Philippines, and Thailand) increased their share of exports to the United States in more capital- and technology-intensive products.

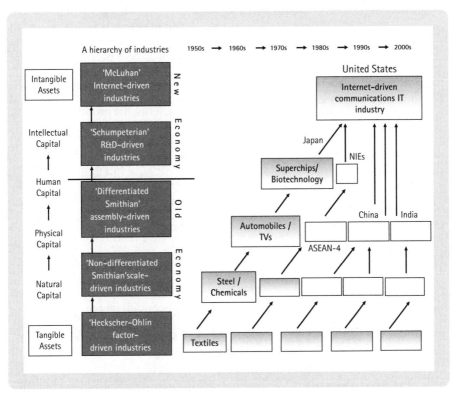

Figure 24.5. Leaping Techno–Economic Paradigms (adapted from Ozawa *et al.*, 2001)

While China's comparative advantage in all labor-intensive industries is increasing and ASEAN 4 countries decreasing, what is of more concern to these countries is China's growing comparative advantage in an increasing number of capital-intensive industries. China's mix of exports currently overlaps most with exports from Indonesia and Thailand, but the overlap in exports is less between China and the more advanced economies of East Asia for the time being. 'This provides breathing space for these economies but...overlap is growing for them too. The competition is bound to intensify in a number of product groups unless countries make determined efforts to diversify their mix of products, to raise the technological thresholds in existing product categories, and to increase their trade in services' (Yusuf, 2003: 25).

The progress of trade and technological development experienced in East Asia is divided into four stages by Yusuf (2004: 4–6), who elaborates the wider international production relations inherent in skill development:

- *Labor-intensive light manufacturing:* In the 1960s Hong Kong, South Korea, Singapore, and Taiwan began investing in light, labor-intensive manufacturing industries, whose products quickly penetrated price-sensitive markets in Western countries.
- *Upgrading by newly industrialized economies:* Export-led growth in light manufacturing was joined in the 1970s by South-East Asian countries, and by 1980 by China. Meanwhile, the Asian countries that were first to industrialize moved into more capital-intensive and skill-intensive manufacturing, attracting a rising flow of foreign direct investment from the West. Multinational corporations began dispersing production of components to overseas subsidiaries in Asia.
- *Global production networking:* By the end of the 1980s East Asia was drawn into a developing web of relationships involving production, trade, and FDI. 'Japanese multinational companies are building a regional division of labour that emphasises technology-intensive prototype production in Japan and mass production of standardised products in Asia' (Hatch, 2003: 31). Rapid increases in trade, FDI, and corporate restructuring in the 1990s made the light manufacturing sectors of East Asia coextensive with company activities in Japan, the United States, and Europe. Large multinational companies trading in automobiles, electronics, office equipment, and optical instruments invested in production facilities, to be followed by their parts suppliers.
- *Technological deepening:* With further trade liberalization, intensifying competition from China in both product markets and for FDI, and an increasing emphasis on scale, a fourth stage in East Asian development was predicated on technological specialization and deepening. A clear illustration of the benefits of the rapid acquisition of technological capability is provided by China, which emerged in the space of ten years to become the fourth largest trading

nation in the world, and the second largest producer of information technology hardware.

Yusuf (2004: 8) highlights the rigors of this pursuit: 'For more than a decade, upgrading has been the mantra of East Asian middle-income economies. As they have collectively struggled to reach the next rung of the ladder, economies in the region have often only succeeded in extending the embrace of commodification.' The normal trajectory of economic development is to begin with labor-intensive light industries such as textiles, to develop heavy industries such as steel and petrochemicals, then differentiated assembly industries such as electronics. Innovation-intensive industries such as biotechnology and supersemiconductors are the foundations of the new knowledge economy, followed by knowledge-based businesses associated with software production, multimedia, and other products based on intellectual capital. A critical question—one that is especially pertinent from a human capital perspective—is whether it is possible to accelerate economic development by missing some of these stages. Is it possible—as Singapore has successfully attempted—to upskill the workforce by intensive programmes of education and training, thus developing the levels of human capital required to equip them for the next phase of development in the global economy? Japan is now on the threshold of a new fifth stage, led and driven by the digital revolution—most notably the Internet—producing *abstract goods* or *conceptual goods*. The Asian NIEs are swiftly catching up with Japan. Although they remain some way behind in R&D-intensive industries, they are stepping up their investment in R&D. The ASEAN 4 countries are still largely in the non-differentiated scale-driven industries, though they have entered, with some success, the labor-intensive, standardized low-end segments of the assembly-based differentiated industries of computer chip assembly and low-end consumer electronics. Meanwhile, the giant economies of China and India have made the greatest strides of all, and both are overtaking the ASEAN 4. China is well on its way to entering the assembly-based industries stage, including automobiles and consumer electronics, taking advantage of its huge domestic markets that can attract foreign multinationals and technologies. Since economic liberalization India has attracted significant multinational investment in R&D centers located in high technology clusters, and progressed as the back-office data-processing center of business across the world.

The impact of the Internet could alter the dynamics of catch-up and compete among Asian economies. The NIEs are adapting to the Web as decisively as is Japan, and are investing in broadband telecommunication networks. Moreover, unlike the previous linear and sector differentiating progression of structural upgrading in which a new industry becomes dominant without significantly affecting the older generation of industries, the Internet-based new economy industries impact upon all of the older generation of industries in areas of management, production, procurement, distribution, and customer services.

Transaction-intensive sectors, such as finance, telecommunications, distribution, and government, are even more dramatically impacted. As the skills associated with web-based services and social computing begin to infuse the more advanced Asian economies as extensively as in the West, the possibilities of greater innovation in the region become more real.

24.7 GLOBAL AND REGIONAL INTEGRATION

Integration is increasing at the global level, developing more competition as freer trade displaces previously protected domestic markets. At the regional level, Japan is no longer the economic driver of East Asia that it was in the recent past, and China is emerging both as a promising market and fierce competitor. As the technological revolution intensifies, the organization of production is transformed by the growth of foreign direct investment (FDI)—the emergence of international production networks bringing together component suppliers, assemblers, supply chain managers, and buyers in dynamic and changing relationships. In this competitive environment China has relied heavily on FDI for inward technology transfer, and the changes in China's exports and imports have correlated with changes in inflows of FDI. In the 1980s FDI was concentrated in labor-intensive industries, by the 1990s they shifted to capital-intensive industries, and this trend continues. Most of China's FDI inflows come from the European Union, Japan, and the United States, but a significant proportion also originates in the newly industrializing economies. Many Japanese firms have moved their production and procurement to China in the medium term to take advantage of lower production costs, to supply the expanding domestic market, and to supply parts to major customers. A significant share of recent flows are into industries producing flat-screen televisions, DVD players, LCD monitors, plasma display panels, laptop computers, and digital cameras, which will significantly augment China's manufacturing capability in higher-technology areas. This shift in high-tech production from Japan (and the United States) to China will continue to develop (Yusuf, 2003: 26). As China becomes more attractive for such relocation of production, other East Asian economies, particularly the ASEAN 4, are experiencing difficulty in attracting the additional FDI inflows needed to upgrade their industries. As Yusuf (2003: 26) argues: 'If China successfully transforms itself from the *factory of the world*, to the *design laboratory of the world* by using direct investment by Japanese corporations in research and development facilities, the pressure on Southeast Asian economies will sharpen further. For the ASEAN nations, this could drastically heighten the urgency of developing new and differentiated products and services.' Such pressures will clearly increase the pressure on ASEAN nations to invest in knowledge-based industries and in the human capital required to develop, manage, and run them.

24.8 COMMODITIZATION OR DIFFERENTIATION

Another powerful influence upon the East Asian economies is the ongoing transformation of the structure of world production in industries such as automobile parts and consumer electronics. In a process of deverticalization, leading firms now outsource virtually all of their manufacturing operations, and restructured value chains have created geographically dispersed global production networks dominated by large contract manufacturers. Many contract manufacturers have their headquarters in the advanced industrial countries, but have specialized production facilities throughout the world, including in East Asia. These international production networks now orchestrate as much as two-thirds of all trade in commoditized manufactures. East Asian firms need to extract the best returns possible from participation in production networks, to develop their own differentiated products in order to avoid being marginalized, and to realize their technological potential in niche markets (Yusuf, 2003: 27). The formula for economic growth in the past thirty years in East Asia has been derived from high rates of capital accumulation, technological change, and the influx of young educated workers. Yusuf (2003) argues that as the proportion of working-age population begins to decline, it is only a leap in the region's technological capability that will permit continued advance toward catching up with the Western economies.

The escape from cut-throat competition in commodity markets is through design skills and innovation: to move from competition based on the cost of cheap factor inputs, to competition based on the high value added of design. These skills enable firms to differentiate their products and, in some instances, to create demand for entirely new products with a new technology that disrupts previous patterns of consumption. The added value provided by successful research and design can provide the returns to finance further growth. The countries in the region are assimilating this lesson. China alone is increasing its R&D spending to 1 percent of GDP, and when adjusted for purchasing power parity it has become the third highest investor in R&D after the United States and Japan. This initiative has received a considerable boost from 400 research centres in China established by multinational companies.

Innovative and creative human capital will be critical to the regional economies of the near future. To achieve this qualitative improvement in human capital, better innovation systems and channels for regional and global collaboration are necessary. The investment in education during the 1990s yielded high returns, but it was education geared toward a factor-intensive model of the economy. Today, schools need to equip students not only with technical skills but with creative capabilities to question and learn independently. East Asia needs to nurture business, professional, and entrepreneurial skills to foster the development of the service activities at the basis of the new economy. (Spurred by the growth of ICT services, in Hong Kong, Singapore and Taiwan services account for 60 percent of GDP, and in the other countries of the region services form around 40 percent of GDP.) With the exception of Hong Kong, Japan, Singapore, and Taiwan, gaps in business skills are evident in the region, and even Japan's level of legal, accounting, and financial skills falls short of other OECD countries.

When the economies of East Asia concentrated on manufacturing and served as suppliers to major US or European corporations, the shortage of professionally skilled human capital was not as apparent. But as these economies attempt to commercialize research and development, and firms seek to develop, design, and market new products independently with their own brand names and package services with higher value-added services, together with manufactured products to raise profit margins, the gaps in professional skills become critical (Yusuf, 2003: 30). East Asian economies recognize their weaknesses in professional and managerial skills and are attempting to educate an elite of managers overseas, to build joint venture universities and business schools with leading US and European partners, and to invest in the development of world-class universities and research institutions at home. (In an ironic exercise Jiatong University launched an international university ranking index to allow it to measure its own progress, which over time has become one of the most influential performance indices influencing the development of Western elite universities.)

24.9 DEVELOPMENT TOWARD KNOWLEDGE-BASED ECONOMIES

The World Bank, in a study funded by the Japanese government, once characterized East Asia's economic performance as *The East Asian Miracle* (World Bank, 1993: 1), describing its economies as the High Performing Asian Economies (HPAEs). Though in the ensuing decade East Asia remained the global leader in terms of growth rates, since the financial crisis of 1997/8 and in increasingly open, volatile, competitive, and connected global markets, the region has struggled to sustain the pace of earlier development. The challenge is for the East Asian economies to become more innovative. The critical question in this context is how the East Asian economies might achieve the transition from high-tech industries towards the knowledge-based economies which they aspire to become. The momentous

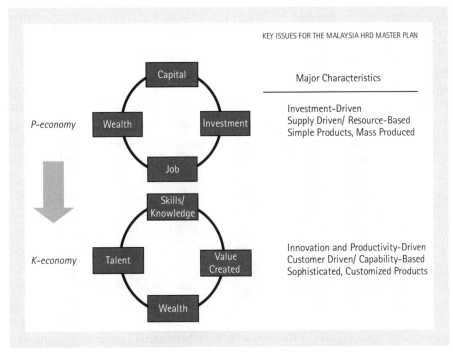

Figure 24.6. The Shift from a Production Economy to a Knowledge Economy

transition is to move from a supply-driven production economy of simple mass-produced products, to an innovative, customer-driven knowledge economy, where human capital in the form of creative human capability brings rewards (Figure 24.6). Can other East Asian countries (and indeed other developing countries) follow the lead of Japan, Singapore, Taiwan, Korea, and Hong Kong and assert their creativity at the forefront of the knowledge economy?

24.9.1 India's Successes in Information Technology Services

India has not been able to significantly increase its share of manufactured exports like its East Asian neighbors. However, in recent years it has made unprecedented progress in exports of information technology services, and more recently in business process outsourcing. India was until fairly recently falling seriously behind the economic development of China, but the success of its service exports has brought some hope and confidence about the future to this vast country. Over the last decade India's market share of service exports has tripled, rising to 1.5 percent of world services exports. After China, India is the largest services exporter among the developing countries. Meanwhile, services have become an increasingly large

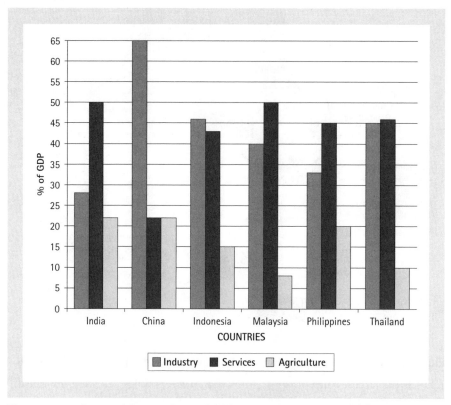

Figure 24.7. Sectoral Comparison of GDP across Countries 2001 (adapted from table 4.14 in Reserve Bank of India, 2004; Thirlwell, 2004: 87)

proportion of total Indian exports, with their share rising from 20 percent in 1990 to more than 30 percent in 2002 (Thirlwell, 2004: 43). India's reliance on services to forge its future distinguishes it from the other East Asian economies that have developed manufacturing and services together (Figure 24.7).

India has become a world leader in the export of IT services, including on-site service contracts and off-site software support, ahead of Ireland, the United States, Germany, and the UK. This often places Indian exporters in direct competition with enterprises in developed economies. India has achieved growing market penetration in the United States, which is the destination for two-thirds of Indian software exports. More than half the Fortune 500 companies are outsourcing to India, including AOL, Citigroup, Dell, Hewlett-Packard, HSBC, and J. P. Morgan Chase (Thirlwell, 2004: 45; Dossani and Kenney, 2003). Multinational providers of services have followed, moving an increasing share of their work to low-cost offshore facilities (providing offshore outsourcing services through FDI and affiliated trade in services). With

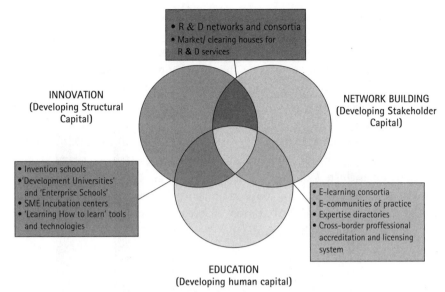

Figure 24.8. Leveraging Knowledge Assets through Clusters (adapted from Tallisayon, 2006)

hundreds of thousands of qualified IT professionals joining the labor force each year, India has the largest concentration of information technology skills in the world.

24.9.2 High-Tech Clusters

International experience suggests that the most intensive innovation occurs in industrial clusters in urban communities that have capability, infrastructural support, and other amenities. It is not possible for East Asian governments to wish into existence these high-technology clusters, though every government has adopted ambitious policies for information and communication technology developments (see Appendix?). Japan, Singapore, and Taiwan have laid the groundwork for such clusters by combining local capacity and international linkages forged through trade, FDI, and the movement of knowledge workers. Other countries such as China, Korea, and Malaysia, each of which has a base in high-tech manufacturing industries, are attempting to induce clusters that fuse manufacturing capability with research and producer services. The expensive, high-risk, state-sponsored approach involves investing heavily in a transport and communications infrastructure, serviced land, research facilities, and providing incentives for high-tech industries to locate in the designated area. More promising environments are open urban milieux that cultivate creativity, offer opportunities for collaboration with firms in other clusters that support innovation, and invite the circulation of human capital from overseas. One advantage of East Asia is the large diaspora of skilled workers participating in leading North American clusters of innovation, who have acquired intangible capital, business contacts, and financial wealth. As in the development of Hong Kong, Singapore, and Taiwan, these individuals can be the nuclei for cluster development in East Asia—providing there is a welcoming institutional environment. Many Chinese and Indian technological entrepreneurs would be happy to return to their country of origin, if the opportunities to achieve their business potential there are real rather than illusory. The lifeblood of dynamic clusters is the continuing innovation of firms, and the constant networking among them. Knowledge assets may be cross-leveraged through regional clusters of education, innovation, and network building (Figure 24.8). The possibility of creating local versions of wireless networked communities, engaging in the continual collaboration enabled by social computing, is actively being pursued in Asia (ADB, 2006, 2007).

24.10 Conclusions

The East Asian economies led by Japan, and more recently and spectacularly China and India, have demonstrated a huge potential for developing human capital, and achieving great strides forward in economic growth and social development. The question is whether this model of rapid growth may be extended to the rest of the developing world that has in recent times struggled simply to stand still. The inescapable conclusion is that in terms of economic development most of the rest of the developing world is between a rock and a hard place. While the economic stasis of absolute poverty is damaging to the economic vitality and cultural integrity of large parts of the developing world, the alternative of an endless struggle with unbalanced terms of trade in resources and commodity production is not providing the increased prosperity and contentment that was promised. Until the terms of international trade, investment, aid, and debt are resolved in a more balanced way, much of the developing world will be left reflecting on what might have been regarding their progress towards a knowledge economy (Roberts, 2009).

For those few economies in East Asia and elsewhere that have been successful in developing the human, economic, and technological capital for the ongoing pursuit of a knowledge economy, there will continue to be the demanding task of encouraging the institutions and the business and educational relationships that will match them equally with advanced industrial countries of the West. 'To a significant extent future competition will essentially be competition between alternative firm-level learning and innovation systems. While these are constructed by firms, they depend increasingly on external assets and relationships' (Scott-Kemmis, 2008: 47). This will involve, more than any other factor, a concentration on developing the human capital of people while allowing people the freedom to define their own objectives and ideals.

References

ACEMOGLU, D., JOHNSON, S., and ROBINSON, J. (2005). 'Institutions as the Fundamental Cause of Long-Run Growth', in Philippe Aghion and Steven Durlauf (eds.), *Handbook of Economic Growth* (Amsterdam: Elsevier), 386–414.

Asian Development Bank (2006). *Ubiquitous Networked Society and the Knowledge-Based Economy* (Manila: ADB).

——(2007). *Moving Towards Knowledge Based Economies: Asian Experiences* (Manila: ADB).

BAIROCH, P. (1982). 'International Industrialisation Levels from 1750–1980', *Journal of European History*, 2: 268–333.

BAKER, D. P., and HOLSINGER, D. B. (1996). 'Human Capital Formation and School Expansion in Asia: Does a Unique Regional Model Exist?', *International Journal of Comparative Sociology*, 37: 155–73.

BARNEY, J. (1991). 'Firm Resources and Sustained Competitive Advantage', *Journal of Management*, 17(1): 99–120.

BOWMAN, M. (1969). 'Economics of Education', *Review of Educational Research*, 39(5): 641–70.

CHAMINADE, C., and EDQUIST, C. (2006). *Rationales for Public Policy Intervention from a Systems of Innovation Approach: The Case of VINNOVA*, CIRCLE Electronic Working Paper Series Paper, 2006/04.

CLARKE, T. (1999). 'The Development of Management Education in China', *Education and Training*, 41(6–7): 273–6.

DEDRICK, J., and KRAEMER, K. (2005). *New Product Development in a Global Knowledge Network: The Notebook PC Industry* (Irvine, Calif.: Personal Computing Industry Center, University of California).

DOSSANI, R., and KENNEY, M. (2003). *Went for Cost, Stayed for Quality? Moving the Back Office to India* (Berkeley Roundtable on the International Economy, Working Paper 156, University of California at Berkeley, Aug.).

DUNNING, J. H. (2006). 'Towards a New Paradigm of Development: Implications for the Determinants of International Business Activity', *Transnational Corporations*, 15(1): 173–228.

EASTERLY, W. (2001). *The Elusive Quest for Growth: Economists' Adventures and Misadventures in the Tropics* (Cambridge, Mass.: MIT Press).

EVANS, P. (2007). *In Search of the 21st Century Developmental State* (University of California, Berkeley, Working Paper, 27 July).

——and STAVETEIG, S. (2006). *21st Century Industrialisation and Development in the Global South: The Chinese Case in Comparative-Historical Perspective* (University of California, Berkeley, Working Paper, 17 Jan.).

FREEMAN, C. (1995). 'The "National System of Innovation" in Historical Perspective', *Cambridge Journal of Economics*, 19: 5–24.

GEORGHIOU, L., SMITH, K., TOIVANEN, O., and YLÄ-ANTTILA, P. (2003). *Evaluation of the Finnish Innovation Support System* (Helsinki: Ministry of Trade and Industry Publications, 5/2003; pp. 38).

GOUJON, A., and SAMIR, K. C. (2006). *Past and Future of Human Capital in Southeast Asia: From 1970 to 2030* (Vienna Institute of Demography, Working Papers, July).

GRANT, R. (1996). 'Toward a Knowledge-Based Theory of the Firm', *Strategic Management Journal*, 17: 109–22.

GUNTER, G. B., and HOEVAN, R. (2004). *The Social Dimension of Globalisation* (Working Paper, 24, World Commission on the Social Dimensions of Globalisation; Geneva: International Labour Office).

HATCH, W. F. (2003). 'Agenda for Asian Regionalism: Industrial Harmonisation, Not Free Trade', *Japanese Economy*, 32(2): 86–97.

HELPMAN, ELHANAN (2004). *The Mystery of Economic Growth* (Cambridge, Mass.: Harvard University Press).

HOFF, KARLA, and STIGLITZ, JOSEPH (2001). 'Modern Economic Theory and Development', in Gerald Meier and Joseph Stiglitz (eds.), *Frontiers of Development Economics* (New York: Oxford University Press).

KRUGMAN, P. R. (1987). 'Is Free Trade Passé?', *Journal of Economic Perspective*, 1(2): 131–44.

—— (1989). *Exchange-Rate Instability* (Cambridge, Mass.: MIT Press).

—— (1992). 'Does the New Trade Theory Require a New Trade Policy?', *World Economy*, 15(4): 423–42.

—— (1994). 'The Myth of Asia's Miracle', *Foreign Affairs*, 73(6): 62–78.

—— and VENABLES, ANTHONY J. (1995). 'Globalization and the Inequality of Nations', *Quarterly Journal of Economics*, 110(4): 857–80.

LINGLE, C. (1997). *The Rise and Decline of the Asian Century* (Hong Kong: Asia 2000).

LIU, G., ZHANG, S., and ZHANG, Z. (2010). *Investing in Human Capital for Economic Development in China* (Singapore: World Scientific Books).

LUCAS, R. E. (1988). 'On the Mechanics of Economic Development', *Journal of Monetary Economics*, 22(1): 3–42.

MADDISON, A. (2000). *The World Economy: A Millennial Perspective* (Paris: OECD).

MIZRAHI, Y. (2004). *Capacity Enhancement Indicators* (Washington, DC: World Bank Institute).

NG, P. T. (2008). 'Educational Reform in Singapore: From Quantity to Quality', *Educational Research for Policy and Practice*, 7(1): 5–15.

O'DOHERTY, D., and ARNOLD, E. (2003). *Understanding Innovation: the Need for a Systemic Approach* (The IPTS Report, 71; Seville: IPTS).

OECD (2001). *Competencies for the Knowledge Economy* (Paris: OECD).

—— (2003). *Human Capital Formation and Foreign Direct Investment in Developing Countries* (Working Paper, 211; Paris: OECD).

OZAWA, T., CASTELLO, S., and PHILLIPS, R. J. (2001). 'The Internet Revolution, the McLuhan Stage of Catch-up, and Institutional Reforms in Asia', *Journal of Economic Issues* (Lincoln: Association for Evolutionary Economics Fiscal Office), 35(2): 289–98.

PITELIS, C. (2009). 'The Sustainable Competitive Advantage and Catching-up of Nations: FDI, Clusters, and the Liability (Asset) of Smallness?', *Management International Review*, 49(1): 95–120.

PORRITT, J. (2007). *Capitalism as if the World Matters* (London: Earthscan).

PORTER, M. (1990). *The Competitive Advantage of Nations* (Basingstoke: Macmillan).

—— KETELS, C., and DELGADO, M. (2007). 'The Microeconomic Foundations of Prosperity: Findings from the Business Competitiveness Index', in A. Lopez-Claros, M. E. Porter, X. Sali-i-Martin, and K. Schwab, *The Global Competitiveness Report 2006–2007* (Houndmills, Basingstoke: Palgrave Macmillan).

RICARDO, D. (1966). *Economic Essays*, ed. with introductory essay and notes by E. C. K. Gonner (new York: A. M. Kelley).

ROBERTS, J. (2009). 'The Global Knowledge Economy', *Critical Perspectives on International Business*, 5(4): 285–303.

RODRIK, D. (2004). *Growth Strategies* (Working Paper, Kennedy School of Government; Cambridge, Mass.: Harvard University).

—— SUBRAMANIAN, A., and TREBBI, F. (2004). 'Institutions Rule: The Primacy of Institutions over Geography and Integration in Economic Development', *Journal of Economic Growth*, 9: 131–65.

ROMER, P. M. (1986). 'Increasing Returns and Long-Run Growth', *Journal of Political Economy*, 94(5): 1002–37.

——(1990). 'Endogenous Technological Change', *Journal of Political Economy*, 98(5): 71–102.

——(1994). 'The Origins of Endogenous Growth', *Journal of Economic Perspectives*, 8: 3–22.

SCOTT-KEMMIS, D. (2008). *Review of the Australian Textile, Clothing and Footwear Industry*, ii. *Industry Policy Frameworks for a Knowledge Economy* (Canberra: Commonwealth of Australia).

SEN, A. (1994). 'Well-Being, Capability and Public Policy', *Giornale degli Economist e Annali di Economia*, 53: 333–47.

——(1999). *Development as Freedom* (New York: Knopf).

SHAPIRO, H., and TAYLOR, L. (1990). 'The State and Industrial Strategy', *World Development*, 18(6): 861–78.

SORENSON, O. (2003). 'Social Networks and Industrial Geography', *Journal of Evolutionary Economics*, 13: 513–27.

SPENDER, J.-C. (1996). 'Competitve Advantage from Tacit Knowledge? Unpacking the Concept and its Strategic Implications', in Bertrand Moingeon and Amy Edmondson (eds.), *Organisational Learning and Competitive Advantage* (London: Sage Publications), 56–73.

STABER, U. (2001). 'The Structure of Networks in Industrial Districts', *International Journal of Urban and Regional Research*, 25: 537–52.

STIGLITZ, J. (2001). 'Foreword', in K. Polanyi (ed.), *The Great Transformation: The Political and Economic Origins of our Time* (Boston: Beacon Press).

TALISAYON, S. D. (2006). *Paradigm Shifts for Survival in the Knowledge Economy* (Paranaque Citz, Philippines: Centre for Conscious Living Foundation).

TALLMAN, S., JENKINS, M., HENRY, N., and PINCH, S. (2004). 'Knowledge, Clusters, and Competitive Advantage', *Academy of Management Review*, 29: 258–71.

TAN, C. (2008). 'Globalisation, the Singapore State and Educational Reforms: Towards Performativity', *Education, Knowledge and Economy*, 2(2): 111–20.

TAYLOR, M., and LEONARD, S., eds. (2002). *Embedded Enterprise and Social Capital* (Aldershot: Ashgate).

TEECE, D. (2000). *Managing Intellectual Capital* (Oxford: Oxford University Press).

THIRWELL, M. P. (2004). *India: The Next Economic Giant* (Lowy Institute Paper 01; Double Bay, NSW: Lowy Institute for International Policy).

TILAK, J. G. G. (2002). *Building Human Capital in East Asia: What Others Can Learn* (Washington, DC: World Bank).

UNCTAD (2007). *World Investment Prospects Survey 2007–2009*. URL: http://www.unctad.org/en/docs//wips2007_en.pdf (accessed May 2010).

UNESCO (2007). *Global Education Spending Concentrated in a Handful of Countries* (Fact Sheet 3; Geneva: UNESCO Institute for Statistics, Oct.).

UZZI, B. (1997). 'Social Structure and Competition in Interfirm Networks: The Paradox of Embeddedness', *Administrative Science Quarterly*, 42: 35–67.

WERNERFELT, B. (1984). 'A Resource-Based View of the Firm', *Strategic Management Journal*, 5(2): 171–80.

Werner International (2007). 'International Comparison of the Hourly Labor Cost in the Primary Textile Industry 2007', *New Twist*, 3 (18 May). URL: http://www.werner-newtwist.com/en/newsl-vol-003/index.htm (accessed May 2010).

World Bank (2006). *The Knowledge Economy, the KAM Methodology and World Bank Operations* (Washington, DC: World Bank Institute).

World Trade Organization (2007). *World Trade 2006: Prospects for 2007*. URL: http://www.wto.org/english/news_e/pres07_e/pr472_e.htm#fnt8 (accessed May 2010).

YOUNG, A. (1994). 'Lessons from the East Asian NIE's: A Contrarian View', *European Economic Review*, 38: 964–73.

YUSUF, SHAHID (2003). *Innovative East Asia: The Future of Growth* (Washington, DC: World Bank).

—— (2004). 'Competitiveness through Technological Advances under Global Production Networking', in Yusuf *et al.*, 2004a: 1–34.

—— and EVENETT, S. J. (2002). *Can East Asia Compete* (Washington, DC: World Bank).

—— ALTAF, M. A, and NABESHIMA, K, (eds.) (2004a). *Global Production Networking and Technological Change in East Asia* (New York: Oxford University Press).

———————(eds.) (2004b). *Global Change and East Asian Policy Initiatives* (New York: Oxford University Press).

CHAPTER 25

......

THE FUTURE OF HUMAN CAPITAL

AN EMPLOYMENT RELATIONS PERSPECTIVE

......

THOMAS A. KOCHAN

ADAM SETH LITWIN

25.1 INTRODUCTION

......

The development and effective utilization of human capital serves as an increasingly vital source of value and competitive advantage for individual firms as well as for the economies in which they operate. While access to fertile land, raw materials, financial capital, and physical technologies may have been the dominant sources of competitive advantage in agrarian and industrial-era economies, knowledge, learning, and a set of reinforcing employment practices are the critical requirements to transform the term 'knowledge economy' from rhetoric to reality. In fact, research has demonstrated rather clearly that even all those observed performance and welfare gains that at first appear to be driven by state-of-the-art computers and information technology (IT) can just as well be ascribed to the human and organizational capital that makes those technologies so effective (Brynjolfsson and Hitt, 2003, Brynjolfsson et al., 2002).

The preceding chapters in this volume do a thorough job of showing how theories of human capital moved from their early-stage emphasis on individual, supply-side decisions regarding investments in education and training, to debates over when and why firms might share some of the costs of investing in workforce development, to more recent views on the relationship between human capital, social capital, firm strategies, and organizational design. We build on these points about the changing roles of individuals and firms, but add another: the importance of considering how *employment relationships* are changing and how labor-market institutions that have historically played key roles in addressing human capital-related challenges are now, too, eroding. As such, we pose a paradox. Just as human capital is growing in importance to individuals, firms, and national economies, many of the changes taking place in employment relationships and labor-market institutions are actually weakening both the incentives and the pressures on individual firms to invest. Resolving this paradox will require broadening the firm-centered approaches that dominate current analysis of human capital to give greater weight to extra-firm relationships, labor-market institutions, and the role of the state in overcoming market failures and encouraging business strategies that emphasize human capital as a source of competitive advantage. In line with this argument, this chapter draws on the employment relationship—not firms nor workers—as its unit of analysis.

It is not surprising that most theories of human capital treat the firm as the key unit of analysis, given the deep imprint that Becker (1964 [1993]) left with his early efforts to distinguish between general and specific human capital. It is especially understandable for research that focuses on American institutions and practices. Ever since the passage of the New Deal employment policies of the 1930s, firms have been assigned central roles in the delivery and financing of a variety of labor-market services,[1] including the provision of workforce training and development (Osterman *et al.*, 2001). Most of the chapters in this volume reflect this emphasis by exploring how individuals and firms allocate the costs and share the benefits of human capital, incorporating human capital development into alternative theories of the firm (such as transaction cost, resource-based, agency, entrepreneurial, and knowledge-based perspectives), and how human capital plays into emerging research on social capital, organizational capabilities, learning, and human resource strategies and architectures. But, as Chapters 12, 22, and 23 each suggest, firm-centric theories, particularly those founded upon the neoclassical economics framework, need to more fully take into account how firm boundaries, strategies, and practices relate to other institutions in society. This is particularly important given the changes in employment relationships that are acting to reduce the labor-market functions served by individual employers. In short, the central argument of this chapter is that a more up-to-date theory of the changing nature of employment relationships is needed to understand whether and how human capital is to serve as a source of competitive advantage in a modern economy—even one as decentralized as that of the US.

In the sections that follow we introduce a basic theoretical framework used to guide employment relations theory and research, and outline several assumptions about the nature of that system that have implicitly guided development and use of human capital within that system during the height of the industrial era—essentially the four decades after enactment of the New Deal legislation of the 1930s. Then, we note how changes in this system pose difficulties for the traditional actors and institutions to continue to perform their functions of developing and making full use of human capital today. Finally, we suggest a set of changes in organizational practices, labor-market institutions, and public policies that will be needed in order to realize a human capital or knowledge-driven economy. We undertake all of this by relying on three particular human capital-related issues that challenge our existing understanding of the way that employment relationships function: human capital investment and development, work–life integration, and technologically engendered changes in work.

25.2 BASIC FEATURES OF AN EMPLOYMENT RELATIONS SYSTEM

Much of researchers' understanding of the employment relationship has been shaped by Dunlop's concept of an 'industrial relations system' (Dunlop 1958 [1993]). According to Dunlop, workers and their representatives bargain implicitly or explicitly with their employers to determine a wide set of observable outcomes encompassing everything from wages to work structures to workplace norms. These interactions, and the resulting 'web of rules', were influenced by three aspects of the bargaining context: the technological characteristics of the work itself and of the wider society, the economic factors impacting upon labor, product, and factor markets, and the locus and distribution of power in society. As an illustration, imagine a major technological breakthrough allowing for easy substitution of capital for labor. Workers would find it difficult to maintain their wages and employment, unless, perhaps, one of the components of the new capital were to witness an inordinate price increase. Therefore, the system would have to process these two opposing forces—potential efficiencies arising from technological change and the potential costs attendant to capital substitution—as it recalibrated to a revised set of outcomes. Extensions to Dunlop's original framework make it useful for explaining a wide range of strategic decisions (for example, Budd, 2004; Kochan et al., 1984)—such as the choice to produce inhouse or to outsource, or the choice to use technology in a way that is 'upskilling' or in a way that is deskilling (Hunter et al., 2001). Among the attractive features of this framework is its respect for market forces and the forces of technological change, but insistence that these forces alone cannot and should not determine outcomes.

Perhaps most remarkable about the original framework is its perceived stability. The roles of employee and employer were clearly defined—unlike in today's economy that acknowledges the ubiquity of self-employment, contracting, and contingent work, among other unconventional arrangements. In Dunlop's world, the parties assumed one another a permanent fixture of the relationship—a sometimes disagreeable partner with whom they would have to engage in order to weather cyclical or structural changes in the world around them. Intensified competition for the company's product, for example, impacted both parties. Changes in production standards meant that factories and workers might need to be retooled or retrained. But, through it all, the employment relationship would weather the storm, internalize the costs and the benefits of resulting adjustments, and partition them across workers and firms. We argue that this industrial relations system, which today we might call an 'employment relations system' or a set of work arrangements, can no longer be assumed an effective processor of the environmental changes affecting the development and use of human capital, even as we transition into an economic era in which it serves as the chief driver of value and competitive advantage. We turn next to identifying the set of assumptions that underpin our existing notions of the employment relationship—assumptions that must be changed if we are to effectively leverage human capital.

25.2.1 Inherited Assumptions Underpinning the Employment Relationship

Whether or not we realize it, researchers and policy-makers bring a set of assumptions to bear on their study of the employment relationship. By and large, these assumptions go unstated and unnoticed until systems that once behaved reasonably well in light of the assumptions—maybe an outlier here or an anomaly there—start to produce as many unexplainable outcomes as they do explainable ones. Our central argument is that the very future of human capital hinges on a large-scale recasting of several key assumptions regarding the employment relationship, away from those developed in the context of an industrial economy to a new set that promotes competition on the basis of workers' productive skills and accumulated knowledge.

The first assumption regarded the geographic scope of competition. Industrial-era theories of employment relations, Dunlop (1958 [1993]) included, assumed that national economies were self-contained. Therefore, it was reasonable for states to set and enforce minimal standards for wages and working conditions and for unions and other labor-market institutions to effectively 'take wages out of competition' (Commons, 1909). Firms may not have welcomed these regulatory floors or the pressures associated with unions and collective bargaining, for example, but these policies and institutions did help to level the competitive playing field within both product and labor markets. Second, clear boundaries were drawn between the economy on the one hand, and households on the other. Their only intersection in the labor market was the dominant male wage-earner, or 'breadwinner'. His wages and benefits were the family's primary support, complemented by the contributions of wives and mothers to non-economic, 'home production'—a role to which they were assumed to be just as committed as men were to their paid work. Third, the job held by the male head of household was assumed to be full-time, long-term, stable, and usually with a very large industrial employer. The fourth assumption dealt with these employers, assuming them to be corporations housing clear, well-understood hierarchies of 'managers' and 'workers' within, and well-defined boundaries between themselves and the external product, labor, and capital markets in which they participated. One consequence of this was that anybody who 'worked for' the firm was an employee, and not a contingent worker, a contractor, nor any other classification that today we might refer to as 'non-traditional'. Finally, out of the New Deal regulations and institutional arrangements emerged an implicit social contract in which long tenure and good performance in an organization were rewarded with wages and employment security that generally grew in tandem with profits and productivity. This social contract served as the glue holding the entire system together.

As noted above, the constellation of institutions that make up incumbent employment systems once effectively internalized many of the costs and benefits of a functioning labor market, including those associated with three areas that are critical to the development and effective use of human capital—phenomena that we will use to illustrate how the system is changing. These tasks are (1) human capital investment and development, (2) utilization of human resource investments in the labor market, with particular emphasis on the changing role of women and work–life practices and policies, and (3) organizational strategies and practices that serve as complements needed to generate the full benefits from human capital—in particular, the role of technology and technological change. Examination of these phenomena reveals the gaps in our present approach to the employment relationship.

25.2.2 Human Capital Investment and Development

Investments in education and training are obviously critical to economies founded upon human capital—a point driven home by the previous chapters in this volume. However, as Blair notes in her chapter, the earliest pronouncements of what came to be regarded as human capital theory—most notably, Becker (1964 [1993])—theorized that much of the human capital required of workers would be systematically underprovided by the normal functioning of a competitive labor market. At the time, however, casual observation, not to mention data, repudiated the theory (for example, Berg,

1970 [2003]). Many employers offered what could only be categorized as general training—confident that their employees, the objects of their investment, would remain with them long enough to deliver anticipated economic benefits. In this way, employment arrangements even managed the provision of continuing education and the training of adult workers. Thus, as the chapters in Part II of this volume emphasize, a deeper and more nuanced theory of the relationship of human capital and firm behavior was needed to explain this seemingly irrational behavior on the part of employers.

The problem that Becker's theory addressed was that of 'poaching'—a phenomenon forestalled by the once-prevailing stability of employment relationships. But what happens when employment relationships cannot be assumed so stable? To the extent that a single firm invests in training and development, or what is now being called 'life-long learning', and to the extent that some or all of the skills developed are general enough to have value on the external labor market, competitors can 'poach' these workers, leaving the investing employer to bear the costs while the recruiting employer gains the benefits of the newly formed human capital—just as Becker theorized. The way that firms mitigated this market dilemma in the industrial era was through the social contract described above. Firms implicitly promised long-term employment opportunities within their organizations in which employees would gain greater status, job security, income, and retirement benefits, and thus have incentives to stay with the firm. These promises were partly based on trust and norms, but were also reinforced by practices that Doeringer and Piore (1971) labeled 'internal labor markets' (ILMs).

ILMs were a common way of structuring work in the industrial era. In their purest form, the firm initially appoints workers at the bottom rung of a tall, rigidly defined job ladder, ascending in title, wages, and responsibilities according to an accepted set of rules, norms, and customs within the firm. Each function or department has its own ladder, and workers are not expected to cross functions—let alone jump off of one firm's ladder and onto another's. In fact, with this model, job tasks are clearly delineated and arranged in such a way that each job prepares the incumbent for the next, higher job he or she will be holding. Were a worker enticed by another employer, he or she would be reluctant to give up their accrued benefits and seniority, so they became loyal, long-term employees. In the event of an economic slowdown, employers would not want to lay off the human capital in which they had invested, lest they create empty rungs in well-functioning job ladders. This made for loyal, long-term employers. Therefore, as long as ILM structures were stable, a great many employers provided workers with the sort of general training that should have made their workers ripe for poaching. Under the stylized version of the employment relationship described above, an expectation of long-term employment among both employers and employees engendered a level of certainty regarding which parties would benefit from workers' increased productivity—the employer providing the training and the worker in whose mind the newly created human capital would reside. Just how the incremental surplus would be split between labor and capital was probably not completely settled *ex ante*, but workers, often with the help of their unions' role in collective bargaining, could anticipate their accruing some share of these productivity gains in the form of real wage increases. What is more, these investments on the part of firms actually reinforced the strength of existing employment relationships, as employers were more likely to hold onto excess labor through cyclical slowdowns. As noted above, laying off a worker, aside from its violation of norms, meant forgoing any and all future returns to the firm's investment.[2]

Workers also absorbed human capital in informal ways as they moved through their respective ILMs. Promotions arose, in part, from one's willingness to accept and pass on largely firm-specific skills. Furthermore, more-senior workers felt protected from competition from below, and were thus willing to train those employees on lower rungs of the job ladder. What resulted was an efficient system for training and retraining workers (Osterman and Burton, 2005)—a system that did not even need to appear explicitly on the firm's books.

Firms, however, did not necessarily invest in human capital purely of their own volition—a point often underemphasized in standard economic models of the firm as well as in the more recent transaction-cost, resource-based, and agency models discussed in this volume. Organized labor, for its own part and sometimes in conjunction with firms, played an active role in maintaining and growing the economy's human capital stock. Industrial unions leveraged their bargaining power to demand that workers' training be kept up to date. Some of this training, as we will discuss, was specifically intended to protect against employee displacement resulting from capital substitution. However, in the presence of job security provisions, employer-funded 'upskilling' also served the firm's interests. Along a parallel but separate track, craft unions such as those encompassing plumbers, electricians, and other building trades developed and funded apprenticeship programs, often in partnership with industry-wide employer organizations as well as the state. In sum, the institutions that scaffolded the employment relationship bolstered human capital formation in ways unimaginable under standard neoclassical assumptions of a 'spot market' for labor.

25.2.3 Work–Life Integration

Perhaps less obvious, but equally important to the healthy functioning of a human capital-intensive economy, are the ways it manages the integration of labor's working and non-working lives.[3] The term 'work–life integration' most often refers to the costs exacted upon workers and their families from the intensification of the demands placed on them by their employers. Surprisingly, however, there is little discussion in the human capital literature of the fact that many economies have allowed a significant portion of their human capital investment to be underutilized because of assumptions and practices concerning the appropriate division of labor between men and women. This becomes an even bigger problem now than in the past as a clear majority of university degrees in the US are awarded to women, bringing the stock of this one particular form of human capital to within sight of gender equality (US Bureau of the Census, 2008).

We have already seen the benefits of long-term employment for human capital formation. Another upshot of long-term employment was a perception among employers that corporate investments in workers' non-work lives would bring returns to the firm. This view was most notably illustrated in 1913, by Henry Ford's introduction of the five-dollar day—part of a larger benefits package that included what we think of today as profit-sharing. The argument was that by the payment of a higher wage, not only would turnover be reduced, but male employees would earn enough to care for their families (Jacoby, 1985). This way, workers' wives, whom Ford also presumed to be the mothers of workers' children, could attend to home and family duties. That these wages were also high enough for his workers to afford his product was no accident. Suffice it to say that it was beneficial for employers to set wage levels sufficiently high such that the income of a single family member— the man—could dovetail with a woman's full commitment to 'home production' in meeting the needs of family life. In the US it also meant the provision of health and retirement benefits to fill in the gaps left by government programs—a practice later reinforced by public policy. This sort of solution was highly presumptive with respect to workers' preferences regarding the household division of labor, but it implicitly guided employment relations practices for much of the industrial era. It had the negative effect, however, of underutilizing the human capital investments which society made in women's education. Not surprisingly, women were system-atically less likely to gain access to employer-sponsored education and training opportunities (Lynch, 1992). This was less of a problem for the overall economy, however, as long as women were willing to specialize in homework and view their paid labor-market activities as secondary to their husbands'. As the educational attainment of women increased and family structures became more varied, the demands to modify this 'male breadwinner' model of employment intensified. Thus there gradually developed the pressure to develop better work–life policies that allow women and men to fully utilize their human capital in the paid labor force.

There are a number of reasons why labor-market forces cannot solve this problem on their own. Drago and Hyatt (2003) point out that a market failure occurs in the production of work family benefits similar to that of human capital investments. Left purely to the market, firms will not provide a sufficient level of benefits to facili-tate work–life integration. An individual employer will generally opt not to offer on-site childcare, for example, because they (and those employees without children) would absorb its full costs. That is, prospective employees anticipating demand for the benefit would flock to the firm, but would probably leave the firm once they no longer needed the services of on-site childcare. Therefore, a program that may well provide a net social benefit would prove unprofitable to individual employers. Of course, if all employers offered or contributed equally to the provision of this benefit, prospective workers would spread themselves more or less evenly across the firms, and the problem would vanish.

Aside from some sort of legal mandate, another way to deal with market failures is via coordination through collective bargaining that spreads common rules or patterns across competitors. This point, too, has been underdeveloped in most theoretical models and empirical studies of human capital. Collective bargaining facilitates work–life integration in a number of ways. To the extent which it boosts salaries and workers' expectations of long-term financial security, it softens the opportunity cost attendant to one's reallocation of time and energy from work to non-work activities. Union wage structures, characterized by the 'rate for the job' mantra, also standardize pay and benefits. In conjunction with rigid, transparent rules regarding staffing and promotions, this system for wage determination guards against the sort of 'rat race' that ensues in workplaces in which pay and promotions are determined solely by individual-level and often crude measures of performance, such as 'billable hours' (Landers *et al.*, 1996, 1997).

Alternatively, some unions such as the Harvard Union of Clerical and Technical Workers (HUCTW) negotiate explicitly for these benefits. In its contract with Harvard University, it prioritized the delivery of work and family benefits to its members, securing thirteen weeks of paid maternity leave (extremely generous by US standards) with flexibility to use additional time accrued through unused vacation and sick days. Other unions have negotiated with multiple employers to construct more far-reaching programs. For example, the Service Employees International Union (SEIU) Local 1199 in New York City responded to its members' demands for childcare benefit by negotiating with several employers for the creation of an omnibus program jointly funded and administered by labor and management. It now includes over 350 employers, providing childcare centers, tuition vouchers, and even a summer camp for about 8,000 children every year.[4]

Government's role with respect to work–life integration is to 'remove from competition' those aspects of the employment relationship deemed valuable from a social standpoint that could fall victim to market forces. For example, one can argue that even if an individual employer does not benefit from encouraging working parents to take leave around the birth of a child, the long-term benefits to the child, the working parent, the present and future employers of the working parent, and the foregone long-term costs to the state 'net out' to a positive social benefit. Moreover, to the extent that effective work–life policies allow more continuous attachment to the labor force among women, prior public investments in their education and development should reap higher rates of return and potential skill shortages should be reduced. There is tremendous cross-country variation in the degree to which states have undertaken this responsibility by mandating or funding various forms of paid and unpaid leave for childbirth, child-rearing, elder care, and so on, with the US and Australia lagging behind other advanced industrialized nations with respect to these sorts of progressive policies. With some national exceptions, it is fair to say that even under the old social contract of the employment relationship, governments abdicated much of their policy-making responsibilities to employers, who themselves pushed the costs onto the families of their employees. Nonetheless, the employment relationship processed these issues in such a way that working people could afford to work a reasonable number of hours each week without abdicating non-work responsibilities and commitments.

25.2.4 Technological Change

In the industrial era, technology and technological change were largely viewed as capital substitution through automation, resulting in a debate over the net economic and social effects of technological change. To the extent that firms felt committed to their workers, the automation decision rested, in part, on the costs of redeploying labor to other parts of production still requiring labor input. In this way, decisions regarding new technologies, on the one hand, and training and retraining, discussed above, became inextricable. Furthermore, any particular manifestation of new technology could end up being harmful or beneficial to workers, depending upon how the innovation worked its way through the employment relations framework. That is, a particular machine was not in and of itself 'upskilling' or deskilling.

Unions recognized, as one of their chief goals, the protection of workers from the adverse impact of technological changes, including the substitution of power-driven equipment for human strength or investments in machines that are faster and less prone to need repair. Contrary to what some may believe, outright opposition of unions to technological change was just one of many ways in which unions protected their members. In most cases, union leaders envisaged some path by which the rank and file could capture a share of the incremental gains resulting from the new technology. Frequently, union negotiators would elicit a job security pledge from employers in exchange for a promise that workers would be encouraged to embrace the new technology. This allowed managers the freedom, within this one constraint, to decide how labor should be redeployed as well as the nature and scope of programs for training and retraining the incumbent workforce. Unions also bargained for the creation of so-called 'Automation Funds'—the most well-known of which resulted from the mechanization of the meat-packing industry in the 1960s (Shultz and Weber, 1966). With seed money provided by Armour & Co., the fund, administered by a joint labor–management committee, undertook extensive examination of the adverse effects of 'modernization', yielding a number of creative solutions to keep workers whole. Aside from training and a program of interplant transfers, the committee embarked on an aggressive placement program, going so far as to visit prospective employers and to make the case for hiring former meat-packers. Programs like this one foreshadowed more extensive programs negotiated by the United Auto Workers (UAW) and the International Association of Machinists (IAM), among others, two decades later.

The public sector has the toughest role of all with respect to workplace technological change. On the one hand, it must maintain a regulatory regime that encourages product market competition, in part, on the basis of technological and production innovations. On the other hand, it has to pick up where existing market and institutional forces leave off with respect to maintaining workforce readiness and dispersing costs associated with technological displacement. As noted above, the responsibility falls on the public sector to realign the system providing workers with general skills training—in this case, the foundational skills required to interact with the new technology or to meet the skill demands of other employers. There are a number of ways to socialize the costs of technological progress. For example, the use of experience rating with respect to unemployment/redundancy benefits places some of the displacement burden on those employers benefiting from new technologies, and some of the remaining share onto those taxpayers presumably benefiting as consumers from the new technology. Laws such as the Worker Adjustment and Retraining Notification (WARN) Act in the US, or the Transfer of Undertakings/Protection of Employment (TUPE) Regulations in the UK, though meant to apply to a broader set of reasons for displacement, exemplify the type of regulations meant to mitigate technological displacement. They do so by providing workers with either severance pay or with time to begin the search for new employment. Finally, it is government's responsibility to fashion and enforce the set of procedures by which workers can unionize, availing themselves of the benefits of collective bargaining in this area, described above. In sum, the institutions defining the employment relationship were able to ensure that steady technological progress came not at the expense of any one party, but instead benefited workers, employers, and society at large.

25.3 SIGNS OF STRESS ON INCUMBENT EMPLOYMENT SYSTEMS

The social contract that held the industrial-era employment system together was far from perfect. Even at its best it was predicated, in large part, on employers' ability to push a great many costs onto women. And it depended on employer behaviors that lasted only as long as labor was strong enough to demand them (Kochan *et al.*, 1984; Jacoby, 1985). Customers also shouldered costs arising in the course of the three phenomena outlined above. In particular, a smaller number of producers with market power—a hallmark of the industrial era—could leverage product market power resulting from relatively inelastic demand for goods produced. Nonetheless, it is only through the social contract's unraveling that we begin to understand the assumptions on which it was based, and there is ample evidence that this process is well under way. Consider the differences in the behavior of America's largest employer before and after the unraveling. General Motors (GM) was America's largest private-sector employer from the 1950s through the 1970s. Its 1950 contract with the UAW provided an 'annual productivity factor' of 2 percent (3 percent in later years) as a way of rewarding workers for productivity increases, over and above regular cost-of-living adjustments. The firm also introduced pensions, health insurance, and joint training funds, establishing a standard that its competitors had little choice but to meet. Thus, GM served as a force for incrementally ratcheting up employment conditions and living standards. Today, Wal-Mart serves as America's largest, private-sector employer. Like GM in prior years, it provides shareholders with demonstrated growth and profitability, and its competitors likewise face pressure to follow the company's employment model (Dube *et al.*, 2007). However, the standard that Wal-Mart sets differs substantially from the standard established by GM in the 1950s. It pays wages that are 30 percent below the national average, and less than half its employees are covered by health insurance or retirement benefits. It has adamantly resisted unionization, and has found itself embroiled in suits over gender discrimination in pay and promotions, refusal to comply with statutory laws regarding overtime pay, and even well-documented cases of locking overnight cleaning crews into their stores (Lichtenstein, 2006).

This contrast highlights some of the longer-term trends revealing cracks and now outright gaps in employment systems. The surge of blue-collar layoffs beginning in the first half of the 1980s signaled that employers were willing to abdicate their historical duty to shield workers from market vicissitudes. A similar increase in layoff rates for white-collar workers came in the early 1990s, and hinted that ILMs may have begun to change for these workers as well. These layoffs had a source over and above intensified product market competition. Management's middle layers, in particular, found that their roles in communication and coordination could be substituted for with ever-cheapening computing power. The diffusion of IT also contributed to the growth in non-traditional, explicitly short-term and *ad hoc* forms of employment.

Without a long-term mindset, employers no longer view the formation and maintenance of human capital as their responsibility (Cappelli, 1999), implying, as Berg (1970 [2003]) has argued, that Becker's propositions regarding general training may have finally found some support in the data. The resulting training gap, aside from its obvious consequences for the economy, proves problematic for an additional reason. Employers actually set skill requirements and choose the technological tools that workers must learn to use. In other words, employers not only had the incentive to train—which now must be internalized some other way—but also had information on the composition of training demands, beneficial to the entire economy.

The widening distribution of incomes offers the most obvious manifestation of the ensuing general skills gap (Autor *et al.*, 2008). What is more, the adoption of new technologies, namely IT, in the workplace appears to be one of its chief causes, producing a phenomenon which economists label 'skill-biased technological change' (SBTC) (Acemoglu, 2002; Krueger, 1993). SBTC refers to the widening of the income distribution with respect to workers' stock of general human capital, typically measured as years of education. According to this theory, increases in earnings inequality result from the introduction of new technologies—computers and other forms of IT—which then increase demand for the highly skilled workers who use them. Just as employers increase their demand for highly skilled workers, they find it easier to substitute the new, inexpensive technology for their low-skilled workers, further exacerbating earnings differentials with respect to skill. Therefore, it appears that at the very time employers are abdicating what had been their responsibility to provide general human capital, technological change has actually made some of this human capital increasingly indispensable to both firms and workers.

Even this perverse consequence resulting from our outmoded, industrial era employment system could potentially be forestalled by the presence of trade unions. Depending on the particular circumstances, unions would probably accept, if not encourage, management's embrace of IT. However, they would also work to negotiate employment security as well as programs for training, retraining, and the redeployment of low-skilled workers. This would enable the technology to deliver its intended increases in productivity while spreading the costs of technological adjustment. However, in the wake of the precipitous decline in trade union density across Anglo-Saxon economies, most workers cannot rely on collective bargaining in this way. The result has been a crisis of life-long learning—potentially crippling for an economy rooted in human capital.

The absence of unions as a countervailing power is felt in yet another way. In the industrial era it was assumed that technological change would naturally result in capital substitution were it not for the strong tactics and demands of trade unions. In this way, collective bargaining dislodged notions of technological determinacy. When unions held sway over employers, firms had little choice but to undertake a 'high-road' strategy with respect to technological change. If firms wanted to adopt new technology, they generally had to find a way to do it with their existing workforce. As noted above, this meant that new technology brought increased investments in human capital. However, it also meant that labor would receive a prenegotiated share of the gains resulting from the technology, leaving the remainder of the pie—however big or small—to the firm's owners. Therefore, investments in technology actually drove managers to better manage all production inputs, including labor.[5] This meant, among other things, reorganizing work to make optimal use of the technology, incentivizing workers, and often empowering them with increased shop-floor authority to use the technology as they saw fit. Those plants that followed this path, introducing new technologies alongside innovative employment practices, indeed performed better than plants which attempted to manage without workforce buy-in or work reorganization, revealing performance complementarities occasioned by simultaneous investments in both human and technological capital (MacDuffie, 1995). Moreover, those plants that took the 'low road' were generally forced to compete on price (Arthur, 1992). As previous chapters have shown, when firms can draw on less expensive labor from developing countries, this is much less likely to be a source of sustainable competitive advantage relative to competition rooted in product quality or some other form of product differentiation.

It is with respect to work–life integration that the strains on legacy employment systems are perhaps most acute. After all, 'family-friendly' policies or other attempts at so-called 'flexibility' did not appear at GM until late in the 1990s, long after the firm's reign as model employer had passed. The public sector has only recently taken action in Australia, and is yet to do so in the US. Nonetheless, the challenges of work–life integration appeared relatively contained through the 1970s, due largely to the plurality of mothers and wives willing to specialize in home production. In the US, 70 percent of mothers in two-parent families now work in the paid labor force. Women with children in families near the median income have added, on average, 535 additional hours (about thirteen weeks) of paid work per year since 1979—an increase of nearly 56 percent! Men in this same category also saw increases, though much smaller in magnitude, netting out to an 18 percentage point jump in the number of annual hours worked per family. Given that three-quarters of the increases in family incomes come from the additional work hours of wives and mothers, it is safe to say that women have been used as an economic 'safety valve' over the last two decades (Mishel *et al.*, 2007). Indeed, employers mitigate the effects of trading off time at home for time at work by introducing 'family-friendly' benefits. However, these benefits are disproportionately made available to managers and professionals (Kochan, 2005). Even for these white-collar employees, career concerns and workplace culture have discouraged their use (Baird and Litwin, 2005; Eaton, 2003).

25.3.1 Revisiting Assumptions

Contrasting GM and Wal-Mart has crystallized much of what has been detailed earlier in this volume on the distinctions between industrial economies and human capital or knowledge economies. Those chapters also detail the causes, not just the consequences, of the transition. What is clear for us, however, is that the basic assumptions underpinning the employment relationship require revision.

Globalization—particularly the dissolution of borders with respect to the movement of capital, labor, and product—undermines the power of individual nations to regulate their labor markets in ways that encourage the right kinds of competition. Employers are correct when they argue that artificial floors on wages, benefits, and working conditions challenge their ability to compete in the product market. Thus, in one sense, former Wal-Mart CEO H. Lee Scott is right to dismiss our comparisons to the GM of an earlier era.

Some well-meaning critics contend that Wal-Mart should be setting the pace for wages and benefits for the entire economy, just as a unionized General Motors was said to have done in the postwar period, helping usher in the great American middle class that this country is so proud of and rightfully so. The facts are that retailing doesn't perform that same function in the economy as GM does or did. Retailing has never occupied the top tier of wages in this country, or in any country. (Greenhouse, 2005)

It is also true that many employers, particularly in the service sector, now create opportunities for those other than the full-time, long-term, 'ideal worker' envisioned in an earlier era, perhaps appealing to second and third earners—homemakers and students—in their households. This begins to compensate for the fact that full-time positions often pay too little to support a family. Finally, it is now the case that firms grow and shrink their employment rolls in response to market shocks—layoffs or redundancies. But they also do so in response to temporary and immediate demands for specific skills: human capital. Due in great part to IT, these human capital demands can often be more easily and more conveniently met not by establishing a conventional 'inhouse' employment relationship, but by outsourcing—taking advantage of one of the new, harder-to-define forms of employment assumed away in the conventional picture of employment. And it is the various forms in which these 'human capitalists' present themselves—independent contractors, freelancers, or temporary/contingent workers—that most obviously breaks the mold formed by existing assumptions. If they are not employees, how can they bargain collectively? What rules govern their interactions with firms, guaranteeing the rights and benefits more easily delivered under the held-over model of employment? More specifically, how will the economy once again cultivate labor's knowledge, skills, and abilities? How will it alleviate the stress, frustration, and insecurity attendant to emergent employment systems? And how can economies ensure that new technologies—particularly IT—allocate gains to a wide range of stakeholders? How managers and policy-makers respond to these sorts of questions determines the future of human capital, and begins with a thorough recasting of the assumptions underpinning the employment relationship.

25.4 RECASTING WORK ARRANGEMENTS FOR A HUMAN CAPITAL-INTENSIVE ECONOMY

So, how can we encourage the right work arrangements for this post-industrial, human capital-based economy? The answer must begin by highlighting the assumptions that require change as economies move from a more national-based industrial economy dominated by male breadwinners, to a global knowledge-driven economy with a diverse workforce and varied family arrangements. However, we first consider the one assumption that fits employment systems old and new the centrality of trust. We use 'trust' here in its broadest sense to mean the ability of two or more parties to share strategic or valuable information with each other without fear that it will be used to undermine one's interests. This type of trust is essential to sustaining productive interactions both within and across organizations. It is trust itself that has decayed and must be restored if organizations and national economies are to transition from industrial-era shareholder-dominated corporations to knowledge-based, human capital-centered companies capable of thriving under the new paradigm. Without trust, employers would have to abandon much of the human capital 'value proposition' articulated in previous chapters. For example, one way that human capital drives value is by pushing decision-making authority out to the front lines, empowering workers to use their own discretion to solve problems and to meet customer needs. This transforms the role of supervisor to one of coach and mentor, himself or herself guided by the idea that those closest to the work and to the customer are best positioned to make key decisions. It also requires that the organization and its managers respect and reward employees based on their contributions of human capital to the firm's goals. In this volume, Chapters 11 and 15 touch on the range of empirical substantiation for the performance effects of innovative employment practices that now abounds in the literature.[6] The importance of trust also carries over into supplier relations. MacDuffie and Helper (2006) have demonstrated that an important part of Toyota's competitive advantage over US auto companies lies in the trust which the company has built in supplier relationships—trust that allows for information-sharing and joint efforts to improve products and processes. The alternative—focusing solely on price reductions as one might with spot-market transactions—led to lower trust relationships, lower quality, and further loss of competitiveness in this industry. The implication is that trust continues to matter as a source of value, even when human capital is delivered by 'suppliers' rather than by employees *per se*.

Organizations, alternatively, can forgo the implementation of innovative employment practices, instead maintaining a 'command and control' or 'low road' approach in which workers defer to their managers for instruction and withhold their knowledge, expertise, and ideas. While unions may no longer be able to pressure firms into taking the 'high road' business strategy—a deliberate choice on the part of managers and their organizations—will be a key determinant of whether or not the new economy generates more efficient and more equitable outcomes than is currently the case. Empirical research conducted in retail banks (Hunter *et al.*, 2001; Autor *et al.*, 2002; Hunter and Lafkas, 2003), call centers (Batt, 1999, 2002), and machine shops (Kelley 1990), among other settings, has shown that management shapes how similar or identical forms of IT are applied in production, either to boost workers' skills, productivity, and earnings, or to reduce labor's power and role in production. IT can play an important role in promoting a knowledge economy by making it relatively inexpensive to push previously centralized information to frontline workers (Brynjolfsson and Mendelson, 1993). This enacts aforementioned complementarities between human and technological capital—complementarities that obtain even where technology allows for highly standardized work if, for example, variation exists in customers' expectations, needs, and potential value to the organization. Likewise, complementarities obtain where the technology generates output that requires human interpretation before this information can be communicated to the customer (Batt, 2002). Under these circumstances, attempts to deploy the technology without adopting the human capital elements of the new work system—usually some form of decentralized decision-making, team-based production, and incentive pay—generate little or no performance benefit (Brynjolfsson *et al.*, 2002; Bresnahan *et al.*, 2000, 2002). The lesson is that while unions are no longer able to pressure firms into taking the 'high road', firms ought to be encouraged by the prospect of complementarities to make this choice on their own. From either macroeconomic or organizational perspectives, it is clear that complementarities between human capital and IT rather than computers *per se* have been the real engine of economic growth (Black and Lynch, 2004; Bartel *et al.*, 2007).

All of these fruits of a human capital-centered economy turn, not surprisingly, on workers being well-trained and well-prepared for their new roles. It is therefore somewhat ironic (and unfortunate) that the old employment model was better poised to provide workers with human capital. As noted above, the onus fell largely on employers willing to invest in workers, based on mutual expectations of a long-term employment relationship. Given the decline in expected duration of employment as well as the increasing share of work done outside the boundaries of traditional employment, it is no longer a safe bet for workers to rely on their employers in this way. Thus, more of the investment burden now falls on individuals, extra-firm labor-market institutions, and government.

Trade unions, as noted above, have historically played an active role in training initiatives. Where they remain, many continue in this effort to keep their members' 'current' and employable. The IAM—one of the more pioneering industrial unions on this issue—has worked with one its largest employers, the Boeing Corporation, to develop a number of training programs (Long and Barrett, 2004; Barrett *et al.*, 2003). These are designed around structural and technological changes in the industry—namely, the shift from traditional materials to so-called 'composites', and the firm's goal to devote US production facilities to the high-value-added parts of the fabrication process. Without these training programs, managers would face a discrepancy between the skills they need and those of their incumbent workforce. Likewise, those low-seniority workers made redundant by competitive pressures would at least re-enter the labor market with cutting-edge, in-demand skills.

Unfortunately, the training needs of those working under the less conventional and less permanent arrangements characterizing the new human capital economy are not accommodated by the traditional industrial union model. Indeed, it is this idea that motivates Chapter 12 above, which details two of the ways that firms now go about acquiring human capital rather than developing it inhouse. Of course, that still begs the question of who will invest in and develop this general human capital. These workers must take charge of monitoring and maintaining their own skill sets. However, inspiration for the new types of institutional support comes from two sources: craft unions and professional associations. This is not surprising. Both of these organizational forms, even in an industrial economy, serve the needs of those whose primary contribution to the economy is knowledge rather than physical strength or dexterity. Both serve workers who are likely to feel at least as much of a long-term commitment to their craft or their profession as they do to the actual organization for which they work. Craft unions and professional associations are also well-positioned to maintain and signal high standards and to leverage scale economies in the delivery of training. Perhaps even more critically, these organizations can provide advantage for their members by forecasting technological changes and innovations and anticipating the resulting and ever-changing skill requirements.

Professional associations serving accountants, nurses, and civil engineers, and even lower-skilled occupations such as nurses' assistants and home healthcare attendants, provide good models of 'continuing education' (Kochan, 2005).[7] So do craft unions, with their well-developed apprenticeship systems.[8] Indeed, increasingly, craft unions are extending their reach to provide skills training to previously disenfranchised minorities to prepare them for 'green-collar' jobs in residential construction and building retrofitting (Pollin *et al.*, 2008). This may be one way in which unions and professional associations redefine and reassert their role in the contemporary economy. An additional avenue by which professional associations could assert themselves is as 'representatives' of, or at least suppliers of, resources for those working under non-traditional employment arrangements. The most prominent and successful attempt to undertake this responsibility in the US is a New York City-based group founded as Working Today and now called Freelancers Union. Freelancers Union provides its members with much of what craft unions provide for their members—namely, different forms of health and welfare benefits. Unlike a standard craft union, the Freelancers Union serves those with a wide mix of skill sets. However, the group does provide, among other things, training around issues common to freelancing, such as self-promotion through new media, budgeting for a 'business of one', and legal and tax issues around freelancing.

Finally, how can we ensure that the new economy addresses work–life integration better than it does at present, and more equitably than the institutions that appeared to address these issues in the industrial era? On the one hand, government can enact and fund paid forms of leave around childbirth and other major life events and responsibilities. However, even the most cooperative firms will find career-driven employees reluctant to take advantage of these benefits unless norms support their use. Thus, once again a collective action problem must be faced. This can only be done if employees collectively begin to voice their preferences and needs for flexibility to integrate their work and family responsibilities. While this need not and may not take the form of a traditional union, some functional equivalent of an employee voice mechanism may be required.

25.5 TOWARD THE FUTURE

The message from this reassessment is that significant institutional and policy reform will be needed in economies that want to grow, raise living standards, and achieve a more equitable distribution of income by making full use of all their human capital resources. We have focused on three challenges once addressed by the employment relationship that now require institutional and/or policy changes. The first is that paradoxically, just as human capital is becoming more critical to both individual firms and national economies, the decline in the expected duration of employment relationships and the weakening of union pressures reduces the willingness of individual firms to be a source of human capital investment. As Cappelli *et al.* note in Chapter 12, new external institutions—search firms and temporary help agencies—will need to play a bigger role in identifying and allocating talent. Professional associations and unions will need to expand their training, development, and placement roles. Government policy-makers will need to encourage formation of industry and/or labor-market networks that pool investments in training.

Second, the central role which women now play in the paid labor force implies the need to modify traditional assumptions about work and family life, norms, and expectations to support flexible work arrangements, and public policies to ensure that flexibility is widely available across the labor force. Failure to adapt to changes in work–family patterns risks systemic underutilization and low rates of return on women's human capital.

Third, new technologies need to be implemented in ways that not only deal with worker concerns for potential or real displacement, but in conjunction with changes in work practices needed for these technologies to generate their highest returns. This requires a different mindset—one in which technology and human capital are seen as complements rather than as substitutes.

All three of these changes in turn require new roles for government, employers, and labor organizations. Government will need to play a stronger role in coordinating private actions to overcome the market failures inherent in individual-firm-based human capital investment decisions. Labor unions, professional associations, and other groups that emerge to represent workers, will need to expand their roles as providers of education and training and as networks that link members to changing job opportunities. Finally, employers will need to become more engaged in the networks of firms, associations/unions, educational programs, search firms, and others that are becoming key sources of human capital development and allocation. In short, the key to achieving and benefiting from a human capital-led economy lies in developing modern extra-firm institutions in addition to innovative public policies. Indeed, this is needed to overcome classic market failures that arise from the competitive behavior of firms operating without institutional constraints. Thus, taken together, the changes in the economy, workforce, and workplace practices reviewed here illustrate that a complete theory of human capital and its role in the modern economy requires going beyond firm-centered theories to incorporate the full range of features that constitute an employment relations system.

ACKNOWLEDGMENT

Thanks are extended to Marian Baird for her insights, particularly with respect to work–life integration.

NOTES

1. Chief among these in the US are healthcare, pensions, and paid time off—much less the province of the public sector than they are in other Anglo-Saxon economies.
2. Cappelli's (2004) analysis of the corporate provision of general training shows firms to be concerned primarily with the deleterious effect of layoffs on the firm's stock of social capital, and Nahapiet's Ch. 2 above provides more detail on the intersection of human and social capital.
3. Frequently labeled 'work–family balance', we prefer the phrase 'work–life integration'. This underlines that workers have idiosyncratic preferences for how they allocate their time and energy between work and non-work activities (Rapoport et al., 2002). It also

allows for workers' non-familial but also non-working interests to figure into consideration, for example, community volunteering and civic responsibilities (Gomez and Gunderson, 2003).

4. Kochan (2005) details these and other initiatives.

5. This process, often referred to as the 'union shock effect', is usually attributed to Slichter (1941). However, Verma (2005) points out that Slichter never actually used this phrase.

6. Boselie *et al.* (2005) catalogue much of the empirical work to date in this area, and pay special attention to the varied methodological and theoretical paths taken by researchers.

7. Osterman *et al.* (2001) provide detailed examples of some of the government, institutional, and hybrid arrangements that have emerged in the US.

8. It is also worth noting Autor's (2001) finding that temporary help supply (THS) firms often fund workers' computer training. While this service is welfare-enhancing and particularly valuable to its participants, the model does not readily extend to life-long learning. It is also predicated on workers' self-selection as a signal of their latent ability, suggesting that it would break down entirely were it to be institutionalized as a method for workers to develop their human capital.

REFERENCES

ACEMOGLU, D. (2002). 'Technical Change, Inequality, and the Labor Market'. *Journal of Economic Literature*, 40(1): 7–72.

ARTHUR, J. B. (1992). 'The Link between Business Strategy and Industrial Relations Systems in American Steel Minimills', *Industrial and Labor Relations Review*, 45(3): 488–506.

AUTOR, D. H. (2001). 'Why do Temporary Help Firms Provide Free General Skills Training?', *Quarterly Journal of Economics*, 116(4): 1409–48.

——KATZ, L. F., and KEARNEY, M. S. (2008). 'Trends in US Wage Inequality: Revising the Revisionists', *Review of Economics and Statistics*, 90(2): 300–23.

——LEVY, F., and MURNANE, R. J. (2002). 'Upstairs, Downstairs: Computers and Skills on Two Floors of a Large Bank', *Industrial and Labor Relations Review*, 55(3): 432–47.

BAIRD, M., and LITWIN, A. S. (2005). 'Rethinking Work and Family Policy: The Making and Taking of Parental Leave in Australia', *International Review of Psychiatry*, 17(5): 385–400.

BARRETT, B., FRAILE, L., LITWIN, A. S., and CUTCHER-GERSHENFELD, J. (2003). *Strategies for Workforce Flexibility and Capability: IAM/Boeing St. Louis* (Washington, DC: US Department of Labor Case Study).

BARTEL, A., ICHNIOWSKI, C., and SHAW, K. (2007). 'How does Information Technology Really Affect Productivity? Plant-Level Comparisons of Product Innovation, Process Improvement and Worker Skills', *Quarterly Journal of Economics*, 122(4): 1721–58.

BATT, R. L. (1999). 'Work Organization, Technology, and Performance in Customer Service and Sales', *Industrial and Labor Relations Review*, 52(4): 539–64.

——(2002). 'Managing Customer Services: Human Resource Practices, Quit Rates, and Sales Growth', *Academy of Management Journal*, 45(3): 587–97.

BECKER, G. S. (1964 [1993]). *Human Capital: A Theoretical and Empirical Analysis with Special Reference to Education* (3rd edn. Chicago: University of Chicago).

BERG, I. (1970 [2003]). *Education and Jobs: The Great Training Robbery* (Clinton Corners, NY: Percheron).

BLACK, S. E. and LYNCH, L. M. (2004). 'What's Driving the New Economy? The Benefits of Workplace Innovation', *Economic Journal*, 114: 97.

BOSELIE, P., DIETZ, G., and BOON, C. (2005). 'Commonalities and Contradictions in HRM and Performance Research', *Human Resource Management Journal*, 15(3): 67–94.

BRESNAHAN, T. F., BRYNJOLFSSON, E., and HITT, L. M. (2000). 'Technology, Organization, and the Demand for Skilled Labor', in M. M. Blair and T. A. Kochan (eds.), *The New Relationship: Human Capital in the American Corporation* (Washington, DC: Brookings), 145–84.

—— —— —— (2002). 'Information Technology, Workplace Organization, and the Demand for Skilled Labor: Firm Level Evidence', *Quarterly Journal of Economics*, 117(1): 339–76.

BRYNJOLFSSON, E., and HITT, L. M. (2003). 'Computing Productivity: Firm-Level Evidence', *Review of Economics and Statistics*, 85(4): 793–808.

—— and MENDELSON, H. (1993). 'Information Systems and the Organization of Modern Enterprise', *Journal of Organizational Computing*, 3(3): 245–55.

—— HITT, L. M., and YANG, S. (2002). 'Intangible Assets: Computers and Organizational Capital', *Brookings Papers on Economic Activity*, 2002(1): 137–81.

BUDD, J. W. (2004). *Employment with a Human Face: Balancing Efficiency, Equity, and Voice* (Ithaca, NY: ILR Press).

CAPPELLI, P. (1999). *The New Deal at Work: Managing the Market-Driven Workforce* (Boston: Harvard Business School).

—— (2004). 'Why do Employers Retrain at-Risk Workers? The Role of Social Capital', *Industrial Relations*, 43(2): 421–47.

COMMONS, J. R. (1909). 'American Shoemakers, 1648–1895: A Sketch of Industrial Evolution', *Quarterly Journal of Economics*, 24(1): 39–98.

DOERINGER, P. B., and PIORE, M. J. (1971). *Internal Labor Markets and Manpower Analysis* (Lexington, Mass.: Heath).

DRAGO, R., and HYATT, D. (2003). 'Symposium: The Effect of Work-Family Policies on Employees and Employers', *Industrial Relations*, 42(2): 139–44.

DUBE, A., LESTER, T. W., and EIDLIN, B. (2007). *Firm Entry and Wages: Impact of Wal-Mart Growth on Earnings throughout the Retail Sector* (SSRN Working Paper, 841684).

DUNLOP, J. T. (1958 [1993]). *Industrial Relations Systems* (Rev. edn. Boston: Harvard Business School).

EATON, S. C. (2003). 'If you Can Use them: Flexibility Policies, Organizational Commitment, and Perceived Performance', *Industrial Relations*, 42(2): 145–67.

GOMEZ, R., and GUNDERSON, M. (2003). 'Volunteer Activity and the Demands of Work and Family', *Relations Industrielles/Industrial Relations*, 58(4): 573–89.

GREENHOUSE, S. (2005). 'Wal-Mart's Chief Calls its Critics Unrealistic', *New York Times* (6 Apr.): C11.

HUNTER, L. W., and LAFKAS, J. J. (2003). 'Opening the Box: Information Technology, Work Practices, and Wages', *Industrial and Labor Relations Review*, 56(2): 224–43.

—— BERNHARDT, A., HUGHES, K. L., and SKURATOWICZ, E. (2001). 'It's Not Just the ATMs: Technology, Firm Strategies, Jobs, and Earnings in Retail Banking', *Industrial and Labor Relations Review*, 54(2): 402–22.

JACOBY, S. M. (1985). *Employing Bureaucracy: Managers, Unions, and the Transformation of Work in American Industry, 1900–1945* (New York: Columbia University).

KELLEY, M. R. (1990). 'New Process Technology, Job Design, and Work Organization: A Contingency Model', *American Sociological Review*, 55(2): 191–208.

KOCHAN, T. A. (2005). *Restoring the American Dream: A Working Families' Agenda for America* (Cambridge, Mass.: MIT).

——McKERSIE, R. B., and CAPPELLI, P. (1984). 'Strategic Choice and Industrial Relations Theory', *Industrial Relations*, 23(1): 16–39.

KRUEGER, A. B. (1993). 'How Computers have Changed the Wage Structure: Evidence from Microdata', *Quarterly Journal of Economics*, 108(1): 33–60.

LANDERS, R. M., REBITZER, J. B., and TAYLOR, L. J. (1996). 'Rat Race Redux: Adverse Selection in the Determination of Work Hours in Law Firms', *American Economic Review*, 86(3): 329–48.

—— —— ——(1997). 'Work Norms and Professional Labor Markets', in F. D. Blau and R. G. EHRENBERG (eds.), *Gender and Family Issues in the Workplace* (New York: Russell Sage), 166–202.

LICHTENSTEIN, N., ed. (2006). *Wal-Mart: The Face of Twenty-First-Century Capitalism* (New York: New Press).

LONG, K., and BARRETT, B. (2004). *IAM and Boeing Joint Quality through Training Programs* (Cambridge, Mass.: MIT Labor Aerospace Research Agenda case study series).

LYNCH, L. M. (1992). 'Private-Sector Training and the Earnings of Young Workers', *American Economic Review*, 82(1): 299–312.

MacDUFFIE, J. P. (1995). 'Human-Resource Bundles and Manufacturing Performance: Organizational Logic and Flexible Production Systems in the World Auto Industry', *Industrial and Labor Relations Review*, 48(2): 197–221.

——and HELPER, S. (2006). 'Collaboration in Supply Chains, with and without Trust', in C. Heckscher and P. Adler (eds.), *The Corporation as a Collaborative Community* (Oxford: Oxford University Press), 417–65.

MISHEL, L., BERNSTEIN, J., and ALLEGRETTO, S. (2007). *The State of Working America 2006/2007* (Ithaca, NY: ILR).

OSTERMAN, P., and BURTON, M. D. (2005). 'Ports and Ladders: The Nature and Relevance of Internal Labor Markets in a Changing World', in S. Ackroyd, R. Batt, P. Thompson, and P. Tolbert (eds.), *Oxford Handbook on Work and Organization* (New York: Oxford University Press), 425–45.

——KOCHAN, T. A., LOCKE, R. M., and PIORE, M. J. (2001). *Working in America: A Blueprint for the New Labor Market* (Cambridge, Mass.: MIT Press).

POLLIN, R., GARRETT-PELTIER, H., HEINTZ, J., and SCHARBER, H. (2008). *Green Recovery: A Program to Create Good Jobs and Start Building a Low-Carbon Economy* (Washington, DC: Center for American Progress).

RAPOPORT, R., BAILYN, L., FLETCHER, J. K., and PRUITT, B. H. (2002). *Beyond Work-Family Balance: Advancing Gender Equity and Workplace Performance* (San Francisco: Jossey-Bass).

SHULTZ, G. P., and WEBER, A. R. (1966). *Strategies for the Displaced Worker: Confronting Economic Change* (New York: Harper & Row).

SLICHTER, S. H. (1941). *Union Policies and Industrial Management* (Washington, DC: Brookings Institution).

US BUREAU OF THE CENSUS (2008). *Statistical Abstract of the United States* (Washington, DC: Department of Commerce, Economics and Statistics Administration, Bureau of the Census, Data User Services Division).

VERMA, A. (2005). 'What do Unions do in the Workplace? Union Effects on Management and HRM Policies', *Journal of Labor Research*, 26(3): 415–49.

INDEX

Tsui, A. S. 341, 346–7
Tung, R. L. 99
Turner, J. H. 444
turnover 362–3, 366–7, 369–70

Ulrich, D. 547
uncertainty 196–8, 199–200, 207–8, 240, 243, 255
    imagination and 242
    in representations 246
    presents opportunities 242, 248–9
    see also Knight, F. H.; Knightian uncertainty; Lachmann, L. M.
union shock effect 667 n. 5
unionization 658
    de- 593, 595, 596, 659
unions 653, 655, 656–7, 659, 662–5
United Auto Workers (UAW) 657, 658
United Kingdom (UK) 314, 593, 595, 596, 599, 603, 640
    manufacturing share 621–2
    recruitment in 319
    Transfer of Undertakings/Protection of Employment Regulations 657
    see also Great Britain
United States of America (USA) 309, 532, 591, 592, 595, 596, 603, 631–2, 636
    employment in 658
    employment services industry 311
    exports to 633, 640
    HC acquisition in 318–19
    losing competitiveness 66
    manufacturing share 621–2
    services industry 125
    staffing industry 321–2
    telecommunications industry 300–1
    training in 599
    Worker Adjustment and Retraining Notification Act 657
    workforce 312–13, 314–15, 533, 593, 594, 660
    work-life integration in 655–6, 660
    see also New York; politics of human capital; Silicon Valley
upskilling 293, 594, 602, 635, 649, 653, 656
Utsuda, Shouei 468–9
Utterback, J. M. 557 n. 23
Uzzi, B. 340

Valeyre, A. 593, 595, 596, 611
valuable, rare, inimitable, non-substitutable (VRIN) 229
    /Organization (O) 221, 223, 227
Veblen, T. 193–4, 199, 205, 208, 438

Verma, A. 667 n. 5
Vietnam 621
Vischer, Jacqueline 34–5
Vladimirou, E. 125
Volvo 589
Vroom, V. H. 369
Vryonides, M. 102

W. L. Gore Co. 558 n. 29
Wachter, M. L. 170
Wade-Benzoni, J. M. 345
wage-work bargain 292, 293, 297
Waldman, M. 102
Wallin, Martin 8, 22–3
Wallman, Steven 439
Wal-Mart 658, 660–1
Wang, H. C. 368
Warner Brothers 556 n. 12
Waterman, R. 413
Watson Wyatt 392
Wayne, S. J. 347
Weber, Max 80, 190, 192, 435
Weber, R. 500
Weeks, John 415
Weick, K. 440
Weisbrod, B. A. 188
Weitz, A. 174
welfare
    production regimes 597, 599, 601, 603
    states 597–8, 600, 606, 608
Wenger, E. 111, 591
Wernerfelt, B. 19, 20
Wezel, F. C. 265
White, H. 18, 206–7
Wijnbergen, C. van 612
Williamson, O. E. 9, 15–16, 17, 21, 166, 175, 176, 179, 557 n. 23
    'hold-up' problem of 153
    on bounded rationality 177–8
    on employee/employer opportunism 173
    on HC and employment relation 169–72, 180
    on hierarchy/forbearance 172, 238–9
    on transaction cost approach 60–1
    TCE theory/approach of 167–8, 174, 460
Winter, S. G. 264, 529, 555 n. 3, 557 n. 23
Wittgenstein, Ludwig 202, 437
Wolfson, M. A. 200
Woolcock, M. 80, 84
work
    environment 477
    -life integration 653–6, 660, 665
    tasks 506–8, 512